P. 294 — Interest Rates —

Financial Management

Robert W. Johnson

Purdue University

Financial Management

Fourth Edition

Allyn and Bacon, Inc.
Boston · London · Sydney

Printed in the United States of America

Library of Congress Catalog Card No. 73–142882

ISBN: 0-205-03231-1

Eighth printing ... October, 1975

Contents

v

Part Two/ Planning and Managing Assets

Part Three/ Planning the Financial Structure

Part Four/ Management of Short- and Intermediate-Term Funds

Preface

This book is designed to achieve a specific objective for a certain group of readers. The objective is to provide a theoretical or conceptual framework that a financial manager can use to reach decisions in the real world. The book is intended to serve the reader who is studying the field of financial management for the first time; nevertheless, while the text is not a learned treatise designed to parade mathematical models and theoretical controversies before budding doctoral students, many advanced students and practitioners may find it useful for reviewing major trends in theory and application.

The intended role of the book influences its content. To apply theory to the real world, a financial manager must know what the real world is like. Therefore, I have continued in this edition to reveal enough about the world of the financial manager to enable him to make meaningful decisions. Insofar as possible, I have avoided merely describing the world of finance, but have emphasized an understanding of how and why institutions and practices exist as they do.

Rather than confuse the reader with conflicting methods and models, I have chosen to develop carefully what appears to be the best approach to financial decision-making. In contrast to earlier editions, some of this financial theory is presented in both mathematical and verbal terms. However, I have attempted to avoid model-building for its own sake and to use mathematics as a supplement to the understanding of financial decision-making. The mathematics (or arithmetic) that you will find here is to help rather than to intimidate.

Finally, special effort has been made to present this material in a manner that will personally involve the reader in the fundamental decisions and compromises of the financial manager as he faces choices between risk and return. I enjoy finance. It can be exciting and challenging, but it can be made dry and oppressive. To the extent that this book is both analytical and stimulating, it will have achieved its objective.

Let me note briefly the major changes that have been made from the previous edition. In general, there is a greater emphasis throughout on risk and the balancing of risk versus return. The concepts of utility and wealth are introduced in the first chapter and serve as a basis for a simple valuation model. Here, too, the trade-off of liquidity versus profitability presented in earlier editions has given way to a broader and more useful concept of risk versus return.

Chapter 3 remains as a relatively unique attempt to give the reader a bird's eye view of what financial management is all about, before becoming enmeshed in the details of financial decision-making. A valuation model for the levered firm is introduced here that serves to aid financial decisions in later chapters.

The discussion of capital budgeting has been largely rewritten with a much greater emphasis on net present value and the problems of evaluating capital expenditures under uncertainty. Operational procedures for allocating expenditures under capital rationing are also introduced. The material on cost of capital has been revised extensively to bring in valuation models for common stock and retained earnings.

To make room for new and more analytical material I have attempted to eliminate unnecessary descriptive material in the discussion of short-term financing without sacrificing a meaningful understanding of institutional practices.

The chapter on leasing now contains an operationally feasible and rational model for choosing between leasing and owning assets, an issue that I avoided with care in earlier editions. The discussion of dividend policy has been expanded to include more of the underlying theory. The chapter on mergers and acquisitions has been extensively revised and based in large part on the valuation model first developed in Chapter 3.

In other respects the content of each chapter has been made as current as possible in the light of financial developments since publication of the previous edition. Problems in the text are new. As in previous editions, many of the problem assignments are designed to help the reader understand the complexities of financial decisions. *Self-Correcting Problems in Finance, 2nd ed.* (By Roland I. Robinson of Michigan State University and Robert W. Johnson) provides a thorough, step-by-step review of basic concepts. Those who wish to use cases with the book can obtain a complete and current list of cases related to each chapter from the publisher.

The reception accorded previous editions has been most heartwarming. I have been especially pleased to receive comments and suggestions from some of the students using the book and have answered every such letter. Their comments and those of friends and colleagues using the book have been most helpful in its revision. I am particularly indebted to Bill Lewellen, my colleague at Purdue, and to the students in our MSIA program for their perceptive critiques. One of our doctoral candidates, Carl Sandberg, uncovered several grievous errors and other sins in an early manuscript. Another, Kenneth Riener, is largely responsible for the very thorough index.

Special thanks for aid in the revision of this edition should go to Professors Keith Smith of the University of California at Los Angeles and Charles Haley of the University of Washington for their intensive reviews of the manuscript. As always, the staff of Allyn and Bacon have performed heroically in moving the book from manuscript to market. Throughout the hectic days of revision my secretary, Jeri McIntyre, somehow kept track of me and my other obligations. My patient wife, Mary, managed once again to live compatibly with an author in the throes of a revision — a circumstance she has come to view with the same enthusiasm as a plague of locusts.

In spite of all the help received, deficiencies undoubtedly remain. For these I take full responsibility and urge readers to call them to my attention.

Robert W. Johnson

G.S.I.A. — Krannert Building
Purdue University
Lafayette, Indiana 47907

Financial Management

Part One

Introduction

The Role of the Financial Manager

1

This book is written from the viewpoint of the financial manager—the individual who has a major role in planning a business concern's needs and uses for funds, raising the necessary funds, and then putting those funds to effective use. Because all fields in a business require and use funds, the role of the financial manager is of vital concern to all the various sectors of business management. Because the financial manager plays a part in allocating resources within a firm, the methods and policies that he recommends should be studied closely by economists.

Our objective is to develop the skill of the financial manager, for the more efficient his performance, the more dynamic will be our economy. Because the duties of a financial manager are typically broad and varied, our discussion is likely to become clogged with details pertaining to all his possible functions. To avoid this as much as possible, we shall concentrate our attention on basic principles and theories universally applicable to all legal forms of profit-seeking businesses. If these are fully grasped, the financial manager can proceed to handle particular problems with confidence and skill.

The Role of Finance in the Economy

Insofar as he plays a part in securing funds and allocating them to various uses within a business concern, the financial manager serves as a vital link in the process of resource allocation. We shall see that the financial manager should do for the company what the price system does for the economy. To develop this point we shall proceed in our discussion from the role of the firm, or organization, in our economic system to a certain type of organization operating within this economic system, and finally to a particular function of management within the organization.

Decision-Making in the Modern Firm

Ours is a free enterprise, capitalistic economy. What does this mean? Most importantly it means that resources — material, labor, capital — are allocated in accordance with a free price system. Restricted supplies of goods and services are more or less automatically rationed among consumers through the price system. As prices of automobiles rise, some consumers reluctantly drop out of the market; a decline in prices will encourage additional purchasers. If we wish to describe the operation in more formal terms, we can say that the price system distributes goods efficiently by equating demand and supply. While the price system regulates the distribution of goods already in existence, it also determines what goods will come into being in the longer run. The automobile manufacturer will produce cars only if he believes that consumers will pay him an adequate price. In theory he pushes his operations to the point where the manufacture of one more car would not give him a sufficient return to make its production worthwhile.

The allocation of resources in our economy is automatic, in contrast to other economic systems where some governmental authority decides what amounts of various products and services will be made available. Under our system consumers make their decisions to buy more or less of various products and services largely independently of one another. Similarly, the automobile manufacturer decides on his production schedule without knowing what the candy or soap manufacturer plans, although they are also competing for consumers' dollars. These decisions influence the decisions of all other producers and consumers as well, an effect similar to the vigorous interaction of flying atoms in a cloud chamber, where each atom affects and is affected by all others.

In the early stages of our economic development decisions concerning the allocation of resources to the production of goods and their ultimate consumption were made by the producer-consumer unit — one person, the *entrepreneur*. As a farmer it was he who decided whether to plant corn instead of oats in the back forty acres; it was he who decided whether the corn would be ground into corn meal or used for feed. If he was an artisan, he made and carried out the necessary decisions about the purchasing, producing, and marketing of his products. Because almost every decision of the one-man "firm" was necessarily made in reference to the market, each managerial decision was directly related to all other decisions through the price system. The one-man "firm" who is a producer-consumer is still characteristic of some primitive societies today and, indeed, is found in the modern capitalistic system. Thus the doctor or lawyer presumably devotes his energies and material resources so that his net satisfactions as a producer and consumer are maximized. In other words, if the lawyer worked one more hour, the additional income would be less satisfying than the hour of leisure sacrificed; the purchase of one additional law book would give less joy than the brandy foregone.

The industrial revolution has changed the individualistic and self-sufficient way of life of many producer-consumers. Markets have grown, and production processes are more complex and require more in the way of capital equipment. As his market widened, the artisan found that it paid to subdivide his work in order to turn out more of his products. New products were developed which could be produced economically only with large aggregations of capital equipment and workers to operate the equipment. These developments necessitated the formation of organizations or firms suited, in terms of the amount of assets and people involved, to the mass production of goods.

In its relations with other firms and consumers the firm in the capitalistic economy still operates under the price system. The products and services it turns out and the level of its operations are largely determined by the prices (costs) of the factors (land, labor, and capital) used in producing these goods and services, and by the prices consumers are willing to pay — or by the quantity consumers are willing to buy at the prices set by the firm.

However, within the firm important changes in the decision-making process have taken place: it has become fragmented and it has been removed from intimate contact with the price system. First, the increasing scale and complexity of the business organization has forced a division of the managerial functions. Decision-making areas are often marked out according to the functional nature of the decision — for example, purchasing, production, personnel, marketing, and finance. Second, allocation of resources within the firm is not handled "automatically" through a free price system, as in the market outside of the firm. Instead, the allocation must be made by orders emanating from the chief operating officer in response to advice from the various functional specialists.

The fragmentation of decision making within the firm has important implications for the training and development of those individuals who are to operate the firm. Although the organizational structure of the firm limits the decision-making areas of each senior officer, the nature of the decisions involved are frequently not as neatly categorized as the organizational structure. Thus the decision concerning the allocation of funds to a new lathe or to more salesmen involves the areas of production and marketing as well as finance. The multifunctional nature of the decisions faced means that each of the senior officers must have a basic understanding of the other areas of management. In other words, the sales manager, production manager, and others should have some familiarity with the principles of financial management. Similarly, the financial manager should reciprocate by attaining some basic knowledge of the other fields.

The lack of the free price system within the firm may impede its efficient operation, because it is difficult to make and to evaluate decisions concerning the allocation of resources. For example, the chance of error in attempting to secure funds in the free market outside the firm is less than it would be in allocating the funds within the company. Should he try to borrow long-term funds for a uranium mining venture, the financial manager is likely to be quickly informed in the market place that this type of financing is not suited to the nature of his business. Whether he wishes to or not, he is forced by the market to issue common stock. In his use of funds within the firm he is not subject to such a rigorous market system of checks and balances. It is possible, although we hope not likely, that the sales manager will win out over the production manager simply because he is more articulate or persuasive. Even if he makes a decision between the two petitioners on the most rational grounds, the financial manager can never be sure in retrospect that the production manager should not have had his lathe rather than the sales manager his additional salesmen.

Misallocation of funds within a company damages the health of the economy as well as that of the firm. Departures from the sort of distribution of resources that would have been made under a free price system mean that goods are produced less efficiently than they might have been. In turn this suggests that consumers will pay more for, and receive less of, the final product than would otherwise have been the case. Because some consumers will drop out of the market, the factors used in manufacturing and marketing the product will be paid less than they should and in time will be diverted to other uses. Thus, as the financial manager carries out his various functions which we shall be covering later in detail, he plays a vital role in our economic process. The better he plans his needs, the more aptly he matches the funds he secures to those needs, and the better he allocates those funds within the business, the better our economic system operates.

The Objectives of the Firm

For the financial manager to make wise decisions he must have a clear understanding of the objective of the firm. Is it to maximize sales? The salary of the president? The firm's share of the market? Let us explore the issue with some care, since a precise definition of the objective of the firm is essential to the development of any financial theory.

First, consider the owners of the firm. We must assume that the firm is to be operated for their benefit. Of course, certain parameters, or limits, are set upon how freely we may operate the firm in their behalf. The government may intervene if we pollute the air or water, and we are likely to be penalized if the plant is unsafe. But within the limits set to protect or improve the public welfare, we operate the firm for the owners' benefit.

Owners are likely to have a very diverse set of goals and life styles. Some have a high preference for current consumption—eat, drink, and be merry. Others may be more of the saving type. Some have a greater willingness to assume risk than others. Given these various attitudes, each of the owners attempts to maximize his satisfaction, or the *utility* that he gains from his wealth.

Since this is a very individual and personalized process, we can not design a method of operating the firm that will directly maximize the utilities of the individual owners. Instead, we will have to achieve this ultimate goal by a two-step process. First, we shall assert that maximization of the utility of individual owners is approximately equivalent to the maximization of their wealth. Second, we shall show that in most cases maximization of wealth is equal to maximization of the market value of the owners' equity; that is, their claim on the assets of the firm. Their claim is represented by the common stock of a corporation, by a share in a partnership, or by an ownership interest in a sole proprietorship. The framework of our discussion is shown below.

Maximize owners' utility from wealth	$\cong$	Maximize owners' wealth	$\cong$	Maximize value of owners' interests in the firm

Utility $\cong$ Wealth. If we maximize an owner's wealth, he will be in a position to maximize his own individual utilities in a free market. If he yearns for current satisfactions, he may borrow against his wealth or simply convert part of it into cash and spend it. If he wishes to save for his old age, he may reinvest a portion of the returns generated by his wealth. Whatever his set of preferences, he can adjust them to his own satisfaction within the limits of his available wealth. The greater his wealth, the more optimal is his consumption pattern.

Wealth $\cong$ Market Price. If an individual owns some of the common stock of American Airlines, the management of that company can best maximize his wealth by following a course of action designed to maximize the market price of American Airlines common stock. In some cases this may not be optimal from a given owner's point of view. If he also has large holdings in United Airlines, American's success in maximizing its market price may be at the expense of United Airlines. Thus the owner who holds United may suffer a decline in his wealth. Nonetheless, without knowing and analyzing each investor's investment portfolio, the optimal strategy of the management of American Airlines will be to maximize the aggregate market value of its common stock.

Were the firm a proprietorship or partnership, the objective of management should be to maximize the price that could be obtained in the market for the owners' interests. However, it is often much more difficult in such cases to equate utility, wealth, and market price. The lawyer (a sole proprietor) who selects fine brandy rather than an additional law book cannot actually measure the effect of this choice upon the value of the firm. The ownership interest is not traded daily in the market, as in the case of the common stock of American Airlines. In theory, if he were able to measure the effect of his decision, he would note a slight decline in market value. He has chosen to consume a minute portion of his wealth, and we have no reason to doubt that this is a rational decision.

In this connection it should be noted that there is an underlying assumption that the market price of American Airlines common stock represents a reasonably accurate reflection of the information available about the concern. Thus, an announcement of awards of new routes is assumed to be widely dispersed and the value to American Airlines quickly assessed. Even though the accountants of a firm have a rather wide range of options in recording income and expenses, the assumption is that the market can see through the reported earnings to the underlying cash flows available for reinvestment or distribution to owners. This latter assumption is open to question, since it is very difficult to test whether the·market really penetrates the haze surrounding the reported net profits after taxes.[1] The evidence is not conclusive, but the financial manager should, nonetheless, be guided by what the market *should* perceive and then make every effort to communicate the proper information to the market.

Determinants of Market Value. If the owners' utility is maximized by maximizing the market value of the owners' equity, what factors must management consider in setting about to achieve this goal? Do we maximize the market value by raising the president's salary, by minimizing inventory, or by sponsoring a car in the Indianapolis 500? These are not very likely alternatives, but they may cause us to pause long enough to realize that the answer to the question is not immediately obvious.

Consider for the moment that we have a money machine. What determines its value to us (and to the market). First, the more money it turns out, the greater its value. The greater the cash flow produced by the machine, the more we have to spend on consumption or to reinvest in other money machines, whatever happens to be our preference.

Note the emphasis on *cash* inflows, not reported accounting profits. The relevance of cash flows and the irrelevance of reported profits for our purposes can be grasped quickly when the owner faces simple decisions. Consider a proprietor whose business consists of writing a book on financial management. The publisher might offer to pay $2;000 per year for five years or a cumulated lump sum of $10,000 at the end of the fifth year. Using the proper accrual techniques, the author's accountants would record the same gross income of $2,000 per year under either arrangement. On the basis of reported profits, the author should be indifferent between the two contracts. But he is not. Regardless of the accountant's reports, the annual cash payments are preferable to the delayed lump-sum payment. Cash is crucial; we can not spend or reinvest accounting entries.

Second, the value of the money machine is influenced by the *timing* of the cash it generates. We prefer $2,000 per year for five years to $10,000 at the end of the fifth year simply because we can spend it for consumption or reinvest it that much sooner. *Money has a time value.*

Third, the value of the money machine is determined in part by the risk of obtaining the expected cash payments. There are various possible measures of risk. We shall assume that risk is measured by the variance of possible outcomes; in this case, by the dispersion in the possible level of cash payments by the money machine.[2] Additionally, we shall also assume that owners are

[1] As an example of such an investigation, see Francis A. Mlynarczyk, "An Empirical Study of Accounting Methods and Stock Prices," *Empirical Research in Accounting, 1969*, pp. 63–81. His findings suggest that the market does see through the accounting vagaries in the utility industry, but these findings may not be applicable to industrial concerns.

[2] Recall that the variance of a probability distribution is the weighted mean of the squared deviations from the mean of the distribution, with the probabilities used as weights. The standard deviation, σ, is merely the square root of the variance. This will be used as the measure of risk, although there may be other considerations, such as the skewness of the distribution.

averse to risk; that is, that they prefer a narrow or "tight" distribution of possible outcomes to a disperse or relatively "flat" distribution of possible outcomes.

For example, assume that we have two money machines called roulette wheels. Wheel *A* will pay $1000, whereas Wheel *B* has an expected payoff of $1000 with a probability of one-half, and equal probabilities of paying either $500 or $1,500. The alternatives are depicted below:

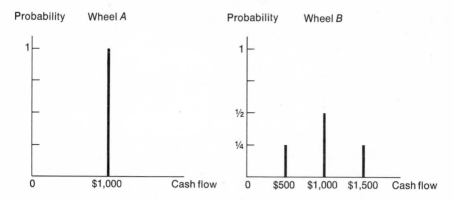

Presumably, you would pay something to take a turn on either wheel, but would you not pay more to take a turn at Wheel *A* than on Wheel *B*?[3] While the expected value of one turn of the wheel is the same in each case ($1,000), most people would prefer the certainty of getting $1000 that comes from the turn of Wheel *A* to the greater variance of possible outcomes faced on Wheel *B*. Although we have one chance in four of an extra $500 from Wheel *B*, there is an equal probability of getting only $500. Getting only $500, rather than $1,000, involves greater pain than the pleasure obtained from the possible gain of $1,500 instead of $1,000. In more formal terms the utility represented by a loss of $500 is greater than the utility of a similar gain.[4]

Now consider Wheels *C* and *D*, which are really business firms. There are many different possible outcomes for the year in question, so that we have a continuous probability distribution over the possible annual cash inflows. Both firms have an expected value (mean) of cash inflows for the year of $1 million, but the variance of the cash inflows of Firm *C* is much less than that of the cash flows of Firm *D*. Other things being equal, the expected cash flow of Firm *C* has a higher value to the owners than that of Firm *D*, because most owners are averse to risk—risk being measured by the variance (or standard deviation) of possible outcomes.

Owners are also averse to variable cash flows because of a fear of bankruptcy. Even if cash inflows average $1 million per year over a period of time, heavy *outflows* in a given year may prevent required payments on debts. As a result the creditors may seize the assets of the firm, leaving the owners empty-

---

[3] If we had unlimited resources and could play the wheel all night, we would be largely indifferent between the wheels. However, in the business world we do not have unlimited resources, and we do not have repeated opportunities to make the same gamble.

[4] If you are indifferent about such trivial amounts, think in terms of thousands of dollars.

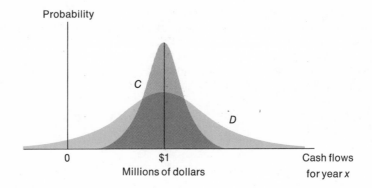

handed. As some statistician once said, one may drown in a stream with an average depth of six inches. So may the shareholders lose their entire investment, even though a firm's *average* cash flows are adequate to meet legal obligations.

Evidence that people are averse to risk is afforded by such phenomena as the sale of fire insurance. Since insurance companies have operating costs and must make a profit, the expected value of a loss to the individual homeowner must be less than the insurance premium he pays. Yet people buy fire insurance because they are averse to the large loss they would suffer, even though it has a relatively low probability. They prefer the certain payment on insurance to the wide variance in possible outcomes that results from being uninsured.

We have now identified the three determinants of the market value of a firm. *Owners prefer more cash to less cash; cash sooner rather than later; and cash inflows that have a small, rather than a wide variance.* Thus the market value of the owners' equity is a function of the *level, timing,* and *variance* of cash inflows. At a later point we shall formalize this relationship as a mathematical model. For the moment it is sufficient to state in general terms the principles that must be followed by the financial manager if he is to meet the objectives of the firm:

1/ The objective of financial management is to maximize the aggregate market value of the owners' equity.

2/ Any decision that affects the amount, timing, or certainty of cash flows available to the owners will also affect the market value of the owners' equity.

Models and Theories

Decision-making involves sorting of important variables from a host of information and identifying their relationship to the decision. For example, a quarterback must decide what play to call on third down. He has a wide variety of information of varying significance; the ability of the opponent's corner back, the strength and direction of the wind, the state of his own center's knee, the condition of the field, and so on. He must decide which of these variables are most important and how they will influence the effectiveness of various plays that he might call. Subject to the perceived constraints, he selects that play which he believes has the best chance of contributing to winning the game. In his mind he develops a model of how the play should operate, given his best estimates of the variables (parameters) that may influence the outcome.

The developers of the SST also use models. They test various configurations in a wind tunnel. In building the miniature models to test, they do not include passenger seats, galleys, and luggage. While these may have some effect on speed, they are not as important as the shape of the wing. Thus the scientists abstract from the many possible variables affecting speed to build a model that captures the most essential parameters. When subjected to various wind speeds, the resulting model tells the engineers how fast the plane should fly with a given configuration, other things being held constant. To the extent that the "other things held constant" influence speed and have not been adequately captured in the model, the estimates of speed will be inaccurate.

Financial managers also use models, either implicitly or explicitly. They are typically mathematical models whose use has been greatly facilitated by the development of computers. Essentially, the financial manager looks at the many variables that might affect a particular decision, determines which are most important, judges the nature of their influence on the outcome of the decision, and constructs a mathematical model to depict the relationships.

In establishing a model of the determinants of the market price of a firm's common stock, we have identified three key variables: the amount, timing, and risk of cash flows. To simplify the analysis we have left out other less important variables that might also influence the market price: the purchase of our shares by a large investment company, release of a market letter touting our stock, the breakdown of a computer, and so on. We simply say that the price of our common stock is a function of three variables:

$$Price = f(amount, timing, and risk of cash flows)$$

As an illustration of the mathematical formulation of a model, let us simplify our basic model even more. Assume that we expect the cash flows to be reasonably level and to extend so far into the future that the stream may be considered as infinite. In that case, we can say that the price is a function of the amount and risk of cash flows. Moreover, we can assert that the larger the amount of flows, the higher the price; and the higher the risk, the lower the price. Now we need some symbols. Let P represent the price; A represent annual cash flows; and k be a percentage rate to reflect the risk. (Call k the *discount rate*.) The higher the risk (variance of possible outcomes) the larger is k. Thus a stream of cash flows that is quite certain might be associated with $k = 6\%$, whereas a very risky stream of cash flows might carry a $k = 15\%$. The relationship can then be depicted as:

$$P = A/k$$

To put numbers into the model, a stream of infinite cash flows of $120 per year in a risk category of 6% would have a price, or market value, of $2,000 [that is, $120/0.06]. Put another way, the cash flows of $120 per year *discounted at 6 percent* have a value of $2,000.

This model tells the financial manager that if he is to raise the market price, other things being equal, he must either increase the level of annual cash flows, *A,* or reduce the risk of obtaining those flows, *k.* Thus the choice is between return and risk.[5]

Note that this discussion is in terms of what the financial manager *should* do. This is because we are interested in the ideal, or *normative* behavior. Should the management of a firm wish to behave in a different manner, development of normative models will provide a basis for judging the cost to the owners of that nonnormative behavior. For example, if management makes a sub-optimal decision that lowers cash inflows, the cost to the owners of that decision can be measured by the difference between the market value of the owners' equity given that decision and the estimated market value given a normative decision.

The other basic type of model is a positive model. It attempts to depict in abstract form how the world *does* behave. Whereas the test of the effectiveness of a normative model is whether or not it enables the financial manager to make better decisions, the test of a positive model is whether or not it enables him to make better predictions. A financial manager would use a normative model to determine the optimal size of an order of rolls of steel, but a positive model to forecast future movements of interest rates. For the most part our discussions will center on implicit or explicit normative models.

Ideally, one might like a global model depicting the interrelationships among all activities within a firm. As a practical matter, we will deal with models reflecting more restricted activities, such as inventory management, investment in fixed assets, and the like. The implicit assumption underlying such models is that other aspects of a firm's financial activities are held constant, so that we can isolate the particular aspect under consideration. Although this may result in solutions that are somewhat sub-optimal in an ideal sense, we will find it a practical approach to making generally sound decisions.

Applicability to "Real World." It is appropriate to ask whether managers do indeed attempt to maximize the market price of their firms' common stock. Although they do not always behave in this fashion, there are forces that encourage such normative behavior. The higher the market price of the firm, the easier it is for it to acquire other firms at attractive prices—or the better price its owners will receive if it is acquired by some other concern. Firms whose

[5] In earlier editions I used the term "profitability versus liquidity." Why the change to return versus risk? Use of the term "return" rather than "profitability" is mainly a matter of taste. There is a danger that "profitability" may connote only reported accounting profits, whereas we are interested in cash flows. It was to avoid this possible confusion that "return" was substituted for "profitability." Use of the term "risk" rather than liquidity" involves more of a conceptual than a semantic change. Liquidity captures only one phase of risk—the risk that a firm will be unable to pay its bills and eventually go bankrupt. Averse as I may be to bankruptcy, I am also averse to the risk measured by the dispersion in possible returns. Faced with a choice between Money Wheel *A,* which will pay me a certain $1000, and Money Wheel *B,* which will pay me either $500 or $1500 with equal probabilities, I will choose Wheel *A.* The choice is not inspired by a fear of a liquidity crisis or bankruptcy; I will be better off in either case. Since the term "liquidity" seemed to reflect only the bankruptcy aspect of risk, I have chosen to use the broader term "risk" to cover both the aversion to bankruptcy and the aversion to dispersions of possible outcomes. Although the latter form of risk is often associated only with variance (or standard deviation), there is no reason to so limit the measurement of risk.

stock is depressed are susceptible to sudden raids by other corporations. Managers of depressed firms are also more likely to find themselves thrown out of office by dissident stockholders.[6] But there is even more direct pressure on many managers to maximize the market value of their firm's common stock. One study of management and ownership in large firms concludes:

> . . . the stockholdings of the senior executives of large publicly-held corporations are much more extensive than is commonly supposed; a considerable portion of their compensation is provided by devices that utilize the firm's stock as the means of payment; and the income attributable to both sources has come to far outweigh that supplied by traditional fixed-dollar awards.[7]

Thus the desire to be in a favorable position to acquire other firms, the fear of being taken over by more successful outsiders, and self-interest combine to force most managers to seek optimal decisions. The measure of the optimal decision is afforded by our model, which depicts the market price as a tradeoff between return (how much cash, and how soon) and the risk (how much variance of possible cash flows).

The Role of the Financial Manager. The balancing of risk and return in order to maximize the market price of the owners' equity constitutes the basic role of the financial manager of the firm—as well as the basic analytical framework of this book. A "safe" return is also a low return, because risk-averse investors bid up the prices of assets producing cash flows with a low variance. By bidding up the price, they naturally lower the rate of return earned on the asset. In contrast, investors will demand a higher return as a reward for assuming greater risk. The issue faced by a financial manager in making decisions—such as the purchase of a new lathe—is whether the return is sufficient to justify the risk incurred. If the reward is just barely sufficient, the market price of the firm should remain unchanged. If the return is more than sufficient, the value of the owners' equity should rise.

Functions of Financial Management

In order to maximize the market price of the owners' equity by properly balancing risk and return, the financial manager is involved in three main functions: financial planning, managing assets, and raising funds. Occasionally, he may become involved in some special and non-recurring problems, such as those concerning the combination of one firm with another or the liquidation of a company. Seldom are these various functions entirely the responsibility of the financial manager. Because financial policies usually affect marketing, production, or other departments, additional officers are usually involved in the decision-making process. There is no established pattern, but there are certain functions of financial management that must be performed.

[6] R. M. Duvall and D. V. Austin, "Predicting the Results of Proxy Contests," *Journal of Finance*, 20 (September, 1965), 464–71.
[7] W. G. Lewellen, "Management and Ownership in the Large Firm," *Journal of Finance*, 24 (May, 1969), 320.

Financial Planning

The planning function is one of the most challenging and interesting of all the functions of the financial manager. Because he frequently participates in setting the long-run course of the business, he must start out with a broad, overall view of the operations of the company. He is first concerned with long-run plans for plant expansion, replacement of machinery and equipment, or other expenditures which will cause unusually large cash drains from the business. On the basis of his knowledge of these plans and estimates of sales for the near future, the financial manager must also estimate cash flows into and out of the business over the near future. In developing these plans, or budgets, he must make the best of an imperfect world, for he should recognize that to a certain extent his plans will be upset by external forces over which he has slight control. For example, significant new developments in machinery may force the company to make heavy expenditures on new equipment in order to maintain its position in the industry. A recession or strike may adversely affect profits. Recognition of the uncertainties of life is made not by throwing out the budget but by building sufficient flexibility into financing arrangement to cope with unforeseen developments.

Managing Assets

As he plans the flows of cash, the financial manager must also see to it that funds are invested wisely or "economically" within the business or else returned to the owners. Every dollar invested in an asset, whether current or fixed, has alternative uses. It could be invested in a government bond, thereby providing safety and liquidity, though a low yield. It could be committed to a research development program for new products, a risky venture, but possibly a very profitable one. Or the dollar might be returned to the owners if they could earn a better return at the same risk, or the same return at less risk. This is the trade-off of risk and profitability that the financial manager must compromise in his plans. Planning the flow of funds and deciding upon their most profitable allocation among the various assets are intimately related functions of financial management that are discussed in Part II of this book.

Raising Funds

If his planned cash outflow exceeds his cash inflow and his cash balance is insufficient to absorb the deficiency, the financial manager will find it necessary to obtain funds from outside the business. Just as a firm bids for labor in the labor market and for steel in the market place, so does it seek money in one or another of various markets for money. They are among the most competitive of all our markets, because anyone who has money to invest may enter and bargain with those who are seeking funds. Although much of the demand for and supply of funds meets in New York City, there is really no such thing as a single market for money, any more than there is a single market for labor or steel.

Within these markets funds are available from many sources, under different types of agreements, and for varying periods of time. The financial manager's problem is to obtain the combination that most closely suits the anticipated needs of his business. Types of financing arrangements that are desirable because of their low cost typically involve fixed commitments. Consequently, the attraction of the low cost must be balanced against the risk of not being able to meet the required payments. The future possibilities in the market for funds must be related to the expected financial condition of the company as it might exist six months from now, rather than to its present-day condition. To illustrate, one must decide whether today is a better time to secure funds than six months from now, or whether it is better to obtain owners' funds today than it would be to acquire funds from creditors six months from now. Thus, to the prediction of his business needs that he has already made as part of his function as a financial planner, the financial manager adds a second prediction, one involving the future course of the markets from which he draws his funds. The considerations involved in planning the optimal mixture of different types of funds are discussed in Part III. The acquisition and management of short- and intermediate-term funds are discussed in Part IV, and similar aspects of long-term financing are covered in Part V.

Meeting Special Problems

A final function of the financial manager is to work on those infrequent, but involved, problems that come to pass in the history of a business. Although varied, they have a common core in that they require placing a value on a business, on its securities, or on some portion of its assets. Let us take a proposal for the combination of two firms. Aside from the legal problems of how it should be done, and the economic problems of whether it should be done at all, there remain the financial problems concerning the basis upon which the current owners shall exchange their securities for securities of the new or surviving firm. This requires a determination of the respective values of the securities involved. If things have gone poorly for a concern, the financial manager will be deeply involved in the readjustment or reorganization of the company's finances to stave off eventual failure. Should the adjustments prove inadequate, the financial manager will be there at the death, supervising the final disposition of the firm's remains to the creditors and owners. These special problems are covered in Part VI.

Organization for Financial Management

The foregoing discussion should not be taken to mean that the operations of every company revolve around the financial manager. The sphere of financial management is not clearly defined in practice, and its necessary functions are handled in a great many ways in different forms of organizational structure. Similarly, the top financial officer—be he called treasurer, controller, vice president, or whatever—performs widely varying duties in different companies. The role of the senior financial officer and the extent of his participation in finance functions will vary according to the function or policy involved, the size of the company, his own ability, and those of other officers and directors. To illustrate: In considering a possible new issue of securities, the financial manager may be only one of many to advise the president and the board of directors, and it is the board of directors who will make the final decision. In a small company the financial manager may handle the accounting, pass on credit, aid in public and stockholder relations, and help out the sales manager with important customers, as well as carry on the finance functions we have already discussed.

The Duties of the Financial Manager

In the few studies we have available concerning the role of the financial manager in business, the importance of the financial manager and of the finance function is clear. Most of the reporting firms in one study indicated that the chief financial officer reported to the president or to the president and the board of directors. One half of the companies reported that the financial officer was on the board of directors.[8] The planning function – participation in long-range financial planning and preparation of long-term budgets – was considered by financial officers to be their most important function. Second in importance was supervision of accounting operations. Although this suggests that financial managers must be thoroughly familiar with accounting theory and fundamentals, it also suggests that accountants must become familiar with financial management if they are to attain higher positions in management.

In terms of time spent rather than importance of functions, the typical chief financial officer was most deeply concerned with working capital management. This would include activities such as accounting operations, credit and collection, contacts with commercial banks and other suppliers of short-term funds, and preparation of budgets. Most financial officers covered in the survey recognized that such decisions as how to finance needs for additional funds would have a lasting effect upon the long-run fortunes of the firm. In addition to these functions, financial officers reported that their time was consumed by such varied activities as supervising cashiers, advising on dividend policy, and handling public relations, pensions and welfare, and stockholder relations. No set pattern emerged, and there was considerable disparity in the amount of time different financial officers spent on the listed activities. We must conclude, then, that in addition to training in accounting and finance, the financial manager should be prepared to accept some assignments only dimly related to his field of specialization.

Growing Importance of the Financial Manager

In recent years financial managers have achieved increasing recognition and higher status in business concerns. The chief financial officer used to be regarded as part of the staff, with promotions to the presidency coming from the line officers. Today we find that financial managers are more and more frequently chosen to head giant corporations because of their deep involvement in broad policy areas. More than most top officers, the financial manager has become concerned with all of the functional areas of business, as well as groups

[8] J. Fred Weston, "The Finance Function," *Journal of Finance*, 9 (September, 1954), pp. 265–82.

and agencies outside of the company. The reasons for this growth in his importance and the widening scope of his duties lie in the increased scale of operation of business firms, their greater complexity, and the longer time-span for planning.

Business firms grow both in response to increasing markets and through mergers and acquisitions. While the growing concentration of assets in the hands of large corporations has important social and economic implications, it also means that the financial managers of these concerns have larger responsibilities. For example, business expenditures for new plant and equipment rose from about $29 billion in 1955 to an annual rate of over $81 billion in mid-1970. Most of these expenditures involved evaluation by financial managers. Mergers, acquisitions, tax problems, and anti-trust matters also accompanied the growth in the size of business firms and called upon the skills of financial management.

The merger movement and widespread diversification of products has greatly increased the complexity of operating business firms. Instead of one-product firms, we have multi-product, multi-divisional companies. This change has required a substantial increase in the amount and speed with which information is collected in order to control these diverse operations. Since computers play an important role in gathering and processing the information, financial managers must learn their strengths and limitations. In many companies the financial manager heads the computer center.

Rapid technological developments, coupled with the large-scale investments made by business firms, call for more long-range planning than was characteristic of earlier years. In contrast with the accountant, who is more concerned with keeping the score on past operations, the financial manager is more likely to be involved in projecting needs and sources of funds for several years into the future. As chief budget officer, he may tie together the long-range projections of marketing, production, and other functional areas of the business firm. Again computers are powerful aids. For example, he can pretest plans by simulation on a computer, so that unfortunate results of a given set of plans can be discovered and avoided.

Thus there are outstanding opportunities in financial management today. The problems faced are often complex and demanding, but the rewards, financial and otherwise, can be great for those who enjoy challenges.

Questions

1/ Contrast the process of resource-allocation in our economy with that in a managed economy, such as that of Russia.

2/ To what extent do we abolish or supplement the free price system in time of war or other national crisis? Why is this done?

3/ Some companies attempt to apply a "free market test" to certain internal decisions. For example, branch plants may be required to compete with outside companies to serve as a source of supply for the main plant. In what other areas of intra-firm decision making does management attempt to apply a market test?

4/ An illustration is provided demonstrating the difference in actual cash inflows and the annual revenues that would be properly recorded by an accountant. Cite a number of instances where there would be differences between actual cash *outflows* and recorded expenses.

5/ Suggest cases in which the interests of management of a corporation might conflict with those of the common stockholders.

6/ If you are currently working for a business firm, prepare a chart showing the position of your senior financial officer in the organization structure.
   a. What are his major responsibilities?
   b. How are decisions involving other departments reached?
   c. What is his background?

7/ If a company has several branch plants, should there be a financial manager for each plant, or just one in the home office, or both? How should you divide the responsibilities between branch and home office?

Problems

1/ You are gambling with two three-sided dice, sides numbered 1, 2, and 3. You are to bet $1 on each throw. What minimum payoff would you demand to bet on the sum of the dice equaling six? What minimum payoff would you require to bet on the sum of the dice equaling four? Explain the difference.

2/ You are offered two games—one with a 3-sided die and the other with a 6-sided die. In the first instance, every time an amount greater than two shows, you receive $10; for an amount less than two, you pay $10. In the second case, you receive an amount equal to $10 times the amount by which the face exceeds three (thus a five gives you $20); or pay $10 times the amount by which the face is less than four. Thus a two costs you $20. What is the expected value of each game? Which is the more attractive to you? Why?

3/ a. The Webb Manufacturing Co. is expected to pay dividends of $2.25 per share for the foreseeable future, although these annual payments are by no means certain. Investments of equivalent risk are yielding 9%. What should be the market price of a share of Webb common stock?
   b. The firm plans to enter a new line of business that promises both greater returns, but, as one might expect, more risk. If it embarks on the new project, the expected value of future dividends to share holders will be $3.50 per share, but the greater variance of possible returns will place the company in a 12% risk class. Should the new venture be undertaken? Explain.
   c. At what level of prospective dividends per share would Webb stockholders be indifferent as to whether or not the new project were undertaken?

Selected References

ANTHONY, R. N., "The Trouble with Profit Maximization," *Harvard Business Review,* 38 (November–December, 1960), pp. 126–34.

COASE, R. H., "The Nature of the Firm," *Economica,* 4 (November, 1937), pp. 386–405.

COLE, A., *Business Enterprise in Its Social Setting.* Cambridge: Harvard University Press, 1959.

DONALDSON, G., "Financial Goals: Management vs. Stockholders," *Harvard Business Review,* 41 (May–June, 1963), pp. 116–29.

DYMENT, J. J., "Financial Planning with a Computer," *Financial Executive,* 38 (April, 1970), pp. 34–35ff.

HARTMANN, H., "Managers and Entrepreneurs: A Useful Distinction?" *Administrative Science Quarterly,* 3 (March, 1959), pp. 429–51.

KAMERSCHEN, D. R. "The Influence of Ownership and Control on Profit Rates," *American Economic Review,* 58 (June, 1968), pp. 432–47.

LARNER, R. J., "The 200 Largest Nonfinancial Corporations," *American Economic Review,* 56 (September, 1966), pp. 777–87.

LEWELLEN, W. G., "Management and Ownership in the Large Firm," *Journal of Finance* 24 (May, 1969), pp. 299–322.

MARGOLIS, J., "The Analysis of the Firm: Rationalism, Conventionalism, and Behaviorism," *Journal of Business,* 31 (July, 1958), pp. 187–99.

MARTING, E. and R. E. FINLEY, *The Financial Manager's Job.* New York: American Management Association, Inc., 1964.

MCCORMICK, W. F., "The Corporate Treasurer's Role," *Financial Executive,* 31 (January, 1963), pp. 27–29ff.

MLYNARCZYK, F. A., "An Empirical Study of Accounting Methods and Stock Prices," *Empirical Research in Accounting,* 1969, pp. 63–81.

MOAG, J. S., W. T. CARLETON and E. M. LERNER, "Defining the Finance Function: A Model-Systems Approach," *Journal of Finance,* 22 (December, 1967), pp. 543–55.

MONSEN, R. J. and A. DOWNS, "A Theory of Large Managerial Firms," *Journal of Political Economy,* 73 (June, 1965), pp. 221–36.

"The New Power of Financial Executives," *Fortune,* 65 (January, 1962), pp. 81–85ff.

SHUBIK, M., "Approaches to the Study of Decision-Making Relevant to the Firm," *Journal of Business,* 34 (April, 1961), pp. 101–18.

SIMON, H. A., "Theories of Decision-Making in Economics," *American Economic Review,* 49 (June, 1959), pp. 253–83. A survey article with a very complete bibliography.

The Environment of Financial Management

2 Because a financial manager operates within a legal environment characteristic of his company, it is worthwhile to study the characteristics of the three basic forms of business organization: proprietorships, partnerships, and corporations. The form of organization selected will have considerable impact upon such matters as our ability to obtain funds, payments of earnings to owners, and the risk borne by owners. Of particular importance will be the effect of taxes upon the income available to the owners. Almost every major business decision has important tax implications, and the decision concerning the form of business organization is no exception to this rule. While no one will become a tax expert after reading this chapter, we may create some demand for tax experts.

Forms of Business Organization

While the majority of business organizations are sole proprietorships, corporations are by far the dominant form of organization if we give weight to their income and assets. In most lines of business sole proprietorships and partnerships outnumber corporations, but corporations usually account for the greater portion of receipts from sales and services (Table 2-1). There are sharp differences among different lines of business. In terms of numbers, sole proprietors dominate the agriculture, retail trade, and service businesses. But in terms of sales, corporations dominate the manufacturing, transportation, and communication fields and account for a majority of business receipts in all but agriculture and the service industries.

TABLE 2-1   Importance of Proprietorships, Partnerships, and Corporations in Selected Lines of Business

| | Percentage of Totals Accounted for by: | | | |
	Sole Proprie- tor	Partner- ship	Corpora- tion	Total
Agriculture, forestry and fisheries				
Number	95.4	3.8	0.8	100.0
Business receipts	72.5	10.8	16.8	100.0
Manufacturing				
Number	44.5	9.0	46.5	100.0
Business receipts	1.3	1.1	97.7	100.0
Transportation, communication, and sanitary services				
Number	79.7	4.2	16.1	100.0
Business receipts	5.7	1.2	93.1	100.0
Retail trade				
Number	75.2	9.9	14.8	100.0
Business receipts	26.2	8.0	65.8	100.0
Services				
Number	85.8	6.5	7.6	100.0
Business receipts	36.8	15.7	47.4	100.0

Note: Details may not add to totals because of rounding.
Source: Internal Revenue Service, U.S. Treasury Department, *Statistics of Income, 1966 Business Income Tax Returns* (Washington, D.C.: U.S. Government Printing Office, 1969, p. 5.

Just as corporations are more financially significant than proprietorships and partnerships, so are big corporations more significant than small ones — but again small corporations outnumber the giants. Just under two percent of corporations have total assets of $5 million or more, but among all corporations these account for almost three-fifths of total receipts and for more than four-fifths of total assets.[1] There are two lessons to be gained from these figures. First, the great bulk of corporations are fairly small, so that many have the same financial problems as proprietorships and partnerships. Second, because of the dominant economic impact of their companies, officers and directors of giant corporations have a special responsibility to society, as well as to their employees, creditors, and owners.

[1] Internal Revenue Service, U.S. Treasury Department, *Statistics of Income, 1966, Business Income Tax Returns* (Washington, D.C.: U.S. Government Printing Office, 1969), p. 233.

In most cases we will have a choice among these forms of business organization. (Attorneys may not incorporate while banks and some other financial institutions must incorporate.) Since we have a choice, let us examine the legal characteristics of each form of business and how we would establish each type. Then we will be in a position to compare their relative advantages and disadvantages.

Sole Proprietorship

The *sole proprietorship* is a firm owned by a single person, who holds title to all of the assets and is responsible for the liabilities. The owner receives the profits or suffers the losses incurred in operations. We can establish a sole proprietorship with great ease. Aside from any local licensing requirements for certain types of business (such as barbershops), we need only start up operations.

Partnership

The *partnership* differs from the proprietorship chiefly in that there is more than one owner. The most common form of partnership is the *general partnership,* under which all partners are liable for the debts of the business. Since two or more individuals carrying on a business for profit may be held to be a partnership, even if they have no agreement, it is important to draw up a formal contract among the partners. Among other matters this agreement should specify the capital contributions to be made by the partners, their salaries or other compensation, how profits and losses are to be divided. If there is no agreement, partners share profits and losses equally, regardless of their capital contributions.

Partnerships are almost as easy to form as sole proprietorships. After drawing up the agreement, the partners may find it desirable to file a copy with the appropriate county official as a matter of record.

A *limited partnership* may be formed under the statutes of some states.[2] In such organizations there must always be at least one general partner, who has all the rights and responsibilities of the general partners described above. However, there are also one or more individuals designated as limited partners, who may not exercise any managerial rights but may share in the profits to an extent specified in the partnership agreement. Most important, the liability of a limited partner for losses and debts is restricted to the amount of his original contribution. Thus creditors of the partnership may not proceed against his personal assets.

Corporation

A *corporation* is a creation of the law. It is a legal entity that is empowered to own property, to contract debts, and to engage in certain activities. The classic definition usually quoted is that of Chief Justice Marshall in 1819:

[2] This is the customary form of organization used for Broadway plays and musicals. The "angels" (the people who put up the money) are made limited partners, while the playwright, producer, and possibly others are general partners. The agreements usually specify that the angels must be repaid their investment before sharing subsequent earnings with the general partners.

> A corporation is an artificial being, invisible, intangible, and existing only in contemplation of law. Being a mere creature of law, it possesses only those properties which the charter of its creation confers upon it, either expressly, or as incidental to its very existence. [*Dartmouth College v. Woodward,* 4 Wheaton (U.S.) 518 (1819).]

This definition should not obscure the fact that there are real, live people who have joined for a common purpose through the means of the corporation. The corporation is simply a remarkable device that permits this group of people to act and be treated as a single person.

How do we form a corporation? The first step is to select the *state of incorporation.* The choice depends primarily upon the state in which we plan to do business and the liberality of the state's laws pertaining to the corporation that it charters. Delaware is a favorite state of incorporation due to a combination of liberal laws and a large body of case law that establishes precedents for almost any corporate legal matter. There are also some differences among the states in the fee or organization tax charged for incorporation and in the annual franchise tax. Since these are relatively small in any case, they are not very influential in affecting the state of incorporation.

Once the state of incorporation is chosen, we must file a *certificate of incorporation* with the proper state official, usually the secretary of state. This specifies such matters as the name of the corporation, the location of the principal office, purposes, the amount of stock authorized, names and addresses of the incorporators and those subscribing to the stock, and the length of time for which the corporation is being formed.

When this document and the accompanying fees are accepted by the state official, he issues a *charter.* This document sets forth the relation between the state and the corporation as expressed in the general corporation laws of the state and the specifics of the certificate of incorporation.

The permissive nature of charters granted by Delaware is illustrated by the Certificate of Incorporation of Houdaille Industries, Inc.:

ARTICLE III

The nature of the business or purpose to be conducted or promoted is:

To engage in any lawful act or activity for which corporations may be organized under the General Corporation Law of Delaware.

Without in any way limiting the generality of the foregoing, to engage in any and every kind of business enterprise, venture or activity, whether manufacturing, sales, service or otherwise; to design, invent or develop; and to buy or otherwise acquire, sell or otherwise dispose of, and otherwise deal in and with real and personal property of every kind and character, tangible and intangible.

Before a corporation begins business, one other step is necessary. There must be a preliminary meeting of the incorporators or stockholders at which they adopt the *bylaws.* These are a set of regulations for the internal management of the corporation that specify such matters as the issuance and transfer of stock, the time and place of stockholders' and directors' meetings, and the selection and qualifications of directors, officers, and various committees.

Selection of the Form of Organization

Many factors determine the selection of the form of organization. Some of these have to do with finance, but others relate to the owners' attitudes toward risk and control. We shall see later that these same factors influence the types of funds selected to finance a company.

Suitability

The form of organization selected should be suitable to the amount and type of funds needed to finance the company. Thus, the Ma-and-Pa Grocery Store may not find the corporate form of organization suitable to its financial needs, while a company that plans to manufacture steel might find the corporate form of organization essential to obtain the necessary funds. Let us examine the aspects of proprietorships, partnerships, and corporations that influence their ability to raise funds.

Liability of Owners for Business Debts. Both sole proprietors and partners are fully and personally liable for business debts of their companies. In contrast, because a corporation has a legal existence separate from its owners, the latter have limited liability. In this respect they are like limited partners. Once they have fully paid for their shares in the corporation, they are not required to make further payments to the corporation or to its creditors. For this reason many find it much more attractive to be a stockholder in a corporation than a proprietor or partner. However, the owner-manager of a small corporation is likely to find that limited liability is more characteristic of textbooks than real life. Creditors may ask him personally to endorse the promises to pay off his corporation, so that he adds his personal assets as backing to the assets pledged by the corporation.

In the case of proprietorships and partnerships the right of business creditors to proceed against owners' personal assets is subject only to the *rule of marshalling of assets.* Under this rule business creditors have first claim on the assets of the business, and personal creditors have first claim on the personal assets of the owner. If the assets of the business are insufficient to satisfy the business creditors, they may proceed against any personal assets that remain after the claims of personal creditors have been satisfied. Consequently, when he has substantial personal assets, the prospective owner may elect to incorporate the business. Otherwise an incompetent partner might incur on behalf of the business excessive debts for which he would be personally liable. While creditors must levy against all partners, they may collect from any one. That partner may then try to collect from the other partners, but this is difficult if your partners are both incompetent and penniless.

Transferability of Ownership. Another reason that it may be less difficult to raise funds for a corporation is the relative ease of transferring ownership. A sole proprietor who wishes to sell his interests may have to search long and hard to find a buyer. If he wishes to sell only part of his equity, he must seek a suitable partner. A partner cannot transfer his interest to another by sale, gift, or will without the consent of all other partners. Partners remaining in the business have the right to choose their partners and need not accept the buyer which a retiring partner may have found for his share. There is value in marketability, and the poor marketability of ownership interests in proprietorships and partnerships hinders one's ability to raise funds for these types of organization.

In contrast, the stockholder of a corporation does not need the approval of other owners to sell his shares. He may sell all, or a portion, of his holdings without disturbing the continued existence of the corporation. If he holds shares in a large corporation, he probably can estimate the market price of his shares and sell them within a few minutes. While shareholders of small, family-owned, or *closed corporations,* as they are called, have the legal right to dispose of their shares as they choose, they may have almost as much difficulty finding buyers as do proprietors and partners. There are about 1,470,000 taxable corporations, but only some 2,800 have issues of securities traded on exchanges in the United States.[3] Possibly 4,000 to 5,000 stocks are traded in the over-the-counter market. Consequently, only a small fraction of corporations have securities that are readily marketable, although these few corporations hold the great bulk of corporate assets.

Permanence. Prospective investors are also interested in the continuity of the business. A proprietorship ceases with the death, withdrawal, or retirement of the proprietor. A partnership is legally terminated upon the withdrawal, death, bankruptcy, or insanity of any one of the partners. In many of these cases it may be necessary to liquidate the business to raise the cash to pay the share of assets due the partner or his heirs. Such a forced liquidation may substantially reduce the values of all the partners' holdings. Thus the uncertain life of a proprietorship and partnership also hampers the raising of funds from owners and creditors.

In contrast, a corporation may receive a perpetual charter or a charter for 20 to 40 years that is easily renewed. The legal existence of a corporation is not jeopardized by the withdrawal or death of any of its owners. When a stockholder dies, his shares go to his heirs.

In summary, the limited liability of owners, the transferability of ownership interests, and the permanence of the corporate form of business organization represent substantial advantages for raising large amounts of money. For these reasons we find most large businesses are incorporated. Some of these advantages dwindle as the size of business decreases, so that it may become as difficult to raise funds for a small corporation as for a proprietorship or partnership of equal size.

Income

Effect of Taxes on Employee-Owners. The owners of a business are interested in the total package of financial benefits that they can derive from a business. Because the owners of many small businesses are also the managers, the benefits they can receive as officers may be as important to them as the payments

---

[3] Securities and Exchange Commission, *34th Annual Report, 1968* (Washington, D.C.: U.S. Government Printing Office, 1969), p. 67.

they receive as owners. The form of business organization materially affects the tax position of the arrangements.

The essential point of difference is that corporations may treat stockholder-employees as employees for federal income tax purposes, whereas proprietorships and partnerships may not treat owners as employees. This means that owner-employees of corporations may obtain fringe benefits, such as stock option plans, trusteed benefit plans, and various types of insurance plans, and treat the cost of these plans as a tax-deductible expense to the corporation. However, if the same firms were organized and taxed as proprietorships or partnerships, the expenses of these plans would not be deductible for tax purposes. An example may help to clarify the point. With trusteed benefit plans (pension plans, profit-sharing plans, and stock-bonus plans), the employer may deduct the cost of the plan in computing the taxable income of the corporation. However, the employee does not pay personal income taxes until he actually receives cash payments from the plan. Thus he defers taxes from years of high earnings to retirement years when earnings are low and subject (he hopes) to lower tax rates. Moreover, he pays no tax during the intervening years on any earnings of the plan. To be eligible for this tax treatment the plan must be non-discriminatory; that is, it must not be for sole benefit of officers, shareholders, supervisors, or highly compensated employees. It must be available to a very substantial portion of all employees. Deductions may also be made under prescribed rules for group life insurance premiums, group hospitalization and medical care premiums, and payments made under wage continuation, accident, or health plans.

Where employees do not already participate in these fringe benefits, they would, in order for the cost to be deducted for tax purposes, have to be included in any plan that would also cover the owner-employees. This might be too expensive. However, if employees already have these benefits or will shortly have them, incorporation provides a means of giving the owner-employees the same benefits with a tax-deductible expense.

Effect of Taxes on Value of Firm. Recall our "simplified" model of the value of a firm's residual equity: that is, the ownership interests of a sole proprietor or general partner, or a corporation's common stock:

$$P = A/k$$

Income taxes affect the value, P, in two ways. First, the government (especially the Federal government) siphons off part of the cash flows through taxes. In view of this unpleasant fact of life, owners are really interested in cash flows *after taxes*. Naturally, they wish to minimize the amount taken by the government (thereby maximizing after-tax cash flows, A), or at least to postpone the taking. Our current simplified model is not equipped to determine the value to the owners of such postponement. Second, the government may alter the variance of cash flows after taxes, thus affecting the risk faced by owners and the percentage rate, k, used to reflect the risk. For example, there are organizations called Small Business Investment Companies which are permitted more favorable tax treatment of losses on their investments than other corporations. This provision reduces the downside risk for investors in SBICs, which are typically rather risky ventures. The lower variance of possible after-tax cash flows (a lower *k*) thus makes them more attractive (a higher *P*) to investors than they might otherwise be. This is by design, since the government wishes to encourage investments in small businesses through the SBICs.

These effects of income taxes on cash flows require that we have some understanding of basic tax provisions, although we can do no more than skim the surface. We shall consider only two aspects: the relative level of Federal income taxes on proprietorships, partnerships, and corporations and the special tax treatment of capital gains and losses.

(1) *Federal income tax.* Proprietors and partners must pay personal income taxes on their shares of the business income whether that income is received or allowed to remain in the business. Individuals in high personal tax brackets thus find it very difficult to accumulate sufficient earnings after taxes to reinvest and finance rapid growth. An illustration of the personal tax rates applicable to taxpayers filing joint returns is shown in Table 2-2. By "taxable income" we mean total income from wages, salaries, and other sources, less business and personal deductions, and less exemptions for dependents.

The corporate income tax rate is 22 percent on the first $25,000 of taxable income (normal tax) and a total rate of 48 percent on taxable income in excess of $25,000 (normal tax of 22 percent plus surtax of 26 percent). On a taxable

TABLE 2-2   Tax Rate Schedule for Married Taxpayers Filing Joint Returns, 1969

Dollar Amount of Taxable Income		Dollar Amount of Tax	
Not over $1,000		14% of the taxable income	
Over	*But not over*		*of excess over*
$1,000	$2,000	$140, plus 15%	$1,000
$2,000	$3,000	$290, plus 16%	$2,000
$3,000	$4,000	$450, plus 17%	$3,000
$4,000	$8,000	$620, plus 19%	$4,000
$8,000	$12,000	$1,380, plus 22%	$8,000
$12,000	$16,000	$2,260, plus 25%	$12,000
$16,000	$20,000	$3,260, plus 28%	$16,000
$20,000	$24,000	$4,380, plus 32%	$20,000
$24,000	$28,000	$5,660, plus 36%	$24,000
$28,000	$32,000	$7,100, plus 39%	$28,000
$32,000	$36,000	$8,660, plus 42%	$32,000
$36,000	$40,000	$10,340, plus 45%	$36,000
$40,000	$44,000	$12,140, plus 48%	$40,000
$44,000	$52,000	$14,060, plus 50%	$44,000
$52,000	$64,000	$18,060, plus 53%	$52,000
$64,000	$76,000	$24,420, plus 55%	$64,000
$76,000	$88,000	$31,020, plus 58%	$76,000
$88,000	$100,000	$37,980, plus 60%	$88,000
$100,000	$120,000	$45,180, plus 62%	$100,000
$120,000	$140,000	$57,580, plus 64%	$120,000
$140,000	$160,000	$70,380, plus 66%	$140,000
$160,000	$180,000	$83,580, plus 68%	$160,000
$180,000	$200,000	$97,180, plus 69%	$180,000
$200,000		$110,980, plus 70%	$200,000

income of $35,000, the corporate income tax could be calculated as follows:

$25,000 × 0.22 = $ 5,500   (Average rate: 10,300/35,000 = 29.4%)
 10,000 × 0.48 =   4,800
$35,000 $10,300

It is no easy task to compare the relative tax advantages of a partnership (or proprietorship) and a corporation. Rather than provide superficial examples, it seems preferable to suggest the nature and complexity of the problem. Other things being equal, the objective is to minimize the present value of future tax payments. This requires, first, an estimate of income. On this basis we can then judge the personal income taxes to be paid by the proprietor or individual partners over time, given the different levels of their incomes, personal deductions, and exemptions for dependents. Alternatively, we can examine the flow of income through the corporation:

Corporate Income Before Payments to Owners
   Minus: Salaries to owners (subject to personal income taxes)
   Minus: Fringe benefits (some subject to personal income taxes at a later date)
   Minus: Interest payments on any borrowings from owners (subject to personal income taxes)
   Equals: Income before taxes
   Minus: Corporate income taxes
   Equals: Net income after taxes
   Minus: Dividends (subject to personal income taxes)
   Equals: Retained earnings

Comparison of this total tax bill (both corporate and personal) to the total tax bill of the proprietorship or partnership requires analysis of the salaries, fringe benefits, method of financing, and dividend policy. Moreover, it is important not to take only one year, but to make some projections for the future.

The analytical problem is further complicated, since some corporations may elect to be taxed as partnerships. Stockholders pay personal income taxes on their proportionate share of the corporation's income before taxes, even though they may not receive any payments. The essential objective of this provision is to avoid the double taxation illustrated above, whereby the stream of corporate income is subject first to the corporate income tax and then to the personal income tax on dividends. It would be advantageous to elect this option when the owners desire to withdraw a substantial portion of the profits of the corporation. Thus owners retain the tax advantages of the corporate form of organization, such as the tax-deductible fringe benefits,[4] while gaining a possible tax advantage in being taxed as a partnership. A corporation may elect not to be taxed if it is a domestic corporation (i.e., chartered by the Federal or a state government) with only one class of stock held by not more than ten shareholders. All shareholders, including any subsequent new shareholders, must consent to the election. It is apparent that a large number of small corpora-

---

[4] However, amounts set aside under qualified pension plans are taxed to the owner-employee as ordinary income to the extent that they exceed 10 percent of the compensation paid or $2,500, whichever is smaller.

tions, especially those that are closely held, could comply with these requirements. Once made, an election is effective for subsequent years unless a new shareholder objects, or all shareholders consent to revoke the election, or the corporation ceases to meet the conditions required to make the election.

(2) *Taxation of capital gains and losses.* The special treatment accorded gains and losses realized on the sale of capital assets affects both the after-tax income of individual investors (sole proprietors, partners, and corporate shareholders) and the annual cash flows generated by corporations. A *capital asset* of an individual would include any securities or business interests, while a capital asset of a business firm is defined as property used in the business but not held for resale. Thus stocks and bonds owned by a chemical company for investment purposes are capital assets, but not when held for sale by a securities dealer.[5] When a capital asset is sold, a short-term gain is realized if it has been held for six months or less. Long-term capital gains or losses are recorded on capital assets held for more than six months. Individuals and corporate taxpayers must first net short-term gains and losses and then long-term gains and losses. The total net gain or loss is then determined by merging the net short-term gain or loss with the net long-term gain or loss.

Whereas any resulting net short-term gain is treated as "ordinary income" and taxed at the full rate, net long-term gains are given more favorable treatment. An individual may either count only one-half of the long-term capital gain and then apply his normal tax rate, or he may choose to pay 25 percent of the gain.[6] It is clear that a taxpayer will elect the first option if his marginal tax rate is below 50 percent and the second option if his marginal rate is above 50 percent. In much the same vein, a corporation will pay between 22 percent and 30 percent of its net long-term capital gains, compared to tax rates on ordinary income ranging from 22 percent to 48 percent.

Other things being equal, the favorable treatment of long-term capital gains leads investors and corporations to seek capital gains in preference to ordinary income. In evaluating common stock, shareholders would normally prefer a given cash flow in the form of a long-term capital gain than as taxable income. However, a shareholder faces the same problem of income versus risk as the corporate financial manager. Current cash dividends are valuable for the very reason that they *are* current and less risky than some future and uncertain capital gain that might be realized by selling the common stock. Similarly, the financial manager of a corporation may be faced with a choice between current, but relatively certain, income taxed at 48 percent versus uncertain future capital gains taxed at 30 percent, or even higher if rates are later changed. Thus the tax laws have an important effect upon the trade-off between risk versus return.

Risk

The unlimited liability borne by proprietors and partners affects more than the availability of financing. Even if an owner could finance a new business without

---

[5] There are special rules for determining capital gains or losses on depreciable assets, such as machinery. Some part of any gain on a sale may be treated as ordinary income and some part as a capital gain. For a fuller explanation of this and other tax matters see *Tax Guide for Small Business* and *Your Federal Income Tax*, both publications of the Internal Revenue Service.

[6] Ultimately, such treatment will be limited to the first $50,000 of an individual's capital-gain income.

outside help, he might still choose the corporate form of organization. Assume a man is going to operate a fishing boat for charter. If he tends to lose a tourist overboard now and then, he might not want to subject his personal assets to damage suits. To avoid this he could incorporate his enterprise and reduce his personal risk. Thus the act of incorporation skews the distribution of possible returns by eliminating the downside risk of a catastrophic loss of personal assets. On the other hand, if he has few personal assets, incorporation may not be worth the bother and expense. Although the bankruptcy laws of the states vary, many of his personal assets may be exempt from seizure by creditors. Consequently, if he is poor enough, he may not need to incorporate to protect his personal assets.

Control

A sole proprietor or partner can be sure that he will retain control or at least partial control of a business. A partner can even force an end to the partnership rather than share control with some individual whom he does not like or trust. In contrast, those in control of a corporation today may find themselves suddenly on the street tomorrow. Where the officers own less than half the voting stock, control of the corporation may be gained by outsiders. For example, one day in May, 1970, the management of Hartford Fire Insurance Company woke to find that International Telephone and Telegraph Corp. was making a public offer to exchange its preferred stock paying $2.25 per share in dividends for Hartford's common stock, then paying $1.40 per share in dividends. Though management may urge rejection of such offers, it may still ultimately lose control over the affairs of the business.

Corporations are also more subject to external control from government agencies than are proprietorships and partnerships. In large part, this results from the greater size and economic power of many corporations, plus the fact that the corporate mechanism was used in the early trust movement and in other attempts to gain monopoly power. Moreover, the separation of management and ownership characteristic of large corporations has raised concern that managers may not be fulfilling their responsibilities to the owners or their full range of obligations to society. Consequently, we have a body of rules and regulations that were designed to curb abuses of power by large corporations but that also affect the operations of small corporations.

Maneuverability

How quickly can the business organization respond to changes in its environment or to internal needs? The sole proprietor needs to consult no one. If he has an opportunity to buy property or to change his line of business, he can seize the chance immediately. Partners, on the other hand, may need to consult other partners, while corporate officers may need to obtain approval from their directors, possibly even their stockholders. It may be necessary to amend the bylaws before action can be taken. Of course, the speed of decision depends partly on the size of the organization, but the form of organization also establishes certain rules and regulations that affect the maneuverability of management.

Timing

There may be some tax advantage to starting a new business as a proprietorship and then incorporating at a later date. Individuals and corporations may carry a net operating loss back to reduce the taxable income of the three preceding years and forward to the five succeeding years. It is not at all uncommon for a new business to suffer losses in its early years, or even to fail. If a new business is established as a corporation, the losses during its first year can only be spread forward for five years. If it is established as a proprietorship, the loss can be spread over eight years (back three and forward five) to reduce the taxable personal income of the owner. This may have the effect of substantially reducing the tax payments of the owner during the early, crucial years.

Our development of general principles and theories of finance relates to all three of these forms of business, although it should be recognized that the application of principles will vary somewhat with the legal form of business involved. Since the corporation is particularly suited to the gathering and harboring of resources necessary to the mass production of many goods and services found in our industrial economy, some emphasis will be given to financial policies as they are developed in this legal medium.

It must be stressed that the proprietorships, partnerships, and corporations with which we deal are basically similar, in that they are firms whose owners are seeking to maximize the value of their residual interests (see Chapter 1). These business firms hold a collection of assets which are subject to the claims of two groups of people: *creditors,* that is, individuals or firms to whom money is owed; and *owners,* who claim whatever amount of assets is left unclaimed by the creditors. Let us not allow the legal form of business organization to obstruct our analysis of the effects of various financial policies upon these two groups. Policies do not affect the corporation as such any more than they affect as such a partnership or proprietorship. *Policies* injure or benefit creditors or owners, not the legal form. "A corporation is an artificial being, invisible, intangible, and existing only in contemplation of law." It feels no pain.

Summary

A financial manager must adjust to his environment or attempt to change it. At the inception of a new business he may influence the form of organization—proprietorship, partnership, or corporation. While unincorporated businesses far outnumber corporations, the latter dominate American business in terms of volume of sales and assets. Selection of the form of organization depends first upon the personal characteristics of the owners: their personal assets, attitude towards risk, desire to be assured of control, and aversion to the paperwork required of corporations. Each form of organization has inherent advantages. The corporate form is more suitable to raise large amounts of money because of the limited liability of owners, the ease of transferring shares, and its permanence. It shields the personal assets of owners from business claims. Yet proprietorships and partnerships offer advantages in assured control and maneuverability, and they may carry important tax advantages to a new business if it experiences losses in its early years. Tax considerations play a dominant role in this, as in many other areas of financial management. While the intricacies of personal and business taxes cannot be discussed adequately here, it should be clear that the form of organization can significantly affect the after-tax income of the owners. As financial managers, we must constantly be alert to the tax implications of decisions and ask before we act.

Questions

1/ How do you explain the large proportion of sole proprietorships in the agriculture, retail trade, and service business?

2/ If the owner must endorse the notes of his corporation to borrow, is there any remaining advantage to his limited liability?

3/ Beginning after 1963, the normal corporate tax rate was cut from 30 percent to 22 percent, while the total rate on taxable income over the surtax exemption was progressively cut from 52 percent to 48 percent.
   a. Other things being equal, what was the probable effect of this change upon the form of business organization selected by business firms?
   b. What are the economic implications of the proportionately greater reduction for small corporations and the general reduction for all corporations?

4/ Without specific reference to tax tables, under what circumstances would you think it advisable for a corporation to be taxed as a partnership?

5/ What is the purpose of loss carry-back and carry-forward provisions?

6/ Assume that expected pre-tax cash flows of a business firm are normally distributed.
   a. If it is a proprietorship or partnership, what is the effect of the graduated personal tax rates (Table 2-2) upon the expected after-tax returns of the owners?
   b. If it is a corporation, what is the effect of the corporate tax rates upon the expected after-tax returns available for reinvestment or distribution to the owners?
   c. Given that owners are risk averse, what conclusions can you draw concerning the effect of the tax structure upon investors' willingness to undertake risky investments?

Problems

1/ At what level of taxable income would the corporate income tax and the personal income tax paid by a sole proprietor filing a joint return (Table 2-2) be equal? Would you necessarily conclude that above this point he should incorporate and below this point maintain a sole proprietorship? Why or why not?

2/ What is the Federal income tax payable by a corporation with a taxable income of $30,000; of $60,000? What is the percentage of the tax to the taxable income in each case?

3/ You and the other shareholder of a small corporation are considering the desirability of electing to be taxed as a partnership. You hold equal amounts of the common stock. The taxable income of the corporation is $35,000, and the entire income after corporate income taxes is paid in dividends. Assume that both partners have allowable deductions and exemptions from gross income equal to $3,350 each and that the income received from the business is the only source of income for each. Each files a joint return. What effect would the adoption of the election have on (a) the total dollar amount of taxes paid by both owners and the corporation and (b) the average tax rate paid? (Ignore the dividends credit.)

Selected References

ARSHT, S. S. and W. K. STAPLETON, "Delaware General Corporation Law: 1969," *Business Lawyer*, 25 (November, 1969), pp. 287–98.

"Close Corporation," *Law and Contemporary Problems*, 18, (Autumn, 1953).

DAVIES, R. M. and M. H. LAWRENCE, *Choosing a Form of Business Organization*. Durham, N.C.: Duke University Law School, 1963.

GIBSON, G. D., "Selecting the Form of Entity for a Small Business," *Business Lawyer*, 18 (November, 1962), pp. 100–113.

HETTENHOUSE, "Cost/Benefit Analysis of Executive Compensation," *Harvard Business Review*, 48 (July–August, 1970), pp. 114–24.

HOLZMAN, R. S., *Tax Basis for Managerial Decisions*. New York: Holt, Rinehart, and Winston, Inc., 1965.

LEWELLEN, W. G., "Executives Lose Out, Even with Options," *Harvard Business Review*, 46 (January–February, 1968), pp. 127–42.

MAER, C. M., JR. and R. A. FRANCIS, "Whether To Incorporate," *Business Lawyer*, 22 (April, 1967), pp. 571–76.

RABY, W. L., *The Income Tax and Business Decisions*. Englewood Cliffs, N.J.: Prentice-Hall, Inc., 1964.

"The Role of Corporate Taxation in the American Economy." *American Economic Review* (Papers and Proceedings) 44, (May, 1954), pp. 486–542.

SMITH D. T., *Effects of Taxation: Corporate Financial Policy*. Boston, Mass.: Graduate School of Business Administration, Harvard University, 1952.

"Tax Reform," *American Economic Review*, 53 (May, 1963), pp. 314–59. Papers by D. T. Smith, R. A. Musgrave, N. B. Ture, J. F. Due, E. R. Rolph, and C. A. Hall, Jr.

Risk versus Return: An Overview

3

In the first chapter we concluded that as financial managers our normative objective is to maximize the value of the owners' equity. In attempting to achieve this result, we are faced with a trade-off between risk and return. Usually, a high expected return for equity can be gained only at the cost of assuming a high risk on the behalf of owners. A "safe" return is also very likely to be a low return. If we are the owners of the business, we must decide whether we wish to eat well or sleep well.

Before plunging into the details of financial management, let us first gain an overview of the process. Not only will this be helpful in itself, but it will also provide a preview of the material in the coming chapters and show its relevance to the basic task of the financial manager.

To focus attention on the fundamental issues, let us make two simplifying assumptions. First, let us assume that expected profits or earnings are equal to expected cash flows. The example to be used is constructed so that it works out that way.[1] Second, let us assume a happy world in which there are no income taxes. This is not consistent with the discussion of Chapter 2, but it will simplify the initial discussion if we do not have to bother with taxes.

Consider that we have $100. We have borrowed $20 from our brother-in-law at 5 percent, largely because he does not know that current money rates are a good deal higher, and have put up $80 of our own money. Since we have available an old shack by the road, we decide to set up a hot dog stand. We spend $100 for hot dogs and operating costs and eventually over the year sell them for $110. Exhibit 3-1 is a diagram of the cash-flow system of our hot dog stand.

EXHIBIT 3-1   An Overview in a No-Tax World

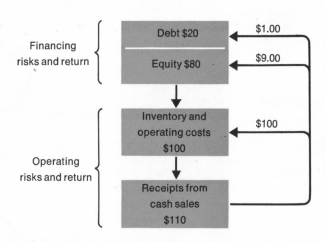

(Obviously, all of these figures could be made larger and more realistic simply by adding zeros.) At the end of the year we have $110, of which we reinvest $100 in the business. (Of course, in actual practice this is a continual process during the year.) From the remaining $10, we give $1 [5% × $20] to our brother-in-law and keep $9. The return on our initial equity investment is 11.25 percent [$9/$80]. This return is a product of two factors. First, we produce $10 of earnings on the invested assets of $100. This was an operating return derived from running the hot dog stand. Second, the manner in which we divided the $10 between creditors and owners affected the owner's return. Based upon the return on total assets, the firm earned 10 percent [$10/$100], but we somehow managed to produce a higher rate of return for the owners. Therefore, the ultimate return of 11.25 percent for the owners was a product of operating and financing activities, each of which involved risk. Let us examine the factors that determine the operating return and the financing return and the accompanying risks.

---

[1] For many financial decisions the distinction between cash flows and reported profits (accounting income) is critical. See especially the discussion of capital budgeting in Chapter 8. However, as we shall see in Chapter 22, over the long life of a firm, estimates of future profits after taxes may be reasonably close to expected cash flows. Therefore, in developing a model for the value of the firm, we may use expected income as a proxy for expected cash flows. In this chapter we assume expected profits and expected cash flows to be equal simply to avoid a discussion which is best treated later in Chapter 22.

Operating Risk and Return

When we start a dollar on its way through the cash-flow system by investing it in inventory, we hope that it returns to the cash reservoir accompanied by some additional pennies. These additional pennies represent the amounts that customers are willing to pay over and above our out-of-pocket costs for the product. The more pennies that come back for each dollar the happier we are. Also the more times we can send that dollar back through the system within a given time period, the happier we are. Our joy is thus a product of the pennies collected per dollar and the number of trips each dollar makes through the cash-flow system during a given time period. We shall refer to these basic determinants of the rate of return from operations as *margin* and *turnover.*

There are three factors that affect margin and turnover: *sales, net operating income,* and *net operating assets.* These data can be readily identified on most income statements and balance sheets.

Sales. It would be preferable to use net sales rather than gross sales, which would normally include some returns and allowances.

Net operating assets. These are all the assets (net of allowances for bad debts, depreciation, and so on) used in the operation of the business to produce the normal, operating income. In contrast, we would class as a non-operating asset a piece of property leased to another party or securities held for long-term investment purposes. The sum of the operating and non-operating assets is equal to total assets. We shall be concerned with the *turnover of operating assets,* that is,

$$\frac{\text{Sales}}{\text{Net operating assets}} = \text{Turnover}$$

Net operating income. This includes all net income before taxes produced by operating assets and excludes any items of non-operating income, such as rental income from leased property, and non-operating expenses, such as interest payments. In other words, the operating assets produce a stream of income known as operating income, and the nonoperating assets produce a stream of income known as non-operating income. In most cases there are few, if any, non-operating assets, and there is something to be said for focusing our analysis on our success in producing earnings in our main line of business. We are concerned with the *net operating margin* (or "margin" for short), which is defined as the ratio of the net operating income to sales, and with the final result, the *earning power,* the ratio of net operating income to the net operating assets. In other words,

$$\frac{\text{Net operating income}}{\text{Sales}} = \text{Net operating margin}$$

$$\frac{\text{Net operating income}}{\text{Net operating assets}} = \text{Earning power}$$

The more we make on each dollar of sales and the more sales we make for each dollar of operating assets, the greater will be our rate of return on each dollar of operating assets. (If we were keeping our books on a cash basis, we would say, "The more we accumulate on each trip of the dollar, and the more trips per dollar, the greater will be the rate of cash accumulation in relation to the total number of dollars in the various operating assets.") We may make this truism even more impressive by putting it into a formula:

$$\text{Earning power} = \text{Margin} \times \text{Turnover}$$

$$\frac{\text{Net operating income}}{\text{Net operating assets}} = \frac{\text{Net operating income}}{\text{Sales}} \times \frac{\text{Sales}}{\text{Net operating assets}}$$

More concisely,

$$EP = Y/O = Y/S \cdot S/O, \text{ where} \tag{3-1}$$

EP = earning power, or rate of return on total operating assets;

Y = net operating income before taxes;

S = net sales; and

O = net operating assets.

Let us apply this formula to our hot dog stand. Assume that of the initial $100 of invested capital, we use $80 for hot dogs and retain $20 in cash for making change and meeting emergencies.[2] Our annual sales are $110. If we can agree that a fair salary for the owner-operator would be $20, we are left with an annual net operating income of $10.

Income Statement

Sales		$110
Operating expenses:		
Cost of goods sold	$80	
Salary	20	100
Net operating income		$ 10

Balance Sheet

Assets		Liabilities & Equity	
Cash	$20	Liabilities	$ 0
Inventory	80	Owners' equity	100
		Total liabilities	
Total assets	$100	and owners' equity	$100

Fitting these figures into the formula, we find that our margin is 9.09 percent, our turnover 1.1 times per year, and our earning power, 10.0 percent per annum.

Earning power	=	Margin	×	Turnover
EP	=	Y/S	×	S/O
10/100	=	10/110	×	110/100
10.00%	=	9.09%	×	1.1

[2] At the end of the year after payment of salaries we would have $90 in cash, so that average net operating assets for the year are $95; i.e., $\frac{\$90 + \$100}{2}$. However, it is simpler to use the $100 figure for our illustration.

If we are willing to invest $100 to obtain an expected annual cash flow of $10 over the foreseeable future, what does this say about the risk that we perceive in this venture? Because we are in a no-tax world, the net operating income, Y, is the same as the annual cash flows, A. If the venture is worth just $100 to us and no more, the value of the firm, V, is $100, and we have

$$V = A/k = Y/k$$

$$\$100 = \$10/k$$

$$k = 0.10 \text{ or } 10\%$$

As an aside, suppose that we believe that the cash flows are quite certain, so that the discount rate, k, should be only 8 percent. If the asking price for the firm is still only $100, we have found a $25 bargain. Our estimated value is $125 [$10/0.08] compared to the purchase price of $100.

Let us assume, however, that we do not have a bargain, but merely a fair investment offering an earning power, EP, of 10 percent. How do we go about improving this earning power? Clearly, we must do something to change either the annual cash flows or the investment in operating assets, if we are to produce an earning power greater than the rate of return of 10 percent demanded for investments of this grade of risk. Since the change in earning power must be the product of a change in either margin or turnover, or both, our attention must then be directed towards these components of earning power:

$$\Delta Y/\Delta O = \Delta Y/\Delta S \cdot \Delta S/\Delta O$$

However, we must not incur any investment in the hot dog business that earns less than 10 percent; that is, $\Delta Y/\Delta O \geq k$. Moreover, we need to be wary of changes in margin or turnover that might involve *more* risk than 10 percent. Such changes demand additional earning power to make them worthwhile.

A detailed veiw of the components of margin and turnover is presented in Exhibit 3-2, a chart generally associated with the DuPont Company. Prime control over the net operating margin is usually considered the role of cost accounting. The financial manager is more directly concerned with decisions affecting working capital and fixed assets, as shown in the lower half of the diagram. These aspects of earning power are covered in Chapters 5–8. Estimates of investments in working capital and fixed assets are merged with estimates of sales and operating expenses by the financial manager into various budgets, the subject of Chapter 9.

Given this background, let us now consider how we might go about improving the earning power of our business, subject to the constraints set forth above.

1. **Methods of Improving Margin.** We can better the margin in two ways: (a) by raising sales more than operating expenses, or (b) by cutting operating expenses more than sales.

a. *Increasing sales more than expenses.* By hiring a helper or by offering larger hot dogs at a higher price we might be able to increase sales in relation to expenses. Possibly by offering customers a wide variety of condiments we can raise the price of hot dogs so that sales increase to $120. If our stock of

EXHIBIT 3-2   Relationship of Factors Affecting Earning Power

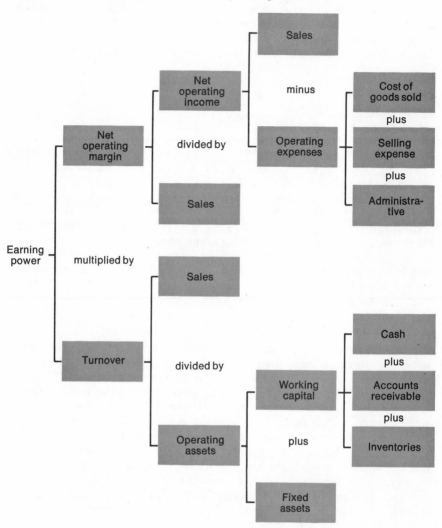

condiments requires an investment of $9, our operating assets rise to $109 and turnover remains unchanged. However, since the rise in sales exceeds the increase in condiments used ($5), our margin and earning power rise substantially. If we can properly assume that there has been no change in the risk of doing business, the value of the firm rises to $150.00 [$15.00/0.10]. The $9 investment in condiments amply meets our constraint that $\Delta Y/\Delta O \geq 10$ percent:

$$\Delta Y/\Delta O = \$5/\$9 > 0.10$$

1a. *Improve margin by increasing sales more than expenses*

		Before		After
Sales		$110		$120
Operating expenses:				
Cost of goods sold	$80		$80	
Salary	20		20	
Condiments used	0	100	5	105
Net operating income		$ 10		$ 15
Net operating assets		$100		$109
Margin		9.09%		12.5 %
Turnover		1.1		1.1
Earning power		10.0 %		13.76%

b. *Reducing expenses more than sales.* There are various means of cutting operating expenses without suffering a corresponding reduction in sales. We may find that sales are so few during certain hours of the day that it does not pay to keep the stand open. By closing during these hours and reducing our salary by $5 (and working elsewhere during this time), we may sell fewer hot dogs, and so reduce sales by 10 percent to $99 and cost of goods sold to $72. This will permit us to lower our investment in net operating assets to $92: $20 in cash and $72 in inventory. Since the $11 decline in sales is accompanied by a $13 drop in operating expenses, our net operating income is better by $2 and earning power has increased to 13.04 percent, in spite of a slight decline in turnover.

1b. *Improve margin by reducing expenses more than sales*

		Before		After
Sales		$110		$99
Operating expenses:				
Cost of goods sold	$80		$72	
Salary	20	100	15	87
Net operating income		$ 10		$12
Net operating assets		$100		$92
Margin		9.09%		12.12%
Turnover		1.1		1.08
Earning power		10.0 %		13.04%

It might be noted that in both of these cases, (1a) and (1b), a change in sales affects the turnover rate. However, in these illustrations that change is less significant than the improvement in the margin.

There are many examples of the application of one or the other of these two methods of improving the margin. Meat markets find that the selling prices of boneless meat may be increased by more than enough to offset the added labor cost required to remove the bones.[3] A grocery discount store is able to cut prices, but still maintain earning power because he may "cut the number of items he carries to perhaps 6,500 from the normal 8,000. Often, too, he shortens trading hours to keep down labor costs. Generally, the lower prices prove a potent appeal."[4] The approach suggested in (1b) above was followed by

[3]"Make Bigger Profits with Boneless Cuts of Meat," *Progressive Grocer,* January, 1961, pp. 68–69.
[4]"The Grocery Business," *Forbes,* 104 (November 1, 1969), p. 36.

Champion Paper & Fiber Co., which dropped "nearly 100 different grades of paper to concentrate on the 20% that provide about 80% of profits."[5] Although this method may not be as heart-warming to the owners as an increase in sales, the greater rate of return should provide some soothing effect.

2. **Methods of Improving Turnover.** There are two methods by which we may attain a higher turnover of operating assets: (a) raise sales relatively more than operating assets, or (b) lower operating assets relatively more than sales.

a. *Increasing sales relatively more than operating assets.* We may expand our stand or offer hamburgers as well as hot dogs. By offering credit, we might expand annual sales to $132. The expansion is not an unmixed blessing, since we need a bookkeeper at $4, and accounts receivable build to $10, with a consequent rise in the investment in net operating assets to $110 from $100. Although the margin remains constant, the earning power is increased by reason of the higher turnover.

2a. *Improve turnover by increasing sales relatively more than operating assets*

		Before		After
Sales		$110		$132
Operating expenses:				
Cost of goods sold	$80		$96	
Salary	20	100	24	120
Net operating income		$ 10		$ 12
Net operating assets		$100		$110
Margin		9.09%		9.09%
Turnover		1.1		1.2
Earning power		10.0%		10.9%

Since $\Delta Y/\Delta O = \$2/\$10 > 10$ percent, the investment in accounts receivable is worthwhile if there is no significant change in the risk of doing business. Whether a change in risk occurs depends upon the nature of the receivables. If a number will prove uncollectible (largely from our relatives), future cash flows will be more variable than in the days when we demanded cash on the barrelhead. But even if k goes to 11 percent, the value of the firm improves:

$$V = \$12/0.11 = \$109.09$$

Thus if 11 percent represents an "outer-limit" guess of the change in variability in earnings and risk of the venture, the offer of credit appears worthwhile.

An application of this means of improving turnover is the substitution of jetliners for piston-engined airliners. Because of their greater speed and capacity the jets are capable of producing three times as much gross revenue as the fastest piston-driven plane.[6] Improvement of turnover is also sought by the manufacturer who introduces better scheduling of production in order to increase production and sales without raising operating assets. A retailer may substitute fast-moving items for stock with a lower turnover and improve his overall turnover and earning power.

[5]"Papermaker Takes Stern Measures," *Business Week,* June 24, 1961, p. 73.
[6]*Wall Street Journal,* October 15, 1958, p. 1.

b. *Reducing operating assets relatively more than sales.* On the other hand, we could reduce our investment in operating assets by paring cash or inventory. Reduction of cash involves a liquidity risk, the danger that we may run out of cash and not be able to pay our bills on time. Too great a reduction in cash will make the firm more risky by placing it several steps nearer bankruptcy. If we can arrange with our supplier to deliver more frequently without raising the price of hot dogs, we can cut our inventory level. In effect, our supplier is carrying our inventory, although we also increase our risk of running out of stock and losing sales. Let us say that a combination of reduced cash and inventory enables a decrease in operating assets to $80 from $100. Now we can withdraw $20 from the business and put it to work elsewhere, while the remaining $80 will earn 12.5 percent.

2b. *Improved turnover by reducing operating assets relatively more than sales*

		Before		After
Sales		110		$110
Operating expenses:				
Cost of goods sold	$80		$80	
Salary	20	100	20	100
Net operating income		$ 10		$ 10
Net operating assets		$100		$ 80
Margin		9.09%		9.09%
Turnover		1.1		1.38
Earning power		10.0%		12.5%

The same effect is achieved when a manufacturer relies on his suppliers for inventory. It may improve earning power to buy frequently in small lots from a steel warehouse rather than to purchase large lots less often directly from the steel producer, even though the factory price is lower than the warehouse price. The advantage of lowered inventories also explains in part the movement of canmakers to manufacture cans in the plants of their large customers. Not only is turnover higher, but savings in handling and shipping costs improve the margin. Obviously, some portion of the greater earning power is sacrificed in the form of lower prices to the brewers.[7]

3. **Changes Affecting both Margin and Turnover.** Usually a change in policy that affects the margin will also affect the turnover. This is particularly true when we change our selling price. For example, we might try lowering our selling prices with the hope of increasing our turnover enough to offset the decline in margin. The basic issue is how much we will increase sales, or, as the economist would say, how elastic is our demand. Taking a leaf from the book of the discount groceries, we might also eliminate slow-moving items from our line so that inventories do not rise as rapidly as sales. A possible result is depicted below. The final decision will depend upon our estimate of chances of bettering sales to that extent and the possibilities of increases in costs that might accompany the higher sales.

[7]"Canmakers Head off Do-it-yourself Packers," *Business Week,* September 20, 1969, p. 53.

3. *Possible effect of decrease in price on earning power*

	Before		After	
Sales		$110		$160
Operating expenses:				
Cost of goods sold	$80		$127	
Salary	20	100	20	147
Net operating income		$ 10		$ 13
Net operating assets		$100		$120
Margin		9.09%		8.13%
Turnover		1.1		1.33
Earning power		10.0%		10.83%

The fruits of experimentation with the margin and turnover are clearly evident in the rise of the discount house. In order to increase sales the discount house reduces prices below those charged by stores that levy a traditional, full-cost markup. Discounters often lease their buildings and fixtures and spend considerably less than traditional merchants to furnish their stores.

TABLE 3-1   Earning Power and Leverage in Selected Industries (Dollar amounts in billions)

	Manu-facturing	Retail Trade	Electric and Gas Companies
Income statement items:			
(A) Sales	$503.0	$183.9	$25.9
(B) Earnings before taxes (EBT)	$ 41.9	$ 5.0	$ 4.4
(C) Earnings after taxes (EAT)	$ 24.4	$ 3.4	$ 2.5
Balance sheet items:			
Current liabilities	$ 84.0	$ 24.0	$ 6.8
Long-term debt	65.9	13.1	39.4
(D) Capital stock & retained earnings	221.6	31.2	34.1
(E) Total assets/liabilities and capital	$371.5	$ 68.3	$80.3
Earning power:			
Net operating margin (B/A)	8.4%	2.7%	17.0%
× Turnover (A/E)	1.36 times	2.69 times	0.32 times
= Earning power (B/E)	11.3%	7.3%	5.5%
Financial leverage:			
Percentage of EBT to owners' equity (B/D)	18.9%	16.0%	12.9%
Percentage of EAT to owners' equity (C/D)	11.0%	10.9%	7.3%

Source: Internal Revenue Service, U.S. Treasury Department, *Statistics of Income, 1965 U.S. Business Tax Returns* (Washington, D.C.: U.S. Government Printing Office, 1968), pp. 243, 245, 247. Total assets include a small amount of non-operating assets, and net operating income includes some non-operating items.

The combination of high sales and low investment in operating assets give the discount houses a very high turnover of operating assets. At the same time discounters cut expenditures on credit services, delivery, and great numbers of sales people. As a result they hold expenses to about 20 percent of sales, compared to 35 percent for more traditional stores.[8] The combination of high turnover and controlled margin has enabled discount houses to gain a very respectable earning power. By the same token, when turnover drops during recessions, some discounters find it difficult to survive.

If the earning power of assets is relatively low in one field and high in another (after allowances for differences in risk), investible funds will eventually flow from one to the other. This movement of funds will tend to equate the earning powers of businesses, even though they may be in different lines of endeavor (but equally risky). For concerns to have similar earning powers we must expect to find that those with a relatively high turnover have a relatively low margin and, conversely, that those with a low turnover have a high margin. This tendency is demonstrated in Table 3-1, which shows composite data for corporations in three major industries in a recent year. The low net operating margin (2.7 percent) for the retail trade as compared with manufacturing is offset in part by a much higher turnover, so that in the end the earning powers are more similar. The highest margin and the lowest turnover are found in the electric power and gas industry. In spite of the very low turnover the high margin produces an earning power about equal to that of the retail trade. We would expect it to be somewhat lower, because shareholders face less risk. We shall see in the following section how the financial managers in the electric power and gas industry are able to convert an earning power on assets of 5.5 percent into a rate of earnings before taxes on the owners' equity of 12.9 percent.

Financing Risk and Return

The second step toward maximization of the present value of the owners' investment is to arrange sources of funds so that the owners obtain as high a return as possible out of the earnings of the business without assuming undue risks. We shall see, however, that certain risks are involved in this process, and that we will have to compromise between income and risk.

Let us return to our hot dog stand. In the original case (Exhibit 3-1) we had $10 of net operating income, of which $1 was used for interest on the debt, while the remaining $9 was allocated to the owner's equity. Although the return on total operating assets was 10 percent, the return on the owner's equity was 11.25 percent [$9/$80]. Somehow we have magnified the earning power of the firm to produce a higher return on the owner's equity. The difference between the earning power of 10 percent and the return on the owner's equity of 11.25 percent is produced by *financial leverage*. If we let the rate of return on the book value of the owner's equity be designated as K and the leverage factor as L, then

$$K = EP \cdot L \qquad (3-2)$$

[8] *Business Week*, December 1, 1962, p. 80.

Solving for L we have

$$11.25\% = 10\% \ (L)$$

$$L = 1.125$$

In other words, in this case the earning power is magnified by 1.125 times to produce the rate of return on the book value of the owner's equity.

Source of Financial Leverage

Where does the leverage factor of 1.125 come from? Had the owners furnished all of the funds for the business, the rate of return on their equity would have equaled the earning power, or 10 percent. In this case, however, we furnished only 8/10ths of the total funds, while our brother-in-law furnished the remaining fraction. Based upon our contributions to total capital, we should have received 8/10ths of the $10 earnings, or $8. In terms of the $20 that our brother-in-law furnished he should have received 2/10ths of the earnings, or $2. However, our contract with him required us to make fixed maximum payments of only $1. In this manner we gained an extra benefit by the difference between his "financial-structure" share of the net operating income and the amount that we were obligated to pay him.

To put it another way, we borrowed from our brother-in-law at 5 percent and put his money to work at 10 percent. As residual owners we received the extra $1 we made on the use of his money. The funds that we invest and the earnings that we allow to remain in the business is termed our *equity*, or interest in the assets. Since it is on the strength of this equity that we are able to secure money from an outsider, we are said to be *trading on the equity*—that is, we have financed a portion of the assets of the company with funds bearing a limited return. The term more commonly used in financial circles is *financial leverage*. The legal form of the business does not affect the existence of leverage. *The important factor in obtaining leverage is that we are utilizing funds for which we are paying a limited* (i.e. *fixed*) return.

The *leverage factor* represents the ratio of the earnings actually received by the residual owners to the amount they "should" have received based solely on their proportionate contribution of funds to the business. This ratio can be reduced to a formula by letting Q equal the proportion of total assets financed by the residual owners' equity. Earnings actually received by the owners is the sum of their financial-structure share, QY, *plus* the difference between (a) what the creditors' financial-structure share would be, $(1 - Q)Y$, and (b) what they *actually* receive in interest, I. Thus the ratio of what the residual owners actually receive to their share produced by the financial structure, or the leverage factor is:

$$L = \frac{QY + [(1 - Q) \ Y - I]}{QY} \tag{3-3}$$

Inserting the data from our example, we then have

$$L = \frac{(0.8)(\$10) + [(1 - 0.8)(\$10) - \$1]}{(0.8)(\$10)} = \frac{\$8 + \$1}{\$8}$$

Now we can see how the financial managers of the electric power and gas companies shown in Table 3-1 were able to convert an earning power of 5.5 percent on total assets into a rate of earnings before taxes on capital stock and retained earnings of 12.9 percent. They used favorable financial leverage. They had almost $1.35 of debt for every $1 of capital stock and surplus. Because the rate of earnings on the investment of the residual owners was improved by leverage, we can conclude that the creditors were paid less on the money they invested than the corporations earned on these funds. As we shall see later, the creditors are willing to put up with this apparently unfair treatment because their prior claim on earnings and assets reduces their risk of loss.

Unfavorable Financial Leverage

Looking at equation (3-3), we can see that leverage need not always be favorable for the residual owners. In this example $(1 - Q)Y > I$, but that may not be so. Had our brother-in-law drawn a hard bargain and insisted on interest payments of 12 percent, the financial leverage would have been unfavorable, because interest payments would have been $2.40 [12% × $20], whereas the earnings on his share of the financial structure would have been only $2. In this case the leverage factor would have been:

$$L = \frac{(0.8)(\$10) + (1 - 0.8)(\$10) - \$2.40}{(0.8)(\$10)} = 0.95.$$

Thus the earning power of 10 percent would have been levered *down* into a lower rate of return on the owner's equity; that is,

$$K = EP \cdot L = 0.10 \times 0.95 = 0.095, \text{ or } 9.5\%.$$

This is an important point. Through the use of leverage we fix a rate of return that must be paid on invested funds before any payments can be made to the residual owners. When we earn more than that rate, the excess goes to the residual owners who thereby earn a higher rate of return than they would have without the use of leverage. When we earn less than the rate we pay for funds, the owners must make up the difference out of their share of the earnings. They then would be better off with no leverage.

Determinants of Leverage

What determines the size of L? We can see this better by simplifying equation (3-3)[9]:

$$L = \frac{1}{Q}\left(\frac{Y - I}{Y}\right). \tag{3-3a}$$

The two factors influencing financial leverage are apparent in the two terms of the equation. First, the lower the ratio of residual owners' equity to total funds supplied $(1/Q)$, the higher the leverage factor. In contrast, if the residual owners supply all the funds, we have a leverage factor of one. Second, the lower

[9]This is the form developed by Pearson Hunt, "A Proposal for Precise Definitions of 'Trading on the Equity' and 'Leverage'," *Journal of Finance*, 16 (September, 1961), pp. 379–81.

the proportion of operating income devoted to interest payments $\left(\frac{Y - I}{Y}\right)$, the higher the leverage factor. It would be highly desirable not to have to pay anything for borrowed funds, both because of the favorable leverage and the reduction of risk of going bankrupt. (We could still go bankrupt through inability to repay the debt when it comes due.)

These determinants of the leverage factor are covered in greater detail in later chapters. The proportion of assets that should be financed by creditors and by owners' equity is examined in Part III: Planning the Financial Structure. The various arrangements that we make with suppliers of funds are examined in Part IV (Managing Short- and Intermediate-Term Funds) and Part V (Managing Long-Term Funds).

Introduction of Taxes

Since taxes are present in the real world, let us now consider their effect. Assume that we incorporate our small business, issuing eight shares of common stock to represent our $80 investment. Let us assume that at our scale of operations the corporate tax rate is 25 percent. The beauty of debt is that the interest is a tax-deductible expense. At the 25 percent rate, this does not make a big difference, but it helps:

Effect of tax-deductible interest

	Without interest as a deductible expense	With interest as a deductible expense
Net operating income	$10.00	$10.00
Interest expense		1.00
Earnings before taxes	10.00	9.00
Taxes (25%)	2.50	2.25
Earnings after taxes	7.50	6.75
Interest expense	1.00	—
Earnings available for common stock	$ 6.50	$ 6.75
Rate of return on book value of common equity	8.13%	8.44%
No. of shares of common stock	8	8
Earnings per share (EPS)	$ 0.81	$ 0.84

The extra 25 cents available for the owners is a result of the fact that the corporation paid 25 cents less in the way of income taxes because of the tax shield provided by the $1.00 interest charge. In effect the government absorbed one-fourth of the interest charge and the owners the rest. Clearly, at the tax rates of 48 percent applicable to larger enterprises debt becomes even more attractive.

Adjustment of formula (3-3a) for taxes is very simple. Let us be very erudite and let the Greek letter *theta*, θ, represent one minus the tax rate; that is 75 percent in this case $[1 - 0.25]$. This is the after-tax rate of cost of interest or other expenses to the owners. Leverage adjusted for taxes, L_a, is then:

$$L_a = \frac{1}{Q} \frac{(Y - I)}{Y} \theta. \qquad (3\text{-}4)$$

The combined effect of earning power and financial leverage upon the after-tax rate of return on the book value of the residual owners' equity, K_a, can then be shown as

$$K_a = EP \cdot L_a, \quad \text{or as} \qquad (3\text{-}5)$$

$$K_a = EP \cdot L \cdot \theta. \qquad (3\text{-}5a)$$

Using the data in our example:

$$K_a = (0.10)(1.125)(0.75) = 0.084375, \text{ or } 8.44\%$$

What is the effect of financial leverage upon the value of the firm? Before the introduction of taxes, we discounted the infinite and constant stream of cash flows generated by an unlevered firm (no debt) at a pretax discount rate, k. Since we now wish to convert all data to an after-tax basis, we should discount the after-tax cash flows, $Y\theta$, at the after-tax rate, k_a. As a reflection of the applicable tax rate, this discount rate must be 7.5 percent, rather than the pre-tax rate of 10 percent. The value of the unlevered firm, V, can be seen to be:

$$V = Y\theta / k_a$$

$$= \frac{(\$10)(0.75)}{0.075} \qquad (3\text{-}6)$$

$$= \$100$$

Now let us determine the value, V_L, of the levered firm. The levered firm is generating total cash flows of $7.75 (compared to the previous $7.50) to be distributed in part to creditors ($1.00), with the remainder being available to the owners ($6.75). It is producing the same cash flows as it did before ($7.50) *plus* an extra $0.25 that is a direct result of the government's permitting us to deduct interest on the bonds for tax purposes. The probabilities of generating the $7.50 are the same as in the case of the unlevered firm; nothing has changed in that respect. Consequently, that portion of the $7.75 should be discounted at k_a, as before. But the extra $0.25 falls into a different category of risk. It is as certain as the tax shield provided by the interest payment — which, in turn, is as certain as the interest payment itself. The risk associated with the interest payment is best measured by the market yield on the bonds. Hence, the stream of cash flows produced by the tax shield should be discounted at the market yield on the bonds to determine the value of that tax shield to the firm. Let the annual interest payment on the bond be designated iD, where i is the yield on the bonds (in this case, 5 percent) and D is the dollar amount of bonds outstanding (in this case, $20). Our payments to the Internal Revenue Service are lower by the corporate tax rate, call it t_c, *times* the interest on the bonds, iD:

$$\begin{aligned} \text{Tax shield provided by interest payments} &= iDt_c \\ &= (0.05)(\$20)(0.25) \\ &= \$0.25 \end{aligned}$$

Given that this stream is as certain as the interest payments on the bonds, the value to the firm of this stream can be shown:

$$\text{Value to firm of tax shield} = \frac{iDt_c}{i} = Dt_c$$

To bring it all together, the value of the levered firm is equal to the value of the unlevered firm *plus* the value of the tax shield provided by any interest payments on debt:

$$V_L = \frac{Y\theta}{k_a} + Dt_c \qquad (3\text{-}7)$$

Since $\theta = 1 - t_c$, this can also be expressed as

$$V_L = \frac{Y(1 - t_c)}{k_a} + Dt_c \qquad (3\text{-}7a)$$

This is an important conclusion. We will have use for this valuation model of the firm in later chapters.

Filling in the data from the case at hand, we have

$$V_L = \frac{(\$10)(0.75)}{0.075} + (\$20)(0.25)$$

$$= \$105.$$

Therefore, the introduction of debt into the financial structure has raised the value of the firm to $105 from $100. Since the bondholders are limited in their claim to $20, the extra $5 of the value of the firm should be reflected in the market value of the common stock. As we shall see in greater detail in Chapter 11, this is not an unlimited money tree that we have discovered. The basic reason will become apparent in the next section of this chapter.

Risk of Financial Leverage

The income advantages of financial leverage make it very tempting. Why should we put up as much as $80 of the $100 needed for our hot dog stand: Why not borrow $60 from our brother-in-law at 5 percent (thus paying him $3), invest only $40 for four shares of common stock, and sit back and rake in the additional earnings per share of about 47 cents?

Effect of added financial leverage

	Proportion of total assets financed by residual owners' equity (Q)	
	At Q = 0.8	At Q = 0.4
Net operating income (Y)	$10.00	$10.00
Interest expense	1.00	3.00
Earnings before taxes	9.00	7.00
Taxes (25%)	2.25	1.75
Earnings available for common stock	$6.75	$5.25
Rate of return on common equity	8.44%	13.125%
No. of shares of common stock	8	4
Earnings per share (EPS)	$0.84	$1.31

The relationship between net operating income (Y) and earnings per share (EPS) is shown in Exhibit 3-3. Since there are no taxes paid on losses, the slope of the function changes at the point where net operating income is just sufficient to cover the interest expense. There are two main points worthy of note in Exhibit 3-3. First, the earnings per share will be higher with the larger portion of debt in the financial structure when net operating income is above $5. Thus if we expect net operating income to range above that level, the return available for the residual owners will be improved by using $60 of debt. Second, observe the effect of financial leverage upon the variance of earnings per share. To illustrate, if the net operating income ranges from $0 to $10, the possible range of earnings per share is from $−0.13 to $0.84 with low financial leverage ($Q=0.8$), whereas with the higher financial leverage ($Q = 0.4$), for the same range of net operating income, earnings per share range from $−0.75 to $1.31.

EXHIBIT 3-3   Relation of Earnings per Share to
Net Operating Income

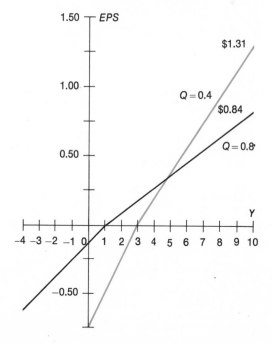

This is a very important point. Financial leverage magnifies the fluctuations in earnings available for the residual owners. When net operating income rises, the earnings of the residual owners increase at a faster rate than without financial leverage; when net operating income falls, the earnings of residual owners decline more rapidly. But this very fact means that we are again faced with a trade-off between risk and return. Although the return for the owners from favorable financial leverage is better than without leverage, the owners assume *added risk* because of the greater dispersion of possible returns. To illustrate this point, consider that there is a probability distribution of possible net operating incomes shown in Exhibit 3-3, ranging from $0 to $10. This probability distribution function is then transformed into a probability distribution over earnings per share, assuming low and high leverage. Since we are using variance as the measure of risk, comparison of the probability distribution functions for $Q = 0.8$ and $Q = 0.4$ (shown on the vertical axis in Exhibit 3-4) shows clearly that the use of greater financial leverage entails a higher risk for the residual owners. Thus the higher returns produced by the greater financial leverage above net operating income of $5 are offset in part by the greater risk involved.

EXHIBIT 3-4   Effect of Financial Leverage upon
Variance of Earnings per Share

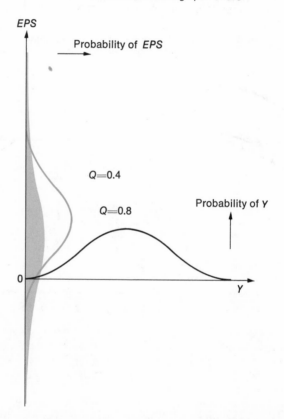

In addition to causing a wider dispersion in possible earnings per share, the greater dependence upon debt in the financial structure adds to the risk of bankruptcy. Interest is a fixed obligation that must be paid, regardless of the level of earnings. Also, debt comes due—as the Penn Central discovered—and we need cash to repay debt. Since it is easier to generate $20 in cash than $60, we face a smaller risk of bankruptcy with the lower level of debt.

Summary

The value of the residual owners' equity in a firm depends upon two factors: (1) their expected cash flows and (2) the dispersion of possible flows around the expected value—return versus risk. Decisions that affect earning power and financial leverage may affect both of these factors. Earning power is a product of margin and turnover. Much of our concern in the next part will be devoted to planning and managing the operating assets that influence the turnover, although decisions in this regard frequently influence the margin as well. Very often, increases in the earning power may be achieved only by assuming added risk. The earning power may be magnified into an even higher rate of return for the residual owners through the use of financial leverage; that is, through the use of funds for which a fixed, maximum rate of charge is paid. However, the use of financial leverage widens the dispersion of possible earnings per share, thereby increasing the risk to the residual owners. Thus the financial manager must balance the chance of making greater profits for the owners against the greater variability of returns and the greater danger of bankruptcy.

Questions

1/ In an effort to persuade the public that its profits were "reasonable" a grocery chain reported that it earned (net) only 1¢ on every dollar of sales. A railroad reported it earned only 6¢ on every dollar of assets. Comment on the suitability of these two approaches as measures of reasonable profits.

2/ A consulting firm studying grocery stores discovered that the gross margin on frozen foods ranged up to 29 percent, compared to 19 percent for groceries. While grocers cut margins on stable items to build traffic, they had tended to leave prices unchanged on frozen foods. Yet about 20 percent of the items accounted for 60 percent of the sales in the frozen food department. Would you recommend any changes in the price structure of frozen foods? If so what changes? If you recommend a change, would you change all prices equally?

3/ At one time Parsons College announced reductions in tuition, room and board charges running from 9 percent to 32 percent for students attending the summer semester in addition to the other two semesters during the regular academic year. Explain in terms of margin and turnover the purpose of this proposal. (*Wall Street Journal,* March 24, 1966, p. 8.)

4/ "The average railroad car spends only an hour and 15 minutes a day doing its job—that is, actually moving with something in it." (*Business Week,* December 18, 1965, p. 123.) What effect does this have upon earning power? What remedial efforts have you observed? To what extent are improvements in earning power offset by added risk?

5/ Using Exhibit 3-2, explain why many small retailers accept bank credit cards from their customers.

6/ Explain in terms of margin and turnover why grocery stores have taken on lines traditionally carried by drug stores.

7/ Is a consumer wise to use financial leverage by buying his car and home on time? Why or why not?

8/ In June, 1970, Indiana Gas Company offered consumers the opportunity to pay for their gas consumption by paying equal dollar amounts for the next eleven months (based upon estimates of normal usage), with any remaining debit or credit balance to be settled in the twelfth month. If there is no adjustment in rates of charge, trace the effect of the change upon the rate of return for the common stockholders of Indiana Gas.

Problems

1/ Study current periodicals, such as *Business Week* and the *Wall Street Journal,* to find examples of changes in policy which will affect the earning power of a company. If you are currently working for some company, what recent changes in policy have been made which will affect its earning power?

2/ a. Two companies both report earning powers of 10 percent. Company A has a margin of 2 percent and Company B a margin of 20 percent. What are the turnovers for Companies A and B?

b. Operating assets and sales for two firms are shown below. What margin will each company have to obtain to secure an earning power of 15 percent?

	Sales	*Operating Assets*
A	$100	$ 50
B	100	400

3/ In October, 1957, Mr. Dwight P. Joyce, chairman and president of The Glidden Company, Cleveland, Ohio, announced that cash prizes would be awarded to division managers doing the best overall job in managing their capital. The prizes, net after 18 percent withholding tax, were to be: 1st, $4000; 2nd, $2500; 3rd, $1250; 4th, $750. His letter to the division managers says in part:

> What is required to win this contest? I am predominantly looking for the manager who makes the most improvement in capital utilization—the manager who reduces his inventories and receivables, *but* at the same time maintains or increases his sales and profits. . . . In judging winners, I am going to lay particular stress on use of liquid capital—that is, cash, receivables, and inventory. These are directly controllable by you. How well did each manager use these assets in generating sales? In other words, what happened to his turnover of liquid capital?
>
> I am also going to evaluate your turnover of fixed plant investment. While a manager cannot radically change his investment in plant, it is his responsibility to utilize this capital investment to its fullest capacity.
>
> In addition to examining these capital turnover factors, I am going to pay close attention to your profits and profit margins. It isn't sufficient to utilize capital to generate a tremendous sales activity, unless those sales

actually result in adequate profits. In other words, the winner is going to be the manager who does the best job or makes the most improvement in utilizing his capital to produce a maximum profit.

In comments to the press on the Money Management Contest Mr. Joyce pointed out that Glidden pays about $56,000 in interest payments on each $1 million of borrowed money.

a. If inventories are reduced by $3 million as a result of this contest, would you say the contest has "paid for itself"?

b. If you were a judge of the contest, what specific accounting information would you use, and how would you use it, to award first prize?

4/ The following data (in billions of dollars) are available for two industries:

	Alpha	Beta
Income statement items:		
(A) Sales	$54.57	$41.89
(B) Earnings before taxes (*EBT*)	6.89	1.21
(C) Earnings after taxes (*EAT*)	3.86	0.78
Balance sheet items:		
Current liabilities	7.95	2.34
Long-term debt	9.86	1.17
(D) Capital stock & retained earnings	41.12	4.14
(E) Total assets/liabilities and capital	$58.43	$ 7.65

a. Complete the table in the manner shown in Table 3-1.

b. One of these firms is a composite of "food stores" and the other of "petroleum refining and related industries." Which is Alpha and which, Beta? How did you reach your conclusion?

5/ The sources of funds of two corporations are shown below. If a corporate income tax rate of 30 percent is assumed, what is the rate of earnings after taxes on the common stockholders' equity in each case when net operating income (as determined before interest and taxes) is as follows: 19_1, $8000; 19_2, $5000; 19_3, $10,000; 19_4, $15,000.

A

4% bonds	$ 40,000
Common equity	60,000

B

| Common equity | 100,000 |

6/ Assume that a corporation's sales are $20,000,000; net operating expenses, $18,000,000; and net operating assets, $6,000,000. Its operating assets have been financed with $2,000,000 in 9 percent debt and 40,000 shares of common stock. The firm is in the 40 percent tax bracket. Compute the rate of return after taxes on the residual owners' equity and the earnings per share by preparing an income statement. Confirm the accuracy of your first calculation by using formula (3-5a).

7/ Look up in Moodys or Standard and Poors *Manuals* the latest annual reports for Niagara Mohawk Power Corporation, R. H. Macy & Company, Inc., and

Union Carbide and Carbon Corporation. Prepare the information requested for each company.

a. Compute the margin, turnover, and earning power (before interest and taxes). Explain differences and similarities you find in your results.
b. Show the major sources of funds classified by: short-term debt, long-term debt, preferred stock, and common stock and retained earnings. The total sources of funds should be equal to total assets.
c. Compute the percent earned before taxes on the total long-term debt, preferred stock, and common stock and retained earnings.
d. Compute the percent earned before and after taxes on the equity of the common stockholders (common stock and retained earnings). How important is financial leverage in affecting the earnings on the equity of the common stockholders?

8/ If you are currently working for some company, make these same calculations for your concern and be prepared to compare your results with those of other firms.

Selected References

BODENHORN, D., "A Cash-Flow Concept of Profit," *Journal of Finance,* 19 (March, 1964), pp. 16–31.
DEARDEN, J., "The Case Against ROI Control," *Harvard Business Review,* 47 (May–June, 1969), pp. 124–35.
SOLOMON, E., *The Theory of Financial Management.* New York: Columbia University Press, 1963.

Part Two

Planning and Managing Assets

Financial Analysis

4

One of the most important functions of the financial manager is that of planning. In order to make plans he must first be able to ascertain his company's immediate position. Like a doctor, he needs to know the condition of his patient before prescribing a course of action. You would not launch a financially weak company on a program of expansion and heavy promotional activity any more than you would send out a patient with heart trouble to do two hours of road work each morning. In other words, plans must fit the financial capabilities of the concern. The financial manager must therefore know how to analyze the concern's position before he can estimate its capabilities.

⅃ Financial analysis may proceed from two points of view: external and internal. The first approach is that of an outsider, a creditor or owner. Since they have provided funds in the past and will very likely be asked to commit even more, the financial manager must examine from their point of view the data that they will have available about his company. We should not need to be reminded that creditors and owners are motivated by considerations of risk versus return. Do the concern's financial statements present the sort of picture that will encourage present creditors and investors to continue support of the company? Is it a good enough picture to attract new funds? Given the financial position of the company, what sorts of funds can be attracted? With the risks indicated by analysis of the financial statements, what sort of returns must be offered to attract more funds to the company, or even to retain existing commitments?

This external analysis is based upon existing financial statements; that is, statements that are historical. In developing his own internal financial analysis the financial manager must prepare more detailed internal planning statements that look to the future. These plans must, of course, be consistent with the strengths and weaknesses revealed in the external analysis. In addition, they depend upon forecasts regarding needed levels of cash, accounts receivable, inventory, and fixed assets—the subject matter of the following four chapters. Thus it will be in Chapter 9 that we will tie together the internal financial analysis through the preparation of budgets. These budgets will enable the financial manager to prepare an estimate income statement and balance sheet, or *pro forma* statements. The expected results depicted in these *pro forma* statements should then be examined from an external point of view to see if the creditors and owners will be satisfied, if not thrilled, with the results.

Approach to Financial Analysis

The Use of Ratios

Financial analysis involves a number of hazards. Probably the foremost problem is that the analyst tends to concentrate on the ratios or percentages as ends in themselves, rather than on what they are supposed to show. If we consider the many different items on a balance sheet and income statement, there are literally hundreds of possible permutations and combinations of these figures. Rather than engage in an encyclopedic tabulation of all of these ratios, it is better to have in mind a concept of what we are trying to learn about the firm's position, and then use or devise the appropriate comparisons. If we concentrate on the purpose of our analysis, we should not have to commit to memory the titles and formulas for a vast number of different ratios.

Let us say that the financial manager is considering the viewpoint of a current or prospective trade creditor. What is important to the short-term creditor? He wants his bill paid and he wants it paid within thirty days. Earnings projected over the next 12 months or next five years are relatively immaterial to him; at least he hopes he will not have to depend on long-run earnings for payment of his bill. He will consider whether the cash flow from current assets will be sufficient to pay current liabilities on time. To judge the ability of our company to meet its current obligations, common sense should lead us to compare the current assets to the current liabilities. Although it may display great erudition on our part to be able to refer to this as the "current ratio," it is more important to know the significance and limitations of this ratio than to know its title.

Mathematical Problems in the Use of Ratios

Financial analysis depends to a great extent on the use of ratios. Because a ratio is a comparison of two figures, a numerator and a denominator, we cannot be sure, when comparing one ratio to another, whether differences are a result of changes in the numerator or in the denominator or in both. To illustrate this point let us consider the company whose condensed balance sheet is shown below:

Current assets	$12,000	Current liabilities	$ 6,000
Fixed assets	20,000	Long-term liabilities	5,000
		Proprietor, capital	21,000
	$32,000		$32,000

At the moment the current ratio is 2:1, which is computed as follows:

$$\frac{\text{Current assets}}{\text{Current liabilities}} = \frac{\$12,000}{\$\ 6,000} = 2:1$$

There are five main types of change that could bring about an apparent improvement in the current ratio from 2:1 to 2.5:1.

1. **Sell Fixed Assets.** Funds released from fixed assets may be used either to reduce current liabilities or to increase current assets. In either case the current ratio is improved. In the examples below it is assumed that the assets are sold at their book value.

(a) *Use funds to reduce current liabilities.*

Current assets	$12,000	Current liabilities	$ 4,800
Fixed assets	18,800	Long-term liabilities	5,000
		Proprietor, capital	21,000
	$30.800		$30,800

(b) *Use funds to increase current assets.*

Current assets	$15,000	Current liabilities	$ 6,000
Fixed assets	17,000	Long-term liabilities	5,000
		Proprietor, capital	21,000
	$32,000		$32,000

2. **Issue Long-Term Debt.** Acquisition of long-term funds would enable the company to improve its current position, either by reducing current liabilities or by increasing current assets. Although the current position is improved, the added burden of the long-term debt may only postpone a financial crisis.

(a) *Use funds to reduce current liabilities.*

Current assets	$12,000	Current liabilities	$ 4,800
Fixed assets	20,000	Long-term liabilities	6,200
		Proprietor, capital	21,000
	$32,000		$32,000

(b) *Use funds to increase current assets.*

Current assets	$15,000	Current liabilities	$ 6,000
Fixed assets	20,000	Long-term liabilities	8,000
		Proprietor, capital	21,000
	$35,000		$35,000

3. Use Current Assets to Reduce Current Liabilities.

Current assets	$10,000	Current liabilities	$ 4,000
Fixed assets	20,000	Long-term liabilities	5,000
		Proprietor, capital	21,000
	$30,000		$30,000

It might be noted in connection with this last example that if the current ratio were originally quite low, it could be "improved" by additional short-term borrowing. If current assets were $3000 as compared with current liabilities of $4000, the current ratio would be 0.75:1. This would rise to 0.83:1 if we borrowed $2000 and invested the money in current assets. We can also observe from cases 1 (a) to 2(b) that the current ratio is usually improved more by the application of funds to the reduction of current liabilities than to an increase in current assets. In this example a decrease of $1200 in current liabilities produces the same effect on the current ratio as an increase of $3000 in current assets.

Although all of these different types of change are capable of producing a "better" current ratio, they are not all equally beneficial to a company's financial position. In fact some changes, such as the increased use of long-term debt or the sale of fixed assets, could represent a worsening of a company's financial position.

Because ratios by themselves are frequently misleading, it is important to keep in mind the overall position of the firm and changes in the dollar amounts of items on the financial statements. One good procedure is to plot important financial data directly on a ratio (semi-log) chart. In this manner we can compare the rates of growth of assets to sales, major costs to revenues, earnings after taxes to net worth, and so on. For many analysts such charts may be more meaningful than tables of various ratios.

Selection of Standards

Finally, there is the problem of what standards to use in comparison with the ratios developed for a given company. If we find that our company has a current ratio of 2.5:1, is it "too high" or "too low"? Although we may not reach any certain conclusion, we can suggest that the farther a given ratio is from some standard, the more likely does it represent an unusual variation that warrants further study. The problem is to determine what standard to use. There are two sources of standards: industry standards and historical standards. Both should be used whenever possible.

Industry Standards. First, we may compare the ratios developed for a given company with ratios for other concerns of about the same size in the same industry. Such comparisons must be made with care. As more and more firms diversify, it becomes increasingly difficult to identify them with given industries. For example, The American Machine and Foundry Company makes cigar wrapping machines, bicycles, automatic pin spotters, radar equipment, and pretzel machines. It is clearly not possible to identify it as a whole with any single industry. Yet proper classification by industry is important because there are wide differences in the financial ratios characteristic of different industries. Even within the same industry, ratios for individual companies will differ markedly according to the size of the company and the services which it performs. Among firms in an industry there are almost always differences of some sort—size, credit terms given and received, type of customer served, cost structures, accounting methods, and so on. For example, the operation of drugstores vary from combination luncheonette-variety stores to "old time" apothecaries. These differences between industries and among firms within the same industry should make it clear why it is futile, and even dangerous, to use universal rules of thumb—such as a 2:1 current ratio—as a standard in evaluating the position of a company. Each firm in an industry is, in a sense, unique. Comparison with industry ratios thus provides only a general analytical framework. Nonetheless, marked differences between a company's ratios and the average for similar companies within the industry should serve to raise questions concerning the suitability of policies which affect the ratios studied, although it may turn out that there are perfectly acceptable reasons for the differences.

When it is possible to classify a concern by industry, there are numerous sources of "standard" industry ratios to use as a basis of comparison:

Dun and Bradstreet. Since 1931 "D & B" has prepared "fourteen important ratios for seventy-two lines of business activity." They are published annually in *Dun's Review and Modern Industry* and are also available in booklet form from Dun and Bradstreet. These ratios are particularly useful because they represent a large sample of companies and are given for the upper quartile, median, and lower quartile. Some selected ratios for a recent year are shown in Table 4-1. Note the wide variation among industries and among firms within the same industry.

Trade associations. Many trade associations prepare detailed profit and loss statements and balance sheet ratios. For example, the National Hardware Association and the National Retail Furniture Association provide extensive balance sheet and income statement analyses for their members.

Government agencies. The Small Business Administration, the U.S. Department of Commerce, and some state departments of commerce publish business studies. Many of these studies cover small businesses, and they frequently include various standard financial ratios. Another useful source is *The Quarterly Financial Report for Manufacturing Corporations* published by the Federal Trade Commission and the Securities and Exchange Commission. This sample survey provides an income statement and balance sheet for all manufacturing corporations, classified by both industry and asset size.

Robert Morris Associates. This association of bank credit men publishes *Statement Studies* annually. Eleven ratios are provided for about 200 lines of business as well as a percentage distribution of items on the balance sheet and income statement. Many commercial banks and some libraries have these studies.

Accounting Corporation of America. This concern publishes the *Barometer of Small Business* semi-annually. The publication provides aggregate balance sheet figures and rather extensive income statement data for different regions and for concerns grouped by volume of sales. The studies are based on direct reports from over 9000 business units in 52 types of business.

National Cash Register Company. The Marketing Services department has

Table 4-1 Selected Dun and Bradstreet Quartile Figures

Line of Business (and Number of Businesses)	Current Assets to Current Debt (Times)	Average Collection Period (Days)	Net Sales to Inventory (Times)	Total Debt to Tangible Net Worth (Percent)	Net Profits on Net Sales (Percent)	Net Profit on Tangible Net Worth (Percent)
Manufacturing Lines:						
Airplane parts and	2.26	29	8.4	60.0	7.01	22.67
accessories (53)	1.78	39	5.9	93.5	4.44	16.67
	1.36	55	4.2	127.1	2.92	8.10
Meat packing	4.20	10	47.5	38.6	1.58	13.65
plants (98)	2.51	13	29.9	83.6	0.99	8.04
	1.46	15	20.3	141.7	0.31	4.05
Wholesale Lines						
Groceries	3.04	9	15.8	92.8	0.99	11.69
(224)	2.08	14	10.7	151.4	0.54	6.42
	1.61	21	8.1	233.6	0.22	2.71
Lumber and						
construction	4.00	33	11.1	57.4	3.07	11.51
materials (160)	2.36	46	6.9	100.9	1.45	6.73
	1.71	62	5.9	135.5	0.59	2.83
Retail Lines						
Grocery stores	2.59		22.5	59.0	1.75	14.95
(138)	1.86	a	16.5	94.1	1.05	9.58
	1.38		12.9	146.8	0.58	5.38
Lumber and other						
building materials	6.25	41	8.2	46	3.10	9.01
dealers (217)	3.33	55	5.2	73.4	1.86	4.95
	2.11	77	4.0	121.0	0.39	0.98

a Not computed. Necessary information as to division between cash sales and credit sales was available in too few cases to obtain an average collection period usable as a broad guide.

Note: Figures shown are for upper quartile, median, and lower quartile.

Source: *Key Business Ratios in 125 Lines 1967* Dun & Bradstreet, Inc.

compiled from various trade associations and other sources expense percentages for 57 lines of business. Some of the tables are not dated.

Other sources. Many bankers are in a position to provide standard ratios for particular industries. For example, the First National Bank of Chicago has for several years made available semi-annual financial data drawn from their reports of a sample of sales finance and consumer credit companies. In some lines of business suppliers may be able to offer suggested standards. Trade journals frequently carry discussions of operating and financial ratios.

Historical Standards. A second standard that the financial manager should use to analyze the financial position of his company is the past record of the company. Such a comparison is important because no one firm can be expected to produce ratios equal to the average ratios for a sample of companies from the industry. We need ratios that reflect the size and age of our particular company, so that we may then determine whether its position is improving or getting worse. Even this approach is not infallible, because the size and the nature of the company's business may have changed over time. Mechanical servitude to a mass of ratios is never a substitute for good judgment.

Illustrative Analysis

Short-Term Analysis

The financial manager may ask, "Is it realistic for me to seek additional bank or trade credit? How does my company look to present or prospective short-term creditors?" As we shall see later, the approach which will be taken here may also be adopted in analyzing the statements of prospective customers seeking credit. The difference lies in the amount of information the financial manager has concerning his own business and that which he has concerning a customer.

Since the foremost concern of short-term creditors is to be paid promptly, the first step in their analysis of our financial statements centers on the relation of current assets to current liabilities and the rapidity with which receivables and inventory turn into cash in the normal course of the business. Because current creditors are generally unwilling to wait out a number of cash turnover cycles in order that the company might generate sufficient profits, the immediate source of cash for the payment of bills must be that obtained from cash sales or by the collection of accounts receivable. Indeed, if suppliers are not paid on time, they are quite likely to shut off further shipments, and this action would forestall any chance of the company to generate profits to pay its obligations. In other words, the key question is whether or not the normal circulation of funds from cash to inventory to accounts receivable and back to cash continues unabated. Restrictions on this flow at any point will very likely reduce the level of supportable operations and cause a "hardening of the financial arteries" which could result in insolvency and failure. As a second step in their analysis, present or prospective creditors will be interested in the proportion of the assets they are financing in relation to the proportion the owners are financing. The smaller the proportion of assets they are financing, the more those assets can drop in value before the creditors' position is threatened and the less they may lose should the firm become insolvent.

For the purposes of our discussion we shall examine the statements of the Moore Lumber Company, a lumber and building supply wholesaler located in a large midwestern city. The statements shown in Table 4-2 are those for the beginning and end of a four-year period during which the dealer's business expanded rapidly. This expansion was so gratifying to the owner that he was not entirely aware of some of the financial implications of his aggressive merchandising tactics.

Statement of Balance Sheet Changes. The financial manager may gain initial insight into his position by studying balance sheet changes. The changes revealed provide clues to problems that require further analysis by the use of ratios and by study of comparative rates of change of accounts on the financial statements. The statement of balance sheet changes may be developed into a

TABLE 4-2   Financial Statements of the Moore Lumber Company

	Balance Sheets			
		Four Years Ago		Current Year
Assets:				
Cash		$ 28,000		$ 7,100
Accounts receivable		170,100		236,800
Inventory		157,200		246,100
Total current assets		$355,300		$490,000
Building and equipment	$67,100		$74,800	
Allowance for depreciation	18,200	48,900	26,100	48,700
Other assets		18,500		23,700
Total		$422,700		$562,400
Liabilities and Capital:				
Notes payable—trade		—		$ 14,800
Accounts payable—trade		$ 61,700		125,700
Notes payable—bank		25,000		60,000
Other liabilities		18,300		26,100
Total current liabilities		$105,000		$226,600
Mortgage (5%)		16,200		9,600
Proprietor, Capital		301,500		326,200
Total		$422,700		$562,400

	Operating Statements			
		Four Years Ago		Current Year
Net sales		$1,583,600		$1,932,700
Opening inventory	$ 148,800		$ 237,900	
Purchases	1,344,300		1,688,900	
	$1,493,100		$1,926,800	
Less: Ending inventory	157,200		246,100	
Cost of goods sold		1,335,900		1,680,700
Gross margin		$ 247,700		$ 252,000
Operating expenses:				
Selling and delivery	93,500		98,000	
Salaries	46,900		50,600	
Other	75,900	216,300	84,100	232,700
Operating margin		31,400		19,300
Interest expense		1,800		2,900
Net profit		$ 29,600		$ 16,400

Note: Figures have been rounded to the nearest hundred.

very elaborate (and more precise) source and application of funds statement.[1] For our purposes, however, we shall ordinarily find it sufficient to use a statement of balance sheet changes such as that shown in Table 4-3.

[1] See Robert H. Gregory and Edward L. Wallace, "Worksheet for Funds Statements Problems," *Accounting Review*, 28 (January, 1952), pp. 88–97.

TABLE 4-3   Statement of Balance Sheet Changes of the Moore Lumber Company

| | Work Sheet | | | |
	Four Years Ago	Current Year	Change Debit	Change Credit
Cash	$ 28,000	$ 7,100		$ 20,900
Accounts receivable	170,100	236,800	$ 66,700	
Inventory	157,200	246,100	88,900	
Building and equipment	67,100	74,800	7,700	
Allowance for depreciation	(18,200)	(26,100)		7,900
Other assets	18,500	23,700	5,200	
	$422,700	$562,400		
Notes payable – trade	–	14,800		14,800
Accounts payable – trade	61,700	125,700		64,000
Notes payable – bank	25,000	60,000		35,000
Other liabilities	18,300	26,100		7,800
Mortgage (5%)	16,200	9,600	6,600	
Proprietor, capital	301,500	326,200		24,700
	$422,700	$562,400	$175,100	$175,100

Statement of Balance Sheet Changes

Sources of Funds

Charges to income which did not require cash (depreciation)		$ 7,900
Increase in liabilities:		
Notes payable – trade	$14,800	
Accounts payable – trade	64,000	
Notes payable – bank	35,000	
Other liabilities	7,800	121,600
Increase in net worth		24,700
Total		$154,200

Uses of Funds

Increase in assets:		
Accounts receivable	$66,700	
Inventory	88,900	
Building and equipment	7,700	
Other assets	5,200	$168,500
Decrease in liabilities:		
Mortgage		6,600
Total		$175,100
Excess of uses over sources		$ 20,900
Net reduction in cash balance		$ 20,900

This statement should not be regarded as a historical representation of the flow of funds discussed in the preceding chapter. It shows merely the changes in assets, liabilities, and net worth that have taken place over a period of time—a month, a year, five years, or whatever period is selected. The period chosen should represent some stage in the life cycle of the business. It might be a period of growth or of decline, or of seasonal upswing or downswing. If an interval of several years is to be studied, it is easier to interpret changes with one statement based on the balance sheet of the first and last year rather than with a series of summaries based on the balance sheets for each of the years covered.

In general terms the summary shown indicates the *sources of funds* as obtained from:

1/ a decrease in assets,
2/ an increase in liabilities,
3/ an increase in net worth (e.g., through retained earnings or additional investment),

and *uses of funds* as applied to:

1/ an increase in assets,
2/ a decrease in liabilities,
3/ a decrease in net worth (e.g., losses, payment of dividends, withdrawals by partners or proprietors).

Despite the fact that it does not represent a precise historical flow of cash, the statement of balance sheet changes provides a useful starting point by directing our attention to possible trouble spots in the Moore Company's financial status. Note the decline in cash of almost $21,000. We must carefully examine the liquidity position of the firm. This change significantly reduces its bill-paying ability. We should also determine whether the considerable growth in accounts receivable and inventory is justified by an increase in sales. The investment in plant and equipment appears to be modest, but we should be sure that lease obligations are not hiding commitments in fixed assets. A danger signal is raised by the increase in liabilities. Whereas net worth has grown by $24,700, liabilities have risen by $121,600. On the surface, this appears to be an unbalanced financing of the growth. We will have to determine if this method of financing brought the company into line with industry practice, or whether Moore is relying too heavily on his creditors for financing. Of particular concern is the growth in money owed suppliers: Notes payable, trade and accounts payable, trade. This appears to confirm our worries about the decline in cash. Moreover, when we see "Notes payable, trade" spring up on the balance sheet, it may be a sign that trade creditors are sufficiently concerned about the company's ability to meet its bills that they are demanding written evidence of the debt in the form of promissory notes. We will have to take special pains to examine the currency of trade payables when we turn to analysis of the various ratios. Let us move to this next step in financial analysis, now that we have a better idea of possible soft spots.

Current Ratio (computed by dividing the current assets by the current liabilities). This is a rough measure of a company's ability to meet its current debt. It should be distinguished from *net working capital,* which is determined by subtracting current liabilities from current assets. An unusually low current ratio indicates that a company may face some difficulty in meeting its bills; an unusually high current ratio suggests that funds are not being used economically within the firm. There may be excessive amounts of inventory on hand, some of which may be obsolete or slow-moving. The amounts of accounts receivable may be excessive, or there may be large idle cash balances. By the use of some of the ratios described below a more accurate analysis of the company's current position may be obtained. As we suspected, the liquidity of the Moore Lumber Company has deteriorated somewhat over the past four years, as evidenced by the decline in the company's current ratio from 3.38:1 to 2.16:1. But the ratio is not badly out of line with the median current ratio for lumber and building material wholesalers (Table 4-1).

	Four years ago	*Current year*	*Industry average*
Current ratio:	$\dfrac{\$355,300}{\$105,000} = 3.38$	$\dfrac{\$490,000}{\$226,600} = 2.16$	2.36

In connection with the decline in liquidity another question might arise. Assume that the company's mortgage agreement specifies that the current ratio must not be allowed to fall below 2:1. A logical question is: How much more short-term debt can the company acquire before violating this provision? This will take some high-powered algebra. Let x equal the added amount of short-term debt and assume that the proceeds are used to acquire various current assets. Then we can set up the following relationship:

$$\frac{490,000 + x}{226,600 + x} = \frac{2}{1}$$

$$x = 36,800$$

The accuracy of the result can be checked by adding $36,800 to present current assets and current liabilities and showing that the new current ratio is indeed 2:1.

Quick Ratio, or Acid-Test Ratio (computed by dividing the sum of cash, accounts receivable, and marketable securities by current liabilities). Since this comparison eliminates the inventories from consideration, it serves as another check on the adequacy of the current ratio. It is a measure of the extent to which cash and "near cash" cover the current liabilities. As we might expect, Moore's has declined from 1.89:1 to 1.08:1.

	Four years ago	*Current year*
Acid test ratio:	$\dfrac{\$198,100}{\$105,000} = 1.89$	$\dfrac{\$243,900}{\$226,600} = 1.08$

Required Days Measure (calculated as shown below). The current ratio and the quick ratio are deficient in that they are historical and compare a given stock (certain current assets) to another stock (current liabilities). The creditors of Moore are fortunate that the quick ratio is greater than 1:1. If the receivables are sound, they may expect their bills to be paid without undue delay. When the quick ratio is lower, creditors must look both to the liquidation of cash and receivables and to cash generated internally by the operations of the business.

The required days measure is designed to estimate the number of days that the creditors will have to wait for payment.

Assume that the cash and receivables of the Moore Lumber Company were just slightly less than the current level, say $221,700. This would fall $4,900 short of meeting the current liabilities of $226,600. Since this is a sole proprietorship, Moore needs to withdraw some cash to make payments on his income tax. Study of Table 4-3 suggests that annual depreciation expense is about $2,000. Thus a rough estimate of cash generated by operations appears as follows:

Net profit (Table 4-2)	$16,400
Less: Estimated personal tax payments	3,600
	12,800
Add: Expenses on the books that did not require payment of cash (depreciation)[2]	2,000
Estimated annual generation of cash	$14,800

How many days will be required for the cash generated by operations to make up the deficit on current liabilities of $4,900? Apparently, about one-third of a year ($4,900/$14,800 = 1/3). We can be more precise by using the formula shown below:

$$\frac{\text{Required days}}{\text{measure}} = \frac{\text{Current liabilities} - \text{Quick assets}}{\text{Annual cash generated from operations}} \times 360 \text{ days}$$

$$= \frac{\$226,600 - \$221,700}{\$14,800} \times 360 = 120 \text{ days.}$$

As with the other ratios, the trend in this statistic would be worth observing over time. Given the actual data for the Moore Lumber Company, it is not of immediate concern. However, Moore's quick ratio is moving towards 1:1, and it is clear that if the current liabilities should come to exceed cash and receivables, the rate at which cash is currently generated by the business is not sufficient to give creditors a comfortable feeling.

Receivables Turnover (computed by dividing annual sales, preferably credit sales, by the average or year-end trade accounts receivable). The purpose is to measure the liquidity of the receivables. If the annual rate of turnover is six times, this means that, on the average, receivables are collected in two months; if the turnover is four times, we must wait an average of three months for the return of our funds invested in receivables. An alternative computation that provides the same kind of information is to determine the average daily credit sales, and then divide this average into the accounts and notes receivable outstanding to determine the average collection period. The receivables turnover of the wholesaler has declined slightly, so that on the average it now takes 45 days to collect receivables as compared to an earlier collection period of 39 days. The change is not great, and we cannot place too much faith in its magnitude since we have available only a year-end rather than an average figure for accounts receivable. We may conclude that the worsening of the current posi-

---

[2]This will be explained more fully in the next chapter.

tion cannot be attributed in any large part to lax collections on our accounts receivable. In this case the wholesaler was selling to his customers in the expectation that they would pay their bills within 30 days. (His terms were "net 30.") Although collections are a little slow in relation to Moore's credit terms, they are not much worse than those commonly experienced in that line of business, as shown by the Dun and Bradstreet data in Table 4-1.

	Four years ago	*Current year*
Receivables turnover:	$\dfrac{\$1,583,600}{\$\ 170,100} = 9.31$ times	$\dfrac{\$1,932,700}{\$\ 236,800} = 8.16$ times

$$\text{Average collection period:} \quad \frac{\$1,583,600}{360} = \frac{\$4,399 \text{ credit}}{\text{sales per day}} \qquad \frac{\$1,932,700}{360} = \frac{\$5,369 \text{ credit}}{\text{sales per day}^3}$$

$$\frac{\$\ 170,100}{\$\ \ \ 4,399} = \frac{39 \text{ days}}{\text{collection}} \qquad \frac{\$\ 236,800}{\$\ \ \ 5,369} = \frac{44 \text{ days}}{\text{collection}}$$
$$\text{period} \qquad\qquad\qquad\qquad \text{period}$$

$$\text{Or: Average collection period} = \frac{\text{Accounts receivable} \times 360}{\text{Annual credit sales}}$$

	Four years ago	*Current year*

$$\frac{\$170,100 \times 360}{\$1,583,600} = \frac{39 \text{ days}}{\text{collection}} \qquad \frac{\$236,800 \times 360}{\$1,932,700} = \frac{44 \text{ days}}{\text{collection}}$$
$$\text{period} \qquad\qquad\qquad\qquad\qquad \text{period}$$

If we have available only credit sales for the past quarter, the collection period should be based on 90 days, rather than 360 days. Assume that credit sales during the previous quarter were $466,000. Then, the collection period is calculated:

$$\frac{\$236,800 \times 90}{\$466,000} = 46 \text{ days.}$$

When a company has experienced a sharp growth in sales or when its sales are seasonal, care must be used in applying the receivables turnover test. If sales have increased in the months preceding the end of a fiscal year, the year-end accounts receivable appearing on the books will reflect those enlarged sales. Comparison of these accounts receivable with sales for the entire year will be misleading. The level of sales for the entire year is not representative of the much higher rate of sales experienced in the last few months of the year. If the figure for year-end receivables is used, the calculated receivables turnover figure will appear to be low. In this case, it would be better to compare sales to a monthly or quarterly average of accounts receivable. If sales are seasonal, such as those of a department store, it may not be objectionable to compare the receivables turnover ratio from one year to the next, so long as the fluctuations in sales are about the same each year. It would clearly be inappropriate to compare the receivables turnover ratio of one department store as of July 31 with that of another store as of January 31.

As with our other ratios, this one may also be too high or too low. An unusually high turnover of accounts receivable for our particular line of business

---

[3] By custom, 360 days is more often used than 365 days. It really makes very little difference.

may indicate an unnecessarily tight credit policy that is hurting sales by driving away our slow-paying customers. We may be selecting only the best customers, or we may be insisting on unusually strict payment terms. If this situation exists, it may also be reflected in a low turnover of inventory and in a low ratio of sales to operating assets. In contrast, an unusually low turnover of accounts receivable would indicate a congestion of funds in this asset that would cut down on the available flow of funds for reinvestment in inventory.

A more exact measure of delinquency on accounts receivable is found by "aging" the accounts. This is a process of classifying the amount owed on each account according to the period that it has been outstanding. Presumably the largest dollar amount of accounts receivable of our lumber wholesaler would be current: that is, outstanding less than 30 days. The remaining accounts could be classed as outstanding 30 to 60 days, 60 to 90 days, and over 90 days.

Inventory Turnover (computed by dividing cost of goods sold by the average inventory).[4] Here we are seeking to determine how rapidly funds flow through the inventory pool and how current is that inventory. The turnover figure gives us an idea as to whether the inventory is deficient or excessive in relation to our volume of sales. The wholesaler's annual inventory turnover has declined from 8.7 times to 6.9 times.

	Four years ago		*Current year*	
Inventory turnover:	$\dfrac{\$1,335,900}{\dfrac{\$148,800 + 157,200}{2}}$	$= \begin{matrix}8.73\\ \text{times}\end{matrix}$	$\dfrac{\$1,680,700}{\dfrac{\$237,900 + 246,100}{2}}$	$= \begin{matrix}6.95\\ \text{times}\end{matrix}$

An unusually low or declining inventory turnover suggests various possibilities. The manager of each firm makes a compromise between being out of stock on occasion and tying up funds in inventory. A decline in inventory turnover indicates that in making this compromise, he has been leaning more towards keeping a full stock on hand. When the turnover is unusually low, it also suggests that there may be obsolete or, at least, slow-moving stock on hand. It calls to mind a drugstore owner who could never turn down a request for an item. No matter what was requested, he would order a dozen or a gross to fill an order for one or two. At his liquidation sale, he was able to offer one of the most varied inventories ever found in a drug store. Had he paid closer attention to his inventory turnover figure, he might not have become another statistic of business failure.

An unusually high inventory turnover is not all to the good either. In a manufacturing concern, efforts to maintain an especially high turnover of raw material may be penalized by running out of items so that production lines are shut down. A high turnover of finished goods may indicate that we are losing profitable sales because we are too frequently out of stock. Some customers follow a practice of buying a certain mixture of products from a company. If we try to sell them just the fast-moving items from the mix, we may not sell them anything. Or we may achieve a high turnover by reducing the selling price of our product. Whether or not this policy is in the long-run interests of the firm

---

[4]If the figures for opening and closing inventories are not available, the average cannot be computed; in this case it is necessary to use closing inventory.

will depend upon the earning power achieved. Sales must be profitable. Contrary to some opinion, you cannot lose a little on the sale of each item and make it up on the volume.

Days Purchases Outstanding (computed by dividing the trade payables by average purchases per day). This ratio is analogous to the average collection period for accounts receivable. Rather than indicate whether Moore's customers are "slow pay," it shows whether Moore is slow pay. All trade payables, both open account and notes payable, should be included in the calculation. The formula is shown below:

$$\text{Days purchases outstanding (or average payment period)} = \frac{\text{Accounts payable} \times 360}{\text{Annual purchases}}$$

Four years ago

$$\frac{\$61,700 \times 360}{\$1,344,300} = 17 \text{ days}$$

Current year

$$\frac{\$140,500 \times 360}{\$1,688,900} = 30 \text{ days}$$

Moore is almost twice as slow in paying his accounts as he was four years ago. His increasingly illiquid position hurts his profits, since he has undoubtedly been losing cash discounts for prompt payment.

If we agree that the buildup of inventories and receivables through the use of trade debt is the basic cause of the present weak current position, is this weakness likely to continue? At its present level of sales, the company probably cannot reduce its accounts receivable in order to lower its liabilities, because the turnover of accounts receivable does not seem unusually low by the standards of either the industry or this firm's historical experience. If the company could manage an annual inventory turnover of 8.73 times, as it did four years ago, the average inventory could be reduced from the current year's level of $242,000 to about $192,500.[5] This would allow a corresponding reduction in liabilities. Earnings are accumulating at an annual rate of about $16,000, but these earnings are subject to the personal income tax levied on the proprietor's income. Therefore, earnings will not accumulate rapidly enough in the short run to produce a significant reduction in current liabilities and increase in net worth. Any further expansion of sales will probably require an even larger investment in current assets and possibly in plant as well. Thus, to a considerable extent, the company may have to totter along with its present weak current position, unless the owner is willing to invest more funds in the business or bring in new owners with additional equity funds.

Debt to Net Worth (computed by dividing the total debt of the business by tangible net worth).[6] This ratio shows the dollars the creditors have put up in relation to the dollars the owners have put up. In this case we are relating the

---

[5] The $192,500 figure is obtained by dividing the current cost of goods sold ($1,680,700) by the "desired" turnover of 8.73 times.

[6] Tangible net worth is obtained by deducting from the net worth the amounts shown for such intangible assets as goodwill, patents, copyrights, and organizational or development expenses. In a sole proprietorship or partnership the net worth is the amount of capital held by the owner or by the partners.

total short- and long-term debt to net worth (including preferred stock, if any). To refresh our memories, the *net worth* of a corporation is the sum of any outstanding preferred stock, common stock, surplus, undivided profits, and any surplus reserve, such as "reserve for contingencies." As we can see, the lumber and building supplies wholesaler is relying heavily on his creditors for funds, more so now than in the past. Formerly the creditors provided 40 cents for every dollar the owner supplied; now they have put up 72 cents for every dollar contributed by the owner.

	Four years ago	*Current year*
Debt to net worth	$\dfrac{\$121,200}{\$301,500} = 0.40{:}1$	$\dfrac{\$236,200}{\$326,200} = 0.72{:}1$

Intangible assets are deducted from net worth for two reasons. First, it is usually difficult to determine their actual value in terms of the earning power that they contribute to the company. Second, some intangible assets, such as goodwill, are often of value to the company only if it continues as a going concern. Since the ratio of debt to net worth is chiefly a measure of creditors' protection in the event of liquidation, any assets that would not contribute to this safety should be excluded from consideration. These are generalizations; when intangible assets have commercial value apart from the company, they need not be deducted from net worth.

If the ratio of debt to net worth is one to one, the assets could decline 50 percent in value before threatening the actual solvency of the business. With a ratio of two to one, creditors are financing two-thirds of the assets. Thus assets could lose only one-third of their value before bringing on insolvency. The stability of the value of the assets depends on the liquidity of the assets and the certainty of the stream of income derived from the assets. Thus companies with a high proportion of "money good" assets, such as sales finance companies and commercial banks, can tolerate a high ratio of debt to net worth. By "money good" assets we mean assets, such as instalment notes receivable and short-term business loans, which are readily collectible and turn rapidly into cash in the normal course of business. Similarly, firms such as electric light companies can borrow more in relation to net worth than steel companies, because the stability and relative certainty of their earnings supports a fairly constant asset value.

A debt-to-net-worth ratio that is too high tells the financial manager that his chances of securing additional borrowed funds are slight, or that additional funds will cost more. Indeed, pressures from creditors may soon restrict his activities in many other respects as well. For example, investments in fixed assets and dividend payments may be limited by direct or implied objections from creditors. It is also possible to have too low a ratio of debt to net worth. Either short-term or long-term debt may be inadequate. If we need funds for just a few months out of each year to finance a seasonal bulge in inventories and accounts receivable, it is usually better to borrow the money for a short period of time rather than have the owners supply these funds. Should the owners furnish the funds to meet the seasonal bulge, this extra money would very likely lie idle in the cash reservoir for most of the year. As we have seen in the preceding chapter, it may be advisable to incur long-term debt in order to provide an adequate rate of earnings for the owners. If we can borrow at 8 percent and put the money to work at 14 percent, the owners benefit by the financial leverage. Although it may give the financial manager a righteous feeling of security not to have any borrowed funds, he may not be developing the rate of earnings on the owner's investment that he could with a less puritanical attitude.

Long-Term Analysis

The financial manager may also be concerned with how well the business is doing in the eyes of those who have furnished or who may furnish long-term funds. Included in this group would be creditors who agree to provide funds for more than a year, and proprietors, partners, or corporate owners who invest in either preferred or common stock. Insofar as it affects the ability of the company to meet current payments on the debt or to pay cash returns to owners, the short-term position discussed in the preceding section is of concern to these long-term creditors and investors. However, for ultimate repayment of the debt and for continued payment of interest and dividends, these groups are more directly interested in the long-run profitability of the company. Whereas a bank loan to finance a seasonal bulge in inventory is repaid when cash is generated by a reduction of the bulge, a long-term debt is repaid either from the profits accumulated through the years or by replacement with other debt or additional owners' equity. Only if the record of the company's earnings is attractive will investors wish to purchase new securities to replace the old.

Coverage Ratios. Each of the long-term creditors or owners will concentrate his attention on that portion of the earnings to which he is entitled. Present or prospective bondholders will examine the operating statements to see how adequately their interest return is covered by the earnings that are available for interest. The figure for *times-interest-earned* may be obtained by dividing the earnings before interest and taxes by the annual interest charges.[7] If more than one issue of bonds is involved in the analysis, the interest charges of each issue under study should be combined with those of any others of equal or senior standing. Let us assume the following situation:

(A)	Gross revenues	$2,800,000
(B)	Cost of goods sold plus operating expenses	800,000
(C)	Income from operations	$2,000,000
(D)	Interest on first mortgage bonds	500,000
(E)		$1,500,000
(F)	Interest on second mortgage bonds	200,000
(G)	Net income before taxes	$1,300,000

If we should mistakenly compute the times-interest-earned coverage for each issue separately, it would appear that the second mortgage bond issue is in a stronger position than the senior issue. Interest charges on the first mort-

---

[7] Some writers prefer to deduct Federal income taxes from the amount available for interest, on the grounds that this gives a figure which represents the earnings available for interest from the owners' standpoint. For this reason, the analyst needs to make clear just what figure he is using.

gage bond issue are covered 4 times (C/D).[8] The $1,500,000 available after the interest expense of the senior issue covers the interest charges of the second mortgage bond issue by 7.5 times (E/F). This is clearly misleading because a junior issue cannot be better protected than the senior issue. Therefore, to compute the times-interest-earned on the second mortgage bonds we should use the overall method: that is, we should combine the interest charges on both bond issues and compare this combined obligation to the flow of funds available to meet these charges. Thus the interest coverage on the second mortgage bonds is only 2.86 times $\left(\dfrac{C}{D+F}\right)$. This overall coverage figure is of greatest significance to the financial manager, because it indicates that a decline in earnings before interest and taxes of $1.86 out of $2.86, or 65 percent, will eliminate the margin of protection for the long-term creditors as a group. The interest charges on any proposed issue of bonds should be added to existing interest charges to judge its safety. If a new bond issue is contemplated, it would be desirable to add to the interest charges already carried those which would be added by the proposed bond issue.

In addition to interest payments there may be other fixed charges, such as rental or lease payments and *sinking fund* payments. The latter are periodic payments that are required to reduce the principal amount of the debt. While frequently required on corporate bond issues, a more familiar example of sinking fund payments may be found in installment loans and most home mortgages. These are customarily arranged so that part of each payment is for interest and the remaining part serves to reduce the outstanding balance of the principal. The latter portion of the payment is also a sinking fund payment.

Since the sinking fund is merely a repayment of debt, it is *not* a deductible expense for income-tax purposes. Because our times-fixed-charges-earned calculation is to be on a before-tax basis, we must blow up the sinking fund payment to a before-tax basis as well. To do this we ask: What must be the before-tax income, Y, that is just sufficient to cover the after-tax sinking fund payment? Recalling that θ is equal to one minus the tax rate $(1-t_c)$, we have

$$\theta Y = \text{Sinking fund payment } (SF)$$

$$Y = SF/\theta$$

For example, if the required annual sinking fund were $62,400, and the corporation's tax rate were 48 percent, the pre-tax cost of the sinking fund would be $120,000 [$62,400/0.52]. If annual lease payments (a tax-deductible expense)

---

[8]There is obviously a relationship between the familiar "times interest earned" and the leverage factor, L, discussed in the previous chapter. Recall that Q is the proportion of assets financed by the residual owners' equity; Y is earnings before interest and taxes; and I is the dollar amount of interest on the debt. We found the leverage factor

$$L = \frac{1}{Q}\left(\frac{Y-I}{Y}\right).$$

Let times interest earned equal $Y/I = T$. Solving this expression for Y, we obtain $Y = IT$. Substituting this in the expression for the leverage factor, we have

$$L = \frac{1}{Q}\left(\frac{IT-I}{IT}\right) = \frac{1}{Q}\left(\frac{T-1}{T}\right).$$

were $160,000, the calculation of *fixed charge coverage* would be as shown below:

$$\text{Fixed charge} \atop \text{coverage} = \frac{\text{Earnings before interest and taxes}}{\text{Interest} + \text{Lease payments} + \dfrac{\text{Sinking fund payment}}{\theta}}$$

$$= \frac{\$2,000,000}{\$700,000 + \$160,000 + \$62,400/0.52} = 2.04$$

Alternatively, this calculation may be based upon annual cash flow generated before taxes, rather than just earnings before interest and taxes (*EBIT*). The addition to *EBIT* in the numerator of the ratio would come mainly from charges against income, such as amortization and depreciation expenses, which were non-cash charges. This form of the calculation matches an estimate of the cash inflows to the required cash outflows for interest, lease payments, and pre-tax cost of sinking fund payments.

Calculation of coverage ratios is made more complex when *preferred stock* is present in the financial structure. Preferred stock is an ownership interest, but annual dividend payments are usually limited to a stated level. Dividends on the preferred stock must be paid before any share of earnings is paid to the common stockholders who are, of course, the residual owners.

If we are looking at the company from the point of view of a present or prospective preferred stockholder, we are interested in the coverage of preferred dividends. There are two possibilities: (1) there may be no long-term debt preceding the preferred stock; or (2) there may be both preferred stock and long-term debt outstanding.

(1) If there is no long-term debt, the coverage of dividends on preferred stock must be based upon the earnings *after* taxes, since this is the stream of earnings available for preferred dividends. The figure for *times-dividends-earned* may then be obtained by dividing the net income after taxes by the dividend requirements of the preferred stock issue under study, combined with the dividend requirements of any other issues of preferred stock of equal or senior standing.

(2) If both bonds and preferred stock are outstanding, we may treat the preferred stock as if it were a very junior bond issue. With this approach, the coverage of preferred dividends can be calculated by dividing the earnings before interest and taxes by the sum of the interest charges on bonds and dividends on preferred stock. This method fails to deduct taxes before the preferred dividends, but it is suitable in practice if clearly defined and used consistently.[9]

The figure determined for times-interest-earned or for the dividend coverage on preferred stock is a measure of the probability of obtaining the agreed rate of return. Again, the standards that would be used to judge the adequacy

[9]A more refined approach would consider the pre-tax position of interest charges and the after-tax position of preferred dividends. Let Y = net income before income taxes; I = interest on bonds; P = preferred dividends; and t = the tax rate. Then

$$\text{Coverage of } P = \frac{Y(1-t)+I}{P+I(1-t)}$$

The numerator expresses earnings after taxes, but before payments on bonds and preferred stock; the denominator is the sum of preferred dividends and the after-tax cost of bond interest.

of the coverage would be determined by comparing the figure with that of other firms in the same industry and with the historical record of the company.

The residual owners (proprietor, partners, or common stockholders) will view the earnings available to them in a number of ways. The sole proprietor is interested in the dollar amount remaining to him; partners in their respective shares of the earnings; and common stockholders in the dollar amount available to them after all senior charges and after Federal income taxes. Quite frequently, the earnings available to the common stockholders are divided by the number of shares outstanding to derive a figure for *earnings per share.* This figure may then be compared to the price per share quoted in the market to derive a *price-earnings* ratio. Thus if the quoted market price were $24 and annual earnings per share were $2, we would say that the price-earnings ratio was 12:1.

To determine the proportion of these earnings that they actually receive in the form of dividends, residual owners may calculate the *payout ratio:* that is, the ratio of dividends per share to earnings per share. The same result would be obtained by dividing total dividend payments on common stock by the total amount of earnings available to the common stock after any preferred dividends.

Residual owners should also compare the dollar amount of earnings available to them with their equity in the business. This is a measure of management's success in achieving the profitability objective of the residual owners. The rate of return is determined by the following formula:

$$\frac{\text{Return on}}{\text{residual equity}} = \frac{\text{Earnings after taxes minus any preferred dividends}}{\text{Net worth of residual owners}}$$

In a corporation the net worth of residual owners would be equal to the common stock plus retained earnings, and in a proprietorship and partnership it would equal the capital of the owners.

Having determined the rate of return on his equity, the present or prospective owner will inquire into the origins of that return by examining the turnover of operating assets, the operating margin, the earning power and the financial leverage.

Let us apply this analysis to our lumber and building supply wholesaler. In this case the rate of return on his residual equity has dropped considerably from 9.82 percent ($29,600/$301,500) to 5.03 percent ($16,400/$326,200). Whereas Moore had been doing rather better than the median firm in this line of business (Table 4-1), he is presently not significantly better than "average." What has brought about this decline? First consider earning power:

	Margin	$\times$	*Turnover*	$=$	*Earning power*
Four years ago	$\dfrac{\$\ \ 31,400}{\$1,583,600}$	$\times$	$\dfrac{\$1,583,600}{\$\ \ 422,700}$	$=$	$\dfrac{\$\ \ 31,400}{\$422,700}$
	1.98%	$\times$	3.75	$=$	7.43%
Current year	$\dfrac{\$\ \ 19,300}{\$1,932,700}$	$\times$	$\dfrac{\$1,932,700}{\$\ \ 562,400}$	$=$	$\dfrac{\$\ \ 19,300}{\$562,400}$
	1.00%	$\times$	3.43	$=$	3.43%

The marked decline in earning power is a product of a slight drop in turn-over of operating assets and a sharp cut in operating margin. The lowered turnover is associated in part with the slower turnover of inventory that was noted earlier in the chapter. We must look further to ascertain the cause of the decline in the net operating margin.

Composition of Earnings. Since the basic reason for the decline in earnings of this company is the drop in the net operating margin from 1.98 percent to 1.00 percent, let us turn to a more detailed investigation of this factor. It is useful to prepare a percentage analysis of the operating statement, as shown in Table 4-4. What we have done here is to take each item on the operating statement as a percentage of net sales. Once again we can compare these percentages with those of other firms in the same business and with the experience of this company over time.

TABLE 4-4   Percentage Composition of Operating Statement of the Moore Lumber Company

	Operating Statements		Percentage Composition	
	Four Years Ago	Current Year	Four Years Ago	Current Year
Net sales	$1,583,600	$1,932,700	100.00%	100.00%
Cost of goods sold	1,335,900	1,680,700	84.36	86.96
Gross margin	$ 247,700	$ 252,000	15.64%	13.04%
Operating expenses:				
Selling and delivery	93,500	98,000	5.90	5.07
Salaries	46,900	50,600	2.96	2.62
Other	75,900	84,100	4.79	4.35
Total operating expenses	$ 216,300	$ 232,700	13.65%	12.04%
Net operating margin	31,400	19,300	1.98	1.00
Interest expense	1,800	2,900	0.11	0.15
Net profit	$ 29,600	$ 16,400	1.87%	0.85%

We may start by examining the *operating ratio,* which is the percentage of total operating expenses plus the cost of goods sold to net sales. The difference between the operating ratio and 100 percent is the net operating margin; in the current year the operating ratio is 99 percent and the margin is 1 percent. Since the operating ratio of this business has increased, we should look further at two main elements: the cost of goods sold and the operating expenses. In re-lation to net sales the cost of goods sold has risen from 84.36 percent to 86.96 percent. Or we could say that the *gross margin* has dropped from 15.64 percent to 13.04 percent. This change may be attributed either to a rise in the cost of goods sold without a corresponding increase in the selling price of those goods, or to price reductions in an effort to get a greater volume of sales. In this particular instance, the latter reason was the more important. In an effort to increase his turnover the owner sacrificed his margin, and the sacrifice was probably unwise. Operating expenses have declined from 13.65 percent to 12.04 percent of net sales. For reasons which we shall examine in greater detail later, one would expect certain of these costs to remain fixed and, therefore, to decline as a percentage of sales as volume increased. It might be added that the operating statements shown summarize many expense items that were available in greater detail in the books of the company. Consequently, in actual practice the financial manager had the opportunity to study these income and expense accounts more closely than we have here. Nonetheless, it is clear that the main cause for the lowered rate of return on the owner's equity is the decline in the gross margin.

Value of Financial Analysis

For the most part we have undertaken our analysis of the financial position of the firm from an external point of view, although there are obvious implications for internal financing. It is reasonable to ask whether such financial analysis works. Do financial ratios successfully predict financial difficulties? Research on this question is difficult, since the weakening of a financial ratio should set in motion actions that will enable the firm to avoid failure. In spite of such problems, research has revealed a significant difference in the means of financial ratios for failed and nonfailed firms. Of special importance is the deterioration of the financial ratios of failed firms for several years prior to bankruptcy.[10] This result emphasizes the importance of following trends in financial ratios, as we have done with Moore Lumber Company.

A more powerful use of financial ratios is to examine them in combination. For example, an increasing ratio of debt to net worth is less alarming if the quick ratio is rising than if it is falling. Taking the various ratios together, we gain a better idea of the health of the firm than if we examine each independently. We have attempted to relate the ratios to each other as we have moved through the analysis of Moore Lumber Company and will provide a concluding summary in the following section. Such a judgmental consideration can be reinforced by statistical techniques that give joint consideration to several ratios. These procedures—multiple regression and discriminant analysis—promise an even more effective use of ratios.[11]

Summary

At the outset of this chapter we stated that financial analysis was a first step in financial planning. Since we have taken this first step concerning our lumber

[10] W. H. Beaver, "Financial Ratios as Predictors of Failure," *Empirical Research in Accounting, Selected Studies, 1966* (Institute of Professional Accounting, January, 1967), pp. 80–81.

[11] E. I. Altman, "Financial Ratios, Discriminant Analysis and the Prediction of Corporate Bankruptcy," *Journal of Finance*, 23 (September, 1968), pp. 589–609.

and building supply wholesaler, let us indicate the impact of this analysis upon his plans for the future. First of all, from the viewpoint of his short-term creditors, his current position has worsened. His current ratio has declined and is below the median for his line of business according to the D & B ratios. Examination of his turnover of receivables and inventory reveals that both have slowed, but that most of his difficulty lies with his inventory turnover. The creditors' position has further weakened because they are financing a higher proportion of the total assets than they did four years ago.

How can he improve his current position? Since his poor cash position was associated with a slower inventory turnover, he examined his inventory and discovered a number of lines that he had taken on in an effort to expand sales were slow-moving and, in a few cases, obsolete. He plans to sell these items, even at a loss if necessary, to reduce his inventory and improve his cash position. As his cash position betters, he can reduce his current debt and better his ratio of debt to net worth.

Let us now look at the effect on his plans of our long-term analysis. The mortgage holder is in no danger, since the times-interest-earned coverage is ample. To the owner the most important factor in our long-term analysis is the lowered rate of return on his own equity. This seems to stem largely from his abortive effort to improve his turnover by cutting prices. Once he weeds out his slow-moving items, his turnover may improve to the point where he is making a satisfactory rate of return. However, at present he plans to be less liberal in his pricing policies. These plans will undoubtedly be aided by the current upturn in building activity in the area.

Questions

1/ Is it possible for a business to be making ample profits and be unable to pay its bills on time? Explain.

2/ Is it possible for a company to have a current ratio of 3:1 and be unable to pay its bills on time? Explain.

3/ What is the relative importance of inventory turnover to a delicatessen and to a dry cleaning establishment?

4/ To compute inventory turnover, cost of goods sold is divided by the average inventory. Why would not the figure for net sales be just as good as cost of goods sold?

5/ In what fields of business would you expect to have a relatively low percentage of net profits to net sales? A relatively high ratio? Why should these differences exist?

6/ What differences would you expect to find in the times-interest-earned figures for debt issues of a manufacturing concern and an electric utility? How would you justify these differences?

Problems

1/ The Broadstreet Men's Clothing Store has current assets of $50,000 and current liabilities of $25,000. Taking each transaction independently, compute the effect on the current ratio and net working capital of each of the following transactions. Do not cumulate the results.

a. A $2000 government bond is purchased.

b. New display cases are purchased for $1,000 cash.

c. $5000 of merchandise is purchased on trade credit.

d. Payment of $5000 is made on accounts payable.

e. Accounts receivable of $6000 are collected.

f. $40,000 is borrowed on the basis of a 10-year mortgage placed on the company's property.

g. The proprietor withdraws $10,000.

h. $15,000 is borrowed from the bank on a short-term basis and used to pay a note maturing in five years.

i. Two delivery trucks are sold for a total of $5000.

j. Allowance for depreciation is increased by $3000.

2/ The Downtown Department Store had an inventory (cost) of $350,000 on February 1, 1971, and $450,000 on January 31, 1972. Its sales for the fiscal year ending January 31, 1972, were $3,000,000. Average markup on selling price was 30 percent. Compute the annual rate of inventory turnover.

3/ The following are the financial statements of the Pilcher Products Corp.

Balance Sheet — December 31, 1971

Cash		$ 60,000
Accounts receivable		230,000
Inventories		170,000
Property and equipment	$600,000	
Less allowance for depreciation	190,000	410,000
		$870,000
Accounts and notes payable — trade		$ 95,000
Notes payable — bank		24,000
Accrued liabilities		16,000
Estimated Federal income tax liability		21,000
First mortgage, 6% bonds, due in 1992		150,000
Second mortgage, 6% bonds, due in 1987		50,000
Common stock — $5 par value; issued and outstanding 50,000 shares		250,000
Capital surplus		25,000
Reserve for plant expansion		65,000
Retained earnings		174,000
		$870,000

Note: There has been no change in the amount of bonds outstanding during 1971.

Income Statement
Year ended December 31, 1971

	Cash	Charge	Total
Net sales	$209,000	$863,000	$1,072,000
Cost of sales:			
Inventory of finished goods—1/1/71		94,000	
Cost of goods manufactured		780,000	
Inventory of finished goods—12/31/71		(103,000)	771,000
Gross profit on sales			$ 301,000
Selling expenses		160,000	
General expenses		73,000	233,000
Net operating profit			$ 68,000
Interest expense			11,000
Net income before Federal income tax			$ 57,000
Federal income tax (estimated)			21,000
Net income			$ 36,000

From the Pilcher Products Corp. financial statements compute the following:
a. Current ratio
b. Acid test ratio
c. Average number of days' charge sales uncollected
d. Average finished goods turnover
e. Ratio of debt to net worth
f. Number of times first mortgage bond interest was earned (before taxes)
g. Number of times second mortgage bond interest was earned (before taxes)
h. Fixed charge coverage. Lease payments included in "General expenses" total $5,000, and sinking fund payments on the two bond issues total $12,000.
i. Earnings per share of common stock
j. Net operating margin
k. Turnover of operating assets
l. Earning power
m. Rate of return before taxes on owners' equity
n. Rate of return after taxes on owners' equity
o. Operating ratio
p. Gross margin (percentage of net sales)

4/ a. The ABC Corporation reports purchases of materials for the year of $1,200,000 and outstanding accounts payable of $200,000. How many days of purchases remain unpaid?
b. The XYZ Corporation reports purchases of materials for the quarter of $400,000 and outstanding accounts payable of $110,000. How many days of purchases remain unpaid?

5/ The following is a condensed balance sheet for the Y Corporation:

Current assets	$ 700,000	Current liabilities	$ 200,000
Fixed assets	800,000	Fixed liabilities	500,000
		Net worth	800,000
	$1,500,000		$1,500,000

Income before interest and taxes, $76,000; interest charges on fixed liabilities, $16,000.

a. How much additional fixed assets could be financed with short-term credit before reducing the current ratio to 2:1?

b. How much additional inventory could be purchased on trade credit before reducing the current ratio to 2:1?

c. How much cash would need to be applied to the reduction of current debt to increase the current ratio to 5:1?

d. How much additional long-term debt could be issued at an annual interest cost of 5%, if it is desired to cover fixed charges by at least three times and to have a debt-to-net-worth ratio not in excess of 1:1?

6/ The Boquist Manufacturing Corporation is planning to form a subsidiary to manufacture ball-point pens. The firm will establish the subsidiary with an $800,000 investment in the subsidiary's common stock. The vice-president — finance wishes to prepare a pro forma balance sheet for the subsidiary based upon various average ratios for this type of business that he has gleaned from published sources. Using the limited information that he has available (shown below), prepare the balance sheet.

These are the only items on the balance sheet. Show computations.

Assets	*Liabilities and Capital*	
Cash	Notes and accounts payable	
Accounts receivable	Common stock	$800,000
Inventory		
Plant and equipment		

Turnover of operating assets (based on year-end figures): 1.5 times
Average collection period (based on 360-day year): 40 days
Gross profit percentage: 30 percent
Inventory turnover (based on year-end inventory): 4 times
Debt to net worth: 0.5:1
Acid test ratio: 0.80:1

Selected References

ALTMAN, E. I., "Financial Ratios, Discriminant Analysis and the Prediction of Corporate Bankruptcy," *Journal of Finance,* 23 (September, 1968), pp. 589–609.

BEAVER, W. H., "Financial Ratios as Predictors of Failure," *Empirical Research in Accounting, Selected Studies, 1966* (Institute of Professional Accounting, January, 1967), pp. 71–111.

BIERMAN, H., "Measuring Financial Liquidity," *Accounting Review,* 35 (October, 1960), pp. 628–32.

BOWLIN, O. D., "The Current Ratio in Current Position Analysis," *Financial Analysts Journal,* 19 (March–April, 1963), pp. 67ff.

EITEMAN, D. K., "A Computer Program for Financial Statement Analysis," *Financial Analysts Journal,* 20 (November–December, 1964), pp. 61–68.

FOULKE, R. A., *Practical Financial Statement Analysis.* 5th ed. New York: McGraw-Hill Book Co., 1961.

GREENLEAF, R. W., *An Introduction to Corporate Financial Statements,* Rev. ed. Indianapolis: Orchard House Press, 1965.

HELFERT, E. A., *Techniques of Financial Analysis.* Homewood, Illinois: Richard D. Irwin, Inc., 1963. Very helpful in a number of areas.

HORRIGAN, J. O., "Some Empirical Bases of Financial Ratio Analysis," *Accounting Review,* 40 (July, 1965), pp. 558–68.

JACKENDOFF, N., *A Study of Published Industry Financial and Operating Ratios.* Philadelphia, Pa.: Bureau of Economic and Business Research, Temple University, 1962.

JAEDICKE, R. K. and R. T. SPROUSE, *Accounting Flows: Income, Funds, and Cash.* Englewood Cliffs, N.J.: Prentice-Hall, Inc., 1965.

JOHNSON, G. L., "Funds-Flow Equations," *Accounting Review,* 41 (July, 1966), pp. 510–17.

MASON, P., "Cash Flow Analysis and Funds Statements," *Journal of Accounting* 111 (March, 1961), pp. 59–72.

ROBINSON, R. I. and R. W. JOHNSON, *Self-Correcting Problems in Finance.* 2nd ed. Boston: Allyn and Bacon, Inc., 1970. Provides excellent reinforcement of analytical tools in many areas of text.

WALTER, J. E., "Determination of Technical Solvency," *Journal of Business,* 30 (January, 1957), pp. 30–43.

Management of Cash

5

Let us pause for a moment to see where we are in the planning process. The financial manager is something like the captain of a ship who hopes to make his way towards England. This is his objective. As we have seen, the financial manager's objective is to maximize the value of the owners' equity. Just as the captain of the ship must know where he is before setting a course for England, so must the financial manager know his position before developing his plans to attain his objective. The study of our present position and how we reached that position has been the subject of the preceding chapter.

Once he knows his starting point, the next step for the captain is to be sure that his ship is "in control." There is little point to planning an ocean voyage with a faulty rudder or a wasteful engine that will use up the oil before arrival. When he is confident that his ship will operate efficiently, he is in a position to chart his course and estimate his needs for fuel, supplies, and labor. He can then check the adequacy of these plans by evaluating the anticipated condition of the ship upon its arrival. Will the trip have been profitable? Will fuel and supplies be sufficient to meet unforeseen storms? Finally, given these estimates of needs, he can set out to provision the ship.

In somewhat salty terms, this is the financial manager's task. He must first assure himself that internal policies are consistent and that they will economize the use of assets: cash, accounts receivable, inventory, and fixed assets will reflect the desired trade-off between risk and return. This is the subject of these next four chapters. The minimum cash balance required, credit and inventory policies, and plans for purchasing major items of plant and equipment must then be fitted together in a master plan for the "voyage" into the coming period. This integration of various plans and policies is achieved by preparing budgets (Chapter 9). In the process of drawing up budgets, the financial manager may discover that some of the policies concerning management of assets need to be revised. For example, credit policies that slow collections on accounts receivable or an inventory policy that allows a substantial accumulation of funds in inventory may conflict with the required minimum cash balances or with needs for new machinery. The budget process forces a compromise between such conflicting policies. After he has prepared his budget, the financial manager will draft a projected income statement and balance sheet so that he can judge the expected condition of the enterprise upon its arrival at the end of the budget period. This evaluation will employ many of the same financial tests discussed in the last chapter. The results of this step may force still another re-evaluation of policies and procedures followed in the management of assets, and of the budgets prepared to implement these policies.

The relative importance of each of the various major types of assets varies considerably from one major industrial group to another (Exhibit 5-1). Thus management of cash assumes greater importance in manufacturing than in public utilities. Management of receivables is particularly significant in construction and the wholesale trades. As we might suspect, inventories are a large proportion of assets in the wholesale and retail trades, and fixed assets dominate the assets of public utilities. We shall see in Chapter 10 that variations in types of assets financed are matched by differences in methods of financing.

Tracing Cash Flows

A conception of the cash flow within a business is vital to our understanding of cash management. That we may better visualize this flow of cash through a business, let us consider Exhibit 5-2. In somewhat mechanical fashion this chart compares the flow of cash to the flow of water through a plumbing system, with various reservoirs along the way. Because we need cash to pay bills, the focus of interest is on the cash reservoir—the cash on hand, or cash balance. Into this reservoir cash flows intermittently from issues of securities and from borrowing. These are external sources of cash.

Closely allied to the cash reservoir is the "near-cash" reservoir. Here we find temporary cash surpluses invested in various short-term securities that will be discussed at the end of this chapter. In large corporations flows between the cash and near-cash reservoir may occur almost daily.

EXHIBIT 5-1   *Composition of Assets by Major Industrial Groups*

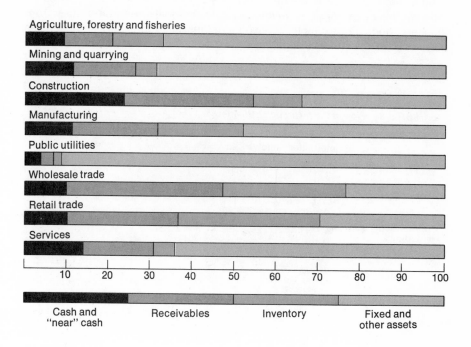

The second source of cash inflow into the cash reservoir is internal, that is, from cash sales and collections on accounts receivable. Any cash realized immediately from the sale of inventory flows directly into the cash reservoir. More frequently, inventory is sold on credit, so that a pool of receivables is built up, and it is not until payments are received on these accounts that cash is returned to the central reservoir. Presumably this inflow of cash is fairly regular, although some companies receive the bulk of the cash proceeds from their sales at the beginning of each month or in some particular season. Others, such as ship-, building concerns, may receive cash payments on contracts at much longer intervals.

There are also intermittent flows of cash from the reservoir to parties outside of the business for interest, dividends or withdrawals by owners, income taxes, repayment of debt, and retirement of other securities. At various intervals cash may be used to purchase fixed assets. Finally, there is a more regular flow out of the cash reservoir into inventories of materials and supplies, wages, and selling and administrative expenses. To assure a steady flow of material onto the production line, it is necessary to keep on hand a supply (reservoir) of raw materials. These flow into work-in-process and from there, with the addition of labor and other expenses, into finished goods inventory. (To simplify the exhibit these inventories are not shown separately.) It is not always necessary that we maintain these reservoirs of raw materials, work-in-process, and finished goods. For example, service industries, such as advertising agencies, may not have inventories of significant size.

EXHIBIT 5-2   Flow of Cash Through a Business

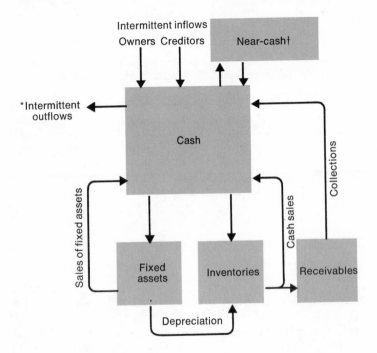

*Intermittent outflows
    Interest
    Income taxes
    Withdrawals by owners
    Repayment of debt
    Retirement of other securities

†Short-term marketable securities, such as U.S. Treasury bills, commercial paper, and certificates of deposit.

Consider the successive flow of funds through the reservoirs of a retailer. In early fall he must build his supply of cash and near-cash, most likely by borrowing from his bank. Then he uses these funds to build his inventories. As these are drawn down during the Christmas buying season, his accounts receivable swell. Finally, in January, he converts his receivables to cash, repays his bank, and diverts any temporarily idle funds into near-cash investments until he is ready to repeat the cycle for the Spring season.

Depreciation

Because it is a cause of confusion, special mention should be made of the frequent reference to depreciation as a "source of cash" or "source of funds." Strictly speaking, in accounting terminology, *funds* are net working capital: that is, current assets minus current liabilities. This is the sense in which we shall use the term in this section. (Later on it will be convenient to use the term as synonymous with "cash," a usage that is common in the field of finance.) The amount of funds generated from operations is frequently calculated to provide a rough estimate of cash generated by operations.

We have seen that at various intervals a company gives up cash in return for fixed assets, such as a machine. Over time it expects to recover the cost of the machine through the sale of products, just as it expects to recoup the cost of raw materials that are a part of the finished product. Since the machine is not immediately used up in the same way that raw materials are used up in the product, it is necessary to allocate a portion of the cost of the machine to each item coming off the production line. This is most frequently done by spreading the original cost of the machine over its estimated service life and then charging the estimated cost of each year's service to the items produced during that year. In pricing and selling its product, we are seeking to recapture immediate and out-of-pocket costs, such as labor and materials, and other costs which were "out-of-pocket" some time ago. This latter group of costs is represented by the fixed assets, and the portion of the original cost that we are charging against the current year's sales is termed *depreciation.*

Rather than claim that depreciation is a "source of funds," it is more accurate (but more long-winded) to say that funds are generated to the extent that revenues from sales exceed expenses that use funds currently. Let us illustrate this by assuming that an energetic entrepreneur invests $500,000 in a fireworks factory. The factory is to be depreciated at the rate of $50,000 per year for 10 years. After the first year of operation, the income statement (before taxes) might appear as shown below:

Sales		$200,000
Materials, labor, and other expenses paid	$80,000	
Depreciation	50,000	130,000
Operating income		$ 70,000

What was the amount of funds generated before taxes by operations? Funds were provided by sales ($200,000) and funds were paid out on materials, labor, and other expenses ($80,000). But funds were not used for depreciation; during the year nobody wrote out a check for $50,000 to "depreciation." Consequently, we could prepare a brief statement as shown below:

Funds Provided by Operations:

Funds provided from sales	$200,000
Expenses that currently used funds	80,000
Net funds provided by operations	$120,000

To emphasize that depreciation in and of itself is not a source of funds, let us now assume that at the beginning of the second year, somebody lights a cigarette in the fireworks plant. Diligent search subsequently fails to turn up any trace of the uninsured plant. Can management still count on funds being generated to the extent of $50,000 per year through depreciation charges? Obviously not. Funds generated by sales are $0; net funds provided by operations are $0.

Is it possible to increase funds provided by operations by increasing the charge for depreciation? This is not possible, but it *is* possible to increase the funds generated *after* taxes. Let us see why this is so. Assume that in the first year of operations management was faced with a choice between two methods of depreciating the plant. During the first year one would provide a charge of $50,000, the other a charge of $90,900.[1] Income statements under the alternative methods would appear as follows:

	Method A		Method B	
Sales		$200,000		$200,000
Materials, labor, etc.	$80,000		$80,000	
Depreciation	50,000	130,000	90,900	170,900
Operating income		$ 70,000		$ 29,100
Taxes (40%)		28,000		11,640
Net profit after taxes		$ 42,000		$ 17,460

By recasting this statement, we can see that funds generated from operations remain unchanged under either method, but that funds generated after taxes are greater under Method B *because of the tax shield provided by the larger depreciation expense:*

	Method A	Method B
Funds provided:		
Funds provided from sales	$200,000	$200,000
Expenses that currently used funds	80,000	80,000
Funds provided by operations	$120,000	$120,000
Tax payments	28,000	11,640
Funds provided after tax payments	$ 92,000	$108,360

Under Method B, depreciation charges are large in the early years, but small in the later years. For example, depreciation charges would amount to only $9091 in the tenth year. The tax shield provided by the depreciation will lessen each year, so that taxes paid each year will rise. Thus if tax rates remain unchanged over the period, the corporation will pay the same total taxes. If this is so, what is the advantage of using accelerated methods of depreciation? The answer lies in the time value of money. We would rather have money now than in the future. We would prefer to make small payments on taxes now rather than later, because we can use the cash that we do not pay out in taxes to invest in the business. In essence, we have an interest-free loan from the government, and that is a very pleasant arrangement.

[1] This is approximately the charge that would be provided by the sum-of-the-digits method of depreciation, whereby 10/55 of the plant is depreciated the first year, 9/55 the second year, and so on to the tenth year, when 1/55 of the plant is depreciated. (The sum of the digits 1 through 10 is 55.)

A word of warning. This discussion has been in terms of depreciation reported for tax purposes. A corporation may use accelerated depreciation for tax purposes and straight-line depreciation for reporting income to its stockholders. In recent years several corporations have switched from accelerated to straight-line depreciation for reporting purposes. For example, by switching to straight-line depreciation, American Seating Company was able to report net income per share in 1966 of $2.03, whereas if it had continued on an accelerated basis reported earnings per share would have been only $0.69.[2]

Relation of Cash Flows to Income Statement

If we end a fiscal year with more in the cash reservoir than at the beginning of the year, this excess does not necessarily equal the profits for the year. This is because accountants keep the books on an accrual, not a cash basis. In seeking to measure net income, accountants recognize that to record income and expense items according to the period in which the check was received or the bill paid distorts the picture. It is clearly misleading to charge against this year's income the cost of a machine whose services will still be available during the following five years. To meet this sort of problem the accountant tries to allocate income and expense items to the fiscal period during which they were respectively earned or incurred. In many cases this means that in his income statement the accountant must overlook the fact that the cash for these items came in or went out of the business during some other fiscal period. Consequently, in the preparation of an income statement he takes some of the real cash flows that have gone into and out of the cash reservoir within the current year and reallocates them to other time periods. In addition he takes cash flows that occurred during other fiscal periods and charges them to the current year. Because of these adjustments the profit the accountant shows and the cash generated from operations are rarely the same.

Changes in Cash Balances

The job of the financial manager would be greatly simplified if the inflow and outflow of cash from the reservoir balanced each other. But they rarely do. It is not enough that they balance out at the end of the year. If the outflow is sufficiently greater than the inflow during some interval within the year the financial manager may be unable to pay his bills. To avoid this unhappy situation he may adjust to changes that lower his cash balance by securing additional funds from outside the business or by reducing accounts receivable, inventory, and fixed assets. In other cases he may oppose proposals made by other department heads because of unfavorable effects upon the cash flow. Some of the changes in cash flows within the business are a result of external forces over which the financial manager has relatively little control. Other changes occur because of shifts in various policies within the firm. Let us consider the events or policy changes that might cause the level of funds in the cash reservoir to rise or to fall.

[2]John H. Myers, "Depreciation Manipulation for Fun and Profits," *Financial Analysts Journal,* 23 (November–December, 1967), p. 121.

External Factors. The level of the cash on hand will rise if the cash inflow from cash sales and collections on accounts receivable is greater than the cash outflow going into materials, labor, other costs, and taxes. As we have seen, this accumulation of cash does not necessarily mean that the company is making a profit in the accounting sense. A rise in the level of cash or near-cash could occur if the sales of the company should decline in response to a seasonal or cyclical decrease in economic activity. As fewer and fewer sales are made, we cut our production. This allows us to cut our cash outflow for direct labor and other costs and to reduce our inventories of raw material and work-in-process. That is, as items move from these two inventory reservoirs, we do not replace them. To support our lower level of sales, we can stock a smaller inventory of finished goods. Finally, the lower level of sales gives rise to a smaller amount of accounts receivable. Thus the supplementary reservoirs of materials and supplies, goods-in-process, finished goods, and accounts receivable are gradually depleted and are not replenished at the same rate. In general, to the extent that we lower the levels in these reservoirs, we raise the level in the cash and near-cash reservoirs.

The level in the reservoir of cash would be lowered in the normal course of business if the cash outflow were greater than the cash inflow. This would be characteristic of an expanding business or one operating in an inflationary economy. Although production and sales might be expanded by increasing the rate of flow through the pipelines, it is unlikely that any prolonged rise in sales could be achieved in this manner if inventories are maintained at their old levels. A rapid rate of drainage from the supplementary tanks of raw materials, work-in-process, and finished goods increases the likelihood of interruptions in production and delivery because of shortages in needed times. Unless the additional sales are cash sales, accounts receivable are almost bound to rise. As expansion presses against the productive capacity of the firm, additional flows of cash into fixed assets will become necessary. With the rise in the levels in these various reservoirs the level of cash in the central tank is likely to decline. The rate at which cash is generated is insufficient to counterbalance the rate of outflow necessary to build up the levels in the various reservoirs of inventories, accounts receivable, and fixed assets. Unless the reservoir of cash was overflowing to begin with, it will be necessary for the firm to turn to outside sources to replenish the level in the cash reservoir.

Internal Factors. Since decisions in most areas of a business will have an impact upon the cash flow, it is important that the financial manager be able to recognize and forecast the financial effects of policy changes in marketing, production, purchasing, personnel and so on. Many of these decisions require a balance between risk and return. Where the effect is significant, he should have a part in reaching the final decision.

A change in marketing policies may affect the rate or timing of cash inflows and outflows. For example, a large advertising campaign will require an immediate cash outflow, but it may be some time before the effects of the campaign are felt in the form of an increased cash inflow from sales. The addition of new products to the company's line may mean more sales and profits in the long run, but to the financial manager it also means larger amounts of cash tied up in inventories and accounts receivable. A decision to pay salesmen on a commission basis will tend to match the cash outflow on their salaries to the cash inflow from collections. If we pay them a flat monthly rate, we will be faced with a cash outflow for salaries that may not be adequately balanced by an inflow from collections during slack seasons. It may well be desirable from the point of view of the sales manager to pay regular salaries in order to keep his staff. The only point to be made is that this policy has a certain drawback in terms of contributing to a lack of balance between cash inflow and outflows.

Production decisions also affect cash flows. Among the more obvious effects would be the drainage of cash to acquire additional fixed assets. Or let us say that management is considering leveling out seasonal peaks in production by manufacturing for inventory during the slack seasons. To make such a decision, top management would consult the labor relations department to determine the effect of such a policy on labor; the production department to determine the effects of the policy on production costs; the sales manager to ascertain the possibility of forecasting sales accurately and the likelihood of model or design changes that would make the inventory obsolete. The financial manager might well point out that during the slack season more cash would be flowing out of the cash reservoir into the inventory of finished goods than would flow back into the cash reservoir from collections of receivables. The risk of having obsolete inventory must be weighed against the lower costs and greater returns that might be obtained by level production.

Purchasing decisions may also have an impact upon financial management. For example, the purchasing agent may be able to obtain a substantial quantity discount if he buys three months' supply at a time rather than one month's supply. However, the financial manager must be consulted to see whether or not he can finance the additional two months' worth of inventory. The final decision will be made by top management in the light of factors such as the forecasts of sales and prices, availability of storage space, the cost and availability of funds, the risk of absolescence, and the return to be gained from quantity discounts.

Even decisions in the personnel area may affect the inflow and outflow of cash. For example, if employees are paid twice a month instead of once a month, cash will flow out more rapidly. In other words, whereas the firm had previously "borrowed" the employees' services for a month before paying for those services, the company will now borrow the services for only two weeks before paying for them. Higher wage rates or the creation of fringe benefits will cause cash to flow out of the reservoir more rapidly than before, and other adjustments will have to be made if the level of cash in the reservoir is to be maintained.

In general, accounting decisions are probably least likely to affect the flow of cash through the business except when decisions affect the amount of Federal income taxes and other taxes to be paid. For example, a decision to treat an expenditure as a current expense rather than as an investment in an asset may slightly lower the amount of the income tax for the current year, but there is no immediate effect at the time upon the cash flow in the business. However the accountant treats the expenditure on his books, it is a cash outflow to the financial manager and it has correspondingly reduced the level of cash in the cash reservoir. Similarly, the accountant may go through various gyrations to allocate expenses among the different products turned out by the company. Although the decisions of this nature may be important in enabling top management to decide which products to manufacture, they have little effect on the immediate cash flow picture.

From this discussion it should be apparent that policy decisions in practically every area of the business may have an impact upon the reservoir of cash because they affect the rate and timing of flows into and out of the reservoir. Consequently, these decisions cannot be reached without the assistance of the financial manager. The more strapped the company is for funds, the greater weight must be given his advice. For a firm that is "cash-poor," maintenance of liquidity in order to reduce risk of bankruptcy is more important than increased profits. Unfortunately, while such a situation restricts freedom of action in marketing, production, purchasing, and other functions within the business, it also limits the ability of the financial manager to obtain funds on reasonable terms. While the maintenance of a liquid position is necessary to the payment of bills, it is also a prerequisite to the acquisition of additional funds from outside the business. As Petrarch said, "There is no place so strong but that an ass laden with gold will find his way in."

Managing Cash Efficiently

Now that we understand how cash flows through a business, how do we manage cash in order to maximize the market value of the owners' equity? There are two aspects. First, we manage cash efficiently. Insofar as possible and desirable, we speed cash flows into the firm and delay cash flows out of the firm. While we have the use of idle cash, we attempt to obtain the highest return on its investment, consistent with a low level of risk. This first aspect of cash management is the business of this section. The second aspect is more fundamental. Given that we are as efficient as possible in handling and investing cash, how do we achieve an optimal balance among alternative uses of cash in order to maximize the value of the net revenue from cash management? This is the much more complex matter that will be analyzed in the following section on managing cash optimally.

Controlling Cash Flows

Speeding Collections of Cash. Even if we cannot persuade our customers to pay their accounts more rapidly, we can often shorten the period that elapses between the time a customer signs a check and the moment we have the use of the funds. To understand this, let us consider our customer in Phoenix, Arizona. We are in New York. After he deposits the check in the mail in Phoenix, it takes about four days to arrive in New York. We need a day to process the check. Technically we do not have the use of the funds as soon as we deposit the check in our bank, but should wait two days for the check to clear through our bank and through the Federal Reserve banking system to the bank of our customer in Phoenix. About seven days after our customer dropped the check in the mail we would have the use of the funds. Thus there are funds floating around for at least a week that our customer cannot use and which we cannot use either.

How can we shorten this interval? One procedure would be to have the checks deposited to our account before we process them, rather than afterwards. We might have our customers forward checks to a lock box in a post office in New York and arrange with the Guaranty Trust Company in New York to pick up these checks, credit them to our account, and advise us of the name of the customer, amount of check, and any other necessary information. We would thus enter this information on our records after the check was on its way through the clearing process.

An alternative would be to move the lock box out west. We can establish a lock box in the post office in Tucson for all of our accounts in the southwest. Customers in this area will then be instructed to send their payments on account to our lock box in Tucson, and a Tucson bank of our choice will remove the checks daily and credit them to our account. We could instruct the Tucson bank to remit balances over a certain amount by wire to our New York bank. By this procedure we might reduce the time interval from the mailing of the check to our use of funds from seven to two days. In other words, we would reduce the "float" by five days. The savings may be considerable. Using this technique, Bendix Corporation has reduced outstanding receivables by two to three days and has "permanently wrung $6 million to $8 million out of them."[3]

The optimal number and location of lock boxes may be estimated by computer simulation or by analytical techniques that approximate the solution.[4] To illustrate the possible savings from one lock box, assume that our annual sales amount to $36 million, average daily collections amount to about $100,000. An average reduction of float of five days would free a gross amount of $500,000 for use elsewhere in our business. Since the Tucson bank would expect us to maintain a deposit to pay for the cost of its services, the net amount of funds freed would be somewhat less. An illustrative calculation is shown below:

Float in central collection system (7 days)	$700,000
Less: Float in regional collection system (2 days)	200,000
Gross funds freed from collection system	500,000
Less: Added funds in regional bank balances to compensate for lock-box services	200,000
Net funds freed	$300,000

There are other benefits to be derived from this system in addition to the reduction of float. Because checks are collected faster, we learn of dishonored checks and weak credit situations sooner. A considerable amount of our own check-handling procedures is transferred to the Tucson bank. Because of the size of its operations, it may be able to handle the task more efficiently than we can. Furthermore, we have achieved better control over incoming cash and considerably reduced the chances of fraud. There are also more intangible benefits obtained through use of the regional bank for credit information and as

[3] *Wall Street Journal*, June 3, 1969, p. 36.

[4] F. K. Levy, "An Application of Heuristic Problem Solving to Accounts Receivable Management," *Management Science*, 12 (February, 1966), pp. B-236-44.

a possible source of loans. The disadvantages of the system lie in the charges made by the bank for its services and the costs and problems of converting to the system. However, if net added annual costs total as much, let us say, as $9000, our annual cost of freeing these funds is only three percent. It is difficult to raise $300,000 at a lower annual cost.

If very large payments are involved, it may be economical to spend additional money to speed the cash to the till. When Ralston Purina was paid a large settlement in Puerto Rico, a messenger was sent there to pick up the check and fly to New York to deposit it so that the funds could then be wired from the bank to headquarters in St. Louis.[5]

Delaying Disbursements of Cash. If we are purchasing materials on terms of 2/10, n/30, we obviously should pay suppliers if at all possible by the tenth day in order to obtain the 2 percent cash discount. However, there is no advantage to paying the account on the second day, rather than the tenth day. By delaying payment until the last day, we are able to have the use of those funds for an additional eight days. The same effect is achieved if we have our divisions requisition funds only as they need them, so that withdrawals from the central checking account will be made just before the disbursement of funds by the division.

Actual disbursement of funds may also be delayed by the use of drafts, a practice that is becoming increasingly popular. A draft is merely an order drawn by one person upon another party (usually a bank) to pay a third person. A check is a draft, but there is an important difference. Whereas we should have the funds in the bank when we draw the check, we must provide cash to meet a draft only when it is presented by our bank to us for payment. For example, American Telephone and Telegraph Co. uses drafts for almost all types of payment. Assume that an employee is paid by draft on a Friday. He deposits it in his local bank. Experience has shown that the draft will not reach AT&T's New York bank until Wednesday or Thursday of the following week. On the day that it is presented by the bank to AT&T, the company has until 3:00 P.M. that afternoon to inspect the draft and to deposit funds to cover it. If AT&T paid employees by check, it would have to have the funds available in the bank on payday; by the use of drafts it obtains the use of these funds for almost an additional week. When payrolls amount to several million dollars, this delay in cash outflow represents a substantial source of funds. However, banks find that drafts involve considerably more handling costs than do checks, and some are levying charges of 20 to 50 cents a draft.

Concentration Banking. A pamphlet from a large bank asks, "Is your company's inventory of money stored in too many places?"[6] Concentration banking is a process of moving scattered inventories of deposits from several collection banks to one or a limited number of concentration banks. Once deposits are gathered in one place the financial manager can control and employ the funds more effectively. For example, the Sun Oil Company requires its district offices to deposit funds daily in local banks. Simultaneously with the deposit, each

[5] "How Business Lives Beyond Its Means," *Business Week,* November 15, 1969, p. 76.
[6] "Cash Mobilization Program," The Northern Trust Bank, Chicago, Illinois.

district office sends a depository transfer check to the main-office bank. The main bank credits Sun's account and clears the check back to the district bank through the normal processes. If larger amounts are involved, it becomes economical to use a wire transfer. Sun freed funds "with a minimum earning of $50,000 a year" by this process.[7] Rather than have its district offices initiate the transfers to concentrate balances, the depository banks could have been instructed to transfer automatically any funds in excess of a specified minimum.

Investing Idle Cash

Instead of permitting temporarily idle funds to remain in our checking account, we should invest those funds in securities that are "near-cash" or reduce outstanding debt. If funds are invested, the securities chosen must be safe and readily marketable. For the sake of an additional percentage point or so in return, we cannot afford to risk loss of a portion of the principal that we will urgently need in the business at a later date. Adherence to this objective clearly rules out purchase of common stocks. It should also rule out purchases of long-term corporate and even government bonds. Changes in interest rates affect the market prices of long-term bonds much more than those of short-term obligations. For example, any financial manager that purchased 25-year, $3\frac{1}{2}$ percent government bonds at $890 in August, 1966, found those same bonds

TABLE 5-1   Interest Yields Available on Short-Term Investments, Mid-1970

Type of Security	(Annual Percentage) Market Yield
Treasury bills	
3-month maturity	6.54
6-month maturity	6.66
Commercial paper	
Prime, 30- to 270-day maturity	8.625–8.75
Finance co. paper placed directly,	
30- to 89-day maturity	7.75
Prime bankers acceptances, one- to 180-day maturity	7.75–8.00
Certificates of deposit	
30–89 day maturity	7.75–8.00
90–179 day maturity	6.75
180 days and longer	7.00
Federal agency issues, 6-month maturity	
Federal Land Bank	6.99
Federal Home Loan Bank	7.16
Tax-exempt securities	
Aaa	6.80
Baa	7.40

Sources: *Federal Reserve Bulletin* and *Wall Street Journal.*

[7] C. B. Axford, "Bank-Corporate Ideas for Improving Cash Management," *Burroughs Clearing House,* 52 (May, 1968), p. 73.

selling for $820 just six months later. Losses on this scale could force major revisions in a company's plans, as well as in the office of the financial manager.

There is a wide variety of securities that would be suitable for our investment portfolio. An indication of the annual yields provided by these different investments is provided in Table 5-1, although the spreads between yields may vary substantially over time in response to changes in the money and capital markets. Let us examine briefly the essential characteristics of these investments.

U.S. Treasury Bills and Notes. Probably the most useful securities for temporary investment of idle funds are U.S. Treasury bills. These are issued weekly by the Treasury with maturities ranging from 91 days to one year. They are readily marketable, even in very large amounts. Treasury notes have initial maturities of from one to five years, although needs for shorter maturities can be met by purchasing notes in the market as they approach maturity. Occasionally the yields on notes may be slightly lower than on bills with about the same maturity date, because holders will usually receive rights to exchange their present securities for a new issue at maturity.

Commercial Paper. A second alternative is the purchase of high-grade commercial paper; that is promissory notes issued by large, established corporations. Beginning in 1964, a number of large commercial banks led by the First National Bank of Boston also began to issue short-term unsecured promissory notes, generally in denominations of $1 million or more. More recently, the large bank-holding companies have also issued commercial paper.

Among the most useful form of commercial paper for large corporate investors are the notes sold by the major finance companies through their own offices. Since these are available for any maturity up to 270 days, we can very precisely time their maturity in relation to our needs for funds. Thus we can arrange to buy paper that will mature just a day before a payment is due on corporate income or social security taxes. The yield on high-grade commercial paper is usually somewhat above that available on short-term government securities.

Certificates of Deposit. Beginning in early 1961, commercial banks began to issue negotiable certificates of deposit, or CDs. Designed by the banks to recapture corporate deposits, these represent receipts for time deposits and offer yields that vary according to maturity and the size and financial reputation of the issuing bank. New York banks offer CDs for time periods of from less than 90 days to 360 days in denominations of $1 million and up, but banks in other cities are willing to sell denominations as small as $100,000 at a somewhat higher yield than offered by the major banks.

Although the yield on CDs purchased directly from banks is limited by Regulation Q administered by the Federal Reserve Board,[8] higher yields may be available by purchasing CDs in the secondary market. While a few small banks have had some unfortunate experience in being unable to redeem CDs

---

[8]Restrictions on maximum rates payable on large CDs of 89 days or less were removed in 1970. The effect is evident by comparing yields on certificates of deposit in Table 5–1.

when they matured, an active market for CDs continues. In mid-1970 there were over $13 billion outstanding.

Bankers Acceptances. An importer of goods is usually not required to pay for them immediately. The seller may send him an order to pay, a draft, with, say, a three-month maturity. If the seller wishes to be particularly certain of being paid, he may ask that the buyer have the draft "accepted" by a commercial bank. By this process the bank guarantees the payment of the draft at maturity, and the buyer gains ready access to credit (after payment of an appropriate fee to the banker for the service). Once accepted by the bank, the draft becomes a "banker's acceptance." If the seller does not wish to wait for his funds for three months, he can readily sell it in the marketplace.

With the growth in international trade the volume of bankers acceptances outstanding has grown rapidly to almost $5.6 billion in mid-1970. Bankers acceptances generally offer somewhat higher yields than Treasury bills, but are a very safe form of short-term investment.

Repurchase Agreements. Generally referred to as RPs, repurchase agreements are arrangements whereby a corporation buys a large amount of Treasury obligations from a bond dealer for a few days (frequently over a weekend), with the understanding that the dealer will then repurchase the securities at an agreed price. Thus the corporation aids the dealer in carrying his inventory of bonds and obtains in return a yield that usually is slightly above the available yield on a Treasury obligation of similar maturity.

Other. Federal agencies, such as the Federal Land Banks, Federal Home Loan Banks, and others, are authorized to issue securities. Although they are not guaranteed by the U.S. Government, they are highly regarded as short-term investments. Yields offered are slightly higher than those on Treasury bills of similar maturity, but the spread has narrowed in recent years.

Still other possible media for short-term investment of idle funds are the securities issued by state and local governments. Since these have the added advantage of being exempt from Federal corporate income taxes, the market yields are somewhat lower than on Treasury bills. However, the yield after taxes may be higher.

Some corporate treasurers have had good results by investing in high-grade preferred stocks, while others have experimented with Mexican commercial paper, foreign securities, and time deposits in Japanese banks. In these cases the added income may more than offset the risk of price fluctuations.[9] These departures from the more common forms of short-term investments thus offer both higher yields and more sleepless nights.

Balancing Alternative Uses

Given that we have devised means of controlling cash inflows and outflows efficiently, and given that the portfolio of near-cash is producing the best yield consistent with the low risk desired, how do we then proceed to achieve an

---

[9] P. F. Anderson and R. D. B. Harman, "The Management of Excess Corporate Cash," *Financial Executive,* 32 (October, 1964), pp. 26–30ff. See also *Wall Street Journal,* November 5, 1963, p. 1.

optimal balance among alternative uses of cash in order to maximize the value of the owners' equity? Let us examine the decision variables. Over some planning horizon we must determine what values to maximize and then the constraints that govern the achievement of that objective.[10] Let us examine these three aspects of managing cash.

Planning Horizon

Do we establish plans for managing cash for a day, a month, or five years? There are really two decisions required. First, how long into the future should we project cash flows? Generally, the longer the period, the higher the probability of making errors in forecasting. Probably an annual projection of cash flows is adequate. The sufficiency of a particular planning horizon can be tested by determining whether or not changes in the length of the horizon materially affect the actions that would be taken during the first segment of the planning period. Second, how should the planning period be segmented? Should it be broken into days, weeks, or months? The finer the segmentation, the higher the probability of making errors in forecasting. To illustrate, the variance of actual net cash flows in relation to the expected value on the 118th *day* in the future is likely to be much greater than the variance in relation to the expected value of the fourth *month*. It is true, however, that we may be able to make quite accurate estimates on a daily basis for the coming week. Therefore, a logical procedure would be to specify plans on a daily basis for the next week, then on a weekly basis for the following two or three weeks, and, finally, on a monthly basis for the remainder of the year.

It is important to recognize that plans should be flexible. The only firm commitment is the action called for on the first day of the plan. The results of that day may require readjustments of the remainder of the plan. Consequently, sound cash management calls for a rolling forecast. For example, General Electric "estimates cash positions daily for a week ahead and then weekly for several weeks ahead."[11] In addition to updating its weekly forecasts, Tenneco, Inc. recasts its monthly projections every three months.

Objective Function

It is all very well to state that our objective is to maximize the market value of the owners' equity, but in managing cash what do we maximize that will lead to this result? Let us assume that we have established a planning horizon of one year. Essentially, we wish to produce as much additional money in the till at the end of the year as possible. This assumes that any cash generated by our activities during the year is recycled to earn additional returns. We can refer to the additional money accumulated at the end of the year as the *net terminal value* or *horizon value*. This value is a result of three decision variables: returns from payments on debts, net returns from investments, and the cost of interest

[10]The discussion is based on the linear programming model set forth by Yair E. Orgler, *Cash Management* (Belmont, Calif.: Wadsworth Publishing Co., Inc., 1970), pp. 47–118.

[11]"How Business Lives Beyond Its Means," *Business Week,* November 15, 1969, p. 74.

paid on short-term loans. Thus our purpose is to maximize the following objective function:

$$\text{Net terminal value} = f \left(\begin{array}{c} \text{Return from} \\ \text{payments} \end{array} + \begin{array}{c} \text{Net yield from} \\ \text{near-cash} \end{array} - \begin{array}{c} \text{Interest paid} \\ \text{on short-term} \\ \text{loans} \end{array} \right)$$

Returns from payments includes the cash discounts that are available when we pay our bills by a specified time. (As indicated earlier, credit terms of 2/10, net 30 days indicate that we can deduct two percent from the face of the invoice if we pay it by the 10th day.) If management should decide to delay payments on accounts payable even beyond the 30-day period, we should attempt to make some estimate of the cost of such delays and charge this cost of a poor credit standing against the net terminal value. Returns from payments also include any savings that can be achieved by prepaying outstanding loans.

The net yield from near-cash investments differs from the gross yield by transaction costs; that is, the cost of buying and selling the securities. The more transfers between cash and near-cash, the higher will be such costs.[12]

The cost of short-term borrowed funds is also a decision variable. To the extent that management decides to rely more heavily on this source of funds, the interest costs will offset the gains to be achieved by prepayment of debt and investment in near-cash.

Constraints

Management is subject to a number of constraints in maximizing the terminal value of its cash-management activity. Some are imposed upon the firm by various institutional arrangements; others are a product of internal policies. We can measure the cost (or benefits) of these latter type of constraints by measuring the terminal value of the objective function, given various changes in the policies under investigation.

Short-Term Financing. A firm is customarily limited in the amounts that it can borrow from commercial banks or other suppliers of short-term funds. Of course, our current position as reflected in the current ratio, quick ratio, and other measures discussed in the preceding chapter will determine the restrictiveness of such constraints upon our cash management. Frequently, constraints on one type of financing are related to other sources of funds. For example, large corporations may issue short-term, unsecured promissory notes, called *commercial paper,* so long as those issues are adequately backed by standby credit arrangements at commercial banks.

Near-Cash. Obviously, in making our plans we are constrained by the fact that we cannot sell more securities than are scheduled to be available at any point during the planning period.

Minimal Cash Balance. A minimal level of cash balance is required to compensate banks for the services that they perform in collecting checks and handling

[12] For a discussion of the proper balancing of yield from securities and transfer costs, see M. H. Miller and D. Orr, "A Model of the Demand for Money by Firms," *Quarterly Journal of Economics,* 80 (August, 1966), pp. 413–35.

payroll accounts and other disbursements. We should try to balance the per-item costs of these various services against the earnings that the bank can receive on our deposits in order to assure their adequacy in compensating the bank for these services. With respect to this type of service the objective is to reduce bank balances to the level where the costs of the services equal the return the bank can earn on the deposit; the extra cash can then be invested elsewhere to improve earnings. (Remember that commercial banks cannot pay interest on demand deposits.)

As we shall see later in greater detail, banks may also require certain balances (called "compensating balances") when they make short-term loans. Thus if we arrange to borrow $100,000 from a bank, we might be required to maintain on the average not less than $15,000 of available funds in our checking account with the bank. Bankers are also becoming more sophisticated in balancing the costs of their services against their earnings from deposits, and may, therefore, institute added service charges if our deposits are not large enough.

Finally, we can expect banks to offer a number of services for which they do not levy a specific charge, but which are nonetheless very valuable. Bankers often act as a clearinghouse of financial information, so that they may put us in touch with new customers, sources of additional capital, and possible candidates for merger or acquisition. In addition they often provide credit information on potential customers. Since banks are also profit-seeking institutions, we should seek to compensate them for these "free" services by maintaining adequate balances.

Management may decide that the minimal level of deposits required to satisfy the banks is not adequate to the needs of the company. This decision depends in part upon the anticipated variance of actual from expected cash flows. The greater the variance, the more likely is management to insist upon retaining additional balances in cash or near-cash. But the relationship of the size of the cash balance to the risk of being caught short is not linear. If the minimum level required by the bank is $50,000, we may substantially reduce the risk of insolvency (inability to pay bills) by increasing our cash balance to $100,000. However, another $50,000 increase to $150,000 may bring only a very slight further reduction in the risk. Thus there are diminishing marginal returns from increasing the cash balance. A second factor influencing the size of the "extra" cash balance is management's willingness to accept risk. Some may be quite willing to run on the thin edge of disaster, whereas others may demand a large cushion of safety.

Cash Flows. During every period cash flows into or out of the firm. The consequent changes in the cash balances constrain the ability of the cash manager to pay bills and to make short-term investments. Many cash flows, such as receipts from accounts receivable and payments on accounts payable, taxes, salaries, and wages, cannot be quickly or substantially influenced by managerial policies. In particular, the more immediate are such payments, the less readily can management change the constraint in order to improve the terminal value of cash management. Consequently, the final formulation of a cash budget, as explained in Chapter 9, is reached only after much prior testing of alternative courses of action. Once the policies are instituted, many cash flows in the near future are substantially "locked in" and thereby serve as effective constraints upon the ability of the financial manager to better the terminal value of the objective function through cash management.

Other. Our ability to manage cash may also be influenced by other constraints, such as limits on the current ratio or net working capital (current assets minus current liabilities) imposed by lenders or by management. Departure from accepted financial ratios may have a costly effect upon the terminal value. As illustration, REA Express, Inc. was able to negotiate a reduction in its net working capital requirements only by doubling the rate that it was paying for its bank loan.[13]

In simple terms, then, the financial manager tries to do the best he can over a defined planning horizon to maximize the terminal, or horizon value of the returns obtained from making payments on debts, from the net yield on near-cash investments, while deducting the cost of short-term borrowings. In pursuing this objective he is subject to several constraints, some of which are partially within his control or the control of other functional managers. He must juggle these constraints to the extent possible and desirable, while considering the risk preferences of management. In each case he should test to see whether a change in the value of a constraint is offset by a shift in the value of some other constraint or in the costs and revenues represented by the decision variables in the objective function.

Summary

Management of cash is particularly important because it brings into sharp focus the trade-off between risk and return faced by the financial manager. If cash is not available to meet bills as they come due, the ultimate risk is faced: the risk of bankruptcy.

Because we frequently use financial statements prepared by accountants, it is necessary to have a clear understanding of how cash flows are measured and why reported earnings do not match cash flows. Indeed, it is very easy to go broke while making a profit.

There are two stages to the management of cash. First, we should manage cash and near-cash efficiently. This is a matter of reducing waste: the "float" of cash represented by incoming collections, payments made sooner than necessary, scattered deposit balances, and excessive and unrewarding balances in checking accounts. This stage includes efficient management of near-cash in order to produce the highest return consistent with a low risk. Second, given efficient handling of cash flows and balances, we can turn to the principal task of cash management: maximization over some planning horizon of the terminal value of the accumulated returns from payments and investments, less the interest costs of short-term financing. In view of the numerous, interrelated constraints involved, this is not a trivial task.

[13] "REA Tries to Avoid Penn Central Route," *Business Week,* June 27, 1970, p. 39.

Questions

1/ Most individuals keep their records on a cash flow basis rather than on an accrual basis. How are these personal cash flows affected by the withholding of personal income taxes (rather than their payment in a lump sum); by changes in wage receipts from a weekly to a monthly basis; by the use of consumer credit? What other changes affect your personal cash flows?

2/ For what sorts of business is the cash generated from operations likely to be large relative to sales? Do these same businesses characteristically use long-term debts as a source of funds?

3/ Let us assume there are two accountants keeping the books for a business. One keeps the books on a cash basis and the other keeps the books on an accrual basis: that is, he allocates expenses and income to the fiscal periods in which they were incurred or earned. At the end of 50 years would there be a significant difference in the total earnings before taxes reported by the two accountants? Why or why not?

4/ Trace the effects of a decline in the price level on the level of investment in inventories, accounts receivable, and fixed assets, and the net effect on the level of cash.

5/ Trace carefully the immediate and long-range effects upon cash balances of the firm instituting the following changes in policies:
   a. It was reported that Deering, Milliken & Company, a major textile company, had shortened its credit terms on man-made fibers from 60 to 30 days. What is the effect on its cash flow and the cash flow of its customers?
   b. At one time Scotts developed a plan to finance dealers' inventories of grass seed and fertilizers. Dealers were shipped inventories, but were billed only for the amounts that they actually sold. *Wall Street Journal,* May 8, 1967, p. 16.
   c. A Cleveland Manufacturer, Curtis Industries, Inc., had been supplying dealers west of Salt Lake City from a public warehouse in Oakland, California. Goods were shipped to California by truck. This system was dropped in some instances in favor of direct shipment to the customer by air freight from Cleveland. It was reported that under the old system the warehousing, handling, and shipping costs for sending a 1500-pound cargo from Cleveland to Seattle came to $530.32, or $73.79 more than the cost of air freight.
   d. In the latter part of 1956 IBM announced it would offer for sale as well as rental its electronic accounting and data-processing machines. For example, one machine would rent for $55 a month and sell for $3400. Trace the effect of this on the cash flow of IBM and its customers who decide to purchase, rather than rent, the machines.
   e. Over the weekend Schick, Inc., fired its 1200 wholesalers and announced that it would take over the distribution of its shavers through a sales subsidiary. Board chairman Chester G. Gifford announced that

the company was increasing its sales force by four times. "We think that the manufacturer must get closer to the retailer," said Mr. Gifford. *Wall Street Journal* (February 24, 1959).

f. Under new depreciation schedules announced by the Internal Revenue Service in 1961, textile companies will be able to depreciate the cost of certain machinery over 15 years or less, compared with 25 years required in earlier depreciation schedules.

g. Ford Motor Co. announced that buyers of diesel-powered tractors between January 1 and March 31 would be refunded one-half of the first six-months' fuel supply. The tractor buyer would be obligated to keep records of fuel purchases during the first six months. In contrast, International Harvester pays winter purchasers of tractors and other farm equipment 6 percent interest on the down payment from date of purchase to the spring plowing season.

h. The government is also concerned with cash management. In the *20th Annual Report* of the Joint Financial Management Improvement Program, it was noted (p. 29) that "In the Department of Health, Education, and Welfare, the National Institutes of Health converted from an automatic quarterly advance system for about 1,500 grantees to a monthly grantee cash request system." What is the effect on the U.S. Treasury?

6/ During 1968, a number of steel companies changed their method of depreciation from accelerated to straight-line for reporting to the shareholders, although the accelerated method was retained for tax purposes. An example of the effect of this shift was reported in *Business Week* (November 2, 1968, p. 130):

Steel's new accounting

Third-quarter earnings per share

	Reported in 1967 [with accelerated depreciation]	Reported in 1968 [with straight-line depreciation]	1968 [if reported on accelerated basis]
Republic	$1.03	$0.72	$0.53
Jones & Laughlin	0.68	0.05	−0.29
Allegheny Ludlum	0.96	0.19	0.07
Armco	0.72	1.15	0.92
Inland	0.63	0.97	0.75

a. What is the effect of the change upon cash flows?

b. Why do you suppose the change was made?

7/ Review Exhibit 5-1. How do you explain the significant differences among industries in the relative proportions of cash, accounts receivable, inventory, and other assets (largely fixed assets)?

8/ What would be the effects on the cash balances maintained by business if the absence of a highly developed commercial banking system made it impossible for businesses to borrow to meet seasonal needs? What would be the effect on the general level of economic activity?

9/ There was introduced in the state legislature of Alabama a bill to invest excess funds of the state in interest-bearing time deposits and short-term U.S. government securities. At the time the bill was introduced the state was reported to have "a total of $89,457,673 on deposit in 100 banks scattered throughout the state." Evidently these were demand deposits. The Alabama Bankers Association attempted to defeat the bill, partly on the grounds that the investment of state funds should not be placed in the hands of an investment committee, as proposed by the bill, but should be left in the hands of the state Treasurer. "She . . . is now empowered to do it by law and has been handling the job satisfactorily all along." (*American Banker* [July 1, 1959], p. 2.)

a. Evaluate the arguments in this dispute.

b. If possible, find out what is done with temporarily idle funds by your state Treasurer. See "Investment of Idle Cash Balances by State and Local Governments, Supplement to Report A-3," Advisory Commission on Intergovernmental Relations, Washington, D.C., 20575 (1965). Single copies obtainable without charge.

10/ In discussing the financial policies of Federated Department Stores, Inc., John F. Lebor, Vice President, stated, "We try to make our major capital expenditures in the spring—that is, any expansions such as buildings or improvements." John F. Lebor, "Financing Modern Retailing," *Advanced Retail Management* (New York: Fairchild Publications, Inc., 1957), p. 45. How would you explain this policy?

Problems

1/ The C. P. Bliss Manufacturing Company, Buffalo, N.Y., is considering using a lock box system for its customers in California. At present its credit sales to that area amount to about $21,600,000. Establishment of a lock box in San Francisco would enable the company to reduce its collection float from 8 days to 2 days. The bank in San Francisco will expect the company to maintain a minimum balance of $70,000. The net additional annual cost of adopting the system will be $1,200. Base calculations on a 360-day year.

a. What is the net amount of cash that will be freed for use elsewhere in the business?

b. What is the annual percentage cost of the funds released from the float?

2/ D. H. Blair & Co., a Wall Street securities firm, suggests that corporate treasurers might even buy preferred stocks on margin; that is, on credit. The interest cost on borrowings is a tax-deductible expense, while corporations pay tax on only 15 percent of dividend income received on preferred stock. (Thus on a $100 dividend income, Federal corporate income taxes are applicable to only $15 of the income.) Assume that the corporation is taxed at 48 percent.

a. With margin requirements at 50 percent, and preferred dividends of 6.75 percent, what is the net after-tax yield on preferred stock, assuming that the corporation borrows half the cost of the security at 6.5 percent?

b. With margin requirements of 70 percent and preferred dividend yields of 6.40 percent, what is the net after-tax yield on preferred stock, assuming that the corporation borrows 30 percent of the cost of the security at 6.8 percent?

c. Look up in the *Federal Reserve Bulletin* current margin requirements, yields on preferred stocks, and bank rates on large, short-term business loans, and calculate the after-tax yield on preferred stock, assuming that that the corporation borrows the maximum amount permitted by the margin requirement.

3/ You are financial manager for a company that has $10 million of idle funds to invest; the full amount will be needed in about 90 days. By reference to financial periodicals, e.g. the *Federal Reserve Bulletin* and the *Wall Street Journal,* prepare a recommendation to the board to directors for the investment of those funds. Be specific concerning the earnings to be expected and the risks involved.

Selected References

ORGLER, Y. E., *Cash Management.* Belmont, Calif.: Wadsworth Publishing Co., Inc., 1970. A very good general presentation.

Managing cash flows

CALMAN, R. F., *Linear Programming of Cash Management: Cash Alpha.* Cambridge, Mass.: MIT Press, 1968.
DONALDSON, G., "Strategy for Financial Emergencies," *Harvard Business Review,* 47 (November–December, 1969), 67–79.
LEVY, F. K., "An Application of Heuristic Problem Solving to Accounts Receivable Management," *Management Science,* 12 (February, 1966), pp. B-236-44.
Searby, F. W., "Use Your Hidden Cash Resources," *Harvard Business Review,* 46 (March–April, 1968), pp. 71–80.

Investing excess cash

ANDERSON, P. F. and R. D. B. HARMAN, "The Management of Excess Corporate Cash," *Financial Executive,* 32 (October, 1964), pp. 26–30ff.
The First Boston Corporation, *Handbook of Securities of the United States Government and Federal Agencies.* Published annually.
HEEBNER, A. G., *Negotiable Certificates of Deposit: The Development of a Money Market Instrument.* New York: Institute of Finance, New York University, 1969.
JONES, R. H., "Face to Face with Cash Management: How One Company Does It," *Financial Executive,* 37 (September, 1969), pp. 37–39.
Money Market Instruments. Cleveland: Federal Reserve Bank of Cleveland, 1965. An excellent booklet.
Money-Market Investments: The Risk and the Return. New York: Morgan Guaranty Trust Company, 1964.
ROBINSON, R. I., *Money and Capital Markets.* New York: McGraw-Hill Book Company, 1964.
ROSS-SKINNER, J., "The Profitable Art of Handling Cash," *Dun's Review and Modern Industry,* 79 (May, 1962), pp. 38–41ff.

Determining optimal cash balance

ARCHER, S. H., "A Model for the Determination of Firm Cash Balances," *Journal of Financial and Quantitative Analysis,* 1 (March, 1966), pp. 1–11.

BAUMOL, W. J., "The Transactions Demand for Cash: An Inventory Theoretic Approach," *Quarterly Journal of Economics,* 66 (November, 1952), pp. 545–56.

BRUNNER, K. and A. H. MELTZER, "Economies of Scale in Cash Balances Reconsidered," *Quarterly Journal of Economics,* 81 (August, 1967), pp. 422–36.

MILLER, M. H. and D. ORR, "A Model of the Demand for Money by Firms," *Quarterly Journal of Economics,* 80 (August, 1966), pp. 413–35.

————, "The Demand for Money by Firms: Extension of Analytic Results," *Journal of Finance,* 23 (December, 1968), pp. 735–60.

WHALEN, E. L., "An Extension of the Baumol-Tobin Approach to the Transactions Demand for Cash," *Journal of Finance,* 23 (March, 1968), pp. 113–34.

Management of Accounts Receivable

6 Policies concerning the management of accounts receivable again involve a trade-off between risk and return. To the extent that we extend lenient terms and grant credit to marginal customers, we tie up funds in receivables and jeopardize our own ability to pay bills.[1] But we also make it easier to sell our products and improve our profits. The principles involved in managing receivables in order to maximize the value of the firm is the subject of this chapter.

We should also be looking ahead to the discussion of budgeting at the end of this section. Policies concerning credit terms and collection efforts will determine how rapidly cash will flow in, thereby affecting our cash budget. Projected income statements will similarly be affected through the influence of credit decisions on sales and losses from bad debts.

---

[1] A recent case in point was provided by Topas Computer Corp. and its subsidiary, Allied Data Processing, Inc. When they were forced to suspend operations, the president observed, "We have been victims of the current liquidity crisis. . . . we have been unable to collect substantial receivables or to obtain needed financing." *Wall Street Journal,* July 13, 1970, p. 22.

Notes and accounts receivable exceed holdings of cash and "near cash" in many lines of business, notably in the construction and retail and wholesale trades (Exhibit 5-1). A particularly important development has been the rise in the proportion of accounts receivable to sales over the past several years (Exhibit 6-1). This change has been a product of more lenient terms and, in some years, slower collections on receivables. While it is a development that has caused some concern among economists about the quality of credit, it has also served to focus attention on the need for better management of accounts receivable.

EXHIBIT 6-1   Percentage of Accounts Receivable to Sales of Manufacturing Corporations, 1959-1970

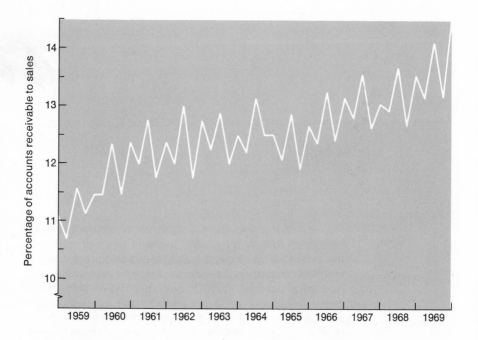

Source: Federal Trade Commission & Securities and Exchange Commission, *Quarterly Financial Report for Manufacturing Corporations.*

Determinants of the Level of Receivables

The level of accounts receivable is a function of the volume of credit sales and the collection period; that is the length of time receivables remain uncollected. The collection period is affected by the various policies controlling the acquisition and collection of receivables. While such policies also influence the absolute level of credit sales as well, the latter is probably more subject to general economic conditions. Since the financial manager cannot control general

economic conditions, he will influence the level of accounts receivable principally by controlling acquisitions and controlling collections.

What should be the financial manager's objective in managing receivables?
Let us return to our basic valuation equation. Recall that for the time being we
are dealing with a firm that is financed entirely with common stock and has a

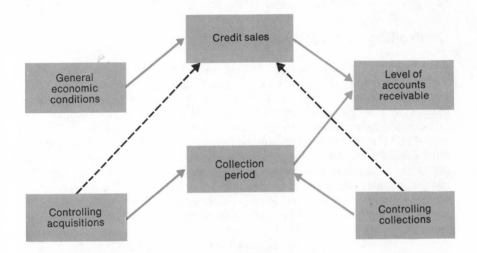

constant annual cash inflow, A. On the assumption now that these are after-tax
cash flows, the value of the firm is shown as follows:

$$V = A/k_a \tag{6-1}$$

where again k_a is the after-tax discount rate for an unlevered firm within this
particular risk category.

A change in credit policy will typically affect both the level of annual cash
flows and the level of cash invested in receivables. This latter amount is *not* the
same as the amount of receivables reported in the accounting records. Part of
the book investment in receivables represents noncash expenses, such as
depreciation. Another portion of the reported amount includes allocated share
of fixed charges, such as the president's salary, that do not change with variations in credit sales. To set policies for managing receivables we are concerned only with the differential annual cash flows ΔA and the change in *cash
investment in receivables* ΔR brought about by a variation in policy. A good approximation of ΔR is likely to be the change in variable costs.

Assume that the change in credit policy does not significantly change the
variance of the cash flows — that is, the risk category of the firm remains the
same. A change in credit policy is acceptable only if the resulting difference in
the value of the cash flows is at least as great as the change in the required
investment in receivables:

$$\Delta A/k_a \geq \Delta R. \tag{6-2}$$

The extent by which the change in the present value of the cash flows,

$\Delta A/k_a$, exceeds with cash investment necessary to generate the changed flows, ΔR, is called the *net present value, NPV:*

$$NPV = \Delta A/k_a - \Delta R. \qquad (6\text{-}3)$$

In essence, we should not undertake any change in credit policy unless the net present value is positive. Let us examine the policies affecting acquisition and collection of receivables to see how they affect the value of the firm.

Controlling Acquisitions of Receivables

What principles should guide us in determining our procedures and policies for granting credit? Consider the credit-granting process. There are five basic steps. First, we must set our credit terms. Second, we must develop some idea of the quality of credit applicant that we are willing to accept; that is, some "cut-off point" in terms of risk. Third, we must investigate each applicant. Fourth, on the basis of the information obtained in our investigation, we must estimate the probability that the customer will pay his bills. Does this customer belong to the group of applicants where the chances are one in ten of not paying, or to the group where the chances are one in twenty of not paying? Finally, by comparing our estimate of the credit-risk group to which the applicant belongs with our pre-determined cut-off point, we decide whether or not to accept the applicant. Thus if our investigations suggest that the chances are one out of ten that the customer will not pay, we will reject the credit applicant if we have previously decided not to accept this degree of risk. Since this process cannot be reduced to the precision of mathematical probability in games of chance, credit policies and decisions must depend to a considerable extent upon the sound judgment of the credit manager or financial manager. However, these policies and decisions will be more valid if he understands the theoretical or conceptual framework within which he must operate.

Setting Credit Terms

Should we decide to grant credit, we are faced with the selection of the period for which we will grant credit and the size of any cash discount we will allow for early payment. If we set our terms at "net 30," we notify customers that they should pay within 30 days and we automatically rule out those who seek terms of "net 60." Changing the cash discount from 2%/10 days to 3%/10 days may attract new customers who are able to take advantage of the discount, but it will not lure those who cannot pay in 10 days.

Although the length of the credit period and the size of the cash discount are frequently set by the customs of the industry, there is no reason to follow custom blindly.[2] Possibly by increasing our cash discount we may shorten the collection period and attract new customers. Offsetting these advantages is the higher discount on invoices—a cash loss on old, as well as new, accounts. The decision rests upon the relative change in the cash investment in receivables compared to the difference in value of cash inflows from collections.

[2]Dwayne Wrightsman, "Optimal Credit Terms for Accounts Receivable," *Quarterly Review of Economics and Business,* 9 (Summer, 1969), pp. 59–66.

In some lines of business we may offer goods either for cash or on credit. Obviously, the credit customer is receiving a more attractive package or mix of goods and services than the cash customer. Should we charge the credit customer more than the cash customer? Although department stores did not make a price distinction between cash and credit customers for many years, there has recently been a widespread movement to levy additional charges on the unpaid balances of credit customers. From the point of view of the financial manager the question is whether or not the possible loss of sales resulting from the charge will be offset by the income from the credit charges and the income earned on any funds freed from the accounts receivable reservoir.

Deciding the Acceptable Grade of Risk

How do we determine what grade of risk we will accept? As we move from groups of customers who are very likely to pay their bills to customers that are less likely to pay their bills, we do two things: we change our cash inflows from collections and increase our cash investment in receivables. The amount added to our cash inflows is equal to the additional sales over time, less added collection costs and any amounts uncollected. Note that we say "sales over time." A $50 order cannot be viewed as only a $50 order; we must consider the present value of the future volume of sales that might be obtained from this customer if we accept his initial order. Obviously this is a difficult estimate to make. The amount added to expenses consists of those production, administrative, and selling costs that are increased because the order is accepted, plus added collection costs.

Observe that we are speaking of *added,* or *incremental,* revenues and costs. When we sell something for $100, the additional costs attributable to this sale may be only $60. The balance of $40 might represent profits and fixed expenses, such as the president's salary and depreciation, which would exist whether or not we make this particular sale. Consequently, in considering whether to sell to a group of customers with a 10 percent risk of nonpayment, from a conceptual point of view we can prepare an estimate of added annual income and expenses as follows:

Added sales by accepting 10% risk group		$2,000
Amounts uncollected (10%)		200
Added receipts		1,800
Added production and selling costs (60% of sales)	$1,200	
Added collection costs	300	
Added expenditures		1,500
Net annual incremental cash flow		$ 300

By accepting this riskier group, we add $1800 to our receipts and $1500 to our expenditures. In spite of the credit losses involved on these accounts, we can better our annual net cash flow by $300.[3]

Is it worthwhile to seek the extra $300? This depends upon how much we will have tied up in these accounts and the return we expect to earn on our

[3] This would not be so if, by accepting this risk group, we turned down orders from customers who involved less credit risk. However, such a policy would be most unrealistic.

investments. If these accounts turn over about four times a year, average receivables outstanding in this group will amount to about $500 ($2000/4). But this is not our direct investment in these accounts. Since added costs, including collection costs, amount to 75 percent of sales ($1500/$2000), our out-of-pocket investment in the average receivables comes to $375. If the added cash flows produced by the new accounts are appropriately discounted at a rate of 15 percent, and if we expect these incremental cash flows to be produced at a level rate over a long period of time, we can calculate the net present value, NPV, of the proposed investment in added receivables as shown below:

$$NPV = \Delta A/k_a - \Delta R$$

$$NPV = \$300/0.15 - \$375 \tag{6-3}$$

$$= \$1625.$$

The net present value will be less if we expect to part company with this class of customer in a year or so.

We can push on into even poorer grade credit risks until the point where the added cash investment in receivables, ΔR, is equal to the incremental value of the discounted cash flows, $\Delta A/k_a$. However, as we proceed on this path, we are also increasing the variance of the expected cash flows and, thereby, the risk faced by the owners of the firm. Not only are R and A changing, but k_a may be changing (increasing) as well. In evaluating the point at which greater leniency no longer increases the value of the firm, we are forced to consider many factors, including the behavior of credit losses and collection costs, the turnover of the receivables, the period of time we expect to deal with the newly-acquired customers, and the increasing risk exposure to which we are subjecting the firm.

As our output changes in relation to capacity, we are likely to change our credit policy. If we are operating at 50 percent of capacity during a recession, we add chiefly material, direct labor costs, and collection charges when we sell to riskier credit applicants. (We should recognize that during a recession the general credit-worthiness of our customers may decline.) When we recover from the recession, customers of this grade of risk may no longer be acceptable. To accommodate their orders we will have to add to our plant capacity. If this additional cost exceeds the revenues they supply, we might reject their orders. In other words, at various levels of operations, there are different sets of incremental costs. Consequently, our credit policy probably should change with our level of activity. As production declines we let in more and more marginal applicants; as production approaches capacity, we begin to weed out those customers who are least likely to pay their bills. However, this process should not be exaggerated. In spite of such changes in our credit policies, receivables will probably decline in a recession (and rise in prosperity) with the general movement in sales.

Investigating the Credit Applicant

We must now sort out those credit applicants who meet our standards from those who do not. Let us first consider trade credit: that is, credit granted by one business concern to another. We receive an order for $100 of grinding wheels from the XYZ Manufacturing Company in Painted Post, N.Y. What do we know about this company? Nothing. We have never had an order from this concern before. How can we obtain enough information to judge its credit-worthiness?

There are two factors that limit the extent of our search for information — time and cost. We cannot take a month to investigate the customer, because he would soon tire of waiting for the grinding wheels and place his order else-where. Nor can we spend a lot of money in the process of investigation. This again is a matter of matching incremental costs and revenues. Within limits the more we spend, the more information we obtain, although there is probably a diminishing marginal return from such expenditures. Thus there comes a point when the incremental costs of credit investigation exceed the possible reduc-tion in credit losses. On $100 orders this point is reached rather quickly. If we are setting credit policy on such orders for a large company, we might allow only a very cursory investigation. Concerns which pass this brief check will be granted credit; those that do not will have their orders shipped "cash in ad-vance" or C.O.D.

There are many sources of information that may be used in granting trade credit. Their use will depend upon the nature of our business and the economi-cal limit of credit investigation costs.

Dun and Bradstreet, Inc. This well-known concern has had more than 130 years of experience in the field of credit reporting. Among its many services, two are of primary importance to the credit manager, the *reference book* and written *credit reports*. Although the reference book is published six times a year, subscribers may elect to obtain the book less frequently or to obtain a reference book covering only a certain region. Close to three million business firms of all types are listed alphabetically according to state and town. Through a system of letters, numbers, and symbols, information is provided concerning the line of business, the range of the company's estimated net worth, and D&B's estimate of the credit standing of the firm. The latter two estimates make up the "rating" of the firm. Thus a D&B rating of F3 would indicate a concern with a net worth of $10,000 to $20,000 with a composite credit appraisal of "good." For example, going back to our credit policy on $100 orders, we might be willing to ship to any customer on open account so long as he had a D&B credit rating of F3 or better. Other miscellaneous information is also provided in the refer-ence book.

Should we desire additonal information, we could ask for a credit report. A fairly simple form of report is illustrated in Exhibit 6-2. Of special significance to the financial manager is the section on "trade," which shows the record the prospective customer has established with other suppliers. "HC" indicates the highest amount of credit that particular supplier has extended in the past. "Owe" shows the amount currently owed to that supplier; "Ppt" means the cus-tomer is prompt in his payments; and, most important, "Disc" means that the customer has been discounting: that is, paying in time to earn a cash discount. This information is based upon the ledger experience of creditors of this com-pany. By *ledger experience* or *ledger history* we mean the running record of transactions and credit balances with each customer. Introduction of electronic

EXHIBIT 6-2 Dun and Bradstreet Report

SIC	NAME & ADDRESS			STARTED	RATING
34 61	803-4520 ARNOLD METAL PRODUCTS CO ARNOLD, SAMUEL B., OWNER	CD 13 APR 21 196- N METAL STAMPINGS		1947	D 1½
	53 MAIN STREET SOUTH DAWSON MICH	TEL215-000-0000	TRADE SALES WORTH EMPLS	DISC-PPT $177,250 $42,961 8	

SUMMARY SALES ARE INCREASING THROUGH SUB-CONTRACT WORK AND PROFITS ARE BEING EARNED AND RETAINED. A SATISFACTORY FINANCIAL CONDITION IS MAINTAINED.

TRADE

HC	OWE	P DUE TERMS		SOLD
3000	1500	2-10-30	Disc	Over 3 yrs
2500	1000	2-10-30	Disc	Over 3 yrs
2000	500	1-10-30	Disc	Old account
500	500	2-10-30	Disc	Over 3 yrs
1000		30	Ppt	Over 3 yrs to 3-6-
500	500	30	1st sale	

Apr 1 196-

FINANCE Statement Dec 31 196-

Cash	4,870	Accts Pay	6,121
Accts Rec	15,472	Notes Pay Curr	2,400
Mdse	14,619	Accruals	3,583
Total Current	34,961	Total Current	12,104
Fixed Assets	22,840	Notes Pay Def	5,000
Other Assets	2,264	NET WORTH	42,961
Total Assets	60,065	Total	60,065

Net sales 196- $177,250; Gross profit $47,821; net profit over and above drawings of the owner $4,204. Inventory valued at lower of cost or market. Reserve for doubtful accounts $1,508. Reserve for depreciation $6,912. Fire insurance merchandise $15,000; fixed assets $20,000. Annual rent $3,000, lease expires January 1 196-.
Signed Apr 21 196- ARNOLD METAL PRODUCTS CO by Samuel B. Arnold, Owner
Johnson Singer, CPA, South Dawson
------O------
Sales increased last year due to increased sub-contract work and this trend is reported continuing. Arnold bought new equipment in September at a cost of $8,000 financed by a bank loan secured by a lien on the equipment payable $200 per month. With increased capacity he has been able to handle a larger volume.
On April 21, 196- Arnold stated that for the first two months of this year volume was $32,075 and operations continue to be profitable. Collections are made promptly and operations are adequately financed.
Medium to high four figure balances are maintained at a local depository where an equipment loan is outstanding and being retired as agreed.

OPERATION Manufactures light metal stampings for industrial concerns and also does some work on a sub-contract basis for aircraft manufacturers. Terms are 30 days net. Owner is active and has five production, two office employees, and one salesman. LOCATION: Rents a one-story cinder block building with 5,000 square feet of floor space located in an industrial section. Premises are orderly.

HISTORY The trade style was registered by the owner January 10, 1947 and is used for general business purposes.
Arnold, born 1908, married, was graduated with a B.S. degree in Mechanical Engineering from Lehigh University in 1931. Employed 1931-1940 by Industrial Machine Corporation, Detroit, and from 1940-46 as production engineer by Aerial Motors, Inc., Detroit. He started this business in 1947 with $7,500 derived from savings.
4-21-6- (803 PRA)

data-processing equipment makes these data much more difficult to obtain, so that credit manager may have to base credit decisions on other information.[4]

Other Specialized Agencies. For certain lines of business other credit-reporting agencies perform a service similar to that provided by D&B. For example, the National Credit Office specializes in credit reports in the textile field, as well as for manufacturers of paints, leather products, and certain other products. Similar mercantile credit agencies operate in other specialized fields.

[4]Robert W. Johnson, "More Scope for Credit Managers," *Harvard Business Review*, 39 (November–December, 1961), pp. 109–20.

Credit bureaus. The National Association of Credit Management furnishes a credit interchange service. Participating firms provide their local bureaus with a list of their customers. When an inquiry is received concerning the payment habits of some company, the credit bureau seeks reports from each of that firm's suppliers and prepares a summary of the information. Reports on credit experience are available at both the local and national levels.

Banks. As we indicate in the preceding chapter, a bank may provide valuable credit information. Thus if our company were located in Chicago, we could request our bank to ask one of its correspondent banks in New York state to check on the credit standing of our customer in Painted Post. Although we would obviously not do this for a $100 order, we might very well do so for a large, important order. Bank credit information may be especially useful if we wish a particular question answered, such as whether or not the customer has pledged his inventory or receivables to secure a loan.

Financial Statements. While financial statements are usually available in the credit reports of Dun and Bradstreet and other similar agencies, we may desire more detailed or more recent information. To obtain the latest balance sheet and income statement of a credit applicant, we can write directly to the customer. Although some will still take offense at this approach, this reaction is fortunately becoming less common. Some credit managers refuse credit to any concern that does not provide its financial statements upon request.

Other Sources of Information. If the expected value of the information warrants the added time and expense, additional insights may also be obtained by personal interviews and visits of our firm's salesmen to the credit applicant. Occasionally information may also be sought from trade associations, better business bureaus, chambers of commerce, attorneys, and investment manuals. Our own collection experience with a customer is an especially valuable basis for reassessing his credit-worthiness. In a sense each grant of credit is a means of buying information about a customer's payment habits. With each timely collection we may raise the probability of his continuing to be an acceptable risk.

Retail concerns are involved not with trade credit, but with consumer credit. This form of credit includes direct loans to consumers extended by financial institutions such as commercial banks and personal finance companies, as well as credit extended to individuals for the purchase of consumer goods. Because the amounts involved are frequently small, costs of investigation must be limited. Furthermore, since customers will not wait long for a loan or for delivery of the merchandise, credit investigation must be rapid. Rather than use mercantile credit agencies, we can turn to local retail credit bureaus to check the customer's payment habits. The growth of regional and national credit agencies providing consumers' credit records from computers has been a logical accompaniment to the rapid growth of consumer credit. If the amount involved is fairly large, we might also check the customer's bank to obtain a general idea of the size of his deposit or whether his relationships with the bank have been satisfactory. The most important source of information is the customer himself. Our credit application form might require him to provide information concerning his place of employment, the number of years employed, his position and salary, the size of his family, his residence and the number of years he has lived at that address, whether he owns his home or rents, and his other obligations.

Analyzing the Customer's Credit-Worthiness

We have determined the degree of credit risk we are willing to accept, and we have gathered an economical amount of information concerning the customer. Now we must determine whether he falls above or below our limit of acceptability.

In mercantile credit the decision concerning the customer's degree of credit risk is often a matter of judgment. First, we are interested in his willingness to pay his debts on time as revealed in his record of payments to other suppliers. Second, we must determine his ability to pay as reflected in his financial statements. Here we will rely primarily upon an analysis of his short-term position: current ratio, acid test ratio, turnover of receivables, days' purchases outstanding, and inventory turnover (review Chapter 4). Although we may be impressed with his profits, we will probably be unwilling to wait until our customer generates sufficient funds through retained earnings to pay our bill.

Other factors bearing on a customer's ability to pay are his business experience, the intensity of competition, and general economic conditions. It is particularly difficult to determine whether to grant credit to new businesses because of the lack of any historical record.

In the case of consumer credit, broad experience has enabled some companies to develop more precise measurements of risk. To enable inexperienced credit men to judge applicants, these companies have instituted a point system which gives so many points for the number of years the applicant has worked for the same company, the number of years at the same address, and so on. These credit-scoring systems have been developed by analyzing past credit records and determining statistically the characteristics that most sharply distinguish between "good" accounts and "bad" accounts, as shown in the diagram below.

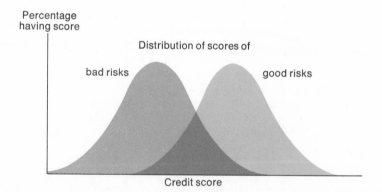

(The statistical procedures used are multiple regression or discriminant analysis.) The weights accorded various characteristics provide the basis for the scores. The weights are chosen so as to "best" distinguish between good and bad credit risks. The total score required for acceptance is based upon the probability of a consumer with that score of paying his debt, the income available if he does pay, and the collection costs and loss involved if he does not pay. Similar systems have been successfully developed in the trade credit area as well. Although old-time credit men dispute the value of the system, it appears to represent a worthwhile attempt at statistical decision-making. However, we should sympathize with the credit man who sees his years of experience being replaced by an adding machine.

Once we have extended trade or consumer credit, continued grants of credit to the same customer may be handled in a more routine fashion. Annual reports submitted by the customer should be reviewed systematically, as well as any major changes in credit ratings reported by Dun and Bradstreet. Quite commonly we set a line of credit for the customer, although we usually do not tell him what that line is. Instead, we use the line to control our internal operations through the "exception principle." So long as the customer's debt to us remains below that line, his account may be handled by some lowly clerk or, better yet, by a computer. The clerk or computer merely asks whether or not the new order would push his debt to us above the line of credit. Only if it does, need the account be brought to the attention of the credit manager. At this time, the credit manager may call for a credit report or other additional information to determine if an increase in the line of credit is justified.

Accepting or Rejecting Applicant

Given information concerning a customer's credit-worthiness, what do we do next? We have a three-way choice: (1) Grant the credit; (2) reject the application; or (3) postpone the decision to seek further information. At a later stage alternative (3) branches again into the same three choices.[5] The selection of alternative (3) depends upon our estimate of the probability that further information will change the credit decision that would be made in the absence of such information. Let us illustrate the principle involved. Assume that without any added data we would reject the application. If that decision should be wrong, we will lose the cash flows over the years that could have been obtained from the account. This is an opportunity cost. Conversely, the "cost" of accepting a bad credit risk is simply the firm's cash investment in the single receivable, since the loss occurs only once. For additional information to have any value to us, it must be sufficiently powerful to change the decision from "reject" to "accept." Therefore, we must take the product of the probability of obtaining such information and the value to us of reversing an incorrect decision and weigh that product against the cost involved in securing the additional information.

To put it in simple terms, if you were betting $5 on the outcome of a baseball game between the Mets and Cubs, you might not do much more than look

[5] For a fuller development of this analysis, see Dileep Mehta, "The Formulation of Credit Policy Models," *Management Science,* 15 (October, 1968), pp. B-30-50.

at a few batting averages and the track record of the two teams in previous encounters. But with a bet of $50,000, you would spend a considerable amount of time and money collecting information about the two teams before deciding which one to support. Nonetheless, there comes a point when you must bet, let's say on the Mets, and not pay more money to investigate the strengths of the teams. Once you had, for example, discovered that the entire starting lineup of the Cubs was down with the flu, the probability of your changing your bet because of additional information would be quite low. Therefore, the expected value of any more information would likely be below the cost of its acquisition.

Controlling Collections of Receivables

Just as the extension of credit requires more knowledge and experience than can be communicated in these few pages, so does the collection of accounts receivable. Let us focus our attention on principles involved rather than on any detailed exposition of collection procedures. Again we return to incremental costs and revenues. Ordinarily the costs of any additional collection effort should not exceed the additional revenues that may be gained from this effort. To put it in simple terms, we usually should not spend $10 to collect a $5 account. More formally, the probability of collection times the amount to be collected should exceed the anticipated collection expense. For example, assume a debt of $500 is outstanding. By spending $50, we believe that we can generate the following collection probabilities:

Probability	×	Amounts collected	=	Expected value
0.7		$ 0		$ 0
0.2		100		20
0.1		200		20
1.0				$40

If that is the gloomy outlook, the value of the firm will be higher if we write the account off now.

The probability of being paid is not solely a function of collection effort. The interval since any payment was received, as well as the other factors that enter into a credit score, influence our assessment of the likelihood. Just as credit scoring systems are developed from historical records, so can the probabilities of collection be estimated by statistical evaluation of our collection experience.[6]

This principle is difficult to apply, because collection efforts on a given account affect not only the amount squeezed from that customer but future sales to that customer and future collections from others as well. Thus if we are overly aggressive in dunning some customer, he may switch his business to one of our competitors. We may be delighted to transfer our collection problems to our competitors, but of course we also transfer the accompanying sales revenue. Rather than develop a reputation as a "soft touch," we should sometimes be

[6]M. Mitchner and R. P. Peterson, "An Operations-Research Study of the Collection of Defaulted Loans," *Operations Research*, 5 (August, 1957), pp. 522–45.

willing to spend more than the possible incremental revenue to collect an individual account. For example, sales finance companies are willing to go to considerable expense to track down "skips"; that is, individuals who finance a car on time and then disappear with the car. Since they cannot afford to encourage this practice, finance companies find it economical in the long run to use every means available to find the skip and bring him to justice.

Besides maintaining an efficient collection department, we may also assure the conversion of a major portion of receivables into cash through the use of *credit insurance.*[7] Credit insurance is designed to protect manufacturers, wholesalers, and advertising agencies from unusual credit losses. Just as we might insure our plant against fire, so we might insure our accounts receivable against extraordinary losses. If a bank extends a loan secured by our accounts receivable, it may require that we insure those accounts and name the bank as beneficiary.

Because our selling prices should be adequate to cover normal credit losses, credit insurance is not designed to protect us against that normal, or *primary loss.* In other words, since it is virtually certain that a given percentage of our sales on credit will prove to be uncollectible, we cannot obtain insurance against this loss. Thus, if the experience of the industry and our own experience indicate that our credit losses will normally amount to $\frac{1}{4}$ of 1 percent of sales, this amount is established by the credit insurance company as our primary loss. Should that be, let us say, $11,000, our agreement with the insurance company would specify that we must bear the first $11,000 of total credit losses during the year. Because a loss of this amount is almost certain on the average, we would presumably have to pay the insurance company an $11,000 premium to assume this loss. It is for this reason that our credit insurance policy will apply only to those credit losses in excess of $11,000.

With respect to the transfer of abnormal credit losses to the insurance company there are two limiting features. To prevent our granting credit recklessly, the insurance company will require that we participate in 10 or 20 percent of the net loss suffered, depending upon the risk involved. This is called "coinsurance." Second, the insurance company will also limit its coverage on individual accounts to an amount which is related to the credit rating of the customer at the time of shipment. To illustrate, the credit insurance company may limit its coverage to $10,000 on each of our accounts receivable with a D&B rating of "E2" at time of shipment. Should the amount owed by such an account be $10,000, the most we could lose on the account (over and above primary loss) would probably be $1000, assuming 10 percent coinsurance. If the amount owed were $15,000, the insurance company would admit $10,000 of this account for coverage purposes and assume 90 percent of this, or $9000 in the adjustment. Thus we could lose up to $6000 on this account.[8] The net amounts collected from the debtor after the adjustment would be distributed on a pro

---

[7] Such insurance is obtainable from the American Credit Indemnity Company. The discussion in this section is based primarily on information made available by that company.

[8] Assume that our primary loss is $11,000; and losses and coverage on three accounts were as follows:

	A	B	C
Coverage	$10,000	$5,000	$2,500
Loss	8,000	7,000	2,000

rata basis as respective interests appear; in this example, 10 percent to us and 90 percent to the insurance company.

The effect of credit insurance is apparent in the diagram below. Essentially, credit insurance reduces the expected loss, because the insurer absorbs a substantial portion of losses above normal (the shaded area under the probability distribution function). Whether or not the insurance is desirable depends upon (1) the relation of the insurance premium to the change in the expected cost of losses and (2) management's aversion to risk.

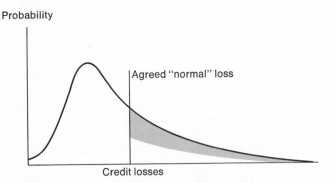

The cost of credit insurance averages about $\frac{1}{10}$ of 1 percent of sales. The desirability of assuming this expense depends upon an individual company's circumstances. When sales are largely to uninsurable risks, credit insurance may be unavailable or overly expensive. To sell only to insurable accounts or only within the limits provided on insurable accounts may mean an uneconomical restriction of credit sales. If accounts are widely diversified and the company soundly financed, some financial managers may not use credit insurance, although premiums are smaller when the risk is smaller. However, if we are not in a strong financial position or are selling to a relatively few large accounts, credit insurance may be especially desirable. To put it another way, the greater the risk that failure of a few important accounts could cause our financial downfall, the more attractive is credit insurance.

Evaluating Management of Receivables

There are two possible sources of error in managing accounts receivable. We may be so restrictive in setting terms, granting credit, and collecting amounts

---

With these limits the amount of loss admitted on these accounts would be as follows:

A	$ 8,000
B	5,000
C	2,000
	$15,000

If our coinsurance were 10 percent, $1,500 would be deducted from the $15,000, leaving $13,500. Since our primary loss would be deducted from this amount, we would collect $2500 from the insurance company ($13,500–$11,000).

due that we unnecessarily increase the costs of our credit department and stifle sales. On the other hand, we might be so lenient that our loss of liquidity and increase in bad debts outweigh incremental revenues from sales and savings in the costs of the credit department.

Evaluation of the performance of the credit department is difficult. The turnover of accounts receivable is probably too coarse a measure to provide effective control. A more refined control device is the aging of accounts receivable. When this had to be done by hand, it was a major undertaking. With the use of computers, accounts receivable can now be aged monthly and a tabulation of past due accounts provided as well. The aging might appear as shown below:

Period outstanding	Accounts receivable outstanding	Percentage
Less than 30 days	$198,200	83.7
30 to 60 days	23,300	9.8
60 to 90 days	12,100	5.1
Over 90 days	3,200	1.4
Totals	$236,800	100.0

The aging schedule provides only an indirect means of judging collection experience. A more direct procedure is to calculate a distribution of collections by the age of the account at the time of collection. Thus we could determine the percentage of our sales that were paid within 30 days, 30 to 60 days, and so on. Finer breakdowns could be obtained if necessary. If management wishes a summary figure, we could determine the mean age of collection at the time of collection.[9]

These methods of evaluating the management of accounts receivable have a common problem. They measure two things at once: efficiency of granting credit and efficiency of collecting past due accounts. If our terms and credit standards are lax, the pressure is on the collection staff to speed the flow of funds through accounts receivable. If we are niggardly in granting credit, we may not even need a collection department. Consequently, while we should use the overall measures of performance, we should also develop means of following the activities of those who grant credit and those who collect on accounts receivable.

One possible measure of performance of the credit granting department is the percentage of orders rejected to credit sales. If we seem to be rejecting an unusually high percentage of orders, we may question whether our terms are too lenient or whether our standards are too tight. Possibly by offering 60-day terms we are attracting such a large number of unacceptable customers that our rejection rate is high. This situation might be remedied by offering terms of net 30 to all customers. On the other hand, if our terms are like those of our competitors, the fault may lie in too rigid credit standards. There will be no black-and-white answer. Basically, we are only seeking information, which, together with other pieces of information, will better enable us to evaluate the performance of the credit department.

The activities of the collection staff can be followed, but probably not evalu-

[9] For a more complete discussion, see Haskel Benishay, "Managerial Controls of Accounts Receivable: A Deterministic Approach," *Journal of Accounting Research,* 3 (Spring, 1965), pp. 114–32.

ated. When we fail to collect from a customer, can we attribute this loss to poor credit evaluation or poor collection procedures? Measures such as the percentage of collections to accounts receivable and percentage of bad debts to credit sales are helpful if carefully used. There is very likely to be a seasonal movement in these percentages. Possible more useful is the percentage of monthly collections on past due accounts to the accounts past due at the beginning of each month. This measure focuses attention more sharply on the fruitfulness of collection activities.

So long as we understand the role of the credit department, our evaluation will be realistic, even though it may not be precise. Other measures than those suggested here may readily be developed. When taken all together, the various measures may present a picture of undesirable restrictiveness or leniency. Thus an unusually low turnover of receivables in relation to the turnover characteristic of our industry, a negligible rejection rate, a high proportion of past due accounts, a low collection ratio, and a low percentage of collection on past due accounts, would strongly suggest the need for a tightening of credit standards and collection procedures. As always, the problem is to determine on the basis of historical and industry whether or not our percentages and ratios are unusually high or low.

Summary

The management of accounts receivable involves many complex and interrelated decisions. By setting our terms of sale, we define in a loose sense the general market that we would like to serve. We must then select the customers from that market to whom we are going to grant credit. This first involves a decision on the acceptable grade of risk. Then we must evaluate credit applicants against this standard. If they pass the test and are given credit, the final step is to collect the amounts owed.

These decisions involve risk and uncertainty. We can never know precisely when or whether a given customer will pay. The best that we can do is to have some idea of the probability that he will pay. When we lower credit standards, we both lower the probability of collection and raise the costs of collection. These negative results must be weighed against the positive gains in incremental revenue and the expected value of the added net return compared to the required added investment in ourstanding accounts receivable.

Questions

1/ How might the credit terms offered by a high fashion dress shop differ from those offered by a dress shop offering low-priced lines?

2/ Would you say that the department store that does not make a separate charge for credit is discriminating against the cash customer in favor of the credit customer? Do stores discriminate among groups of customers in any other respect? Why do they not eliminate this discrimination?

3/ Until recently automobile manufacturers sold to dealers on cash terms and required payment when the automobile was delivered to the dealer. This practice was characteristic of the industry from its infancy. Why do you suppose this trade practice came about? What changes do you think will occur now that two manufacturers offer 15-day terms?

4/ A credit jeweler sells under such terms that the down payment on an article is always equal to at least the cost of the article to him. Would you say that he can set his credit standards to accept relatively high risk or relatively low risk customers? Explain.

5/ A high proportion (60–70 percent) of loans to consumers by personal loan companies is made to former customers.
   a. What differences would you expect to find in the costs associated with credit in an expanding company and a static company?
   b. What savings might be achieved if the expanding company buys loan offices of existing concerns rather than sets up new offices of its own?

6/ The XYZ Corporation requests a $10,000 loan from a bank and also orders $10,000 of materials from another manufacturer.
   a. Would you expect to find any difference in the thoroughness of the credit investigation by the bank and by the supplier? Why? Explain.
   b. Would you expect the bank and supplier to have different credit standards? Why or why not?

7/ What might the following suggest to you as financial manager?
   a. An unusually low rejection rate on credit applications and an unusually high percentage of accounts past due.
   b. A normal rejection rate and turnover of accounts receivable, but an unusually high percentage of bad debts to credit sales.
   c. An unusually high rejection rate, an unusually high turnover of accounts receivable, and an unusually low percentage of bad debts to credit sales.
   d. An unusually low rejection rate, an unusually high turnover of accounts receivable, and an unusually low percentage of bad debts to credit sales.

8/ "Yesterday we fired our credit manager. During his term of office he let credit losses rise from $\frac{1}{4}$ of 1% of sales to $\frac{1}{2}$ of 1% of sales — a doubling of our losses." Do the data cited justify his dismissal? If not, what additional information would you wish to have before deciding whether to fire (or promote) him?

9/ The following statement was presented by a consultant to a large accounting firm at a national operations research meeting:

> "In short, the loan officer must distribute his resources among the various uses open to him in such a way that material costs are held down and net income maintained or improved — to *minimize loan risk* and to *maximize loan profit.*"

Discuss.

Problems

1/ The sales manager estimates that sales could be increased 10,000 units by selling to a group of less credit-worthy customers. The credit manager estimates that credit losses from this group will amount to 5 percent of sales and that additional collection effort attributable to this group will cost $5000. The plant is operating at about 60 percent of capacity (120,000 units). Balances outstanding in the marginal accounts will average $20,000.

The accountant prepares the statement shown below and advises against selling to this additional group. Do you agree? Support your position.

Selling price per unit		$7.00
Cost of goods sold:		
Materials	$1.75	
Direct labor	2.15	
Factory overhead*	1.40	5.30
Gross margin		1.70
Selling expenses**	0.60	
Administrative expenses	0.55	1.15
Net profit per unit		$0.55
Profit on 10,000 units		$5,500
Credit losses (5% × $70,000)	$3,500	
Additional collection costs	5,000	8,500
Net loss by selling to poorer grade of customer		$3,000

*Heat, light, power, salaries of foremen, supervisors and other indirect labor. Production could rise substantially before these costs would be affected.
**Salesmen are paid salaries, not commissions. No change is contemplated in other fixed selling expenses, such as advertising and administration.

2/ The Woycik Manufacturing Corp. sells on terms of net 30 days, but accounts are usually paid in 50 days on the average. Annual sales are $13,600. What is the firm's accounts receivable on the balance sheet?

3/ The Ames Manufacturing Corporation produces an inexpensive clock. Sales are at a level of $200,000 per year, but could be more than doubled with current production facilities. The suggestion has been made that the firm be more lenient in its credit policies. It is currently selling to risks categorized as A, B, and C. The credit manager has prepared the information shown below for lower risk classes. The data shown are for each class by itself; that is, the $40,000 increase in sales to Class E would be over and above the sales made to Class D. Ames is financed entirely by common stock, and the credit manager estimates that it should earn at least 20% on a before-tax basis (k). In this particular instance he knows that his calculations will be simpler if all are done on a before-tax basis.

Risk class	Estimated increase in sales	Estimated days outstanding receivables	Expected rate of default and collection costs
D	$30,000	60	5%
E	40,000	72	7
F	45,000	80	9
G	40,000	90	11
Selling price per unit	$2.00		
Direct, out-of-pocket costs per unit	1.80		

What additional risk classes, if any, should the credit manager add to present sales?

4/ We have a credit insurance policy which provides for a primary loss of $20,000 and a coinsurance feature of 10 percent on rated accounts. Coverage on each account in the following classes is limited as follows:

C	$1\frac{1}{2}$	$25,000
D +	$1\frac{1}{2}$	20,000
D	$1\frac{1}{2}$	15,000
E	2	10,000

During the year four accounts become insolvent. The D&B rating at the time of shipment and the amount of loss is shown below:

C	$1\frac{1}{2}$	$13,000
D +	$1\frac{1}{2}$	3,000
D	$1\frac{1}{2}$	20,000
E	2	10,000

How much will we collect from the insurance company on the basis of this information?

Selected References

ALTMAN, E. I., "Financial Ratios, Discriminant Analysis and the Prediction of Corporate Bankruptcy," *Journal of Finance,* 23 (September, 1968), pp. 589–610.

BECKMAN, T. N. and R. BARTEL, *Credits and Collections in Theory and Practice.* 8th New York: McGraw-Hill Book Co., 1969.

BENISHAY, H., "Managerial Controls of Accounts Receivable: A Deterministic Approach." *Journal of Accounting Research,* 3 (Spring, 1965), pp. 114–32.

_____, "A Stochastic Model of Credit Sales Debt," *Journal of the American Statistical Association,* 61 (December, 1966) pp. 1010–28.

BERANEK, W., *Analysis For Financial Decisions.* Homewood, Ill.: Richard D. Irwin, Inc., 1963, Chapter 10.

BIERMAN, H. Jr. and W. H. Hausman, "The Credit Granting Decision," *Management Science,* 16 (April, 1970), pp. B-519–32.

BOGGESS, W. P., Screen-Test Your Credit Risks," *Harvard Business Review,* 45 (November–December, 1967), pp. 113–22.

BOWEN, R. L., JR., "Application of Margin Rates to Credit Analysis," *Management Accounting,* 48 (November, 1966), pp. 26–31.

FRIEDLAND, S., *The Economics of Corporate Finance.* Englewood Cliffs, N.J.: Prentice-Hall, Inc., 1966, Ch. 4.

GREER, C. C., "The Optimal Credit Acceptance Policy," *Journal of Financial and Quantitative Analysis,* 2 (December, 1967) pp. 399–416.

JOHNSON, R. W., "More Scope for Credit Managers," *Harvard Business Review,* 39 (November–December, 1961), pp. 109–20.

MARRAH, G. L., "Managing Receivables," *Financial Executive,* 38 (July, 1970), pp. 40–44.

MEHTA, D., "The Formulation of Credit Policy Models," *Management Science,* 15 (October, 1968), pp. B-30–50.

MITCHNER, M. and R. P. PETERSON, "An Operations-Research Study of the Collection of Defaulted Loans," *Operations Research,* 5 (August, 1957), 522–45.

MYERS, J. H. and E. W. FORGY, "Development of Numerical Credit Evaluation Systems," *Journal of American Statistical Association,* 58 (September, 1963), 799–806.

SOLDOFSKY, R. M., "A Model for Accounts Receivable Management," *Management Accounting,* 47 (January, 1966), pp. 55–58.

TINGLE, J. O., "Financial Assistance as a Typing Product—Fortner Enterprises v. U. S. Steel," *Business Lawyer,* 25 (November, 1969), pp. 121–32.

WELSHANS, T., "Using Credit for Profit Making," *Harvard Business Review,* 45 (January–February, 1967), pp. 141–56.

WRIGHTSMAN, D., "Optimal Terms for Accounts Receivable," *Quarterly Review of Economics and Business,* 9 (Summer, 1969), pp. 59–66.

Management of Inventory

7 Management of inventory deserves special attention on three counts. First, inventory comprises a significant segment of total assets for a number of business concerns, especially those in the retail trade (Exhibit 5-1). Second, since inventory is the least liquid of current assets, errors in its management are not quickly remedied. Third, changes in the levels of inventory have important economic effects. During periods of declining sales inventories may not be replenished, so that further impetus is given to a drop in gross national production. During other periods inventories may be built up at a more rapid rate than sales. These movements are unstabilizing and the resulting "inventory cycles" are a matter of deep concern to economists and businessmen. To the extent that good financial management minimizes these variations, the economy will be more stable.

There is considerable evidence that modern methods of managing inventories have, in recent years, cut the size of inventories in relation to sales (Exhibit 7-1). To a considerable extent the better control of inventories may be attributed to the use of computers which can both test the effect of various inventory plans by simulation and operate the inventory model selected. By feeding current data on sales and inventory levels of a particular item into a computer, we can determine within seconds how soon we may need additional inventory and to what level the stock should be built. Other forces are also at work. Ability to keep inventories in check is assisted by better inventory controls of suppliers, so that they can deliver more promptly. Greater centralization of warehousing, with the use of air freight in some cases, can reduce the size of total inventories. While these changes have improved the turnover of operating assets for individual companies, we can expect a more widespread benefit if better inventory control in prosperous times cushions the shock of future recessions.

Let us begin by noting that there are several different types of inventory: supplies, raw materials, goods in process, and finished goods. *Supplies* are usually defined as items that are used in the operation of the business but do not go into or become incorporated in the final product. Mop heads would be classified as supplies (unless we were manufacturing mops). *Raw materials* are the materials, sub-assemblies, or other items brought in from other plants or purchased from suppliers, which become a part of the final product. Goods in transit from raw materials to finished goods are considered as *goods in process,* while the completed product is termed *finished goods.* To develop a full under-

EXHIBIT 7-1.   Inventories Compared With Monthly Sales*

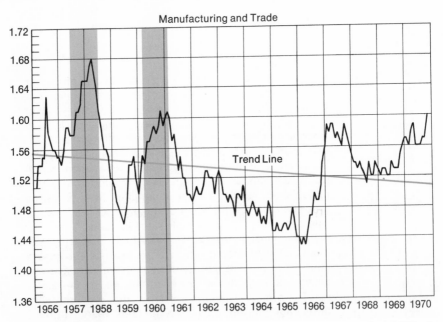

Ratios based on seasonally adjusted data.
Shaded areas represent periods of business recessions as defined by the National Bureau of Economic Research.

Source: U.S. Department of Commerce

Prepared by Federal Reserve Bank of St. Louis

standing of inventory management, we shall consider a manufacturing concern, although the concepts also apply to other types of business.

Determination of the "right" amount of inventory requires a balancing of the costs and risks of carrying inventory against the benefits derived from having the inventory available. As we increase our inventories we must reach a point where the additional costs associated with that increase outweigh the additional benefits obtainable. While we shall not attempt to develop many elaborate formulas to calculate the optimum level of inventory, we shall suggest the concepts and principles involved in determining inventory policy.

Cost of Inventory

Let us consider first the total costs associated with carrying inventory and then those costs which may vary with the level of inventory. The tabulation below provides a fairly complete picture of inventory costs:[1]

Cost of capital
    Inventory
    Equipment to handle and store inventory
Cost of space occupied
    Depreciation, maintenance, rental
    Taxes
    Heating, utility costs
    Janitorial labor
Inventory service costs
    Taxes on inventories
    Insurance
    Pilferage
    Deterioration
    Costs of ordering
    Labor costs of receiving and stocking
    Inventory records and bookkeeping costs
Inventory risks
    Risk of decline in price
    Risk of changes in style or other causes of obsolescence

Estimates of total costs of carrying inventory generally range from 15 to 30 percent of inventory value: that is, if we put $100 into inventory at the beginning of the year, it will cost from $10 to $30 to carry it to the end of the year. For purposes of planning the levels of inventory, we are interested only in the variable portion of those costs: that is, in those costs that would be affected by our plans. In general, costs related to the space occupied remain fixed in the short run, regardless of normal variations in inventory. Depreciation expense continues whether the storage areas are used or not. Elements of the inventory service costs are also fixed, but for the most part these costs and the cost of the funds tied up in inventory will vary with the dollar level of the inventory.

[1] Adapted from U.S. Steel Supply Division of U.S. Steel, "Value Analysis at Work,"

Although each company must examine its own costs, we shall assume for purposes of discussion that these variable or planning costs vary directly with the dollar amount of inventory carried.

In practice it is very difficult to judge the risk of losses on inventory that will result from declines in price or obsolescence. Rather than consider these as a portion of the variable costs, it may be wise to evaluate these risks separately. In this way management can readily vary the inventory policy by setting the approximate level at "30 days' sales" or "60 days' sales." Thus if management expected costs of materials to rise, it might instruct the purchasing department to stock enough raw materials to support 60 days of production. However, when we later prepare our budgets, we may find that we do not have sufficient cash to sink into an extra 30 days of inventory. In addition, we are in business to manufacture some product, not to speculate in commodities. While the line between "shrewd buying" and "inventory speculation" is difficult to draw, we should recognize when we have departed from the field of production to that of speculation. (Our banker is likely to call a halt to the process before we do.) Once we move into inventory speculation, the conceptual framework for inventory policy which is advanced here will no longer apply.

If large amounts of commodities are carried in inventory, it may be possible to reduce losses from price fluctuations by *hedging*. Briefly, this is a process of entering into futures contracts to sell the commodity or some product derived from the commodity at a certain price. Theoretically, when a flour miller buys wheat, he might at the same time enter into a futures contract to deliver wheat at a given price. Should the price of wheat decline, he is likely to lose on the wheat he owns, but will offset that loss through a gain on the futures contract. Although practice seldom jibes with theory, the miller will probably have smaller annual inventory losses (and profits) if he hedges than if he does not hedge. In some cases a bank may require that the inventory be hedged before it grants a loan to a company which carries large amounts of inventory.

Functions of Inventory

Why do we need inventory? What functions does it serve? In short, what are the benefits of having inventory, and do these benefits increase in direct proportion to increases in the level of inventory? Finally, at what point do the benefits begin to cost more than they are worth?

Some inventories are unavoidable. All or a portion of the goods-in-process inventory is unavoidable. At the moment we count the inventory, some will be in the machines, or in the process of going from one machine to another, or in transit from the raw materials storeroom to the production line or from the production line to the finished goods warehouse. If we are to have any production at all, inventory in transit is unavoidable. However, we can often minimize this inventory by better production scheduling and by more efficient organization of the production line. As an alternative we could consider subcontracting part of the work, so that we place the burden of the goods-in-process inventory on the subcontractor. Sometimes inventory in transit is allowed to accumulate in order to ease difficulties of production scheduling and planning. If this is a conscious policy, it may be acceptable; too often it is a lazy man's way out of a fairly demanding task.

The rest of the inventory in supplies, raw materials, goods in process, and finished goods is maintained for one fundamental purpose. Basically we maintain inventories because they enable us to perform the functions of buying, manufacturing, and selling at different rates. As one writer has put it, "inventories serve to uncouple successive operations in the process of making a product and getting it to customers."[2] In other words, inventories enable us for short periods to produce at a greater rate than we buy materials, or vice versa; or to sell at a greater rate than we produce, or vice versa. Our problem is to determine at what point the benefits derived from uncoupling the functions of buying, production, and sales are exceeded by the costs of carrying the inventory. But let us now examine in greater detail the functions performed by inventories.

Lot-Size Stocks

Other things being equal, we would like to see the functions of purchasing, producing, and selling performed at those rates that are most efficient for the process involved. For example, it may be most economical to buy 100 mop heads at a time, even though they are used most effectively at the rate of two a week. Rather than buy at the rate of two a week, or use them at the rate of 100 a week, we "uncouple" the buying and using functions by stocking an inventory of mop heads. In this fashion we can both buy and use them at the most efficient rate. Keep in mind, however, that we are achieving efficiency in these areas at the cost of carrying that inventory.

Similarly, for the sake of efficiency, we may wish to uncouple sales and production. Our production costs per unit may be lowest if we produce 1000 sauce pans per hour for a week and then shut down and set up the line to produce 1000 frying pans an hour for another week. Since our sales will not follow that same pattern, we shall be forced to carry a finished goods inventory of sauce pans and frying pans. Again, at what point do the costs of carrying that inventory eat up the savings from the longer productions runs?[3]

We can be reasonably sure that we will not continue to lower the cost per unit at the same rate as we purchase or produce items in larger and larger lots. Lower costs per unit typically come about because we spread certain fixed costs, such as set-up time and depreciation on machinery, over a larger and larger number of units. As the size of a production run increases, these savings become progressively smaller. Therefore, while the costs of carrying inventory may rise approximately in direct proportion to the dollar value of the inventory, it cannot be said that the savings from purchasing or producing in large lots increase in direct proportion to the size of the lot.

Now let us balance the costs of carrying inventories of raw material against the benefits obtained from purchasing in large lots, rather than small. The same

[2] John F. Magee, "Guides to Inventory Policy," *Harvard Business Review*, 34 (January–February, 1956), p. 51.
[3] Examples might also be developed wherein production takes place at a greater rate than purchasing, and sales at a greater rate than production.

conceptual approach applies to the weighing of the costs of carrying inventories of finished goods against the benefits obtained from long, rather than short, production runs. In either case our problem is the same: at what point do the additional costs of carrying more inventory outweigh the additional savings that might be obtained from ordering, or producing, in larger amounts?

The conceptual approach to the problem is illustrated in Exhibit 7-2. The exhibit is based upon the following assumptions with reference to an item in the inventory of raw materials:

Annual inventory carrying charge (i.e. variable cost) = 20% of average dollar value
Purchasing cost per order = $8
Requirements for year = 2000 units
Price per unit = $1

(A) Order size	100	200	400	500	1000	2000
(B) No. of orders $\dfrac{2000}{(A)}$	20	10	5	4	2	1
(C) Average inventory $\dfrac{(A)}{2} \times \$1$	$50	$100	$200	$250	$500	$1000
(D) Total carrying cost 20% × (C)	$10	$20	$40	$50	$100	$200
(E) Total ordering cost $8 × (B)	$160	$80	$40	$32	$16	$8
(F) Total cost (D) + (E)	$170	$100	$80	$82	$116	$208

EXHIBIT 7-2   Relation Between Size of Order and Cost of Carrying Inventory

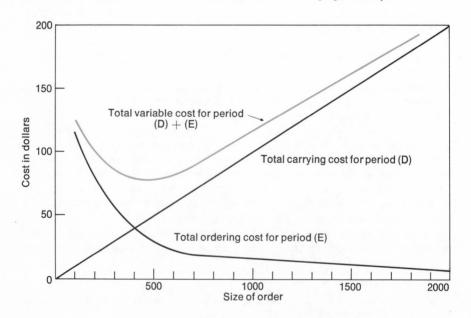

Both the tabulation and exhibit show that the most economical operation would be five orders of 400 units. Should we have four orders for 500 units, we would reduce our total purchasing costs by $8, but add $10 to our costs of carrying inventories. Since the additional costs exceed the additional savings, it would not be economical to push our order size to 500 units. On the other hand, it would not be economical to try to reduce our average inventory by making ten orders for 200 units. While this would cut our carrying cost by $20, it would raise our ordering costs by $40.

Determination of the most economical order quantity may be made through the use of a formula,[4] in which (for this chapter only):

Q = order quantity (in units)

R = requirements of the item for the period (in units)

S = purchasing cost per order

P = price paid per unit

I = annual inventory carrying charge as a percentage of the average inventory value

Then the economical order quantity (E.O.Q.) is $\sqrt{\dfrac{2 \times R \times S}{P \times I}}$.

With the figures in Exhibit 7-1, E.O.Q. $= \sqrt{\dfrac{2 \times 2000 \times 8}{1 \times 0.2}} = 400$

units. Application of the formula becomes somewhat more difficult if quantity discounts are involved, although the principle is the same.

Because of the time and labor involved in making the calculations, it is not desirable to determine the E.O.Q. for each item of inventory. Examination of inventories will usually reveal that a few items make up a relatively large percentage of the total inventory value. For these items use of E.O.Q. probably does not provide sufficiently close control. Instead, more constant attention to rate of use, suppliers' lead times, and stocks on hand is needed to reduce inventory to a minimum and yet not interfere with production. With high-value items the size and timing of each purchase order is a separate decision.

---

[4] The formula is easily derived. To the notations shown, add the following:

T = total annual cost

N = number of orders per year

x = size of an individual order in units

$x/2$ = average number of items in inventory over time

Then, $T = PR + SN + I(xP/2)$
Since $N = R/x$, we can substitute for N;

$$T = PR + RS/x + I(xP/2)$$
$$dT/dx = -RS/x^2 + IP/2$$

Setting this equal to 0, and solving for x;

$$-RS/x^2 + IP/2 = 0$$
$$IPx^2 = 2RS$$
$$x = \sqrt{\frac{2RS}{IP}}$$

Since the second derivative is greater than zero for all possible values of x, this is a minimum.

With inventory items in the middle range of value it is often desirable to determine the E.O.Q. for each item. When stocks reach a certain predetermined minimum, an order is placed for that quantity. Since the curve depicting total variable costs is quite flat near the E.O.Q. point, no great increase in costs is involved if we depart slightly from the E.O.Q. to gain a more convenient size of purchase or production order.[5] The E.O.Q. and order point must be reviewed regularly. If there are fairly large numbers of items in the medium-value class, it may be desirable to set up tables or charts based on carrying charges and ordering costs so that a clerk may determine the E.O.Q. from them.

On items that are large in number, but make up only a small percentage of the total dollar cost of the inventory, it is probably not worth the effort to develop such precise controls. Miscellaneous items, such as nuts and bolts which can readily be obtained from a nearby mill supply house, can be controlled in a more mechanical fashion. For example, some companies use two bins. When one is empty, an order is placed for a new stock. However, such variations in the application of the principle do not destroy its validity.

Safety Stocks

A portion of inventory is maintained to absorb random fluctuations in purchasing, production, or sales. Thus, even though we purchase 400 units at once, we would ordinarily not time our orders so that we would run out of that item just as the order is to be delivered. Instead, we will keep some stock to use in maintaining an even flow of production in case the supplier is slow in delivery or the material does not meet specifications. Safety stocks in the form of goods in process provide a continual flow of materials through the machines in spite of occasional delays at one stage or another in the process. Finally, safety stocks would also be maintained in finished goods. To avoid making customers wait for delivery we would not plan so closely that a production run of some item would be completed just as the last of that item is shipped from the finished goods warehouse.

If we assume that inventories are used at an even rate, we might diagram the relation of new orders (or production runs) and the safety stocks of raw materials (or finished goods) as shown in Exhibit 7-3.

Assume that the safety stock is 100 units and that E.O.Q. is 1000 units. If we use 50 units per week and two weeks normally elapse from the time the order is placed to delivery, the *order point* should be set at 200 units. When the inventory reaches 200 units, we would place an order for 1000 units.[6] By the time that order arrives two weeks later, our inventory would be reduced to 100 units. If the order does not arrive on time, we can dip into our safety stocks for two weeks. Our problem is to determine the size of the safety stock.

To develop the principles involved, let us concentrate our attention on the factors determining the size of safety stocks of raw materials and finished goods. Although the considerations may again be expressed in a formula, we shall be content in this case to develop an understanding of the concepts. Management

[5] Arthur Snyder, "Principles of Inventory Management," *Financial Executive*, 32 (April, 1964), pp. 13–21.
[6] An alternative procedure is to order at regular intervals and adjust the size of the order to the rate of usage.

EXHIBIT 7-3   Changes in Level of Inventory Over Time

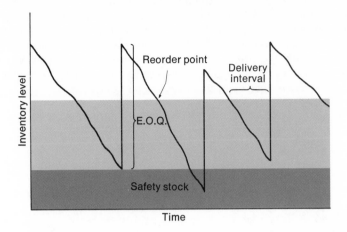

must consider the probabilities of running out of stock, the size of inventory in relation to delays in production or delivery of orders, and the relation of the costs of carrying inventory to the costs of being out of stock.

Risk of Being Out of Stock. The risk of being out of stock depends upon the size of the safety stock and the variance in the flow of incoming orders. Other things being equal, the smaller the safety stock, the larger the risk of being out of stock. (As we shall see later, the relationship is not linear.) The larger the variance in the size and frequency of incoming orders, the higher the risk of running out of stock. Put another way, the greater the risk of having a string of frequent, large orders, the higher should be the safety stock to avoid running out of stock.

Variations in incoming orders should be absorbed to a considerable extent by the safety stocks. That is their purpose. If there is a random increase in the rate of use of some item, we should allow the safety stock of that item to be drawn down, rather than place rush orders to replenish the inventory. Otherwise, the costly emergency orders are likely to result in surplus stocks of the item.

Size of Inventory in Relation to Delays from Being Out of Stock. Can we say that the larger our safety stocks, the smaller the danger of holding up production or delivery to a customer? That is, if we are only "half safe" with a stock of 200 units, are we 100 percent safe with a stock of 400 units? Unfortunately, this is not the case. For illustration let us consider the safety stocks of finished goods. Since we have little control over the items or quantity our customers order, it is virtually impossible to eliminate "out-of-stocks." Although we reduce the number of delayed orders by increasing the inventory of finished goods, we do not reduce them in proportion to the increases in inventory. In fact it would take an infinitely large inventory to eliminate delayed orders, and even the sales department would not advocate that policy.

Experience concerning the relationship between inventory size and delayed orders suggests that it is somewhat as shown in Exhibit 7-4. As indicated in the exhibit, an increase in inventory investment from $50 to $100 effects a marked reduction in the percentage of delayed orders, from about 44 percent to 24 percent. However, a corresponding improvement is not obtained if we increase the investment further. An inventory investment of $300 will result in 5 percent of orders being delayed, whereas an additional investment of $200 will be required to reduce delayed orders to 2 percent.

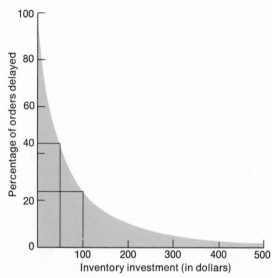

EXHIBIT 7-4   Relation Between Percentage of Delayed Orders and Dollars invested in Inventory

In practice it is very difficult to determine the precise relationship of the level of service to customers and the size of inventory. Records of the frequency of "stock-outs" at different levels of inventory may shed light on the relationship. When this approach is not possible management must determine some normal service level to customers. Thus if the practice of the industry is to provide delivery within one week of receipt of an order, and "normal" weekly sales are determined to be 10,000 units, then our safety stocks plus our weekly production should be set at a level sufficient to meet this demand. Management must then be willing to delay shipment on orders when weekly sales rise so far above the normal level of 10,000 that safety stocks are completely depleted.

Relation of Costs of Carrying Inventory to Costs of Being Out of Stock. Since we have already discussed the costs of carrying inventory, we may turn our attention to the costs of being out of stock. In the case of raw materials, the costs of being out of stock may be the costs of shutting down the production line. In some continuous-process industries, such as a steel mill, this may be very high. We should also consider the costs of emergency purchase orders and the costs of pressing our suppliers to deliver. Costs of being out of stock of finished goods show up in lost sales and emergency production orders. The cost of these lost sales is the revenue they would have added over and above the expense they would have added. If we are in an industry where prompt delivery is an important form of competition, we will have to maintain larger stocks in relation to sales than would be the case in an industry where competition centers on other aspects, such as price and quality. There is considerable room for judgment. For example, we cannot tell what sales are lost through our gaining a reputation for being out of stock or slow on delivery. Customers gradually drift away without making their reasons explicit. Nonetheless, an important first step is the recognition by management that there are costs of being out of stock, and that these costs may be considerable.

The ultimate decision concerning the level of delayed orders that will be tolerated is up to management. An inventory investment of $300 will result in 5 percent of orders being delayed. Is it worth the additional investment of $200 to reduce delayed orders to 2 percent? Will the slight betterment of relationships with customers justify incurring the additional costs associated with the higher level of inventory? That is, management should not push investment in safety stocks beyond the point that the added costs of carrying that inventory exceed the savings gained by avoiding delays in filling orders. At this same point any reduction in safety stocks would cut costs of carrying inventory less than the resulting increase in the costs of being out of stock. In short, at this point the variable costs of being out of stock and of carrying inventory are equal. Since it is difficult and time-consuming to estimate this point, greatest effort should be directed to those inventory items which account for a significant dollar value of the total inventory and to those which are especially critical to the maintenance of an even flow of production and sales. For example, a manufacturer of box board might pay particularly close attention to his stocks of waste paper and to special and expensive grades purchased from distant suppliers. Ample stocks of essential bearings would also be maintained to prevent a sudden and costly shut-down of the mill.

Anticipation Stocks

Many business concerns cannot aim to have fairly constant levels of inventory throughout a year, but must build up inventories because of seasonal factors. Steel mills in Buffalo, N.Y., must accumulate inventories of iron ore during the summer months to keep production going during the winter when the lake freighters cannot bring in ore. Because canners and other food processors must pack when the crops are available, they build up large stocks of finished goods. Manufacturers of toys, lawn mowers, and Easter hats usually find it necessary to accumulate stocks in advance of their selling season. Inventories which are in addition to the safety stocks and are designed to carry a business through a seasonal bulge in purchasing, production, or sales can be termed anticipation stocks.

The first step in the determination of anticipation stocks is to prepare a forecast of sales by period. Incorporated in this forecast should be an estimate of the probable degree of error in the forecast. It is often useful to compare our past forecasts with actual results so that we can judge our probable error. If the chances of error are great, if the opportunities for recovery from a poor estimate are small, and if the penalties of error are large, we shall want to build ample anticipation stocks. Assume that (1) experience has shown that our estimates of seasonal movements in sales are often wide of the mark; (2) our lead time from production to finished product is six weeks; and (3) the industry practice is to provide immediate delivery to customers. If we err in estimating sales, as is likely, we have little opportunity to overcome any inventory shortage by rushing through a production order in time to provide the desired level of customer service. About the only way out of this unpleasant situation is to maintain rather large safety and anticipation stocks of finished goods.

On the other hand, if production can be rapidly adjusted to sales, our anticipation stocks need not be as high. Consider a short-order cafe; it maintains very little in the way of an inventory of finished goods but relies on a hot griddle to bring finished goods into line with demand. In other industries customers do not expect immediate delivery, so that adjustments of production to demand may be made by expanding or contracting the delivery time. This situation would, in large part, be true of the machine tool industry.

One method of adjusting plans to the degree of probable error is to set up two sales schedules, one representing the "most probable" estimate and the other an estimate of the highest expected level of sales. The latter should not be somebody's wild dream, but a forecast of the highest that can reasonably be expected. If the chances and penalties of error are great and opportunities of recovery from bad guesses are poor, production and inventory schedules should be more closely related to the "high" than the "most probable" estimate. If the contrary situation holds, then schedules should be more attuned to the "most probable" estimate.

Our guiding principle in planning the level of anticipation stocks is to minimize the combined cost of being out of stock and the costs of carrying inventory. The concept may be illustrated with the use of some very simple figures (Table 7-1). Assume that we have made an estimate of the units of sales (demand) for each period. The word "period" is used to indicate that we must prepare estimates of sales and production not by months but by production days. In this manner we take into account the fact that production days in March exceed those in February. To simplify the illustration, planned production, sales, and inventories for only six periods are shown.

Sales vary from 20 to 80 units per period. By using inventories to uncouple production from sales, we can obtain the advantages of level production at the cost of carrying additional inventory. If we plan to produce 50 units every period, our inventories will rise as high as 50 units, or 40 units in excess of our assumed safety stocks of 10 units. Over the entire six periods we will carry a total overstock of 100 units for one period, or, to put it another way, we will maintain an inventory of 100 unit-periods in excess of the safety stocks. On the assumption that it costs $1 per unit to carry it in inventory for one period the inventory carrying cost of the level production plan is $100.

At the other extreme, we might plan to produce strictly in accordance with the sales pattern. Under this system there would be no overstock. If actual sales follow planned sales, we should end each period with our minimum safety stock of 10 units. This production pattern may be undesirable for several reasons. It may even be impossible if we do not have the capacity to produce 80 units per period (the maximum level of demand). As a compromise between

TABLE 7-1   Determination of Level of Anticipation Stocks

Period	1	2	3	4	5	6	Total
Planned sales (units)	50	40	20	50	80	60	300
A. *Level Production*							
Planned production	50	50	50	50	50	50	300
Inventory (end of period)[a]	10	20	50	50	20	10	
Safety stocks	10	10	10	10	10	10	
Inventory in excess of safety stocks	0	10	40	40	10	0	100 unit-periods

Cost of carrying one unit one period = $1
Cost of anticipation stocks for level production = $100

	1	2	3	4	5	6	Total
B. *Variable Production*							
Planned production	50	40	40	50	60	60	300
Inventory (end of period)[a]	10	10	30	30	10	10	
Safety stocks	10	10	10	10	10	10	
Inventory in excess of safety stocks	0	0	20	20	0	0	40 unit-periods

Cost of carrying one unit one period = $1
Cost of anticipation stocks for variable production = $40

[a] Assuming opening balance of 10 units.

level production and full seasonal production we might adopt the production and inventory schedule shown in the lower half of Table 7-1. In this case production varies from 40 to 60 units per period, and the anticipation inventory is reduced to 40 unit-periods. Against the carrying cost of inventory ($40) we must balance the added costs of the fluctuations in production. With variable rather than level production there may be costs of overtime, layoffs, training, and so on. Should these costs exceed the $60 saving in inventory carrying cost that resulted from adopting the variable production plan, it would be unwise to accept this proposal. Intangible considerations concerning morale and relations with the union might also enter the decision-making process. By experimentation with various alternative production plans (or by more elaborate mathematical manipulations), we aim to develop a production pattern that will meet our seasonal demand with the desired degree of safety and keep our combined production and inventory carrying costs at a minimum.

Once production and inventory schedules have been adopted, the plans must constantly be checked against actual experience. Should sales rise above expectations, safety stocks may be drawn down and production schedules increased. Again it should be emphasized that the safety stocks should be used rather than allow the full impact of the higher sales to be felt by the production schedule. The object is to permit a relatively smooth adjustment in production schedules. If action is taken too quickly, or if the adjustment in production schedules is too large, we may find that inventory builds up so rapidly that production schedules must be cut back sharply. With a poor inventory control system it is possible to magnify, rather than minimize, in production schedules the fluctuations in sales.

When lead time is long and the season short, we may have no opportunity to replenish stocks if we err in our estimates of sales. Orders lost then are lost forever. This would be the case of the manufacturer of toys. Moreover, if he errs on the other extreme and overstocks, he will probably have to reduce prices sharply to clean out his inventory after Christmas. Although this is sometimes termed a "crash problem," it represents only a more extreme version of the general problem of determining anticipation stocks. In these crash problems the penalties of substantial errors on either side are usually greater than in industries with a less intense seasonal movement in sales.[7]

Evaluation of Management of Inventory

An overall measure of the effectiveness of inventory policies may be obtained by calculation of the turnover of inventory, as explained in Chapter 4. Since this is a very broad measure, it may conceal a multitude of problems. More precise evaluation of the management of inventory is achieved by relating the process of evaluation to the objectives of inventory management. Among the more important objectives are the control of stock-outs, obsolescence and spoilage, and inventory costs. If these costs are deemed important to control, the accounting system or other records must be designed to show our success in affecting these aspects of inventory management. For example, it is often useful to know when we ran out of stock of an item and how long we were out of stock. The consequences of being out of stock are usually much more difficult to measure. In evaluating the management of inventory, we must recognize that some stock-outs will have to be tolerated in preference to the costs of maintaining a larger inventory.

Another aspect of the evaluation of management of inventory is a check of actual against planned performance. Before we criticize a high percentage of delayed orders, we must determine whether the plans were poorly laid or whether well-laid plans were not followed. Consequently, we need to check estimates of demand, both to improve future estimates and to adjust inventory plans to variations in actual sales. Our plans call for various amounts of inventory at different stages in the flow of goods from raw materials to finished goods. Are the proper amounts of materials where they are supposed to be? If not, why not? Can action be taken to bring inventories into line with plans, or do the plans need revision? In large part this is a control function, but it is essential that control be effective if we are to evaluate our success in the management of inventory and to improve that management in the future.

Summary

Investment in inventories is costly. Among some types of business the investment in inventories is so large and risks of loss so great that considerable attention must be concentrated on its management.

[7] For an excellent discussion of the crash problem see John F. Magee, *Production Planning and Inventory Control* (New York: McGraw-Hill Book Co., 1958), pp. 157–61.

As with the management of accounts receivable, management must balance the costs of increases in the levels of inventory against the benefits that will be realized from those increases. While most of the benefits will be realized in the short run, there will probably be long-run effects on sales and profits if the company gains a reputation for prompt service.

There will always be idle stocks of inventory, and the aim of management should not be to reduce these to zero. Stocks grow because it is frequently more efficient to purchase, produce, and sell in large lots. Some stocks must be maintained to allow for unforeseen changes — failure of a supplier to deliver on schedule, a sudden increase in demand, a breakdown of some machine. Finally, some stocks are maintained to meet forthcoming demand. Because the level of inventories may be adjusted rapidly, anticipation stocks are accumulated largely to meet seasonal increases in demand. Development of a system to make optimal inventory decisions and to facilitate the detailed management of inventory is greatly aided by the use of computers.

Questions

1/ Trace the effect on raw materials, goods in process, and finished goods inventories of the following developments:
   a. Greater standardizations of parts.
   b. More refined and accurate forecasts of sales.
   c. Faster shipping time to and from the factory.
   d. Expectations of increases in the price level.

2/ "The ideal of the manufacturer is to have raw material flow directly through process into consumption without any necessity whatsoever for stock or storage. Of course that ideal can never be attained. However, the degree to which we approach it is the measure of good management. All inventory control, all refinements of business, all flexibility of ordering points and ordering lots are based upon this concept of approaching as nearly as possible to a zero inventory in actual practice — to the elimination of all inventories other than the work legitimately in process." Oscar Grothe (Vice President, White Sewing Machine Company), "Coordinating Purchasing and Inventory Control," *The Management Review,* 18 (August, 1929), p. 262. Would you agree with this statement? Explain your position.

3/ One means of reducing carrying cost of inventory is to have suppliers carry much of the inventory of raw materials and customers carry much of the inventory of finished goods.
   a. In each case how might this result be achieved? Give some examples.
   b. What are some of the possible costs of transferring inventory burden to suppliers and customers?

4/ Does an individual consumer maintain lot-size, safety, and anticipation inventories? Explain and illustrate.

5/ Although Japanese department stores gross only 20 percent, as compared to about 36 percent for American stores, they are able to earn about the same percentage of net profit (3 percent). In part this is attributable to the fact that the Japanese stores can take more risks on merchandise because they have passed the warehousing function to wholesalers and are able to order in small quantities as needed. ("Tokyo Opens Fifth Avenue Shop," *Business Week* [October 25, 1958], p. 54.)

   a. Why do you suppose that stores in the U.S. do not adopt the same practice? Can the Japanese store on Fifth Avenue, N.Y., adopt this practice?

   b. What are the effects of this practice on earning power? (Review Chapter 3.)

6/ Which inventories (in transit, lot-size, safety, and anticipation) will be affected, and how, by the following changes:

   a. Elimination of quantity discounts by a major supplier.

   b. Establishment of a steel warehouse in the community, where none previously existed. We previously found it necessary to purchase most requirements from the mill.

   c. Increased use of air freight in preference to rail in shipping goods to customers.

   d. Establishment of a policy of shipping goods on consignment to important customers.

   e. Substantial discounts are offered distributors by a lawn mower manufacturer for firm orders placed in November and December. (What is the effect on the inventories of the manufacturer?)

7/ Is it ever justifiable financially for a retail store to sell merchandise for less than cost (other than as a "loss leader")? Explain.

8/ Consider a fuel oil company and a manufacturer of expensive power lawn mowers. Which is likely to have a higher level of anticipation stocks in relation to sales? What factors will enter into the determination of the level of these stocks?

9/ A retail store estimates its inventory requirements by comparing the quantities on hand at the end of each month with those at the beginning of each month. Thus if the beginning inventory of an item were 500; purchase orders received, 800; and inventory at the end of the month, 700; it would be determined that the monthly rate of use was 600 units. Similarly, if opening inventory were 400 and the item was out of stock at the end of the month, the monthly rate of usage was calculated to be 400. Appropriate adjustments are made for seasonal movements in sales. Have you any improvements to suggest? Explain.

10/ We are a manufacturer of toys. Management closely controls the relation of the dollar value of finished goods inventory to sales. Comparison with similar companies indicates that our inventory of finished goods is somewhat higher in relation to sales than typical for the industry. Yet we have experienced a number of stock-outs and have had to dispose of some items at distress prices in late December. What is wrong? What improvements can you suggest?

11/ It is general practice to require a filling station operator to pay for gasoline at the time of delivery. Because many operators are pressed for funds, they rarely order a full tank-truck at a time. Texaco, Inc., is testing a newly developed "black box" which is positioned between the pumps and storage tanks. It can be programmed to release 1000 gallons at a time upon insertion of a coded punched card. Texaco retains title to the gasoline in the tank. When the operator wishes to replenish his supply, he sends the money for units of 1000 gallons, and Texaco telephones him to provide the code number to release for his use the desired number of gallons.

    a. What are the benefits of this plan to Texaco and to the operators of the gas stations?

    b. Trace the effects of the plan on the earning power of Texaco and the operators.

Problem

The J. W. Edwards Manufacturing Company buys large quantities of raw material X at $2.00 per unit. The company's bookkeeper has determined the following cost associated with carrying the inventory of this product. Item X constitutes about 10 percent of the raw material inventory, and there is little variation in its use from week to week.

    Estimated annual cost of funds invested in average inventory: 16 percent. Depreciation and property taxes on space occupied: $4000 annually (based on floor space; there is no alternative use for the space at present).

    Estimated direct costs per purchase order: $9.00.

    Estimated requirements for one year: 60,000 units.

    a. What is the economical order size and number of orders?

    b. Assume that we desire a safety stock of 850 units of this item.

If it takes about one week to secure delivery, at what level of inventory should a reorder by placed? Show calculations.

Selected References

BERANEK, "Financial Implications of Lot-Size Inventory Models," *Management Science,* 13 (April, 1967), pp. B-401–8.

FETTER, R. B. and W. C. DALLECK., *Decision Models for Inventory Management.* Homewood, Illinois: Richard D. Irwin, Inc., 1961.

HADLEY, G. and T. M. WHITIN., *Analysis of Inventory Systems.* Englewood Cliffs, N. J.: Prentice-Hall, Inc., 1963.

MAGEE, J. F., "Guides to Inventory Policy," *Harvard Business Review,* 34 (January–February), pp. 49–60 (March–April); pp. 103–16; (May–June) 1956, pp. 57–70. An excellent summary of many of the principles developed more fully in his book.

————, *Production Planning and Inventory Control.* New York: McGraw-Hill Book Co., 1958.

NADDOR, E., *Inventory Systems.* New York: John Wiley & Sons, Inc., 1966.

SNYDER, A., "Principles of Inventory Management." *Financial Executive,* 32 (April, 1964), pp. 12–21.

STOCKTON, R. S., *Basic Inventory Systems: Concepts and Analysis.* Boston: Allyn and Bacon, Inc. 1965.

Techniques in Inventory Management. New York: National Association of Accountants, Research Report No. 40, 1964.

VIENOTT, A. F., Jr., "The Status of Mathematical Inventory Theory," *Management Science,* 12 (July, 1966), pp. 745–77. You will need a good deal of math. Also provides a good bibliography.

Management of Fixed Assets: Capital Budgeting

8

Probably no area of decision-making by financial managers is more important to the success of the firm than the evaluation of capital expenditures. What do we mean by a *capital expenditure?* How do we distinguish between operating expenditures and capital expenditures? Conceptually, there is really no difference. We spend money for labor and materials in the hope that we will realize some return on our investment. Similarly, we spend money for executive development or a new building with the same aspiration in mind. The distinction between the two expenditures is that we expect to realize a return from the outlays on labor and materials with a few months, whereas the benefits from a new building may be forthcoming over a period of many years. More or less arbitrarily we define an operating expenditure as one whose principal benefits are gained within a year, and a capital expenditure as one whose benefits are realized over a period longer than a year. Plans for capital expenditures are incorporated in a *capital budget,* and the process of evaluating proposed capital expenditures is termed *capital budgeting.*

A capital expenditure usually gives rise to a fixed asset on the balance sheet. It is evident from Exhibit 5-1 that the effective management of these fixed assets is a dominant problem for many companies. Over four-fifths of the assets of public utilities are fixed, as are about two-thirds of the assets of concerns engaged in agriculture, forestry and fisheries; mining and quarrying. Not quite half of the assets of manufacturing concerns is made up of fixed assets.

Not only is capital budgeting of fundamental significance to the firm, but it also is of great importance to the economy as a whole. Variations in business investment in plant and equipment are generally regarded as being one of the decisive factors in causing swings in general business activity. Too often investment decisions are made in a setting of black pessimism or giddy optimism. Capital budgeting is based upon unemotional appraisal of the long-range monetary and non-monetary benefits of capital expenditures. Since transient moods should have no part in the process, intelligent capital budgeting may lead to a more stable level of business activity. In fact the shrewd financial manager may be able to take advantage of others' unwarranted pessimism by buying equipment at low prices at the bottom of a recession in order to be better prepared to secure sales on the upswing.

Outlays on fixed assets differ from investment in current assets in three important respects. First, the expenditures planned are often (but not always) of considerable size. In contrast, proportionately smaller amounts are usually involved in a decision to extend credit to a particular customer or to stock more of an item of inventory. Second, these latter decisions can be reversed within a few months, whereas capital expenditures represent long-term investments that often involve forecasts extending for several years into the future. Third, investments in current assets very seldom change the overall riskiness of the firm. Such commitments usually keep the firm in its current line of business, whereas a capital expenditure may take the company into a entirely new field of endeavor. Where a new investment involves a risk that is significantly different from that characterizing the existing firm, we will need to make additional adjustments that were not deemed necessary when we were discussing investments in current assets.

Let us now set forth the "plan of attack" for this chapter. The "raw materials" for proper evaluation of a capital expenditure are estimates of cash flows associated with that outlay. Hence, our first step will be to estimate the outflows of cash required by a capital expenditure and the subsequent inflows that it will generate. The underlying concept involved in capital budgeting is that money has a *time value;* that is, that a dollar to be received tomorrow does not have the same present value as dollar received today. The development of an understanding of this widely-applicable concept will be our second task. Given estimates of cash flows and a clear grasp of the time value of money, we will then be in a position to appraise the various techniques for evaluating proposed capital expenditures. Finally, we will introduce procedures for dealing with those projects whose risk differs from that characteristic of the firm.

Measurement of Cash Flows[1]

Why does our interest focus on cash flows and not the profit reported by the accountant? The answer is quite simple. To make additional profit, we must have *cash* to reinvest, but there is no assurance that we will have the accountant's reported profits available in the form of cash. We may have more, or we may have less. Reasons for differences between cash flows and reported accounting income were discussed in Chapter 5. For capital-budgeting purposes our main interest in the accounting records will be to ascertain how the accountant treats certain items of income and expense for tax purposes.

Each proposal for capital expenditure involves two flows of cash: (1) the net outflow of cash required by the new investment, and (2) the net annual inflow of cash as a result of the new investment. The validity of any capital budgeting procedure is dependent upon the accuracy of our estimates of these flows.

Initial Investment Required

Let us assume that we are considering the purchase of a machine that will reduce the direct cash outlay (after tax adjustments) on labor and material costs over the next three years. This reduction of cash outflow is just as beneficial as an increase in cash inflow. To evaluate the desirability of purchasing the machine we must first determine the net cash outlay necessary to produce the enlarged stream of cash benefits. All cash receipts and expenditures associated with the acquisition of the new machine must be considered. We should include as part of the investment any necessary increases in cash, accounts receivable, and inventory. Let us say that the new machine costs $10,500 and the freight is $500. In addition it costs $1000 to prepare a special foundation for the new machine. This gives us a total depreciable cost of $12,000. Were there no old machine involved this would be our initial investment.

When the new machine is a replacement for an existing piece of equipment, we must make further adjustments to determine our initial investment. To keep matters simple, let us say that both old and new machines have expected economic lives of three years and may be depreciated on a straight-line basis over that period. Assume that the old equipment has a book value of $3000, but can be sold for only $1500. For the sake of simplicity, let us further assume that the tax saving on the book loss would amount to $500.[2]

How should we treat the disposal of the old machine? We must imagine that we are at a fork in a trail. On the lower part of the trail we keep the old ma-

---

[1]For a more detailed exposition of the remaining material in this chapter, see Robert W. Johnson, *Capital Budgeting* (Belmont, Calif.: Wadsworth Publishing Co., 1970).

[2]A gain from the sale of personal property, such as a machine, must be reported as ordinary income unless the depreciation accumulated since 1961 is less than the gain. In that case, the gain equal to the balance as a capital gain. If personal property, such as a truck, is traded in on a new business property, no taxable gain or loss is usually recorded. The tax treatment of gains and losses on sale of real property is even more complicated. For simplicity we will specify a tax rate or amount on gains or losses from sale of fixed assets in illustrations and problems. As a practical matter, one should consult a tax expert or be one.

chine. In this case we will realize no immediate return from its sale, but we will preserve the annual tax shield afforded by its depreciation ($3000/3 = $1000). On the upper fork of the trail we buy a new machine for $12,000 and gain an annual tax shield of $4000. Upon disposal of the old machine we may realize some cash return from the sale (in this case $1500), and we will have a lower ($500) tax bill, because we sold the machine at a taxable loss. Consequently, our net initial investment associated with the proposal "Buy new machine; sell old" is $10,000 (−$12,000 + $1500 + $500). We must remember to make adjustments in future cash flows to reflect the differences in tax shields offered by depreciation on the two machines.

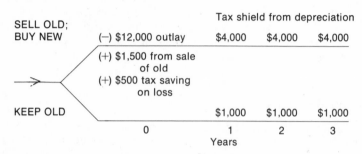

If we must sell the old machinery at a loss, should not the loss (net of tax benefits) be charged against the purchase of the new machine? Does not the adoption of the proposal cause the loss? The answer to both questions is "no." The loss on the old machine involves no outflow of cash; it is only a bookkeeping entry. Therefore, the loss does not constitute any drawback to the purchase of the new machine. Instead, the loss should be attributed to the purchase of the old equipment. Maybe we purchased unwisely. Maybe we should have depreciated the old machinery at a faster rate. Nonetheless, the errors associated with the old equipment should not be visited upon the new machine. Whatever investment we have in the old machinery is a *sunk cost.* Whether we have recovered that sunk cost over the period that we have owned the machinery is a matter of history.

Possibly a few questions may clarify the principle involved. If you paid $10,000 for an oil well that went dry the day after you bought it, would you charge the $10,000 cost against your next investment? Would you say that your next $10,000 investment would have to be doubly profitable in order to recover your dry hole cost—otherwise you would not invest? If you would normally be satisfied with a 10 percent rate of return, would your next $10,000 have to earn 20 percent? Obviously not. The book losses on old investments should not burden proposed new investments.

There will be instances (though not in this example) when we will find it necessary to consider an *opportunity cost* as part of the initial required investment. Assume that we already have some steel reinforcing rods lying about that could be used in the foundation for the new machine. Since we do not have to buy them, there is a great temptation not to charge them to the initial investment. However, we should ask: What is the next best alternative use for the rods? If we are told that they would otherwise be sold and return an after-tax cash flow of $300, that amount should be considered as part of the initial required investment.[3] Even though we did not spend $300, use of the rods requires that we forego an opportunity to gain $300.

Differential Flows of Cash

The second step is to calculate the future net changes in cash flows resulting from the capital expenditure. In this process it is fundamental that we consider only the *changes* that we will make in cash inflows and outflows. If we keep the old equipment, cash flows will remain unchanged. Our purchase of a new machine will cause some change in future cash flows, and this change or differential is the sole matter of our concern. Possibly the new machine will allow us to reduce our labor costs or use a cheaper material, so that the cash outflow will be lowered. Maybe the new machine will enable us to turn out a greater volume, so that more cash will flow into the business. In any case *we are concerned only with the differential flows of cash resulting from the purchase of the new machine.*

Let us illustrate the determination of possible benefits resulting from its purchase. Assume that we have two unskilled workers, each earning $5000 a year, operating two old machines. If the proposed purchase of one new machine will enable us to produce the same volume as with the two old machines, but with only one worker, we can reduce our cash outflow for direct labor by $5000 annually. To this saving we might add $500 from possible lowered expenditures on repairs and reduced losses on scrap resulting from the more modern equipment. Thus the total reduction in cash outflow in our example is $5500.

The substitution of one machine for two will very likely reduce the amount of floor space required for machinery. Let us assume that we free 1000 sq. ft. of floor space, although we have no other use for the space and are unable to lease it to somebody else. Assume that the rent on the factory is allocated to each department at a rate of 20¢ per square foot. Does this mean that one of the benefits derived from the purchase of the new machine is an annual saving of $200? Of course not. By the installation of the new machine we have in no way changed the cash outflow on rental payments. Since we have no alternative use for the floor space that has been saved, there will be no increase in cash inflow either. The department concerned may "save" $200 per year because of the reduced charge to the department for floor space. However, for the company as a whole there is no change in net cash inflow resulting from the additional space that has been made available. The $200 should not enter into the calculation of the differential flows of cash resulting from the acquisition of the new machine.

[3] For *decision-making purposes* we need to know the after-tax cash flows that would have resulted from the sale of the rods. In contrast, for *accounting purposes* a quite different figure may be capitalized as part of the book cost of the new machine. The accounting problems are nontrivial, but their resolution will affect the allowable depreciation on the new machine. These complexities explain why opportunity cost was not directly incorporated in our example.

The purchase of new machinery might bring about increased cash receipts while cash expenditures remain relatively constant. We could replace the two old machines with two new ones and hope that the doubled production will be followed by doubled sales. This may not prove to be the case. Our market may be so limited that we cannot readily increase sales. If the additional volume can be moved only by increased advertising expenditures, these extra cash outflows must be deducted from the annual benefits derived from the new machines. On the assumption that manufacturing expenses remain unchanged, calculation of the annual differential flows of cash resulting from increased output might appear as shown below:

Additional sales revenue		$18,000
Additional advertising expenses	$2,000	
Additional salesman	8,000	
Additional expenses		10,000
Additional taxable income		$ 8,000

A further word must now be said about the effect on these calculations of income taxes (see Chapter 2). Since we were concerned with the differential cash flows under various alternatives, we must determine the differential payments on income taxes under the alternatives. The annual cash benefit adjusted for the differential tax payment gives us our *net cash benefit after taxes*.

To illustrate this point, let us return to our original proposal of buying a new machine for $12,000 to replace an old machine with a book value of $3000. If we find that estimated savings before taxes in labor, materials, and repairs with the new machine will amount to $5500 annually, we can construct a table to determine the net savings after taxes. Essentially, we are keeping two sets of books, one on an accounting or accrual basis and the other on a cash flow basis:

		On books	Cash flow
Savings in labor, material, and repairs		$5,500	$5,500
Depreciation on new machine	$4,000		
Less: Depreciation on old machine	1,000		
Additional depreciation expense		3,000	
Additional taxable income		2,500	
Increase in income tax (40%)*		1,000	1,000
Net additional income after taxes		$1,500	
Net annual cash benefits after taxes			$4,500

*Assumed tax rate.

Note that the initial investment ($10,000) and the depreciable book cost of the machine ($12,000) are different. This is often the case. Were the proposal to require an additional commitment of funds to accounts receivable and inventory, the initial investment might exceed the book cost of the equipment.

Where are we now? We have calculated the initial after-tax cash investment required ($10,000) and the annual net cash benefits after taxes for three years ($4500). This can be shown as:

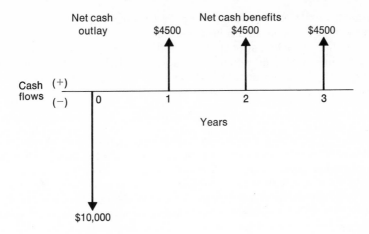

It should be emphasized that this stage of the analysis is the key to success in capital budgeting. Unless the input of estimated cash flows is accurate, the output will be misleading, no matter how sophisticated we make our subsequent manipulations.

But now we have a problem. The total cash benefit received over the three years is $13,500 (3 × $4500). Would this investment be as attractive if the pattern of cash benefits were $2500 the first year, $4500 the second year, and $6500 the third year? The total return is still $13,500. Instinctively, we feel that we would prefer to have our cash benefits sooner, rather than later. But how much more attractive is the first time pattern of cash benefits than the second time pattern? To evaluate investment proposals that generate cash benefits at future periods of time, we must consider the time value of money.

Time Value of Money

We have all heard the expression, "A bird in the hand is worth two in the bush." This refers to the time value of birds, but the principle involved is equally applicable to money. If offered a choice between a dollar today and a dollar a year from now, most of us would choose a dollar today. Clearly, a dollar a year from now is less valuable than a dollar today. Why is this so? As individuals we may reply that the dollar today will give us immediate pleasure in the form of a date or a movie. Immediate pleasure is preferable to postponed pleasure.

However, we must look at this problem from the point of view of the financial manager of a business concern. He prefers the dollar today, not because of the immediate pleasure he will gain, but because he can put that dollar to work within the company and earn some return on it. Should he choose to receive the dollar a year from now, he will forgo the money he might earn over the course of the year on the present dollar. In the words of the economist, there is an *opportunity cost* involved in passing up the earnings that would be obtained by using the present dollar in the firm over the year.

Were this a constant stream of cash inflows of $4500 per year for an infinite period of time, we could again use the valuation formula first introduced in Chapter 1 and simply discount that cash flow at some after-tax rate—say 10 percent—to find the present value of the flows:

$$\$4500/0.10 = \$45,000$$

But in this case we are to receive cash benefits of $4500 for only three years. The valuation formula that we have found convenient to use up to this point is no longer applicable. We are dealing with cash flows to be received for a limited period of time, rather than for an infinite period, as previously assumed.

The present value of a three-year flow of $4500 must be considerably less than that of an infinite series of $4500 inflows. How do we proceed to determine the present value of cash flows to be received for a finite period? At the outset we can agree that we would not ordinarily relinquish today's dollar in exchange for a promise that it will be returned a year from now. We will want our dollar back *plus* some payment for its use. If we think that we should receive 10 percent for the intended use of our money, today's dollar should be returned a year from now with an additional 10¢. Thus $1.00 invested at 10 percent today would be worth $1.10 a year from now. To put it another way, the *present value* of $1.10 a year from now, discounted at 10 percent, is $1.00. This is a bit awkward, however. We are seldom going to be called upon to give the present value of $1.10 a year from now; we are much more likely to be faced with the problem of calculating the present value of $1.00 received a year from now, or some multiple of $1.00. Thus we would like to know what amount, invested at 10 percent, will cumulate to $1.00 a year from now. As it turns out, $0.909 invested at 10 percent will be worth $1.00 a year from now ($0.909 + 10% × $0.909 = $1.00). In other words, the present value of $1.00 a year from now, discounted at 10 percent, is $0.909.

If today's dollar is worth $1.10 a year from now, it should be worth even more two years from now. Today we invest a dollar at 10 percent; at the end of the first year we reinvest $1.10 at 10 percent. Consequently, at a rate of 10 percent, compounded annually, a dollar today is worth 1.21 at the end of the second year. Alternatively, we could say that $1.00 two years from now has a present value of $0.826: that is, if $0.826 were invested at an annual compound interest rate of 10 percent, it would amount to $1.00 at the end of the second year. This is proved below:

	Amount invested first of year	Interest earned at 10% on amount invested	Amount available at end of year
1st year	$0.826 × 10% =	$0.083	$0.909
2nd year	0.909 × 10% =	0.091	1.00

Thus we can construct a small table showing the present value of $1.00 received one year from now and two years from now, in each case assuming an interest rate of 10 percent.

Years hence	Present value at 10% of $1 received at end of the year
0	$1.00
1	0.909
2	0.826

Fortunately, we need struggle no longer to develop our own table; the necessary tables are readily available. A portion of a "present value table" is shown in Appendix A-1. The relatively simple mathematics underlying the table is shown in the accompanying material.

If the present value of $1.00 received a year from now is $0.909 and the present value of another $1.00 received two years from now is 0.826, what is the present value of a stream of cash benefits of $1.00 at the end of year 1 and year 2 discounted at 10 percent? Clearly, the present value of a dollar a year for the next two years is $0.909 + $0.826 or $1.735. (Because of differences due to rounding, it is actually 1.736.) There will be occasions when we will wish to evaluate a series of receipts. For this purpose we will use Appendix A-2, which shows the present value of $1.00 received annually for a specified number of years. A series of equal payments over time is called an *annuity*.

Both Appendices A-1 and A-2 assume that the cash benefits are received at the *end* of each period of time. Other tables are available that assume that the cash benefits are available continuously throughout the year. Moreover, Appendices A-1 and A-2 could be used to evaluate income streams received monthly or semi-annually. Instead of the time periods being years, they can be considered as months or half-years. Rates of return would then be monthly or semi-annual rates, but could readily be converted to or from annual rates.

Evaluation of Capital Expenditures

There is a considerable array of methods for evaluating capital expenditures. We will consider first the two procedures that employ the time value of money. In this discussion we shall consider that all new capital expenditures are just as risky as those investments currently held by the firm. Then we will review briefly two other methods that do not consider the time value of money. Space is devoted to these two latter techniques primarily because they are still in use, either as sole criteria for evaluation or as supplements to one of the two methods employing the time value of money. Over time they should become more of historical than practical interest.

Before examining the two approaches employing the time value of money, we need to review the principles that should determine the discount rate to be used in the process of evaluation. Let us first recall the role of the discount rate under the assumption that we are dealing with an unlevered firm and then see what changes occur when this restrictive assumption is relaxed.

Review: Restricted Assumptions

Let us recall the discussion in Chapter 1. We wish to maximize the utility of the residual owners. This is best facilitated by maximizing their wealth, which in turn is a reflection of the market value of their equity holdings. Up to this point we have restricted our discussion to the very simple case of an unlevered firm having nothing but common stock outstanding. If constant, infinite, after-tax cash flows, A, are assumed, the market value, V, of the firm has been shown as:

$$V = A/k_a .$$
(8-1)

Should we wish to focus attention on k_a, the after-tax discount rate (and we do), formula (8-1) can be reshaped as shown below:

$$A/V = k_a .$$
(8-2)

If estimated annual cash flows are $6000, and the aggregated market value of the common stock is $50,000, then k_a is 12 percent [$6/$50].

Since we are assuming that estimated future cash flows are given, variations in the market value of the firm can be seen to determine k_a: the lower V, the higher k_a, and vice versa. The important point is that k_a is a *market rate;* that is, it is established by the residual owners through the price that they are willing to pay for the shares of the common stock. *Management does not set k_a; it is set in the marketplace.* How do owners set the market price of the stock? Very simply. They examine other investment opportunities. If this stock offers a yield that is too low in view of the risks involved, they will sell the stock, thus lowering its price until the yield rises enough to justify assuming the risk. (Recall that we measure the degree of risk by the variance of the expected annual cash flows, A.) If the stock offers a return that is high in relation to other investment opportunities of similar risk, the market price of this stock will be bid up until the yield drops to the point where it is commensurate with the risk.

Now: Relaxed Assumptions.

Let us now relax the rather strict assumptions that we are dealing with a firm having only common stock outstanding. Let us consider any firm, however it may be financed. This firm also has an opportunity cost, but it is not as easy to measure as in the more rarefied case just discussed. But there surely must exist some rate *established by the market* that represents an opportunity cost for investments of the grade of risk characteristic of the firm. Investments of the same degree of risk that yield less than this rate will depress the market price of the stock; investments yielding more will raise the market price of the stock. To designate this more generalized opportunity cost we shall use the symbol, ρ (the Greek letter "rho").[4] It is the equilibrium rate of return that will leave the firm's shareholders just as well off after the new investment as before. This equilibrium rate, or opportunity cost, may thus be viewed as a hurdle rate for capital expenditures. But if this is the minimum rate demanded of capital expenditures (of the same risk class), it may also be viewed in the other light. Through the prices that they pay for various types of the firm's securities, investors must establish an aggregate *cost of capital* for the firm. If risk is held constant, any new investments should earn no less than this aggregate rate. In short, *the hurdle rate, or opportunity cost, is the cost of capital, ρ.* Just as in the case of

[4]It's good form to use a few Greek letters now and then. Besides, this is frequently used to designate the cost of capital.

k_a, the identity of the opportunity cost and the cost of capital is brought about by the efficiency of the marketplace. Should investors find better yields elsewhere on equally risky opportunities, they will sell their shares, thereby depressing the market price and raising the cost of capital.

Measurement of the cost of capital is not a trivial task. Since we cannot do everything at the same time, we will assume for the purposes of this chapter that the cost of capital, ρ, has been estimated from market data and proceed to show its relevance to capital budgeting. In essence, we generate a need for knowing the cost of capital in this chapter and will then show how to calculate it in Chapter 11. Approached in this fashion, Chapter 11 becomes much more exciting.

Net Present Value

Assume that we have a proposed capital expenditure, costing c dollars. The question is whether it is worth the cost; that is, whether the present value of the anticipated cash flows is more or less than the required outlay. Since we are assuming that the new investment is as risky as current investments, the appropriate discount rate is the firm's current cost of capital, ρ. If we let A_t represent the after-tax cash flows generated by the new investment in year t, the present value of those cash inflows, E, can be calculated as follows:

$$E = \frac{A_1}{(1+\rho)} + \frac{A_2}{(1+\rho)^2} + \cdots + \frac{A_n}{(1+\rho)^n}, \quad \text{or} \tag{8-3}$$

$$E = \sum_{t=1}^{n} \frac{A_t}{(1+\rho)^t}, \quad t = 1, 2, \ldots, n. \tag{8-3a}$$

Note that formula (8-3) is merely the mathematical expression of Appendix A-2. For example, the present value of $1 per year for two years, discounted at 10 percent can be shown as:

$$E = \frac{1}{(1+0.10)} + \frac{1}{(1+0.10)^2}$$

$$= 0.909 + 0.826$$

$$= 1.736$$

Clearly, we should not pay more than E for the expected stream of cash flows produced by any given asset, because that asset would then yield less than the opportunity cost, ρ. Thus E is a "hurdle price;" if we cannot buy it for that price, or less, we should not buy it. Should we be able to acquire the asset for less than E, we have a bargain and should be able to raise the market value of the firm by the difference between E and the acquisition cost, c. This difference is, of course, the *net present value, NPV:*

$$NPV = E - c \tag{8-4}$$

$$NPV = \sum_{t=1}^{n} \frac{A_t}{(1+\rho)^t} - c, \quad \text{or more simply} \tag{8-4a}$$

$$NPV = \sum_{t=1}^{n} A_t (1+\rho)^{-t} - c. \tag{8-4b}$$

Let us illustrate the process. Assume that our cost of capital net after taxes has been estimated at 10 percent. The cash benefits net after taxes of a $10,000 investment have been estimated at $4500 per year for three years. Using Appendix A-2, we find that the present value of this stream of income discounted at 10 percent is $11,192.

$$2.487 \times \$4,500 = \$11,192 = E$$

Exactly the same process is sometimes presented as summing the present values of the outlays on the investment and the present value of the cash proceeds expected from the investment. If the resulting *net present value* is greater than zero, a net gain will be realized from the investment. Thus we have:

Present value of outlays (C)	$-10,000
Present value of proceeds (E)	+11,192
Net present value (NPV)	$ 1,192

To put the matter another way, $11,192 is the upper limit of the price we would be willing to pay to acquire this machine. The figure of $1192 represents the "bargain" we are obtaining, in that it is the amount over and above the purchase price that we would be willing to pay.

This particular approach may be useful when we find it necessary to make investment outlays during the first few years of the life of the project. This would be typical if we were building a large plant and making progress payments. We would then have to calculate the present value of the outlays, as well as the present value of the proceeds from the investment. In all of our illustrations we have assumed that the required cash outlays occur in the first period.

Some proponents of the present value approach convert the results into a *profitability index, desirability index,* or *benefit-cost ratio* by dividing the present value of the net cash benefits by the present value of the cash outlays required. For example, the profitability index for the $10,000 machine would be 1.12:

$$\frac{\text{Present value of net cash benefits}}{\text{Present value of outlays}} = \frac{E}{C} = \frac{\$11,192}{\$10,000} = 1.12$$

Where the object is to determine whether the proposed expenditure should be immediately rejected or not, this step is unnecessary. So long as the net present value is greater than zero, the proposal is worth considering. The profitability index may be suitable for selecting among conflicting proposals, although when there are substantial differences in the initial outlays required it may be desirable to take the conflicting proposal with the highest net present value. To a considerable extent the profitability index appears to be an attempt to make the present-value approach more meaningful to management. It is a matter of dispute whether this objective is achieved, or whether the profitability index is merely an "eccentric perversion."[5] In some cases use of the profitability index will lead to the selection of one project with a lower *NPV* than that of an alternative that is rejected.[6]

[5] A. J. Merrett and Allen Sykes, *The Finance and Analysis of Capital Projects* (New York: John Wiley & Sons, Inc., 1963), p. 150.

[6] H. M. Weingartner, "The Excess Present Value Index—A Theoretical Basis and Critique," *Journal of Accounting Research*, 1 (Autumn, 1963), pp. 120–21.

Discounted Rate of Return

This method of evaluating capital expenditures is also known by such names as internal rate of return, investor's method, and time-adjusted return. Recall that under the net-present-value method just described we arrived at an expected value in dollars, E, given expected annual net cash benefits, A_t, and a predetermined cost of capital, p. The rule was to accept the project if it had a positive net present value; that is, if $E > c$. The unknown was the present value of the net cash benefits, E. Under the discounted-rate-of return approach the cash flows are again known, but the unknown is the annual rate of return, r, earned on the initial cash outlay, c. In short, we must solve the following for r:

$$c = \frac{A_1}{(1+r)} + \frac{A_2}{(1+r)^2} + \cdots + \frac{A_n}{(1+r)^n}. \tag{8-5}$$

$$c = \sum_{t=1}^{n} A_t(1+r)^{-t} \tag{8-5a}$$

Essentially, solution of equation (8-5) requires that we find that value of r which will make the *NPV* of the project equal to zero. Whereas E was the highest price the firm could afford to pay for any given project under the present-value approach, r should be no less than the firm's cost of capital. If the discounted rate of return earned, r, is greater than the cost of capital, p, the market value of the owners' equity—and consequently their wealth—will be raised by acceptance of the project.

Calculation of Discounted Rate of Return. Let us return to Appendix A-2. Assume that we are told that if we will invest $2.106 in some venture, we will receive $1.00 a year for three years, and nothing thereafter. On our investment of $2.106 we receive a total of $3.00—a return of our original investment plus a compounded annual return. But what is that annual discounted rate of return? We know the future stream of cash flows (A_t) and the investment (c) required to achieve the income, but we would like to know the rate of return, or yield (r). The answer must lie somewhere in the "3-year line" of Appendix A-2. As we move along this line, we find that the rate that just equates an annual return of $1.00 a year for three years to the required investment of $2.106 is 20 percent. That is to say:

$$\$2.106 = \frac{\$1.00}{(1+0.20)} + \frac{\$1.00}{(1+0.20)^2} + \frac{\$1.00}{(1+0.20)^3}$$

Let us apply this technique to determine the rate of return on our $10,000 machine. We can estimate the rate of return by a series of successive approximations; that is, by making guesses at its value.[7] We wish to find that one rate that will equate the stream of $4500 net cash benefits for three years with the present required investment of $10,000. Let us see if a rate of 16 percent works.

[7] Since cash flows are uniform, we could enter Appendix A-2 more directly. We know that some factor (x) from the table, multiplied by the annual net cash benefits, must equal $10,000. Therefore:

$$4{,}500x = 10{,}000$$

$$x = 2.222$$

We know that the rate of return must fall between 16 and 18 percent, since the factor 2.222 falls between 2.246 and 2.174 on the "three-year-line" in Appendix A-2.

From Appendix A-2 we see that the present value of $4500 received annually for three years and discounted at 16 percent is $10,107:

$$2.246 \times \$4,500 = \$10,107$$

This tells us that if we were to invest $10,107 in return for $4500 a year for three years, the annual rate of return would be 16 percent. However, we do not need to invest this much money; our net investment is only $10,000. Therefore, the true rate of return that we will receive must be more than 16 percent. Let us try 18 percent. Using Appendix A-2 again, we find that the present value of $4500 received annually for three years and discounted at 18 percent is $9783:

$$2.174 \times \$4,500 = \$9,783$$

This calculation tells us that if we were to invest $9783 in return for the specified cash benefits, the rate of return would be 18 percent. Because we actually must invest more than $9783, the rate to be gained must be less than 18 percent, but more than 16 percent. Moreover, it must be closer to 16 percent, because the actual required investment of $10,000 is closer to $10,107 than to $9783. We can approximate the actual rate by interpolation:

	Discounted rates of return	Present values	Present values
Appendix A-2	16%	$10,107	$10,107
	r%		10,000
Appendix A-2	18%	9,783	
Differences	2%	$ 324	$ 107

The data could be diagrammed as shown below:

Present value	$9,783	$10,000	$10,107
Rate of return	18%	r%	16%

$$\frac{\$107}{\$324} \times 2\% = 0.7\% \qquad 16\% + 0.7\% = 16.7\%$$

Observe that the calculated rate is, as we expected, closer to 16 percent than to 18 percent. In other words, a net cash inflow of $4500 at the end of each year for three years is equivalent to a discounted rate of return of about 16.7 percent compounded annually on an initial net investment of $10,000. We can easily check the validity of this figure, as shown below. To obtain great accuracy, we shall use a rate of 16.66 percent, rather than the rate rounded off to one decimal point.

	Amount invested first of year		Interest at 16.66% earned on amount invested		Amount available at end of year	Amount withdrawn at end of year
1st yr.	$10,000	+	$1,666	=	$11,666	$4,500
2nd yr.	7,166	+	1,194	=	8,360	4,500
3rd yr.	3,860	+	643	=	4,503	4,500

The difference between $4503 and $4500 is small considering the amounts involved. If the true rate been used, no difference would have resulted.

Another way of viewing the table above would be to consider that we have deposited $10,000 with a rather generous banker who has agreed to pay almost 16.7 percent, compounded annually, on all deposits. At the end of each year we withdraw $4500 after the bank has calculated the interest on our account. Our last withdrawal of $4500 at the end of the third year just empties the account. (The $3 difference is for "service charges.")

Rate of return can also be applied in situations in which the net cash benefit is not the same in each year. This is frequently the case. If the machine we propose to buy is estimated to have some salvage value at the end of the third year, this cash return (net after taxes) should be added to the net cash benefit of that year. The introduction of a basic new product may bring increasing returns as it gains public acceptance. For example, this might have been the case with the proposal to purchase a machine for $10,000 which in three successive years would produce net cash benefits after taxes of $2500, $4500, and $6500, respectively. The proposal to invest $10,000 to obtain annual net cash inflows of $4500 for three years offers a higher rate of return, however. Even though the total dollar return is the same in both cases, the yield on the capital investment is about 16.7 percent for the level net cash benefits, as compared to slightly over 14 percent for the machine with the delayed cash benefits. To obtain this latter rate, we must make successive approximations from Appendix A-1 and then interpolate if necessary. Although computer programs are available to perform this series of approximations very quickly, it is important to understand what the computer is up to. By making successive approximations, we find that the 14 percent rate is very close to the actual discounted rate of return:

14% rate

0.877 × $2,500 = $ 2,193
0.769 × 4,500 =   3,461
0.675 × 6,500 =   4,388
$10,042

Comparison of Net Present Value and Discounted Rate of Return

If we have ample funds available and are evaluating a single proposed capital expenditure, use of either net present value or discounted rate of return should give the same decision. If the net present value is positive, the discounted rate of return will also exceed the cost of capital, so that the project should be accepted. If *NPV* is negative, acceptance will penalize the stockholders, unless there are some non-quantifiable benefits to be derived from the expenditure. Only if a project has intermittent cash *out*flows over its life-time are we likely to run into problems by using the discounted-rate-of-return method, and such projects are relatively rare.[8]

However, we are seldom called upon to evaluate a single project in isolation, Often, we must rank projects that are *mutually exclusive;* that is, acceptance of one automatically rules out acceptance of others. For example, if we are considering three different types of computer, acceptance of one means that we will reject the other two. In addition, we may be faced with a choice among

---

[8] In solving for *r* in equation (8-5), we are really solving for the roots of a polynomial of degree *n*. If there are several changes of sign we may obtain more than one root; that is, more than one discounted rate of return. This disconcerting turn of events can always be avoided by using net present value.

projects that is forced by *capital rationing.* By this we mean that the dollar investment required by acceptable projects (positive *NPV's*) is greater than the amount that management is willing or able to budget for capital expenditures. Management may decide to ration capital in the short run in order to avoid the sale of additional securities in a depressed market or to maintain the current level of dividend payments. In addition to these rational justifications for a capital-rationing situation, management may simply have an unreasoned fear of assuming debt. Rational or not, in the real world there is capital rationing, and we must devise means to rank projects under such circumstances. When the existence of mutually exclusive projects or capital rationing requires that we rank projects, the net-present-value method is superior to the discounted-rate-of-return procedure.

The inherent difficulty involved in ranking projects can best be illustrated by examining the *size disparity problem.* This is occasioned by major differences in the initial outlays on proposals for capital expenditures that must be ranked. An extreme example will illustrate the underlying dilemma. If you had an either-or choice between earning a 25 percent return on $1000 for one year or a 50 percent rate of return on $1 for one year, which would you choose? Since most people would prefer ending the year with an extra $250 as opposed to an extra 50¢, we can see that a decision based upon the discounted rate of return would have been unfortunate. Let us see why this is so.

Consider projects A and B shown below. Although both offer a rate of return greater than the cost of capital and have positive net present values, we cannot accept both, either because they are mutually exclusive or because we are constrained by capital rationing.

Project	Initial outlay	Net cash benefits end of first year	Discounted rate of return	Net present value @ 10%
A	$10,000	$11,500	15%	$453.50
B	$22,000	24,860	13%	$597.74

It should be somewhat disconcerting to observe that the ranking provided by the discounted rate of return and by the net-present-value approach are not the same. This difference arises because of an implicit assumption concerning the reinvestment opportunities available for the extra $12,000 that would be available if project A, rather than B, were selected. Should we opt for project A, there is an implicit assumption that the extra $12,000 can be reinvested in some other project for at least the same rate of return as earned by project A; namely 15 percent. This is both unlikely and, more important, theoretically incorrect. In purchasing our securities, investors have set market prices which have established a cost of capital of 10%. So long as we stay in this class of risk, we should pursue capital expenditures down to the point where they yield 10 percent (but no less). If our stockholders have thus established our *marginal return* at 10 percent, we cannot assume that our marginal investment opportunities yield 15 percent. Since our owners rank alternative investments in this risk class using a rate of 10 percent, our ranking will be suboptimal if we use some other rate.

Let us make the proper theoretical assumption that the extra $12,000 can be reinvested in some project C at the marginal rate of 10 percent. Then the terminal value at the year's end of that investment strategy will be $24,700:

(1) Project	(2) Initial outlay	(3) Discounted rate of return	(4) Earnings end of year	(5) Net Cash benefits end of year (2) + (4)
A	$10,000	15%	1,500	11,500
C	12,000	10%	1,200	13,200
A + C	$22,000		Terminal value	$24,700

But examination of our prior text table shows that acceptance of project B would provide a higher terminal value of $24,860. Thus the net-present-value approach correctly ranks the two projects. Whereas use of the discounted rate of return implicitly assumes reinvestment at the calculated rate of return, ranking by use of net present value implicitly assumes reinvestment at the cost of capital. These implicit assumptions do not stem from the means used to calculate rate of return or net present value. They arise only in a ranking procedure, when we must decide implicitly or explicitly what is done with cash flows made available by the choice of one project over another. The same kind of implicit assumption arises when two projects show a time disparity in the generation of cash flows; as indicated in the diagram below:

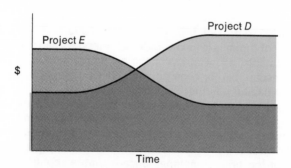

As in the case of size disparity, the issue is the alternative use of the differential cash flows generated by the two projects. In reality this is merely a special case of the size disparity problem.

Use of net present value is particularly appropriate when we are faced with capital rationing, so that we must select from among a "bundle" of projects, all of which would be acceptable if we just had more money to invest. Even though the discounted rates of return on all projects being examined are above the cost of capital, these percentage yields provide only part of the necessary data about the projects. We have only rates and no usable information about the dollars involved. We cannot relate the array of rates to the change in the market value of the owners' equity that would result from acceptance of any given subset of projects. We can obtain this information by using net present value.

To illustrate the point, consider Table 8-1, which lists a number of proposals available for acceptance. Capital rationing restrains our budget to $300. Which projects should be selected?

TABLE 8-1　　Equal-Risk Proposals for Capital Expenditure

Project	Outlay	Cash Inflow End of Year	NPV @10%	Discounted Return of Return
F	100	120	$ 9.08	20%
G	100	119	8.17	19%
H	100	112	1.81	12%
I	200	232	10.89	16%
J	300	354	21.79	18%

Examination of the rates of return is not very illuminating. The 18 percent return on project J is nice, but is it as good as, say, the 20 percent return from project F, coupled with the 16 percent return from project I? A much better approach is to determine the net present values of all possible subsets of proposals that will use up the $300 available:

F, G, H $19.06*　H, I $12.70
F, I　　$19.97　　J $21.79
G, I　　$19.06

*$9.08 + $8.17 + $1.81

This array shows very quickly that we will raise the value of the firm most by investing the $300 in project J. Obviously, the solution is more difficult when a very large array of projects is involved. Nonetheless, we can see that the optimal solution is attainable, especially with the aid of a computer, whereas it would not be readily accessible (or even optimal) if we employed the discounted rate of return under capital rationing.[9]

Although the discounted-rate-of-return and net-present-value approaches have the crucial advantage of recognizing the time value of money, they do not at present possess the advantage of being widely employed in all industries. Rougher techniques are used, sometimes because they are reasonably suitable to the needs of the firm, sometimes because more sophisticated techniques are not understood by management, and sometimes because management is still in process of training and educating its personnel in the use of rate of return or present value. The other two approaches most commonly used—payback and average rate of return—have their usefulness, but suffer from the fundamental deficiency that they ignore the time value of money. Let us examine each briefly.

Payback

The *payback* period is the length of time necessary for the sum of the annual net cash benefits to equal the initial investment. Thus a machine requiring a net

[9] This analysis deliberately avoids the issue of multi-period budgets. Capital expenditures in one year may draw funds from the following year, although funds are also generated by accepted projects. We should recognize that the problem exists, but it is not readily solved operationally.

cash outlay of $15,000 will be "paid for" in three years, if the cumulated annual cash savings after taxes equal $15,000 at the end of the third year. This approach has three major deficiencies. First, it ignores variations in the rate at which net savings are realized. For example, we might have two different $15,000 machines, whose annual net cash benefits (after taxes) would be as follows:

	A	B
1st year	$7,000	$3,000
2nd year	5,000	5,000
3rd year	3,000	7,000

Although both machines are "paid for" in three years, the investments are not equally desirable because of the time value of money. The more rapid return of the initial investment in the case of machine A makes it more desirable than machine B from the standpoint of profitability. The degree of superiority of A over B can be measured by determining the rate of return on the investment or the net present value.

Second, the payback approach fails to consider any stream of income extending beyond the payback period. Let us assume that we decide that any investment must pay for itself within two years, or we will not make it. On this basis a $10,000 machine that returned $5000 a year for only two years might be purchased. We would be forced to reject a proposal to buy a $10,000 machine that would return $4000 a year for five years. This decision would not maximize the market value of the owners' equity.

Third, the payback method has no means of adjusting for the different scales of investment. It provides a measure of the rate at which an investment is returned and, therefore, is not a useful device for selecting from among an array of projects under capital rationing.

The payback approach has its uses. If the firm is desperately short of cash, the financial manager may use the payback method to emphasize investments that produce a quick return of cash funds. Industries characterized by instability, uncertainty, and rapid technological change may adopt the payback approach on the grounds that the future is so unpredictable there is no point in projecting differential flows of cash beyond two years.

Average Rate of Return

The *average rate of return* (or *accounting rate of return*) may be defined as the percentage of the average annual net income after taxes to the average investment over the life of the project. This is not based upon cash flows, but upon the reported accounting income. Assume that an investment of $10,000 in a machine is expected to produce average net profits after taxes of $1400 per year for four years. In addition we must invest $2000 in inventory and accounts receivable necessary to support the project. The return of $1400 per year must be related to the average investment in the project over its life. The investment in inventory and receivables will be constant over the four years, but we will gradually recover the $10,000 initially invested in the machine. If we assume straight-line depreciation, our investment in the machine will decline year by year from $10,000 to $7500 to $5000 to $2500, and finally to $0 (assuming no scrap value). Consequently, our average investment in the project over the five years is only $7000:

$$2,000 + \tfrac{1}{2} (\$10,000 + \$0) = \$7,000$$

By comparing the average annual return after taxes to the average investment, we can compute the average rate of return on the investment:

$$\frac{\$1,400}{\$7,000} = 20 \text{ percent after taxes}$$

This measure of profitability is adequate if income streams are relatively constant and if there is no need for accurate comparison with other average rates of return or with the cost of capital. It is used as a practical operating tool by many business firms. However, as with the previous method, the time value of money is ignored. The return on average investment is stated to be 20 percent, whether most of the total net income of $5600 is earned in the first year or in the fourth year. This is an important deficiency.

If the cash flow is fairly uniform, and the capital project has a negligible salvage value, the methods discussed above may provide satisfactory estimates of the true rate of return. If the expected life of a project is greater than twice the expected payback period, the reciprocal of the payback provides a reasonably satisfactory estimate. Thus, if the payback is four years and the total expected life is ten years, the payback estimate of the rate of return is $\frac{1}{4}$, or 25 percent. The true rate of return for any level stream of receipts with these characteristics is 22.5 percent.[10] If the anticipated life of the project is less than twice the payback period, the average rate of return provides the better estimate.

Evaluation of Risk

Up to this point we have based all calculations upon the expected value of cash flows. But there is obviously a range of possible *NPV*'s, of which the expected *NPV* is only one. There are many causes of variance in the expected net present value (or expected discounted rate of return). Predicted savings may be affected by the dispersion of future labor rates and prices of materials. Cash inflows generated by plant expansion will vary with future selling prices and volume of sales. Even the cash outlay on new plant and equipment is subject to a frequency distribution over a possible range of values. Taken together, these factors produce a probability distribution function over the net present value. The wider the dispersion of possible outcomes (i.e. the greater the variance or standard deviation), the greater the risk involved in the project.

Why do we care about risk? We are concerned because selection of capital expenditures based upon their net present values without adjustment for risk may not, in fact, maximize the market value of the residual owners' equity if there are significant differences in risk among the projects. Variations in pos-

[10]Myron J. Gordon, "The Payoff Period and the Rate of Profit," *Journal of Business* (October, 1955); reprinted in Ezra Solomon, *The Management of Corporate Capital* (Chicago: The Free Press of Glencoe, 1959), pp. 48–55. However, for any given project "the deviation of the payback reciprocal from the internal rate also decreases as the [discounted] rate [of return] increases." Marshall Sarnat and Haim Levy, "The Relationship of Rules of Thumb to the Internal Rate of Return: A Restatement and Generalization," *Journal of Finance*, 24 (June, 1969), p. 481.

sible outcomes, coupled with aversion to risk, could lead to situations in which owners would prefer project K to project L. In spite of project L's higher expected NPV, the uncertainty of the outcome may outweigh the difference in the expected NPV's.

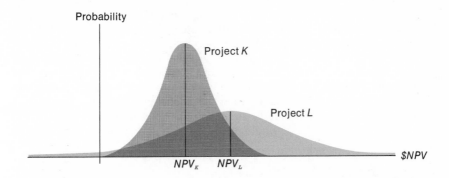

Whether a given investor will prefer project K to L will depend upon his aversion to risk and the difference between the expected NPV's. The attitude of investors in general towards the probability distributions diagrammed above will be expressed in the costs of capital of firms making the products associated with projects K and L. Because investors are risk averse, the cost of capital of firm L will be higher than that of firm K. We are thus informed by the market that we must consider risk in capital budgeting.

In using the firm's cost of capital, ρ, to discount cash flows to compute net present value, we are already recognizing the degree of risk characteristic of the firm's activities. If we are firm K, no additional cognizance need be taken of the risk on more K-type projects. It is when somebody brings in an L-type project—or any other project where the associated risk, is significantly different from that of existing projects—that the need arises to give special consideration to risk.

Just how to give this "special consideration" is a matter of considerable controversy in financial literature. There are two basic approaches (which are not mutually exclusive). One method of dealing with risk is to describe the level of risk in some fashion, so that management may reach an intuitive judgment about the proposed capital expenditure. A second approach is to devise a means of systematically allowing for risk in ranking proposals.

Methods of Describing Risk

One way of describing risk is to make clear to management the assumptions underlying the various estimates leading to a final expected net present value (or discounted rate of return). Since management finds downside variation from the expected NPV painful, it may be useful to calculate the maximum possible loss that the firm could suffer if the fates should conspire to produce the worst possible outcome. Some investments may be partially recoverable. A dress manufacturer that bets on midi's when mini's are "in" can at least cut a few inches off and survive. But pity the manufacturer who bets on mini's when midi's are in. His inventory has virtually no salvage value.

Another way of conveying to management a sense of the dispersion of possible outcomes from an investment is by sensitivity analysis. This is a process of determining the effect upon net present value of possible variations in the factors used to estimate after-tax cash flows. Not only does this indicate the range of possible dispersion in NPV, but it also identifies those parameters that are most influential in determining NPV. Attention may then be focused on making accurate estimates of these factors.

If we can make a sensitivity analysis, we may also be able to assign probabilities to the possible values of the factors affecting the NPV of a project. Given these assigned estimates, we should be able to construct a probability distribution function over possible values of the net present value, as shown in the diagram for projects K and L. Such distributions can be generated by use of the computer, although it would obviously be economical to do so only for major projects.[11]

Methods of Allowing for Risk

Although it may be very helpful to describe the level of risk to management, it might be better if we could design a procedure for systematically adjusting for risk. Of the two basic approaches of allowing for risk, the risk-adjusted discount rate appears to have the greater operational applicability.[12]

If we are in the business of manufacturing product K, our firm has a cost of capital that reflects the risk of that endeavor. Should we decide to diversify into product L, our firm's cost of capital is not appropriate for discounting the cash flows generated by that investment. It has a higher risk. How much higher can be determined by calculating the cost of capital of firms engaged in the business of making product L. Thus there is a unique cost of capital for every proposed capital investment.[13] It is the rate that the investment must earn in order to leave the market value of the owners' equity unchanged. If the project is in the same risk class as that of the firm, the current cost of capital, ρ, is the appropriate cost of capital. However, if we are evaluating a project that is in another risk class, we should discount its cash flows using a different, risk-adjusted cost of capital.

---

[11] See D. B. Hertz, "Risk Analysis in Capital Investment," Harvard Business Review, 42 (January-February, 1964), pp. 95–106.

[12] An alternative is the certainty-equivalent approach. Managment is asked to view the risks associated with generating a particular cash flow in a given year and to estimate the certain cash flow that would be just as attractive as the uncertain cash flows. By repeating the process for each year's cash flows over the life of the project, management generates a series of certainty-equivalent cash flows, which may then be discounted at a default-free rate to determine a certainty-equivalent NPV. The rule is then to take the subset of projects with the highest aggregate certainty-equivalent NPV if under capital rationing, or all positive NPV's if not. The theoretical attractions of this approach seem outweighed by the operational difficulties of generating certainty-equivalent cash flows. For further discussion, see Johnson, op. cit., pp. 124–26.

[13] It has been argued that we must consider the covariances among possible outcomes of proposed capital expenditures and of proposed projects with existing projects. However, investors can generally achieve their own diversification. Their ability to diversify means that they will not pay anything extra to the firm to perform this same function (other than to reduce significantly the risk of bankruptcy). In view of the diversification investors can achieve in their own portfolios, we should be able to treat projects as risk independent and not be concerned with covariances among projects and among proposed and existing projects. For a fuller discussion see Johnson, op. cit., pp. 131–37.

To illustrate application of this approach, assume that our product is canned soup. We are considering a diversification program that will take us into the electronics business, one with more excitement, but also more risk. Because of capital rationing we must choose between investing $100,000 in expansion of soup-manufacturing facilities (project *K*) or committing an equal amount in a small electronics plant (project *L*). Cash flows from the added soup facilities are expected to be $18,000 per year for ten years; from the electronics business, $22,000 per year for ten years. Valued at the firm's current cost of capital — say 8 percent — the investment in the electronics operation appears to be much more desirable:

	8% P. V. factor	Annual cash flows	PV	NPV
K	6.710	$18,000	$120,780	$20,780
L	6.710	22,000	147,620	47,620

Projects valued at 8%

However, examination of the cost of capital of electronics firms suggests that a more suitable cost of capital for that higher risk is about 14 percent. If we do not earn at least this much on the electronics investment, the market value of our common stock will decline. Using this risk-adjusted cost of capital, we find that the net present value of the investment in electronics (*L*) is lower by almost $32,900. Given the adjustment for risk, the investment in the soup kitchen is more attractive:

Project L at 14%

	14% P. V. factor	Annual cash flows	PV	NPV
L	5.216	$22,000	$114,752	$14,752

Again, this is an either-or choice. Were we not restricted by capital rationing, both investments would be desirable, since the risk-adjusted *NPV* is positive in both cases.

If there are a large number of projects under consideration, the procedure is essentially the same. For proposals that represent a continuation or support of the firm's current activities, the current cost of capital should be used to discount cash flows. Cash flows of projects whose risk (dispersion of possible outcomes) is significantly different from that of the firm's current risk class should be discounted at costs of capital characteristic of the industries represented. Once the risk-adjusted *NPV*'s have been determined, we must find that subset with the highest aggregate *NPV* if the firm is subject to capital rationing. Otherwise, all projects with positive *NPV*'s that are not mutually exclusive may be accepted.

Organization and Control

The organization for carrying out capital budgeting procedures and controlling capital expenditures varies from company to company. In a small company all proposals for capital expenditures may be submitted to the president and board of directors, if any, for consideration. Frequently, in a large company the exception principle is employed. A department head may be authorized to approve expenditures up to $10,000; a plant manager, payments up to $50,000; and the president, capital expenditures up to $200,000. Other proposals are submitted to a budget committee headed by the president. This committee evaluates the proposals in terms of their costs and benefits and in relation to the availability of cash. The final recommendation for various capital expenditures is usually submitted to the board of directors for approval.

The planning period will also vary, depending in part on the ability to forecast future demand for the company's products and in part on the nature of the capital expenditures involved. An electric utility can extend its planning horizon five or ten years. Economic forecasts of power consumption are likely to be a good deal more reliable than forecasts of the sales of automobiles or washing machines. Furthermore, because of the time necessary to bring new plant and equipment into operation, electric utilities must make long-range plans if they are to have the power available when needed.

Once a capital expenditure is approved, an appropriation may be set aside to cover that estimated expenditure. If the financial manager is charged with the control of capital expenditures, it will be his responsibility to obtain progress reports on the project. Should the funds be draining away at a faster rate than anticipated, it may be necessary to ask for a supplemental appropriation or a more penurious director of the project. Regular progress reports are necessary in order to revise financial plans as needed. Some sort of report is customarily submitted at the completion of the project: that is, when the machine is finally in place or the building ready for occupancy. At this point the appropriation is closed.

Probably the most important step in the control process is an evaluation of the results of the proposal. What was the final cost in relation to the anticipated cost? Did the benefits realized match up the projected gains?[14] We need some systematic review of the results of capital expenditures for two principal reasons. For one thing, if department heads know that we check results, their original proposals are likely to be more realistic than they might otherwise be. More important, we should be able to learn from our past errors and so improve our capital budgeting processes. Where did we err? Did the machine cost more than anticipated? What expenditures did we forget? Where were our assumptions wrong?

Summary

Capital budgeting probably spells the difference between success and failure for many business concerns. Regardless of the size of the company or the level at which the decisions are made, the principles should be the same. We are committing a sum of money today in return for an expected stream of net cash benefits in the future. Evaluation of the desirability of a particular project re-

[14]Determination of the cash benefits realized is sometimes difficult because accounting records are not prepared on a cash basis.

quires that we give greater weight to income that is to be received in the near future. We must consider the time value of money. The two methods of evaluating capital expenditures that take into account the time value of money are net present value and discounted rate of return. When projects are mutually exclusive or the firm is operating under capital rationing, projects must be ranked. For this purpose the net-present-value approach is superior to the discounted rate of return. When projects are compared, net present value carries the implicit assumption that differences in cash flows are reinvested at the cost of capital. In addition the change in the value of the firm may be measured directly by comparing the NPV's of various subsets of projects.

Because investors are averse to risk, we must consider differences in the risk (variance of possible outcomes) among proposed capital expenditures. A rather brief excursion into this complex area suggests that recognition of risk can best be achieved by discounting cash flows at risk-adjusted rates. If a proposal does not change the risk class of the firm, the current cost of capital is suitable. In contrast, if a project's risk differs from that of the firm, its cash flows should be discounted at a risk-adjusted rate derived by measuring the cost of capital of firms in the proposed new line of business.

Questions

1/ From a theoretical standpoint, would you classify the following as operating or capital expenditures? Explain your decisions.
   a. The annual salary of the company's attorney.
   b. The costs of a patent infringement suit to protect the company's patent on one of its major products.
   c. The costs of moving machinery around to gain a more efficient plant layout.
   d. The costs of a six-week training program for a new employee.
   e. The costs of a picnic for the employees.
   f. The costs of a small pilot plant that will be in operation for less than a year.

2/ From recent periodicals obtain reports of a capital expenditure undertaken by a business firm. Describe the decision taken and the forecasts that were necessarily involved in reaching that decision. Comment on the relative degree of certainty of the various forecasts involved.

3/ We pay a consultant $1000 to study the desirability of installing some new equipment. When he submits his analysis and recommendation, should we add his fee to the cost of the new machine in order to determine the desirability of purchasing it? Explain your answer.

4/ Which of the following should be charged to or deducted from the cost of a new machine for capital budgeting purposes? Explain your decisions. (Ignore taxes in all cases.)
   a. The book value of the old machine is $3000.
   b. The old machine can be sold for $1000.
   c. The book loss on the old machine will be $2000.

d. It will cost $300 to dismantle and remove the old machine.

e. It will cost $200 to install some special wiring for the new machine.

f. It will cost $500 to train the operators of the new machine.

g. Additional investment of $8000 in accounts receivable and inventory will be required.

5/ A railroad is considering reduction of passenger service between two points. There are two possible approaches: to reduce the number of cars per train or to reduce the number of trains per day. Discuss the two proposals, indicating clearly the costs that you believe would be reduced under each:

a. Fuel costs

b. Salary of the crew

c. Maintenance of track

d. Salary of signalmen

e. Terminal expenses

6/ Since costs are "sunk" once a capital expenditure is made, what is the value of checking the results of these investment decisions?

7/ Beginning in 1961 textile manufacturers were permitted to depreciate textile machinery more rapidly for tax purposes than in earlier years. Assume that textile manufacturer A uses discounted rate of return or net present value to evaluate capital expenditure proposals, and that manufacturer B uses average rate of return exclusively. Given the change in tax treatment, will there be any difference between manufacturer A and B in their willingness to purchase new equipment? Explain.

Problems

1/ Calculate the following:

a. The present value of $9000 to be received at the end of 10 years, discounted at 14 percent.

b. The present value of $3000 for 8 years, discounted at 10 percent.

c. The present value of $3000 for 5 years, discounted at 10 percent.

d. The present value of $2000 for 5 years, discounted at 10 percent.

e. The present value of $2000 for 5 years, followed by $3000 for an additional 3 years, all discounted at 10 percent.

2/ Two conflicting proposals of equal risk have been made for the purchase of new equipment. The data on each are given below:

	A	B
Net cash outlay	$8,500	$6,000
Salvage value	0	0
Estimated life	5 yrs.	5 yrs.
Net cash benefits before depreciation and taxes		
1–3 yrs.	2,500	1,500
4–5 yrs.	2,000	1,500

Assume straight-line depreciation and a corporate tax rate of 40 percent. Cost of capital is assumed to be 10 percent. Provide the necessary computations to rank each project in terms of:
a. Discounted rate of return
b. Net present value and profitability index
c. Payback
d. Average rate of return.
How do you explain any differences in the ranking?

3/ A machine now in use has a book value of $1800. It can be sold for $2500, but could be used for three more years, at the end of which time it would have no salvage value. A new machine can be purchased at an invoice price of $14,000 to replace the present equipment. Freight-in will amount to $800 and installation cost, $200. Because of the nature of the product manufactured, it also has an expected life of three years, and will have no salvage value at the end of that time. With the new machine expected direct cash savings amount to $8000 the first year and $7000 in each of the next two years.

Corporate income taxes are at an annual rate of 40 percent, and the tax rate applicable to gains or losses on sales of equipment amounts to 30 percent. Both the present and proposed equipment would be depreciated on a straight-line basis over three years. Cost of capital is assumed to be 10 percent. Each question below should be considered independently.

a. On the basis of the above assumptions, compute the discounted rate of return after taxes on the investment and the net present value.
b. Assume now that the prospective salvage value of the machine at the end of the third year is estimated to be $1800, and that straight-line depreciation is calculated on this basis. If all other assumptions remain as in (a), what are the discounted rates of return and net present value?
c. Assume that an additional $2000 must be invested in accounts receivable and inventory during the three years, but that this will be freed at the end of the third year. If all other assumptions remain as in (a), what are the discounted rates of return and net present value?
d. Assume that the company employs the sum-of-the-years'-digits method of depreciation: that is, $\frac{3}{6}$ of the initial cost is taken as depreciation the first year, $\frac{2}{6}$ the second, and $\frac{1}{6}$ the third. If all other assumptions remain as in (a), what are the discounted rates of return and net present value?

4/ At the bankruptcy sale of the Hotel St. George (Brooklyn, N.Y.), Vantor Properties, Inc., submitted two bids, one for $2,300,000 in cash and the other for $2,500,000, with $900,000 to be paid in cash immediately and the balance payable over four years in equal installments. (*Wall Street Journal,* January 23, 1964, p. 6).

If the seller accepts the installment payments rather than "cash on the barrel head," what is the implicit rate of return he obtains from the larger total payment? Assume that the installment payments are made at the end of each year.

5/ Assume that a firm with a cost of capital of 12 percent must choose between two mutually exclusive projects having cash flows as shown below:

Project	Initial outlay	Annual net cash benefits for 5 years
A	$6,000	$2,000
B	10,000	3,165

a. Compute the net present value and discounted rate of return for each project.
b. Compute the *marginal* discounted rate of return available on the incremental investment of $4,000 in project B.
c. In the absence of capital rationing, which project should be selected? Why? How do your findings in (b) relate to the conclusions that you draw from (a)?

6/ Assume that a firm with a cost of capital of 10 percent must choose between the two mutually exclusive projects having cash flows as shown below:

Project	Initial outlay	Annual net cash benefits 1	2	3
X	$10,000	$7,000	$4,000	$2,000
Y	10,000	2,000	4,000	8,200

a. Compute the net present value and discounted rate of return for each project. Why is there a difference in ranking? In the absence of capital rationing, which project should be selected? Why?
b. Management wishes to measure the sensitivity of the net present value to variations in cost of capital. To provide such an analysis prepare a chart showing present value on the vertical axis and cost of capital on the horizontal axis. Plot the *NPV*'s of projects X and Y, given a range of cost of capital from 0 percent to 24 percent. What does this information convey to management?
c. On the chart prepared in (b) above, note the cost of capital at which X and Y have a *NPV* of $0. Compare these results with those obtained in (a) above. What does this tell us about the relationship of *NPV* and discounted rate of return?

7/ The Sartoris Manufacturing Corp. has a number of capital investment proposals available, but its capital budget is limited to $500.
a. Given the information about the projects shown below, which should be selected?

Project	Outlay	NPV
A	$100	$26
B	100	18
C	100	16
D	200	40
E	200	36
F	300	60

b. Now assume that projects A and B are mutually exclusive. Which projects should be selected?

c. Under the assumptions given in (b), how much would the value of the firm increase? How much would it have increased had it not been limited by capital rationing? How much has capital rationing cost the owners of the firm?

8/ Consider the following two projects:

Initial outlay	5 years	Annual net cash benefits for 10 years	20 years
$10,000	$2,374	$1,490	$1,018
10,000	3,054	2,070	1,687

a. Estimate the annual rate of return by using the reciprocal of the payback period. E.g., if the payback is 4 years, its reciprocal is 1/4 and the estimated rate of return is 25 percent.

b. Compute the discounted rate of return.

c. By comparing your results in (a) and (b) above, what conclusions do you draw concerning the relationship of the reciprocal of payback and the discounted rate of return?

9/ The H. G. Fraine & Co. is planning to build a warehouse. Two possibilities are being considered:

Plan A. Build a small warehouse now and enlarge it later. The present construction cost will be $300,000, and the expected cost of the enlargement, to be paid for at the end of the fifth year, will be $200,000. Maintenance during the first five years will amount to $5000 per year, also payable at the end of each year.

Plan B. Build a large warehouse now at a cost of $400,000. Maintenance is estimated at $8000 per year for the first five years.

Assume that the cost of capital is 10 percent and ignore any tax aspects. Using net present value and discounted rate of return, evaluate the relative desirability of the two plans. (*Hint:* To calculate the rate of return, determine the added investment required by Plan B and the differences in annual net cash flows that will result from its adoption. Do not be alarmed by negative cash flows.)

10/ Hettenhouse Hot Shops is a small chain of short-order restaurants. Management is considering investing $50,000 either in another hot shop or in a feed and grain business. Annual cash flows from the hot shop are estimated at $12,400, whereas annual cash flows from the feed and grain business are estimated at $10,500 — in each case for a 10-year period.

a. Initially, Hettenhouse estimates his cost of capital in the hot shop business to be 15 percent. On this basis, what is the net present value of each of the two investments, and which would be chosen?

b. However, upon reflection he realizes that the feed and grain business is less risky. Study of market data on feed and grain companies suggests that a reasonable estimate of cost of capital for this line of endeavor is 10 percent. With this added consideration of risk, which is the more attractive investment?

Selected References

Note: There is a large body of literature in this area. Many fine articles have been omitted to conserve space. My apologies to the authors.

ARROW, K. J. and R. C. LIND, "Uncertainty and the Evaluation of Public Investment Decisions," *American Economic Review,* 60 (June, 1970), pp. 364–78.

BAILEY, M. J. "Formal Criteria for Investment Decisions," *Journal of Political Economy* 67 (October, 1959), pp. 476–88.

BERNHARD, R. H., "Mathematical Programming Models for Capital Budgeting—A Survey, Generalization, and Critique," *Journal of Financial and Quantitative Analysis,* 4 (June, 1969), pp. 111–58.

BIERMAN, H. and S. SMIDT, *The Capital Budgeting Decision.* New York: Macmillan Co., 1966.

BROWN, H. P., "The Present Value Theory of Investment Appraisal: A Critical Analysis," *Bulletin Oxford University Institute of Economics and Statistics,* 31 (May, 1969), pp. 105–31.

CHEN, H. Y., "Valuation under Uncertainty," *Journal of Financial and Quantitative Analysis,* 2 (September, 1967), pp. 313–25.

EDGE, C. G., *A Practical Manual on the Appraisal of Capital Expenditure.* Hamilton, Ontario: Society of Industrial and Cost Accountants of Canada, 1964.

ELTON, E. J., "Capital Rationing and External Discount Rates," *Journal of Finance,* 25 (June, 1970), pp. 573–84.

FARRAR, D. E., *The Investment Decision under Uncertainty.* Englewood Cliffs, N.J.: Prentice-Hall, 1962.

GONEDES, N. J., "A Test of the Equivalent-Risk Hypothesis," *Journal of Financial and Quantitative Analysis,* 4 (June, 1969), pp. 159–78.

HERTZ, D. B., "Investment Policies that Pay Off," *Harvard Business Review,* 46 (January–February, 1968), pp. 96–108.

————, "Risk Analysis in Capital Investment," *Harvard Business Review,* 42 (January–February, 1964), pp. 95–106. A non-mathematical exposition of the approach used in the article by F. S. Hillier.

HILLIER, F. S., "The Derivation of Probabilistic Information for the Evaluation of Risky Investments," *Management Science,* 9 (April, 1963), pp. 443–57.

JOHNSON, R. W., *Capital Budgeting.* Belmont, Calif.: Wadsworth Publishing Co., 1970.

MAO, J. C. T. and J. F. HELLIWELL, "Investment Decisions under Uncertainty: Theory and Practice," *Journal of Finance* 24 (May, 1969), pp. 323–38.

MERRETT, A. J. and A. SYKES, *The Finance and Analysis of Capital Projects.* New York: John Wiley & Sons, Inc., 1963. An excellent presentation.

MOAG, J. S. and E. M. LERNER, "Capital Budgeting under Imperfect Market Conditions—A Systems Framework," *Journal of Finance,* 24 (September, 1969), pp. 613–22.

QUIRIN, G. D., *The Capital Expenditure Decision.* Homewood, Ill.: Richard Irwin, Inc., 1967.

ROBICHEK, A. A. and S. C. MYERS, "Conceptual Problems in the Use of Risk-Adjusted Discount Rates," *Journal of Finance,* 21 (December, 1966), pp. 727–30.

SALAZAR, R. C. and S. K. SEN, "A Simulation Model of Capital Budgeting under Uncertainty," *Management Science,* 15 (December, 1968), pp. B-137–60.

SARNAT, M. and H. LEVY, "The Relationship of Rules of Thumb to the Internal Rate of Return: A Restatement and Generalization," *Journal of Finance,* 24 (June, 1969), pp. 479–90.

SOLOMON, E., Ed., *The Management of Corporate Capital.* Chicago: The Free Press of Glencoe, 1959. An excellent collection of articles pertaining to Chapters 8 and 11. For the most part, articles in this collection are not listed elsewhere in this bibliography.

SOLOMON, M. B., Jr., "Uncertainty and its Effect on Capital Investment Analysis," *Management Science,* 12 (April, 1966), pp. B-334–39.

SWALM, R. O., "Capital Expenditure Analysis—A Bibliography," *Engineering Economist,* 13 (Winter, 1968), pp. 105–29.

_____, "Utility Theory—Insights into Risk Taking," *Harvard Business Review*, 44 (November–December, 1966), pp. 123–36.

TEICHROEW, D., A. A. ROBICHEK and M. MONTALBANO, "An Analysis of Criteria for Investment and Financing Decisions under Certainty," *Management Science*, 12 (November, 1965), pp. 151–79.

TERBORGH, G. W., *Business and Investment Policy: A MAPI Study and Manual*. Washington, D.C.: Machinery and Allied Products Institute and Council for Technological Advancement, 1958.

TUTTLE, D. L. and R. H. LITZENBERGER, "Leverage, Diversification and Capital Market Effects on a Risk-Adjusted Capital Budgeting Framework," *Journal of Finance*, 23 (June, 1968), pp. 427–44.

WEINGARTNER, H. M., "Capital Budgeting of Interrelated Projects: Survey and Synthesis," *Management Science*, 12 (March, 1966), pp. 485–516.

_____, "The Excess Present Value Index—A Theoretical Basis and Critique," *Journal of Accounting Research*, 1 (Autumn, 1963) pp. 213–24.

WILSON, R., "Investment Analysis under Uncertainty," *Management Science*, 15 (August, 1969), 650–64.

Preparation of Budgets

9

We are now in a position to draw together the various policies that we have established for the management of assets, and to project their effect upon the financial position of the company in the light of forecasts of sales. Given the policies concerning the management of assets, the level of sales will determine the required amounts of cash, accounts receivable, inventory, and fixed assets. For example, if we have a policy of carrying inventories equal to twice expected sales, a forecast of sales of 10,000 units for the month of April will call for a projected inventory of 20,000 units at the end of March. The aim of the budget process is to enable us to project the results of this combined effect:

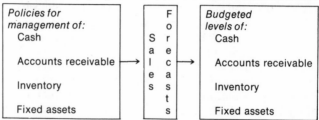

Policies for management of:	Sales	Forecasts	Budgeted levels of:
Cash			Cash
Accounts receivable			Accounts receivable
Inventory			Inventory
Fixed assets			Fixed assets

Estimates of sales depend upon external and internal factors. First, the economic outlook for the nation and for our industry will affect the level of sales. Our competitive position will then determine our expected share of the available market. Second, policies concerning the management of assets affect sales. Our credit policies influence the segment of the market secured; our inventory policies, the frequency of delays in filling orders; and policies concerning capital expenditures, the quality of the product and our ability to fulfill delivery commitments.

The integration of these factors with policies relating to management of assets is accomplished by the preparation of *budgets*—formal, written plans in words and figures setting forth the expected path of the company over some specified period. In nautical terms the budgets correspond to the course charted for a ship. It seems entirely logical to prepare such a plan for an ocean voyage, but there are still many businesses willing to set sail with vague and vacillating policies on the management of assets and high hopes for sales, but without concrete plans.

Why Plan?

Were it not for the large number of business failures, it would seem ridiculous to ask, "Why plan?" However, a fairly large proportion of financial difficulties, particularly those that beset small businesses, seems to arise from a failure to plan. Certainly, a good number of failures would be avoided through planning. There are relatively few planned failures, but innumerable unplanned ones.

To Encourage Thinking Ahead

Probably the most important reason for planning is that it forces people at all levels of management to think ahead. If we do not make people think ahead, they are very likely to live in the past. By this we mean that they will consciously or unconsciously project historical experience into the future. But what was true for last year may not be true for the coming year. To assume without investigation that the future will always duplicate the past is to have no plan at all.

Financial embarrassment is most acute when it is least expected. If we know in January that we are going to have to borrow additional funds in June, we have six months to investigate various sources of funds. Because we plan, we have alternatives. Because we have alternatives we can bargain one source against the other and secure our funds under the most favorable conditions. If we wait until the latter part of May to discover that we need funds in June, our alternatives are likely to be fewer. Because the time we have to investigate possible sources of funds is shorter, we will uncover fewer sources. There will be fewer sources available for discovery in any case. Over a six-month period the market for loanable funds may change quite markedly, with many prospective lenders entering and leaving the market. Within a period of a few weeks there may be only one or two sources available and willing to make the sort of loan we need. The urgency of our need leaves us in a poor bargaining position with respect to these lenders. In addition, our very lack of financial plans tags us as deficient in the field of financial management. If prospective lenders do not shy away entirely, they will at least drive a hard bargain to protect themselves against our inadequacies.

Because plans are necessarily estimates, some who are impressed with the apparent accuracy of historical accounting statements are likely to throw up their hands in despair and allege that there is no point in planning. Plans are admittedly inaccurate; therefore, why go through the process of doing something you know is incorrect? There are two answers to this. First, almost all business decisions involve an element of forecasting. If we decide to raise the price of hot dogs, we are making certain assumptions as to the future reaction of the market to the increased price. Decisions to add a new line or a new salesman involve predictions of the future profitability of the line and productivity of the salesman. Although these forecasts are almost never 100 percent accurate and are, in fact, sometimes quite wrong, management cannot shy away from making decisions because of the inherent risks of prediction that are involved. The errors and problems which develop from not making plans are likely to be considerably greater than those which evolve from the necessary inaccuracies in making plans.

A second answer to those who complain about the inaccuracies of financial plans is that plans once made are not supposed to be static guides which must be slavishly followed. When a storm blows the captain off the course which he originally plotted for England, he plans a new course. In the same way the financial manager must be ready to revise his plans if some unexpected economic storm upsets his plans. In fact his original planning process should have provided room for alternative courses of action. The greater the uncertainty of the future, the more flexible should be the company's financial plans. If we have formed a company to develop and market a new product, it would probably not be wise to plan to build a plant and buy the necessary equipment. The chances of error in estimating the sales of a wholly new product are too great, the error of estimate too large. Because of these uncertainties our financial plans may call for leasing plant and equipment or for hiring another manufacturer to carry on the initial production. We would not permanently commit any more of our funds than absolutely necessary until we have gained enough experience to lessen the risks of prediction. Most horseplayers would not sink their whole bankroll on a horse that had never run a race before, but some small businessmen are willing to commit their entire life savings to a product that has never been sold before.

To Encourage Coordinated Thinking

We saw in Chapter 3 that almost every policy decision in such areas as production, marketing, purchasing, and personnel has financial implications. Planning forces the heads of these various departments to project the financial impact of their decisions upon the rest of the company. No one department head can act independently. Even if his plans do not directly concern another department, they will affect all departments indirectly by influencing the flows of cash into and out of the business and by affecting the profitability of the company. Financial planning is the integrating force that helps each department head see the impact of his decision upon the functions of other department heads. Properly organized, the procedures for development of plans can be one of the most effective coordinating and training devices in a business firm.

To Develop Standards for Future Performance

Without plans our standard or measure of performance almost automatically becomes based on historical standards. We sold $21,000 of our product in June of this year, but only $20,000 in June of last year. Give the sales manager a bonus; we are doing better. But are we? What if we used a different standard, a standard of what sales *should be* rather than what they happened to be last year? If we had made specific plans for this year, we would certainly have made a forecast of sales. A period of rising incomes and improving economic conditions might have led us to predict sales for June of $23,000. If our economic forecasts turn out to be approximately correct, we can then see that the sales manager has turned in a relatively poor performance by producing sales of only $21,000. In spite of the fact that he has done better than last year, he has probably allowed us to slip behind our competitors so that our share of the market has diminished. Thus plans provide reasonable standards against which we may gauge our performance. Although not precisely accurate gauges, these plans are more accurate than the standards we would obtain by haphazardly adopting last year's performance as this year's measure of success. Past records help to set new standards for future performance, but they should not necessarily serve as standards themselves.

To Control Actions of Subordinates

Not only do we use budgets as a standard to measure performance, but we also set budget goals to guide actions of subordinates. If the budget is properly prepared, variations from the budget (either above or below) call attention to areas that may require remedial action. By devising some system of rewards and penalties, we may attempt to force employees to adhere to our budget, although this is more difficult than might appear. People can devise ingenious schemes to "beat the budget," but their actions may not improve the company's earning power.

The Nature of Budgets

A *budget* is nothing more than a written plan expressed in terms of units or dollars, or both. In essence, it is a model that represents the effect of varying levels of activity (input) upon costs, revenues, and cash flows (outputs). Because of their great problems of coordination and control of performance, large firms are likely to have more detailed and elaborate budgets than small companies. For example, Sun Oil Company has developed a corporate financial model that enables management to make long-range plans by testing the outcomes of various strategies and activities. To illustrate, the ultimate impact upon the cash budget, income statement, and balance sheet of different price strategies can readily be simulated on the computer and the results made quickly available to management.[1] Such corporate financial models are a first step towards ultimate development of an overall management information system.

Relation to Functions of Financial Manager

By the preparation of budgets the financial manager plans the balancing of risk and return designed to maximize the present value of the owners' investment. His estimates of cash flows and profits are based upon forecasts of sales. However, plans for sales must in turn be tempered by their suitability to cash resources and their desirability from the point of view of profits. Thus we have a mutually determined system. We cannot calculate our cash flows and profits until we have an estimate of sales, but we cannot reach a final estimate of sales until we have tested the effect of planned sales upon cash flows and profits. For example, an expansion of sales must be predicated upon the availability of funds to finance the necessary growth in plant and equipment, accounts receivable, and inventory. The proposed addition of a new line may cause liquidity problems or make no worthwhile contribution to the expected rate of return to the owners. Consequently, the final budget drawn up for a company usually represents the product of a number of false starts, revised estimates, and agonized reappraisals. The advantage of being able to test alternative strategies quickly with a computerized financial model are obvious.

Period Covered by Budgets

Probably the best, and most inconclusive, answer to the question of how long a period should a budget cover is "long enough." That is, the budget should cover a period of time long enough to make possible effective planning.

When considering plans for plant expansion, long-term debt management, and dividend policy, we need to develop long-range budgets extending for as long as five or ten years. As one illustration, a decision to construct a large plant involves long-run forecasts that the end product can be sold profitably over some period of years. As the customers of Consolidated Edison in New York City have discovered, it then takes several more years from the conception of a new plant to its final completion and breaking-in period. The first year of this long-range budget then provides key data for the annual budget.

Planning for short-term borrowings and investments, purchases, labor payments, and so on is usually modelled in a one-year budget. To make estimates for a period of much longer than a year involves greater risks of error in our estimates. The longer the period, the greater the chance that our plans will be upset by such factors as changes in economic conditions, development of competing products, shifts in our costs, and changes in consumers' tastes. There are disadvantages to having a budget period that is too short. We run the danger of failing to take into account important events which lie just beyond the period covered by the budget. If we plan sales and income for January, we may over-

[1] George W. Gershefski, "Building a Corporate Financial Model," *Harvard Business Review*, 47 (July–August, 1969), pp. 61–72.

look a buildup of inventory required in February or a bank loan which must be repaid in March. Budget periods that are too short also impose a heavy task on those involved in preparing budgets. It takes considerably less effort to prepare a budget for a year and review it quarterly than to prepare new and separate budgets for each quarter. Finally, budget periods that are too short may lead to the same degree of error in forecasting as budgets that cover much longer periods. For example, in the preparation of a budget for a retail store it may be as difficult to estimate sales accurately for a week as for three years. For short periods of time exogenous factors such as a snow storm, a local strike, or a strong promotional effort by a competing store may drastically affect sales. These factors "average out" over a longer period of time so that a prediction of sales for three months may be much closer to the mark than a forecast of sales for the coming week.

Long-Range Budget

The basic objective of a long-range budget is to determine the effect upon financial requirements of various alternate plans. Basically, long-range planning involves making estimates of a series of future balance sheets in order to see what financial requirements remain unfulfilled over and above planned short-term debt, expected retention of earnings, and existing long-term debt and capital stock. The "gap" must be filled with additional long-term debt, capital stock, and reduction in payments to owners. If these sources are insufficient, planned sales and plant expansion must be curtailed to fit perceived availability of financial resources.

The regression method of projecting balance sheets is sometimes a useful procedure. The first step is to plot for each of several years the historical relationship of various assets and liabilities to sales. It is not advisable to plot balance-sheet items that are established more by company policy than by sales. Such items are investments, long-term debt, preferred stock, and common stock. To illustrate the procedure, accounts receivable and current liabilities of the Jos. Schlitz Brewing Company have been related to sales for each year, 1960–1969. Thus the 1969 "point" for accounts receivable in the upper panel of Exhibit 9-1 represents accounts receivable of $24.8 million plotted against the vertical axis and net sales of $418.8 million plotted against the horizontal axis.

The second step is to draw a line of average relationship through the resulting scatter diagram. This regression line may be fitted by eye or more precisely by mathematical calculation. It may be linear, as in Exhibit 9-1, or nonlinear. As can be seen in the exhibit, the "fit" is very good for current liabilities and was good for accounts receivable until 1968–1969, when a change in credit policy occurred.

The third step is to prepare forecasts of sales for each year over the planning horizon. As will be seen in the discussion of short-term budgeting, sales forecasts may be derived from a number of sources. The economic process of preparing such forecasts is beyond the scope of this discussion.

EXHIBIT 9-1   Scatter Diagrams, Jos. Schlitz Brewing Company

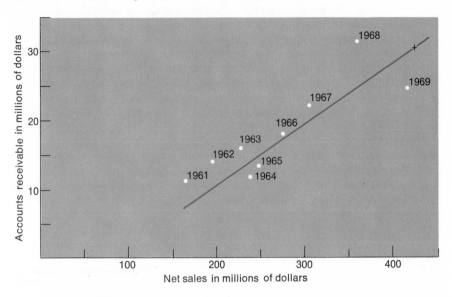

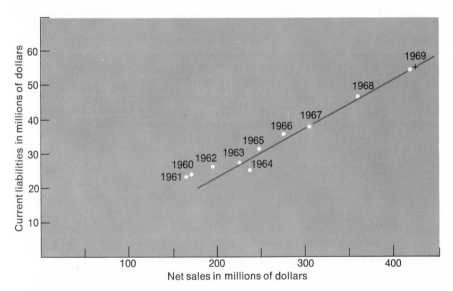

The fourth step is to project levels of accounts receivable and other assets, as well as the level of current liabilities and retained earnings. For example, if the estimate of sales for 1970 were $425 million, our corresponding estimate of accounts receivable would be about $30.5 million; and for current liabilities,

$55 million. The coordinates of the 1970 estimate are shown by (+) in Exhibit 9-1. (Until we understood more about the changed policy relating to accounts receivable, we would be uneasy about that estimate.)

The fifth step is to determine the financial needs over the coming years based upon the gap between the derived estimates of financial needs (assets) and resources. Thus if our 1970 estimate of assets exceeded by $25 million the sum of projected current liabilities and retained earnings, plus existing long-term debt and capital stock, we would have to make plans for additional long-term financing or else pare our expansion plans. The same process would, of course, be iterated for subsequent years. Also, the entire process could be carried out through the use of a computer. Again, our purpose is to explain what the computer might do for us, rather than treat it as a wonderous "black box" that does mysterious things, such as preparing long-range budgets.

The final step is to determine how long-term funds should be raised to meet financial requirements. This is the subject of the following chapters.

The Cash Budget and Related Budgets

Meaning

In essence, the cash budget is an attempt to predict over a given time period the various entries in our checkbook: that is, the deposits to and withdrawals from our bank account. Our principal aim is to discover whether at any time there will be insufficient funds on hand to cover the checks we would like to draw. To avoid becoming overwhelmed in details, we classify the anticipated deposits and withdrawals under various headings, such as collections from accounts receivable and payments for raw materials. We then balance the withdrawals against the deposits, so that we show our expectations of either a net increase or decrease in our cash balance by the end of the period of time selected.

Preparation

The first step in the preparation of the cash budget is the selection of the period of time to be covered by the budget. The considerations involved in this decision were discussed earlier in this chapter. The financial manager must next consider to what extent he will break the overall time span into smaller segments. Let us say that he decides to construct a cash budget to cover a period of six months. On the one hand, he could prepare a statement showing the expected receipts and disbursements of cash for the entire six months. On the other hand, he could make up a statement which would show the anticipated cash receipts and disbursements for each month or week within the six month period. The predicted net change in the cash balance at the end of the six months would be the same under either budget. The difference between the two forms of budgets lies in the information supplied on the fluctuations in the cash reservoir level during the time span covered by the budget.

The next step in the preparation of a cash budget is to estimate sales.

There are two basic approaches to this problem, and both should be used wherever possible. Under the *internal approach* management may ask the sales department to develop from within the department an estimate of sales for the forthcoming six months. This is a "grass roots" approach. Each salesman is asked to determine how much he will be able to sell during the forthcoming period and to break down his estimate by customer and by product line. By cumulating these individual reports, the sales manager is able to prepare an estimate of sales by product line and in total.

The *external approach* bases a forecast of sales upon an analysis of economic factors. For example, the sales of building material will be closely associated with new housing starts. If we were producing gypsum board, we might first obtain forecasts of the number of housing starts over the next six months. Given the projected number of housing starts, we should be able to estimate on the basis of our historical experience the millions of board feet that would be sold. This estimate would be adjusted for any trend in the size of houses or in the use of gypsum board per house. Projections of the dollar amount of sales would be developed from the estimates of volume and anticipated price levels. Having the estimate for the total sales of gypsum board in the United States, we could then judge how much our company might sell. Our expected share of the market would be affected by anticipated changes in capacity, price, quality, styling, sales effort, salesmen's incentives, and any new lines to be added. Our competitors' probable reactions to any such innovations will also affect our share of the market. The final estimate of sales must be what we can reasonably expect to achieve, and not an inflated goal for the sales department.

Since the internal and external estimates will probably not agree, the next step is to develop a sales budget which represents a reasonable compromise between the two estimates. This is a matter of experience and judgment, with special attention to the past accuracy of each of the two approaches. From the final forecast for the half year, we can then prepare sales budgets for each month within the period if necessary. These monthly estimates would depend upon customary seasonal fluctuations in our sales—that is, we might ordinarily make 10 percent of the first half year's sales in January, 13 percent in February, and so on. We must also consider the number of "trading days" in each month. Thus, if we are selling men's shoes, we will clearly be open for sales for fewer days in February than in March.[2]

To illustrate the subsequent steps in the preparation of a cash budget, let us now turn to Table 9-1. This table shows the sales, production, inventory, and purchasing budgets which provide necessary information for the cash budget. The illustration is purposely kept very simple in order to explain the principles of budgeting rather than to provide a model set of budget forms. As we go along, we shall point out some of the complexities that would be involved in the preparation of a budget for a larger or more complex business. Let us assume that our firm is producing a single product. We expect that sales for the first six months of the year will total 105,000 units at $1 per unit and rise from 5000 in

[2] For a discussion of time series analysis for short-term forecasting see John Neter and William Wasserman, *Fundamental Statistics for Business and Economics*, 2nd ed. (Boston: Allyn and Bacon, Inc., 1966), pp. 671–708.

TABLE 9-1   Sales, Production, Inventory, and Purchasing Budgets

	Jan.	Feb.	March	April	May	June
	Units					
Finished Goods						
Beginning inv.	2,000	13,000	21,000	23,000	25,000	19,000
Production	16,000	16,000	20,000	22,000	22,000	22,000
Total	18,000	29,000	41,000	45,000	47,000	41,000
Shipments	5,000	8,000	18,000	20,000	28,000	26,000
Ending inv.	13,000	21,000	23,000	25,000	19,000	15,000
Raw Material						
Beginning inv.	17,000	17,000	21,000	23,000	23,000	23,000
Purchases	16,000	20,000	22,000	22,000	22,000	20,000
Total	33,000	37,000	43,000	45,000	45,000	43,000
Used	16,000	16,000	20,000	22,000	22,000	22,000
Ending inv.	17,000	21,000	23,000	23,000	23,000	21,000

	Jan.	Feb.	March	April	May	June
	Dollar Amounts					
Finished Goods[a]						
Beginning inv.	$ 1,200	$ 7,800	$12,600	$13,800	$15,000	$11,400
Production	9,600	9,600	12,000	13,200	13,200	13,200
Total	$10,800	$17,400	$24,600	$27,000	$28,200	$24,600
Shipments	3,000	4,800	10,800	12,000	16,800	15,600
Ending inv.	$ 7,800	$12,600	$13,800	$15,000	$11,400	$ 9,000
Raw Material[b]						
Beginning inv.	$ 6,800	$ 6,800	$ 8,400	$ 9,200	$ 9,200	$ 9,200
Purchases	6,400	8,000	8,800	8,800	8,800	8,000
Total	$13,200	$14,800	$17,200	$18,000	$18,000	$17,200
Used	6,400	6,400	8,000	8,800	8,800	8,800
Ending inv.	$ 6,800	$ 8,400	$ 9,200	$ 9,200	$ 9,200	$ 8,400

[a] 60¢ per unit.
[b] 40¢ per unit.

January to a peak of 28,000 in May. This information is shown in Table 9-1 opposite the heading, "Shipments."

The effect of inventory policies for finished goods is the next consideration. Shall we attune our production to our rate of sales, or shall we attempt to have a more constant level of production? Let us assume that we have established some inventory policy, and that the application of sales forecasts to that policy produces the data for inventory levels and required production schedules to restock finished goods inventory (see Table 9-1).

The total flows into and out of the finished goods inventory for the entire six months are shown on the following page.

Opening inventory, January 1	2,000 units
Added by production	118,000
Goods available for sale	120,000
Goods sold	105,000
Ending inventory, June 30	15,000

The forecast of sales and the decision on monthly production automatically determines the monthly inventories of finished goods (Table 9-1). For example, we enter January with an inventory of 2000 units. With production scheduled at 16,000 units and shipments (sales) at 5000 units, we necessarily add a net of 11,000 units to our inventory, so that we enter February with 13,000 units on hand. The finished goods are valued at 60¢ per unit, composed of 40¢ for materials, 10¢ for labor, and 10¢ for factory overhead, including depreciation. Thus our finished goods inventory at the end of January is valued at $7800 ($0.60 × 13,000).

As indicated in our discussion of inventory management in Chapter 7, the size of the raw material inventory depends upon production plans and the "safety margin" desired between the amount stocked and the amount expected to be used. Let us assume that, after considering these factors, we decide to enter each month with 1000 more units of raw material on hand than necessary to take care of estimated production for the month. Thus we enter February with 17,000 units of raw material to support February's production of 16,000 units. Once we have made our policy with respect to the raw material inventory, our schedule of purchases automatically follows. If we enter February with 17,000 units and plan to use 16,000 in production, a balance of 1000 units will remain. In order to enter March with the 21,000 units necessary to support that month's production of 20,000, we must purchase an additional 20,000 units in February. Thus we derive our schedule of purchases.

The sales, production, inventory, and purchasing budgets shown in Table 9-1 are the core of any budget system. From these plans may be derived various supplemental budgets for manufacturing expenses, distribution costs, administrative expenses, or other associated items of expense and income. Since expenditures for research and development and for capital equipment will ordinarily be fairly independent of sales for a six-month period, the preparation of these budgets may be made apart from the sales and production budgets.

So far we have been talking chiefly about expenditures in the accounting sense. For example, the 10¢ per unit charge for factory overhead is an allocated, average charge that includes depreciation expense. There are thus two problems in translating this accounting figure into cash flows. First, the actual outflows of cash for factory overhead may not parallel the factory output in units, and, second, the depreciation expense is not a monthly outflow of cash. The total factory overhead is estimated at $11,800 (118,000 units × 10¢). Of this amount, let us assume that $1300 is depreciation. *This will not appear in the cash budget.* The remaining $10,500 of factory overhead is spread according to actual anticipated cash payments for heat, light, power, factory supervision, and so on. Since production is higher in the last three months, we assume that the cash payments amount to $1700 per month for the first three months and $1800 per month for the last three months.

The final allocation of cash inflows and outflows by months is illustrated in the work sheet in the top half of Table 9-2. First, let us consider receipts from sales. For the sake of simplicity, it is assumed here that the sales of one month are collected in the following month: that is, $8000 in cash is collected in March from payments made on the accounts receivable which originated in February. In actual practice more accurate estimates of the rates of collection can be made. For example, experience may show a fairly reliable ratio of collections to accounts receivable outstanding at the beginning of each month. We may find that, of the accounts created in any one month, 75 percent are collected within 30 days, 20 percent within 30–60 days, and the remainder in 60–90 days. Estimates of collections may also be adjusted downward to take into account probable losses from bad debts. The ultimate collection rate will, of course, depend largely upon the terms granted customers, the energy of our collection department, and the economic conditions in the industry.

Payments on purchases of raw material will also lag behind the period in which purchases were made. It is assumed here that we are purchasing materials on terms of 2/10 EOM n/30. This means that the $8000 of materials purchased in February must be paid for within the first ten days of March in order to receive a 2 percent cash discount. In this case, the net payment to suppliers in March would be $7840. It is also assumed that the capital budget calls for the purchase of a piece of equipment in March, with payment of the $1000 to be made at the end of April.

In a larger company the monthly allocation of wages, direct factory expense, administrative expense, and selling expenses would be based upon separate budgets for each of these expense categories. Each of these separate budgets would be derived from the production budget set forth in Table 9-1. We have assumed here that our monthly wage expense is 10¢ per item produced. However, if we wish to introduce greater accuracy, we should adjust the monthly wage payments for the number of pay days within the month. For example, if April has only four pay days and May has five, total wage payments in the latter month would be one-fourth higher in spite of the fact that the level of production remains the same in each of these months. The degree of accuracy sought will depend, in large part, upon the stringency of the cash position. Assumptions on other payments are implicit in Table 9-2. Were this a corporation, provision would be made in the cash budget for payment of income taxes and dividends. A sole proprietor or partners might also count on making some cash withdrawals during the period.

The final result of these anticipated cash receipts and disbursements is shown in the Operating Transactions section of the cash budget in Table 9-2 Although we begin January with a cash balance of $7400 and expect to finish June with a balance of $10,236, we show a deficit in the cash reservoir of $10,292 at the end of March. Essentially this cash shortage arises because we have planned a buildup of inventory in advance of expected sales. Faced with the information in this cash budget, management has two alternatives if it wishes to maintain the projected level of sales: it must either change its plans and not accumulate inventory, or else secure additional funds from some source outside the business.

Since the cash budget in our example has been made especially simple,

TABLE 9-2   Cash Budget

	Jan.	Feb.	March	April	May	June
			Work Sheet			
Receipts						
1. Sales	$ 5,000	$ 8,000	$18,000	$20,000	$28,000	$26,000
Collections on accounts receivable	4,800[a]	5,000	8,000	18,000	20,000	28,000
Payments						
1. Purchases	6,400	8,000	8,800	8,800	8,800	8,000
Payments on accounts payable	5,880[b]	6,272	7,840	8,624	8,624	8,624
2. Wages	1,600	1,600	2,000	2,200	2,200	2,200
3. Direct factory	1,700	1,700	1,700	1,800	1,800	1,800
4. Admin. expenses	700	700	700	800	800	800
5. Selling expenses	900	900	1,300	1,400	1,400	1,400
6. Purchase of equip.			1,000			
Payment for equip.				1,000		

	Jan.	Feb.	March	April	May	June
			Cash Budget			
Operating Transactions						
Receipts:						
Collections	$ 4,800	$ 5,000	$ 8,000	$18,000	$20,000	$28,000
Payments:						
Payments on accounts payable	5,880	6,272	7,840	8,624	8,624	8,624
Wages	1,600	1,600	2,000	2,200	2,200	2,200
Direct factory	1,700	1,700	1,700	1,800	1,800	1,800
Admin. expenses	700	700	700	800	800	800
Selling expenses	900	900	1,300	1,400	1,400	1,400
Payment for equip.				1,000		
	$10,780	$11,172	$13,540	$15,824	$14,824	$14,824
Net monthly cash gain (loss)	(5,980)	(6,172)	(5,540)	2,176	5,176	13,176
Cash balance, E.O.M. 12/31 $7,400	$ 1,420	($4,752)	($10,292)	($8,116)	($2,940)	$10,236
Financial Transactions						
Cash balance, B.O.M.[c]	$ 7,400	$ 1,420	$ 1,248	$ 2,708	$ 7,884	$11,060
Borrowings (repayments), B.O.M.	0	6,000	7,000	3,000	(2,000)	(8,000)
Total	$ 7,400	$ 7,420	$ 8,248	$ 5,708	$ 5,884	$ 3,060
Net monthly cash gain (loss)	(5,980)	(6,172)	(5,540)	2,176	5,176	13,176
Cash balance, E.O.M.[d]	$ 1,420	$ 1,248	$ 2,708	$ 7,884	$11,060	$16,236
Cumulative borrowings, B.O.M.	0	$ 6,000	$13,000	$16,000	$14,000	$ 6,000

[a] Accounts receivable, December 31.
[b] Accounts payable, December 31, less 2% cash discount.
[c] Beginning of month.
[d] End of month.

it may be worthwhile to note the other items that might appear in a cash budget. Observe that each item represents an actual receipt or disbursement of cash.

Cash receipts:
    Collections on accounts receivable
    Cash sales
    Disposal of fixed assets
    Loans or sale of securities
    Miscellaneous: e.g., rent, interest, dividends
Cash disbursements:
    Accounts payable
    Payroll (wages and salaries)
    Factory expenses
    Administrative and selling expenses
    Purchase of fixed assets (from capital expenditures budget)
    Income taxes
    Retirement of loans or securities
    Payments of interest
    Payments of dividends or withdrawals by owners

We have observed that the financial manager may not believe it necessary to prepare a monthly forecast of cash receipts and disbursements. An estimate of cash flows for the entire six-month period may be sufficient. There are two approaches to this simplified form of cash budget—the projected balance sheet and the adjusted income statement. Both have a serious defect in that they do not reveal differences in the timing of inflows and outflows of cash.

The *projected balance sheet method* is based on a comparison of present and future balance sheets. While the budget process usually includes the preparation of an estimated or pro forma balance sheet from the cash budget, the estimated balance sheet can be constructed by a short-cut method. Estimates of inventory and accounts receivable will be related to our forecasts of sales and the customary relationship of these accounts to the level of sales. For example, if sales were expected to be $200,000 for the first half of the year and the *annual* turnover of accounts receivable was eight times, we could estimate that accounts receivable on June 30 would be about $50,000.[3] Fixed assets will be increased by any new investments, and the allowance for depreciation will grow by the normal depreciation charges. As sales and purchases change, so will accounts payable. Retained earnings and liability for income taxes will depend upon estimated profits. In this fashion we could estimate with some degree of accuracy each item on the balance sheet for June 30—that is, each item except cash. The cash balance would be "forced" by subtracting total estimated assets from total estimated liabilities and capital. A negative or inadequate cash balance would indicate a need for additional funds as of that date.

The *adjusted income statement method* starts from the income statement

---

[3] If the annual turnover is eight times, then the turnover for six months would be four times, assuming a fairly constant level of sales. (If sales were not fairly constant, this method of estimation should not be used anyway.) Since turnover is found by dividing sales by accounts receivable, accounts receivable may be calculated by dividing sales by the turnover, or $200,000/4 equals $50,000.

instead of from the balance sheet. To the anticipated net income are added charges against income that do not absorb cash, such as depreciation. Other additions to cash which would not appear on the income statement would result from decreases in assets and from increases in liabilities and net worth. For example, if we anticipate collecting $220,000 from accounts receivable and expect sales of $200,000, accounts receivable will decline $20,000 during the period. This decrease in accounts receivable represents a source of cash in addition to the reported profits. The next step is to subtract expected cash drains which would not be covered in the income statement. Loss of cash would result from increases in assets and from decreases in liabilities and net worth. For example, the purchase of equipment would not appear in the income statement, but would drain funds from the cash reservoir. The repayment of debt would cause an outflow of cash which would not be reported on the income statement. The net change in the cash balance from the beginning to the end of the period is then the result of the addition to the net profit of these cash inflows and the subtraction of the various cash outflows. From the change in the cash balance the financial manager can estimate the amount of any additional funds he may need to secure. The approach can probably best be summarized by the following tabulation. Obviously most items are mutually exclusive: that is, if the amount of accounts receivable decreases, it will be shown as an addition to cash and not appear as a deduction from cash.

Estimated net profit (as reported by accountant)
Add:
  Decreases in assets
    Depreciation
    Accounts receivable (excess of collections over sales)
    Inventory
    Deferred charges
    Sale of investment securities
    Sale of plant and equipment
  Increases in liabilities
    Accounts payable and other current liabilities
    Sale of long-term debt
  Increases in net worth
    Sale of securities; additional investment by owners
Subtract:
  Increases in assets
    Accounts receivable (excess of sales over collections)
    Inventory
    Deferred charges
    Purchases of investment securities
    Purchases of plant and equipment
  Decreases in liabilities
    Accounts payable and other current liabilities
    Repayment of long-term debt
  Decreases in net worth
    Retirement of securities
    Dividends; withdrawals by owners
Net increase or decrease in cash balance

Use of Cash Budget

Planning for Borrowing. The cash budget in Table 9-2 shows that we will find it necessary to begin borrowing, possibly from a bank, in February. Our decision on how much to borrow at that time will depend upon the size of our expected cash deficit and the minimum balance of cash that we wish to keep on hand (Chapter 5). If we assume that a minimum balance of $1000 would be satisfactory, borrowings of $6000 will carry us through the month and leave us with a month-end cash balance of about $1250. The impact of our plans for borrowings is shown in the section of the cash budget that is headed *Financial Transactions.*[4] The $10,292 deficit shown for the cash balance at the end of March under "Operating Transactions" suggests that total borrowings of $12,000 would carry us through that month and would represent our maximum needs for the first half of the year. However, this is not the case. If we look at the cash flows during the first ten days of April, we can estimate collections of about one-third of the previous month's accounts receivable, or about $6000. Roughly one-third of the expenditures for wages, direct factory costs, administration, and selling will be paid out as well. This amounts to $2070. We have assumed that the equipment is to be paid for at the end of April. However, *all* the accounts payable must be met by April 10 (that is, within the discount period) if we are to receive our 2 percent cash discount. Thus we have:

Cash inflow:		$ 6,000
Cash outflow:		
Accounts payable	$8,624	
Other	2,070	10,694
Cash loss in first 10 days of April		$ 4,694
Cumulative cash deficit at end of March		10,292
Cumulative cash deficit by April 10		$14,986

In other words, the cash deficit as of April 10 will be almost $7000 greater than the deficit on April 30. To assure a minimum cash balance of $1000 during April, we must borrow a total of $16,000. Borrowings must be planned to meet the greatest need at any one time during the six-month period.

Planning for Repayment of Debt. A lender will wish to know not only how much we desire to borrow, but when he will be repaid. In this case the cash budget shows that, if all goes according to plan, the last $6000 of the loan can probably be repaid on July 1. This is an important piece of information, since some types of lenders, such as banks, would find this sort of loan attractive. Others, such as insurance companies, would not. Planning for the repayment of debt thus helps to formulate our plans for borrowing and also provides some assurance to the lender that he will be repaid. Repayment of any existing debt should be scheduled in the *Financial Transactions* section of the cash budget.

Planning for Payments to Owners. As we shall see later, the owner of this business anticipates making a very fine profit. However, the cash budget shows that withdrawal of any of the profits during this period would serve only to in-

[4] This section could be made into a separate financial budget. The variety of budgets used depends on the needs of the company and the imagination of the financial manager.

crease his cash problems. He might be able to withdraw some cash by the end of June, although the desirability of this would depend upon the information developed in the cash budget for the last half of the year. Any other payments, such as dividends on preferred stock or interest on debt, would also be scheduled in the appropriate month in the *Financial Transactions* section. The interest cost of the bank loan has been omitted in this example to simplify matters.

Planning for Efficient Use of Cash. The financial manager seeks to put his cash to work as profitably as possible without jeopardizing his liquidity function. The cash budget provides the mechanism for meeting this dilemma. One of the most profitable uses of cash is to pay bills within the discount period. If for no other reason, this application alone justifies preparation of the cash budget, since it both enhances credit reputation and, most important, saves a considerable amount of money by taking advantage of cash discounts. Our cash budget shows that with adequate borrowed funds we will be able to take our cash discounts by paying within the tenth day of each month.

If we were in a more affluent position, the cash budget might also show periods of time during which we would have more cash on hand than needed. From the budget we could estimate the amount of the excess cash and the period of time we would have the excess. These funds would then be available for the types of investment discussed in Chapter 5.

Projected Financial Statements

Once detailed budgets have been prepared, a final step in the budget process is to examine the position of the company as it will appear at the end of the budget period. This analysis will be based upon a projected, or pro forma, income statement and balance sheet. The tools of analysis may be those described in Chapter 4.

Projected Income Statement

We have predicted that sales for the next six months will be 105,000 units at $1 per unit (Table 9-3). In practice the figure for cost of goods sold ($63,000) would be derived from a detailed schedule summarizing the costs of raw material used, direct labor costs, and indirect manufacturing expenses. In our simple example, the figure for raw materials used has been obtained from the inventory budget (Table 9-1) and direct labor and direct factory expenditures from the cash budget (Table 9-2). Depreciation has been assumed at $1300 for the six months. Thus it will cost $70,800 to turn out 118,000 units, or 60¢ per unit. Of the total amount available (120,000 units), 15,000 remain in inventory, and 105,000 are sold. Thus the cost of goods sold amounts to $63,000 (105,000 × 60¢).

Our planned expenditures for administration and selling are in the form of cash, so that the six-month totals shown in Table 9-3 represent the sum of the

TABLE 9-3   Pro Forma Income Statement, January 1 to June 30

Sales			$105,000
Cost of goods sold:			
Inventory, January 1		$ 1,200	
Cost of goods manufactured:			
Raw materials used	$47,200		
Direct labor	11,800		
Direct factory	10,500		
Depreciation	1,300	70,800	
Total		72,000	
Inventory, June 30		9,000	63,000
Gross profit			42,000
Administrative expense		4,500	
Selling expense		7,300	11,800
Operating profit			30,200
Purchase discounts taken[a]			936
Net profit			$ 31,136

[a]As will be noted in Chapter 12, a more desirable accounting procedure would be to deduct purchase discounts from the cost of raw materials, so that purchase discounts received are not treated as income. The method was not used here to facilitate comparison of this table to Table 9-1.

monthly figures appearing in the cash budget. The purchase discounts may be derived by comparing the scheduled purchases with the budgeted cash payments on accounts payable, as shown in the cash budget. The end result is an estimated net profit for the proprietor of $31,136. In a large company each item in the pro forma income statement would be supported by one or more detailed budgets. The amount of detail will depend in part upon the importance of planning various expenditures and the costs involved in the planning process. There is no one set of planning statements that will suit all companies.

Projected Balance Sheet

The capstone on the budgetary process is the preparation of a pro forma balance sheet (Table 9-4). Let us see how each of the figures on the projected balance sheet of June 30 is obtained.

The cash balance is the final figure shown on the *Financial Transactions* section of the cash budget. The accounts receivable represent the sales for June; it is assumed that no collections have been made. The amounts shown for inventories can be obtained from the inventory budgets. If we go back to the cash budget, we will see that we purchased additional equipment in March, so that the gross amount of equipment on hand will rise from $26,000 to $27,000. However, from the pro forma income statement we find that estimated depreciation for the six-month period is $1300; this charge raises the allowance for depreciation from $8200 to $9500. Consequently, the net amount shown for machinery and equipment declines by $300.

On the other side of the balance sheet, the figure of $6000 for the notes payable to the bank is obtained from the *Financial Transactions* section of the cash budget. It will be recalled that the note can probably be repaid on July 1. Accounts payable represent purchases made in June and not yet paid for. The amount of $63,136 shown for the proprietor's capital account is the sum of the opening balance in his account, $32,000, and the profit for the period as shown on the pro forma income statement ($31,136).

TABLE 9-4   Balance Sheet, December 31, and Pro Forma Balance Sheet, June 30

		Dec. 31		June 30
Assets				
Cash		$ 7,400		$16,236
Accounts receivable		4,800		26,000
Inventories:				
Raw material		6,800		8,400
Finished goods		1,200		9,000
Machinery and equipment	$26,000		$27,000	
Allow. for depreciation	8,200	17,800	9,500	17,500
Total assets		$38,000		$77,136
Liabilities and Capital				
Notes payable—bank		—		$ 6,000
Accounts payable		$ 6,000		8,000
Proprietor, capital		32,000		63,136
		$38,000		$77,136

With the pro forma income statement and balance sheet in hand, we can analyze the results in the manner suggested in Chapter 4. Does our balance sheet of June 30 represent an improvement over that of December 31? Does the percentage composition of our income statement suggest areas where we might reduce costs? Will our creditors be encouraged or discouraged by the results six months from now? These planning statements are probably more important to analyze than historical records. If we do not like what we find, we still have a chance to do something about it.

Limitations of Budgets

Errors in Estimates. It should be emphasized again that in preparing a cash budget we are painting with a broad brush. These are estimates which depend to a great extent upon the accuracy of the original estimates of sales. For this reason it is somewhat ridiculous to carry out the monthly figures to the last dollar as we have done in these tables. Such refinement gives a misleading air of accuracy to our budget; it would be preferable to round the amounts to the nearest $10 or $100. It was not done here so that the reader might check the calculations if he were so inclined.

The lack of accuracy also means that the financial manager should periodically review actual performance against the budget. If the variation is substantial, it may require adjustments in the budget for future months. Budgets are guides, not substitutes, for good judgment. Because predictions are seldom entirely correct, the budgets that are derived from these predictions must be administered with some discretion and understanding of their limitations.

Time Segments Covered. Even if we take account of the fact that budgets are estimates, we need to keep in mind that the period covered by the estimates may be inappropriate. That is, there are certain inherent limitations in the mechanics of preparation. The cash budget shown in Table 9-2 breaks down a six-month period into monthly segments. To have prepared a summary estimate of total cash inflow and outflow for the entire half year would have been at least misleading and possibly fatal. Even with a monthly breakdown we found that the figures were misleading because during the first ten days of each month funds flowed out of the cash reservoir much more rapidly than they flowed in. Because of the credit terms received from suppliers in this case, it might have been wise to prepare the cash budget for the period January 10–February 10–March 10, and so on. The financial manager should not become so impressed, or intimidated, by the apparent reliability of the figures on a cash budget that he fails to maintain a properly suspicious attitude.

Human Problems. The budget will be prepared and operated by human beings. This poses many problems, especially at the time a budget system is introduced. To many people in a business organization the budget may represent a challenge to their status. For example, the production manager may be accustomed to preparing his own schedules; now this is no longer a function left to his discretion. Not only that, but the central office will be using the budget system to check on his performance and may ask embarrassing questions if his performance is not in accord with the budget. Thus, by introducing a budget system, we are probably taking away certain rights, and humans characteristically resist such changes. Most groups are more adept at unseen resistance to change than is management at enforcing change.

Summary

It has been said that the ability to plan separates man from animal. A less debatable statement may be that planning frequently distinguishes business success from business failure. By encouraging thinking ahead in a coordinated fashion, the budget process is a management tool useful to all phases of business operations. Not only do budgets enable management to anticipate forthcoming problems, they also serve as standards for performance as the business moves forward.

There is no set formula for the form, detail, or periods covered by budgets. Each budget system must be designed for the situation at hand, bearing in mind the character of the company, its position, and the nature of the plans involved. Ordinarily the budget system will be most detailed in those aspects of operations most important to the firm's success. If cash is short, the cash budget will receive closest attention. If advertising is a major key to success, the advertising budget will be prepared and examined with special care. A very small company might have its budget written on a slip of paper. In contrast, the annual budget for the United States Government is a tome running to thousands of pages. The period covered by the budget will vary with the nature of the plans involved and with the degree of accuracy possible in the preparation of estimates.

A cash budget is an essential tool to the financial manager in his liquidity objective. It is based upon production, inventory, and purchasing budgets, which are derived in turn from the sales budget. By predicting the flow of funds into and out of the cash reservoir, the financial manager is able to determine the amount of any outside funds required and the period they will be needed. On the other hand, he may anticipate excess cash, which might be put to profitable use within the company.

The culmination of the budget process is the preparation of the pro forma balance sheet, which represents the position of the company at some point in the future if the plans set forth in the cash budget and pro forma income statement (and all their supporting and supplementary budgets) are realized. Analysis of this statement and the pro forma income statements should reveal whether or not the plans represented in these statements will lead the company along the path desired by management.

Questions

1/ What predictions are involved in a decision to:
   a. drop an item from a line?
   b. pay a guaranteed annual wage?
   c. buy rather than lease a plant?
   d. substitute a machine for labor?

2/ A large portion of the revenues of International Business Machines Corp. are obtained from long-term leasing contracts. If a substantially higher proportion of revenues were obtained from direct sales, would revenues be easier to forecast? Explain.

3/ Of seasonal and cyclical fluctuations in business, which do you believe is the easier to forecast with reasonable accuracy a year in advance? Why?

4/ What procedures would you use to estimate sales for the coming year of the following:
   a. diapers?
   b. $15 fountain pens?
   c. college textbooks?
   d. road graders?

5/ "Periodic reviews make the original budget worthless." Comment.

6/ A businessman brags to you that he has plenty of money in the bank; there-fore, he does not need to prepare a cash budget. Comment.

7/ How can management vary the timing of cash receipts and disbursements? Cite specific examples.

8/ Do the estimated net profits after taxes for a fiscal year represent the net addition to the cash balance for the period? Discuss in detail.

9/ How is budgeting related to "margin times turnover equals earning power"?

10/ How is it that the company shown in the illustration in this chapter was able to make such a handsome profit and still needed to borrow during the six months?

Problems

1/ Assume you have been asked to prepare a cash budget for the Better-Value Store for the period August 1 to January 31. In estimating the seasonal cash requirements make the following assumptions:
    I. a. Sales are 40% for cash, 60% on open book account.
       b. Of the credit sales, 75% are collected in the first month following the sale and 25% in the second month following the sale.
       c. Gross profit margin on sales averages 20%.
       d. All inventory purchases are paid during the month in which they are made.
       e. A basic inventory of $10,000 (cost) is constantly maintained, and the store follows the policy of purchasing enough additional inventory each month to cover the following month's sales.
       f. A minimum cash balance of $2000 is to be maintained by the store.
       g. "Accrued wages and salaries" and "other current liabilities" remain unchanged.
       h. Any additional financing needed will be in multiples of $1000.
       i. This is a sole proprietorship.

II.   Balance Sheet, August 1

Cash		$ 5,100	Accrued wages	
Accounts receivable		14,700	and salaries	$ 600
Inventory (cost)		26,000	Other liabilities	2,000
Furniture			Capital	59,200
& fixtures	$20,000			
Allow for				
depreciation	4,000	16,000		
		$61,800		$61,800

III. Past sales: June $18,000; July $20,000.

IV. Sales budget

August	$20,000	November	$40,000
September	26,000	December	50,000
October	24,000	January	18,000
		February	16,000

V. Monthly expenses

Wages and salaries:

August	$1,400	November	2,000
September	1,600	December	2,000
October	1,600	January	1,400

Rent: $400 per month
Depreciation: $150 per month
Other expenses: 1% of sales

Required:

(1) Prepare a work sheet and cash budget similar to that shown in Table 9–2.
(2) Indicate clearly the maximum amount of necessary borrowings. When will it be possible to repay the loan?
(3) Prepare a pro forma income statement and balance sheet.
(4) Various simplifying assumptions have been made. If they were removed how would the planning by the management of this company become more complicated?

2/ An automobile agency has been formed to sell new cars. Monthly sales are expected to be $140,000. About 60 percent of these sales will be made on instalment. For planning purposes it is estimated that on these sales the down payment will be 25 percent and the average term of instalment notes 36 months. Management is considering holding the instalment paper rather than selling it to a sales finance company or bank. However, before making the decision, it wishes to know the maximum amount that will eventually be invested in this paper. Prepare this estimate for management, showing all calculations.

3/ Construct a chart, showing on the *x*-axis disposable personal income and on the *y*-axis the net profits before taxes of the Sherwin-Williams Company (manufacturers of paint). The data shown below may be used, but should be brought up to date, using the *Federal Reserve Bulletin* and investment manuals.

a. Draw a free-hand line to show the average relationship between disposable personal income and the net profit before taxes of Sherwin-Williams Company. (Since the profits are reported for fiscal years ending August 31 and disposable personal income for years ending December 31, there is an implicit suggestion that disposable personal income lags behind profits. An alternate approach to this problem would be to plot the profits for 1967 against disposable personal income for 1966, and so on.)

b. How do you explain unusually wide variations from your line of average relationship?

c. Estimate disposable personal income for the coming year and net profits before taxes for the Sherwin-Williams Company.

Year	Disposable personal income (billions of dollars)	Net profits (millions of dollars)
1951	227.5	19.51
1952	238.7	17.49
1953	252.5	20.32
1954	256.9	21.31
1955	274.4	23.75
1956	292.9	27.50
1957	308.8	30.00
1958	317.9	27.93
1959	337.1	32.81
1960	349.9	29.43
1961	364.7	28.73
1962	384.6	28.51
1963	402.5	29.89
1964	431.8	33.62
1965	473.2	36.76
1966	511.9	38.76
1967	546.5	34.14
1968	590.0	36.27
1969	629.7	30.47

d. Would you expect to find a closer relationship between new construction and the net profits of Sherwin-Williams Company? Why or why not?

4/ If a firm's average collection period is 40 days, and daily credit sales are $20,000, what would you estimate for accounts receivable on the balance sheet?

5/ Assemble the balance sheets and sales for the past 11 years for a selected (or assigned) manufacturing company. Set aside the most recent year and prepare scatter diagrams (as in Exhibit 9-1) for cash, accounts receivable, inventory, fixed assets (net), current liabilities, and retained earnings with sales. In each diagram fit a line of average relationship. A freehand "fit" is satisfactory, and a straight line will probably suffice.

Given the known sales for the most recent year, estimate from your regression line the amounts that will be outstanding of the various assets, current liabilities, and retained earnings. Insert these data into an estimated balance sheet for the most recent year. Assuming that investment, any deferred charges, long-term debt, and capital stock remain constant, bring your estimated balance sheet into balance with a "plug" figure labelled "additional long-term financing" or "additional short-term investments," depending upon the need.

Now, in adjoining columns enter the actual balance sheet data for the most recent year. How well did you do? Can you explain the cause of any substantial discrepancies?

Selected References

ARGYRIS, C., "Human Problems with Budgets," *Harvard Business Review,* 31 (January–February, 1953), pp. 97–110.

GERSHEFSKI, G. W., "Building a Corporate Financial Model," *Harvard Business Review,* 47 (July–August, 1969), pp. 61–72.

_____, *The Development and Application of a Corporate Financial Model.* Oxford, Ohio: Planning Executives Institute, 1968.

HAGAMAN, T. C., "Forecasting in Financial Planning," *Financial Executive,* 36 (July, 1968), pp. 28–30ff.

IJIRI, Y., J. C. KINARD, and F. B. PUTNEY, "An Integrated Evaluation System for Budget Forecasting and Operating Performance with a Classified Budgeting Bibliography," *Journal of Accounting Research,* 6 (Spring, 1968), pp. 1–28.

KNAPP, R. A., "Forecasting and Measuring with Correlation Analysis," *Financial Executive,* 31 (May, 1963), pp. 13–19.

LERNER, E. M., "Simulating a Cash Budget," *California Management Review,* 11 (Winter, 1968), pp. 79–86.

MITCHELL, W. E., "Cash Forecasting," *Controller,* 28 (April, 1960), pp. 162–66ff.

NETER, J. and W. WASSERMAN, *Fundamental Statistics for Business and Economics,* ch. 15–17. Boston: Allyn and Bacon, Inc., 1961.

SUSSMAN, M. R., "A Note on the Implications of Periodic 'Cash Flow'," *Journal of Finance,* 17 (December, 1962), pp. 658–62.

WESTON, J. F., "Financial Analysis: Planning and Control," *Financial Executive,* 33 (July, 1965), pp. 40–42ff.

Part Three

Planning the Financial Structure

Alternative Methods
of Financing

10

Our financial plans show the amounts of funds needed over some future period of time. As indicated by our cash budget, some needs for funds may be relatively temporary because seasonal liquidation of inventory and receivables will generate the cash necessary for the repayment of creditors. In contrast, funds employed for capital expenditures will often be committed to the business for many years. In other words, our plans for funds should cover both the amount required as well as the period over which these funds will be needed. On the basis of the plans developed in the cash budget and the budget for capital expenditures we should be able to prepare an estimate of the assets that will appear on one or more pro forma balance sheets.

Knowing the amount and duration of the need is only the first major step. We must now consider what types of funds to seek in order to meet these needs. As shown by our pro forma income statement, some profits may be generated through operations. Should these be retained in the business or paid out to the owners? Will retained earnings prove sufficient to meet our needs, or must additional funds be obtained from outside the business? There is some mix of debt and equity funds that is best suited for our company. Consideration of the factors that will determine this mix is the purpose of this and the following chapter. Once we know what types of funds we are looking for, our next step will be to study where we might obtain financing of this sort and under what terms it might be available. Consideration of the acquisition of funds is the subject of Parts IV and V of this book.

Characteristics of Debt versus Equity

We have a choice between two basic instruments, or arrangements for financing: debt and equity. Although we will be discussing various specific forms of debt and equity in greater detail later, we need to note at this point the basic characteristics of each. Debt, of course, is the obligation incurred by borrowing. Equity is the owners' share of the assets. There are four distinguishing features: maturity, claim on income, claim on assets, and right to voice in management.

Maturity

Debt comes due; it must be repaid at some time specified in the agreement between the company and its creditors. The distinction among short-, intermediate-, and long-term debts lies in the time for which contracts are written. Thus short-term debt is scheduled to mature within one year, intermediate term debt in 1–10 years, and long-term debt in a period longer than ten years. As we shall see in later chapters, these definitions are rather arbitrary. If the debt is not paid when due, the creditors may seize assets or even force the liquidation of the company, depending upon the terms of their agreement with the company.

Equity has no date of maturity. When owners invest in a company, there is no agreement that they will have their initial investment returned. If an owner wishes to regain his investment, he must either find another buyer for his share in the company, or liquidate the company. Whether or not he regains his original investment depends upon the fortunes of the company and his bargaining ability.

Claim on Income

There are three aspects of the claims on income that distinguish debt from equity—the priority of the claim, the certainty of the claim, and the amount of the claim.

Priority of Claim. The claims of creditors are prior to the claims of owners. All obligations to creditors must be met first, and in some instances owners may not withdraw profits if those withdrawals would jeopardize the prior claims of the creditors.

While the claims of creditors on the company's income are prior to those of all groups of owners, the claims of preferred owners on income usually precede those of residual owners. In this connection two types of preferred owners have been noted. In some partnerships there may be limited partners, and in corporations there may be preferred stockholders. The residual owners in the partnership are the general partners, while in the corporation they are the common stockholders. Dividends (*not* interest) must be paid on the preferred stock in accordance with the agreement before any distribution can be made to the common stockholders. Similar arrangements are frequently found in the case of limited partnerships.

Certainty of Claim. If the company has promised to pay interest on the debt, it must pay the interest regardless of the level of earnings, or face legal action.[1] The interest payments are a *fixed charge.* Payments to owners are termed *withdrawals* in the case of proprietorships and partnerships and *dividends* in the case of corporations. In the first instance, the payment is at the discretion of the owner or partners; in the second, at the discretion of the board of directors (which is elected by the stockholders). Whether the ownership interest is preferred or residual, there is no promise on the part of the company to pay, although the owners always hope for the best.[2]

Amount of Claim. Interest payments on debt are limited to a certain fixed amount. The bank receives, let us say, 8 percent and no more on its loan to us, regardless of how profitable (or unprofitable) the company may be. In return for their prior claim on income, preferred stockholders generally agree to limit the amount of their annual claim. Assume that we have outstanding a $8 preferred stock. Once we have paid the preferred shareholders $8 per share (plus any back dividends not paid in earlier years if the preferred stock is "cumulative") we need pay them no more. Any remaining earnings can then be paid to the common stockholders. The common stockholders thus have a claim to any income left over after the exercise of the prior claims of creditors and any preferred stockholders. The amount of income available will vary from year to year, so that residual owners have no reason to expect regular dividends. However, as we shall see later, directors frequently try to establish a regular dividend pattern, so that the percentage of earnings paid out as dividends may vary substantially from year to year.

Claim on Assets

Creditors and owners seldom invest in a company with the expectation that they will participate in its ultimate liquidation. Nonetheless, their relative fates in time of trouble are necessarily of some concern. Whereas claims on income are significant with respect to a going concern, claims on assets are usually important when a company gets into difficulty, especially when the assets are being liquidated. The claims of creditors on assets are always prior to those of owners, and the claims of preferred owners are usually superior to those of residual

---

[1] There is a form of debt called *income bonds* which is an exception to this generalization. Interest must be paid on income bonds only if it has been earned.

[2] In a few instances limited partners may force liquidation of the partnership if their original investment has not been repaid by the end of a specified period of time.

owners. In return for this prior position, the creditors agree to seek no more than the principal they have loaned us, plus any unpaid interest. Limited partners and preferred stockholders and generally restricted to recovering an amount approximately equal to their original investment. Last in line are the common stockholders. They can have whatever is left, although the bones have usually been picked rather clean by the time they arrive on the scene. Unfortunately for the residual owners, assets seldom have the value in liquidation that they have with a going concern.

Right to Voice in Management

Creditors have no direct voice in the management of a company, although they may place certain restrictions in the loan agreement on management's activities. Even without written agreements creditors have a certain degree of control, because we know we cannot count on their continued support if we poorly manage the affairs of the company. Nonetheless, if a proprietor or various partners are incompetent, creditors cannot vote them out; they can only withhold their credit. Similarly, creditors have no vote in determining the board of directors of a corporation. In actual practice, of course, there are no restrictions on the rights of the creditors to voice their disapproval if they believe a concern owing the money is being mismanaged. Although they are entitled to speak freely, there is very little they can legally do about it until continued mismanagement results in a default on payment of interest or principal.

Preferred owners may or may not have any voting control. Limited partners are specifically prohibited from having a voice in management. Generally, preferred stockholders do not have the right to vote for members of the board of directors. However, if the financial affairs of the company have deteriorated to such an extent that a certain number of quarterly dividends on the preferred stock have not been paid, the preferred shareholders are often given the right to elect a minority (occasionally a majority) of the members of the board of directors. This is a process known in financial circles as closing the barn door after the horse has been stolen.

In most cases then, the power to choose the management rests with the residual owners. In the case of a corporation this power is exercised through voting for the board of directors, who in turn appoint the management. In the case of a proprietorship or partnership, the owners usually are the managers. It seems reasonable that the residual owners should have control. Since they have the last claim on income and assets, their risk is greater than that of creditors or preferred owners. They could hardly be expected to invest their money in a business under these terms unless they had the power to control its affairs.

The basic methods of financing available to a business concern and the major sources from which funds might be obtained are summarized at the bottom of Exhibit 10-1. Since we will use the term later on, let us note that *capital structure* means the total intermediate- and long-term debt plus the net worth. Current liabilities are the only type of funds shown excluded from the definition. Our purpose is to explain the reasons for the variations in types of funds employed by the major industrial groups shown. For example, why do companies engaged in mining and quarrying obtain about three-fifths of their funds in the form of net worth, while public utilities finance just over two-fifths of their needs in this manner? Why do concerns engaged in construction and in wholesale trade rely on short-term debt so heavily?

EXHIBIT 10-1   Composition of Liabilities and Net Worth by Major Industrial Groups

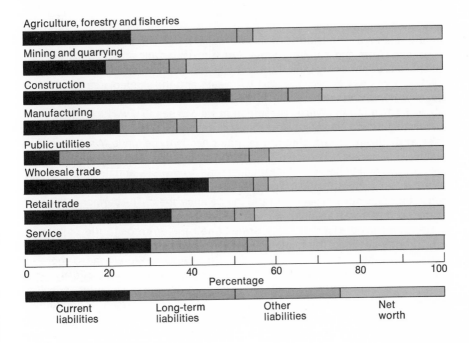

Source: U.S. Treasury Department, Internal Revenue Service, *Statistics of Income, 1965, U.S. Business Tax Returns,* pp. 242-249.

Factors To Consider in Planning Methods of Financing

There are certain common, and often conflicting, elements or criteria involved in determining the methods of financing assets. Because each company's situation is different, the weight given these elements in making the decision varies according to conditions in the economy, the industry, and the company. However, the freedom of management to adjust the mix of debt and equity in accordance with these criteria is limited by the availability of the various types of funds that are sought. Even though management may decide that it wishes to borrow more, the suppliers of funds may conclude that this would involve too much risk. Consequently, the plans that management ultimately makes in the light of these factors often involve a compromise between its desires and conditions imposed by the suppliers of funds.

Suitability

This refers to the compatibility of the types of funds used in relation to the nature of the assets financed: that is, the types of funds obtained must be consistent or in harmony with the kinds of operating assets employed.

Let us consider our estimated or pro forma balance sheets. In our cash budget we have made plans for seasonal expansion in inventories, accounts receivable, and any other current assets. Also incorporated in the cash budget are any planned acquisitions of fixed assets. These expenditures are derived, of course, from the capital budget. For discussion purposes let us diagram these plans as shown in Exhibit 10-2. The unshaded area represents the planned levels of fixed assets over the next two years and the shaded area the planned levels of current assets.

From this rather stylized presentation we can see that we have made plans for an expanding business, and that we will require larger amounts of both fixed and current assets. One further point needs to be made. We can observe that even in our slack season there are still some current assets on hand. At no time are we completely out of cash, accounts receivable, and inventory. Therefore, some of the so-called "current assets" are really "fixed assets" in the sense that they never disappear from the balance sheet. The permanent portion of the current assets is indicated by the area between the solid line separating current and fixed assets and the dotted line running through the bottoms of the troughs showing the minimum current assets employed. As the business expands we need more "permanent" current assets. We will need more inventory to assure delivery; the increased sales will almost automatically result in higher accounts receivable; and we will probably require a larger "cushion" of cash in the bank. In practice the distinction between permanent and temporary assets is not as clear as it might seem from the diagram. Nonetheless, the distinction exists and will affect the types of funds we seek to finance those needs.

As a general rule, it is desirable to finance the permanent assets, including "permanent current assets," with permanent funds. Just as in the case of "permanent current assets," there are "permanent current liabilities." It would be most unusual for the firm not to have any accounts payable or accrued liabilities. (These are shown in the cross-hatched area of Exhibit 10-2.) The particular mixture of equity, long-term debt, and "permanent current liabilities" used to finance permanent assets will depend upon other factors to be considered later. The reason for financing permanent assets with permanent funds relates to the cash flows obtained from the assets. A fixed asset provides services over a number of years. Through the use of these services and the sale of our product or services we obtain a cash inflow which includes a recovery of a portion of our investment in the fixed assets (depreciation). By the very nature of the assets involved, the recovery of our investment in fixed assets is usually a slow process. Consequently, it would be unwise to promise to repay a creditor

EXHIBIT 10-2   Relation of Need for Funds to Types of Funds Used

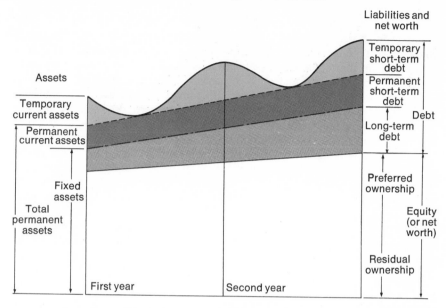

who has financed fixed assets at a rate faster than we are able to obtain cash inflows from those assets. Of course, in practice we do not segregate fixed assets and say that the flows from certain fixed assets go to certain creditors, and the flows from other fixed assets go to other creditors. We consider assets as a group. The point remains, however, that companies with proportionately large amounts of fixed assets customarily rely on similarly large amounts of permanent funds in the form of long-term debt or equity.

The higher the proportion of temporary current assets, the greater our need for short-term debt. Thus the large proportion of current assets in the construction and wholesale trades explains the heavy reliance on short-term debt in these industrial groups. When accounts receivable and inventory contract, we would like to be able to use our excess cash to repay debt. It would be most unprofitable to pay interest on a loan when the borrowed funds are resting idle in the bank. If we financed our temporary current assets with owners' funds or long-term debt, the idle cash balances would represent a very unprofitable investment of their money. Therefore, one of the objectives of the financial manager will be to finance temporary current assets with flexible short-term debt that may be expanded or contracted with corresponding fluctuations in the assets.

Risk

Any business is subject to fluctuating sales, which in turn may lead to equal or even greater variations in the earnings available for owners. For purposes of discussion assume that we are dealing with a corporation. The common stockholders are averse to risk as measured by variance in expected returns. They face two forms of risk: business risk and financial risk. First, as we have seen earlier, given the same expected earnings per share, owners prefer to purchase (make a bet on) those shares that have a "tight" probability distribution on earnings to those shares having a wider variance. In other words, given the same expected return, the expected utility of the shares with a narrow variance is higher than that of those shares with a wide variance of possible earnings per share. To put it still another way, owners are unwilling to accept a wide variance unless it is offset by a higher expected level of earnings. Thus the balancing of risk versus return becomes a choice between sleeping well and eating well. The individual trade-offs between risk and return made by investors are, of course, ultimately reflected in the market prices of corporate securities.

But there is a second form of risk: the risk of bankruptcy. Earlier in this chapter we saw that the residual owners are last in line in their claims on income and assets. When we assume debt, we take on two fixed obligations; first, to pay interest on the debt and, second, to repay the principal. Quite frequently repayments on the principal of the debt are made annually through *sinking fund payments.* Our risk is measured by the likelihood that expected fluctuations in sales will reduce us to such an illiquid position that we cannot meet interest and any required sinking fund payments on the debt. This is our risk of bankruptcy.

In analyzing these risks, we must recognize that fluctuations in sales result in fluctuations in earnings available for the residual owners and, most important, that the variations in sales are *magnified* by two forces that we will call operating leverage and financial leverage. A knowledge of the basic reasons for this magnification is important as a guide to deciding how much debt to include in our capital structure. Understand, however, that these are techniques used to convey information to management about risk, rather than being decisional tools.

Operating Leverage. The role of operating leverage can best be explained by use of a break-even chart, which relates the general effect of the level of output upon income and expenses and, therefore, upon net operating income (Y). If we examine the operating costs of a company, we will find that some of them change in direct proportion to variations in output. When output rises 10 percent, these costs also rise 10 percent. A baby food manufacturer would probably find that his costs of fruit and vegetables are *variable costs:* that is, the more he produces, the more he must spend for these items. Other variable costs might be direct labor and the cost of the containers. Other costs are *fixed costs* in that they do not change with variations in the level of output. The president of our baby food company is rather unlikely to lower his salary when production drops. Probably the costs of supervision, heat, light, and depreciation are also fixed costs.

Finally there is a group of costs that do not change in direct proportion to changes in the volume of production, but nonetheless do vary somewhat with output. For example, if output declines substantially, we may cut a few foremen from the payrolls and let the remaining foremen supervise more lines. Such mixtures of variable and fixed costs can usually be separated into their components, as shown on the following page.

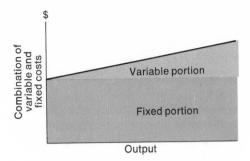

Segregated and variable costs may then be combined on a chart to show the behavior of the total costs with variations in output (Exhibit 10-3). We could put the variable costs on top of the fixed costs. However, for reasons which will be apparent later, we will put the fixed costs on top of the variable costs.

EXHIBIT 10-3   Break-Even Chart

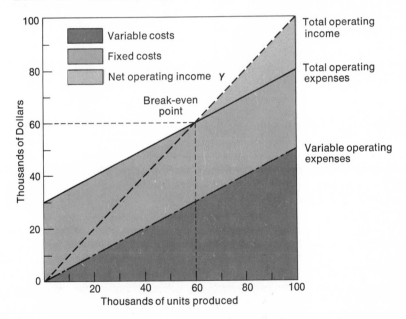

The total expense line is the same in either case. On the chart we have added a line for "total income," which shows the total sales revenue at each level of output, assuming goods are sold at $1 per unit.

What does the chart tell us? As output ranges from 0 to 100,000 units, variable costs move from $0 to $50,000. Regardless of the level of output, we have a group of expenses that remain constant at $30,000. When these fixed costs are added to variable costs, we find that total expenses vary from $30,000, when there is no production,[3] to $80,000, at an output of 100,000 units. Since total income at this level of output is $100,000, the profit is $20,000. However, at lower levels of output the margin between total income and total expenses narrows. Finally, at an output of 60,000 units the total income from sales is just equal to the total expenses. This is the *break-even point.* We can show this in figures as well:

Total income:	60,000 units × $1.00 = $60,000	
Total expenses:		
Fixed		$30,000
Variable	60,000 units × $0.50 =	30,000
		$60,000

Below the break-even point we will report an operating loss; the lower the level of output, the greater the loss.

The break-even point (*BEP*) is determined by the level of fixed costs and the spread between the selling price and variable cost per unit. It may be found directly by use of the formula shown below:[4]

$$BEP = \frac{F}{p - v} \qquad (10\text{-}1)$$

where F = the dollar amount of fixed operating costs,
p = the selling price per unit of output and
v = the variable costs per unit of output.
Using the data in the example, we have:

$$BEP = \frac{\$30,000}{\$1.00 - 0.50} = 60,000 \text{ units.}$$

As indicated by the expression, an increase in fixed costs or a narrowing of the difference between selling price and variable costs will raise the break-even point.

Were there no fixed costs, there would be no break-even point and no operating leverage. The importance of the fixed costs is that they induce a variance in net operating income (Y) that is greater than the variance in sales. Just as the fulcrum that provides financial leverage is the fixed payment for the use of funds, so the fulcrum that creates operating leverage is the fixed charges for various services, including those provided by the fixed assets (depreciation). Let us illustrate this point. First, assume a very simple, discrete probability distribution over three possible levels of sales, as indicated at the top of Table 10-1. With the income and expenses given above and a tax rate of 50 percent to keep the arithmetic simple, earnings after taxes will be those shown in Part A of the table. Under the assumption that our firm is financed entirely with 400 shares of common stock, the expected earnings per share can be seen to range from $1.88 to $10.63.

---

[3] As we shall see later, this is not very realistic.
[4] The formula is easily derived. Let *BEP* equal the volume of sales (in units) at the break-even point. Then:

$$F + v(BEP) = p(BEP)$$

Solving for *BEP* will produce equation (10-1).

TABLE 10-1   Variations in Operating Leverage

Probability of Sales		$\frac{1}{4}$		$\frac{1}{2}$		$\frac{1}{4}$	
A							
Net sales @ $ 1/unit		$63,000		$70,000		$77,000	
Variable costs @ $0.50	$31,500		$35,000		$38,500		
Fixed costs	30,000	61,500	30,000	65,000	30,000	68,500	
Net operating income		1,500		5,000		8,500	
Taxes (50%)		750		2,500		4,250	
Earnings after taxes		$750		$2,500		$4,250	
Earnings per share		$\frac{\$750}{400} = \$1.88$		$\frac{\$2,500}{400} = \$6.25$		$\frac{\$4,250}{400} = \$10.63$	
B							
Net sales @ $ 1/unit		$63,000		$70,000		$77,000	
Variable costs@ $0.80	$50,400		$56,000		$61,600		
Fixed costs	9,000	59,400	9,000	65,000	9,000	70,600	
Net operating income		3,600		5,000		6,400	
Taxes (50%)		1,800		2,500		3,200	
Earnings after taxes		$1,800		$2,500		$3,200	
Earnings per share		$\frac{\$1,800}{400} = \$4.50$		$\frac{\$2,500}{400} = \$6.25$		$\frac{\$3,200}{400} = \$8.00$	

With net sales of $70,000 it is possible that the same net operating income of $5,000 could have been generated with a different mixture of fixed and variable costs. For example, we might have used more direct labor and less specialized machinery. Part B of Table 10-1 shows the net operating income and earnings per share produced by the same levels of sales, but with fixed costs at $9,000 and variable costs at $0.80 per unit. Now expected earnings per share range from $4.50 to $8.00.

The probabilities of achieving various levels of earnings per share (*EPS*) under the two different cost structures are shown in Exhibit 10-4. Comparison of the results of high operating leverage (A) with low operating leverage (B) shows that a higher operating leverage creates a wider variance in expected returns for the owners. Since the expected values of both distributions are identical,[5] we would prefer the tighter distribution represented by the cost structure shown in Part B, all other things being equal.

The difference between the two distributions shown in Exhibit 10-4 arises because the cost structure shown in Part B creates a different and lower break-even point. Although the difference between selling price and variable costs has narrowed, fixed costs are much lower. As a result, the break-even point under Part B is only 45,000 units compared to 60,000 units under Part A.[6]

[5] The expected values of both distributions are identical: $\frac{1}{4}(\$1.875) + \frac{1}{2}(\$6.25) + \frac{1}{4}(\$10.625) = \$6.25 = \frac{1}{4}(\$4.50) = \frac{1}{2}(\$6.25) + \frac{1}{4}(\$8.00)$. Do not assume from the example that it is undesirable to introduce machinery to replace labor. It pays when the higher expected return more than offsets the greater variance in expected returns.

[6] $BEP = \dfrac{\$9,000}{\$1.00 - \$0.80} = 45,000$ units

EXHIBIT 10-4   Effect of Variations in Operating Leverage

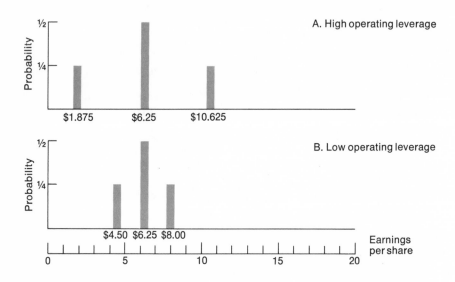

Although Exhibit 10-4 very graphically depicts the impact of different break-even points on the dispersion of possible outcomes, it will be helpful to have a specific measure of operating leverage. We are interested in the rate of increase in net operating income in response to an increase in sales. We base the calculation on the change in net operating income, rather than earnings per share because we wish to isolate the effect of operating leverage from financial leverage. As shown in Part A of Table 10-1, an output of 70,000 units produces net operating income (Y) of $5,000, while an output of 77,000 units (10 percent higher) produces a net operating income of $8,500 (70 percent higher).[7] We shall define the *degree of operating leverage* at a point as the ratio of the percentage increase in net operating income, Y, to the percentage increase in output. In this case we have:

$$\text{Degree of operating leverage at 70,000 units} = \frac{\text{Percentage increase in } Y}{\text{Percentage increase in output}} = \frac{70\%}{10\%} = 7.0$$

In other words, from this point the rate of increase in Y is 7.0 times the rate of increase in output. Because these are assumed to be straight-line relationships, this statement holds true for any percentage increase. Thus a 5 percent increase in output will generate a 35 percent increase in Y; a 15 percent rise in output, a 105 percent increase in Y, and so on.

Since it would be laborious to prepare a table such as that shown above to determine the degree of operating leverage at any point, it is easier to use the

[7]Earnings before interest and taxes, or *EBIT*, differs from net operating income (Y) only if there are non-operating income or expense items, other than interest expense. In the absence of such items, net operating income equals earnings before interest and taxes, or $Y = EBIT$. As a practical matter, it usually makes very little difference which item is used in calculating the degree of operating leverage.

simple formula shown below. In this case $T =$ the number of units produced at the point for which the degree of operating leverage is being calculated; $p =$ the selling price per unit; $v =$ the variable costs per unit; and $F =$ the total fixed costs. Then:

$$\text{Degree of operating leverage at } T = \frac{T(p - v)}{T(p - v) - F}. \text{[8]} \qquad (10\text{-}2)$$

Using our data from Table 10-1, we have the degree of operating leverage (*DOL*) at 70,000 units:

$$\frac{70,000(\$1.00 - 0.50)}{70,000(1.00 - 0.50) - \$30,000} = 7.0$$

When the break-even point is known, the degree of operating leverage may be calculated as shown below:[9]

$$DOL \text{ at } T = \frac{T}{T - BEP} \qquad (10\text{-}3)$$

Given our example, we have:

$$DOL \text{ at } 70,000 \text{ units} = \frac{70,000}{70,000 - 60,000} = 7.0$$

This form of expression emphasizes the essential relationship of the degree of operating leverage to the break-even point. The farther the firm operates from its break-even point, the lower the degree of operating leverage. For example, were the firm operating at an output of 120,000 units, *DOL* would be only 2.0.[10]

Financial Leverage. Variations in net operating income are magnified into still greater fluctuations in earnings per share by the use of financial leverage. Financial leverage is employed whenever funds are obtained in return for a limited payment, whether that be interest on debt or dividends on preferred stock. Although some financial analysts do not include short-term debt in evaluating leverage, its effect is the same as that of long-term debt, although its existence may be more transitory.

To illustrate the effect of financial leverage on the variability of earnings available for the residual owners, let us assume that our corporation needs

---

[8] Let ΔT be the change in units produced. Since fixed costs are constant, the change in net operating income is $\Delta T(p - v)$, and the rate of change in net operating income is $\frac{\Delta T(p - y)}{pT - vT - F}$. The rate of change in output is $\Delta T/T$. Then the ratio of the change in net operating income to the change in output must be

$$\frac{\frac{\Delta T(p - v)}{pT - vT - F}}{\frac{\Delta T}{T}} = \frac{\Delta T(p - v)}{T(p - v) - F} \cdot \frac{T}{\Delta T} = \frac{T(p - v)}{T(p - v) - F}$$

At the break-even point, $T(p - v) = F$; since the denominator in the fraction is then zero, the degree of operating leverage is undefined.

[9] By solving (10-1) for F, we find: $F = (BEP)(p - v)$. Substituting this result in (10-2) and simplifying, we have the result shown in (10-3). I am indebted to Professors Robert S. Himes, Eamon Kelly, and M. Richard Sussman for taking the time to point this out in correspondence.

[10] $\frac{120,000}{120,000 - 60,000} = 2.0$

$40,000. We may either use no leverage and meet our needs by selling 400 shares of common stock at $100 per share (as presumed in Table 10-1), or employ $20,000 of 8 percent bonds and 200 shares of common stock at $100 per share. In this second case, let us assume that there are no non-operating income or expense items other than the $1600 interest on the bonds, so that the net operating income (Y) is the same as earnings before interest and taxes ($EBIT$). If there were these other items, we would base our calculations on $EBIT$.

Given the Y of $5000 shown earlier in Part A of Table 10-1, (high operating leverage), how do earnings per share vary in response to the introduction of financial leverage? From that table we can see that when Y was 70 percent higher, so were earnings per share (EPS). But in Table 10-2, Part A, we can see that *with* leverage, a 70 percent increase in $EBIT$ results in more than a 100 percent shift in EPS — from $8.50 to $17.25. Thus the use of financial leverage increases still further the dispersion in expected EPS that was first introduced by operating leverage.

TABLE 10-2   Variations in Financial Leverage

Probability of Sales	$\frac{1}{4}$	$\frac{1}{2}$	$\frac{1}{4}$
Sales	$63,000	$70,000	$77,000
A			
$Y = EBIT$ (Table 10-1)	1,500	5,000	8,500
Interest (I)	1,600	1,600	1,600
Earnings before taxes	(100)	3,400	6,900
Taxes (50%)	0	1,700	3,450
Earnings after taxes	(100)	1,700	3,450
Earnings per share	$\frac{(100)}{200} = (\$0.50)$	$\frac{1,700}{200} = \$8.50$	$\frac{3,450}{200} = \$17.25$
B			
$Y = EBIT$ (Table 10-1)	3,600	5,000	6,400
Interest (I)	1,600	1,600	1,600
Earnings before taxes	2,000	3,400	4,800
Taxes (50%)	1,000	1,700	2,400
Earnings after taxes	1,000	1,700	2,400
Earnings per share	$\frac{1,000}{200} = \$5.00$	$\frac{1,700}{200} = \$8.50$	$\frac{2,400}{200} = \$12.00$

The combined effect of operating and financial leverage on the variance of *EPS* is shown in Exhibit 10-5. The greatest risk (variance) is produced by combining high operating leverage with high financial leverage (A-2). The lowest risk is present when there is both low operating leverage and no financial leverage (B-1). Under Part B, introduction of leverage both raises the expected value of EPS and enlarges the variance (B-2). Clearly, we will sleep better under B-1, but eat better under B-2.

As in the case of operating leverage, it will be useful to have a specific

EXHIBIT 10-5   *Effect of Variations in Operating Leverage and Financial Leverage*

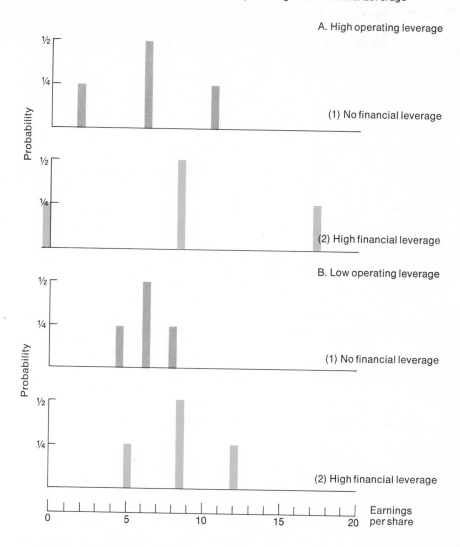

measure of the degree of magnification produced by financial leverage at any given level of Y (Y = EBIT by our assumptions). We shall define *degree of financial leverage* at a point as the ratio of the percentage increase in *EPS* to the percentage increase in *Y*.

From Part A of Table 10-2 we have:

$$\text{Degree of financial leverage at } Y \text{ of } \$5000 = \frac{\text{Percentage increase in } EPS}{\text{Percentage increase in } Y} = \frac{103\%}{70\%} = 1.47$$

In other words, from this point the rate of increase in *EPS* is 1.47 times the rate of increase in *Y*. Because these are straight-line relationships, this statement holds true for any percentage increase in *Y*. Thus a 10 percent increase in *Y* will generate a 14.7 increase in *EPS*.

To determine the degree of financial leverage more directly we can use the simple formula shown below:

$$\text{Degree of financial leverage} = \frac{Y}{Y - I} \quad [11] \qquad (10\text{-}4)$$

where I = interest on debt in dollars.

Substituting our earlier figures from Table 10-2, Part A, we have:

$$\begin{array}{l} \text{Degree of financial} \\ \text{leverage at } Y \text{ of} \\ \$5000 \end{array} = \frac{\$5000}{\$5000 - \$1600} = 1.47$$

In words rather than symbols, the formula tells us that the degree of financial leverage at a point is the ratio of net operating income to net operating income before taxes, but after interest charges. Because the interest charge is the fulcrum that provides the financial leverage, an increase in interest charges relative to *Y* will increase the degree of financial leverage, and vice versa. To put it another way, the lower is the coverage of interest charges, the higher is the degree of financial leverage. As times-interest-earned improves, the degree of financial leverage declines.

It may also be observed that the combined effect of operating and financial leverage is the product of the degree of operating leverage and the degree of financial leverage, or 10.3 (7.0×1.47).[12] As we can see in the last two columns,

---

[11] Let ΔY be the change in *Y*. Since interest costs remain unchanged, the change in the dollar amount of EPS is $\frac{\Delta Y(1 - t)}{N}$, where t is the corporate income tax rate, and N is the number of shares of common stock outstanding. The percentage increase in EPS is then

$$\frac{\dfrac{\Delta Y(1 - t)}{N}}{\dfrac{(Y - I)(1 - t)}{N}} = \frac{\Delta Y}{Y - I}$$

The rate of change in *Y* is $\Delta Y/Y$. Then the ratio of the percentage increase in EPS to the percentage increase in *Y* at *Y* must be

$$\frac{\dfrac{\Delta Y}{Y - I}}{\dfrac{\Delta Y}{Y}} = \frac{\Delta Y}{Y - I} \cdot \frac{Y}{\Delta Y} = \frac{Y}{Y - I}$$

When $Y = I$, the denominator in the fraction is then zero, and the degree of financial leverage is undefined.

[12] The combined effect of operating and financial leverage may be calculated directly by use of the formula shown below:

$$\text{Combined effect of operating and financial leverage at } T = \frac{T(p - v)}{T(p - v) - F - I}$$ in which T = the number of units produced at the point for which the combined effect is being calculated; p = the selling price per unit; v = the variable cost per unit; F = the total fixed costs; and I = the dollar amount of interest charges. In the case illustrated we have:

$$\frac{70,000(\$1.00 - 0.50)}{70,000(\$1.00 - 0.50) - \$30,000 - \$1,600} = \frac{\$35,000}{\$3,400} = 10.3.$$

in Table 10-2, Part A, a 10 percent variance in output (sales) from $70,000 to $77,000, would generate an increase in earnings per share from $8.50 to $17.25 — a shift of 103 percent.

In summary, variations in sales will result in magnified changes in net operating income because of operating leverage. Use of financial leverage will generate a still wider variance in earnings per share of common stock. The variance induced by operating and financial leverage reduces the expected utility of the corporation's stream of earnings to its shareholders, because they are typically risk averse. However, the unfavorable aspects of variance may be more than offset by a higher level of expected earnings per share. Ultimately, excessive variance can bring significant risks of bankruptcy — inability to meet required payments on the debt. This risk places an outer limit on the firm's ability to obtain borrowed funds in the market.[13]

Income

One of our objectives in planning the types of funds to use is to provide a high income for the residual owners. To determine whether financial leverage is favorable or not we must study the effect of various levels of debt upon earnings after taxes of common stock. The same approach is applicable when an issue of preferred is contemplated. However, because interest on debt is a tax-deductible expense and dividends on preferred stock are not, debt is more desirable than preferred stock from the standpoint of income. If income taxes take 40 percent of net profits, the after-tax cost to common stockholders of 8 percent bonds is 4.8 percent (0.60 × 8 percent). The after-tax cost of 8 percent preferred stock is still 8 percent.

It will be useful to have a means of communicating to management the effect on earnings per share of variations in the capital structure. As a matter of practice it is customary to relate EPS to earnings before interest and taxes (EBIT). As a starting point, we would like to know the level of EBIT at which earnings per share of common stock are the same, regardless of the mix. We shall define this level as the *indifference point*. Keep in mind that, while residual owners are indifferent at this point as to income, they are certainly not indifferent about risk.

The indifference point may readily be seen in Exhibit 10-6, which is based on Part A of Tables 10-1 and 10-2. An additional function has been added to show the relationship between EPS and EBIT on the assumption that $10,000 of 8 percent bonds had been issued, along with 300 shares of common stock. In studying this exhibit, we must keep in mind that two factors are held constant in our example: the dollar amount of funds obtained ($14,000) and the interest rate on bonds (8 percent).

Under any of the three alternative mixes of debt and equity, the indifference point is at an EBIT of $3200.[14] At this level, earnings per share of common stock

---

[13] This discussion has been in terms of accounting income, rather than cash flows. A more sophisticated approach would be to base estimates of debt capacity on cash flows.

[14] The indifference point may be computed by formula.

Let x = earnings before interest and taxes at the indifference point.

N_1 = number of shares of common stock outstanding if only common stock is issued;

N_2 = number of shares of common stock outstanding if both bonds and common stock are issued;

EXHIBIT 10-6   Analysis of Financial Leverage

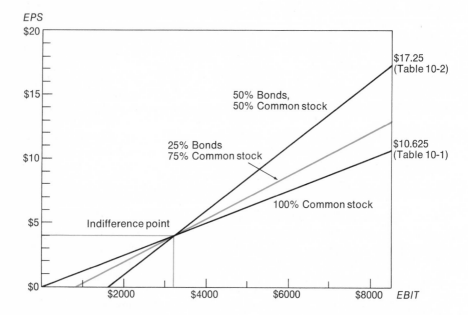

are $4.00. Above that level of income, the earnings per share available for common stock will be greater if 8 percent bonds are issued; below that level of income, the owners' income will be greater if no bonds are used. This is easily

---

N_3 = number of shares of common stock outstanding if both preferred and common stock are issued.

I = dollar amount of interest on bonds

P = dollar amount of preferred dividends

t = corporate income tax rate

For a newly-formed corporation, the indifference point may be computed by the following formulas:

$$\text{Common versus bonds:}\quad \frac{x(1-t)}{N_1} = \frac{(x-I)(1-t)}{N_2}$$

Applying this formula to the unlevered and levered corporations in Tables 10-1 and 10-2, we have:

$$\frac{0.50x}{400} = \frac{0.50(x-1600)}{200}$$

$$x = \$3200$$

$$\text{Common versus preferred:}\quad \frac{x(1-t)}{N} = \frac{x(1-t)-P}{N_3}$$

If a corporation already has bonds outstanding, we may let I_1 = dollar amount of interest paid on existing debt and I_2 = dollar amount of interest paid on additional debt. Also let N_1 = number of shares of common stock outstanding if additional bonds are issued. The indifference point may be determined by the following formula:

$$\frac{(x-I_1)(1-t)}{N_1} = \frac{(x-I_1-I_2)(1-t)}{N_2}$$

understood if we stop to think that $3200 *EBIT* represents an 8 percent return on total funds employed of $40,000. Therefore, if earnings are below that level, we are paying more to use the bondholders' money than we are earning on it before taxes, and the owners suffer correspondingly. Financial leverage is unfavorable. Above the indifference point we are earning more on the bondholders' money than we are paying for it, and thereby benefiting the common shareholders.

Although Exhibit 10-6 is a convenient means of displaying the effects of financial leverage upon *EPS,* we should bear in mind that the other aspect of leverage—risk—is omitted from this presentation. Even if we believe that on the average *EBIT* will be above the indifference point, we cannot design a capital structure that is too heavy with debt. At some point the added risk outweighs the possible added income.

Control

Another consideration in planning the types of funds to use is the desire of the residual owners to maintain control of the company. As we saw earlier in this chapter, creditors have no voice in the selection of management, and preferred owners have none, or very little. If we obtain funds from creditors or preferred owners, we sacrifice little or no share of our control of management. To put the matter another way in reference to our example, we may have a choice between controlling a million-dollar company with an investment of $40,000 or an investment of $20,000. If we have only $20,000 ourselves, we face the alternative of raising the additional amount needed from nonvoting creditors or preferred stockholders, or from additional voting common stockholders.[15]

There is no question of who is in control in a proprietorship. The owner is the manager, and his freedom of control is unquestioned. In fact, this is probably one of the reasons he is in business for himself. His unwillingness to bring in any outsiders to share his control may also hamper his ability to raise additional funds. Legally, partners have an equal voice in management, although minor decisions in specific areas may be delegated to various partners. In a corporation each common stockholder is entitled to vote in proportion to the number of shares that he owns. As we have seen, preferred stockholders may also have a vote at times. Usually the majority rules, although it may take more than a majority for certain specified decisions.

If the main object of the owners is to maintain control, it might appear advisable to raise any necessary additional funds from creditors or preferred owners. This is not always the case. As we have seen, if we borrow more than we can service or repay, the creditors may seize the assets of the company to satisfy their claims. In this case we lose all control. It might be better to sacrifice a measure of control by some additional equity financing rather than run the risk of losing all control to creditors by employing too much debt. Similarly, we may be able to issue additional preferred stock only with the promise that, if we fail to pay their dividends, we will allow the preferred stockholders to elect a majority of the board of directors. In this case the preferred stock may be less desirable than additional common stock.

[15] There is a form of nonvoting common stock that is becoming increasingly scarce.

Maneuverability. This refers to our ability to adjust our sources of funds upwards or downwards in response to major changes in needs for funds. We have indicated that short-term debt allows adjustments in sources of funds to seasonal swings in current assets. However, the overall needs for funds may undergo drastic shifts over a period of years.

Basically we seek maneuverability in order to have as many alternatives as possible open when we need to expand or contract our total funds employed. Not only does it enable us to use the type of funds that is most readily available at any given time, but it also enhances our bargaining power when dealing with a prospective supplier of funds. To illustrate, let us say that we have borrowed so much in the past that we are top-heavy with debt; now we wish to obtain some additional funds. Even though borrowed funds may be generally available at very low interest rates, we may not be able to obtain any. Prospective lenders look askance at our balance sheet and at our income in relation to fixed charges. Instead of being able to borrow on favorable terms, we may be forced to seek equity money at a time when equity money is generally scarce. Furthermore, the prospective suppliers of equity funds recognize that we have no alternative but to strike a bargain with them. We cannot say that if we do not obtain equity funds on favorable terms, we can always borrow some. We can only protest that if the bargain is too unfavorable we will cancel our plans for expansion.

Not only do we wish "elbow room" to expand, but we also desire maneuverability on the downside. Maybe we would like to dispose of certain assets and use the proceeds from their sale to reduce our liabilities or to pay back the original investment of the preferred owners. Maybe we now regard some past agreement as a very unfortunate bargain and would like to get out of it. Since debt always has a date of maturity, this type of funds automatically provides us with this type of maneuverability. On the other hand, we may not wish to wait until the debt matures to eliminate it, and there is no obligation to return the investment made by the preferred owners. To provide the desired maneuverability, we should try to incorporate in the agreement with the suppliers of these funds a provision that we can *call* the debt or preferred stock. This simply means that with adequate notice we can repay the creditors or preferred stockholders, although we may have to give them a premium in addition to their original investment. Whether or not they will agree to this sort of arrangement will depend upon our respective bargaining powers at the time we make the agreement.

Timing

Closely related to maneuverability in determining the types of funds used is the factor of timing. An important consequence of maneuverability is that it enables us to seize opportunities that will allow us to minimize the total cost of debt and equity funds. Frequently very substantial savings may be obtained by proper timing of a security issue. For example, between early 1968 and the end of 1969, the average yield on industrial bonds rose about three percentage points. By floating a $300 million bond issue in 1968 rather than 1969, a corporation would have saved $9 million per year over the life of the issue.

Considering timing as the sole criterion in our selection of sources of funds over the business cycle, we seek to shift from short-term to long-term debt in the early stages of recovery from a recession. At this point long-term rates are likely to be low, and we will need these funds later to finance additions to permanent fixed and current assets. It is better to make this switch early and freeze the low-cost long-term debt into the capital structure. Although the cost of short-term borrowings at a later stage in the recovery will probably exceed the cost of long-term borrowings, the rate on long-term borrowings will probably have increased as well. Moreover, it may then be more difficult to market long-term bonds without granting special privileges to the bondholders.

As recovery progresses the ratio of price to earnings of the common stock is likely to rise, so that eventually it may be desirable to issue additional common stock. By timing the sale of common stock in order to obtain as much as possible per share, we minimize the number of shares necessary to raise a given amount of funds. In turn, this minimizes the dilution of future cash flows per share. Sale of common equity also expands the equity base to provide maneuverability for later issues of debt during the next recovery phase of the business cycle.

Of course, timing is not the only consideration. At times funds will be needed and must be obtained, even if they are relatively costly. We must still maintain a proper balance between debt and equity, and may find it necessary to forgo adding "cheap" debt to the capital structure if we are already top-heavy with debt. Agreements with existing bondholders may prevent our replacing a relatively expensive bond issue with one that requires lower interest payments. Thus timing in obtaining funds is excerised within limits imposed by the timing of needs for funds, the extent of maneuverability, and existing agreements with creditors and owners.

Evaluation of Determining Factors

The decision as to the types of funds to employ represents a compromise among the factors of suitability, income, risk, control, maneuverability, and timing. We shall assume that the compromise is to be made with the best interests of the residual owners in mind. The compromise is reached within a certain environment, which is composed of the economy, the industry, and the company itself. We frequently have little control over this environment. Let us discuss the significant aspects of this frame of reference which must be considered in arriving at the final financial plan.

Characteristics of the Economy

When we determine a financial plan today, we are going to have to live with it for some period of time. Consequently, any financial plan involves certain predictions of the economic outlook. It is better to make these forecasts consciously as part of the process of financial planning, rather than to assume automatically that today's economic situation will persist tomorrow.

Level of Business Activity. If the level of business activity is expected to increase, it may mean that our needs for assets and the funds with which to finance their acquisition will also grow. An outlook for rapid expansion puts a premium on maneuverability in setting our financial plans. As we shall see, the impact of expected changes in the general level of business activity will have markedly different effects upon different industries.

Money and Capital Markets. Although detailed discussion of the nature of money and capital markets must wait until Chapter 16, the outlook for the cost and availability of different types of funds is of great significance. It is of special importance with respect to the income factor in determining the types of funds to employ. Should we feel that borrowed funds will become costly or scarce, we may wish to raise our degree of financial leverage immediately. An expected decline in interest rates may encourage us to postpone borrowing, but to keep in a maneuverable position in order to take advantage of cheaper money later on.

Tax Rates. Since the interest cost on borrowed funds is a tax-deductible expense, increases in the applicable tax rates raise the desirability of debt in relation to other types of funds from the point of view of income. In a sense the income tax has legislated a higher proportion of debt to equity for American business than would otherwise exist. The greater financial leverage is acceptable so long as the economy preserves enough stability to permit business firms to meet payments on the debt.

Personal income tax rates affect the payment of dividends by corporations. Stockholders do not pay personal income taxes on their share of a corporation's earnings, but do pay taxes on any portion of the earnings distributed as dividends. Consequently, increases in personal income tax rates tend to encourage the retention of earnings by some corporations and a greater reliance on retained earnings for financing growth. The balance struck between debt and equity will depend in part upon the relative levels of corporate income tax rates and personal income tax rates.

Characteristics of the Industry

Seasonal Variations. Industries with wide seasonal movements in sales are likely to need relatively large proportions of flexible short-term borrowings. Considerations of the suitability of the types of funds to the assets financed will probably be of special importance to such enterprises as retail department stores and manufacturers of toys, fertilizers, and women's clothing.

Cyclical Variations. The sales of some products are fairly immune to changes in the level of national income. In economic terminology we would say that these goods have a low *income elasticity*. Industries dealing with nondurable consumer goods (food) or with inexpensive items (paper clips) or with items in habitual use (cigarettes) are likely to find the variations in their sales less than the movements in national income. Sales of products with a high income elasticity are subject to wider variations than the national income. This would be true of such items as refrigerators, machine tools, and most capital equipment. During one year of the depression in the 'thirties the total output of one manufacturer of locomotives was precisely one locomotive.

Maneuverability and risk become major factors to consider in planning the types of funds to use if an industry's sales vary widely over a business cycle. Room must be left for easy and rapid expansion or contraction of funds used. Given wide fluctuations in sales, it may prove unwise to add much financial leverage to existing operating leverage. Moreover, there is the risk of not being able to meet the required payments in the lean years. A large debt issue maturing during some future year of depression could spell the end of the company.

Nature of Competition. The nature of competition within the industry will also affect the weight given the various factors that influence the sources of funds used. For example, in the dress industry much of the competition is based on style. Because styles are unpredictable and transitory, profits are equally so. Firms in this business commonly emphasize equity over debt because of the excessive risk of not being able to meet payments on borrowed funds.

At the other extreme we have public utilities, which are relatively free from intra-industry competition. (By a public utility we mean a company involved in the production or sale of electricity, gas, water, transportation services, or telephone services.) A company that provides electricity to a given area generally has an exclusive right to provide the service. Without the inroads of competitors its profits are likely to be more stable and predictable than in industries which are not granted monopoly powers. This stability of earnings helps to explain the emphasis such companies have been able to place on the use of financial leverage.

Stage in Life Cycle. Industries are born; they grow; they mature; and, finally, they frequently decline. In the early days of the radio manufacturing industry many companies entered the field. Because the rate of failure was high, only a few went on to participate in the rapid growth of sales that finally ensued. Ultimately most homes had electricity and one or more radios. Sales of sets became more dependent upon the demand for replacement, and the industry had reached maturity. Whereas the industry had been fairly resistant to changes in the level of business activity during its period of growth, sales were now more dependent upon population growth, replacement, and movements in national income. If these companies had not turned to the manufacture of television sets, they might now be passing through a period of relative decline or senility.

How does the stage of the life cycle of the industry affect the weight assigned the factors of suitability, risk, income, control, and maneuverability? If the industry is in its infancy, the rate of failure will be high. The main source of funds is risk capital, frequently obtained through the services of promotors who specialize in searching out investors willing to undertake a speculative venture. We would do well to avoid seeking funds which require any fixed payments. The risk outweighs the attractions of financial leverage. During the period of rapid growth, special attention may be paid to maneuverability to assure that as we grow we are able to obtain funds when needed and under acceptable terms. When the industry has reached maturity, we must be prepared to meet the financial impacts of wider seasonal and cyclical swings in sales. If the outlook is for a long-term decline in business, we should build a financial structure that will allow for easy contraction in the sources of funds used.

Regulation. The types of funds used by public utilities are rather closely supervised by various regulatory bodies. To illustrate the sorts of limitations imposed, let us consider the electric light and power companies and the railroads. Some electric power companies operating in more than one state are subject to regulation by the Securities and Exchange Commission. The rules of this federal agency have influenced the financing of electric power companies to some extent by generally limiting, to companies under its jurisdiction, the use of long-term debt to 50 percent of the capital structure and preferred stock to 25 percent of the capital structure. Because of the much greater variations in their earnings, railroads finance a much smaller proportion of their needs with long-term debt.

By limiting the rates that may be charged, regulatory commissions affect the earnings of these enterprises and thus, indirectly, the types of funds they can obtain. The commissions may also require an electric utility or railroad to provide service that is unprofitable. For example, railroads may not discontinue trains or portions of their lines without permission from the Interstate Commerce Commission. Such limitations on earnings may make it difficult for the business concern to obtain additional funds on attractive terms.

Custom. In addition to the specific dictates that regulatory commissions lay down for public utilities, tradition has established certain rules of thumb for the capital structures of companies in many fields. For example, it is suggested that industrial concerns in general should limit their long-term debt to the amount of net working capital (current assets less current liabilities) and to 50 percent of the depreciated value of assets. Furthermore, earnings after income taxes should cover the interest payments on the debt by not less than three times.[16] Standards relating to specific manufacturing, wholesale, and retail trades have developed in part from the publication of average ratios for different industries by Dun and Bradstreet and the Robert Morris Associates. If we depart significantly from these standards, we may find it more difficult or costly to obtain funds. In a sense the burden of proof is on us to explain why our ratio of debt to net worth or coverage of interest charges should be out of line with the average for the industry.

Characteristics of the Company

Form of Organization. As explained in Chapter 2, the form of organization affects the liability of owners for the debts of the firm. Corporations usually find it easier to acquire equity capital than do proprietorships or partnerships, because stockholders risk only their original investment. Additionally, they can often sell their shares to others with relative ease. In general, we would conclude that the corporate form of organization provides a more ready access to

[16] Harry G. Guthmann and Herbert E. Dougall, *Corporate Financial Policy* (Englewood Cliffs, N.J.: Prentice-Hall, 1962), pp. 275–82. The rules cited are for illustrative purposes only; to understand them fully the entire discussion should be studied.

most types of funds. If this is the case, maneuverability looms as a larger problem for proprietorships and partnerships.

Finally, the acquisition of additional equity in a proprietorship or partnership will usually result in a greater sacrifice of control than in the case of a corporation. If we bring in an outsider as a partner, he is very likely to insist upon having a voice in management that is consistent with the investment he has made. In contrast, if we sell common stock to widely scattered stockholders, they will find it difficult to organize in order to seize control.

Size. At the outset we indicated that management's freedom to weigh the factors of suitability, risk, income, control, maneuverability, and timing was limited by the ability and willingness of the market to provide the types of funds desired. Management's freedom of choice is especially limited in the case of very small and very large companies.

Companies that are very small must rely to a considerable degree upon owners' funds for their financing. The corner drug store and the dry cleaners down the block find it very difficult to obtain long-term debt. Even somewhat larger companies cannot afford to split up the types of funds they obtain. Although it might theoretically be desirable for a firm needing $100,000 to raise $30,000 with long-term debt, $20,000 with preferred stock, and $50,000 with common stock, it would be expensive. The costs of marketing these small issues of securities would outweigh any possible advantages. Because they do not have ready access to different types of funds from various sources, small companies are in a relatively poor bargaining position when they seek funds. To counteract this inherent disadvantage small companies must give great weight to the factor of maneuverability. Sources of funds available to a small company are few and far between; we should not risk losing these by building a weak financial structure.

In contrast, very large concerns are forced to employ different types of funds. Because they need so much money, they would find it difficult to satisfy their total needs at a reasonable cost if they restricted their demands to just one type of funds. Consider the problems American Telephone and Telegraph might have faced if it had tried to raise all of its funds by the sale of common stock.

Credit Standing. The higher our credit standing the greater our maneuverability. If our credit standing is poor, our financial planning should aim to improve our credit standing and better our maneuverability. Our credit standing is mainly a product of our liquidity, earnings potential, and record of having met previous obligations. The value and character of the assets that we have to pledge as security are of secondary importance. In part, credit standing is also determined by the general ability and reputation of management. Unfortunately, it is much easier to lose a good credit standing than to regain it.

Assurance of Control. Proprietors and partners have little doubt that they will continue to control the management of their companies. The significance owners accord to improving control in the case of a corporation is related to the firmness of their grasp upon the reins. This will be dependent in part upon the relations of the company with stockholders, the distribution of the stock, and the method used in voting. Happy and scattered stockholders are an aid to the continuation of control. As we shall see later, methods of selecting members of the board of directors have also been devised to minimize the impact of indignant stockholders.

Management of small corporations must also give special attention to the factor of control. If the firm's common stock were publicly available, it might be relatively easy for a larger concern or some financial pirate to buy a controlling interest. Consequently, owners are likely to hold on to their stock and favor growth on the basis of debt, preferred stock, or retained earnings rather than through the issue of additional shares of common stock. Even if this policy means that growth will be slow, owners of many small concerns prefer a gradual growth to the risk of losing control.

Summary

In financing assets, we have a choice among various methods of financing. To simplify matters we have considered only the basic features of debt and equity as related to maturity, claim on income, claim on assets, and voice in management. When we come to discussing these types of funds in greater detail, we shall see that there are many variations in the bargains that are made between the companies seeking funds and those that supply them. However, such modifications do not change the basic distinctions we have made between debt and equity.

The mixture of debt and equity that will ultimately be used represents a compromise between the combination we would like to employ and the ability and willingness of the market to supply such funds. Our determination of the most desirable mix of debt and equity is affected by considerations of suitability, risk, income, control, maneuverability, and timing. The relative weights assigned these factors will vary widely from company to company, depending upon the general economic conditions, the characteristics of the industry, and the particular situation of our own company. Financial theory has not developed to the point that when data relative to these considerations are fed in one end of a computer an ideal financial structure will pop out of the other. Consequently human judgment must be used to resolve the many conflicting forces in laying plans for the types of funds to be sought.

Questions

1/ Under what circumstances would a company's total costs vary directly with output (that is, with a 10 percent increase in output, total costs would rise 10 percent)? Would this firm have a break-even point? What sorts of business enterprise approach this situation?

2/ What is the general effect on the break-even point of the following changes in policy?
   a. Selling prices are decreased.

    b. Instead of leasing our store for $10,000 annually, we decide to purchase land and a building on which the annual depreciation charge will be $12,000.

    c. A savings in labor cost reduces variable costs per unit.

3/ In each case in question 2, assume that the company operates above the break-even point both before and after the indicated changes in policy. Explain the effect of the changes upon the degree of operating leverage.

4/ Let us assume we are operating an automobile repair shop. A major cost of operations is labor. We can pay the mechanics $2.20 an hour for the time they actually work, or a flat payment of $2.00 an hour, regardless of whether or not work is available. Discuss the effect upon the break-even point, operating leverage, and possible financing of the two alternatives.

5/ One of the latest trends in the mechanics of carrying on business is an increasing lack of flexibility with an increase in the process associated with automation. The president of a large chemical company recently pointed out that almost one half of the company's employees were salaried and that almost one half of the hourly employees were engaged in services and maintenance. Explain the problems from the point of view of the financial manager of such increasing inflexibility in costs.

6/ Eastern Air Lines has inaugurated a "shuttle service" between Boston, New York, and Washington that requires no reservations. Eastern claims that its break-even point is 50 percent of capacity, because the Constellations used in the service are largely depreciated. In contrast, the break-even point on a new jet, costing $5–$6 million, is said to be around 60 percent (*Wall Street Journal,* August 21, 1961, p. 6).

    a. Does this suggest that it is more profitable for airlines to operate older equipment? Why or why not? Discuss.

    b. Does this suggest that, once a piece of equipment is fully depreciated, the price charged for its services may be reduced? Discuss.

7/ a. Jet aircraft are much more efficient than propeller-driven planes; that is, they can produce many more passenger revenue miles per hour. Moreover, about 50 percent of airline costs are fixed. What effect do you believe the introduction of jets and the rise in airline travel had on the airline industry's break-even point and *EBIT*? Is your answer consistent with your response to (6) above?

    b. The CAB in 1960 set a standard return on total funds employed (debt plus equity) of 10.25 percent. Given this decision and your analysis in (a) above, would you expect airlines to use a high or low proportion of debt to equity? Explain.

    c. What dangers are inherent in this situation for the airlines? (Based on "T.W.A.: Prosperity But No Peace," *Fortune,* 72 [July, 1965], pp. 122 –25ff.)

8/ Some restaurants are offering "twofers"—a "special ticket that enables a diner to buy two meals, excluding liquor, for the price of one." Explain in terms of break-even analysis the financial reasons for this merchandising plan. (*Wall Street Journal*, September 5, 1962, p. 4.)

9/ What sort of capital structure would you propose for a corporation if your primary objectives were to:
   a. Maximize the possible income for common stockholders.
   b. Assure control with a minimum investment.
   c. Minimize fluctuations in earnings per share on common stock.
   d. Prepare for a later issue of long-term debt.
   (Explain your answers in each case.)

10/ Which would have a higher proportion of permanent current assets—a grocery store or a college bookstore? Explain.

11/ Some economists believe that swings in business activity may not be so wide as in earlier years. If this is so, what effect is this greater economic stability likely to have on the types of funds used by American business?

12/ Under the practice of "price leadership" an important firm initiates a price change, which is then followed by other companies in the same industry.
   a. What differences might you expect to find in the capital structures of the "leader" and "followers"?
   b. What differences in typical capital structures within the industry might you expect to find if the industry was characterized by greater price competition?

13/ An appliance dealer who sells furnaces and heaters is considering selling air conditioners as well. What effect might this decision have on the types of funds he uses?

14/ In the past Montgomery Ward financed its accounts receivable and property directly with its own capital. However, during 1959–60, Montgomery Ward Credit Corp. was established to acquire a large portion of the accounts receivable of the parent corporation. Similarly, Montgomery Ward Real Estate Corp. was set up to finance future acquisitions of real estate. What reasons can you suggest for handling Montgomery Ward's financing partly through specialized subsidiaries, rather than entirely by the parent company? ("Montgomery Ward: Prosperity Is Still Around the Corner," *Fortune,* 62 [November, 1960], p. 220.)

15/ In the comparison of operating revenues of telephone companies and electric utilities, it has been observed that wages amount to 40 percent of revenues for the telephone company, but only 20 percent of revenues of electric utilities. Wage costs are probably more inflexible in the case of the telephone company. Net operating income amounts to about 15 percent of revenues and 25 percent of revenues for telephone companies and electric utilities, respectively. About 80 percent of all households now have telephones, and a higher percentage of revenues are coming from long distance services than in earlier years. Using these facts, explain the differences that might be justified between the capital structures of telephone companies and electric utilities. (Gilbert Burck, "Is A.T.&T. Playing It Too Safe?" *Fortune,* 62 [September, 1960], p. 282.)

Problems

1/ We have the following information available for Companies A and B:

	Company A		Company B	
Units produced and sold		25,000		25,000
Revenues		$100,000		$100,000
Variable costs	$25,000		$50,000	
Fixed costs	50,000	75,000	25,000	75,000
Net operating income		$ 25,000		$ 25,000

a. What is the break-even point for each company?
b. What is the degree of operating leverage for each company at 25,000 units?
c. How do you explain the differences that you observe between these companies' break-even points and degrees of operating leverage?

2/ Rework Part A of Tables 10-1 and 10-2 on the assumption that variable costs are $0.60 per unit and fixed costs $23,000. Keep all other assumptions the same.
a. Determine the degree of operating leverage and the degree of financial leverage, given sales of $70,000. Explain differences in your results from similar calculations in the text.
b. What is the product of the degree of operating leverage and the degree of financial leverage? Demonstrate the relationship of this product to the difference in sales and *EPS* at sales of $70,000 and $77,000.
c. Prepare a break-even chart, as shown in Exhibit 10-3.
d. Calculate the break-even point and check that result against the break-even point shown in your graph in (c) above.
e. Prepare an exhibit, as shown in Exhibit 10-6, depicting the relationship of *EPS* to *EBIT* of the unlevered and levered corporation.
f. Calculate the indifference point and check that result against the in-difference point shown in your graph in (e) above.

3/ The J. R. Longstreet Corporation manufactures only one product. Its fixed costs total $180,000, and variable costs amount to $1.50 per unit. The items are sold at $3.00 per unit.
I. a. Prepare a diagram showing the company's break-even point, using Exhibit 10-3 as a model.
b. Prove the break-even point shown in your chart mathematically (see equation (10-1)).
c. Assume that the company is operating at a level of 140,000 units and that sales rise by 10 percent to 154,000 units. What is the percentage increase in net operating income? Use these figures to compute the degree of operating leverage.
d. Using formula (10-2), compute the degree of operating leverage for the following levels of output: 140,000 units, 150,000 units, and 180,000 units.
II. (In this and the following sections, show all computations.) Assume

that variable costs rise to $1.60 per unit, but that fixed costs and selling price remain as originally indicated.

    a. What is the new break-even point?

    b. What is the degree of operating leverage for the following levels of output: 140,000 units, 150,000 units, and 180,000 units.

    c. How do you explain the differences that you observe between results in parts I and II?

III. Assume that fixed costs rise to $195,000, but that variable costs and selling price remain as originally indicated in Part I.

    a. What is the new break-even point?

    b. What is the degree of operating leverage at 140,000 units, 150,000 units, and 180,000 units?

    c. How do you explain the differences that you observe among your results in parts I, II, and III?

IV. Assume that the selling price is increased to $3.30 per unit, but that fixed and variable costs remain as originally indicated in Part I.

    a. What is the new break-even point?

    b. What is the degree of operating leverage at 140,000 units, 150,000 units, and 180,000 units?

    c. How do you explain the differences that you observe between your results in parts I and IV?

4/ The E. A. Nelson Corp. is considering lowering its selling price on product Y. The following information is available on the costs of producing and the income from selling the product:

Sales revenue (75,000 units @10)		$750,000
Variable costs (75,000 units)	$450,000	
Fixed costs	200,000	650,000
Net operating income		$100,000

To assist management in reaching a decision, the financial manager has prepared a table to show the percentage increase in volume necessary to maintain a net operating income of $100,000 on the item with decreases in price of 5%, 10%, and 15%.

Decrease in selling price (%)	Volume necessary to produce profit $100,000 (units)	Increase in volume required (units)	Percentage increase in volume required (%)
5%			
10%			
15%			

    a. Complete the table.

    b. How do you explain the variations in the percentage increase in volume necessary to maintain a profit of $100,000? (That is, why is not the percentage increase in volume required for a 10% decrease in price just double the percentage increase in volume required for a 5% decrease in price?)

5/ The R. H. Raymond Corporation has 10,000 shares of common stock outstanding.[17] Last year's income statement is summarized below along with four partial pro forma statements reflecting different assumptions regarding a new plant. In all instances, one million dollars must be raised and the new plant will cost one million dollars.

		Pro Forma			
		Sell 5,000 shares of stock		Sell 6% Bonds	
	Actual 1971	Optimistic	Pessimistic	Optimistic	Pessimistic
Sales	$500,000	$1,000,000	$600,000	$1,000,000	$600,000
Variable Operating Expenses	150,000	300,000			
Marginal income	$350,000	$ 700,000			
Fixed operating expenses	230,000	400,000	400,000	400,000	400,000
Net operating profit	$120,000				
Interest	-0-				
		$	$	$	$
Net profit before taxes	$120,000				
Federal income tax (50%)	60,000				
		$	$	$	$
Net profit	$ 60,000				
Earnings per share	$6	$	$	$	$

Assume that you are the financial vice-president of Raymond Corporation. Your assistant started the above projection using last year's financial report and projections of sales and fixed expenses sent to you by the sales and production departments.

Required: Complete the tabulation and draft a memorandum to the board of directors in which you explain that by selling bonds instead of stock the firm would be trading on the equity. Be sure to explain what this means and use the tabulation as an illustration. Assume that a copy of the tabulation will accompany your memorandum.

6/ The directors of the J. R. Longstreet Corporation (Problem 3) are considering the methods of financing the corporation. Initially, $600,000 will be needed. Some of the directors wish to finance the needs by issuing 6,000 shares of common stock. Another group believes that the corporation should issue $300,000 of 10% bonds and raise the remaining $300,000 by selling 3,000 shares of common stock. Assume federal income taxes are at a rate of 40%.

I. a. Prepare an indifference chart showing the earnings after taxes available per share of common stock at various levels of earnings before interest and taxes (*EBIT*).

b. Prove the indifference point shown in your chart mathematically. (See footnote 14).

[17] I am indebted to Professor Robert H. Raymond for this problem.

c. Compare earnings per share (*EPS*) under the two proposed capital structures if *EBIT* is $50,000 and $70,000. How do you explain the differences in your results?

II. Assume that the 10% bonds are used along with the 3,000 shares of common stock.

a. Initially the company is expected to operate at a level of 160,000 units, so that *EBIT* will be $60,000. If *EBIT* should rise by 10 percent, what will be the percentage increase in earnings per share of common stock (*EPS*)? Use these figures to compute the degree of financial leverage at *EBIT* of $60,000.

b. Using the formula given, compute the degree of financial leverage for the following levels of *EBIT*: $48,000, $60,000, and $132,000.

III. Assume that the bond-stock capital structure is to be used and that sales rise by 10 percent to 176,000 units from 160,000 units. (Selling price is $3.00 per unit; variable costs, $1.50 per unit; and fixed costs total $180,000.)

a. Compute the percentage increase in *EPS*.

b. What is the degree of operating leverage at 160,000 units?

c. Multiply the degree of operating leverage at 160,000 units by the degree of financial leverage at *EBIT* of $60,000. Their product is the combined effect of operating and financial leverage. Show that this agrees with the result you obtained in Part (a) of this section.

7/ The percentage composition of the sources of funds for selected groups of corporations are shown below. The industries represented are textile mill products, communication, apparel and accessories (retail), and credit agencies other than banks. Identify each industry from the data supplied and explain how you reached your decision.

	A	B	C	D
Short-term debt	70.1%	33.6%	21.2%	10.5%
Long-term debt	18.8	13.0	12.4	30.8
Preferred stock	0.6	3.0	2.7	1.2
Common stock & surplus	10.5	50.4	63.7	57.5
	100.0%	100.0%	100.0%	100.0%

Selected References

BATY, G., *Initial Financing of the New Research-Based Enterprise in New England.* Boston: Federal Reserve Bank of Boston, Research Report No. 25, 1964.

BIERMAN, H., Jr., "Risk and the Addition of Debt to the Capital Structure," *Journal of Financial and Quantitative Analysis,* 3 (December, 1968), pp. 415–26.

DONALDSON, G., *Corporate Debt Capacity.* Boston: Graduate School of Business Administration, Harvard University, 1961.

————, "New Framework for Corporate Debt Policy," *Harvard Business Review,* 40 (March–April, 1962), pp. 117–31.

GHANDHI, J. K. S., "On the Measurement of Leverage," *Journal of Finance,* 21 (December, 1966), pp. 715–26.

JAEDICKE, R. K. and A. A. ROBICHEK. "Cost-Volume-Profit Analysis under Conditions of Uncertainty." *Accounting Review,* 39 (October, 1964), pp. 917–26.

MANES, R., "A New Dimension to Breakeven Analysis," *Journal of Accounting Research*, 4 (Spring, 1966), pp. 87–100.

MAYER, R. W., "Analysis of Internal Risk in the Industrial Firm," *Financial Analysts Journal*, 15 (November, 1959), pp. 91–95.

MEISELMAN, D. and E. SHAPIRO, *The Measurement of Corporate Sources and Uses of Funds*. New York: National Bureau of Economic Research, 1964.

MORGAN, B. W., "Corporate Debt and Stockholder Portfolio Selection," *Yale Economic Essays*, 7 (Fall, 1967), pp. 201–59.

MORRISON, T. A. and E. KACZKA, "A New Application of Calculus and Risk Analysis to Cost-Volume-Profit Changes," *Accounting Review*, 44 (April, 1969), pp. 330–43. Also, see footnotes at beginning for references to other articles on nonlinear breakeven analysis.

ROBICHEK, A. A. and S. C. MYERS, *Optimal Financing Decisions*. Englewood Cliffs: Prentice-Hall, Inc., 1965.

_____, "Problems in the Theory of Optimal Capital Structure," *Journal of Finance and Quantitative Analysis*, 1 (June, 1966), pp. 1–35.

SARMA, L. V. L. N. and K. S. H. RAO, "Leverage and the Value of the Firm" *Journal of Finance*, 24 (September, 1969), pp. 673–78.

SCHWARTZ, E., "Theory of the Capital Structure of the Firm," *Journal of Finance*, 14 (March, 1959), pp. 18–39.

SMITH, G. W., "Decreasing Utility for Money and Optimal Corporate Debt Ratio," *Engineering Economist*, 13 (Winter, 1968), pp. 87–104.

WALTER, J. E., "The Use of Borrowed Funds," *Journal of Business*, 28 (April, 1955), pp. 138–47.

WESTWICK, C. A., "A Graphical Treatment of Gearing," *Journal of Accounting Research*, 4 (Autumn, 1966), pp. 239–44.

Cost of Capital

11   Cost of capital is a subject of great importance to financial managers and economists. In Chapter 8 we first referred to cost of capital as an "opportunity cost" and employed it as the discount rate in the net-present-value approach to evaluation of capital investments. If the net present value of a proposed expenditure is positive, given this opportunity cost, the market value of the firm should rise if the project is accepted. Alternatively, the cost of capital may be used as a "hurdle rate" when evaluating proposed capital expenditures by the discounted-rate-of-return approach. If the expected return exceeds the cost of capital, the residual owners should be better off financially if the project is undertaken.

Second, the cost of capital provides a measure of the effectiveness of the design of the capital structure (Chapter 10). In that chapter we dealt with various means of demonstrating the effect of variations in the capital structure, as well as the factors influencing the design of the structure. Now we need a reasonably precise measurement of the cost of capital. For a given company at a point in time, there are likely to be some capital structures that are better than others. To some extent we can judge their relative merits by measuring the cost of capital.

Finally, the cost of capital and the means used to measure it are significant to the economy as a whole. If measures of cost of capital are defective, so that cutoff rates are generally too high, the economy may not grow as rapidly as it might. Total investment in new plant and equipment will be lower than economically justified. If some firms employ cutoff rates that are too low, they will divert resources from more productive to less productive uses. By the same token, if governmental agencies use incorrect costs of capital in evaluating their capital expenditures, the same unfortunate results follow.[1] Thus, erroneous calculation of cost of capital both hampers the nation's rate of growth and produces suboptimal allocation of resources to meet our economic and social needs.

The purpose of this chapter is to indicate the analytical problems in determining the cost of capital and to demonstrate one approach to this task. It will quickly become apparent that this is not an area of hard and fast rules. Instead, it is a field still in the process of development and subject to a considerable amount of critical discussion. Moreover, any reasonably acceptable approach to determining the cost of capital must depend in part on forecasts. Because of the theoretical problems and the forecasts involved, it is most important that we do not consider the cost of capital to be one particular cutoff point. Rather it is a value encompassed by a broad boundary area. When we say that our cost of capital for a given amount of financing is 10 percent after taxes, we really mean that as net present value approaches zero, or as the discounted rate of return reaches the neighborhood of 10 percent, our examination should be increasingly rigorous. The cost of capital designates a "worry zone;" it is not a refined statistical measure.

Introduction

Having commented upon the crucial importance of the cost of capital, let us now turn to its definition, the assumptions that will underly our discussion, and a description of our plan of attack. In view of the ease of defining the cost of capital, it is disheartening to discover that it is so difficult to determine. Professor Myron Gordon has provided us with an excellent definition: "The cost of capital for a given firm is a discount rate with the property that an investment with a rate of profit above (below) this rate will raise (lower) the value of the firm."[2] Note that cost of capital is linked to the *value* of the firm, specifically, the market value. Thus the financial manager may *measure* his firm's cost of capital, and his policies may *affect* the cost of capital. But the ultimate *determination* of the cost of capital rests in the marketplace and is established by investors who manage their portfolios to achieve what each views as his optimal balance between risk and return.

---

[1] As illustration, see "Interest Rate Guidelines for Federal Decisionmaking," *Hearing* before the Subcommittee on Economy in Government of the Joint Economic Committee, U.S. Cong., 90th Cong., 2nd Sess., January 29, 1968 (Washington, D.C.: U.S. Government Printing Office, 1968).

[2] Myron J. Gordon, *The Investment, Financing and Valuation of the Corporation* (Homewood, Illinois: Richard D. Irwin, Inc., 1962), p. 218.

A basic assumption underlying our discussion of cost of capital is that there is no change in the risk class of assets. Essentially, we will develop a measure of the market's evaluation of the current risk class of the firm. That cost of capital is then applicable only to evaluation of proposed investments that keep the firm in its current line of business and risk class. As pointed out in the discussion of capital budgeting, a proposed investment in a new field that would carry the firm out of its risk class should be judged by using the cost of capital characteristic of firms operating in that new field.

It follows that after we have undertaken a new line of endeavor, the market will re-evaluate our firm and in this process establish a new cost of capital for our firm. For example, many sales finance companies are diversifying into new lines of business. C.I.T. Financial Corporation has acquired companies producing X-ray equipment and greeting cards. While the income of a finance company is relatively stable and its assets (mainly notes receivable) quite liquid, these features are not characteristic of the income streams and assets of manufacturing concerns. Continued diversification along these lines may cause investors to demand higher rates of return and so raise the cost of capital.

We undertake to measure the cost of capital *given* our existing capital structure. Analytical procedures are available for estimating costs of capital with varying capital structures, but would require development of a much more extensive model than space permits.[3] This is probably not too limiting an assumption. Minor changes in the capital structure do not affect the cost of capital greatly. In the real world of capital budgeting, estimates of labor savings, rates of technical obsolescence, and so on are probably subject to greater errors of estimation than is the cost of capital. Second, we can judge the effects of significant changes in our capital structure by measuring the costs of capital of other firms in the same industry which have significantly different capital structures. Therefore, the technique developed here for measuring the current cost of capital of a firm should have immediate applicability for a financial manager in spite of these limiting assumptions.

In developing a measure of cost of capital, we shall first compute the costs of the components of debt and equity. Then we will obtain a weighted average of the costs of the components. Finally, we shall draw some conclusions from the theoretical controversy concerning the effect of changes in capital structure upon the average cost of capital.

Costs of Debt and Equity

In estimating the cost of individual segments of debt and equity, we must keep in mind that we are interested in the cost expressed as a rate *after taxes.* This is because the cost of capital is to be used to compute the net present value of after-tax cash flows or to compare with a discounted rate of return derived from after-tax cash flows. In other words, we wish to compare apples to apples only after the Internal Revenue Service has taken its bite.

[3] I recommend my colleague's book. See Wilbur G. Lewellen, *The Cost of Capital* (Belmont, Calif.: Wadsworth Publishing Company, Inc., 1969).

Long-Term Debt — Bonds[4]

In the case of long-term debt we must again match the net amount that may be received from the issue against the obligation undertaken to make cash payments on the bond: Assume that we can obtain a net of $970 on the sale of a 10-year, $5\frac{1}{2}$ percent bond with a face value of $1000. In return for $970 today we must pay $55 per year for 10 years and $1000 at the end of the tenth year. What is the cost of this contract? There are two methods of estimating the cost: one accurate, the other approximate.

Accurate Method. Our experience with present value tables should lead us to suspect that this same approach is applicable to a precise calculation of the cost of the bonds. This is the case. In general terms, our problem is to solve for i in the equation below:

$$B = \frac{I}{(1+i)} + \frac{I}{(1+i)^2} + \cdots + \frac{I}{(1+i)^n} + \frac{D}{(1+i)^n}, \quad \text{where,} \qquad (11\text{-}1)$$

B = net proceeds of bond issue, or market price of bond,

I = annual dollar amount of interest to be paid on bond,

D = the face (or par) value of the bond, and

n = the number of years to maturity.

Inserting the data from our example, we have:

$$\$970 = \frac{\$55}{(1+i)} + \frac{\$55}{(1+i)^2} + \cdots + \frac{\$55}{(1+i)^{10}} + \frac{\$1000}{(1+i)^{10}}$$

More precise tables are needed for this calculation than shown in Appendix A, especially since most bond interest is actually paid semi-annually. Comprehensive bond tables are available that show the precise yield of the bond described above as 5.90 percent. However, the student of financial management should by now have an understanding of the basic principles underlying the construction of such bond tables.[5]

Approximate Method. For most practical purposes the approximate method will provide a sufficiently accurate estimate of the cost of debt. There are four steps to the approximate method: (1) Estimate the average amount of funds available to us over the ten years; (2) Calculate the average annual cost of those funds; (3) Compute the percentage of the average annual cost to the average amount of funds available; and (4) Adjust this rate to an after-tax basis.

We can receive a net amount of only $970 on the bond because investors believe that our interest payments are inadequate to support a higher price. By

---

[4] The after-tax cost of leases or rental agreements should also be calculated. However, this involves assumptions and computations of considerable complexity. Rather than give an easy, but incorrect, method of determining the cost of capital for leases, it seems advisable to postpone this problem to more advanced levels. For a sophisticated treatment of the problem see Richard F. Vancil, "Lease or Borrow—New Method of Analysis," *Harvard Business Review*, 39 (September-October, 1961), pp. 122–36; and William D. McEachron, "Leasing: A Discounted Cash-Flow Approach," *Controller*, 29 (May, 1961), pp. 213–19.

[5] Calculation of the cost of bonds that must be gradually retired through sinking fund payments is based on the same principle, but involves more tedious computations.

not making larger interest payments we are in a sense "holding back" funds annually from the bondholders. Although we start with $970 available, we accumulate funds through our "holdback" until they reach $1000 at the end of the tenth year. Thus the average amount of funds we will have in use during the 10-year period is $985.

$$\frac{\$970 + \$1,000}{2} = \$985$$

However, we must also take into account as a cost our ultimate obligation to repay an extra $30 over and above the amount that we received. Assume that this extra sum is spread equally over the ten interest payments, so that $3 is added to each payment ($30/10 years = $3 per year). Thus we can assume that we are paying an "average" of $58 per year to borrow an "average" of $985. Our approximate cost of long-term debt *before* taxes is 5.89 percent ($58/$985). We note that this is very close to the cost derived from a bond table.

Similar calculations are required if we receive more than the face amount for a bond. In either case the approximate yield may be calculated with the aid of a simple formula. Assume that the bond is to mature at $1000 in n years. Let B be the net proceeds and I be the annual dollar interest to be paid on the bond. Then we have:

$$\text{Approximate yield} = \frac{I + \dfrac{1,000 - B}{n}}{\dfrac{B + 1,000}{2}}$$

Whether we use the accurate or approximate method, the calculation of the cost of debt should be based upon the *market price* of the firm's debt. Although a company may have issued debt with a low coupon rate at some time in the past, the relevant issue for decision-making purposes is the current cost of debt for the on-going firm. This cost is determined by the price the market is willing to pay *now* for the future stream of cash payments that we promise on our debt.

Tax Adjustment. Since we wish all cost-of-capital rates to be on an after-tax basis, we must adjust the pre-tax interest rate on the bonds downwards to reflect the fact that it is a tax-deductible expense. If we again assume a corporate tax rate of 48 percent, the cost after taxes of the bonds is only 3.07 percent (0.52 × 5.89 percent). This adjustment assumes that the corporation is making a profit, so that the interest expense does serve to lower tax payments.

Preferred Stock

Recall that our agreement with preferred stockholders provides only that we will fulfill our dividend payments to them before paying any dividends to the residual owners—the common stockholders. To determine the cost of preferred stock we need to relate the expected annual dividend, d, to the market price of the preferred stock, P_0. The calculation will assume that there is no requirement that the stock be gradually retired. Although the preferred dividend is not a fixed obligation as in the case of interest on bonds, we would not ordinarily issue preferred stock unless we had every expectation of meeting the dividend payments. Under these assumptions, then, that we face an infinite and level stream of payments, we can determine the cost of preferred stock, k_p, by solving the following equation:

$$P_0 = \bar{d}/k_p \qquad (11\text{--}2)$$

$$k_p = \bar{d}/P_0 \qquad (11\text{--}3)$$

Recall that we have seen this equation before as representing the present value of an infinite stream of level cash flows. To illustrate its application, assume that we have an issue of preferred stock calling for an annual dividend of $3 per share, and that the market price is $40. Using equation (11–2), we find the cost of this preferred stock as follows:

$$k_p = \$3/\$40$$

$$= 7.5 \text{ percent}$$

Observe that this is the cost of capital *after* taxes, since the dividends on preferred stock are not a tax-deductible expense. Consequently, no tax adjustment is necessary.

Common Stock

Calculation of the cost of equity is subject to greater hazards than we faced in determining the cost of debt and preferred stock. For one thing, the returns are more uncertain. For another, the returns are unlikely to be constant, so that we cannot use present value tables that assume level annual flows.

Let us embark on determination of the cost of common stock by considering what determines its market value. A matter of some dispute in the past has been whether the value of common stock is based on earnings or dividends. The consensus has centered on dividends for a very good reason. Shareholders can spend cash dividends, but not reported earnings, certainly not the portion of earnings retained within the firm. Those retained earnings may provide future dividends, but stockholders cannot spend those until they receive them. Just as we evaluate a proposed capital expenditure in terms of the amount, timing, and risk of *cash* flows, so must our shareholders value our common stock in the marketplace.

With this fundamental tenet as a basis, let us consider the case of Western Power Co. Set a planning horizon of one year. What are we buying when we pay $50 for a share of common stock of Western? Assume that the dividend for the coming year is expected to be $3.00 per share, while earnings will be about $4.00. Earnings and prices have been rising at a compound annual rate of about 5 percent. Moreover, investment advisory services studied suggest that this rate of growth may be expected to continue in the foreseeable future. This means that our best estimate is that the market price of Western at the end of the year should be about $52.50 [$50(1 + 0.05)]. Let us insert these data into our familiar present value formula, using as the unknown rate of discount the cost of equity, k_e:

$$\underline{\text{Present price}} = \begin{array}{c}\textit{Present value of}\\ \textit{dividend at end}\\ \textit{of year}\end{array} \quad + \quad \begin{array}{c}\textit{Present value of}\\ \textit{expected market}\\ \textit{price at end of}\\ \textit{year}\end{array}$$

$$\$50 \quad = \quad \frac{\$3.00}{(1 + k_e)} \quad + \quad \frac{\$50(1 + 0.05)}{(1 + k_e)}$$

This may be expressed in general terms as

$$P_0 = \frac{\bar{d}_1}{(1 + k_e)} + \frac{P_0(1 + g)}{(1 + k_e)}, \quad \text{where} \tag{11-3}$$

P_0 = current market price of stock,
$\bar{d}_1$ = expected annual dividend at end of first year,
g = expected annual rate of growth of dividends per share,
k_e = cost of common stock equity.

If we solve this equation for k_e, we can arrange terms to obtain the following result:

$$(1 + k_e)(\$50) = \$3.00 + \$50 + \$2.50$$

$$\$50k_e = \$3.00 + \$2.50$$

Then:

$$\begin{array}{ccccc}\begin{array}{c}\textit{Cost of}\\ \textit{equity capital}\end{array} & = & \begin{array}{c}\textit{Expected}\\ \textit{dividend}\\ \textit{yield}\end{array} & + & \begin{array}{c}\textit{Expected}\\ \textit{capital gains}\\ \textit{yield}\end{array}\\ \\ k_e & = & \dfrac{\$3.00}{\$50.00} & + & \dfrac{\$2.50}{\$50.00}\end{array}$$

Let us put this relationship in general terms to arrive at a fundamental equation for the cost of equity capital:

$$k_e = \frac{\bar{d}_1}{P_0} + g \tag{11-4}$$

The data for Western are precisely those shown above, with the observation that $\$2.50/\$50.00 = 0.05 = g$:

$$k_e = \$3.00/\$50 + 0.05$$
$$= 0.06 + 0.05$$
$$= 11 \text{ percent}$$

In words, the cost of equity capital is the sum of the expected dividend yield and the expected rate of growth.

This was only a one-period example, but it may now be extended on the basis of two assumptions: (1) that the growth rate, g, is constant; and (2) that the growth in dividends at the rate g is expected to continue for an infinite period. We could relax these assumptions later without too much difficulty.

We can restate in general terms the original equation (11-3) for the market price of the common stock as shown below:

$$P_0 = \frac{\bar{d}_1}{(1 + k_e)} + \frac{P_0(1 + g)}{(1 + k_e)} \tag{11-3}$$

$$= \frac{\bar{d}_1}{(1 + k_e)} + \frac{P_1}{(1 + k_e)} \tag{11-5}$$

But just as the current price, P_0, represents the market's expectations of the coming year's dividend and the year-end price, so does P_1, the expected market price at the end of the first year, represent the market's expectations of the *following* year's dividend and year-end price given the growth rate, g. That is:

$$P_1 = \frac{\bar{d}_1(1 + g)}{(1 + k_e)} + \frac{P_1(1 + g)}{(1 + k_e)} \tag{11-6}$$

If we substitute the values shown for P_1 from (11-6) into (11-5), we obtain:

$$P_0 = \frac{\bar{d}_1}{(1 + k_e)} + \frac{1}{(1 + k_e)}\left[\frac{\bar{d}_1(1 + g)}{(1 + k_e)} + \frac{P_1(1 + g)}{(1 + k_e)}\right]$$

$$P_0 = \frac{\bar{d}_1}{(1 + k_e)} + \frac{\bar{d}_1(1 + g)}{(1 + k_e)^2} + \frac{P_1(1 + g)}{(1 + k_e)^2} \tag{11-7}$$

But we note that $\bar{d}_1 = d_0(1 + g)$, and that $P_1 = P_0(1 + g)$. Substituting these values in (11-7), we have:

$$P_0 = \frac{d_0(1 + g)}{(1 + k_e)} + \frac{d_0(1 + g)^2}{(1 + k_e)^2} + \frac{P_0(1 + g)^2}{(1 + k_e)^2} \tag{11-8}$$

We could continue this process by solving for P_2 in terms of expected future dividends and market price. But the point should be clear without becoming boring. We may assert that the current market price is equal to the present value of expected dividends over some planning horizon plus the present value of the market price at the end of that planning horizon. But the price at the end of the horizon is, itself, equal to the present value of still more expected dividends over a still longer planning horizon. In short, by carrying our expectation to infinity, we have:

$$P_0 = \frac{d_0(1 + g)}{(1 + k_e)} + \frac{d_0(1 + g)^2}{(1 + k_e)^2} + \cdots + \frac{d_0(1 + g)^\infty}{(1 + k_e)^\infty}. \tag{11-9}$$

$$P_0 = \sum_{t=1}^{\infty} \frac{\bar{d}_t(1 + g)^t}{(1 + k_e)^t}. \tag{11-9a}$$

This simplifies to a familiar form:[6]

$$k_e = \frac{\bar{d}_1}{P_0} + g. \tag{11-10}$$

[6] $P_0 = \sum_{t=1}^{\infty} \frac{d_0(1 + g)^t}{(1 + k_e)} = d_0 \sum_{t=1}^{\infty} \frac{(1 + g)^t}{(1 + k_e)^t}$

The sum of a geometric progression

$$\sum_{t=1}^{\infty} \frac{1}{(1 + x)^t} = \frac{1}{x}.$$

At this point someone may cry in alarm, "What about the firm, such as Control Data Corp., that does not pay dividends?" How does that fit into the formula for cost of equity capital? Although stockholders may not anticipate dividends in the near future, they must expect dividends at some point. Those expectations are expressed in the expected market price of the common stock at some point in the future. Stockholders are asked to put a lot of faith in the rate of growth, g, which will finally put the corporation in a position to pay out cash dividends. Were the corporation for some odd reason forbidden by its charter from ever paying dividends, stockholders would pay nothing for its common stock. It is no good to say that they will pay *something* in the hope that at some future date the price of the stock will rise in value. It will not rise above zero because in a rational market investors will not pay anything for a certain stream of zero dividends per share.

New Issue of Common Stock. As we shall see later, when a corporation issues common stock to new stockholders, the firm will net less than the current market price.[7] The group (called "underwriters") selling the stock for us will offer it to the public at a price slightly under the current market price in order to sell it promptly. Their compensation, or "spread," will further reduce the amount remitted to the corporation. In addition, the corporation must bear certain legal, accounting, and other issue expenses. Whereas such flotation and underpricing costs are relatively minor in the case of a new bond issue, they can range from about 5 percent to 30 percent in the case of a new issue of common stock.

To adjust for this deficiency in net receipts, we need to make a proportional increase in the calculated cost of common equity. It is a simple matter. If we let k_e' equal the cost of new issues of common stock, then

$$k_e' = \frac{k_e}{1-b}, \quad \text{where} \tag{11-11}$$

b = flotation costs and underpricing.

---

[6] We may define

$$\frac{1+g}{1+k_e} = \frac{1}{(1+x)}, \quad [g < k_e].$$

Then solving for x, we have

$$x = \frac{k_e - g}{1+g}.$$

Applying the rule for the sum of a geometric progression, our initial equation simplifies to

$$P_0 = d_0(1/x) = \frac{d_0(1+g)}{k_e - g}$$

Solving for k_e, we have:

$$k_e = \frac{d_0(1+g)}{P_0} + g = \frac{d_1}{P_0} + g.$$

Alternatively,

$$P_0 = \frac{d_1}{k_e - g}, \quad k_e > g.$$

Based on Lewellen, *op. cit.*, pp. 96–97.

[7] If the entire new issue is sold to existing shareholders, any discount arising in the sale does not affect the cost of common equity, k_e. See A. J. Merrett and Allen Sykes, *The Finance and Analysis of Capital Projects* (New York: John Wiley & Sons, Inc., 1962), p. 83.

As illustration, assume that Western's flotation and underwriting costs on new issues of common stock typically amount to 10 percent of the gross proceeds. We can then find our cost of new common stock to be 12.22 percent:

$$k_e' = \frac{0.11}{1 - 0.10} = 0.1222$$

Retained Earnings

If we assume that the corporation should serve the residual owners, retained earnings are certainly not costless. Had they been paid to the owners as dividends, the owners could have reinvested those returns and obtained additional earnings. Thus there is an opportunity cost involved in retained earnings, and it is this cost that we wish to focus upon.

Consider the issue from the viewpoint of the common shareholders. We observed in Chapter 2 that there are two different tax rates that apply to returns from their investment in common stock. Dividend income is subject to personal income tax rates, whereas capital gains are taxed at the capital gains tax rate, which is half of the applicable normal tax rate, but not greater than 25 percent. Other things being equal, the tax differential makes a yield from capital gains more attractive than a corresponding yield from dividends.

Given the assumed growing stream of cash dividends, the common stockholders of Western anticipate a yield before taxes of 11 percent. If one assumes a 35 percent personal tax rate, their yield after taxes will be 7.15 percent (11.0 × 0.65).[8] Rather than pay out cash dividends, Western could retain the earnings. If these earnings are reinvested within the firm at an adequate return, the market price of the stock should rise in anticipation of future payments of cash dividends. The impact on the common stockholders is twofold. First, if they sell their stock, the realized gain will be subject to a lower tax rate than dividend income. Second, a delay in the sale of the stock will also postpone the cash outflow for the capital gains tax. This makes the income from capital gains even more attractive. Recent economic studies suggest that the differential in tax rates and delay in realization of the gain produces an effective capital gains tax rate of about 10 percent.[9] If we let the cost of retained earnings be designated as k_r, we can see that the after-tax yield of a capital gain must then be $0.9k_r$. For the stockholders to be indifferent between after-tax capital gains and after-tax dividend income, it must be true that

After-tax capital gain	=	After-tax dividend income
$0.9k_r$	=	7.15 percent
k_r	=	7.94 percent

We are now in a position to make a general statement about the calculation of the cost of retained earnings by attaching symbols to the preceding calcula-

---

[8]This is based upon evidence concerning the tax rate applicable to the "average" investor. Vincent Jolivet, "The Weighted Average Marginal Tax Rate on Dividends Received by Individuals in the United States," *American Economic Review*, 56 (June, 1966), pp. 473–77.

[9]Martin J. Bailey, "Capital Gains and Income Taxation," in M. J. Bailey and A. C. Harberger, eds. *Taxation of Income from Capital*, (Washington, D.C.: Brookings Institution, 1969), pp. 11–49.

tions. Let t_p equal the personal tax rate and t_g equal the capital gains rate. The after-tax rates applicable to dividends and capital gains are then, respectively $(1 - t_p)$ and $(1 - t_g)$. The process that we followed above was to solve for k_r, the opportunity cost of retained earnings:

$$
\begin{array}{ccc}
\dfrac{\text{After-tax yield}}{\text{on capital gains}} & = & \dfrac{\text{After-tax yield}}{\text{from dividend}} \\
& & \text{income} \\[2mm]
k_r\,(1 - t_g) & = & k_e(1 - t_p) \\[2mm]
k_r & = & k_e\,\dfrac{(1 - t_p)}{(1 - t_g)}
\end{array}
\qquad \text{(11-12)}
$$

Applying the data from Western directly, we have

$$k_r = 0.11\,\frac{(1 - 0.35)}{(1 - 0.10)}$$

$$= 0.0794, \text{ or } 7.94 \text{ percent.}$$

The Weighted Cost of Capital

The Problem of Joint Costs

We have means of estimating the costs of the various types of funds that might be raised either internally or externally. It would appear relatively simple to estimate how a new machine or plant is going to be financed and then calculate the cost of capital for that investment. Thus if a firm simultaneously invests $5,000,000 in a new plant and equipment and floats a $5,000,000 issue of 8 percent bonds, it might be argued that the cost of capital for *that* investment is 4.2 percent (net after 48 percent taxes). Unfortunately, life is not so simple.

First of all, if we tried to associate each source of funds with a particular investment, we would have the chaotic situation in which a machine might be purchased with a rate of return of 5 percent because it was "financed with debt" during that month, while a machine offering a 20 percent return might be rejected next month because it would have to be "financed by a new issue of common stock." Although the cost of capital may change over time, its level at any one moment should not be dependent upon the current block of new financing.

But there is still another reason why we should view the cost of capital as a joint cost—a cost of a mixture of debt and equity. While a firm does not often float issues of debt and common stock in combination, each issue of debt is nonetheless dependent upon some equity base. An issue of debt increases the likelihood of further equity financing, via either retained earnings or new issues of stock. Even though this particular issue of debt may not unbalance the capital structure, over the long run we must expect to maintain adequate equity to support our borrowings. Similarly, a new issue of common stock is not as expensive as it might appear, since it provides a foundation for future, less costly issues of debt. Our capital is made available on a "package deal" basis, and it is the future cash payments that we must make on the entire mixture of capital sources that constitute our cost of capital.

The Weighting Procedure

The weighting procedure set forth is based upon the assumption that the corporation will continue to finance its needs over time in about the same proportions currently reflected in the market values of each source of funds.[10] Should the firm need $50 million, this does *not* mean that the $50 million offering of securities will be made up of proportionate shares of bonds, preferred stock, common stock, and retained earnings. Instead, we assume that over time these are roughly the proportions maintained, but that we may first float some common stock, later some bonds, while retaining a portion of earnings over the years. If we plan to change the capital structure, neither these weights nor the costs of the components of the capital structure will hold. To judge whether a heavier reliance on debt is desirable, we will have to measure the cost of capital of firms in the same industry (same risk class) that do depend more heavily on debt. Finally, to evaluate future capital expenditures, we must measure the cost of future, or *incremental,* financing. This requires that we measure the cost of new common stock after appropriate adjustment for flotation costs and underpricing.

Calculation of the weighted cost of capital for Western Power is illustrated in Table 11-1, using the costs of the various components of the capital structure developed above. Since common stock and retained earnings are not "quoted" separately in the market, their shares of the total market value of the common stock are based upon their book-value proportions applied to the aggregate market value of $216 million. The weighted cost of capital may be seen to be

TABLE 11-1   Weighted Cost of Capital, Western Power Co.

Capital Structure	Symbol	(1) After-tax Cost of Capital Rate	(2) Market Value*	(3) Proportion	(1) × (3) Weighted Cost
Bonds	i	3.07	$108	30%	0.92%
Preferred stock	k_p	7.50	36	10	0.75
Common stock	k_e'	12.22		20†	2.44
			216		
Retained earnings	k_r	7.94		40†	3.18
			$360	100%	7.29%

*In millions of dollars
†Computed as follows:

	Book Values	Proportion	Allocated Market Value	Proportion of Total
Common stock	$ 60	33⅓% × $216	$ 72	72/360 = 20%
Retained earnings	120	66⅔ × 216	144	144/360 = 40%
Totals	180	100%	$216	

[10] It is only fair to note that there is not universal agreement about whether to use book value or market value for weights. Since we measure costs in reference to the market, it is consistent to derive the weighting system from the market as well.

about 7.3 percent. To calculate the net present value of proposed investments from present-value tables Western might wish to provide a slight "safety margin" and use a discount rate of 7.5 percent possibly 8 percent.

Optimal Capital Structure

Another hotly debated issue in the field of financial management is whether or not there is an optimal mixture of debt and equity for a business firm—and, if so, how to identify that optimal mixture.[11] Recall, that in Chapter 3 we developed a model for the value of a levered firm:

$$V_L = \frac{Y(1 - t_c)}{k_a} + Dt_c, \quad \text{where} \tag{3-7a}$$

V_L = market value of a levered firm,

Y = expected annual net operating income before taxes,

t_c = corporate income tax rate, and

D = dollar amount of debt outstanding.

Although we did not pursue the issue in depth at the time, we at least raised the basic issue: If a little financial leverage is good, why is not more leverage even better? Let us show that equation (3-7a) leads precisely to the conclusion: the more debt the better. We can see why this is so by following forward with the data used in Chapter 3:

$$Y = \$10$$
$$t_c = 25\%$$
$$D = \$20$$

There are also eight shares of common stock outstanding, and total assets are $100. Filling in the data in (3-7a) we found

$$V_L = \frac{(\$10)(0.75)}{0.075} + (\$20)(0.25)$$

$$= \$105.$$

Since the debt has a market value of $20, the remaining aggregate value of the common stock must be $85, or $10.625 per share ($85/8 shares). Our model in equation (3-7a) suggests that an added dollar of debt does not result in a corresponding decline in the total market value of the common stock because

---

[11] Those wishing to review the historical development of theory in this area should turn to the "Selected References" at the end of the chapter. Of particular significance in this respect are the works of Barges, Baxter, Gordon, Vickers, and, of course, the two who initially sparked the controversy and thereby made a major contribution to the field, Franco Modigliani and Merton H. Miller.

of the tax advantage of the debt. Therefore, if $20 of debt is good, $50 should be better:

$$V_L = \frac{(\$10)(0.75)}{0.075} + (\$50)(0.25)$$

$$= \$112.50$$

With $50 of debt, we have only five shares of common stock with an aggregate market value of $62.50 [$112.50 − $50]. Thus the introduction of debt has raised the market price per share to $12.50 ($62.50/5 shares) from $11.625.

As we said in Chapter 3, "this is not an unlimited money tree that we have discovered." As we continue to raise the proportion of debt in our capital structure, two groups become uneasy. First, our creditors recognize that they are being faced with an increasing risk. Given variability in earnings, magnified further by financial leverage, they face a growing risk that the firm may not be able to meet its interest payments. Moreover, debt comes due, and if large amounts mature in a bad year, the firm may not be able to repay. These possibilities add to a risk of bankruptcy, or at least a long and agonizing reorganization. Since creditors are averse to this risk, we find, as noted in Chapter 10, that they have developed various rules of thumb that prescribe debt limits for business firms (as well as for governmental bodies). Such limits are related to the cyclical variations characteristic of the industry, the nature of competition, and the stage in its life cycle, as well as the specific characteristics of the borrower.

But the shareholders also become uneasy as the proportion of debt rises. They recognize that if the firm is unable to meet its obligations to creditors, it faces bankruptcy. As we noted in Chapter 10, the common stockholders are "last on the totem pole" and are likely to be left empty-handed after the firm has worked out its problems in bankruptcy court.

Prospective lenders express their unease, first, by demanding higher rates and more restrictive arrangements, and, finally, by refusing to loan at all. Stockholders demonstrate their unease in the marketplace. If the level of debt becomes oppressive, they discount the anticipated stream of dividends at a higher and higher discount rate, thereby lowering the market price per share. There is not a fixed level of debt to equity at which creditors and owners rebel. It is really more of an area of tolerance, as suggested by the shaded area in Exhibit 11-1. Nonetheless, there are limits on debt imposed by the market, so that the model indicated in equation (3-7a) applies only to the range from zero debt to "too much" debt.

How do we know that we are approaching the point of excessive debt? Our creditors tell us. First, agreements with long-term creditors usually contain restrictions on the amount of debt that can be incurred. Second, even without restrictions, efforts to float additional bonds may meet resistance. Our underwriters may urge that further issues would be unwise and show a persuasive lack of interest in selling the issue for us. If we persist, even in the face of these obstacles, the market will tell us by not buying the bonds.

Finally, how do we know that we have the "right amount" of debt, such that it will minimize our cost of capital and maximize the market value of the firm.

EXHIBIT 11-1   Effect of Leverage on Stock Price

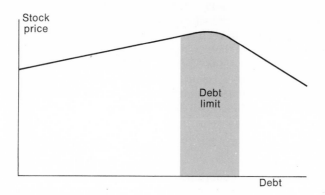

We will never know in any precise sense, but one possibility is to estimate the optimal mixture of debt and equity by determining the cost of capital for other firms in the same industry and risk class. With sufficient care in analysis and an adequate and homogenous sample,[12] we might expect to produce a scatter diagram relating cost of capital, ρ, to the ratio of debt to equity appearing somewhat as shown in Exhibit 11-2. However, it is not entirely clear that this degree of analysis is necessary. As suggested in the exhibit, we can rely on the market to police our trade-off between risk and return very well. Note that the cost of

EXHIBIT 11-2   Relation of Cost of Capital to Financial Leverage

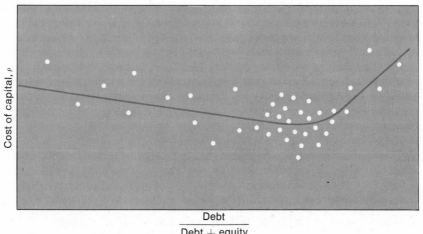

[12]These are not trivial constraints by any means.

258 Planning the Financial Structure

capital declines until we approach our debt limit. Thus, we are unlikely to go far wrong in our efforts to maximize the market value of the owners' equity if we pursue the use of debt until we begin to receive clear signals from creditors and owners that we are approaching our debt limit. Over the years the financial manager should attempt to keep his capital structure within reasonable bounds, such as the shaded "debt limit" range shown in Exhibit 11-1. He will not always be at the limit, since he will raise debt in "lumpy" amounts, it being uneconomical to sell a series of small issues of debt. This policy will both minimize his cost of capital and maximize the market price of the common equity. The latter is, of course, the basic objective of financial management.

Summary

The cost of capital is an opportunity cost established by the market. Its measurement is important both for use in capital budgeting and in the design of a capital structure that maximizes the value of the owners' equity. In our analysis we have assumed (1) that there will be no change in the riskiness of assets, and (2) that the present capital structure will be perpetuated in the same proportions currently reflected in the market value of the components of debt and equity. Estimates of the after-tax costs of debt and equity were also based on market values of the securities. The cost of debt is its yield to maturity, net after taxes, while the cost of preferred stock is simply the ratio of the annual dividend to its market price. The cost of outstanding common stock is that rate which equates the stream of future cash dividends to the market price of the stock, an approach directly analogous to the discounted rate of return. In our model we assumed a constant growth rate compounded annually over an infinite period of time. However, these assumptions could readily be adjusted without changing the premise of the basic model. The costs of additional common stock and retained earnings are derived with relative ease from the estimate of the cost of outstanding common stock. These estimates of the costs of debt and equity are then weighted by the market-value proportions of the capital structure to determine a weighted cost of capital. Since interest is a tax-deductible expense, finding the optimal capital structure turns out not to be an onerous task. The solution is to add debt until it becomes apparent from reactions by creditors and owners that the firm is approaching its debt limit.

Questions

1/ The discussion in this chapter centered on the calculation of the cost of capital for a corporation. Explain how these same principles would be applied to a sole proprietorship. At what points is the task easier, and at what points is it more difficult?

2/ Would you as an individual be willing to borrow funds at 6 percent, so long as you could continue to invest these funds in a franchised hamburger stand with anticipated earnings of 7 percent. Why or why not?

3/ Assume that corporations are classified into various groups according to the risk involved in their particular lines of business. If you observe corporations in a particular homogeneous group, would you expect them all to have about the same cost of capital? Why or why not? What would be the possible causes of any observed differences?

4/ During the latter part of 1970, Flying Tiger Lines, Inc. acquired a substantial interest in the North American Car Corporation, a railroad-car leasing company. Flying Tiger is an air cargo carrier. (*New York Times,* August 20, 1970, p. 51.) What effect do you think that this acquisition will have on Flying Tiger's cost of capital? Explain.

5/ We have suggested that management should decide on expansion by comparing the rate of return on proposed projects with the cost of capital. There are other possible goals that are employed from time to time. Analyze each critically.
   a. Accept projects that increase profit as a percentage of sales.
   b. Accept projects that provide a rate of return greater than the company's present return on capital (earnings before interest but after taxes divided by total long-term capital).
   c. Accept projects whose return is greater than the interest on long-term debt and dividends on common stock.

6/ Trace the effect of the following events upon a corporation's cost of capital and the relative attractiveness of the various possible components of the capital structure.
   a. An increase in federal corporate income tax rates.
   b. An increase in personal income tax rates.
   c. Abolition of the favored treatment of capital gains.
   d. An increased resistance of the economy to cyclical fluctuations.
   e. An increase in speculative interest in common stocks.

7/ Trace the effect of a decline in cost of capital upon capital expenditures. If you were in a policy-making position in government and wished to stimulate investment in plant and equipment, what actions could you take to influence the cost of capital? Explain carefully the nature of the influence.

8/ During a recent fiscal year the following discount rates (costs of capital) were used by Federal agencies to evaluate proposed capital expenditures:

Agriculture, rural electrification program	4.875%
Department of Defense, shipyard program	10.0
Department of Interior:	
Utility program, average risk	12.0
Aquatic living resources	3.1 and 6.0
Indian reservation resources development	3.1
Department of Health, Education and Welfare	
Cancer control	4.0 and 6.0

Analyze the effect of the discount rates used upon the "maximization of society's utility" from these capital expenditures. (*Interest Rate Guidelines for Federal Decision-making.* (Washington, D.C.: U.S. Government Printing Office, 1968), pp. 19–20.)

Problems

1/ In April, 1969, Kentucky Fried Chicken Corp. was selling for about $46 per share with an expected annual dividend of $0.10 per share. If we assume that this venture carries a relatively high risk, so that we may estimate a reasonable k_e at 15 percent, what is the market's estimate of the compound annual growth rate for an infinite time horizon?

2/ The Jos. Schlitz Brewing Company reports the following earnings per share:

1961	$0.71	1966	$1.80
1962	1.00	1967	2.02
1963	1.35	1968	1.73
1964	1.47	1969	2.17
1965	1.48		

At the time the financial vice president was calculating the cost of capital he found the market price of the common stock to be $60 per share. The anticipated dividend was $1.40. Because the firm was well known, he believed that new common stock could be sold at a discount of only 10 percent from the current market price. He planned to assume that his shareholders were on the average in marginal tax brackets of 35 percent and that their effective capital gains rate was 10 percent.

He planned to estimate the growth in dividends from the growth in earnings per share. Since the growth was reasonably steady, he planned to use the relationship: $(1961\ EPS)(1 + g)^8 = (1969\ EPS)$. Given this format, he felt that the growth rate could be estimated from present-value tables—just as he had made estimates of the discounted rate of return for capital-budgeting purposes.

The company had outstanding several issues of debt on which the average rate was about 9.1 percent. The firm was paying taxes at a rate of 52 percent of earnings. The market value was probably very close to the book value.

At the end of 1969, the firm's capital structure was as follows:

Long-term debt	$ 31,032,000
Common stock (issued 9,791,218 shares; par value $7.50)	73,434,000
Retained earnings	123,915,000

Problem: Prepare an estimate of the average cost of capital for the Jos. Schlitz Brewing Company.

3/ Calculate the average cost of capital for some large corporation assigned to you. Assume a corporate income tax rate of 48% unless otherwise notified. The following suggestions may prove helpful.
  a. Review the second paragraph in the previous problem for a clue to the procedure for estimating the growth of EPS.
  b. Bonds. Look up the current price of the bonds, the rate paid, and calculate the yield to maturity by the approximate method. If a bond issue has a sinking fund, assume that all bonds come due on the last maturity.

(This is theoretically incorrect, but it simplifies the calculations considerably.)

c. Preferred stock. Look up the current price of the stock and determine the yield directly from the dividend rate. Ignore any sinking fund requirements.

d. Assume that the expected dividend is equivalent to the dividends for the last 12 months, as reported in the *Wall Street Journal* or other source. Assume that underpricing and flotation costs on a new issue will amount to 10%.

e. Retained earnings. Assume $t_p = 35\%$, and $t_g = 10\%$.

Selected References

ARCHER, S. H. and L. G. FAERBER, "Firm Size and the Cost of Externally Secured Equity Capital," *Journal of Finance,* 21 (May, 1966), pp. 69–83.

ARDITTI, F. D., "Risk and the Required Return on Equity," Journal of Finance, 22 (March, 1967), 19–36.

BARGES, A., *The Effect of Capital Structure on the Cost of Capital.* Englewood Cliffs, N.J.: Prentice Hall, Inc., 1963.

BAUMOL, W. J. and B. G. MALKIEL, "The Firm's Optimal Debt-Equity Combination and the Cost of Capital," *Quarterly Journal of Economics,* 81 (November, 1967), pp. 547–78.

BAUMOL, W. J., "On the Social Rate of Discount," *American Economic Review,* 58 (September, 1968), pp. 788–802. Provides insights on the discount rate appropriate for investment decisions by non-profit and government organizations.

BAXTER, N. D., "Leverage, Risk of Ruin and the Cost of Capital," *Journal of Finance,* 22 (September, 1967), pp. 395–403.

BERANEK, W., *The Effect of Leverage on the Market Value of Common Stock.* Madison: Bureau of Business Research and Service, University of Wisconsin, 1965.

BONESS, A. J., "A Pedagogic Note on the Cost of Capital," *Journal of Finance,* 19 (March, 1964), pp. 99–106.

GORDON, M. J., *The Investment, Financing, and Valuation of the Corporation.* Homewood, Illinois: Richard D. Irwin, Inc., 1962.

LERNER, E. M. and W. T. CARLETON, "The Integration of Capital Budgeting and Stock Valuation," *American Economic Review,* 54 (September, 1964), pp. 683–702.

LEWELLEN, W. G., *The Cost of Capital.* Belmont, Calif.: Wadsworth Publishing Company, Inc., 1969.

MAO, J. C. T., *Quantitative Analysis of Financial Decisions.* Toronto: Collier-Macmillan Canada, Ltd., 1969. Ch. 10–12.

MILLER, M. H. and F. MODIGLIANI, "Some Estimates of the Cost of Capital to the Electric Utility Industry, 1954–57," *American Economic Review* 56 (June, 1966), pp. 333–91.

MODIGLIANI, F. and M. H. MILLER, "The Cost of Capital, Corporation Finance and the Theory of Investment," *American Economic Review,* 48 (June, 1958), pp. 261–97.

_____, "Corporate Income Taxes and the Cost of Capital: A Correction," *American Economic Review,* 53 (June, 1963), pp. 433–43.

PFAHL, J. K., D. T. CRARY, and R. H. HOWARD, "The Limits of Leverage," *Financial Executive,* 38 (May, 1970), pp. 48–50ff.

SCHWARTZ, E., "A Note on the Cost of Capital, Leverage, Dividends and the Corporate Veil," *Southern Economic Journal,* 31 (July, 1964), pp. 58–61.

SLOANE, W. R. and A. REISMAN, "Stock Evaluation Theory: Classification, Reconciliation, and General Model," *Journal of Financial and Quantitative Analysis,* 3 (June, 1968), pp. 171–204.

STIGLITZ, J. E., "A Re-Examination of the Modigliani-Miller Theorem," *American Economic Review,* 59 (December, 1969), pp. 784–93.

TINSLEY, P. A., "Capital Structure, Precautionary Balances, and Valuation of the Firm: The Problem of Financial Risk," *Journal of Financial and Quantitative Analysis,* 5 (March, 1970), pp. 33–62.

VICKERS, D., "The Cost of Capital and the Structure of the Firm," *Journal of Finance,* 25 (March, 1970), 35–46.

WIPPERN, R. F., "Financial Structure and the Value of the Firm," *Journal of Finance,* 21 (December, 1966), pp. 615–34.

Part Four

Management of Short- and Intermediate-Term Funds

Trade Credit and Commercial Paper

12 Once we have decided upon the nature of our need for funds, the next step in financial management is to secure the funds. The chapters which follow cover the sources of funds, and are arranged according to the period of time for which the funds are obtained, beginning with short-term funds and concluding with long-term funds. There are certain inherent limitations to this approach. First of all, there is really no clear-cut line that distinguishes a short-term loan from an intermediate-term loan, or an inter-mediate-term loan from a long-term loan. Furthermore, an arrangement which begins as a short-term loan may become a long-term loan through inability of the borrower to repay in the specified time. Sudden good fortune may convert a long-term financing arrangement into a short-term contract. Second, various financial institutions may be sources of more than one type of funds. For example, banks typically make short-term loans, but many also make loans for five, and sometimes ten, years. In spite of these drawbacks, the division of chapters according to the term of the financing makes sense. The financial manager first determines the type of funds he needs and then seeks to learn what financial institution is likely to provide him with that kind of money. He does not decide to borrow from a bank and then investigate the loan arrangements available for banks.

In Chapter 10 we discussed the various factors determining the types of funds needed. The great variation among companies suggests that any figures showing average proportions of short-, intermediate-, and long-term funds are likely to be rather poor averages. However, it was apparent that manufacturing concerns generally relied more heavily on short-term debt than did utilities, such as electric and gas companies, and corporations in the field of transportation. Even greater reliance was placed on short-term credit by companies in the retail and wholesale trades. In our discussion of the major sources of short-term credit in this and the following chapter, we should keep in mind the principal types of concerns that depend most heavily upon this source of funds.

Meaning and Extent of Use of Trade Credit

Probably the most common form of short-term debt is that which is termed *trade credit or mercantile credit*. Although it may not total to as much in dollars as other forms of credit, practically every firm, whether a sole proprietorship, partnership, or corporation, has some form of trade credit. We may define trade credit as short-term credit extended by a supplier to a buyer in conjunction with the purchase of goods for ultimate resale. By restricting this to short-term credit, we intend to omit arrangements for the installment purchase of machinery and equipment which typically provide for the extension of credit over some period of time. Because we are speaking only of credit extended in connection with the purchase of goods, the definition eliminates direct loans from the supplier to his customer or any loan from one business to another. By the use of the words "for ultimate resale," we are also excluding *consumer credit,* that is, credit given by a retailer to a consumer so that he might purchase goods.

It is somewhat difficult to tell just how much trade credit is used, because compilations of data such as shown in Chapter 10 rarely follow the precise definition of trade credit which has been given here. However, analysis of the data suggests that the firms making the greatest use of trade credit were in manufacturing and the wholesale and retail trades. Some additional data on a much larger sample of manufacturing firms at the beginning of 1970, also reveal that there is a great deal of variation in their use of trade credit.[1] Companies manufacturing apparel and other finished products financed 18.6 percent of their assets from trade credit, and manufacturers of dairy products used trade credit to finance something over 14 percent of their assets. At the other extreme, companies making very little use of trade credit were manufacturers of alcoholic beverages (5.5 percent) and tobacco products (5.1 percent).

It is also generally true that small companies make a relatively greater use of trade credit than do large concerns. Whereas firms with assets under $1 million financed 17.4 percent of their assets with trade credit, those with assets

---

[1] Federal Trade Commission and Securities and Exchange Commission, *Quarterly Financial Report for Manufacturing Corporations* (First quarter, 1970), pp. 12–33.

of $1 billion and over used trade credit to finance only 6.9 percent of their assets.[2] The dependence of small companies on trade credit frequently enables them to obtain funds during periods when short-term money is otherwise both difficult and expensive to obtain. Large corporations typically borrow under favorable terms, then make some of this money available to their customers through the media of trade credit. This is not entirely a friendly, self-sacrificing gesture, of course. By providing additional trade credit when it is needed, the large corporations hope to enable their customers to survive and be suitably loyal.

Forms of Trade Credit

Open Account

The most common form of trade credit is the open account. This can best be explained by tracing its origin. We usually set the process in motion by sending our supplier a purchase order. At the time he ships the order he will send us an invoice which describes the items shipped, their selling price, and the terms of sale. The only evidence our supplier has of the credit that he has extended to us is our original purchase order, the copy of the invoice which he has retained, and an entry in his books to record the receivable. We do not ordinarily provide our supplier with any more formal acknowledgment of our debt to him. The system is advantageous because of its simplicity. It is a mark of the progress we have made as an economy based on credit that the great bulk of trade credit is extended in this somewhat informal fashion.

Trade Acceptance

In a few lines of business the trade acceptance is still used. Let us follow a transaction involving trade credit based on a trade acceptance. After receiving our order and checking our credit, our supplier will ship the goods ordered. However, the supplier will submit through a local bank the shipping documents and a *draft*—an order for us to pay him the amount owed. When we sign this draft, we *accept* it; that is, we formally acknowledge a debt to the supplier payable at some specified date. Upon acceptance, the local bank will turn over the shipping documents that will enable us to obtain the goods ordered. The bank then returns the trade acceptance to our supplier. He may sell it to his bank to secure funds for his own use or he may hold it. In any case, in due time the trade acceptance will be sent to the bank we have designated on the acceptance for collection. The bank will notify us to pay the debt, which we originally acknowledged by accepting the draft, and will remit our payment to the holder of the acceptance, less the bank's usual fee, of course.

What has all this paper work accomplished? Most important, it has given our supplier a legal document that is a clear acknowledgment of our debt to him. We cannot claim we do not owe him the money, or that we do not owe him that particular amount of money, because our signature is there on the face of

[2] *ibid.*, pp. 29 and 33.

the acceptance. The trade acceptance has two other advantages to the supplier. He can use it to raise funds from his own bank if he needs to. In addition, when the time for collection comes he is in a very strong position, for we are very unlikely to damage our credit reputation by failing to pay when notified by the bank. It is one thing to fail to pay an open account promptly, but quite another to ignore the presentation of a trade acceptance by our bank. Clearly the trade acceptance is a fine thing for the supplier, but puts the buyer under rigid requirements. It is for this reason that competition among suppliers for business has tended to rule out the trade acceptance in favor of the open book account.

Promissory Note

A promissory note is an unconditional written promise made by one person to another to pay on demand or at a specified time a certain sum of money to order or to bearer. As used in trade credit, promissory notes almost always call for payment of the debt at some future date, rather than on demand. There are two main occasions for the use of promissory notes in connection with trade credit. In some lines of business, such as wholesale jewelers, milling companies, and dealers in raw and dressed furs, it is customary to use promissory notes in the ordinary course of business rather than open accounts. In other lines of business, if a supplier finds that a customer is well overdue on his account, he may request a promissory note in order to obtain a formal acknowledgment of the debt and a commitment as to the date when it will be paid. Thus the customer gains more time in exchange for his promissory note. This is probably the more common use. Consequently, if "notes payable—trade" suddenly crops up on the balance sheet of one of our customers, we should view this account with a properly jaundiced eye.

The promissory note does not give the creditor any more security than if he had a probable claim in the form of an open account. As in the case of the trade acceptance, it simply reduces the possibility of an argument that the claim exists. Again, when a promissory note is presented through a bank for collection, the pressure on the customer for full and immediate payment is more effective than collection letters from the supplier's credit department. Any promissory notes or trade acceptances would appear on the books of the customer as "notes payable," rather than as accounts payable, which would represent trade credit received on an open book account.

Terms of Trade Credit

There are three possible aspects of trade credit terms that we should understand as an aid to effective use of this form of credit:

(1) The size of the discount, if any, from the invoice price for making cash payment within a specified time period. This discount is termed the *cash discount*. It should be distinguished from the *trade discount* and *quantity discount*. The trade discount is a percentage reduction from the invoice price given to firms at various levels in the channel of distribution. For example, if a manufacturer offers discounts of 40–20 from the list, or invoice, price of

$1.00, it might indicate that the retailer would pay the wholesaler $0.60 ($1 less 40 percent), and the wholesaler would pay the manufacturer $0.48 ($0.60 less 20 percent). The quantity discount is a percentage reduction from the invoice price given for purchasing certain minimum amounts of the item. Thus a discount of 5 percent might be given for buying at least a gross of a particular item.

(2) The period of time within which payment must be made if the cash discount, if any, is to be earned. The period of time is usually fairly short, ten or 20 days.

(3) The period of time which can elapse before payment of the bill if the cash discount is not taken. When no cash discount is offered, it is simply the period allowed for payment of the invoice or bill.

Trade credit terms vary greatly. We shall discuss them in the order of liberality of the period of time given to make payment.

C.B.D. — Cash before Delivery

Because we must pay for the goods before the supplier will ship them, these terms involve no credit at all. When a supplier imposes these terms he either knows nothing about us or he knows our reputation all too well. In fact, if he is so doubtful of our reliability that he uses such terms, he will probably wait until our check clears before making shipment on our order.

C.O.D. — Cash on Delivery

Under these terms the supplier ships the goods by mail or express, and we must pay for the goods before taking possession. The supplier takes the risk that we will not pay and he will have to pay the costs of shipping the merchandise both ways.

S.D. — B.L. — Sight Draft, Bill of Lading Attached

If our supplier elects to sell on these terms, he will ship the goods and send a sight draft and bill of lading to our bank. Because this is a sight draft, we must immediately pay the amount demanded on the face of the draft in order to obtain the bill of lading. These credit terms are characteristically used by meat packers, when shipping carload lots, and by fruit and vegetable canners.

Cash Terms

Odd as it may seem, in mercantile credit "cash terms" involve some extension of credit. Cash terms may be expressed in various ways, such as net cash, net 10 days, and bill to bill. Generally, all of these terms mean that the buyer has a week to ten days to make payment. Thus, by trade custom "net cash" may mean that the buyer has seven or ten days in which to pay the bill. Terms of net 7 days are found on purchases of cigars, cigarettes, and tobacco; fresh fruits and produce; meat and poultry. Retailers frequently purchase butter, eggs, and cheese on terms of net 10 days. When "bill-to-bill" terms are used in these trades, the bill for the previous delivery is collected at the time a new delivery is made. In effect, this is usually equivalent to terms of net 7 days.

Ordinary Terms

Such trade credit terms call for the allowance of a cash discount if the bill is paid within ten or 20 days of the date on the invoice and for payment of the bill in full in 30 or 60 days. A typical example would be the credit terms of 2/10, n/30 offered by wholesalers of plumbing and heating supplies. This means that if the bill is paid within ten days of the date of the invoice, a discount of 2 percent may be deducted from the face amount of the invoice. If the cash discount is not taken, the full amount of the bill must be paid within 30 days. When the buyer is some distance away or the method of shipment is slow, terms may be 2/10, n/30 A.O.G. (arrival of goods). This arrangement affords the buyer the opportunity of inspecting the goods before paying for them. More important, it provides all buyers with equal opportunity to sell the goods and repay the account, regardless of their distance from the point of shipment.

Monthly Billing

In some lines of business where a number of orders may be delivered during a month, it would be uneconomical to keep track of cash discounts on each invoice. Consequently, it is the practice to allow the buyer to make a single payment covering all his purchases during the month. He is entitled to a cash discount if payment is made by a certain date in the following month. For example, manufacturers of leather luggage frequently sell on terms of 2/10, E.O.M. n/30. Latin students sometimes express the same arrangement as 2/10 prox. n/30. "Prox." is an abbreviation for the Latin word "proximo," which as we all know means "the next." Under these terms a cash discount of 2 percent will be allowed on all purchases during March if payment is made before April 10. Payment in full must be made by April 30. Since many merchants would be loath to buy on March 30 and pay for the goods ten days later, it is frequently customary to consider the 25th as the end of the month. By this arrangement merchandise purchased from the manufacturer on March 30 must be paid for by May 10 in order to receive a cash discount; the buyer has thus received trade credit for about 40 days.

In some lines of business the cash discount is so high that it really amounts to a trade discount. For example, many manufacturers of dresses sell on terms of 8/10 E.O.M. Since it would be financial suicide to miss out on such a large discount, buyers would almost universally take the discount, and it ceases to have much meaning as a cash discount. Such terms are found mostly in the apparel trades.

Seasonal Dating

These credit terms are probably as much for the convenience of the supplier as the buyer. They are designed to encourage buyers to send in orders for seasonal goods before the period of peak sales so that the supplier can judge his market and level out his production and shipping activities as much as possible. For example, textbook publishers encourage university bookstores to send in their orders for fall in the early part of the summer with the understanding that shipments on the orders will be made at the convenience of the publisher. In return for this favor, publishers allow terms of n/30 October 1. This allows the bookstore until October 30 to settle its bill, even though it may have ordered and received the books sometime during July. Similar dating arrangements are found on sales of toys and holiday greeting cards.

Consignments

A supplier may be willing to grant us credit for the entire period that we hold goods before their sale. Under this arrangement he would ship us the goods, but retain title to them while we hold them for sale. When we sold the goods, we would send the supplier the amount realized on their sale, less our gross profit; or we might send him the gross amount from sales until we had paid for all the goods consigned to us. We have the right to return any unsold goods to the supplier. By this arrangement the supplier is providing all the financing for inventory. He may be willing to do this because he wants to get a new product on display or because he wants to put on a big sale of some item. These terms are common in the magazine publishing business. Retail stores grant display areas to distributors who stock the magazine racks. Each week the route men collect the cost of magazines sold and take back any periodicals that are out of date.

The variations in trade credit terms make a certain amount of sense. First, the period of credit granted is related to the nature of the commodity. Items having a high turnover, such as meats, groceries, and cigarettes are sold on fairly short credit terms. High style items or merchandise that is in the nature of a fad may carry fairly short terms, because the supplier is not willing to bear the risk of obsolescence. Second, the credit risk involved is reflected in terms. Retail shops in the apparel trades are characterized by a rather high rate of failure. This may explain in part the rather large cash discount allowed; it represents an effort by the supplier to get his money in as quickly as possible. Individual credit applicants who are particularly weak may be forced to buy on C.B.D. or C.O.D. terms. Third, the nature of competition among suppliers is expressed in credit terms as well as in price and service. A few large buyers will probably obtain better credit terms from a large group of sellers than if the situation were reversed. When the product or the seller is new, the granting of easier credit terms than are customary may be one of many methods used by the seller to gain a foothold in the market. During a recession sellers may ease their credit terms in an effort to maintain sales. Finally, the financial strength of the seller relative to that of the buyer is also a determinant of credit terms. Although it might appear that a strong seller could dictate stringent terms, he may succeed only in putting his customers out of business. In some trades the retailers must be carried along by their financially stronger suppliers. On the other hand, if the supplier is especially weak, he may have to restrict his credit terms in order to survive himself. He must speed his inflow of cash, even at the sacrifice of sales and profits. Although relative bargaining strength plays a large part in determining credit terms, neither side can push its advantage to the extent that the other party is forced into financial difficulties.

Cost of Trade Credit

There is both an explicit and implicit cost to the use of trade credit. An explicit cost arises when we fail to pay on time so that we lose our cash discount. Let us assume that credit terms are 2/10, net 30. If the invoice is for $100, the real cost of the goods is $98, and $2 is *added* to the cost as a finance charge if we fail to pay by the 10th day.[3] Because we should pay by the 30th day in any case, we will have used our supplier's funds for an additional 20 days (from the tenth day to the 30th day). The effective rate for those 20 days is 2/98, and there are 365/20 20-day intervals during the year. Thus the true annual cost of missing the cash discount is

$$2/98 \times 365/20 = 0.3724, \text{ or } 37.24 \text{ percent.}[4]$$

Even if no cash discounts are allowed, there is an implicit cost of trade credit. The supplier must set up a credit department to approve our order, to keep the necessary records, to pursue us for payment if necessary, and to cover any losses on bad debts. Our account payable is the supplier's account receivable, and he must secure funds at a cost to carry these accounts. Like all his other operating costs, these costs of granting credit must be covered in the long run by the prices the supplier charges.

There is still another cost of trade credit which should be considered by the financial manager. If our liquidity position is especially weak, we will have to seek out those suppliers that grant the most lenient trade credit terms. No supplier can consistently give unusually lenient terms without incurring additional expenses in his credit department and without having to secure additional funds himself to finance his enlarged accounts receivable. To remain in business he will have to pass these costs on to us in some way. In relation to his less lenient competitors he may possibly charge higher prices, or sell lower quality merchandise, or render poorer service. Thus the supplier will increase our costs in one way or another, and our efforts to preserve our liquidity will be at the sacrifice of our profitability. This is not to say that the decision to seek out lenient suppliers would be a bad one; in fact, if we are to stay in business we may have no other choice.

Reasons for Use of Trade Credit

Cost

If we take all available cash discounts, the use of trade credit ordinarily adds nothing to our costs. For this reason, it is a very desirable form of credit. As indicated earlier, the price we are charged must in the long run cover all the

---

[3] The cost of purchase discounts missed is often incorporated in "Purchases" and carried through to "Cost of Goods Sold," which is a tax-deductible expense. In other cases a separate expense, "Purchase Discounts Missed," may be shown (also tax-deductible). The latter is the preferable procedure, since it sharply highlights the cost of the failure of the financial manager to pay his bills promptly.

[4] This is the mathematical procedure required for disclosure of the annual percentage rate to consumers and farmers under the Consumer Credit Protection Act as specified in the accompanying Regulation Z, Section 226.8(o).

costs of the supplier, including the costs of his credit department. Since the credit cost is already buried in the price, we pay something extra to use the credit only if we fail to take cash discounts offered. If we could find a supplier who would lower the price for immediate cash payment, we could avoid this concealed charge for trade credit. Since this is not ordinarily possible, we finance our purchases through trade credit at "no cost" to ourselves. However, it is only "no cost" in the same sense that the supplier does not make a separate charge for many of the other services that he provides along with the goods he sells.

Since the supplier does not levy a specific additional charge for the use of trade credit, it also follows that it ordinarily costs nothing additional to use trade credit to the fullest extent. If we are buying goods on credit, it is economical to use the full period of the cash discount or, if no cash discount is allowed, the full period of net credit terms. If we are buying on terms of net 30, the price is the same whether we pay on the 5th or the 30th day. We pay nothing extra to use the supplier's money the additional 25 days. Indeed, it adds nothing to our costs at the time not to pay the bill promptly and to use the supplier's credit for 45 days. However, this misuse of trade credit may make it difficult for us to secure credit elsewhere, not only from other suppliers, but from banks and other lenders as well. Consequently, failure to pay bills on time may raise our long-run cost.

Liberality

Many business firms are able to obtain trade credit at times when no financial institution will lend them money. This is particularly true of companies that are small or newly established. Basically, a supplier regards credit as a sales aid. Consequently, he evaluates the cost of liberal credit terms against the costs and effectiveness of other methods of competition, such as price reductions, advertising programs, and bonuses for the salesmen. The supplier makes his profit by selling a "package" which includes the product and various services, such as credit. What he loses by providing credit he can recover by charging a higher price on the product or by cutting other services. Nor does he view each transaction in isolation. Rather than reject our purchase order, he is likely to accept it in the hope that it is the prelude to a steady stream of profitable purchase orders. In contrast, the granting of credit is the main function of a financial institution and, to a considerable extent, each loan must pay for itself. Since the interest charge may be the only source of income on a loan, a lending institution, such as a bank, must choose its loans with care to relate the degree of risk it can afford to assume to the interest charge it can levy. Because its margin of profit is less ample than that of the typical grantor of trade credit, a bank simply cannot afford to assume the same degree of risk. In addition, the loan activities of banks are carefully scrutinized by various state and federal agencies. To satisfy these auditors and to protect their depositors, bankers must be especially cautious in extending credit.

We are also able to obtain liberal trade credit because the supplier does not examine our financial position with the same degree of care that a bank or other financial institution would. Not only is a supplier willing to assume more risk, but he cannot afford to review each credit application in detail. Whereas a bank might have several hundred loans outstanding, a large manufacturer might have thousands of customers scattered all over the country. If he examined the financial statements and operations of each of these customers with the same care that a bank would employ, our supplier would have very low credit losses. However, the level of his sales would probably decline to a point where they would not be high enough to support the high costs of his credit department.

Convenience

It takes very little effort to get into debt when using trade credit. Customarily there are no formal applications to fill out, no notes to sign, and no rigid repayment dates. Should we fail to meet a payment on a promissory note to the bank, we may be forced into bankruptcy. If we are occasionally a little late in paying a supplier, we do relatively little or no harm to our credit reputation.

Flexibility

Trade credit is useful because we can use it when we need it. Accumulation of inventory to meet a seasonal bulge in sales is financed in part by an automatic swelling of trade credit. Then as we enter the selling season we can gradually reduce our accounts payable from collections on our own accounts receivable.

In contrast, a loan secured by a mortgage on our plant and equipment cannot be changed day-by-day to match seasonal movements in inventory. Since trade credit is directly related to inventory and sales, it provides an element of flexibility needed in our sources of funds. Trade credit also contributes to the flexibility of our financing in another sense. Because trade creditors seldom ask that we pledge assets to secure our debts, the use of trade credit leaves our assets unencumbered. We are then in a better position to seek additional funds elsewhere and to offer some of our assets as security. This freedom is not unlimited, however. Should we attempt to secure additional funds by pledging to others a substantial portion of our most valuable and liquid assets, our suppliers may request that they be equally well secured.

Maintaining Trade Credit

The best way to assure continued favorable relations with firms supplying trade credit is to manage our financial affairs properly. In particular this means attention to our liquidity function so that we pay bills when due. It is not only important to our profitability to take cash discounts, but it is also important to our credit reputation to be known as a company that "discounts" its accounts payable. As we saw in the discussion on the management of our own accounts receivable, information on the payment habits of most firms is quite readily available. If we are to continue to secure trade credit, we must see to it that the reports on our own company are favorable.

Relations with trade creditors are also enhanced by a willingness to provide them with information. Many firms make it a practice to send their annual statements promptly to their principal creditors. It is probably even more important to provide full information to credit rating agencies, such as Dun and Bradstreet. Some business managers seem to regard requests for information by Dun and Bradstreet as an invasion of their privacy. They should recognize that their secrecy may encourage suppliers to respect their privacy by extending them no credit.

Excessive use of trade credit is often the immediate cause of business failure. Because it is easy to obtain in relation to most other forms of credit, there is sometimes a tendency to base a company's expansion upon trade credit rather than upon the residual owners' equity. But growth in trade credit is usually inadequate to keep up with the increase in assets in a rapidly expanding concern. Ultimately, accounts become so delinquent that trade creditors call a halt to further extensions; then the company may have no place to turn. Since it has used up its most lenient source of credit, it can hardly expect to be received warmly by less tolerant credit grantors. Consequently, the sequel is often failure; at best it is an agonizing financial readjustment.

Commercial Paper

Commercial paper consists of short-term unsecured promissory notes. The minimum denomination is typically no less than $25,000 and often no less than $100,000 to $1,000,000. The maturity is seldom for more than 270 days, since a longer maturity would require registration of the issue with the Securities and Exchange Commission. Although the volume of commercial paper outstanding more than quadrupled from the end of 1964 to mid-1970, (Exhibit 12-1), it does not provide as much funds to commerce and industry as short-term bank loans. At mid-1970, commercial paper amounted to less than a third of commercial and industrial loans outstanding at commercial banks. This relationship should not obscure the fact that for large companies with an excellent credit reputation, particularly finance companies, commercial paper is an important source of short-term credit.

Sale of Commercial Paper

Commercial paper may be sold through dealers or placed directly. Industrial firms, utilities, small finance companies, and more recently, bank holding companies, sell their paper through dealers, who typically receive a "spread" of $\frac{1}{8}$ of 1 percent on prime paper and $\frac{1}{4}$ of 1 percent on other paper for their marketing services. The market is well-organized and highly impersonal. The treasurer of one utility commented, "I keep the blank forms in my desk, and when I want $10-million or so I just fill out one and send it down to the dealer by messenger."[5]

Large finance companies and some bank holding companies sell their commercial paper directly to investors without the use of middlemen, and are willing to sell notes of any maturity desired from two days to 270 days. Over three-fifths of the paper outstanding at mid-1970 had been sold directly.

[5]"Money Men Put Their Bets on Paper," *Business Week*, July 19, 1969, p. 73.

EXHIBIT 12-1   Commercial Paper Outstanding, by Issuer

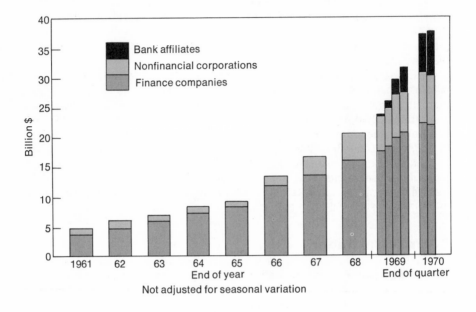

Not adjusted for seasonal variation

Source: U.S. Department of Commerce, Office of Business Economics.

A recent innovation in commercial paper has been *documented discount notes.* Under this arrangement a bank that is short on loanable funds guarantees by a letter of credit the commercial paper to be issued by a small corporate borrower. The contingent liability undertaken by the bank provides the backing necessary for the business firm to sell its paper through dealers.

The principal purchasers of commercial paper are nonbank financial institutions, such as mutual funds, insurance companies, and pension and retirement funds. Other buyers are business corporations with excess funds and commercial banks outside of the money centers of New York and Chicago. The rapid growth of commercial paper in recent years has been a double-edged sword for the banks. On the one hand, corporations with excess funds have withdrawn deposits from the banks to buy commercial paper for its relatively attractive yield. On the other hand, some prospective borrowers have favored commercial paper, rather than bank loans. Thus the rise of commercial paper has cut into the growth of commercial bank deposits and loans. It was partly to answer this threat to their deposits that commercial banks began to issue the certificates of deposit discussed in Chapter 5. However, when the Federal Reserve Board maintains a lower ceiling on CD's than the market rate, funds drain rapidly from CD's into treasury bills and commercial paper.

Role of Commercial Banks

Although commercial banks are not so important as nonbank investors as a source of funds in the commercial paper market, they are significant in another sense. Corporations wishing to sell their commercial paper usually must first have lines of credit at leading commercial banks. For corporations other than large finance companies, unused lines (open-to-borrow arrangements) should equal outstanding commercial paper. This backstop by bank lines is deemed necessary because of the highly impersonal nature of the commercial paper market. Because many issuers of commercial paper simply replace one maturing issue with another, there is always the danger that new buyers may not be found. In such instances the borrower must be able to replace commercial paper with bank loans.

A case in point is the recent Penn Central difficulty. When Penn Central filed a petition for reorganization on June 21, 1970, one of its problems was over $80 million in maturing commercial paper. Since this had been rated "prime" up to three weeks prior to the petition, investors got a bad case of the jitters that led to a sharp turndown of commercial paper outstandings.[6] From the end of May to the end of August, 1970, commercial paper outstandings plunged by $3.2 billion. Those firms with maturing commercial paper had to turn to bank lines to obtain the funds to meet these obligations. One of the more spectacular adjustments was that of Chrysler Financial Corporation, which had about $1.5 billion of commercial paper outstanding at the time. From "normal" daily sales of $100 million, its commercial-paper sales dropped about 40 percent. When the company had used up most of its $650 million of unused bank lines, a group of banks lead by Manufacturers Hanover quickly put together a $410 million package of added bank lines and purchase of receivables that turned the tide and restored confidence in the firm's commercial paper.[7]

Reasons for Use of Commercial Paper

Why do corporations use commercial paper? In the first place it is usually less expensive than short-term bank credit. Most banks require that commercial borrowers retain noninterest-yielding demand deposits equal to 15 to 20 percent of their loan. As we shall see in the next chapter, these are called compensating balances. Because such idle balances may add significantly to the costs of bank loans, the rates shown in Table 12-1 for commercial paper and bank loans are not strictly comparable. On the other hand, some issuers of commercial paper may find it necessary to pay a small commitment fee, say $\frac{1}{4}$ of 1 percent, for the bank lines to backstop their outstanding commercial paper.

Second, the largest finance companies in particular use commercial paper because they have obtained all the short-term loans conveniently available

---

[6] Commercial paper is rated as prime, desirable, or satisfactory by the National Credit Office, a subsidiary of Dun and Bradstreet. It had rated the paper of Penn Central as prime until June 1, 1970, when it changed the rating to "reserved;" that is, the situation was "too ambiguous to base a rating on." *Wall Street Journal*, August 13, 1970, p. 10. Standard and Poors Corp. is now starting a rating service for commercial paper.

[7] "How Banks Rallied on a Loan for Chrysler," *New York Times*, July 7, 1970, pp. 53, 55.

TABLE 12-1   Comparison of Rates on Commercial Paper and Commercial Bank Rates on Short-Term Business Loans (percent per Annum)

| | (averages for year) | | |
Year	Prime Commercial Paper 4- to 6- Months	Finance Co. Paper Placed Directly 3- to 6- Months	Prime Rates Charged by Banks
1965	4.38	4.27	$4\frac{1}{2}$–5
1966	5.55	5.42	$5\frac{1}{2}$–6
1967	5.10	4.89	$5\frac{1}{2}$–6
1968	5.90	5.69	6–$6\frac{1}{2}$
1969	7.83	7.16	7–$8\frac{1}{2}$
1970	7.72	7.23	$6\frac{3}{4}$–8

Source: *Federal Reserve Bulletin*, February, 1971, p. A33.

from commercial banks. Since a national bank may not make loans to any one borrower in excess of 10 percent of its capital and surplus, a large finance company, such as General Motors Acceptance Corporation, eventually runs out of banks that are large enough to provide it with a worthwhile line of credit. The movement to commercial paper was intensified by the shortage of loanable funds at commercial banks in the late 1960's.

A third possible reason sometimes cited for the use of commercial paper is that its use adds to the prestige of the issuer. It seems more likely that the prestige was there before the paper was sold.

Summary

The most commonly used source of short-term funds is trade credit: that is, credit extended by a supplier to a buyer in conjunction with the purchase of goods for ultimate resale. Small companies characteristically make relatively greater use of trade credit than large concerns, although the use also varies considerably according to the line of business involved. The role of trade credit as a form of non-price competition explains in large part the very common use of the informal open book account in relation to the more restrictive trade acceptance and promissory note. While not always explainable, the great variations in trade credit terms are frequently related to the nature of the commodity financed, the risks of loss, and the relative bargaining strengths of seller and buyer. Although trade credit can be ruinously expensive if we fail to take cash discounts, it is otherwise a form of short-term credit that has numerous advantages. Properly used, trade credit adds little to the cost of doing business and is quite readily obtainable. One of the chief advantages of trade credit is that it can be conveniently expanded or contracted as the need arises.

Whereas trade credit is an important source of unsecured short-term credit for small firms, commercial paper assumes a significant role only for large corporations. Although it is typically less expensive than bank borrowings, it is a less reliable source because of the alacrity with which buyers of commercial paper may switch to more attractive investments. For this reason corporations backstop their issues of commercial paper with substantial unused bank lines.

Questions

1/ If you are purchasing on terms of 2/10, n/30, but selling on terms of net 60, what financial problems are created by these differences? What might prevent you from changing the trade credit terms under which you purchase and sell?

2/ Drug manufacturers often sell their products to wholesalers on terms of 2/10, n/30, but wholesalers sell to retailers on terms of 2/10, 10 days E.O.M., n/30. How do you explain this difference?

3/ Manufacturers of knitted outerwear sell to wholesalers on terms of net 10 days, E.O.M., the 25th day of the month being considered as the end of the month. Wholesalers of these items frequently sell to retailers on terms of 8%, 10 days E.O.M. How do you explain this difference?

4/ Paper mills sell to paper wholesalers on terms of 2/30, net 31. What is the effect of such terms? How do you explain them?

5/ If you were a retailer, would you expect a higher or lower markup on goods that you hold on consignment as compared to goods that you have financed? Explain.

6/ If we outlawed all cash discounts, what would probably happen to the general level of invoice prices? Distinguish between those lines of business with very high cash discounts (e.g., 8/10, n/30) and those with "normal" cash discounts (e.g., 2/10, n/30).

7/ Smith, Kline & French, Inc., a wholesale drug company, has announced a plan whereby it will invest the 2 percent cash discount to which a retailer is entitled in the shares of either of two mutual funds selected by the dealer. SK&F also pays the brokerage fees, which would otherwise represent a charge to the dealer of about 8 percent of the amount invested. Dealers who purchase $1500 worth of drugs quarterly from SK&F and pay their bills promptly are entitled to join the plan. An SK&F representative pointed out that most druggists purchased at least $1500 quarterly, but that not all purchases were made from one wholesaler (*Business Week,* September 17, 1960, p. 178).
a. What reasons do you see for the offer of this plan?
b. Would you consider this to be strictly a cash discount?

8/ Some discount stores, and even some college bookstores, operate on a "negative net working capital basis"—that is, they sell the merchandise before they are required to pay for it. What would be their credit position should inventory turnover decline?

9/ On June 23, 1970, the Board of Governors of the Federal Reserve System voted to suspend Regulation Q interest rate ceilings on 30- to 89-day large certificates of deposit (CD's), effective the next day. Why do you suppose the action was taken at that time?

Problems

1/ Compute the direct cost (at an annual rate) of failure to take cash discounts under the following trade credit terms. Assume that the purchaser makes payment on the final due date.
   a. 1/10, n/30
   b. 2/15, n/30
   c. 5/10, n/60
   d. 8/10, n/30

2/ R & J Press gave bookstores a cash discount of 2/10 E.O.M., but not on seasonal dating (October 1). If you placed an order on June 15, what is the implied annual rate if you actually pay on September 30?

3/ You are purchasing furniture on terms of 2/10, n/60. If you are unable to pay by the tenth day, what is the annual rate you are paying for trade credit if (a) you pay on the 20th day and (b) if you pay on the 60th day?

4/ The lumber and building supplies dealer (Table 4-2) was purchasing most of his lumber on terms of 2%, 10 days, after arrival, net 30 days. These purchases represented about 70 percent of his total purchases. If he had failed to take these cash discounts on his lumber purchases in the current year, what would have been his net profit?

Selected References

BAXTER, N. D., *The Commercial Paper Market*. Princeton, N.J.: Princeton University, 1964.

BENISHAY, H., "A Stochastic Model of Credit Sales Debt." *Journal of the American Statistical Association*, 61 (December, 1966), pp. 1010–1028.

CHRISTIE, R. A., "New Developments in the Commercial Paper Market," *Industrial Banker*, 35 (August, 1969), pp. 10–13ff.

COATES, J. P., "Trade Credit: A Case-Study," *Journal of Industrial Economics*, (June, 1965), pp. 205–13.

HUNGATE, R. P., Interbusiness Financing: *Economic Implications for Small Business*. Washington, D.C.: Small Business Administration, 1962.

LEVITT, M. S., "Monetary Theory and Trade Credit: An Historical Approach," *Yorkshire Bulletin of Economic and Social Research*, 16, No. 2 (1964), pp. 88–96.

LIBSEY, R. G. and BRECHLING, F. P. R. "Trade Credit and Monetary Policy," *Economic Journal*, 73 (December, 1963), pp. 614–41.

MELTZER, A. H. "Mercantile Credit, Monetary Policy, and Size of Firms," *Review of Economics and Statistics*, 42 (November, 1960), pp. 429–37.

NADIRI, M. I., "The Determinants of Trade Credit in the U.S. Total Manufacturing Sector," *Econometrica*, 37 (July, 1969), pp. 408–23.

REINHARDT, H., "Economics of Mercantile Credit; A Study in Methodology," *Review of Economics and Statistics*, 39 (November, 1957), pp. 463–67.

SCHADRACK, F. C., Jr., "Demand and Supply in the Commercial Paper Market," *Journal of Finance,* 25 (September, 1970), pp. 837–52.

SEIDEN, M. H., *The Quality of Trade Credit.* New York: National Bureau of Economic Research, 1964.

SELDEN, R. T., *Trends and Cycles in the Commercial Paper Market* (New York: National Bureau of Economic Research, 1963).

WHITE, W. H., "Trade Credit and Monetary Policy: A Reconciliation," *Economic Journal,* 74 (December, 1964), pp. 935–46.

Various studies on management of trade credit are available from the Credit Research Foundation, 3000 Marcus Avenue, Lake Success, N.Y. 11040

Short-Term Loans

13

If we could draw up a balance sheet for every business concern at this point in time, we would probably find that almost all are financing part of their needs with trade credit, whereas a considerable number are not using short-term credit from a bank or other commercial lender. Nonetheless, these more formal short-term credit arrangements are essential to the survival of many business firms. Companies in the retail and wholesale trades depend relatively more on short-term loans from commercial banks than do public utilities, such as railroads and electric companies. Manufacturing concerns use short-term bank credit extensively, although we again need to observe the variations among different industries and companies of different size. A sample of manufacturing corporations of all sizes shows that at mid-1970, they obtained about 5 percent of all their funds from short-term bank loans. Users of relatively large proportions of short-term bank credit were manufacturers of apparel and other finished products (11.5 percent) and leather and leather products (12.5 percent). Manufacturers of iron and steel and petroleum refiners used practically no short-term bank credit.[1] Among these concerns, current assets were also a relatively small proportion of total assets.

Most of this chapter deals with short-term loans provided by commercial banks. Although many of these loans are unsecured, business firms must often pledge or sell some of their assets in order to obtain needed funds. In such cases they may turn to other lenders whose credit standards are less exacting than those of commercial banks. As an alternative to secured short-term loans, some firms may sell their accounts receivable. Finally, there are various other minor sources of short-term credit, some of which are especially important to newly formed business concerns.

Arranging the Loan

The Application

When we request a loan, the lender will ordinarily seek information in three primary areas: personal information on the chief officers of the company, information concerning the business, and information concerning the loan — its proposed use and how and when it will be repaid. If we understand why the lender wishes this information, we can do a better job of furnishing him the right information and be less hesitant about providing it. One of the frequent complaints of lenders is that prospective borrowers are too secretive concerning their business. The relationship between lender and borrower is much like that of a doctor and his patient. Neither the lender nor the doctor is given to gossip about clients, and both must rely on complete frankness from those that they serve.

A lender seeks personal information on the chief officers because he must be completely convinced of our honesty. As one banker remarked to the writer, "We can't afford to take any risk that a borrower is dishonest, because he will probably succeed in cheating us — though he'll cheat us only once. We figure it is a losing game, because he can spend 24 hours a day figuring out how to cheat us, while we can spend only a few hours a month watching him." So far as a lender is concerned, honesty and integrity are absolutes. A reputation for honesty is like virtue; once lost, it is never regained.

Most lenders do not expect to make loans only to prime companies. Were this their standard, there would be very few loans made. However, they do wish to have reasonable expectations of being repaid in the normal course of business. To reach a conclusion on this score a lender will ask to review our historical financial statements as well as our planning statements — cash budget, capital budget (if applicable), pro forma income statement and balance sheet.

A banker, for example, will probably ask that we fill in a rather forbidding form requiring several pages of detailed financial information. An integral part of such a form is a statement similar to that shown in Exhibit 13-1. Observe that we certify that the information is provided "for the purpose of securing credit."

[1] Federal Trade Commission and Securities and Exchange Commission, *Quarterly Financial Report for Manufacturing Corporations* (Second quarter, 1970), pp. 13–27.

This phrase puts the statements submitted under the provisions of the false financial statement laws, which provide that the submission of a false financial statement for the purpose of obtaining credit is a misdemeanor punishable by fine or imprisonment. Further, we agree that in the absence of any information to the contrary ". . . this may be considered as a continuing statement and substantially correct." This means that we should continue to submit financial statements to the bank and that we should tell the bank when any major change in our business takes place between statements.

EXHIBIT 13-1 Typical Statement Required of Corporate Borrower

---

To ANYTOWN NATIONAL BANK

For the purpose of procuring credit from time to time with you for our negotiable paper or otherwise, we furnish the following as a true and accurate statement of our financial condition on .... 19 .... We agree to and will notify you immediately in writing of any materially unfavorable change in our financial condition, and in the absence of such notice or of a new and full written statement, this may be considered as a continuing statement and substantially correct; and it is hereby expressly agreed that upon application for further credit, this statement shall have the same force and effect as if delivered as an original statement of our financial condition at the time such further credit is requested.

If any judgment is entered or any legal action or prosecution is commenced against the undersigned, or if the undersigned becomes financially embarrassed, or on the failure of the undersigned to notify you of any such change in the financial condition of the undersigned as above mentioned, or if the undersigned assigns any accounts or transfers or encumbers any assets which in your opinion materially affects the business or financial condition of the undersigned, then all obligations of whatsoever name, kind or nature held by you upon which the undersigned is obligated as maker or endorser shall at your option, be and become immediately due, notwithstanding the date of payment as fixed by the obligation then held by you, and any credit balance of the undersigned may be applied by you in satisfaction of any such obligation.

Finally, the banker will wish to know what we plan to do with the money in order to determine whether or not the purpose is suitable to the lending policy of the bank. If we plan to buy machinery and equipment with the money, he might argue that certain types of financing other than a short-term bank loan would serve our needs better. It may appear that we plan to purchase inventory for speculative reasons, or there may be other objectionable features to our plans. Of course, this problem should not arise, because before we make the request for a loan, we should have a good idea of whether or not our proposed use falls within the lending policies of the bank.

The Repayment Schedule

A lender wants to know how and when we will repay a loan. In large part repayment is dependent upon the use we plan to make of the loan, and we should request a repayment plan that is suited to the purpose of the loan. To explain this, we need to return to the cash-flow system discussed in Chapter 5.

Loans Repaid in Normal Course of Business. There are basically two sources from which a lender can be repaid in the normal course of business — either from a decrease in current assets or from cash generated from sales. In the difference between these two sources lies the usual difference between short- and intermediate-term credit. Although intermediate-term credit will be discussed in Chapter 14, it is important that the distinction between these two forms of credit be made now.

Short-term loans. On the one hand, a loan may be used to build up the inventory and accounts receivable pools to meet a seasonal bulge in sales. Initially the borrowed funds are invested in inventory and then, as the inventory is sold, in accounts receivable. As we collect on the accounts receivable, funds are returned in the normal course of business to the cash reservoir for repayment of the loan. We should then remain out of debt until we need to finance the next seasonal bulge. Such a seasonal financing program should be revealed in the cash budget.

Intermediate-term loans. On the other hand, a loan may be used to build permanent increases in these pools of current assets or to purchase certain fixed assets. If we were expanding our business, this sort of financing would be necessary. In this case we cannot reduce inventories and accounts receivable to generate funds for the repayment of the loan. Instead, the funds for repayment must come over several years from cash generated from sales. Although net profits after taxes, but excluding depreciation charges and any other noncash expenses, are not an exact measure, they serve as a rough estimate of the annual increment of cash from normal operations. Profit expectations would be revealed in income statement projections (Chapter 9).

Why does a banker or other lender care whether our debt will be repaid within a year or within five years, so long as it is eventually repaid? He has the same cash flow problems that we do. Should he tie up his funds in long-term loans, he might be unable to take care of customers who need funds for only a few months. Consequently, he needs to plan his lending operations to provide an inflow of funds to meet future demands. For this reason it would represent poor planning on our part and sad bank relations to ask for and receive a loan for 90 days, only to rush in on the 89th day and request a year's extension. It would be even worse not to request an extension until the 95th day.

Loans not Repaid in Normal Course of Business. Finally, there are situations in which a lender might extend credit and expect repayment from funds which are not generated in the normal course of business. For example, we may plan to issue some long-term bonds to finance construction of a new plant. Since we make partial and periodic payments to the contractor as construction progresses, we have two alternatives. We might issue the bonds now and invest the extra funds we do not need in short-term government bonds. These would be gradually liquidated to make payments to the contractor. This procedure enhances our liquidity, but not our profitability, because the rate of return on government bonds is usually very low. In contrast, we might borrow from a bank as we need to make payments to the contractor. Eventually, our accumulated debt to the bank would be paid off with funds obtained by the issue of the bonds. This process of replacing short-term with long-term debt is called *funding.* The alternative we select would depend in part upon whether we expect interest rates of long-term borrowings to rise or fall over the period of construction.

Forms of Bank Credit

Credit Line

While the use of the term varies in practice, a credit line is "generally an informal understanding between the borrower and the bank as to the maximum amount of credit which the bank will provide the borrower at any one time."[2] Under this form of arrangement the bank is not legally obligated to provide the credit in the amount agreed upon. However, most banks will honor their informal commitment rather than develop the reputation of being unreliable. As the availability of bank credit lessens during a period of tight money, credit lines become more formalized. In return for a firm commitment banks ask for a fee of $\frac{1}{4}$ to $\frac{1}{2}$ percent a year on the unused portion of the commitment. The size of the fee depends upon the degree of credit stringency and the bargaining power of the borrower.

Credit lines are customarily established for only a year at a time. However, some banks review a borrower's position each time he presents a note to borrow against his line of credit. The bank's officers usually review the line yearly and may adjust it to the changed credit-worthiness of the borrower. This borrowing arrangement explains why the bank expects to be informed promptly of any change in our financial position during the year.

Credit lines are used in two principal ways:

1. The most common use of credit lines is with seasonal borrowing. On the basis of our cash budget we would estimate our maximum borrowings and arrange a credit line for that amount. Because the line is to meet our seasonal needs, we should not have to use the line for one or more months out of each year.

The advantages to the borrower of this arrangement are substantial. Barring any major misfortune, he can proceed to plan his financial affairs with the assurance of being able to call on the bank for loans up to the limit of the line. Moreover, he has had the added benefit of the careful review and approval of his plans by the banker, who is unlikely to view the prospects with quite the same rose-colored glasses worn by the borrower.

2. Credit lines may also be used with such arrangements as revolving credit and with loans to finance equipment and construction. As we shall see in greater detail in this chapter, revolving credit often involves lending against a "pool" of accounts receivable or inventory, with those assets serving as security for the loan. These loan arrangements frequently extend for a period of more than a year and often involve a firm commitment on the part of the bank to supply the credit, subject to certain limitations. We may be in debt to the bank for the dura-

[2] Caroline H. Cagel, "Credit Lines and Minimum Balance Requirements," *Federal Reserve Bulletin,* 42 (June, 1956), p. 573.

tion of the agreement, although the level of our debt would fluctuate with our needs for credit. Some would not use the term "credit line" here, but few banks make a clear distinction.

Single Loan

When we borrow from the bank only occasionally, the bank will treat each loan as a separate arrangement. For example, a new government contract may require that we increase our investment in inventory for a few months. To finance the increase we may arrange for a short-term loan from the bank. Those banks which do not grant lines of credit consider each loan request on its individual merits, even though some borrowers may need seasonal loans every year.

Credit Terms

When we borrow we are making an arrangement that involves a "package" of interrelated terms. Some features reflect our financing needs: the size of the loan and its maturity. While these terms are subject to negotiation, other features are more directly a result of bargaining with the lender. We shall discuss first those terms that are associated with short-term loans from commercial banks: minimum deposit balances and periods during which we are required to remain out of debt to the bank. Next we shall consider terms that are part of the loan-offer function of both banks and other lenders: requirements for security, the cost of the loan, and limitations on financial activities. These loan terms are closely interrelated. If we can provide government bonds as security for a loan, we may be able to obtain a relatively low rate of interest. A long-term loan may require security, whereas a short-term loan may not. Although we must treat these elements separately in this section for the sake of clarity, it is important to realize at the outset that a loan agreement is a bargain covering a mutually related group of services provided by the lender and obligations incurred by the borrower.

At any one time the terms under which credit is made available will differ simply because there are many competing lenders. Some never make loans under certain terms as a matter of policy; others change their lending policies from time to time. For example, one banker may never make unsecured loans for a period of longer than a year. Another banker will ordinarily be willing to grant this type of loan. However, if he feels that the proportion of these loans in his portfolio is already high, he may turn down a request for such a loan from an applicant who would have been acceptable at another time, or he may make the loan only on a secured basis. Although this means that we cannot lay down any uniform rules concerning the policies of various lenders, it also means that a prospective borrower will find it well worth his while to shop around among various lenders until he finds one that suits his needs. The fact that we get turned down on a loan request from one bank in no way means that all banks in our community will reject our request.[3]

---

[3]To illustrate this point, a marginal loan application was presented to 36 bankers in Iowa; 19 rejected the loan, but 17 said that they would make the loan. Robert M. Soldofsky, "Policy Variations in Making Marginal Loans," *Burroughs Clearing House*, 54 (November, 1969), p. 31.

In addition, terms on short-term loans will vary over time as conditions in the money and capital market change. In an era of "tight money" terms will be onerous and stringent. Restricted credit seldom hits borrowers with equal force. Some may find bank loans very costly; others may find them unavailable at any cost. There is some evidence that small borrowers feel the pinch more than large borrowers. Nor do the monetary policies of the Federal Reserve System affect all banks equally. Sometimes banks in Chicago and New York are fairly well "loaned up," while banks in smaller cities have relatively more excess reserves and are actively seeking loans. Consequently, the particular combination of terms that we agree upon with our lender will depend upon his willingness to accept various terms, general credit conditions, and our bargaining strength and ability.

Minimum Balance

An increasingly large proportion of commercial banks require that borrowers maintain deposit balances in some relation to the amount they are borrowing or the amount of the line of credit. These are often called *compensating balances,* because they are a form of compensation to the bank. We would be most likely to face this requirement when borrowing from a large, urban bank, espe-

EXHIBIT 13-2   Loan-Term Indices

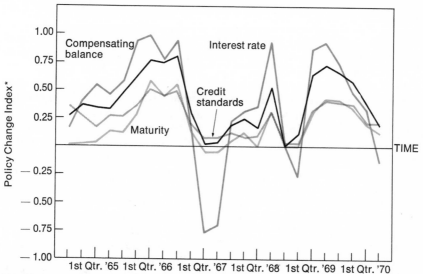

*Fraction of Banks Reporting Firmer Policy Less Fraction of Banks Reporting Easier Policy.

The Board of Governors has conducted the Quarterly Survey of Changes in Bank Lending Practices since September, 1964. The Survey questions bankers about changes in lending policies. The indices show the fraction of banks reporting firmer conditions minus the fraction reporting easier conditions. A positive figure means that, in general, policy was firmer compared to one quarter earlier. A negative figure indicates that easier policy prevailed.

Source: Duane G. Harris, "Rationing Credit to Business: More than Interest Rates," *Business Review,* Federal Reserve Bank of Philadelphia (August, 1970), pp. 4–5.

cially from a bank that customarily grants lines of credit. Compensating balances are demanded very frequently of sales finance and consumer finance companies.

Like other bank terms, compensating balances vary from bank to bank and from time to time. Sometimes the requirement is informal and not specified precisely. Currently banks expect borrowers to maintain deposits equal to 15 to 20 percent of the line of credit. Some banks requiring compensating balances permit customers to average the requirement, generally over a year, in order to adjust to seasonal needs for funds. However, finance companies are seldom permitted this privilege.

Compensating balance requirements are quite sensitive to changes in the availability of loanable funds at commercial banks. When money becomes tight, compensating balance requirements generally move higher, apply to more borrowers, and are more rigidly enforced. This is evident in Exhibit 13–2. During the very tight money period in 1969, a high proportion of bankers reported requiring higher interest rates, more frequent and higher compensating balances, shorter maturities, and higher credit standings of borrowers. New borrowers were subjected to more severe restraints than existing customers.

"Cleanup" of Debt

When a bank grants a line of credit to finance a seasonal expansion in our inventory and accounts receivable, it may expect us to "clean up" the loan each year. In other words, the bank will require us to be out of debt to it for one or more months each year. This cleanup period is proof to the bank that we are using its money only for seasonal expansion. If we are unable to clean up the debt, the bank will have good reason to believe that its funds are being used as a permanent part of our capital structure. In such a case the bank is likely to suggest that we seek other sources of funds for fixed capital and rely on our bank for seasonal needs only.

If we are borrowing from several banks, an individual bank may enforce a cleanup of its loan, but allow us to borrow from other banks during its cleanup period. The argument advanced for permitting this arrangement is that it proves to the bank that we have ample lines of credit to provide for any unexpected need for funds or to cushion the loss of any individual lines of credit. Other banks may require that we not borrow from any banks during the cleanup period. However, they will still allow us to expand other forms of credit, such as trade credit. Thus another reason for the use of the cleanup period is to show the bank that we have a certain amount of "elbow room" in our financing; that is, that we are not using every last bit of credit available to us.

Cleanup of debt is not expected on bank loans extended for more than a year. If the bank is financing our purchase of some new display fixtures for a store, we may sign a note for 36 months. Although we would probably make monthly payments on the note, the bank would not expect us to be out of debt to it until the end of the 36 months. Cleanup periods are ordinarily not required on revolving credit arrangements either.

Security Interest

There are several different types of financial institutions that grant secured loans to business. *Commercial banks* are the most important. In addition, there is a group of *finance companies* that engage principally in financing businesses on a secured basis. They may be distinguished from commercial banks in that they cannot accept deposits, but raise their funds just as any business concern does from issues of securities and from short-term borrowings. Because finance companies often take part in many different types of lending, it is difficult to classify them precisely. *Commercial finance companies* grant loans in return for the pledge of inventory, accounts receivable, or other sound assets. Sometimes a finance company participates with a bank in supplying funds, with the finance company handling the details of the account and the bank providing some portion of the funds. *Factors* specialize chiefly in financing based on accounts receivable; they may make loans on accounts receivable or purchase the receivables. *Old line factors* only purchase accounts receivable. *Sales finance companies* both finance the inventories of dealers in automobiles, appliances, and the like, and buy the instalment notes signed by individuals who have purchased the merchandise on time. We say they are involved in both wholesale and retail financing. These companies often have divisions that engage in inventory and accounts receivable financing for other types of business. *Consumer finance companies* make small loans to individuals in some instances for use in business. They are a relatively unimportant source of funds for business use.

By a secured loan we mean a loan protected by a *security interest*. Under the Uniform Commercial Code (now passed in all states but Louisiana) a security interest is "an interest in personal property or fixtures which secures payment or performance of an obligation." The term *collateral* refers to "the property subject to a security interest." If the borrower does not fulfill his obligations, the creditor may seize the collateral. If the assets are more than enough to satisfy the claims of the secured creditors, the excess realized from their sale must be applied to settle the claims of any unsecured creditors before any payments are made to the owners. Should the pledged assets be insufficient to satisfy the claims of the secured creditors, they share and share alike in any remaining assets with the unsecured creditors to the extent of their unsatisfied claims.

At the outset we should understand that lenders do not "reach for security," as they put it, because they think that a loan will not be repaid. If they thought that, they would not make the loan in the first place. No lender wants to end up being the owner of 80,000 pounds of frozen turkeys or $60,000 of accounts receivable owed by 400 firms scattered across the country. These assets are better than not having any repayment on a loan, but they are nowhere near as pleasant as cash. Bankers may ask for security on marginal loans, rather than turn down the loan applications on an unsecured basis, but they hope that they do not have to seize—and get "stuck" with—the assets pledged.

Let us now consider the various assets that might serve as collateral. Since we are considering only short-term loans, it is understandable that the desired collateral is correspondingly liquid: cash, accounts receivable, and inventory.

Cash. Even though a bank loan may be unsecured by receivables or inventory, the bank still has the *right of offset* against any deposits we may have in the bank. This means that the bank can use the amount we have on deposit to apply against our debts if we default on the loan. Observe in Exhibit 13–1 that ". . . any credit balance of the undersigned may be applied by you in satisfaction of any such obligation." Take the following very simple balance sheet:

Cash (Deposit)	$ 1,000	Bank loan	$ 5,000
Other assets	14,000	Accounts payable	5,000
		Proprietor, capital	5,000
	$15,000		$15,000

Assume the company is unable to meet its bills and is forced to liquidate. The "other assets" bring only $6000, so that the total cash available to settle claims is $7000. Without the right of offset, the bank would share with other general creditors, as shown below:

Cash available to settle claims of creditors		Claims		Final settlement
Cash in bank	$1,000	Bank loan	$ 5,000 × 0.70 =	$3,500
Cash from liqui-dation of assets	6,000	Accounts payable	5,000 × 0.70 =	3,500
	$7,000		$10,000	$7,000

$$7,000/\$10,000 = 0.70$$

The combined claims for $10,000 would be settled for $7000 or for 70 cents on the dollar. The bank would collect $3500. However, with the right of offset, the bank would use the deposit to reduce its claim by $1000 and would share with other general creditors as shown below.

Cash available to settle claims of creditors		Claims after exercise of right of offset		Final settlement
Cash from liqui-dation of assets	$6,000	Bank loan	$4,000 × 0.667 =	$2,666.67
				1,000.00*
		Accounts payable	5,000 × 0.667 =	3,333.33
	$6,000		$9,000	$7,000.00

$6,000/$9,000 = 0.667

*Realized from seizure of bank deposit.

Thus with the right of offset the bank collects a total of $3666.67 as compared with only $3500 without the right.

Accounts Receivable. We may give a security interest to a lender in all or a portion of our accounts receivable. What we have then is a pool of accounts receivable that have been assigned to a lender. Feeding into the pool are newly created accounts receivable resulting from sales. Reductions in the pool result from our customer's payments on account, returns and allowances, bad debts, and overdue accounts. The lending procedures are designed to limit our borrowings to some fixed percentage of the receivables in the pool.

Since the security devices used are relatively standard, the bargaining between lender and borrower centers on the percentage of the dollar amount advanced in relation to the dollar amount of receivables assigned and the interest and service charges. If we are willing to be satisfied with a low percentage advance, we may obtain a slight reduction in the cost of the funds advanced because of the lender's greater margin of protection.

(1) *Percentage of loan value.* Commercial finance companies and factors are typically willing to loan a somewhat higher percentage of the receivables pledged than commercial banks. Loan percentages for commercial finance companies and factors center on 80 percent with a range of 65 to 85 percent. In contrast the advances of commercial banks probably average 75 percent of the face value of the receivables and range from 50 to 90 percent.

In determining the amount to advance, the lender must judge the possible decline in value of the accounts receivable. Failure of our customers to pay their accounts, returns of defective merchandise, and demands for reductions in price because of poor quality will reduce our outstanding receivables. Consequently, the lender must determine whether our customers are good risks and whether they seem to believe that we have an acceptable product. Not only will he check our credit rating, but he will also check that of our customers with some credit agency, such as Dun and Bradstreet. We must expect to provide the prospective lender with an aging of our receivables and a record of our past bad debts and returns and allowances.

(2) *Security devices.* Since procedures followed are similar among the various financial institutions in this field, let us assume that we are borrowing from a commercial finance company. It is still our responsibility to pass on the creditworthiness of our customers. If we err, we suffer, not the finance company. Once we have sold goods on credit to a customer, we assign the account to the finance company. We must warrant that our customer is solvent, that the accounts are genuine, that the amounts owed are not being disputed by our customer, and that we do not owe our customer any money that he can offset against the amount he owes us on the account.

Since the finance company does not notify our customers that we have assigned their accounts, this arrangement is termed *non-notification* financing. This feature may be desirable, because in some lines of business it is still regarded as a sign of financial weakness to "hock" our accounts receivable. Under this form of financing it is our responsibility to make all collections on the receivables. As checks come in to us from our customers, we list them and forward them intact to the finance company to credit to our account.

If we assign a $1000 account and receive a loan of $800, how do we get the other $200 when our customer pays his account? This is our "equity" in the account. If our borrowings from the finance company are not over the 80 percent limit, the finance company will usually send us its check for $200 or, more likely, make weekly or semi-weekly settlements. If we are borrowing more than we should in relation to the pool of receivables, the $200 will probably be applied to reduce our debt to the finance company.

(3) *Interest and service charges.* Because of the detailed handling costs involved, we should expect to pay more for this form of credit than we would on an unsecured loan from a commercial bank. The charges we will pay are determined mainly by the average size of our accounts receivable, the amount and turnover of receivables, and the quality of the receivables. Small accounts with a high turnover require more servicing, and the lender will pass these costs on to us in one form or another. Low quality receivables are likely to be reflected in a high finance charge and low percentage of advance.

Although financing charges may be calculated in a number of ways, we will consider only the annual effective rate. Whereas banks often split the interest and service charges, finance companies ordinarily combine them into one overall finance charge. Charges by commercial finance companies range from a daily rate of "1/15th of 1% [about 24 percent per annum] on small and more marginal accounts to 1./40th of 1% [9 percent annually] on larger and secured but bankable accounts."[4]

An important consideration in the cost of accounts receivable financing is that the interest charge is ordinarily based upon the average *daily* balance outstanding. Although these finance rates may seem high, it is possible that the total cost might be lower than on an unsecured short-term bank loan. A bank may require that we sign a 90-day note for our maximum needs and maintain a compensating balance besides. If our daily needs for funds fluctuate widely, there may be considerable periods when we are paying for, but not using, the borrowed funds. In contrast, on an accounts receivable loan we borrow and pay for funds only when we need them, and even banks do not typically require a compensating balance. To fulfill our profit objective we should examine the total dollar cost of each alternative rather than just the annual rates charged. Moreover, we should keep in mind the principles of financial leverage. If we can put the finance company's money to work at 24 percent, it is a profitable operation, even though we pay the finance company 14 percent for the use of its money.

Inventory. Inventory financing involves the pledge of all or a portion of our inventory as security for a loan. Three considerations of prime importance to the lender will affect the desirability of this form of loan from our point of view as a borrower. The lender must determine what percentage of the cost or market value of the pledged inventory he is willing to lend to us; through what legal device his claim, or lien on the inventory, will be enforced; and the charge to be made for the use of the money.

Since no two lenders will weigh all the factors the same, it may pay us to shop around among various possible lenders with the aim of securing the most desirable mix of funds available, form of security device, and loan cost. Compromise is clearly involved. One lender may be willing to make a loan of 80 percent of our inventory value, but require an expensive or bothersome method of pledging the inventory and charge 10 percent interest. Another lender might make a loan of only 60 percent of inventory value, but offer a very flexible method of pledging the inventory and charge 8 percent interest. Consequently, we must weigh the advantage of having the additional funds against the disadvantage of their higher cost and associated inconveniences.

(1) *Percentage of loan value.* A margin of safety is required by the lender to protect him against a possible decline in the market value of the goods pledged and to cover any costs that will be involved in selling the goods. The amount of loan that can be acquired from most lenders will vary from 50 to 90 percent of the cost or market value of the inventory, whichever is lower. Although it might appear from this that the lender is relying wholly on the collateral pledged, we

[4]Monroe R. Lazere, "Financing Accounts," in M. R. Lazere, ed., *Commercial Financing* (New York: Ronald Press Co., 1968), p. 53.

should emphasize again that the bank or other lender looks first to the credit position of the borrower. If it does not appear that he can repay the loan in the normal course of his operations, he should not expect to obtain one.

(2) *Security devices.* There are two basic methods by which we may use our inventory as collateral for a loan. We may maintain possession of the inventory, or place it in the hands of a responsible third party. As a borrower we may indicate a preference for one or another security device, but the ultimate decision will probably be made by the lender. Among other factors that he will consider are the nature of our inventory, the use to which it is put, and our reliability and integrity.

Inventory in possession of borrower. Sometimes the collateral for a loan is clearly identifiable, just as automobiles may be identified by their serial numbers. With this protection lenders may be willing to advance a relatively large portion of the cost of the goods. For example, a bank may advance an amount equal to 90 percent of the cost of a car to a dealer. This form of financing is commonly called *floor-planning* and applies to all forms of consumer durables.

Under this security agreement the dealer agrees to hold the car and the proceeds from its sale in trust for the bank. The note the dealer signs is a demand note, because as soon as he sells the car, he must immediately return to the bank the amount it has advanced on the car. Obviously, such an agreement would be made only with a trustworthy dealer.

The bank protects its interest in the car and the proceeds of its sale by filing a financing statement with the appropriate public official. This puts the dealer's other creditors on notice that title to the dealer's stock of new cars probably rests with the bank. The bank will also require the dealer properly to insure the cars in its interest. At irregular and unannounced intervals the bank will check the dealer's inventory. The serial numbers on the automobiles are compared with the numbers shown on the security agreement.[5] Either the car should be there, or the proceeds of its sale should be in the hands of the bank. If this is not the case the car has been "sold out of trust," and the dealer is using for his own purposes the cash which properly belongs to the bank. The bank will ordinarily react to this gambit by calling for immediate payment of all amounts owed by the dealer.

In other cases the collateral for a loan is not clearly identifiable, e.g., men's suits in process of manufacture. In this case the security agreement provides for a floating charge or continuing lien on the shifting stock. The security interest applies to the raw materials, goods in process, and finished goods. We are free to sell the suits to some retailer, but the lien then applies to the ac-

---

[5] The writer recalls one instance where a dealer was supposed to have about 40 cars in one location and 30 in another, all pledged to the bank. Instead of checking the serial numbers of each car, the bank's representative counted the cars at the first location. There were 40 on hand. He was then persuaded to go to lunch. After lunch he found 30 cars at the second location. As you may have guessed, they had been driven over from the first location during lunch. The bank experienced a substantial loss.

A more spectacular recent case involved Billie Sol Estes, who allegedly tricked a number of finance companies "into buying $22 million of mortgages on largely non-existent liquid fertilizer tanks." While representatives of the finance companies were checking serial numbers on one side of a field, it was alleged that Mr. Estes' employees "would race about the flat West Texas countryside frantically changing serial numbers on the tanks that really did exist to conform to the numbers on the visitor's lists." *Wall Street Journal,* May 22, 1962, p. 1.

counts receivable generated. Again, so that other creditors can be warned that the lien has been placed on the goods and their proceeds, a financing statement must be filed with the proper state official.

From our point of view this form of security agreement has a number of advantages. It is much more convenient in our production processes to have complete control of the goods. No great amount of paper work is required to take the raw materials out of our own storage facilities and put them into production. Our required periodic reports of receipts and shipments are probably no more onerous than those we would use for our own accounting procedures. Nor is there any third party involved who must be paid to act as custodian for our goods. However, from the lender's point of view this is less desirable than the use of warehouse receipts, which will be discussed later in this chapter. Because the goods are in control of the borrower and not clearly identifiable, a much greater reliance must be placed upon his honesty. The inspections necessary to encourage his honesty are time-consuming and expensive. Consequently, the lender will probably loan closer to 50 percent than 90 percent of the value of the inventory. This type of financing is restricted primarily to commercial finance companies who have had long experience in this specialized form of lending.

Inventory in possession of a third party. From the point of view of the lender the security arrangements just discussed have one overriding disadvantage. The goods remain in the hands of the borrower. As a result a good deal of policing must be done by the lender, and bitter experience has shown that it is impossible to gain complete protection. A much greater measure of safety for the lender is obtained when the goods serving as collateral for a loan are placed in the hands of a third party (warehouseman) who will then issue a document placing security interest in the goods in the hands of the bank (warehouse receipt). Under this arrangement the warehouseman may not release the goods to the borrower unless the bank authorizes the withdrawal. And the bank will ordinarily not authorize the withdrawal unless the borrower pays off a corresponding portion of his debt to the bank.

There are two types of warehouses that may be used: terminal warehouses and field warehouses. A *terminal warehouse* is a public warehouse which rents space to the storer of goods. More recently, *field warehouses* have come into increasing prominence. Instead of bringing the goods to the warehouse, we bring the warehouse to the goods. A field warehouse is set up on the premises of the borrower. The designated storage area is segregated by heavy screening, or some other device, and placed under lock and key in the hands of the warehouse company. The field warehouse may be a storeroom, an oil tank, a pile of coal, logs in a mill pond, or lumber stacked in a lumber yard. The only requirement is that the warehouse company be in "continuous, exclusive, and notorious possession." Various signs are posted around showing the areas under the control of the warehouse company. Frequently, an employee of the borrower familiar with the storage and handling of the inventory is hired by the warehouse company, placed under bond, and put in charge of the storage area.

We would be likely to request a field warehouse rather than a public warehouse arrangement when we need frequent access to the raw materials or finished goods that have been pledged. (Ordinarily goods in process cannot be handled under a field warehouse, because the warehouseman could not maintain adequate control of the materials.) Such arrangements would also be required if the nature of the inventory would prohibit public, or terminal, warehousing. This would be true of the logs in the mill pond.

Finally, no discussion of warehouse receipts would be complete without reference to the famous salad oil case. In this instance it was charged that forged warehouse receipts representing large quantities of oil were used to obtain loans for Allied Crude Vegetable Oil Refining Corp. Apparently, some were issued fraudulently; at least when people began looking for the oil, up to $150 million of it was missing. Some of the tanks in which it was supposed to be stored did not exist either. A number of banks, including some of the nation's largest, suffered substantial losses, and 20 companies were forced into bankruptcy.[6] The scandal in no way invalidates the use of warehouse receipts, but it does suggest a need for more frequent inspections of the warehoused goods by lenders or a requirement by lenders for reports of periodic audits by independent accountants.

(3) *Interest and service charges.* When loans are based on inventory retained by the borrower the interest charge may include a service charge for the costs of checking inventory and assuring compliance with the agreement. The more difficult and time-consuming this task, the higher the combined charge. Some lenders separate the interest and service charge. On inventory loans based on warehouse receipts, interest and service charges are largely separate and distinct. Interest charges are levied by the lender and are related to the size of the loan and credit-worthiness of the borrower. Service charges are levied by the warehouseman and vary with the handling charges and the period the goods are in storage. We would not ordinarily undertake to pledge our inventory unless we planned to continue this arrangement for some period of time. This would be especially true of field warehousing because of the initial costs of establishing such an arrangement. A rapid turnover of inventory will add substantially to the warehousing costs because in-and-out handling charges are frequently more than double the monthly storage charge.

Other Collateral. Many other types of collateral may be pledged to obtain a loan. Commercial banks very frequently make loans to small businesses based upon collateral that is unrelated to the business. This would come about because the business itself has no acceptable assets that may be pledged or because the owner does not wish to reveal information concerning the business. This collateral may consist of securities, passbooks on savings accounts, mortgages on commercial or residential properties, and the cash surrender value of life insurance policies.

If the stocks used as collateral are listed on some stock exchange, a bank may be willing to loan up to about 75 percent of their market value, especially if they are actively traded.[7] With collateral of this quality, the interest charge

---

[6] Mr. De Angelis, president of Allied Crude, pleaded guilty "to three counts of circulating forged warehouse receipts and one count of conspiracy." At last report he had appealed his 20-year sentence. *New York Times,* August 26, 1965, p. 47.

[7] However, loans made for the specific purpose of buying securities come under the margin requirements of the Federal Reserve Board. For example, a loan to purchase stock in the latter part of 1970 could not exceed 35 percent of the market value of the stock at the time of the extension of credit.

may be fairly low and covered in part by dividends received on the stock. Loans on bonds, especially government bonds, may be as high as 80 to 90 percent of the market value, whereas loans on securities that are not listed on an exchange may be only 40 or 50 percent of market value. Securities which are seldom traded are often unacceptable to the bank as collateral. Banks, finance companies, and other lenders are usually willing to loan up to 95 percent of the cash surrender value of life insurance policies.[8] Since loans secured by mortgages on commercial or residential properties usually extend for more than a year, they are really not short-term loans. However, we might note that the percentage advanced will probably range from 50 to 80 percent of the value of the property.

Other Requirements. Even on unsecured loans, a bank or other lender may make various requirements to add to the safety of its loan. If a company has obtained loans from its officers, the bank may require that these loans be *subordinated* to the bank loan. This means that the officers making the loans agree that in case of insolvency, bankruptcy, or liquidation the claims of the bank must be satisfied in full before the officers receive any repayment of their loans to the company. Approval by the bank may be required to raise officers' salaries, to purchase assets, or to repay certain debts ahead of schedule. Withdrawls by the owner or payments of dividends may be restricted by various means. For example, the bank may restrict such payments to earnings, or a portion of the earnings, accumulated from the original date of the loan. In addition, the bank may forbid the withdrawal of earnings that would reduce the current ratio or net working capital below a certain level. To a great extent these requirements are not onerous in that good financial management would call for about the same policies. Clearly the bank does not make these requirements to tell us how to run our business, but to insure that its funds are channeled into proper uses.

Cost

Methods of Determining Interest Rate. Lenders may determine our interest charge in a number of ways. Although interest is seldom an important cost item in most lines of business, it is worthwhile to be able to calculate the true, or effective, rate in order to compare it with the rate levied by alternative sources of funds.

Interest on unpaid balance. This is the simplest method of calculating interest costs, but unfortunately it is probably less common than more complex methods. Under this method we would sign a note promising to repay in one year $1000 plus interest at 6 percent; that is, $1060. The stated interest rate of 6 percent is the same as the true, or effective, rate.

Discount method. This procedure is commonly used by commercial banks.

[8] Long regarded as impeccable collateral, insurance policies have been employed in some recent swindles. The scheme involved bidding up the price of "penny stock" in the over-the-counter market to establish a fictitiously high price. The stock was then exchanged for a paid-up life insurance policy or a surety bond. The insurance policy, or surety bond, was then pledged as collateral for a bank loan. "Whether there's any intention to pay off the loan is incidental." Banks in various parts of the country may have been bilked by as much as $25 million. "Collateral Con Game," *Wall Street Journal*, June 9, 1969, p. 30.

We sign a note promising to pay $1000 in one year. The bank takes the agreed interest charge out in advance and credits our account for $940 ($1000 − $60). At the end of the year it charges our account for $1000. Under this arrangement we have paid $60 for the use of $940 for one year. Our effective rate of interest is not the stated rate of 6 percent, but is $60/$940, or 6.38 percent.

Instalment loans. Banks and other lenders are handling an increasing portion of their loans to small business for the purchases of machinery and equipment and loans as instalment loans. This tendency seems to be especially marked during periods of tight money. Whereas the preceding loan arrangements require a lump sum payment of the principal owed when the note matures, instalment loans usually require monthly payments to reduce the principal. Under the "discount" method, the bank would credit $940 to our account, but we would sign a note for $1000, which we would repay in twelve instalments of $83.33 each. The effective rate is considerably more than 6 percent, because we are making monthly payments on the principal of the loan throughout the year. With each monthly payment we lower the amount that we have borrowed from the bank. Throughout the year we have had the use on the average of only about half of $940. Since we paid $60 to use an average of about $470, the effective rate we are paying is close to 12 percent.[9] This is costly, but we may be happy to pay this rate in order to obtain the loan.

Effect of Minimum Balance on Interest Rate. The minimum balance requirement adds to our costs only if the required balance is higher than that we would normally keep in the bank. If the required balance is higher than we would maintain, the effect is to reduce the amount of the bank loan that we can use and to raise the effective cost of our loan. Assume we obtain a loan for $100,000 at 8 percent per annum, and the bank requires us to maintain a minimum deposit balance of 20 percent, or $20,000. If we would normally keep a balance of only $15,000, we can use only $95,000 of the loan, although we are paying for $100,000. Consequently, the effective annual cost of the money is $8,000/$95,000, or 8.42 percent.

Determinants of Interest Rate. Earlier in this chapter we pointed out that interest rates vary over time with changes in the monetary policies of the Federal Reserve System and the fiscal policies of the Treasury. However, at any given time interest rates charged on business loans vary by industry, by size of loan, and by the maturity of the loan. The relationships are not clear,

[9] If we wished to be more refined, we could estimate the effective interest rate using the constant ratio method:

$$i = \frac{2mD}{P(n+1)}$$

where i equals the annual rate of charge; m, the number of payments in one year (usually 12); D, the interest charge in dollars; P, the principal or cash advance, and n, the total number of payments. In our example above using the "add-on" method:

$$i = \frac{2 \times 12 \times 60}{1,000\,(12+1)} = 11.1\%$$

If the bank uses the discount method, the effective rate would be:

$$i = \frac{2 \times 12 \times 60}{940\,(12+1)} = 11.8\%$$

since each of these factors is related to the other. Local and regional competitive conditions have a measurable effect upon the interest charges we must pay, with short-term bank loans in cities in the Northeast and West generally more costly than similar loans from banks in the Southeast and New York City (Table 13-1). Secured loans often carry a somewhat higher rate than similar unsecured loans because of the additional work involved in administering collateral such as inventory and receivables. Usury laws in most states place an upper limit of 6 to 8 percent on the stated rate that may be charged, although in a number of states the limits are not applicable to corporate borrowers. In recent years of high money rates these archaic laws have caused lenders to shut off credit to those borrowers whose loans would be subject to usury.

TABLE 13-1   Weighted Average Bank Rates on Short-Term Business Loans, May, 1970 (percent per annum)

| | Size of Loan (in/thousands of dollars) | | | | | |
Center	All Loans	1–9	10–99	100–499	500–999	1,000 and Over
New York City	8.24	9.05	8.91	8.53	8.31	8.13
7 Other Northeast	8.86	9.23	9.34	9.01	8.72	8.45
8 North Central	8.44	8.80	8.93	8.78	8.44	8.24
7 Southeast	8.44	8.70	8.77	8.49	8.31	8.15
8 Southwest	8.61	9.10	8.90	8.61	8.32	8.58
4 West Coast	8.42	9.49	9.13	8.72	8.50	8.13

At this time the bank prime rate was 8 percent.
Source: *Federal Reserve Bulletin*, 56 (September, 1970), p. A-32.

Average interest rates are higher on small loans than on large loans; and since small loans generally go to small borrowers, we should add that rates are typically higher for small borrowers than for larger borrowers (see Table 13-1). Much of this variation is understandable when we realize that a bank faces certain fixed costs in granting and administering a loan. It does not take 100 times as much work to grant a $100,000 loan as to grant a $1000 loan; in fact, it may even take less work if the borrower is well-known and with an unsullied reputation. Consequently, these fixed charges are a higher percentage of the principal of small loans than of large loans. In addition small borrowers may be less credit-worthy on the average than large borrowers.

Large companies in well-established industries may be able to borrow from commercial banks at the lowest or *prime rate*. Although the prime rate may remain constant for a considerable period of time, the customers entitled to this minimum rate may vary as credit conditions change. During the very tight money period of 1969, fewer and fewer customers qualified for prime, even though the prime rate was at a very high level (Exhibit 13-3). Since requirements for compensating balances were tightened at the same time, the effective increase in bank rates was higher than revealed by the quoted prime rate.

In periods of tight money, banks and other lenders may seek to increase their return on loans by asking for *equity kickers*. These are typically based on a share in the income from the enterprise financed—possibly stock-purchase

EXHIBIT 13-3   The Prime Rate on Commercial Bank Loans

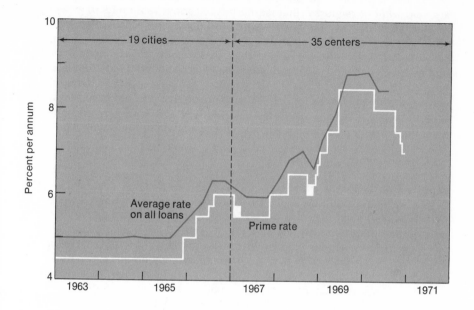

warrants (that is, options on common stock) or an extra payment tied to the performance of the borrowing company's stock. Mortgage lenders quite commonly seek equity kickers, such as a percentage of rental income, in addition to their regular interest return in periods of tight money.

Sale of Accounts Receivable

Old line factors are involved solely in the outright purchase of accounts receivable. Probably not many more than 20 companies limit their activities to purchasing receivables. Most commercial finance companies and factors both grant loans on receivables and purchase receivables, and engage in many other financing activities. In recent years a few commercial banks have entered the field, mainly by purchase of existing factoring concerns.

Procedures

At the outset let us clarify the distinction between loans on receivables and factored receivables. In the first instance the receivables are ours to have and to hold, to pursue and collect, and to lose money on if they are not paid. In the second instance, we sell approved accounts receivable as they are generated, along with all their associated headaches, to the factor. The receivables are sold *without recourse;* that is, the factor cannot require us to make good on any bona fide accounts we have sold him if he is unable to collect the balance owed. If we have obtained a loan on accounts receivable, all the receivables will show on our balance sheet as an asset, with a note to the effect that so many dollars' worth have been pledged against the note that is shown payable to the bank or finance company. If we have sold the accounts receivable, none are visible on the balance sheet, and no note payable appears on the liability side. The only item that will probably appear will be an asset account showing any amount we may still have coming to us from the sale of our receivables to the factor.

The agreement made with the factor is usually written for a year and renewed annually. Either party may cancel on 60 days' notice. When a customer sends us an order we obtain the factor's approval of the customer's credit before we ship the goods. If the factor turns down the account, we may still ship the goods "on department risk," but we know in advance that the factor will not buy that particular account. On the invoice to an approved customer we state that the account has been sold to the factor and that all payments are to be made directly to the factor. Duplicate copies of invoices are sent promptly to the factor.

Why is the notification acceptable under this arrangement if it was not when we obtained a loan on our receivables? Factoring is limited mainly to companies associated with textiles, shoes, furniture, equipment, and certain foods. Because it has been an accepted way of doing business in these fields for years, no stigma attaches to the firm that factors its receivables. In some lines we would be peculiar if we did not factor our receivables.

Interest and Service Charges

To understand the charges made by the factor we should separate the functions he performs. On the one hand, he provides a collection service for our accounts, handles the necessary bookkeeping, and absorbs any bad debt losses that may occur. On the other hand, he may lend us money prior to the time that he is able to collect on the accounts we have sold him. Let us see how he levies his charge for these two functions.

Service Commission. Under the factoring function known as *maturity factoring* the factor provides only the service of collecting the accounts we have sold to him and bearing the risk of credit loss. The factor pays us in full on the maturity date of the invoice. His commission depends upon the services performed and is inversely related to the volume of sales and the average invoice price. Commission rates are higher, the greater the expectancy of bad debts, the longer the credit terms, and the greater the amount of detail work required. Commission rates for maturity factoring range from $\frac{3}{4}$ of 1 percent to 2 percent and probably average somewhat over 1 percent of the invoice.

Cash Advance. Under the arrangement known as *advance factoring* we may draw against the receivables purchased by the factor prior to their maturity.

Since we are in effect selling for cash, the amount of the advance will be the *net* amount of the invoice, after cash discounts, less an amount to cover estimated claims, returns, and other allowances. This method of establishing the amount of the advance should not disguise the fact that an advance by a factor is in essence an unsecured loan, since he already owns the receivables. The factor's interest charge will be above and tied to the prime rate. However, it will be based on daily balances, and no compensating balances are required, as in the case of bank loans.

Reasons for Use

Factoring, as opposed to other forms of borrowing, is especially desirable when we need the services that the factor provides. In a highly seasonal business it is frequently uneconomical to maintain a credit department that will work overtime during a portion of the year and loaf the rest of the time. Because a factor serves many different industries he is able to operate more economically without wide seasonal swings in volume of activity. In industries such as the textile trades, the risks of credit loss are fairly high and credit extension takes considerable skill. Because factors are in a better position to assess the risks than an individual company, we may be able to increase sales more than if we carried the risk of bad debts ourselves. This is especially true in the export business. Thus evaluation of the desirability of factoring receivables should balance any expected added revenues from sales, less the charges for factoring and incremental costs of added sales, against the costs of maintaining our own credit department and the risk of losses on bad debts.

Limitations on the use of factors in terms of average size of account, volume of sales, age of business, and the like are generally the same as those previously indicated for loans on accounts receivable. In addition we have observed that factoring is not characteristic of many lines of business in which it would be a mark of ill repute to be found factoring our receivables. However, this traditional bias has been breaking down. When money is scarce and dear, many concerns turn to factoring and find it a very satisfactory means of financing.

Other Unsecured Credit

Endorsements and Guarantees

When our own credit standing is somewhat inadequate to obtain a loan, we may turn to another individual or company to endorse or guarantee our note to the bank. Small businesses quite frequently obtain funds under this arrangement. If we fail to fulfill our agreement with the bank, the other party must meet the obligation. Although the lender will be concerned with the credit standing of our endorser as well as with ours, he will not make the loan in the first place if he feels that we will default. Banks also provide letters of credit with which a borrower can then obtain funds from another lender, while the bank carries the ultimate credit risk. Of course, the bank charges a fee for this accommodation. A young man just out of college may sometimes get off to a flying start in business if his father is in a position to endorse his note for $100,000.

Loans from Officers, Employees, Relatives and Friends

Although these loans are ordinarily not a source of funds for large companies, they are often used by small businesses. Terms and costs of such loans vary widely, although one advantage is that arrangements are likely to be quite flexible. Maturity dates are often less rigid than that specified by the bank.

Loans from Customers

When we pay the telephone company for a month's service in advance, we are in effect loaning the company money. Various forms of customers' deposits and travellers' checks also amount to loans. The ill-fated manufacturer of the Tucker automobile raised working capital by selling a package of seat covers and other accessories to prospective purchasers of the car. Sometimes progress payments are made to construction firms and advances granted to subcontractors. Universities attempt to collect tuition at the beginning of each semester prior to imparting wisdom to the students. In all these cases, customers are providing a portion of the funds used in the business, frequently at little or no cost to the business. To the extent that business firms can develop such arrangements, their working capital problems are eased.

Loans from Suppliers

Occasionally suppliers provide credit to business in addition to trade credit. For example, a beer distributor may provide a cooler to a tavern, so long as the owner continues to purchase the required brand. Although this is not cash, it relieves the owner of the necessity of using his cash to buy one. Ice cream companies sell freezers to retailers, often at nominal finance charges, with payments made via a small additional charge on each package of ice cream. The large oil companies usually finance the sales made by their outlets on credit cards by crediting the charge slips held by dealers against deliveries of gasoline. In a sense the supplier buys the accounts receivable of the filling station operator so that he is relieved of the burden of carrying them. Such arrangements are most common among small businesses.

Accruals

Accruals represent liabilities for services rendered. They arise automatically because we keep our accounting records on an "accrual basis" rather than a "cash basis"; that is, we charge wages and other expenses to the period in which we receive the services. The counterpart to the charge against income is the creation of a liability account, such as "accrued wages." Funds also accrue from sales taxes, social security taxes, and other taxes before they are turned over to the proper government agencies. Accruals differ from other forms of credit discussed, in that management takes no overt action to acquire accruals.

Summary

Next to trade credit, bank credit is the most widely used form of short-term borrowing. Large corporations often have access to other sources of funds, and very small companies may not be sufficiently credit-worthy to obtain bank loans.

In making application for a loan, we should remember that the lender is fundamentally interested in our integrity (our willingness to repay the loan) and in our managerial talent (our ability to repay the loan). We can best persuade the lender of our acceptability on these counts by being honest with him in all respects and by presenting historical financial statements and planning statements which reflect, respectively, our past success and our ability to make realistic plans.

We must recognize that the basic source of repayment of short-term loans must be the seasonal reduction of inventories and accounts receivable. If the flow of funds from these sources is inadequate, the lender is extending long-term credit. This is not objectionable, but both borrower and lender should be aware of the situation at the time the loan is granted. Long-term loans are usually repaid at a slower rate from the cash generated by sales over several years. In both cases it is important to note that the loan is repaid in the normal course of business without the forced liquidation of any assets.

The terms under which short-term loans are available are as varied as the policies of banks and finance companies. Changing credit conditions also affect lenders and borrowers, although not uniformly. Thus we might face a different package of terms if we go from one lender to another or seek a loan from one month to another. Significant credit terms on a bank loan are requirements for a compensating balance and cleanup period. Other aspects of the loan-offer function are the collateral required, restrictions on operations, and the cost of the loan arrangement.

The riskier our business, the greater is the likelihood that we will find it necessary to pledge some of our assets in order to obtain a loan. From the lender's point of view the most desirable business assets are usually the inventory and accounts receivable. On the one hand, the lender is primarily interested in securing a definite legal claim on the asset against any possible claims of other creditors. Second, he wishes to be assured that the value of the assets does not fall below the amount he has loaned, and that we do not divert to our own purposes the funds realized from the sale of the asset. On the other hand, we would like as much freedom as possible in our use of inventory and accounts receivable. Furthermore, to minimize the cost of the loan we would prefer that the lender engage in a minimum of checking and inspecting the collateral. To put it bluntly, we would like to obtain a loan and then be left to conduct our business as before. Much of our discussion in this chapter has centered on the various arrangements that have been devised as a compromise to the conflicting wishes of lender and borrower.

In the case of inventory loans, a security agreement leaving the inventory in the hands of the borrower provides him greater freedom than the pledge of warehouse receipts. Although it may be more costly, a field warehouse is often more convenient for the borrower than a terminal, or public, warehouse. If we factor our accounts receivable, we are freed from the bother of collections and the risk of bad debt losses. In those industries where "hocking" of receivables is viewed with disdain, a pledge of receivables may be possible, though we have the responsibility for maintaining collections.

Questions

1/ How would the financial analysis and standards of credit-worthiness differ with respect to a prospective trade debtor and a prospective bank borrower?

2/ Consider each of the following circumstances and explain in each case: whether a short-term bank loan is suitable as a method of finance; whether the loan should be handled on a line of credit; whether the bank might reasonably expect a cleanup period.
   a. A hardware distributor wishes to borrow so that he can purchase a carload of lawn mowers in February.
   b. An appliance dealer wishes to borrow so that he can carry the time payment notes of his customers.
   c. A contractor wishes to finance the construction of a house he is building under contract.
   d. In March a small department store which has faced rising prices for some time wishes to borrow to carry inventory and accounts receivable.

3/ Why should commercial bank rates on business loans typically be lower than the effective rates charged on trade credit when cash discounts are missed?

4/ What types of security device would you think suitable to secure a pledge of inventory for the following types of products:
   a. Stocks of nickel, silver, and copper at an electrometal plating company.
   b. Stock of television sets at a discount house.
   c. Piece goods at a men's clothing factory.
   d. Whiskey aging in barrels in a warehouse.
   e. Cases said to contain medium-sized eggs in a refrigerated warehouse.

5/ In each case in question 4, what do you think should be the percentage of the loan to the value of the inventory? How would you determine the value of the inventory? How did you determine your recommended loan value?

6/ In each case in question 4, what special precautions would you take as a lender?

7/ Are trade creditors concerned if we pledge receivables or inventory to obtain a loan from a bank? Why or why not?

8/ Which appears less likely to interfere with our internal operating procedures — a pledge of inventory or an assignment of accounts receivable?

9/ Sometimes the expression is used that a borrower "warehouses his receivables" when he assigns them to a bank or factor to obtain a loan. How is the assignment of receivables similar to and different from pledging warhouse receipts to secure a loan?

10/ How is the current ratio affected by a pledge of accounts receivable as compared with outright sale of accounts receivable to a factor?

11/ How is credit insurance similar to and different from factoring accounts receivable?

12/ Why should the effective annual charge made for financing the instalment purchase of a freezer unit by a grocery store be 18 percent, while the rate for a $100,000 unsecured loan be only 8 percent?

Problems

1/ Review the cash budget shown in Chapter 9.
   a. If you were financial manager of this company, what sort of financing arrangement would you request of the bank?
   b. Will your borrowing plans change if the bank requires a minimum balance of 20% of the amount borrowed? How?
   c. Will your borrowing plans change if the bank requires a minimum balance of 20% of the line of credit? How?
   d. Under the borrowing schedule shown, what is the dollar cost of financing the bank borrowings February through June if the bank charges an effective rate of 8%?
   e. If terms of purchase were 2/10, n/30, what would be the dollar cost of failing to take the cash discounts on purchases during these same months?

2/ You sign a 90-day note for $15,000 discounted at 8% per annum.
   a. What are the proceeds that the bank will credit to your account?
   b. What is the effective rate of interest you are paying on the note?

3/ Assume that you need the full use of $50,000 for 12 months. You can obtain a loan at $8\frac{1}{2}$% without a compensating balance or one at 8% with a compensating balance equal to 20% of the amount borrowed. To simplify calculations, assume that interest is not discounted, but paid at the maturity of the loan. What arrangement would you accept and how much would you borrow:
   a. If you would otherwise maintain no balance with the bank? (*Hint:* let x equal the amount you need to borrow. If the compensating balance were 10%, then $x - 0.10x$ would equal the dollar amount fully available after deduction of the compensating balance.)
   b. If you would normally maintain an $8000 balance with the bank? (*Hint:* you're on your own.)

4/ A business fails and is forced to liquidate. The balance sheet prior to liquidation is shown as follows:

Cash (deposit)	$ 5,000	Bank loan	$12,000
Other assets	40,000	Accounts payable	35,000
		Proprietorship capital	
		(deficit)	(2,000)
	$45,000		$45,000

The other assets bring $25,000 upon liquidation. What would the bank
receive in total payment on its loan:
a. Without the right of offset?
b. With the right of offset?

5/ In order to finance the purchase of a showcase you sign a note for $2400
repayable in 12 equal monthly installments. The bank quotes its rate as
"8½% discount" and credits your account with $2196. What is the approxi-
mate effective annual rate of interest you are paying? Show calculations.
(It will be more accurate if you use the constant ratio formula shown in
the footnote on page 299.)

6/ The balance sheet of the Easyfale Corporation showed the following assets
and liabilities just prior to liquidation:

Cash	$ 3,000	Bank loan	$10,000
Acc't receivable	15,000	Acc't payable and	
Inventory	13,000	other	35,000
Equipment	20,000	Common stock	6,000
	$51,000		$51,000

In liquidation the following amounts were realized:

Cash	$ 3,000	(of which $2,500 was in the bank; bank
Acc't receivable	10,500	has right of offset)
Inventory	7,000	
Equipment	10,000	

The inventory was pledged to the bank to secure its loan.
a. How much does the bank receive in final payment on its loan?
b. What would the bank have received if it had not had a lien on the inventory?
c. What do the trade and other creditors receive in each case?

7/ The Phahl Manufacturing Corporation faces a seasonal expansion of inventory of $80,000 (net of cash discount). The financial manager finds that
the necessary funds will be available through any one of the following
sources:
a. Buy on terms of 2/10, n/60; plan to pay on the 60th day. (*Hint:* Let x
equal the gross purchase price of the goods. Then $x - 0.02x = $80,000$.)
b. Borrow from a commercial bank at 8½ percent per annum.
c. Borrow from another commercial bank at an annual rate of 8 percent
discounted.
d. Borrow on a warehouse receipt from a commercial finance company.
Terms are 10 percent interest per annum, with the loan amounting to

75 percent of the value of the goods. Additional inventory is available to provide adequate collateral. The warehousing charge is a fixed yearly charge of $500 plus a flat charge of 1½ percent of the value of the inventory warehoused.

e. Borrow on accounts receivable from a commercial finance company at a rate of 1/20 of 1 percent per day on the outstanding face value of of the accounts receivable pledged, the loan value of the accounts to be 90 percent of their face value.

(1) If the full $80,000 needed was obtained in each case and the full amount of the loan remained outstanding for 60 days, what would be the effective financing cost (a) in dollars, (b) as an annual percentage? Use a 360-day year, but in the case of parts (b) through (e) base the annual percentage on the assumption that funds will be used for 60 days.

(2) What would be the dollar cost of (e) if the loan were reduced by $20,000 at the end of 20 days and by an additional $10,000 at the end of the next ten days?

8/ The following shows the current asset and current liability position of the H. Stevenson Co.:

Cash	$ 80,000	Notes and accounts	
Accounts rec.	400,000	payable	$1,000,000
Inventory	520,000		
	$1,000,000		$1,000,000

Discussions are being held with an old line factor to consider the possibility of selling accounts receivable to him. Although the factor will not purchase the accounts now showing on the books, he will purchase new receivables on the following terms:

Factor's commission, 1 percent of value of receivables, net after deduction of 2 percent purchase discount. (Company's terms of sale are 2/10, n/30.)

Average payment date of receivables to be considered as 20 days.

Interest at 10 percent per annum is to be charged on amounts advanced by the factor prior to the average due date. The amount advanced by the factor is equal to gross sales, less purchase discounts, less the factor's commission. To simplify calculations it is assumed that returns and allowances are negligible.

Annual credit sales are expected to be $6,000,000.

a. Calculate:
(1) The largest amount that the factor will lend us at any one time on the assumption that sales are level throughout the year.
(2) On the assumption that we borrow all that the factor will advance, what will be the total interest cost?
(3) What will be the total factor's commission?

b. If we had been selling our accounts receivable to the factor, how would our current position as shown above have appeared if the proceeds from the factor had been applied to reduce the current liabilities?

(Assume no amounts are due from the factor.) What is the current ratio with and without the sale of receivables?

9/ Arbaugh's Department Store, Lansing, Michigan, has advertised a "Christmas Gift Club." Under the terms of the offer customers begin making weekly payments of $2 on November 23, 19_1, and complete the 46th payment on October 3, 19_2. Two weeks later they are given certificates redeemable for $100 in merchandise at the Arbaugh Store. (*The State Journal,* October 27, 1963, p. A-14.)

   a. On the basis of this information what is the effective cost of these funds to Arbaugh's assuming that customers use their certificates as soon as they are available (to the nearest percentage)?

   b. On the basis of the above information what is the effective cost to Arbaugh's assuming that customers use their certificates eight weeks after they are available (to the nearest percentage)? *Note:* In (a) and (b) you may find it useful to know that if a is the first term; l the last term; n the number of terms in an arithmetic progression; then s, the sum of n terms, equals $n/2(a + 1)$. Do not worry about compounding the weekly payments, although this might be theoretically correct.

   c. What other factors should be considered in determining whether the plan is profitable to Arbaugh's?

10/ The Greater Lafayette TV Cable Co., Inc. charges $6.40 per month to homeowners that use its cable. However, an individual who pays for one year in advance may deduct 5 percent from the amount of the advance payment. What rate of return would you receive by making this investment? Note that it is an after-tax return. (*Hint:* The return is the same as the cost of not making the payment in advance; i.e. the annual percentage rate charged for making the payment in instalments. Try the constant ratio formula in the footnote on page 299.)

Selected References

BACH, G. L. and C. J. HUIZENGA, "The Differential Effects of Tight Money," *American Economic Review,* 51 (March, 1961), pp. 52–80.

BAXTER, N. D. and H. T. SHAPIRO, "Compensating-Balance Requirements: The Results of a Survey," *Journal of Finance,* 19 (September, 1964), pp. 483–96.

BENSTON, G. J., "Commercial Bank Price Discrimination Against Small Loans," *Journal of Finance,* 19 (December, 1964), pp. 631–43.

DAVIS, R. G. and J. M. GUTTENTAG, "Balance Requirements and Deposit Competition," *Journal of Political Economy,* 21 (December, 1963), pp. 581–85.

"Financing Inventory through Field Warehousing," *Yale Law Journal,* 69 (March, 1960), pp. 663–708.

FLECHSIG, T. G., *Banking Market Structure and Performance in Metropolitan Areas.* Washington, D.C.: Federal Reserve Board, 1965.

FREIMER, M. and M. J. GORDON, "Why Bankers Ration Credit," *Quarterly Journal of Economics,* 79 (August, 1965), pp. 397–416.

GIBSON, W. E., "Compensating Balance Requirements," *National Banking Review,* 2 (March, 1965), pp. 387–95.

GUTTENTAG, J. M., "Credit Availability, Interest Rates, and Monetary Policy," *Southern Economic Journal* 26, (January, 1960), pp. 219–28.

HARRIS, D. G., "Rationing Credit to Business: More than Interest Rates," *Business Review,* Federal Reserve Bank of Philadelphia (August, 1970), pp. 3–14.

HAYES, D. A., *Bank Lending Practices: Issues and Practices* (Ann Arbor, Mich.: University of Michigan, 1964)

HESTER, D. D., "An Empirical Examination of a Commercial Bank Loan Offer Function," *Yale Economic Essays,* 2 (1962), pp. 3–57.

HODGMAN, D. R., *Commercial Bank Loan and Investment Policy.* Champaign, Ill.: Bureau of Economic and Business Research, University of Illinois, 1963.

HURLEY, E. M., "Business Financing by Business Finance Companies," *Federal Reserve Bulletin,* 54 (October, 1968), pp. 815–27.

JAFFEE, D. M. and F. MODIGLIANI, "A Theory and Test of Credit Rationing," *American Economic Review,* 59 (December, 1969), pp. 850–72.

LAUDADIO, L., "Size of Bank, Size of Borrower, and the Rate of Interest," *Journal of Finance,* 18 (March, 1963), pp. 20–28.

LAZERE, M. R., ed., *Commercial Financing.* New York: Ronald Press Co., 1968.

LEVENSON, A. M., "Interest Rate and Cost Differentials in Bank Lending to Small and Large Business," *Review of Economics and Statistics,* 44 (May, 1962) pp. 190–97.

LUCKETT, D. G. and J. D. LAGES, "Bank Lending and Small Business," in *Studies in the Factor Markets for Small Business Firms.* Ames, Iowa: Iowa State University, 1964, pp. 7–45.

PHILLIPS, A., "Evidence on Concentration in Banking Markets and Interest Rates," *Federal Reserve Bulletin,* 53 (June, 1967), pp. 916–26.

"Quarterly Survey of Changes in Bank Lending Practice," *Federal Reserve Bulletin,* 54 (April, 1968), pp. 362–67.

ROBICHEK, A. A., D. TEICHROEW, and J. M. JONES, "Optimal Short-Term Financing Decision," *Management Science,* 12 (September, 1965), pp. 1–36.

ROBINSON, R. I., *The Management of Bank Funds.* Parts III and IV. New York: McGraw-Hill Book Co., Inc., 1962.

SHAPRIO, H. T. and N. D. BAXTER, "Compensating-Balance Requirements: The Theory and Its Implications," *Southern Economic Journal,* (January, 1964).

SWEETSER, A. G., *Financing Goods.* Newton Highlands, Mass.: Albert G. Sweetser, 1957.

TAYLOR, C. T., "Average Interest Charges, The Loan Mix and Measures of Competition: Sixth Federal Reserve District Experience," *Journal of Finance,* 23 (December, 1968), pp. 793–804.

Intermediate-Term Financing

14

As we move from short-term financing to intermediate- and long-term financing, we are making a very fundamental shift in the sources from which these funds must be repaid. When we obtain short-term loans, we typically use this money to finance an accumulation of inventory and accounts receivable. At the end of the season or during cyclical declines we reduce inventories and collect accounts receivable. The conversion of these current assets into cash enables a company to repay its short-term loans. Because short-term funds move into and out of current assets, or *working capital,* as they are called, short-term loans are sometimes referred to as working capital loans.

In contrast, intermediate- and long-term funds are sought more for investment in plant and equipment and permanent current assets (refer to Exhibit 10-2) than for financing seasonal changes in current assets. Because the uses of these funds differ, the sources of repayment are altered as well. Funds obtained from sales of stock and from retained earnings are usually invested permanently; owners receive dividends, but seldom are repaid their original investment. These relatively fixed sources of funds are discussed in Chapters 19 through 21.

Other funds are only loaned to a company, to be returned gradually over a period of years along with regular interest payments. More or less arbitrarily, we have divided these borrowed funds into two classes: intermediate-term (1–10 years) and long-term (over 10 years). Long-term debt financing and leasing will be covered in Chapters 17 and 18. However, our analysis of the role of both intermediate- and long-term borrowing will be clarified if we first understand the sources of repayment. Then we can move to a consideration in this chapter of the reasons for the use of intermediate-term financing and the sources of such funds.

Sources of Repayment

Uses of Funds

A basic requirement of intermediate- and long-term borrowing is that it also be suited to the uses made of the funds. Because funds obtained for longer than one year are used for different purposes, the sources of repayment are different. How are these funds used? Ordinarily, when we borrow funds for long periods, we have two possible investments in mind—purchases of plant and equipment, or permanent additions to our current assets.

Historically, long-term financing and investment in plant and equipment have been closely associated. The rapid increase in mechanization and automation in recent years has forced many companies to seek funds for the equipment necessary to maintain their competitive position. Not only has more plant and equipment been needed, but it has become increasingly expensive. Internal funds (net earnings retained after taxes but before noncash expenses, such as depreciation) have been a more important source of long-term funds than external sources (issues of stock and borrowing).

Permanent additions to current assets are necessary to maintain a long-term growth in sales. Our dollar investment in inventory and accounts receivable is a product of the number of units handled and the price per unit. When sales expand, the number of units grows; during periods of inflation, the price per unit rises. In either case more dollars become committed to inventory and accounts receivable until such time as the trend is reversed.

Repayment of Funds

When borrowed funds are sunk into machinery or permanent additions to current assets, how are they repaid? As we shall see later, funds obtained from intermediate-term debt are typically repaid gradually over the term of the loan. These repayments are ordinarily generated by net profits after taxes but before depreciation. In other words, when we pay back borrowed money, we gradually replace those borrowings with earnings, with the owners' equity.

To sharpen the distinction in the method of repaying short- and intermediate-term borrowings, let us consider the following simple examples. Assume that we begin with a balance sheet as shown below:

Before incurring debt

Cash	$ 10	Current liabilities	$ 40
Accounts receivable	30		
Inventory	40	Proprietor, capital	110
Plant and equipment (net)	70		
	$150		$150

If we assume some short-term debt to finance a seasonal increase in current assets, our balance sheet might appear as follows:

After incurring short-term debt

Cash	$ 15	Current liabilities	$ 90
Accounts receivable	50		
Inventory	65	Proprietor, capital	110
Plant and equipment (net)	70		
	$200		$200

After the season is over and we draw down our inventories and accounts receivable, we should be able to repay the $50 of current debt from the extra cash accumulated. If we assume that profits are withdrawn by the owner, the balance sheet will appear just as it did before incurring the debt. (We assume that as equipment depreciates, it is replaced with new equipment.)

However, we may need to increase permanently the level of our current assets and to purchase additional equipment. In this case, our balance sheet might appear as follows:

After incurring intermediate-term debt

Cash	$ 10	Current liabilities	$ 40
Accounts receivable	40	Long-term	50
Inventory	50	liabilities*	
Plant and equipment (net)	100	Proprietor, capital	110
	$200		$200

*Accountants classify non-current liabilities as "long-term debt." Only the current portions of intermediate-term debt are counted as part of current liabilities.

Usually, the proprietor will maintain his plant and equipment at its new level and allow sufficient earnings to accumulate to repay the debt. It is a two-step operation: momentarily, earnings are retained in the form of cash, and then the cash is applied to a reduction of the debt.

After repaying intermediate-term debt

Cash	$ 10	Current liabilities		$ 40
Accounts receivable	40	Prop., capital	$110	
Inventory	50	Add: retained		
Plant and equipment (net)	100	earnings	50	160
	$200			$200

In order to identify clearly the source of cash for repayment of the debt, we may refer to a statement of cash receipts and disbursements. It is assumed that revenues are $270; cash expenditures, including taxes, are $200; and depreciation expense, $20. The statement would then appear as follows:

Revenues	$270	Replacement of plant and		
Expenditures requiring the use of cash	200	equipment	$20	
		Repayment of intermediate-term debt	50	$70
Cash generated	$ 70	Net addition to cash		0

Observe that after repayment of intermediate- or long-term debt the current assets remain at their new, higher level. In a recession or long-run decline we could reduce the current assets to repay long-term debt. This is hardly an attractive prospect. If the recession is temporary, we will have to rebuild the current assets, possibly on disadvantageous terms.

Consequently, lenders engaged in intermediate- and long-term financing will be much more concerned with our earning power than when they evaluated our financial position for a possible short-term loan. Attention is focused less on the balance sheet, more on our income statement. They attempt to gauge our ability to generate cash over the long run. Earning power thus becomes the main security behind the loan. However, these lenders are still concerned that we maintain a strong current position, because any failure to pay current obligations is likely to involve them in our difficulties as well. There is no diminution in the importance assigned to our character and integrity and to the size of the owner's investment in relation to the total debt to be assumed.

Reasons for Using Intermediate-Term Debt

The nature of our need very largely determines the types of funds sought. We seek debt rather than equity funds for the various reasons covered in Chapter 10: that is, considerations of control, income, and so on. In addition, new equity funds obtained by issuing securities are just not suited to financing occasional purchases of machinery and equipment. We usually do not need very large amounts at any one time, and the initial marketing expense, or acquisition cost, of equity funds is frequently fairly high. To incur this expense for a financial need that may be present for only a few years would be most uneconomical. We would have very little use out of the funds obtained and the expense per year would probably be very high. In terms of its suitability to the nature of the assets financed, debt is more desirable than equity when intermediate-term financing is desired.

Why not use short-term debt? Probably we cannot generate cash rapidly enough to be assured of repaying our obligations within a year. Again, the nature of the assets financed must rule. We need to be assured of having the funds to use for some definite period—and for a period of longer than a year. Furthermore, we may not be able to "afford" additional short-term debt because of its effect on our current ratio. All except the current maturities of intermediate-term debt is classified as a long-term liability. If we use some of the funds obtained to acquire current assets or to repay current liabilities, the intermediate-term debt may materially improve our current position.

If not short-term debt, why not long-term debt? Again, we are up against the nature of the assets financed. If we do not need the money for 20 years, there is no use in paying for it over that period of time. The relatively small amounts often needed, especially by small companies, would be uneconomical to raise in the capital markets. Furthermore, our financing arrangements are made more easily through direct negotiation with a lender, as is typical of intermediate-term financing. Not only that, but the agreements we can make are probably more varied and can be more closely suited to our particular needs than the more formal arrangements reached in the capital markets. Finally, it may be less expensive to take out a term loan than to sell long-term bonds if rates on intermediate-term debt are lower than on long-term debt.

Characteristics of Intermediate-Term Financing

Loans that extend for one to ten years are frequently called *term loans.* A distinguishing feature of such loans is that they are usually *amortized:* that is, regular monthly, quarterly, or yearly installment payments are made which are applied to pay the interest and to reduce the principal of the loan outstanding. Home mortgages are amortized in the same fashion. We pay $80 a month for 20 years. At the beginning most of the $80 goes for interest and very little to reduce the principal, but over the years the proportion of our monthly payment which applies to the principal increases. Occasionally term loans are made to business which call for an extra large payment in the last year. Lenders ordinarily do not view these *balloon notes* too favorably. They have no reason to believe we are suddenly going to have money in the fifth year that we have not been able to generate in the preceding four years.

Intermediate-Term Financing from Commercial Banks

Extent of Use

In considering the role that commercial banks play in intermediate-term financing of business, we must remember that bankers have traditionally favored short-term loans because of the demand nature of their deposit liabilities. However, the needs of their borrowers coupled with their own desire to put money to work during periods of depression and recession have led bankers to make more and more term loans. With the advent of the Federal Deposit Insurance Corporation bankers have also had greater assurance that their depositors would not make mass withdrawals as they did during the early thirties. With the reduced liquidity of their deposits, banks can reduce the liquidity of their assets correspondingly. In addition, bank examiners have recognized the favorable aspects of the amortization feature of term loans. Because the borrower is making regular reductions in principal, the bank is getting its money back twice as rapidly as if it waited for a lump-sum payment on the final maturity date.

In spite of these incentives to adopt term loans, some bankers today are still unwilling to grant loans with an initial maturity in excess of one year.

These same bankers may be willing to extend demand notes or renew short-term notes for several years, although the reasoning behind this policy is a bit difficult to explain. Other bankers limit their term loans in relation to their time deposits or total loans or are unwilling to extend credit beyond five years. In general large banks in large communities grant term loans more frequently than small banks in small communities. At the end of August, 1970, almost 30 percent of the outstanding commercial and industrial loans of about 160 large commercial banks were made under term-loan agreements, with a concentration of such loans in New York and Chicago.[1]

Banks supply term loans to business concerns for two different purposes. First, they extend term loans for investment in permanent current assets and fixed assets, with the expectation that they will be repaid through funds generated from operations. Second, they extend interim credits to "tide the firm over" until it can sell an issue of bonds or stocks. In the latter case the bank will be repaid by the proceeds from the sale of the securities. This interim financing is most commonly used to finance the initial stages of a plant expansion. Under the usual arrangement the borrower can draw down needed funds as construction progresses. Then, near the end of construction, the loan is repaid by the sale of securities in the capital market. Like a seasonal loan, this arrangement economizes on the use of funds, since they are borrowed and paid for only when needed.

Terms

Term loans involve the pledge of collateral more frequently than seasonal, short-term loans. Banks reach for security most frequently on loans to small companies. Almost all term loans with maturities in excess of five years that are made to small businesses are secured. This practice is understandable if we consider the risk inherent in extending credit over this period of time to businesses which are frequently less stable and less protected against competition than larger concerns. Another reason for seeking collateral on term loans to small concerns is the lack of depth of management characteristic of many small companies ruled by one man. Bankers are willing to take liens on a variety of assets—showcases, counters, trucks, laundry and dry cleaning equipment, real estate, inventory, and accounts receivable.

Loans that are to be repaid from earnings may be extended for periods as long as ten years, although tight money markets often cause bankers to shorten the maximum maturity. Average maturities are probably closer to five years. By their very nature interim term loans to finance construction usually mature in two to three years.

Provisions to Prevent Dissipation of Assets, Especially Cash. When a bank has a lien on certain assets, it obviously wishes to be sure that these assets either remain in the business or that it has its loan repaid. The remaining assets provide additional security in case the assets pledged are insufficient. The current position and cash position are especially important if the bank is to receive its instalment payments on the loan. To protect itself on these accounts,

[1] *Federal Reserve Bulletin*, 56 (September, 1970), p. A31.

a bank is likely to make the following requirements in some form or other:

(1)   We must maintain a minimum net working capital (current assets minus current liabilities) and possibly a minimum current ratio. Often the requirement is that withdrawals by owners or payments of dividends are prohibited if they will reduce the net working capital or current ratio below the specified minimum.

(2)   In addition to net working capital requirements, the agreement may prevent our taking too much money out of the business by specifically limiting withdrawals or dividends. For example, withdrawals, payments of dividends, or redemption of capital stock may be restricted to earnings realized after the date the loan was made, or to some percentage of those earnings. We may have to obtain permission from the bank to raise officers' salaries.

(3)   To prevent our disposing of assets, we are ordinarily not permitted to sell fixed assets over a certain dollar amount without approval of the bank. For the same reason we will not be allowed to sell our accounts receivable.

(4)   To prevent our tying up funds in illiquid investments the bank is very likely to require that we obtain its permission before making any investments in fixed assets over a certain dollar amount. Nor will the bank allow us to make loans and advances to others or purchase securities other than U.S. government obligations without its prior approval.

Provisions to Prevent Pledge of Assets to Others. Not only is the bank interested in preventing the dissipation of the assets, but it also wishes to be sure that no outsider obtains a lien on those assets which would reduce the amount that would be realized by the bank in any liquidation. To protect its position, the bank is likely to make the following conditions:

(1)   The agreement will ordinarily contain a *negative pledge clause,* whereby we promise not to pledge our assets to anybody else.

(2)   The more borrowers in the picture besides the bank, the less will be left for the bank in the event of liquidation. Consequently, the bank will restrict additional borrowings in some fashion. In part the requirement that we maintain a minimum net working capital restricts our ability to add to our current liabilities. Long-term borrowings are usually subject to prior approval from the bank. For the same reason, the bank will ordinarily prohibit us from guaranteeing or endorsing an obligation for any other person or company.

Provisions to Assure the Bank of Continued Efficient Management. Since the bank is making a long-run commitment, it is interested in continuation of our present management and in being regularly informed of developments in our company. To achieve this end, the bank will make the following requirements:

(1)   The bank may take out, or require us to take out, insurance on the lives of key officers.

(2)   To keep the bank informed of our status, we must provide audited annual reports and often quarterly or semi-annual reports.

Finally, most agreements include an *acceleration clause.* This states that if we fail either to make the required payments or to live up to the provisions of the agreement the whole of the loan is immediately due and payable. Without such a clause, the bank would have to wait for each instalment payment on the note and sue to collect that. Obviously it is much simpler for the bank to take legal action to collect the entire loan. Furthermore, the acceleration clause enables the bank to step quickly into a situation and forestall further deterioration. When the alternative is immediate payment of the loan in full, we are apt to accept with alacrity any suggestions the bank makes for improving our financial position.

All of these covenants, coupled with the acceleration clause, appear very onerous and oppressive. To some extent we should expect this. If a bank is to let us have the use of its money for periods up to ten years, it is only reasonable that it should seek to protect itself during that period. The apparent harshness of these terms is tempered by two considerations. First, we should recognize that many of the policies required by the bank are only matters of good financial management. Even without specific strictures by a bank, we ought to maintain an adequate net working capital and restrict withdrawals or dividends to reasonable amounts in relation to earnings. Second, there is room for discretion on the part of the bank over the years. Because we are negotiating directly with one lender, or a small group of lenders, we are in a good position to attempt to renegotiate aspects of the agreement that later prove to handicap our operations. It is no more in the bank's interest than in ours to hamper operations so as to reduce our liquidity or profitability. However, we should negotiate from strength: our financial position and past adherence to the terms of the agreement should be above reproach.

We observed in Chapter 13 that the interest charge on bank loans is more closely related to the size of loan than to its maturity. Interest rates on term loans probably average a percentage point higher than those on short-term loans of similar size, although the spread varies with conditions in the money and capital markets. If the loan is handled through the consumer instalment loan department, the effective cost may be 12 percent to 18 percent. A growing practice on large term loans has been to adjust the rate over the life of the loan to variations in the prime bank rate. As an example, in early 1968, Northwest Airlines arranged a five-year, $95 million term loan with 18 banks, with the interest after December 31, 1969, to be at the prime rate plus $\frac{1}{4}$ of 1 percent, but not to exceed 6.5 percent.[2] Since the prime rate was at 8.5 percent by mid-1969, a certain feeling of contentment must have pervaded the financial manager's office at Northwest.

Another factor to consider is whether or not we can repay the loan ahead of time without penalty. If no provision for prepayment is included in our agreement, the bank would be entitled to insist upon its interest for the full period of the loan, even though we repay the loan prior to its scheduled maturity. Rather than adopt this narrow point of view, the bank would be more likely to allow us to prepay the loan without penalty or with only a small penalty, say one percent of the prepaid balance. Sometimes prepayment penalties are levied only if we obtain funds from other lenders in order to pay off the term loan at the bank.

Again it should be emphasized that we are bargaining over a package — a mix consisting of the maturity, terms of the agreement, and the interest to be

[2] *Wall Street Journal,* April 5, 1968, p. 19.

charged. The importance of the various elements of the package will vary among borrowers. We should be willing grudgingly to concede to the bank on those elements of the package that are unimportant to us in return for concessions from the bank on the aspects that are important to us. The final bargain reached will depend upon our financial position, the eagerness of the bank to put its money to work in this sort of loan, and our bargaining ability.

Intermediate-Term Financing From Insurance Companies

Loans of one to ten years duration are not as readily available from insurance companies as from commercial banks. A more common arrangement is for a bank and insurance company to join in financing an instalment loan to a business. Under this arrangement a bank might take the intermediate-term notes maturing in the first five or ten years, while the insurance companies would take the balance, which might extend up to 15 to 20 years. Actually, we would refer to the insurance company's portion of the loan as long-term credit.

Aside from these loans, insurance companies make few loans to small businesses. They are generally not equipped to handle the detailed and costly investigation necessary to develop term lending to small business on a large scale. In addition, a very high proportion of small concerns are unincorporated; and many state insurance laws prohibit loans of this sort to unincorporated firms. Insurance companies are able to play a much more important role in making loans in large amounts and for long terms, although they may still require that these loans be repaid in instalments.

The terms under which life insurance companies make loans are generally similar to those of commercial banks. Sometimes the insurance company requires a borrower to have a line of credit at a commercial bank to be sure that somebody is actively watching the borrower's current position. A requirement that the borrower clean up his bank lines for 30 to 60 days during every 12- or 15-month period is not uncommon, although this is sometimes an onerous requirement and is fought by both bank and borrower.

Equipment Loans from Finance Companies

The trend towards mechanization has resulted in a particularly rapid growth of intermediate-term financing by commercial finance companies for purchases of equipment. The dollar volume of this type of financing is small compared with their accounts receivable financing. However, the dollar amount outstanding is fairly large because the maturities on these loans are considerably longer than on accounts receivable loans.

Because the interest charges of finance companies are typically higher than those of commercial banks, we would be more likely to turn to this source of intermediate-term financing after finding that our needs could not be satisfactorily fulfilled by a commercial bank. Whether or not a finance company will finance the equipment will depend very largely on the estimated earning power of the equipment. Even though our net worth may be small in relation to the obligations incurred, we may still be able to finance the equipment if it will pay for itself and increase the owner's equity. Because finance companies rely primarily on the earning power of the equipment, they will be less concerned with our overall financial position and earnings. Consequently, they have less need to control our general operations through a rather elaborate agreement like that we might make with a bank.

There are two basic methods of financing equipment through a finance company: we can purchase it on instalment or lease it. (Leasing is discussed in Chapter 18.) In each instance we can deal directly with a finance company or indirectly with it through the distributor or manufacturer of the equipment. Observe that this latter arrangement differs from previously discussed forms of intermediate-term financing in which we were always dealing directly with the lender.

The instalment purchase of a piece of equipment, such as a barber's chair, a lathe, or a printing press, is similar to the instalment purchase of an automobile by a consumer. Almost any type of equipment may be purchased on instalment, although it should have a fairly long economic life and be removable. Should the equipment become a fixed part of the real estate of the instalment buyer, it is difficult to repossess. Ordinarily we must make a down payment and sign a security agreement that rests title to the equipment with the holder of our obligation until we fulfill our debt. If we fail to make the required payments, the lender will repossess the equipment.

We are concerned with our terms of purchase—the down payment, the maturity, and the interest charge. The down payment and maturity are interrelated in that the lender tries to adjust these so that our unpaid balance will always be below the resale value of the equipment. For example, if the equipment is highly specialized, its immediate resale value will be low, and the lender is likely to require a high down payment. If the machine depreciates slowly, we may be able to stretch the maturity on our note to five, or even ten, years. Or if we agree to make a relatively large down payment, we may be able to stretch out the maturity, even though the equipment depreciates fairly rapidly. Down payments typically range from 10 to 35 percent and maturities from 12 to 42 months, although longer maturities are available.

Most finance companies now provide that payments may be made in accordance with whatever depreciation system we are using or to fit seasonal movements in sales. The philosophy is that payments for the machine are attuned to the rate at which cash is generated. If we feel that the more valuable portion of the services of a machine are received in the early years of its life, we may use the "sum-of-the-digits" method of depreciation. This system allows us to "bunch" the depreciation expense of the machine in the early years of its life when determining our taxable income. If we are allowed to depreciate the equipment over three years, we may take as a depreciation charge $\frac{3}{6}$ of the initial cost the first year; $\frac{2}{6}$, the second year, and $\frac{1}{6}$, the third year.[3] An example of

---

[3]The sum-of-the-digits plan means that to obtain the denominator of the fraction applicable to the initial cost we add up the number of years involved. Thus, if the machine is depreciated over three years, the denominator is 6 (1 + 2 + 3). In the first year the numerator is equal to the number of years over which the machine is to be depreciated. In the second year the numerator is one less; in the third year, two less, and so on.

fitting payments to seasonal movements in income is provided by the American Machine and Foundry Company. When it finances the purchase of its automatic pinspotting equipment by bowling centers, the company requires only eight monthly payments a year. No payments are necessary during the summer months when bowling centers show less profit.

Because the interest charge is computed on the original upaid balance, we must keep in mind that the true, or effective, rate is about double the stated rate. Since we are making monthly payments on principal, the amount of money we actually have in use over the life of our contract is about half the original balance. Effective annual rates range from 8 to 24 percent.

Intermediate-Term Financing by Government Agencies

Although government agencies have a relatively small role in financing business, there are various lending programs currently in force which may be of great benefit to individual companies. We will consider only the major programs of financial assistance, but there are many other programs ranging from insurance to subsidies to loans and grants.[4]

Government loan programs have certain common characteristics that are worthy of note at the outset. First, the emphasis is on intermediate-term loans; no equity funds are made available directly by government agencies. Second, the government is viewed as a "court of last resort." In most cases to borrow under one of these programs we must be able to show that we have tried and been unable to obtain a loan from banks and possibly other private lenders. In other words, legislatures have not wished to put the government into competition with private lenders. Third, because these agencies are a court of last resort and should receive only marginal applications, a high proportion of those applications are denied. Fourth, loans approved are usually extended at a uniform rate of interest and a rate that is probably below the "market rate" for the grade of risk. In other words an element of subsidy is involved. Fifth, a relatively high proportion of loans are made to manufacturing concerns, a reflection of their needs for funds to carry inventories and to purchase machinery and equipment. Finally, in almost all cases the loans are secured.

Small Business Administration

The most ambitious program currently in force to aid small business is that of the Small Business Administration (SBA). For some time Congress has been sympathetic towards the difficulties faced by small business in raising funds.[5] Although there are a number of advantages to being small, ease of financing is not one of them.

[4] See *Handbook for Small Business: A Survey of Small Business Programs of the Federal Government,* 3rd ed. (Washington, D.C.: Senate Select Committee on Small Business and the House Select Committee on Small Business, 1969).

[5] This sentimental attachment to small business may be more understandable if we consider that there are over 4.6 million small business firms in the United States.

According to section 207 of the Small Business Act of 1953, SBA is empowered to:

> . . . make loans to enable small-business concerns to finance plant construction, conversion, or expansion, including the acquisition of equipment, facilities, machinery, supplies, or materials; or to supply such concerns with working capital to be used in the manufacture of articles, equipment, supplies, or materials for war, defense, or essential civilian production or as may be necessary to insure a well-balanced national economy.

All manufacturing concerns with 250 or fewer employees are considered as "small" and eligible for SBA loans. Firms with between 250 and 1500 employees may be eligible, depending upon the type of industry. Those with more than 1500 employees are not entitled to borrow from the SBA. Qualifications of non-manufacturing concerns are based upon their annual dollar sales.

Credit requirements are similar to those a bank would make for a term loan, only in application they may be somewhat less stringent. If we are applying for a loan, we must be able to show that we have good character, ability to operate the business successfully, a record of past income and future prospects which suggests our ability to repay the loan out of income, sufficient owners' equity, and adequate collateral.

There are two basic types of loans for which we might apply: *direct loans* and *participation loans*. The first type of loan is obtained directly from the SBA. With the second type the SBA participates with a bank in a loan or guarantees payment of part of the loan up to 90 percent. In recent years emphasis has been on participation loans, in part because of opposition by bankers to direct competition by a government agency and in part because of a shortage of funds at the SBA.

While the rate of interest on the SBA's share of a loan is set at a maximum of $5\frac{1}{2}$ percent, a bank may set a rate higher than that on its share of a loan, providing the rate is legal and reasonable. Certainly, the SBA's rate is below the "going market rate" for loans of this size and risk. The greatest amount of credit the SBA can extend to any one borrower is usually $350,000 although on participation loans the total amount we may receive is considerably greater if the bank's share is large. While the average maturity is around five years, the maximum term permitted is usually ten years, generally repayable in monthly instalments.

If we wish a participation loan, our bank will make the application. The SBA has made a valiant and relatively successful effort to reduce the amount of red tape required to obtain a loan. Under the "Simplified Blanket Loan Guarantee Plan," for example, the SBA signs a master agreement with a bank. Issuance or denial of a loan guarantee is provided by the SBA within ten work days, and most of the servicing is handled by the bank.

As a contribution to the antipoverty program, the SBA offers loans for truly small businesses operated by low-income persons or those economically disadvantaged who cannot find other sources of credit. Economic opportunity loans may be made for up to $25,000 at a maximum maturity of 15 years.

Rather than deny the loan because of inadequate collateral, the SBA relies "on the character of the applicant and the projected performance of the firm."[6] As part of the loan agreement, the SBA may require a borrower to undertake management training.

Because public moneys and emotions are involved, certain types of loans may not be approved by SBA. These include loans to "bail out" other creditors; to effect a change in ownership of the business; to speculate in any kind of property; to finance businesses that are involved in gambling or that derive a substantial portion of gross income from the sale of alcoholic beverages.

State Development Authorities

State development authorities use public funds in an effort to attract industry and redevelop depressed areas. They originated in 1955 with the Industrial Park Authority of New Hampshire. The Pennsylvania Industrial Development Authority (PIDA), which was organized in the following year, has served as a model for a number of other states. Loans of the authority may be made only to non-profit community development corporations or foundations. In order to attract a manufacturer to its community the local group builds a plant, which it then leases to the manufacturer at an attractive rental. Of the total cost at least 10 percent must be provided by the local group, up to 40 percent by PIDA, and the remainder through conventional sources based on a first mortgage on the plant. States that have followed in Pennsylvania's footsteps have introduced numerous variations in this basic plan, including loan guarantee programs similar to that of the SBA.

Industrial Aid Bonds

These tax-exempt securities are issued by a city or county to finance the construction of a plant that is then leased to industry. Ordinarily the municipality can secure financing at a lower cost than the manufacturing corporation. Moreover, there are no property taxes on the municipally-owned plant. As a result a corporation may find that it is considerably cheaper to accept this arrangement than to build its own facilities. The bonds are either a general obligation of the city or are backed by the anticipated revenues from the lease on the plant. The rapid growth in the use of industrial aid bonds was sharply curtailed in 1968 by removal of the tax exemption of all issues in excess of $5 million.[7] In view of this change, it is unlikely that they will provide a significant source of funds for business in the future.

---

[6] *Ibid.,* p. 171.

[7] The Federal legislation "also prohibits public financing support of large projects by limiting the capital spending of the recipient firm to a total of $5 million in any one location over a period of 3 years before and 3 years after the issue." Edwin C. Gooding, "The New Status of Industrial Aid Bonds," *New England Business Review* (Federal Reserve Bank of Boston), November, 1968, p. 2. See also, Susan R. Robinson, "Industrial Development Bonds: They're Not What They Used to Be," *Business Review* (Federal Reserve Bank of Philadelphia), March, 1969, pp. 3–8.

Government-Sponsored Credit Agencies

Small Business Investment Companies

Small Business Investment Companies (SBIC's) are not government agencies, but are licensed by the SBA under the Small Business Investment Act of 1958. They are operated by private citizens to provide long-term debt and equity funds for small business, as defined by the SBA.

At the time of formation an SBIC must usually have at least $300,000 paid-in capital and surplus obtained from private sources. Once it has committed a substantial portion of private equity and borrowed funds to small-business loans, the SBA may lend to the SBIC an amount up to two times the capital account of the SBIC. The debt owed the SBA may be subordinated to the claims of private lenders.[8] Thus private individuals might invest $300,000 in an SBIC and borrow an additional $300,000. Upon investment of at least 75 percent of funds, a subordinated loan of an additional $600,000 might be obtained from the SBIC, which, in turn, would support further borrowing from private sources. Avid readers will recognize this as *leverage*.

Only small business concerns, as defined by the SBA, can receive funds from SBIC's. Generally, they must have assets less than $5 million, net worth less than $2.5 million, and average net income after taxes of less than $250,000 over the previous two years. Although SBIC's are permitted to purchase the common stock of a small business, most have provided funds through long-term loans or by the purchase of debentures (unsecured bonds) that may later be converted into common stock at the option of the SBIC. No more than 20 percent of an SBIC's paid-in capital and surplus may be invested in any one small-business concern. However, SBIC's frequently pool their resources to make large loans. Usually loans and debentures carry maturities greater than five years.

Considerable encouragement to the formation of SBIC's is given through special tax privileges. Dividends received by an SBIC on its investment in stocks are exempt from the corporate income tax. Losses realized by the SBIC may be taken as an offset against ordinary income for tax purposes, rather than as a capital-loss deduction. Similarly, investors in an SBIC may report any loss on the stock as an ordinary-loss deduction. This feature is of particular benefit to stockholders in high tax brackets.

In their brief span of existence SBIC's have had a somewhat checkered career. Because of the heavy fixed cost of screening applicants for loans, SBIC's have typically not relieved the financing problems of very small businesses, but have provided funds for larger "small" concerns. While some adjustments have been made in regulations restricting the SBIC's, it seems unlikely that they can be forced into performing a lending function that is uneconomical. Officers of SBIC's have discovered to their sorrow that an extensive sorting is needed to find a few attractive investment opportunities. As illustration, Continental Capital "investigated more than 1,000 possible financings in its first ten years; of

---

[8] Borrowings from the SBA may be up to three times the excess of capital funds above $1 million, provided that 65 percent of total funds available for investment are invested or committed in venture capital investments.

these, about 150 were considered by its directors, and 64 investments were actually disbursed . . ."[9] On the investor's side there has been the unwelcome discovery that a considerable period of time elapses between placing funds with an SBIC and obtaining a profit on the investment. Continental Capital reports an "incubation period" on new investments of about five years.

State Development Credit Corporations[10]

The earliest and most active state development credit corporations were in New England, the first having been established in Maine in 1949. These are private corporations which sell common stock to individuals and nonfinancial corporations. The bulk of their funds comes from commercial banks and other financial institutions which have been permitted by special legislation to pledge a line of credit to these corporations. For example, a commercial bank may be permitted to pledge 2 or $2\frac{1}{2}$ percent of its capital and surplus. Total borrowings of a development corporation may amount to as much as ten times its issued stock and surplus.

Since the purpose of the development corporation is to shore up the economies of the state, business concerns most likely to succeed in obtaining a loan are those needing funds to expand, those offering to establish a plant in an area of surplus labor, and those faced with the alternative of closing and adding to surplus labor.

Almost all loans made are secured, although the degree of protection required is often less ample than might be found on a commercial bank loan.

Intermediate-Term Financing From Suppliers and Manufacturers[11]

Although the total dollar amounts are small compared to total intermediate-term financing, credit extended by suppliers and manufacturers is important in certain lines of business, especially to small concerns. In fact, this form of financing arises for the most part because the supplier or manufacturer is in a stronger financial position than the retailer. To build retail outlets financial assistance over and above normal trade credit is necessary. Hence, these financial arrangements can be considered in large part as marketing devices. For this reason credit standards are often more lenient than those applied by banks and finance companies.

Various arrangements have been devised to enable retail outlets to buy equipment necessary to store or display the products of the distributor or manufacturer. Suppliers of dairy products provide refrigeration equipment which can be paid for over five years. A filling station operator can often finance

[9] NASBIC News (National Association of Small Business Investment Companies), June 26, 1969, p. 4.

[10] The material in this section is based upon Paul S. Anderson, "State Development Credit Corporations," Financing Small Business (Washington, D.C.: Federal Reserve System, 1958), pp. 336–54; U.S. Department of Commerce, "Statewide Industrial Development Credit Corporations and State Development Authorities" (April, 1958); and Edwin C. Gooding, op. cit. (November, 1968).

[11] The material in this section is based in part upon Robert S. Einzig, "Credit from Large to Small Business," Financing Small Business (Washington, D.C.: Federal Reserve System, 1958), pp. 491–92.

equipment through the oil company supplying his products. In both of these cases arrangements may sometimes be made to repay the debt through additional charges on the actual costs of the products purchased by the dealer. Grain companies and sugar refiners provide storage facilities at customers' plants or offer long-term loans so that their customers may purchase their own equipment and facilities.

In other cases the large company finances the retailer's working capital needs. Loans up to ten years are available from subsidiaries of one of the shoe manufacturers, and working capital loans are also available to filling station operators. Qualified automobile dealers may arrange to have 75 or 80 percent of their needs financed from the manufacturer through preferred stock which is then retired over a period of five to seven years.

Sometimes the distributor or manufacturer does not offer funds directly, but guarantees or endorses a dealer's note. A promise by a manufacturer to buy back any unsold merchandise held by a dealer is of material aid to the dealer in financing his inventory through a bank or finance company. A similar principle was involved when Walt Disney financed Disneyland. The 32 concessionaires paid rent for the first and last years of a five-year lease, and the "Disneys then hocked the middle three-year lease expectations at the bank."[12]

Summary

Whereas short-term loans are ordinarily repaid by seasonal reductions in accounts receivable and inventory, monthly payments on interest and principal of intermediate-term debt must usually come from cash profits. A large portion of the increased use of machinery and equipment is financed through term loans, especially among small companies. Insurance companies are more likely to provide long-term funds to large borrowers than intermediate-term loans to small concerns. Those in strong financial positions are often able to obtain term loans from commercial banks, although they must be able to offer security and adhere to fairly rigid requirements to protect the position of the bank. To finance equipment, borrowers in somewhat less fortunate circumstances or those who desire more flexible financing arrangements may turn to commercial finance companies. Equipment may also be purchased on the instalment plan. Borrowers whose applications for term loans are denied by private lenders may be able to obtain a term loan from some government agency or through a private, government-sponsored company. Small companies would naturally look to the Small Business Administration or to a Small Business Investment Corporation. Some firms may finance their plant indirectly through a state development authority, or directly via a lease from a state development credit corporation. Finally, in some lines of business, intermediate-term financing may be obtained from suppliers and manufacturers, who tend to view their financial aid primarily as a marketing device.

In general, as we go from commercial banks and insurance companies, to finance companies, to government agencies, to manufacturers and suppliers, credit standards become more lenient. However, they never become very

---

[12] *Business Week*, July 24, 1965, p. 82.

lenient. We are still expected to have an adequate equity base and to demonstrate managerial ability, integrity, and potential earnings sufficient to repay the loan.

Questions

1/ Would term loans be suitable for financing seasonal accumulations of accounts receivable and inventory? Why or why not?

2/ If an owner will eventually substitute retained earnings for a term loan, why would he not make the necessary addition to equity to begin with and so avoid the term loan?

3/ Under what circumstances might it be desirable to substitute a term loan for short-term borrowing?

4/ A study of loans outstanding at large commercial banks as of August 26, 1970, showed that term loans amounted to 44 percent of total loans granted to the petroleum refining industry, but only 16 percent of loans to firms in the wholesale trade. How do you explain this difference?

5/ What advantage can you see that a borrower might obtain from having a "balloon note"? What disadvantages?

6/ Why should lenders require relatively higher down payments and shorter maturities on loans secured by used equipment than on loans secured by new equipment?

7/ If you are seeking a term loan from a bank at the present time, would you ask for a fixed interest rate, or would you be willing to tie the rate paid to the prime rate? What factors influenced your decision and how?

8/ During what stage of the business cycle would you particularly desire lenient prepayment provisions on a term loan? Explain.

9/ "In most Government credit programs the interest rate is uniform for all geographical areas and for all loan sizes, risks, and maturities. Another characteristic is that the rates change infrequently." (Carl T. Arlt, "Government Loan Programs for Small Business," *Financing Small Business,* Washington, D.C., Federal Reserve System, 1958, p. 270.) Comment on the desirability of this practice from the point of view of public policy.

10/ "The Government loan programs have not been financially self-sustaining; in each case, the income from interest and participation and guaranty fees has not covered costs. . . ." (Arlt, *op. cit.,* p. 275.) Comment on the desirability of this procedure from the point of view of public policy.

Problem

1/ The David Ewert Bowling Corp. is considering financing ten alleys costing a total of $45,000 through the manufacturer. After a 10 percent downpayment the balance may be repaid in 24 monthly instalments of $1856.25. (Based on *Wall Street Journal,* November 18, 1964.)

a. What is the dollar amount of interest charged?

b. What is the approximate rate of interest being charged. (If you wish to to be especially erudite, you may use the formula shown in footnote 9, Chapter 13.)

c. For a business in this risk class, the rate appears to be somewhat low. How do you explain this?

Selected References

BUDZEIKA, G., "Term Lending by New York City Banks," in Federal Reserve Bank of New York, *Essays in Money and Credit* (New York, 1964), pp. 62–66.

CREPAS, K. J. and R. A. STEVENSON, "Are Industrial Aid Bonds Fulfilling Their Intended Purpose?" *Financial Analysis Journal,* 24 (November-December, 1968), pp. 105–9.

DAVLIN, W. R., "State Development Corporations: The Pennsylvania Experience," *Law and Contemporary Problems,* 24 (Winter, 1959), pp. 89–97.

HAYES, D. A., *Bank Lending Policies: Issues and Practices,* Ch. 6. Ann Arbor, Mich.: Bureau of Business Research, University of Michigan, 1964.

HAYES, S. L. and D. H. WOODS, "Are SBICs Doing Their Job?" *Harvard Business Review,* 41 (March-April, 1963), pp. 6–8.

Small Business Administration, *Annual Reports.*

SUSS, F. T., "SBA Small Business Financing Programs," *The Business Lawyer,* 18 (November, 1962), pp. 120–25.

ZEIDMAN, P. F., "The Small Business Investment Company–A Tool for Economic Self-Help," *Business Lawyer,* 21 (July, 1966), pp. 947–63.

Part Five

Managing Long-Term Funds

The Money and Capital Markets

15

As we move from short-term and intermediate-term sources of funds to long-term sources, we find that the arrangements under which funds are obtained are typically more formal. For example, agreements that bind borrower and lender for a quarter-century must be drawn with detailed care. Moreover, the amounts involved are likely to be larger than in the case of short-term credit. Contrast the open accounts under trade credit with outstanding balances of a few dollars with the multimillion dollar issues of bonds and stocks of giant corporations. Many more millions of dollars are retained for reinvestment than are paid out to owners.

In this section we are concerned with obtaining and managing long-term funds. Because timing our entry into the long-term market for funds is of crucial importance, our first order of business will be a careful examination of the market from which these funds are obtainable. The better our understanding of the flow of funds through the money and capital markets, the more likely we are to time an issue of securities so that we obtain terms that are favorable to to the residual owners. The analysis of these markets is the subject of this chapter.

Once we have decided when to issue securities, our next question may be "How?" Consequently, the following chapter will deal with the processes of obtaining money from the capital market. Following that, we can then analyze the various arrangements by which it is possible to obtain long-term funds. These are covered in the remaining chapters of this section.

Characteristics of Money and Capital Markets

Meaning

There are various meanings or definitions of the money market and the capital market. Technically the term *money market* covers only impersonal or stand-ardized forms of short-term credit. Thus the money market is "the active market for money and close money substitutes which financial institutions and others rely upon to provide the liquidity needed in the usual course of their operations. This would not include the bank checking accounts of most individuals or of most business firms; nor would it take in most savings deposits or savings bonds."[1] Some of the principal money market instruments are short-term U.S. government obligations, interbank loans and balances, and issues of U.S. government agencies. Banks and the Federal government have a relatively important role in the organized money market, while large business corporations reach into it by selling their commercial paper and by buying short-term government obligations and commercial paper of other concerns for temporary investment.

In recent years the volume of money market instruments has grown substantially, and daily transactions in the money market now amount to several billions of dollars. Through this market temporary demands for cash by some economic units are quickly and efficiently satisfied by other economic units with short-term, excess balances of cash.

In contrast, within the *customers' market* we have short-term loans arranged directly by business with a lender. The principal lenders in this market are the commercial banks. This is a highly personal sort of market. Tradition, loyalty, ignorance, or lack of bargaining power may weld a borrower to one bank for many years, regardless of seemingly more attractive sources of funds elsewhere.

The *capital market* deals in long-term securities, both debt and equity. Among the instruments traded are U.S. government securities (long-term) and corporate bonds, preferred stocks, and common stocks.

The markets are closely interrelated, because both lenders and borrowers may, within limits, move from one to the other. Commercial banks are especially fluid, as they may shift among U.S. government bills (money market), business loans (customers' market), and corporate bonds (capital market) as considerations of liquidity and profitability dictate. On the other side of the market a large corporation may raise funds by selling commercial paper (money market),

[1] Robert V. Roosa, *Federal Reserve Operations in the Money and Government Securities Markets* (New York: Federal Reserve Bank of New York, 1956), p. 11.

obtaining a direct loan from a bank (customers' market), or by selling bonds or stock (capital market). As we shall see, the interrelationships among the markets and their various segments are complex, ever-changing, and never dull.

Institutions

The institutions involved in the money and capital markets are frequently highly specialized. We shall be dealing with many of them in greater detail later. In part the law forces these institutions to specialize. Commercial banks may no longer participate in the marketing of newly issued corporate securities. Mutual savings banks may not accept demand deposits or make unsecured loans to business. In part, competition forces institutions to specialize. Because the money and capital markets are complex and dynamic you have to be good to survive. There is no such thing as a little mistake on a $100 million bond issue. Since it is usually not possible to be good at everything, institutions and individuals tend to concentrate on fairly narrow aspects of financial operations. Thus we find firms that specialize in marketing new issues of securities for chemical companies, or in selling municipal bonds, or in dealing in U.S. government obligations. Since people within these firms also have specialized roles in these financial operations, the decisions made are typically well-informed and shrewd. Consequently, the money and capital markets generally provide a sensitive and sensible instrument for directing the flow of funds into the hands of business, agriculture, government, and consumers.

Location

Where are the money and capital markets? Actually, they are all over the country, although a good deal of the activities are concentrated in New York. The banker in Sheboygan, Wisconsin, making a short-term loan to enable a farmer to buy some cows is part of the money market. The finance company in Atlanta that finances the purchase of a new car by a carpenter is part of the money market. However, many financial transactions around the country are related to the New York market. The Sheboygan banker very likely has an interbank balance in New York, and the finance company probably borrows from some banks in New York and sells its bonds through some bond houses in New York. Although its importance in relation to other financial centers, such as Chicago and Los Angeles, has probably declined somewhat over the years, New York remains as the leading financial center of the nation.

To seek funds intelligently in these markets requires a broad understanding of their functioning. Only the most general relationships can be covered in this chapter. Indications of the complexities involved may encourage further study, especially concerning the impact on the money and capital markets of monetary and fiscal policies. Fortunately, most financial managers have access to specialized advice in their dealings with the money and capital markets, either from members of the board of directors, from attorneys, or from individuals directly involved in the markets.

Flow of Funds

The extent of participation of large and small businesses in the financial markets varies considerably. Small companies rely principally on the customers' market for those funds that the owners cannot supply. Short-term bank loans and credit granted by suppliers are the two most important outside sources of funds for these companies, although the total dollar amount involved is a fairly small portion of total short-term credit extended to business. These small companies are forced to depend on the customers' market for their external funds because they generally find that the money and capital markets are inaccessible, especially if they are unincorporated (proprietorships and partnerships). For the most part the institutions and practices that have developed in the capital market are most efficient in channeling large amounts of funds to large corporations. The ease with which blocks of securities ranging to $100 million, and sometimes more, are sold in the capital market serves as good evidence of the efficiency of this market.

Because of the dominance of corporations in the money and capital markets and because of the lack of adequate information on sources of funds of unincorporated business, we shall concentrate on the flow of funds through the money and capital markets to corporations. We shall exclude as users of funds banks, insurance companies, and investment companies, since they will be considered as suppliers of funds. At the outset we should also make clear that, except where specifically noted, all estimates of sources and uses of funds appearing in this chapter are on a net, rather than a gross, basis. Thus the *gross* proceeds of newly issued securities may be $100 million, but if $40 million is used to repay other outstanding debts, the *net* funds obtained amount to $60 million.

Relative Importance of Internal and External Funds

To illustrate the functioning of the money and capital markets let us turn to estimates for 1966–70 (Table 15-1). During these eight years non-financial corporations used about $361 billion for purchases of plant and equipment and about $91 billion for increases in gross working capital in the form of inventories, receivables, and miscellaneous assets. From Table 15-1 we can see that $311 billion, or over three-fifths of total funds used, was obtained from internal sources: retained profits and depreciation allowances. Our concern in this chapter is with the remaining two-fifths, about $195 billion, that was obtained for the most part from the capital and money markets. Of this amount about 62 percent was secured from the capital market and the balance from short-term creditors.

Relative Importance of Types of External Funds Obtained

Particularly noteworthy is the fact that these corporations borrowed more than nine dollars out of every ten that they obtained externally. In view of our discovery in Chapter 11 that debt is normally the least expensive component of a firm's capital structure, we should not find this result surprising. However, some

TABLE 15-1   Sources and Uses of Funds of Business Corporations,[a] 1966–1970 (in billions of dollars)

Sources of Funds		
Internal Sources:		
Retained profits		89.3
Depreciation allowances		221.3
Total internal sources		310.6
External Sources:		
Long-term funds:		
Long-term debt	65.7	
Preferred and common stock	12.0	
Net new issues		77.7
Mortgages		22.3
Term bank loans		18.6
Total long-term funds		118.6
Short-term funds:		
Notes and accounts payable[b]		21.1
Short-term bank loans		19.8
Federal income tax liabilities		(1.6)
Other liabilities		36.8
Total short-term funds		76.1
Total external sources		194.7
Total sources		505.3

Uses of Funds		
Plant and Equipment		360.9
Working Capital (gross)		
Inventories (book value)	39.1	
Receivables	40.5	
Miscellaneous	11.5	
Total working capital		91.1
Statistical discrepancy		30.0
Total uses		482.0
Excess of sources over uses		23.3
Net change in cash and near cash		
Cash	2.3	
U.S. government securities	(0.3)	
Open market paper	21.3	23.3

[a] Covers all corporations except banks, insurance companies, and investment companies.
[b] Includes bankers acceptances, commercial paper, finance company paper, U.S. government payables, and trade payables.
Source: Banker's Trust Company, *The Investment Outlook for 1970*, Tables 26, 27. Based on Department of Commerce, Securities and Exchange Commission and Other Financial Data.

portion of the debt was convertible into common stock. Of the net new issues of securities only $12 billion represented issues of preferred or common stocks. Hence a classification of the types of funds obtained externally appears as follows:

Short-term debt	$ 76.1
Long-term debt	106.6
Total debt	182.7
Net new issues of stocks	12.0
Total external funds	$194.7

To a considerable extent this emphasis on debt is balanced by the large amount of retained earnings. With retained earnings as a cushion of equity, corporations are naturally in a position where they can borrow when they go outside the company for funds. In addition the high proportion of debt funds flowing through the various channels to business concerns is a product of the nature of the channels themselves. For reasons which should become apparent later, the institutions that dominate in supplying funds to corporations usually surrender their funds in return for the rights of creditors rather than the rights of owners. The large investment made in plant and equipment (Table 15-1) suggests a need for long-term rather than short-term funds. Furthermore, the period under study was generally characterized by rising prices and rising sales. As a result, businesses were also making relatively permanent investments in higher-priced inventories and receivables. The high corporate income tax rates made long-term debt especially attractive as a means of meeting these needs, because the interest payment on debt was a tax-deductible expense.

The Origin of External Funds

External funds for the use of business, agriculture, government, and consumers originate in credit created by the commercial banking system, in personal savings, and from foreign investment.

Credit Created by Commercial Banks. Credit may be created by the commercial banking system because of the *fractional reserve* system. Essentially this means that a commercial bank does not need to keep on hand $100 in cash for every $100 in deposits. Under the rules of the Federal Reserve System member banks are required to keep only a portion of their deposits as cash in the vault and on deposit with a Federal Reserve bank. To simplify our explanation, let us say that the required reserve is 20 percent. Thus a bank might have the following balance sheet:

First National Bank

Assets		Liabilities and capital	
Cash	$ 100	Deposits	$2,000
Deposit with Federal Reserve bank	400	Capital	300
U.S. government securities	1,000		
Loans	800		
	$2,300		$2,300

If the Federal Reserve bank buys the U.S. government obligation from this bank, the Federal Reserve bank will credit the purchase price of the security ($1000) to the commercial bank's deposit with the Federal Reserve bank. Then the commercial bank will have a reserve of $1400. Since the bank needs to keep only 20 percent of deposits in its reserve, it has excess reserves of $1000, since 20% × $2000 = $400. No interest is paid on the deposit at the Federal Reserve bank. Because banks like to be profitmaking institutions, this bank will probably make a loan of $1000 to somebody. The initial result of making the loan will be to increase the asset, "loans," by $1000 and to increase deposit liabilities by the same amount. In other words when a bank makes a loan to a business, it does not shove currency across the counter, but credits the amount of the loan to the borrower's account. The balance sheet would then momentarily appear:

First National Bank

Assets		*Liabilities and capital*	
Cash	$ 100	Deposits	$3,000
Deposit with Federal Reserve bank	1,400	Capital	300
Loans	1,800		
	$3,300		$3,300

Thus the bank has created credit by loaning an amount equal to its excess reserves. Some business firm now has the use of $1000. Assume that this business firm draws a check for $1000 on its newly created deposit to pay a bill. The recipient of the check deposits it in a second bank. That bank's deposit liabilities are thereby increased by $1000, while the deposit liabilities of the first bank are decreased by the same amount. In the process of clearing the check the Federal Reserve bank transfers $1000 from the deposit account of the first bank to the deposit account of the second bank. This is a much simpler way of handling the matter than for the first bank to wrap up $1000 in currency and send it to the second bank. The balance sheet of the first bank now appears:

First National Bank

Assets		*Liabilities and capital*	
Cash	$ 100	Deposits	$2,000
Deposit with Federal Reserve bank	400	Capital	300
Loans	1,800		
	$2,300		$2,300

Now the second bank has an additional deposit at the Federal Reserve bank of $1000 and an additional deposit liability of $1000. Since it needs to keep only 20 percent, or $200, of the new deposit on reserve, it can lend an amount equal to its excess reserves, or $800; that is, it can create credit on the amount of $800. Just after the $800 loan has been made, the changes in the balance sheet of the second bank would appear as:

Second National Bank

Deposits with Federal Reserve bank	+ $1,000	Deposits	+ 1,800
		(Acquired	1,000)
Loans	+ 800	(Created	800)

In due course the $800 newly created deposit is put to use by the borrower and added to the deposits of another bank. That bank in turn creates credit to the extent of its newly acquired *excess* reserves of $640. By travelling from bank to bank in this fashion, the initial $1000 of excess reserves obtained by the first bank is capable of increasing the flow of credit by $5000, assuming a 20 percent reserve is required. To put it another way, when banks must maintain $1 in their reserves for every $5 in deposits, a rise of $1000 in excess reserves enables the commercial banking system to increase deposits by $5000. Since deposits originate when banks make loans and investments, we can also say that a rise of $1000 in reserves makes possible an increase in loans and investments of $5000.

Personal Savings. Personal savings may be defined as the excess of personal income over consumption expenditures, taxes, and other payments to the government. Over the past several years annual personal savings have grown from about $20 billion to over $50 billion:

1963 – $19.9	1967 – $40.4
1964 – 26.2	1968 – 40.4
1965 – 28.4	1969 – 37.6
1966 – 32.5	1970 I − 44.8 (annual rate)
	1970 II − 51.5 (annual rate)

The relatively stable growth in the rate of personal savings is noteworthy. Should demand for investable funds level off, as it did during the early part of 1967, and individuals continue to supply increasing savings, it would seem likely that users of funds would have to pay less. This is precisely what happened. However, later in 1967 and the following year business firms raised their investment in inventories, plant, and equipment. Individuals made greater use of

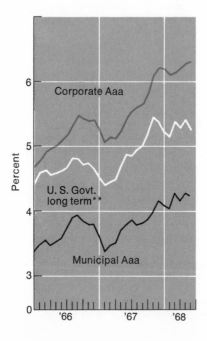

BOND YIELDS

instalment credit and did not increase their rate of saving. The net effect was to bring about an increase in the cost of long-term funds, as may be seen in the accompanying chart. This was also a period of restrictive monetary policy which sharply reduced the flow of reserves into the banking system. This is something of an over-simplification of the forces at work in the period, but the discussion may suggest some of the basic relationships.

Foreign Investment. Funds are also provided in the money and capital markets by foreign investors. Short-term liabilities to foreigners reported by banks in the United States rose to $41.8 billion at mid-1970, from $27.6 billion at the end of 1966. Because funds provided by foreigners are considerably less than those created by the banking system and generated by personal savings, they are not specifically considered in the discussion that follows.

At certain times movements of foreign capital have considerable significance, especially in the money market. Even without movements of these claims, the large short-term liability to foreigners in relation to available monetary gold supplies has been a very important influence upon fiscal and monetary policies. Should short-term money rates in the United States be allowed to fall significantly below similar rates in other countries, foreigners would be likely to withdraw their funds. But further drains of the U.S. gold supply could have a severe impact upon the money supply and the level of economic activity. Consequently, the money managers have a much more difficult task in this decade than they did before the United States became an important international banker. For the same reason, the money managers of business firms also face a more complex world.

Yield differentials on deposit balances in the U.S. and foreign countries have contributed to the growth of the *Eurodollar* market. These are simply deposits denominated in U.S. dollars at commercial banks outside the United States, mostly in Europe. They arise in a number of ways. For example, an English firm (or a U.S. firm) holding deposits in a U.S. bank may transfer those deposits to a London bank. A French manufacturer selling his product in the U.S. may deposit checks drawn on U.S. bank accounts in his bank in Paris.

American companies have found Eurodollars useful to finance working capital needs of their foreign operations. Not only do Eurodollars provide a media for short-term loans and investments, but they may also be tapped by issues of long-term bonds. Thus a U.S. firm may sell dollar-denominated bonds in England. One advantage to business firms in using these markets is that they are relatively free of controls that at times distort financial markets in the United States. As we might expect, the free market reflects more quickly and accurately changes in the money markets. Thus, while state usury laws in the U.S. held down the rates (and supply) of loans, and limits on rates payable on savings deposits restricted their growth during 1969–70, the Eurodollar market flourished at lending rates that were often above 10 percent.

Channels

How do funds created by the banking system and personal savings end up in the hands of business? Let us first consider credit created by commercial banks, which are included among those institutions involved in financing business,

EXHIBIT 15-1   Flow of Personal Savings through Money and Capital Markets to Non-financial Corporations

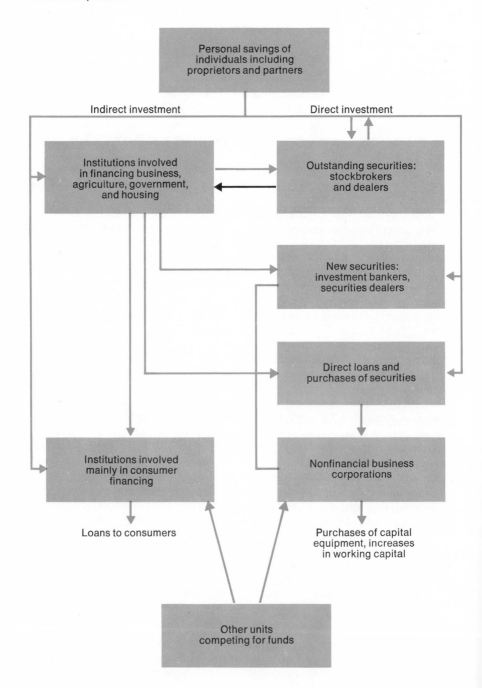

agriculture, government, and residential housing (Exhibit 15-1). Frequently, credit made available through the commercial banking system is extended directly to business firms. At other times banks acquire securities of business corporations through middlemen called investment bankers and securities dealers. Moreover, institutions involved in consumer financing obtain funds from commercial banks either directly or through middlemen. (In order to simplify the exhibit, not all of these flows have been shown.) Finally, expansion of bank credit is ordinarily associated with a rise in personal income, which in turn may result in a higher level of personal savings.

Personal savings are apt to follow a somewhat more circuitous route than credit created by the commercial banking system. As indicated in Exhibit 15-1, they may be invested directly or indirectly. Let us first consider the direct-investment path on the right-hand side of the exhibit. An individual has a three-way choice. First, he may buy securities that are already outstanding. Because these securities are held by some other investor, their purchase does not represent new investment from the point of view of the economy. Somebody who had securities now has cash; somebody who once had cash now has securities. In the market for outstanding securities there is a constant reshuffling of buying and selling. None of this spirited activity represents new investment, because the funds are not channeled into the purchase of new equipment or into investment in working capital. Active markets for outstanding securities, such as the New York Stock Exchange and American Stock Exchange, are important indirect aids to financing business. Corporate securities are more attractive investments when they can be readily sold. However, since it does not furnish new funds to business, the market for outstanding securities will not be considered further. The resale of outstanding securities is indicated in Exhibit 15-1 by means of the black arrow.

Second, an individual may purchase newly issued securities from middlemen, called investment bankers and securities dealers. As we shall see later, this channel is one commonly used in the large-scale marketing of securities.

Third, personal savings can be used for direct loans to business or for purchases of securities directly from business firms. No middleman is involved in such transactions. For example, the Thorp Finance Company sells certain types of bonds directly to investors from its various offices in Wisconsin. Wealthy individuals frequently make direct investments in small corporations.

Now let us turn to the left-hand side of Exhibit 15-1 — indirect investment. As shown in the exhibit, we may group institutions involved in the money and capital markets under two headings:

1. Institutions involved in financing business, agriculture, government and residential housing:
   Commercial banks
   Life insurance companies
   Mutual savings banks
   Fire, casualty, and marine insurance companies
   Corporate pension funds
   State and local government retirement funds
   Savings and loan associations
   Other institutions

2. Institutions involved mainly in consumer financing:
   Sales finance companies
   Consumer finance companies
   Credit unions
   Industrial loan companies
   Consumer credit departments of commercial banks

Individuals make their personal savings available to these institutions by making deposits (commercial banks and mutual savings banks), by purchasing shares (savings and loan associations and credit unions), by paying insurance premiums, a portion of which is invested (insurance companies), and by making contributions to retirement funds (insurance companies and corporate and government retirement funds). Occasionally individuals also purchase securities newly issued by sales finance and consumer credit companies.

Individuals place their savings in these financial institutions for two main reasons. First, the small saver finds it impossible or prohibitively expensive to make direct financial investments. Instead he channels his savings to financial institutions, which accept savings in small amounts and then reinvest them in large amounts. Second, even if he could afford to purchase several hundred dollars worth of some stock, the individual saver would not be able to obtain much diversification. He would be likely to have all his eggs in one basket, a procedure which would not be a sound investment practice. By putting his savings in some financial institutions, he spreads his risk by obtaining a share in at least several hundred different investments.

The financial institutions with which we are primarily concerned are those that direct personal savings into business uses. They have the same three basic alternatives that the individual does in making a direct financial investment. They may purchase securities that are already outstanding, purchase new securities from middlemen, and make direct loans and investments.

The rate at which financial institutions make funds available to business firms does not always match the rate at which they obtain personal savings. If sufficiently attractive investments are not available financial institutions may allow their assets to become more liquid. By this we mean that they permit cash balances and holdings of readily marketable government obligations to grow at a faster pace than loans and investments to business. Thus the flow of funds to business and financial institutions is derived from any credit created by banks and the flow of personal savings to these institutions plus any reductions or minus any additions the financial institutions make in their own pools of liquid investible funds.

Although it is not shown on the exhibit, nonfinancial corporations also furnish funds to each other and to financial institutions. The most common form is the extension of credit by one business firm to another at the time goods are sold. As we saw in Chapter 5, some large corporations also temporarily invest idle funds in the short-term obligations of other corporations, including those of the financial institutions that provide funds to consumers. By adding to their deposits at commercial banks, savings banks, and savings and loan associations, business firms provide funds that these institutions may then make available to other borrowers. In addition some government agencies lend to business concerns funds that the government has borrowed or acquired from taxes. Thus the money and capital markets are tied together with a spider web of channels through which funds flow in all directions.

Relative Importance of Channels

The proportion of external funds that business corporations obtain directly from individuals is quite small. Most of the funds that nonfinancial institutions raised with new security issues in the period from 1966 to 1970 were obtained from various financial institutions. Among the various financial institutions, corporate and state and local pension funds have been the two most important channels through which funds have moved to business corporations via new issues of securities. During the 1966-70 period corporate pension funds purchased over $28 billion of corporate securities, a truly astounding growth. Over the same period state and local pension funds acquired a net amount of about $23 billion of corporate securities, with an emphasis on bonds (Table 15-2). Life insurance companies were third in importance, with a high proportion of their $20 billion investment also being in bonds.

TABLE 15-2   New Corporate Security Issues, 1966–1970 (in billions of dollars)

Net New Issues (TABLE 15-1)[a]	84.1
Bonds and notes	72.1
Stocks	12.0
Increase in Ownership of Bonds	
Life insurance companies	14.6
Mutual savings banks	3.7
Fire and casualty insurance companies	4.7
Corporate pension funds	5.0
State and local government retirement funds	17.0
Total savings institutions	45.0
Commercial banks	0.1
Individuals and others[b]	27.0
Total bonds	72.1
Increase in Ownership in Stocks	
Life insurance companies	5.8
Mutual savings banks	0.8
Fire and casualty insurance companies	3.3
Corporate pension funds	23.1
State and local government retirement funds	5.7
Total savings institutions	38.7
Individuals and others[b]	(26.7)
Total stocks	12.0

[a] Excludes investment company issues, but includes issues of banks and insurance companies. Hence, the difference between the $84.1 billion shown here and the net new issues of $77.7 shown in Table 15–1 is represented by net issues of banks and insurance companies.
[b] Reflects reevaluation of book assets of some holders.
Source: Bankers Trust Company, *The Investment Outlook for 1970.* Tables 10 and 11 compiled from information available from Securities and Exchange Commission; ownership data based on book values of bonds and on purchases less sales, where available, of common stock.

Factors Affecting Flow of Funds

Competitive Nature of the Market

In general the money and capital markets are highly competitive. As we saw in an earlier chapter, the user of funds usually has several alternatives. We may be able to choose among various types of debt and equity funds. We have a choice in the timing of our financing. As we shall see in later chapters, we may also select among various possible suppliers of funds. In general the larger and stronger we are the more alternatives we have.

On the supply side the individual saver also has many choices. He can spend rather than save. He may invest directly or indirectly. In either case he has many different businesses and financial institutions seeking his savings. The financial institutions have many possible uses of their funds too. Competing with business for funds are the U.S. government, Federal agencies, state and municipal governments, foreign governments, and non-profit institutions. Moreover, consumers seek to borrow funds to purchase homes and various consumer durables.

The alternatives available to users and suppliers of funds are real alternatives because there is no product differentiation in the money and capital markets. Money is money. As a user of funds we do not say that we prefer the insurance company's money to the bank's because it has a more attractive shade of green. We are interested in the amount we can secure, the period that we may use it, and the obligations we incur to obtain it. Suppliers of funds are equally realistic and unemotional. Although convenience of location and other factors play a role in determining where individuals place their savings, there is evidently a large group that shops for the highest rate of return available, given a certain grade of risk. Financial institutions are ordinarily highly sophisticated investors.

The different segments of the money and capital markets are thus linked together because both users and suppliers of funds have alternatives. A change in the flows through one channel will ultimately have some degree of influence on flows through other channels.

To a considerable extent these flows are regulated and adjusted by changes in costs of funds. This process can be illustrated by reference to the shifts in the money and capital markets that brought interest rates in the United States by mid-1970 to the highest level in a century. To understand that remarkable, and for some, painful, situation we must examine the developments during the 1960's. Whereas business firms had been able to finance a substantial portion of their needs with internally generated funds during the first half of the decade, the rapid economic expansion of the last half, coupled with inflation forced many companies to turn to external sources of funds (Exhibit 15-2). Credit requirements of state and local governments also grew and added to the pressure on the capital markets.

The already heavy demands on the capital markets were increased after 1965 by a vast expansion in spending by the Federal government, both for defense and non-defense items. Since taxes were not raised to meet these expenditures,

EXHIBIT 15-2   *Corporate Investment and Its Financing*

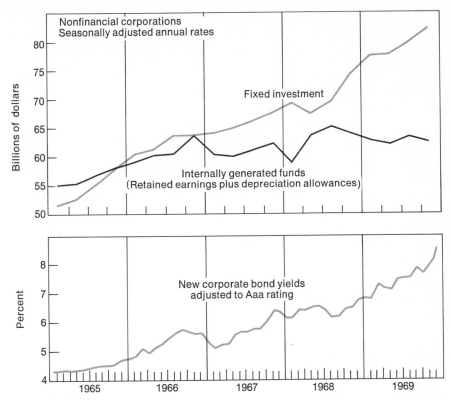

Source: Board of Governors of the
Federal Reserve System

Prepared by Federal Reserve Bank of New York

the budget deficit had to be filled by turning to the money and capital markets.

After a brief, but severe effort to stem the inflationary tide in 1966, The Federal Reserve System moved to a position of ease and made substantial reserves available to the banking system. This expansion of the monetary base added fuel to the inflation and had a two-fold effect on the money and capital markets. On the one hand, borrowers wished to invest in plant and equipment before prices went up even more. At a later date they hoped to repay the debt with "cheap" dollars. On the other hand, lenders were unwilling to sacrifice current dollars except at rates that both compensated them for their normal risks *plus* the loss of purchasing power. Although interest rates rose rapidly during this period, they reached levels that did little more than offset the rapid growth in prices.

Finally, when the Federal Reserve shifted to a position of restraint in 1969, the market was left with the pent-up demands generated by the processes that began earlier in the decade. Reserve requirements were raised and the Federal Reserve sold government bonds in order to maintain pressure upon the reserves of the banking system. This action forced up interest rates (Remember: sales of bonds push *down* the prices and thereby force *up* the yields.)

Under this combination of pressures, there was no place for interest rates to go but up. And up they went. From the end of 1969 to mid-1970, the interest rates on the highest-grade corporate bonds rose from 7.03 percent to 8.48 percent This may not seem like much, but consider the plight of a corporate treasurer who decided to postpone a $50 million dollar issue of bonds, because he thought that the forces pushing up rates would be temporary. By delaying his issue, he cost his corporation $125,000 per year (before taxes) over the life of the bond issue. It is this sort of opportunity for loss or gain that makes it desirable to understand the intricate interrelationships of the money and capital markets. Although changes in costs of funds are sometimes imperfect and slow-moving, they probably provide for a far more effective regulation and fruitful application of the flows through the money and capital markets than any central authority would be able to dictate.

As we shall see in the next chapter the Federal and state governments foster fair competition in the capital market by requiring that corporations offering securities for public sale provide prospective buyers with a considerable amount of information on their affairs. Although this does not mean that securities are purchased solely on their merits, the regulations probably divert some amount of funds from the pockets of fly-by-night operations to sounder uses. Most public utilities are required by state or Federal regulatory authorities to offer their securities for public bidding by investment bankers in an effort to encourage competition for these securities.

Factors Restricting Competition

Discussion in Chapter 10 showed that the users of funds do not have complete discretion in the types of funds they employ. Custom, regulations, and inherent characteristics of the company and its industry limit the free range of choice of management. Somewhat similar restrictions affect the supply side in the money and capital markets.

Regulation and Tradition. Most financial institutions are rather limited in the types of investment they can make, or the sorts of contracts they can accept in return for the surrender of their funds. In addition tradition has established various rules of thumb for these suppliers of funds, just as they have helped establish certain standards for the companies to whom they make funds available. The most important consideration bearing on their investment policy is that they have fixed commitments. Commercial banks, mutual savings banks, and savings and loan associations have promised to return their depositors' savings dollar for dollar. Insurance companies and pension funds have fixed obligations to their policy holders or pensioners. Because of these commitments these financial institutions dare not assume much risk in investing their funds. Safety of principal must be put ahead of the possible rate of return. These institutions would voluntarily restrict such purchases in order to keep the assumed risk within reasonable bounds, even if government regulation did not restrict purchases of common stock in many cases.

In the case of all of these financial institutions custom and principles of good investment management generally decree that an institution not become too heavily committed to one company or one industry. For this reason a sales finance company seeking additional funds might be turned down by a commercial bank, while a less credit-worthy furniture manufacturer would be granted a loan. The banker would argue that he was "loaned up" so far as consumer credit paper was concerned, but that it would not unbalance his loan portfolio to extend credit to the furniture manufacturer. No uniform standards exist among the various financial institutions for the proportions of loans that may be granted to different industries.

Commercial banks traditionally restrict much of their operations to short-term securities and loans and, therefore, are involved chiefly in the money and customer markets. They are on the horns of the same dilemma facing their borrowers—risk vs. return. Although long-term loans may often earn more for a bank, a large proportion of its liabilities are usually in the form of deposits subject to check: i.e., demand deposits. To insure that it can meet these liabilities, banks channel a substantial portion of their funds into short-term loans, although a portion of savings flowing into time deposits is usually directed into mortgages and debt issues of corporations and state and local governments (Table 15-3). Commercial banks are not a direct source of equity funds.

TABLE 15-3   Funds Supplied by Commercial Banks, 1966–1970 (in billions of dollars)

Mortgages	25.0	
Corporate bonds (Table 15-2)	0.1	
State and local government securities	24.0	
		49.1
Investment funds		
Loans to corporate business[a] (Table 15-1)	38.4	
Loans to other business[a]	7.9	
Loans on securities	2.2	
Other loans, net, excluding customer	9.2	
Consumer loans	14.6	
		72.3
Short-term funds		
U.S. government securities	(6.3)	
Federal agency securities	2.4	
Federal government securities		(3.9)
Total funds		117.4

[a] Includes term loans.
Note: Details may not add to totals because of rounding.
Source: Bankers Trust Company, *The Investment Outlook for 1970*, Table 25. Based on data from the flow of funds accounts, Federal Reserve and Securities and Exchange Commission.

Savings banks are mutual institutions which accept savings deposits and reinvest them under provisions of the laws of the state in which they are chartered. Although the laws are gradually being liberalized, savings banks are generally permitted to purchase only small amounts of corporate stocks. Corporate bonds must ordinarily conform to certain statutory requirements to be eligible for investment by savings banks. These financial institutions are a relatively unimportant source of business financing.

Life insurance companies invested five times as much in bonds and mortgages as in common stocks during 1966–70, although many of the mortgages on commercial property probably contained "equity kickers." The balance of debt versus equity has resulted in part from legislation severely limiting their purchases of stock and from the nature of insurance companies' liabilities. Technical aspects of the valuation of their investments have also worked against large purchases of common stocks. Aside from these legal restrictions, life insurance companies do not have a strong incentive to buy common stocks. Since their obligations are fixed in money terms, they do not have to hedge against rising prices through purchases of common stock. Consequently, most of the $50 billion that life insurance companies had available to invest during 1966–70 was placed in debt obligations of one form or another (Table 15–4).

TABLE 15-4   Sources and Uses of Funds of Life Insurance
Companies, 1966–1970 (in billions of dollars)

Sources of Funds	
Increase in admitted assets	49.0
Decrease in U.S. Government Securities	1.6
Total	50.6
Uses of Funds	
Mortgages	14.9
Corporate bonds (Table 15-2)	14.6
Corporate stocks (Table 15-2)	5.8
State and local government securities	(0.1)
Foreign securities	1.0
Policy loans	8.5
Real estate	1.8
Increase in cash	0.0
Other	4.1
Total	50.6

Note: Details may not add to totals because of rounding.
Source: Bankers Trust Company, *The Investment Outlook for 1970*, Table 15. Based on data from Institute of Life Insurance, except data on home mortgages from Federal Home Loan Bank Board.

In addition, because bonds and mortgages have offered higher yields than common stocks for a number of years (Exhibit 15-3), life insurance companies have not been eager to invest inflows of funds in the equity market. To be entirely accurate we should note that the chart depicts only the dividend yield on common stocks and does not include gains or losses from movements in price. The increased role of life insurance companies in the pension business will probably cause some increase in their purchases of equities, but probably not a startling one.[2] The ever-present risk of a sharp decline in common stock prices causes portfolio managers to be wary.

Because they pay Federal income taxes on only 15 percent of their income from dividends, but on 100 percent of their income from interest, *fire, casualty,*

EXHIBIT 15-3   *Stock and Bond Yields*

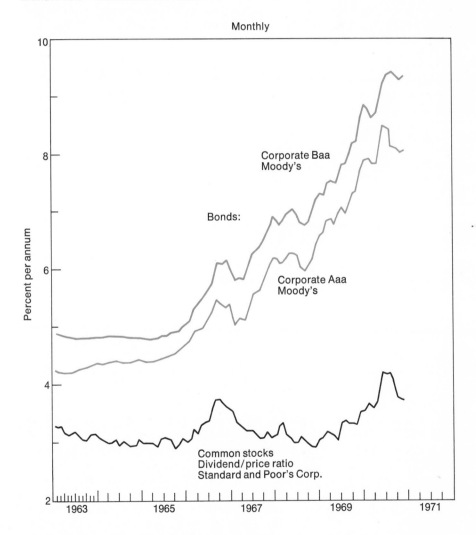

Monthly

Corporate Baa
Moody's

Bonds:

Corporate Aaa
Moody's

Common stocks
Dividend/price ratio
Standard and Poor's Corp.

Percent per annum

BOARD OF GOVERNORS OF THE FEDERAL RESERVE SYSTEM

[2]Orson H. Hart, "Life Insurance Companies and the Equity Capital Markets," *Journal of Finance,* 20 (May, 1965), pp. 358–67.

and *marine insurance companies* favor purchases of corporate stocks to corporate bonds. Since the income received from state and local government obligations is exempt from Federal income taxes, a large proportion of investible funds are directed into the purchase of these securities. The growth of these insurance companies has been much less rapid than that of life insurance companies.

Corporate pension funds are established to provide retirement benefits for a company's officers and employees. Their remarkable growth from 1966 to 1970 has provided almost $35 billion for the financing of business and government (Table 15-5). Over the same period *state and local government retirement*

TABLE 15-5   Sources and Uses of Funds of Corporate Pension
Funds, 1966–1970 (in billions of dollars)

Sources of Funds	
Employer contributions	34.7
Employee contributions	4.2
Investment income	16.1
Total receipts	55.0
Less: benefit payments[a]	19.8
Net receipts	34.9
Uses of funds	
Mortgages	0.9
Corporate bonds (Table 15-2)	5.0
Corporate stocks (Table 15-2)[b]	23.1
U.S. Government and agency securities	(0.3)
Other	6.4
Total	34.9

[a] Includes relatively minor amounts of expenses.
[b] Represents changes in book value of holdings of preferred stock and net acquisitions of common stock.
Note: Details may not add to totals because of rounding.
Source: Bankers Trust Company, *The Investment Outlook for 1970*, Table 16. Based on data from Securities and Exchange Commission on uninsured pension plans. Uses of funds are based on book values.

funds provided an additional $25 billion in investible funds (Table 15-6). The investments of these pension funds are affected by restrictions set at the time they are established. Many funds are administered by the trust departments of banks, which traditionally lean towards bonds, rather than stocks, although this situation seems to be changing. A number of banks have set up special pension funds that have followed a more aggressive investment policy than typical of banks' trust departments. Most of the funds available to state and local government retirement funds were placed in bonds and mortgages. By contrast, managers of corporate pension funds placed almost two-thirds of their net receipts in corporate stocks.

Other financial institutions are less important as sources of funds to finance business. Of increasing prominence are *investment companies* which sell common stock in small amounts to investors and reinvest those funds in

TABLE 15-6   Sources and Uses of Funds of State and Local
Government Retirement Funds, 1966–1970
(in billions of dollars)

Sources of Funds	
Employer contributions[a]	19.8
Employee contributions	11.6
Investment income	9.8
Total receipts	41.2
Less: benefit payments	15.1
Net receipts	26.1
Uses of Funds	
Mortgages	2.7
Corporate bonds (Table 15-2)	17.0
Corporate stocks (Table 15-2)	5.7
U.S. government and agency securities	(0.8)
Other	0.7
Total	25.2
Statistical discrepancy	0.9

[a] Governmental unit.
Note: Details may not add to totals because of rounding.
Source: Bankers Trust Company, *The Investment Outlook for 1970*, Table 17. Based on data from *The National Income and Product Accounts of the United States, 1929–1968*, U.S. Department of Commerce, Tables 3.7, 3.8 and 3.9, and national income supplements in *The Survey of Current Business;* uses of funds data from Flow of Funds Accounts, Federal Reserve.

corporate and government securities. Since they seldom purchase newly issued securities, except those of well-established concerns, they are not a common means of directly channeling personal savings directly to businesses. The types of securities they are able to purchase are limited only by their charter or by their stated objectives. By their purchases of previously issued stocks and bonds, these institutions tend to support the market prices of these securities and make it easier for corporations to secure more funds with new issues. Certain government agencies also provide loans to business within the limits set by Federal or state governments. Other minor sources of funds are personal trusts and, to a very limited extent, savings and loan associations.

Taxation. Various features of Federal and state tax laws affect the free operation of competitive forces in the supplying of funds to the money and capital markets. We have already observed some differences in the impact of taxes upon various financial institutions. The effect of taxes upon the ability and willingness of the individual to provide funds is complex and obscure. On the one hand, an increase in personal income taxes tends to reduce the amount of personal savings that are made available to the money and capital markets. On the other hand, individuals holding stocks may exclude from their gross income $100 of dividend income. This provision encourages the purchase of stocks. Since capital gains are taxed at a lower rate than income from salaries, taxpayers in high income brackets are induced to purchase securities that are likely to show a capital gain. Such prospects would be more typical of common stocks than of bonds.

Still another aspect of our tax laws tends to divert investible funds from businesses to states and municipalities. Since the income from the obligations of these units is exempt from Federal income taxes, individuals and businesses in high income tax brackets may favor these investments to the exclusion of all others. To illustrate, a married taxpayer with a taxable income between $44,000 and $52,000 and filing a joint return would find that a tax-exempt security yielding 5 percent would provide a marginal after-tax income equivalent to a yield of 10 percent from bonds.

Dynamic Factors Affecting the Flow of Savings

Up to this point we have considered influences on the flow of savings that are largely static. Since tradition and laws change slowly, they provide a rather constant setting or framework for our study of the money and capital markets. One of the most fascinating and challenging aspects of the financial manager's job is that he is seeking funds in a market that is constantly changing. Sometimes funds of all sorts are readily available in relation to the amounts demanded. At other times funds from certain channels may be in short supply. These variations also affect the types of funds available. If funds from insurance companies are in short supply, it is likely that long-term debt will also be difficult to obtain. Conversely, if bank lending is restricted, the supply of short-term loans will dry up relative to long-term funds.

An understanding of the money and capital markets and the participating institutions is essential to at least two aspects of a financial manager's job: (1) The balance he chooses between short- and long-term borrowing; and (2) The timing of issues of long-term debt, as well as any preferred stock. The good financial manager will look "upstream" as it were to see what future influx of investible funds may be expected and what demands will be imposed on that inflow. In addition he must also be aware of the impact of general economic conditions and monetary and fiscal policies upon these flows. Let us see how a financial manager should interpret these variables in order to determine the maturity and timing of his borrowings.

General Economic Conditions. Economic theory tells us that in general the flow of funds to business expands during business expansion and contracts during a contraction of business activity. With higher incomes individuals are able to save more. Rising prices and the needs for larger amounts of inventory and receivables to support higher levels of sales lead business to seek additional funds. More plant and equipment may be needed as well. Because funds are generated from investment in fixed assets only slowly, the rate at which funds are released during a recession may not match the rate of absorption during the preceding period of expansion.

There is a tendency (although it is hardly clear-cut) for costs of funds to decline during periods of recession and then to rise during the subsequent recovery. To illustrate, during the slowdown in 1967, the cost of funds, especially short-term funds, tended to decline (Exhibit 15-4). The flow of funds was fairly ample in relation to the needs for funds, and the efforts of lenders to find

EXHIBIT 15-4   Long- and Short-Term Interest Rates

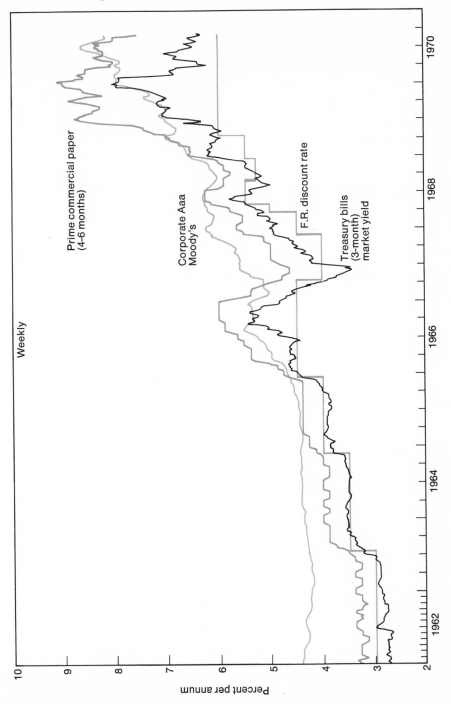

Weekly

Prime commercial paper
(4-6 months)

Corporate Aaa
Moody's

F.R. discount rate

Treasury bills
(3-month)
market yield

Percent per annum

1962   1964   1966   1968   1970

10 9 8 7 6 5 4 3 2

suitable outlets for the flows of personal savings pushed the costs of money downward. When the level of business activity increased, rates for most types of funds rose as well. Funds generated internally did not entirely match the needs for funds during the periods of expansion. Consequently, the spirited bidding for these funds among business, agriculture, government, and consumer forced up the cost of funds. However, the response of interest rates to changes in the level of business activity is not immediate. Studies indicate that both short- and long-term interest rates tend to lag behind other cyclical indicators.[3]

Monetary Policies. Since detailed discussion of the effect of monetary policies on the money and capital markets properly belongs in a separate field of study, we shall consider briefly only two indices that should prove helpful to the financial manager in assaying the effects of Federal Reserve policy upon his borrowing plans.

(1) *Net reserve position.* Essentially, the Federal Reserve System attempts to restrict or expand the credit-creating ability of commercial banks by reducing or enlarging the excess reserves of the banks. Although it is possible to change the percentage required as a reserve against demand and time deposits, the more common practice of the Federal Reserve System is to raise or lower the reserves of banks by purchasing or selling government securities in the open market. Usually, the System restricts its open market operations to certain short-term government obligations. The effect of these operations ordinarily spreads through the commercial banking system to all segments of the money and capital markets.

Indications of a shift in Federal Reserve policy may be noted by studying the net reserve position of the banking system. It will be recalled from the discussion in the early part of this chapter that member banks are required to maintain a certain percentage of their demand and time deposits on deposit with one of the Federal Reserve banks. At any time some banks in the system will have more reserves on deposit than required. These are *excess reserves.* Other banks in the system may have no excess reserves and may be borrowing from a Federal Reserve bank as well. The *net reserve position* of member banks of the Federal Reserve System is determined by deducting borrowings from excess reserves. For example, when money was "tight" at the end of August, 1969, the banking system was operating with *net borrowed reserves* of $992 million, as shown below (in millions of dollars):

Total reserves held	$26,909
Required reserves	26,697
Excess reserves	212
Borrowings at Federal Reserve banks	1,204
Free reserves	$ −992

A year later, there were growing signs of a slowdown in the economy. Although there were still inflationary pressures, the Federal Reserve eased credit somewhat, as shown by the net free reserves (still negative) at the end of August, 1970:

[3] Geoffrey H. Moore, *Statistical Indicators of Cyclical Revivals and Recessions* (New York: National Bureau of Economic Research, Inc., 1950).

Total reserves held	$28,161
Required reserves	28,036
Excess reserves	125
Borrowings at Federal Reserve banks	660
Free reserves	$ −535

This easing of the net reserve placed banks in a better position to extend credit. Over the 12-month period the prime rate dropped to $7\frac{1}{2}$ percent from $8\frac{1}{2}$ percent, and the rate on prime commercial paper fell sharply (Exhibit 15-4).

(2) *Money stock.* A more controversial index of monetary policy is the money stock: private checking accounts and currency in the hands of the public. Some economists, notably Professor Milton Friedman of the University of Chicago, view this as the most important monetary variable. We can observe in Exhibit 15-5 the period of very tight money from June, 1969, through February, 1970, when the money stock actually decreased slightly. As signs of impending recession grew, the expansion of the money stock gave a clue that at least short-term rates might turn down. This quickly became evident in the

EXHIBIT 15-5   Money Stock

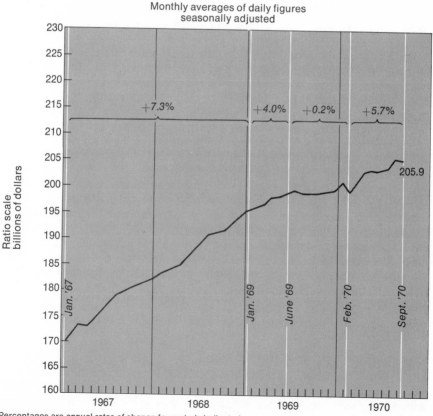

Monthly averages of daily figures
seasonally adjusted

Percentages are annual rates of change for periods indicated.

Prepared by Federal Reserve Bank of St. Louis

yields on prime commercial paper and short-term Treasury obligations (Exhibit 15-4), but a decline in long-term rates was delayed until after midyear.

Viewing these two indices of monetary policy together, a shrewd financial manager might have shifted to a higher proportion of short-term financing during the period in the hope that he could eventually fund these short-term loans at lower long-term rates. These expectations would have been reinforced by an increased flow of personal savings (noted earlier in the chapter) and rising time deposits at commercial banks. However, optimism would surely have been tempered by the large pent-up demand for long-term funds by corporations and state and municipal governments, as well as forecasts of Federal deficits.

Fiscal Policies. At times the "stickiness" of long-term interest rates may be partly explained by fiscal policies: that is, the policies of governmental bodies concerning taxation, borrowing, and expenditures. Because its gross debt exceeds $375 billion, the U.S. Treasury is the most important single borrower in the money and capital markets. Consequently, if it adds to the amount of its outstanding debt, it tends to drain the channels of available funds. As a result, corporate, state, and municipal borrowers find that funds are nowhere near as plentiful or as reasonable as they had hoped.

The Treasury's policies of debt management also have great impact on the money and capital markets. One such policy has been the effort to lengthen the maturities of the outstanding government debt. Thus, even if the Treasury is not adding to the total amount of outstanding debt, it may still have great effect on the financial markets if its reduces its short-term borrowings and increases its long-term debt. In the face of ample funds in the money market, short-term rates may then decline, while heavy borrowing by the Treasury in the capital markets may nudge long-term rates upwards.

Governmental borrowers may be viewed by business as just one more competitor for the flow of funds through the money and capital markets. State and municipal borrowers have an advantage in that purchasers of their bonds do not have to pay Federal income taxes on the interest. The Federal government has an advantage because it has a better credit standing than business firms as a result of its power to tax. When these governmental units spend more than they recover in taxes, they must borrow in the money and capital markets. Conversely, when they take in more than they spend, they are able to repay their debts. The individuals and institutions receiving these payments can then make loans and investments to business, consumers, or other governmental units. Because they issue only debt obligations, the influence of the fiscal policy is felt first in the market for short- and long-term debt. The impact is often considerable.

Summary

In a broad sense we may conceive of the money market as dealing in certain short-term obligations, and the capital market as dealing in long-term debt and equity funds. Nonfinancial corporations turn to the financial markets for about one-third of the funds they use to replace and increase their assets.

These funds have their origin primarily in credit created by commercial banks and personal savings of individuals. On their way to business concerns these funds may flow along many different paths. The rate of flow, its direction, and the paths followed are constantly changing in response to changes in demand and supply as expressed in the availability of funds and in the charges levied for their use. Because money has no brand preference and because the individuals involved in the market are highly sophisticated, funds are generally allocated economically. Although suppliers of funds are hedged about with various legal and self-imposed restrictions, they still have sufficient flexibility and enough alternatives to make the money and capital markets quite competitive. As a result adjustments to changes in economic conditions and monetary and fiscal policies take place almost automatically. To his predictions of his needs for funds, the financial manager must now add his predictions concerning the future flows of funds in the money and capital markets.

Questions

1/ What are the types of financial institutions found in your community? Which are primarily concerned with loans to business and which with loans to consumers? Which are primarily involved in the money market and which in the capital market?

2/ Trace the probable effects on the money and capital markets of the following events. Make your assumptions clear.
   a. Individuals reduce the proportion of savings that they make through commercial banks and increase their savings through corporate pension funds.
   b. Individuals reduce the proportion of savings that they make through mutual savings and commercial banks and increase their savings through life insurance companies.
   c. Individuals cash in their U.S. savings bonds and purchase common stocks.
   d. The Federal government incurs a substantial deficit and finds it necessary to issue in the course of a year several billion dollars of long-term bonds.
   e. Personal income taxes on dividend income are eliminated.
   f. Payments of life insurance premiums are made a tax-deductible expense for purpose of Federal personal income taxes.

3/ Would adjustments of the cost of funds in response to increases in demand for funds be speeded or retarded by the fact that financial institutions were in unusually liquid position?

4/ During recent periods of "tight money," many school boards found the interest cost on bonds to finance the construction of new schools had risen sharply. Some argued that the Federal or state governments should buy school bonds at low interest rates.
   a. Do you believe school bonds should receive special treatment in the capital market?
   b. Do you favor the recommendation made?

5/ What effect does a generally rising price level have on:
   a. The willingness of financial institutions to buy debt or equity securities?
   b. The willingness of individuals to buy debt or equity securities?
   c. The willingness of universities to place endowment funds into debt or equity securities?

6/ In June, 1965, the two largest banks in New York borrowed more than half a billion dollars by selling some 25-year bonds and notes. These issues are subordinate to the claims of depositors, and banks do not need to maintain any reserves behind the debt with the Federal Reserve bank. What is the effect on the money and capital markets of such issues? Be specific in tracing the causes of the change.

7/ During the recent period of tight money the Commission on Mortgage Interest Rates concluded in its report to the President:

"The foregoing analysis of postwar developments in the mortgage market points to the following conclusions: (1) Rising interest rates hurt the mortgage market and homebuilding activity, both by raising the cost and more importantly by curtailing the availability of mortgage credit. Credit availability is curtailed in the mortgage market as savings are diverted from key mortgage lending institutions and as these institutions are attracted to investments other than mortgages. (2) Unduly low FHA-VA interest rate ceilings impose an additional constraint on these sectors, by affecting both the availability of credit—as some lenders shy away from making loans at such low rates—and mortgage demand—since the burden of the resulting discount points inhibits some home sales. . . . (pp. 32–33). . . . the Commission recommends complete elimination of the interest rate ceilings on FHA and VA mortgages. This will permit such loans to be originated at any interest rate that is acceptable to both borrower and lender . . . (p. 68)."

In their dissenting view, two members of the Commission, Representative Wright Patman and Leonor K. Sullivan observed:

"After many months of deliberation, the Commission performed its first assignment by recommending what the mortgage industry itself has requested—the permanent elimination of FHA and VA mortgage interest rate ceilings, so that these rates can go as high as the traffic will bear, regardless of how many families this action prices out of the housing market. (pp. 122–23)" They proposed that, instead of eliminating the 6 percent interest rate ceiling on FHA and VA insured mortgages, the mortgage market should be expanded by moves such as requiring "that pension funds, mutual funds, and other financial sources which benefit from Federal tax concessions, be required as a quid pro quo to assist in meeting housing objectives by devoting an additional 5 to 10 percent of their resources to home mortgages."

   a. Evaluate these conflicting views.
   b. Evaluate the effects of the conflicting proposals upon the cost and availability of long-term borrowed funds for business firms and mortgage funds for homebuilding.

Problems

1/ From Data in the *Federal Reserve Bulletin* prepare a table or chart showing for the past twelve months:
   a. The rates on prime commercial paper, 4- to 6-months.
   b. Corporate bond yields, Aaa.
   c. The net reserve position of the Federal Reserve System.
   d. The total money supply.
   How do you explain movements that have taken place in these interest rates? Consider both the general trend and differences in movements among the three rates considered. Useful source material will be found in the *Federal Reserve Bulletin*, *Monthly Review* of the Federal Reserve Bank of New York, and the *Review* of the Federal Reserve Bank of St. Louis.

2/ Take some personal investment (other than in outstanding securities) that you have made recently in some financial institution.
   a. Obtain the last annual report of that institution and prepare a percentage breakdown of its assets to determine the use to which your funds were put.
   b. Explain the factors that apparently have determined the investment policy of the institution.
   c. What sort of promise did the institution make about the return of your money?

3/ In Moody's *Banks, Insurance, Real Estate, Investment Trust* look up the "Summary of Invested Assets" for Prudential Insurance Company of America for the latest year available. Compare the latest year with the percentage distribution two years ago.
   a. What notable changes have taken place?
   b. How do you explain those changes?

4/ Prepare a 500-word statement explaining the present Federal Reserve monetary policy and how that policy is being implemented. Indicate the general effect of the policy upon the money and capital markets. Useful source material to consult: *Federal Reserve Bulletin, Wall Street Journal, Business Week, Monthly Review* of the Federal Reserve Bank of New York, and the *Review* of the Federal Reserve Bank of St. Louis.

Selected References

BRIMMER, A. F., "Credit Conditions and Price Determination in the Corporate Bond Market," *Journal of Finance,* 15 (September, 1960), pp. 353–70.

Commission on Money and Credit. A library on money and credit, composed of eight volumes on financial institutions and nine on monetary and fiscal policy. Englewood Cliffs, N.J.: Prentice-Hall, Inc., 1962–1963.

"Eurodollars—An Important Source of Funds for American Banks," *Business Conditions* (Federal Reserve Bank of Chicago), June, 1969, pp. 9–20. A bibliography is also available from the Bank.

FRIEDMAN, M., "The Euro-Dollar Market: Some First Principles," *Morgan Guaranty Survey,* October, 1969.

FREUND, W. C. and E. D. ZINBARG, "Application of Flow of Funds to Interest Rate Forecasting, *Journal of Finance,* 18 (May, 1963), pp. 231–48.

GOLDSMITH, R. W., *Financial Intermediaries in the American Economy since 1900.* Princeton, N.J.: Princeton University Press, 1958.

_____, *A Study of Savings in the United States, 1897 to 1949.* Princeton, N.J.: Princeton University Press, 1955. 3 vols. A monumental study covering estimates of savings and national wealth.

GURLEY, J. G. and E. S. SHAW, *Money in a Theory of Finance.* Washington, D.C.: Brookings Institution, 1960.

HANSON, W. C., *Capital Sources and Major Investing Institutions.* New York: Simmons-Boardman Books, 1963.

HART, O. H., "Life Insurance Companies and the Equity Capital Markets," *Journal of Finance,* 20 (May, 1965), pp. 358–67.

HOLLAND, D. M. *Private Pension Funds: Projected Growth.* New York: National Bureau of Economic Research, 1966.

The Investment Outlook. New York: Bankers Trust Company. An annual study of the forces of supply and demand in the capital market.

KESSEL, R. A., *The Cyclical Behavior of the Term Structure of Interest Rates.* New York: National Bureau of Economic Research, 1965. (Occasional paper 91)

LITTLE, J. S., "The Euro-dollar Market: Its Nature and Impact," *New England Business Review* (Federal Reserve Bank of Boston), May/June, 1969, pp. 2–31.

LUDTKE, James B., *The American Financial System.* Boston: Allyn and Bacon, Inc., 1967.

O'LEARY, J. J., "Application of Flow-of-Funds Data to Capital Market Analysis," National Bureau of Economic Research, *The Flow-of-Funds Approach to Social Accounting* (Princeton, N.J.: Princeton University Press, 1962).

MADDEN, C. H., *The Money Side of "The Street."* New York: Federal Reserve Bank of New York, 1959.

MEIGS, A. J., "The Changing Role of Banks in the Market for Equities," *Journal of Finance,* 20 (May, 1965), pp. 368–78.

ROBINSON, R. I., "Forecasting Interest Rates," *Journal of Business,* 27 (January, 1954), pp. 87–100.

_____, *Money and Capital Markets.* New York: McGraw-Hill Book Co., 1964.

ROOSA, R. V., *Federal Reserve Operations in the Money and Government Securities Markets.* New York: Federal Reserve Bank of New York, 1956. A classic.

STONE, R. W., "The Changing Structure of the Money Market," *Journal of Finance,* 20 (May, 1965), pp. 229–38.

VAN HORNE, *Function and Analysis of Capital Market Rates* (Englewood Cliffs, N.J.: Prentice-Hall, Inc., 1970).

_____, "Interest-Rate Risk and the Term Structure of Interest Rates," *Journal of Political Economy,* (August, 1965), pp. 344–51.

WOOD, J. H., "Expectations and the Demand for Bonds," *American Economic Review,* 59 (September, 1969), pp. 522–30.

A "Selected Bibliography on Monetary Policy and Management of the Public Debt, 1947–1960," may be obtained from the library, Board of Governors of the Federal Reserve System, Washington 25, D.C.

Obtaining Funds From the Capital Market

16 Before we discuss the various arrangements under which we may obtain long-term debt or equity funds, we need to examine the methods of reaching into the capital market for these funds. Because such large amounts of money are obtained at one time, various specialized institutions have been developed to facilitate the flow of funds from supplier to user. This specialization substantially benefits both parties; the economist would say that it helps to produce a more perfectly competitive market. Certainly, the securities market is one of the most highly developed and economical channels of distribution in this country. The business concerns that use these specialized institutions to obtain long-term funds are almost always corporations, frequently very large ones. Consider the $200 million debt issue of Weyerhaeuser Company in October, 1970. No one company could have readily supplied this much money; even if it could, it would have been unwilling to concentrate its investments to such an extent. On the other hand, Weyerhaeuser was not equipped to sell these securities piecemeal. It wanted the money in October, 1970 — not in dribbles over the next two years. Weyerhaeuser was able to get its money at one time and yet, by turning to investment bankers, have its securities sold in quantities desired by investors.

We should make clear that in this chapter we are talking only about issues of *new* securities. Except for a brief comment on the regulations of the Securities and Exchange Commission (SEC) concerning the trading of previously issued securities on the organized exchanges, we shall not deal with these *secondary markets.* It should be noted that the existence of good secondary markets is important to the successful sale of new securities. It also provides information to the firm about the probable cost of both debt and equity capital. From the secondary market we thus obtain our estimates of the cost of capital for our firm, as well as for firms in other risk classes.

Role of the Investment Banker

Many financial managers undertake an offering of securities once in their lifetime, if ever. The financial manager is akin to the general practitioner in medicine. He takes care of the day-to-day problems that are closely related to the short- and intermediate-term financial needs of the company, just as the general practitioner takes care of the every-day colds and stomach aches. However, when a major financial undertaking is in the offing, the financial manager is likely to call in a specialist in the field—the investment banker— just as the general practitioner calls in the surgeon when a major operation is required.

To eliminate any possible confusion we should distinguish between investment bankers and commercial bankers. Investment bankers are essentially middlemen who channel funds from those who wish to invest to those who need the funds. If they finance business corporations at all, they do it only for the brief period that may elapse between the time they purchase and sell the corporations' securities. The largest concentration of investment banking houses is found in New York. Commercial bankers engage principally in short- and intermediate-term financing of business, although they do invest in corporate bonds. They are suppliers of funds, and are prohibited by law from functioning as investment bankers for business concerns.

It will aid our understanding of the economic role of the investment banker if we first view his functions in marketing terminology. A corporation issuing securities has something to sell, just as a manufacturer of shirts has something to sell. The problem is to move the securities, or shirts, as economically as possible through channels of distribution to the ultimate consumer. In this process certain basic functions must be performed—investigating, risk-assuming, and selling.

Consider first the investigating or buying function. Usually the shirt manufacturer does not deal directly with consumers. Instead, distributors or centrally-located buying offices place orders with the manufacturer. Their orders depend in large part upon what they think the ultimate customer wants. Thus the buying function is basically that of determining and then communicating the wishes of the consumer in terms of quantity, price, and style to the manufacturer. In the same way the investment banker serves as an informational link between the capital market and the company issuing securities. Because he specializes in studying the market, the investment banker probably does a better job of matching the time of sale, price, and features of a new issue of securities to the desires of the buyers than if the corporation attempted to perform this function itself. Securities thus tailored to the needs of the market will sell readily, so that both the buyer and issuer of securities are economically served.

Second, the manufacturer wishes to sell his shirts at a fair price as soon as possible in order to recover his investment in the inventory of finished goods and return these funds to active use within the business. Once the shirts have moved to a lower level in the channel of distribution, somebody else has money tied up in inventory, and somebody else must bear the risk of any subsequent decline in prices. For the same reason, a corporation selling securities would like to consummate the sale as quickly as possible at a certain, predetermined price. It is economical to transfer the risk of carrying securities to concerns that are skilled in this area and that have or can obtain funds to carry the securities until they are finally sold. This is the risk-bearing function of investment bankers.

Finally, the shirt manufacturer is usually in no position to market the product at the retail level, any more than a corporation issuing securities is able to sell its stocks and bonds to individual investors across the country. Both concerns need other organizations to perform the selling function, to buy in large lots and sell in small lots. Both need somebody to move the shirts or securities to where the customers want them and to encourage the customers to buy them. Since corporations sell new securities only occasionally, their need for somebody else to perform the selling function is especially great. It would be very costly to maintain a selling organization for infrequent issues of securities. The function is performed economically only when many corporations channel their issues through a relatively small group of specialized institutions.

In general, competition forces a close relationship between payments and marketing functions performed. If the risk is small and the selling easy, the share that the distributor and retail dealer receive of the final retail price of shirts or securities will also be small. Furthermore, we need to pay only for those services performed. If a manufacturer can sell several thousand shirts directly to the armed forces, he need not pay for any of the marketing functions described. Similarly, if a corporation can sell $10 million worth of bonds directly to an insurance company, it may be able to avoid using the services of investment bankers. With this analogy in mind, let us now turn to a more thorough examination of the functions performed by investment bankers.

Investigating Function

Let us assume that a company has selected an investment banking house to handle the sale of its securities. (The selection of an investment banker is discussed later in this chapter.) This banker is known as the *originating house.* Sometimes two or three houses work together, in which case they may be called a "nucleus group." The success of an originating house lies in its ability to effect a satisfactory compromise among the interests of the investor, other investment banking houses participating in the issue, and the corporation issuing the securities.

Since the name of the originating house will be associated with the issue, it needs to maintain the long-run goodwill of the investors who will buy the securities. To be sure that the issuing company is sound the banker will undertake an exhaustive study of its financial statements, properties, and management. In drawing up recommended provisions of the security issue, the investment banker will also be certain that the necessary covenants to protect the interests of the investor are provided. (Covenants are clauses in an agreement between lender and borrower that specify obligations or promises.)

Because other investment banking houses will be asked to join in buying the issue, the originating banker must consider their interests (which correspond closely with his own). He is investigating the issuer for them. Their money is riding on his findings. They will want to be sure that the issue is sound and that the time of sale and price of the issue are set so that it will sell quickly. If the originating banker performs well, the other investment bankers will be willing to participate with him in future issues. Better still, they may ask him to participate with them when they originate issues.

Finally, the originating house has important responsibilities to the corporation issuing the security. In recommending the terms of sale, the banker must take care lest he suggest covenants so restrictive that the corporation has little flexibility. He will provide general financial advice both before and after the issue. The originating house will also assist in the preparation of the documents necessary to comply with state and Federal regulations governing the sale of securities to the public.

The most important service of the investment banker to the issuing corporation is in timing and pricing the issue. With respect to the timing of the issue it has been said that:

> It is here, with his feel and judgment of the market, that the top-notch investment banker renders what is perhaps his most important service. The probable state of the general security market at any given future time is a most difficult thing to forecast. Only those with ripe trading experience and the finest kind of general background in financial affairs and practical economics can effectively render service of this character.[1]

The pricing of the issue is also a crucial and delicate aspect of the buying function. Even after all the preliminary investigation, which may take several months, banker and issuer may fail to agree on these terms. On the one hand, the issuer would like to obtain as much for his securities as possible. When bonds are sold, certain claims on income and assets are sacrificed; when stock is sold, present owners may have to share future earnings, claims on assets, and rights to management with others. The issuer clearly would like to obtain as large a sum as possible in return for these sacrifices. Although the investment banker would like to have the market price of the securities rise slightly after they have been sold, he also does not wish to set the initial offering price

[1] *Opinion* of Harold R. Medina, C. J., in the District Court of the United States for the Southern District of New York, Civil Action No. 43–757, p. 54.

PROSPECTUS

$35,000,000

Northern Illinois Gas Company

First Mortgage Bonds, 8½% Series due August 1, 1976

The Bonds will not be subject to redemption prior to maturity.

Application will be made to list the Bonds on the New York Stock Exchange.
Listing will be subject to meeting the distribution requirements of the Exchange.

ESE SECURITIES HAVE NOT BEEN APPROVED OR DISAPPROVED BY THE SECURITIES AND EXCHANGE COMMISSION NOR HAS THE COMMISSION PASSED UPON THE ACCURACY OR ADEQUACY OF THIS PROSPECTUS. ANY REPRESENTATION TO THE CONTRARY IS A CRIMINAL OFFENSE.

	Price to Public(1)	Underwriting Discounts and Commissions(2)	Proceeds to Company(1)(3)
Unit	101%	.941%	100.059%
al	$35,350,000	$329,350	$35,020,650

Plus accrued interest from August 1, 1970.
The Company has agreed to indemnify the several Purchasers against certain civil liabilities, including liabilities under the Securities Act of 1933.
Before deduction of expenses payable by the Company estimated at $87,000.

The Bonds are offered by the several Purchasers when, as and if issued by the Company and accepted e Purchasers and subject to their right to reject orders in whole or in part. It is expected that the Bonds, efinitive fully registered form, will be ready for delivery on or about August 20, 1970.

e First Boston Corporation

Halsey, Stuart & Co. Inc.

Lehman Brothers

Salomon Brothers

The date of this Prospectus is August 11, 1970.

too low. This would reflect on his judgment and might cost him future business.

On the other hand, the investment banker does not wish to price the issue too high. It will be difficult to sell and will sell slowly. He might even have to take a loss in order to move the issue. As we shall see, he is often working on a very narrow margin. Consequently, the investment banker must have a rapid turnover of the securities he handles and can ill afford to take substantial losses.

Pricing begins with the banker's guess of what the market will pay for the securities, given the proposed features of the offering. The banker then works back from this price to determine the price that he will pay for the issue. Basically, he considers the current market prices of other securities of similar quality with similar features. Since these are "seasoned" securities, he is likely to price his new issue a little lower to allow for the fact that the market will have to absorb a sudden flood of the new securities. Observe in Exhibit 16-1 that the price at which the investment bankers hope to sell to the public the Northern Illinois Gas Company $8\frac{1}{2}$% first mortgage bonds was set at $1010 per bond, a capital-raising effort of $35,350,000 in the aggregate. From this price is deducted the gross spread, or compensation to the investment bankers handling the sale of the issue. The larger the spread, the greater the joy of the investment banker and the pain of the issuing corporation. In this case the gross spread was $9.41 per bond, a total spread of $329,350. This sum must then cover all costs of investigating, risk-bearing, and selling the issue and still leave some profit for the investment bankers. The price to the public less the gross spread is the amount the investment bankers have promised to pay to the issuing corporation, in this case $35,020,650. Final agreement on the price to the public and the gross spread is usually reached a few days or few hours before the issue is to be sold to the public. This permits the banker to take into account any last-minute changes in conditions in the capital market.

Risk-Bearing Function

At some stage in the preliminary investigation, the originating house and issuer sign a preliminary agreement giving the banker an option to purchase the securities if they are eventually to be issued. Since no one investment banker would wish to risk buying $35 million worth of bonds for resale, the originating house will ask other investment bankers to join together in a *syndicate* to share the burden (and commission). In the Northern Illinois Gas issue 30 other bankers joined the four firms in the nucleus group (listed in the exhibit) in handling the issue. Usually a certain amount of the investment bankers' commission is paid to the originating house to cover its costs of preparing the issue for the market. The balance is split among all the investment bankers according to the shares they have obligated themselves to buy and resell. As we shall see, a small portion of the commission may then be reallocated to others participating in the selling effort.

When these bankers sign a final agreement with the issuer, they agree to *underwrite* the issue; that is, they agree to deliver to Northern Illinois Gas a check for $35,020,650 seven to ten days after the offering date to the public (August 11, 1970). This is called the settlement date. The risk of not selling the bonds is the underwriters', not Northern Illinois'. Usually each underwriter is responsible for selling only the portion of the securities allocated to him. In this issue the underwriters' shares ranged from $100,000 to $4,200,000. Only in the event that there are certain adverse legal opinions, or if the SEC prevents the sale, or if there is a substantial unfavorable change in the conditions of the market or the company—only in such cases can the underwriters avoid purchasing the issue. Even if they foresee a sizeable loss, they are likely to stay with the issuer rather than earn a reputation for being unreliable.

Because the investment bankers are usually handling the sale of a number of issues, they cannot supply all the funds necessary to carry the issue if it has not been sold by the settlement date. In order to carry the unsold portion in inventory until it can be sold the underwriters will temporarily borrow from commercial banks, using the securities as collateral.

We can avoid paying the investment banker for his risk-assuming function if we ask him to sell our securities on a *best efforts* basis rather than to underwrite them. Under this arrangement the selling price is fixed, but the amount of securities that will be sold at that price is uncertain. A small company may have no other choice; the risk may be so great that the investment banker is unwilling to underwrite the issue. Because some securities may not be sold, this is often an unsatisfactory arrangement for a small company. If it needs $200,000 to build a plant, the job cannot be done with $150,000. Laws in several states provide that unless most of an offering is sold, the investors' money must be returned, less any sales commission paid to the investment banker.

At the other extreme very large corporations occasionally sell their securities on a best efforts, or commission, basis because they feel the risk of not selling the securities is slight. If there is virtually no risk to assume, these corporations are willing to assume it themselves rather than pay the investment banker for the performance of this function.

An illustration of the latter case was the sale of $100 million of debentures by C.I.T. Financial Corporation. The investment banking firm of Salomon Brothers & Hutzler was employed as an agent by C.I.T. and received a commission ranging from $\frac{1}{4}$ to $\frac{3}{8}$ of 1 percent of the principal amount of the debentures sold through its efforts (that is, from $2.50 to $3.75 per thousand dollar bond). The agreement specified that the investment banker "is not required to take or pay for any of the Series Debentures but only to use its best efforts to cause their sale to the public . . . The Corporation has reserved the right to sell the Series Debentures itself and the right to enter into substantially similar agreements with not more than 10 additional agents."[2] No additional agents were used, and the $100 million issue sold out very quickly.

Selling Function

The essence of the investment banker's business is turnover. When he *grosses* only $\frac{9}{10}$ of 1 percent on the selling price, as in the case of the Northern Illinois Gas issue, he must sell a large volume to develop an adequate earning power. If the banker cannot sell an issue before the settlement date, he must still pay

[2]C.I.T. Financial Corporation, *Prospectus* (July 23, 1957), p. 11.

the issuing corporation in full and carry the unsold securities in inventory until he can sell them. He then has his own funds tied up in part of the inventory and is paying interest to a bank to finance the balance. He is missing out on opportunities to participate in other issues and runs the risk of having to sell this one at a loss. If the issue sells slowly, the underwriters may agree to reduce the selling price and take a loss rather than tie up their funds. In large part the investment banker can avoid this predicament by buying, timing, and pricing wisely. However, it is also important to have a strong selling organization.

The formation of a syndicate is desirable not only to spread the risk but to distribute the issue widely and quickly. A large portion of the issue will be sold by salesmen of the underwriters. On these sales the investment banker receives the full amount of the gross spread. Some securities may be allocated to *dealers* all over the country for resale. These local security dealers perform only a selling function and do not underwrite the issue. Their role is similar to that of a broker or manufacturer's agent in marketing other products. For their selling services the dealers receive a discount from the offering price to the public. Since they perform only the selling function and do not assume any part of the investigating function or the risk of underwriting the issue, their spread is less than that of the investment bankers underwriting the issue. For example, on the Northern Illinois Gas issue it was agreed that members of the syndicate could allow a selling concession to certain selected dealers of $\frac{1}{2}$ of 1 percent of the principal amount, out of which these dealers or members of the syndicate could allow a "spread" of $\frac{1}{4}$ of 1 percent to any dealers. In other words, the underwriters purchased each bond from Northern Illinois Gas at $1000.59. Some were sold to "selected dealers" at $1005.59 [that is, $1000.59 + (0.005 \times $1000)]. In turn these dealers were permitted to sell bonds to any other dealers at $1008.09 [that is, $1005.59 + (0.0025 \times $1000)]. All underwriters and dealers sold the bonds to the public at $1010 each.

The selling effort by these underwriters and dealers begins prior to the offering date. An announcement of the forthcoming offering is made to alert the prospective investors. However, the corporation must avoid undertaking a publicity campaign. This is against SEC regulations. Copies of a statement, called a prospectus, filed with the SEC setting forth the basic facts concerning the corporation and the proposed issue are made available to interested investors. The face of this booklet is identical to that shown in Exhibit 16-1, with three exceptions. Because it is not known when the SEC will permit the sale of the securities, no offering date is shown. No price is shown, since that will be set shortly after the offering date. In addition the following statement is stamped in bright red on the face:

A registration statement relating to the securities referred to herein has been filed with the Securities and Exchange Commission, but has not yet become effective. Information contained herein is for informative purposes only, and is subject to correction and change without notice. Under no circumstances is it to be considered a prospectus, or as an offer to sell, or the solicitation of an offer to buy the securities referred to herein. No offer to buy or sell any such securities should be made and no order to purchase the securities herein referred to will be accepted unless and until a registration statement under the Federal Securities Act of 1933 relating to the securities herein referred to has become effective.

Because of the arresting hue of the stamp and the obvious intent of the document, this booklet is referred to as a *red herring*.

The SEC examines the material provided in the prospectus and registration statement as to its accuracy and adequacy; it makes no judgment as to quality or value in relation to price. When the SEC agrees to permit the sale of the securities, the members of the syndicate and dealers are notified that the registration has become "effective." Salesmen then notify prospective investors of the offering price of the issue and seek orders for the securities. With a good issue, proper timing and pricing, and an active selling organization, the securities may be sold within a few hours of the time their sale is permitted by the SEC. Thus all of the $200 million of bonds offered by Weyerhaeuser were sold by late evening of the same day on which they were offered. Yet on the same day Connecticut Light and Power Company's $40 million of $8\frac{7}{8}$ percent bonds received a much less favorable response, and only one-fourth were taken on the first day.[3] When $20 million remained unsold six days later, the underwriters "released the issue;" that is, they ceased attempting to sell the issue at the offering price and sold it at the price necessary to move out the remaining balance. It immediately dropped $1\frac{1}{2}$ points, or $15 per bond — rather more than the underwriters' spread.[4]

In the prospectus for the issue by Northern Illinois Gas there is a statement:

> In connection with this offering, the purchasers may over-allot or effect transactions which stabilize or maintain the market price of the securities offered hereby at a level above that which might otherwise prevail in the open market. Such stabilizing, if commenced, may be discontinued at any time.

In simple terms this means that the managing underwriters may place orders in the open market to buy these bonds should the price tend to drift below $1010. This process of *stabilization* is designed to prevent minor downward price fluctuations resulting from the sudden entry to the market of this $35 million issue. Although it might be viewed as price fixing in violation of antitrust laws, it can hardly be very effective price fixing in view of the many alternative securities available to investors. If the issue has been overpriced, no amount of stabilization will help the underwriters. They will simply keep buying back the bonds they have just sold — surely an exercise in futility. Eventually, they will have to cut loose from their original offering price and let the bonds seek their own level in the market, as in the case of the Connecticut Light and Power issue.

A syndicate is formed for each issue of securities. As soon as a particular issue is sold, the syndicate is dissolved. While a company may employ the same originating house for a number of different issues, the syndicates formed by the originating house usually differ from one issue to the next.

The procedures described above also apply to preferred and common

---

[3] *Wall Street Journal*, October 8, 1970, p. 17.
[4] *Wall Street Journal*, October 14, 1970, p. 23.

stocks. Because of the greater price volatility of common stock, the underwriters typically receive a larger "spread," but they also worry more.

Selection of Investment Banker

The investment banker who finally handles the sales of securities may be selected in one of two ways: direct negotiation or public bid. In the one case we select the firm; in the other case investment bankers bid for our securities.

In direct negotiation two factors tend to limit the degree of competition among investment bankers for issues of securities. First, a concern may allow one investment banker to handle its sales for many years, although it is under no obligation to do so. Second, we should recognize that there is some degree of specialization in the field. For example, Halsey, Stuart & Co., Inc., deals mainly in bonds of utilities; and Morgan, Stanley & Co. in "blue chip" securities, such as those of U.S. Steel and General Motors Corporation. Adherence to one banker and specialization among bankers limit, but certainly do not eliminate, competition among investment bankers.

Either the company or the investment banker may take the initiative in suggesting that an issue of securities be made. When it is known that a large company is considering the sale of its securities, investment banking firms often compete actively to handle the issue. Read what Albert Gordon of Kidder, Peabody & Co., a well-known investment banking firm, has to say on the methods used to obtain business:

> It is our policy to study the field to determine which industries are likely to be in need of funds, or which companies can advantageously refund their securities. Having made those studies, we then decide which companies we might be able to successfully solicit. We try to find weaknesses wherever we can. We go after those weaknesses to the best of our ability. If there is time left over from those situations, we get after other situations.
>
> One cannot go to a company and say merely it would be nice if you did business with us. It is necessary to develop a program, and to present facts and figures that the company is interested in. The preparation of such facts and figures and terms, the development of terms — each situation is different — such development takes a great deal of time, and it would be impossible to solicit every company in the United States. We advertise, we do everything we can to get business. In addition to that, we go after any piece of business we think we have a chance of getting.[5]

The situation is quite different when securities are sold on a bid basis. This method is used on rather standardized issues of securities by public utilities and railroads (as well as by states, cities, school districts, and so on). We may enlist the services of an investment banker to draw up the terms of our offering and to prepare the registration statement for the SEC, but he then is not permitted to bid for the issue. Once we have determined what securities we wish to sell, and when we wish to sell them, we advertise for bids. Under the leadership of one to three firms acting as managers, investment bankers

[5] *Opinion* of Harold R. Medina, C. J., p. 328. (Quoted from testimony of Albert Gordon.)

then form syndicates to bid on the issue. Because a syndicate does not know in advance if it will win the issue, there is very little "advance selling" of the issue. The managers check with leading financial institutions in order to judge the tone of the market and report the results of their findings to the group. Some time before the bid date the issuer holds a meeting to provide essential information concerning the corporation's affairs and financial position to prospective underwriters. An hour or so before the time the bid is due each syndicate meets and agrees upon a final bid, which represents the proceeds the issuer will receive for his securities. The members of the syndicate will also agree upon their offering price to the public and allowances to be made to dealers, although these matters do not constitute part of the bid. At the appointed place, date, and hour, the bids from various syndicates are opened. The securities are awarded to the highest bidder; that is, to the group whose price will give the issuer the lowest net interest cost. Often the securities may be made available for sale on the following day.

Because investment bankers are skilled in judging the market, their bids are generally very close. On a recent offering by Texas Electric Service Company the first and second-place bids were unusually close—a three cent difference for each $1000 bond.[6] The closeness of the bids illustrates the accuracy with which experts are able to judge the market value of a promised stream of cash payments.

With certain exceptions railroads subject to regulations by the Interstate Commerce Commission and public utility holding companies registered with the SEC are required to offer their securities for public bid and to award each issue to the highest bidder.[7] State public utility commissions often have similar requirements. During the recent period of tight money the requirement for public bids was waived in a number of cases when it became apparent that the borrowing firm would receive only one bid, at most.[8]

There is considerable controversy over the desirability of requiring corporations to offer their securities on a public bid basis. The argument for competitive bidding is that it enables the issuer to receive the highest price for his securities. (However, this argument cannot be supported statistically because it is not possible to determine the price that would have been received under other arrangements.) Presumably this favorable price is reflected in lower costs or better services for the customers of the public utilities and railroads.

The other side of the story is that the issuer is giving up some services of the investment banker that are valuable not only to the issuer, but to investors as well. Note that on a competitive bid it is the issuer who sets the time of sale and who draws up the form of security and terms of the issue. Without the specialized knowledge of the investment banker of the capital markets, the time of sale or form of security may be poorly chosen. As a result the company may receive less for its securities than if it had arranged their sale on a negotiated

---

[6] *Wall Street Journal,* October 14, 1970, p. 23.

[7] Issues exempt from this rule are those sold to existing stockholders, sales involving less than $1,000,000, short-term securities and term loans, and other cases of negligible importance.

[8] For example, the California Public Utilities Commission permitted the Pacific Telephone and Telegraph Co. to negotiate terms of a proposed $150 million debt offering with an underwriter of its choice. *Wall Street Journal,* February 12, 1970, p. 26.

basis. Since the issuer draws up the terms of the agreement, the interests of investors may not be adequately protected — or as well protected if the investment banker had prepared the terms. The investment banker cannot afford to undertake an intensive and expensive investigation when he may not win the issue. Finally, when securities are sold in this fashion, the banker has no incentive to make any sales effort before the bid is awarded. If his bid wins, he is likely to favor sales in large blocks to various financial institutions in order to move the issue quickly. In some cases the issuer might prefer wider distribution among individual and institutional investors, to avoid possible concentration of voting control.

Distribution of Securities

Public Offering

In recent years around 60 percent of the dollar amount of all corporate issues (debt and equity) have been sold to the public and the balance directly to financial institutions.

We may distinguish two groups of public buyers. On the one hand, we may sell our securities to the general public without requiring that purchasers have any special relationship to our company. (To avoid registration of the issue with the SEC we may wish to limit the purchasers to residents of one state.) On the other hand, we may limit the purchasers to those who hold securities we have previously issued or to other special groups, such as officers, employees, or customers.

General Public. In the fiscal year ended June 30, 1969, most registered public offerings were made to the general public, rather than to special groups, although it should be noted that the public offerings exclude investment company issues (Table 16-1). The proportion of public offerings to special groups was especially low for debt issues.

TABLE 16-1   Corporate Securities Offered for Public Cash Sale, Year Ended June 30, 1969
(Estimated gross proceeds in millions of dollars)

Registered Under 1933 Act	All Types	Bonds, Notes, Debentures	Preferred Stock	Common Stock
General Public	16,153	10,635	493	5,025
Special groups:				
Security holders	1,043	145	22	875
Other	87	38	—[a]	49
Totals	17,282	10,818	515	5,949

[a]$8,000.
Note: Details may not add to totals because of rounding.
Source: Securities and Exchange Commission, *35th Annual Report, Fiscal Year Ended June 30, 1969* (Washington, D.C.: U.S. Government Printing Office, 1970), p. 188.

Almost all large offerings of corporate securities to the general public are made through investment bankers. On very small issues to the general public the underwriting cost is sometimes prohibitive, or it is not possible to find an underwriter who will handle the issue. Although most investment bankers are not interested in underwriting issues of less than $1 million, a few firms specialize in handling issues of under $300,000. When they are locally well-known and highly regarded, some small companies have successfully sold their own securities to the general public without the aid of an investment banker. Respected and nationally-known companies, such as the American Telephone and Telegraph Company, have also occasionally sold their own securities, especially when new issues are sold fairly frequently.

Special Groups. Some corporations sell securities to officers and employees and occasionally to customers. The use of *stock options,* whereby key executives are given an option to buy a certain number of shares of common stock within a stated period of time at a given price, has become popular. The purpose of the option is to enhance the executive's net income after taxes, as well as to encourage him to improve the fortunes of the company as expressed in the market price of the stock. If certain legal requirements are met, any profit the executive makes by exercising his option and selling the stock may be considered a capital gain. This is then taxed at lower rates than ordinary income. If the market price falls below the option price, the option has no value, of course.

More important in terms of dollar volume are the sales of common stocks to those already holding common stock of the company. If an additional issue of common stock were sold to the general public, the share of the corporation's earnings, assets, and rights to management held by existing stockholders would be correspondingly diminished. Under common law they should be offered the chance to maintain their proportionate interest in the company. This right, termed a *pre-emptive right,* is supported by some state laws as well as in the charters of many corporations.

When securities are offered first to existing stockholders, it is called a *privileged subscription* or *rights offering.* The procedure is fairly simple. After the issue has been approved, we send out notices to stockholders saying that all those who are stockholders as of a certain date may subscribe to additional shares, say one additional share of common stock for each four shares currently held. If the current market price is $55 we might set the subscription price at $50. Then the holder of four shares of common stock will receive one *right* for each of his shares; if he sends his four rights together with $50 to us, we will issue an additional share of stock to him. The stockholder does not have to "exercise his rights" as it is called. Instead, he may easily sell the rights through his broker. However, he usually has only 20 days or so to make up his mind before the rights "expire" and become valueless. Stockholders should either exercise or sell their rights; they *lose* by doing *nothing.*

For a period after the rights offering has been announced the stock will sell "rights on"; that is, a person buying and holding the stock during this interval will be entitled to receive the rights when they are issued. How can the approximate value of the rights be determined during this period? We need to take into account the fact that after the offering there will be 25 percent more shares outstanding than at present. The owner of four shares of stock with a current market price of $55 is entitled to subscribe to one additional share for $50. If he does so, his investment in five shares will total $270 (4 × $55 + $50), or an average of $54 per share ($270/5). With this background we can easily devise a formula to determine P, the theoretical future value of one share of common stock after the offering has expired, using the following notation:

M_1 = the present market price of the stock "rights on"

N = the number of rights (or old shares) necessary to purchase one new share of stock

S = the subscription price of the stock

Then,

$$P = \frac{M_1 N + S}{N + 1} = \frac{\$55 \times 4 + \$50}{4 + 1} = \frac{\$270}{5} = \$54$$

A schematic picture of the theoretical behavior of the price of the stock and value of a right is shown below.

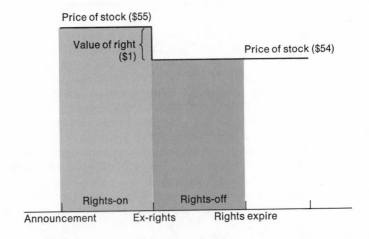

Price of stock ($55)

Value of right ($1)

Price of stock ($54)

Rights-on   Rights-off

Announcement   Ex-rights   Rights expire

Since the holder of four rights is being asked to pay $50 for stock with an estimated future market value of $54, the total value of the four rights necessary to make this "bargain" purchase must be $4 ($54 − $50). Consequently, the value of each right must be $1. This may also be determined by a formula using the notation above and letting V_1 = the theoretical value of one right when the stock is selling "rights on."

Value of right when stock is selling "rights on":

$$V_1 = \frac{M_1 - S}{N + 1}, \quad \text{or} \quad V_1 = \frac{\$55 - \$50}{4 + 1} = \$1$$

We should observe that the holder of four shares of stock really does not receive anything of value when he is issued the rights. Although the rights are worth a total of $4, he will lose $1 per share on the market value of his four shares of stock.

At a certain specified date purchasers of the stock are no longer entitled to receive the rights, and we say that the stock is selling "ex-rights." When the stock loses the right, we would expect its market price to fall by the value of one right, or from $55 to $54. At this time the rights are traded separately from the stock. A purchaser of four rights could buy one share of stock from the company for $50. How much would he pay for the rights? We would expect that he might pay no more than $4 for the rights, or $1 each. Together with his $50, this would bring his total purchase price of one share of stock to $54, the market price of the stock. In other words, after the stock has gone ex-rights, the new market price of the common stock is M_2, and the theoretical value of the rights, V_2, is as follows:

Value of right when stock is selling "rights off":

$$V_2 = \frac{M_2 - S}{N}, \quad \text{or} \quad V_2 = \frac{\$54 - \$50}{4} = \$1$$

In actual practice, the rights may sell for more than $1, because of their speculative attractions. An advance of only $4 in the market price of the stock would about double the value of the rights.

If the market price of the stock should fall below $50 during the brief period the rights are outstanding, our rights offering is in trouble. No stockholder in his right mind would pay us $50 for stock that is available at a lower price on one of the organized exchanges. If we really need the money, we may assure ourselves of receiving it by having the issue underwritten. Under this arrangement, termed a *stand-by commitment,* a syndicate of investment bankers agrees to buy whatever portion of the issue is not purchased by the common stockholders.[9] Of course, there is a charge for this service.

The risk that the rights will not be exercised depends upon a number of factors. (Presumably the greater the risk, the greater the likelihood that we will wish to underwrite the offering and the greater will be the investment bankers' commission.) Investors know it will be some time before we will be able to put the new funds received to work; therefore, for a while the present earnings will be spread over a larger number of shares. Consequently, if the issue is large in relation to the amount of common stock already outstanding, it is likely to depress the price of the stock on the market. We thus run the risk that the market price will fall below the subscription price. Moreover, the size of the offering in relation to existing shares affects the willingness and ability of stockholders to acquire additional shares. An offering of one additional share for each ten held

[9]Underwriters will attempt to hedge their risk by the "layoff technique." When the stock has gone ex-rights, the underwriters will both buy rights on the market and sell the stock "short." By a short sale we mean that the underwriters will sell stock that they have temporarily borrowed from brokers or investors. Then the rights are exercised to obtain stock that is used to make good the borrowed stock. (This is called "covering" the short position.) By this activity the underwriters hope to have as many rights exercised as possible, so that relatively few shares are left for them to buy from the company. Moreover, the shares the underwriters must purchase may have previously been sold by means of the short sales.

is likely to move better than an offering of five additional shares for each ten held. It puts a much greater strain on an investor's wealth and loyalty to ask him to buy five additional shares than to buy only one additional share.

Of great importance is the spread between the market price and the subscription price in relation to the normal variations in the price of the stock and the general market outlook. If the stock is not extensively traded and fluctuates widely in price, we would want to set the subscription price well below the current market price. This would reduce the risk that the market price would fall below the subscription price during the period the rights are outstanding. In setting the spread, we should also consider the general strength of the market, since any general weakness or uncertainty is likely to be felt by all stocks. Should we set too narrow a spread in relation to variations in our own stock and the strength of the general market, we increase the risk that the rights will not be exercised.

Of importance too is the expected rate of earnings from the new capital. The more productive the new funds, the more likely the rights offering will be successful. Finally, the period during which the rights are outstanding should also be considered. The longer the period, the greater the chance of an unfavorable change in market conditions that might force the market price of the stock below its subscription price.

Private Placement

The term *private placement* ordinarily applies to the direct sale of large blocks of securities by corporations to institutional investors. Because of the legal restrictions on investments by these financial institutions, the bulk of private placements are long-term debt issues. The term *direct negotiation,* a form of private placement, will be used here to refer to sales of securities to one or a few investors by small business. Although definitive statistics are lacking, direct negotiation is probably used chiefly for the sale of common stock.

Let us first consider the direct sale of securities by large corporations. About one-fifth of the dollar amount of corporate debt issues was privately placed during the first half of 1970 (Exhibit 16-2), and debt issues comprised almost all of private placements. Purchasers of such issues are mainly insurance companies, pension funds, and, occasionally, commercial banks. If an investment banker is involved, he is engaged for his advice and to find a purchaser for the issue. Since he acts as an agent for the issuer and does not underwrite the issue, his fee is quite small, usually ranging from about $\frac{1}{4}$ of 1 percent to $1\frac{1}{2}$ percent of the principal, depending upon the size of the issue and the amount of effort involved.

Why do corporations prefer to sell their securities directly to financial institutions rather than through investment bankers to the general public? One of the most important reasons for private placement is the greater speed with which the sale may be consummated. On most issues to the public various documents must be deposited with the SEC. A waiting period of several weeks usually elapses while the SEC examines these papers. During this period prices

EXHIBIT 16-2   *Debt Issues, Classified by Method of Offering*

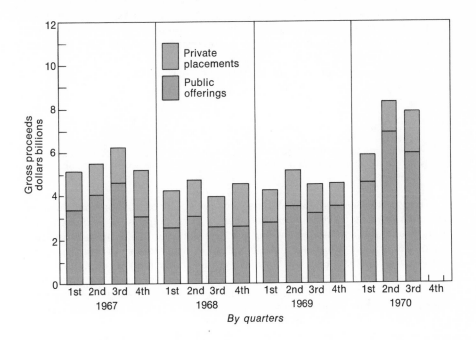

may decline in the market so that the issue cannot be sold at a favorable price. Because privately placed issues do not have to be registered with the SEC, this enforced delay and the resultant uncertainties are avoided. In addition special terms or privileges may be incorporated in the agreement with the financial institution that would be unpalatable to the general public. The terms may be perfectly justifiable, but it is easier to educate a few officers of an insurance company than a host of prospective buyers. For the same reason it is usually easier to make later adjustments in the terms of the contract when the issue has been placed privately. Because companies do not have to prepare registration papers for the SEC or pay registration fees, these expenses are avoided by private placement. However, the prospective buyer is well aware of these savings and may be able to insist on a higher interest rate. The interest premium a borrower pays in the private market may range around $\frac{1}{4}$ to $\frac{1}{2}$ of 1 percent. In periods of tight money a corporation may find that it must also add a "kicker" by giving the financial institution buying its bonds some claim on its common stock.

Small businesses find quite a different approach necessary to tap the capital markets. They are seldom able to reach the capital market through investment bankers, and then only on a "best efforts" basis in most cases. However, when an underwriter is obtained, chances for a successful offering are materially improved.[10] Because of the risks associated with small businesses, especially new companies, most investors are unwilling to make long-term loans to them. Consequently, proprietors of small companies needing long-term funds must usually negotiate directly with investors for equity funds, generally in return for common stock.

If we were operating a small business, where would we seek equity capital? The list of possibilities is large:

> Wealthy individuals, family estates, partners and associates in investment-banking houses, investment-banking firms for their own account, closed-end investment companies, outright venture-capital firms, pension funds, non-financial corporations seeking diversification, dissatisfied corporate officers, wealthy men seeking active management roles, and others.[11]

This rather dry recitation of the sources of equity capital for small business conceals the great difficulty experienced in obtaining funds. As one exceedingly successful small businessman told the writer, in his early days he "beat the bricks" looking for money. He sold stock to his parents, his brother, to anyone who would listen to him. *Venture-capital firms* (that is, companies that specialize in providing funds to small, risky businesses) report that they reject 90 out of 100 applicants after the first interview. Usually management is unbalanced—frequently *good financial management* is lacking! Often a satisfactory growth potential is not evident. Out of the ten firms reaching the second interview, only one or two can offer the requirements necessary to obtain equity financing.

Contrary to what they might fear, many small businessmen do not necessarily have to give up control to obtain equity capital. Most outside investors are not interested in taking over managerial duties, but they do want enough of a "say" in management to protect their interests and a large enough share in the equity to give them a good return on their investment. The anticipated annual rate of return necessary to attract venture capital probably centers on 20 percent.

Cost of Public Offerings

There are two immediate costs involved in selling securities through underwriters to the public. One is the underwriters' commission, which is incorporated in the price paid by the public and is not an expense on the books of the corporation. The other is composed of various expenses borne by the corporation which represent deductions from the gross proceeds. Note that in the case of

---

[10] One study of financing small corporations concluded, "commercial underwriters sold on the average 90 percent of the amount of each issue initially offered while direct promoters succeeded in selling only 50 percent." Daniel Ounjian, "Public Financing of Small Corporations: The Regulation A Market," *New England Business Review* (Federal Reserve Bank of Boston), October, 1966, p. 19.

[11] G. T. Brown, S. H. Miller, L. S. Ritter, and R. I. Robinson, "Availability and Cost of External Equity Capital for Small Business Ventures," *Financing Small Business* (Washington, D.C.: Federal Reserve System, 1958), p. 529.

the $35 million issue by Northern Illinois Gas (Exhibit 16-1), the commission amounted to $329,350 and other expenses to $87,000. Although these may seem like fairly large sums, we should keep in mind that they are fairly negligible in relation to interest costs. If these flotation costs were written off over the 6-year life of the bond, they would amount to slightly under $70,000 per year, as compared to an annual cash payment on interest of $2,975,000 ($8\frac{1}{2}$ percent of principal amount of $35 million).

What makes up the "other expenses"? The SEC has estimated that such expenses would total about $34,000 on a $2 million issue of common stock. Legal, accounting, and engineering fees make up about two-fifths of the total, with printing and engraving, state and federal taxes, and other items making up the balance.[12]

Flotation costs vary according to the type of security, the industry of the issuer, the size of the issue and issuer, and the underwriting risk involved. Flotation costs of common stock are relatively higher than for preferred stock and bonds. In part this difference reflects the fact that common stock is often sold in small blocks to numerous investors scattered across the country. Moreover, there is usually more risk involved in underwriting common stock because the market prices of common stocks vary more widely than in the case of preferred stock and bonds. The costs of flotation are generally somewhat higher for manufacturing corporations than for corporations in communications and electric, gas, and water utilities, although differences narrow for large issues. Again, the higher flotation costs for industrials probably reflect in part the greater underwriting risk associated with selling securities of these concerns. Most noticeable of all are the differences in flotation costs on large and small issues (Exhibit 16-3). Many of the costs of underwriting an issue and a high proportion of the expenses borne by the issuer are fixed. Consequently, these flotation costs are fairly high in relation to the total proceeds of small issues of securities, but often fall to less than 1 percent of gross proceeds on very large corporate issues. It is not at all unusual for underwriting commissions alone on speculative sales of common stock to run as high as 15 percent of the amount raised. In addition underwriters are often given the privilege of buying *warrants* at a nominal price. These give the holder the right to buy common stock at a specified price. For example, Myron A. Lomasney & Co., an investment banker specializing in underwriting venture capital for new companies, "paid $200 for warrants to buy 20,000 shares of BBM Photocopy Mfg. Corp. at $3." When BBM stock later sold for $40, these warrants were worth $800,000, yet the amount of stock floated for BBM by the underwriter was only $300,000.[13]

Government Regulation

Government regulation applies both to the sale of new issues and to the purchase and sale of previously issued securities. Regulation of transactions in existing issues is largely within the province of the Federal authorities, specifi-

---

[12] Securities and Exchange Commission, *Cost of Flotation of Registered Equity Issues, 1963–1965* (Washington, D.C.: U.S. Government Printing Office, 1970), p. 42.

[13] "Small Underwriters Make Big Splash in Market," *Business Week*, September 24, 1960, p. 147.

EXHIBIT 16-3   Total Cost of Flotation of Registered Equity Issues as Percentage of Proceeds, 1963–1965

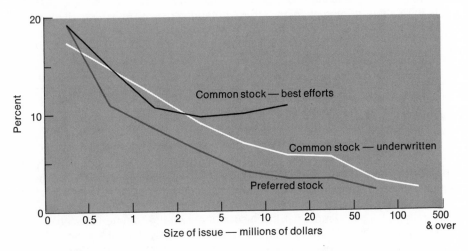

Source: Securities and Exchange Commission, *Cost of Flotation of Registered Equity Issues, 1963–1965* Washington, D.C.: U.S. Government Printing Office, 1970), pp. 13, 30.

cally the SEC, whereas both state and Federal regulations may apply to the sale of new issues.

New Issues

Federal Regulation. Interstate security sales are regulated by the Federal Securities Act of 1933. Securities issued by the following organizations are exempt from the provisions of the act: Federal, state, and municipal governments; common carriers subject to regulation by the Interstate Commerce Commission; commercial banks; certain savings and loan associations; and non-profit institutions. A corporation issuing up to $300,000 of securities needs file only some very elementary information with the SEC ten days prior to the public offering. We have already noted that private placements are exempt.

The basic philosophy of the act is that a prospective buyer should be given full, adequate, and accurate information. Let us see how this is provided. Some time prior to the prospective offering date we must file with the SEC a *registration statement* and a *prospectus*. The registration statement is a rather bulky compilation of all pertinent information concerning our company and its chief officers. The prospectus is a summary of the significant points covered in the registration statement. Without the price and offering date, this is the "red herring" mentioned earlier. With this information, it is a statement that must be given a prospective purchaser of the securities at the time they are offered for sale. If the buyer is unable to understand the prospectus, or does not read it, or reads it and ignores unfavorable information, that is his hard luck. The Federal act does not take on the responsibility for telling the investor what he should or should not buy.

The SEC can prevent the sale of securities until it believes that the registration statement and prospectus contain no misleading statements and omit no significant information. During the fiscal year ending June 30, 1969, a record number of filings with the SEC pushed the median time that elapsed between the date of filing a registration statement and the effective date to 65 days. At the SEC this time was consumed by examining the registration statement, preparing a letter of comment, and reviewing amendments filed by the issuer in response to the letter of comment. Presumably investors used this time to peruse the "red herring."

Most omissions or misstatements in the registration statement are dealt with by means of the letter of comment. If there are material deficiencies the SEC may issue a *stop order* to prevent the sale of the securities until the shortcomings are corrected. To illustrate the matters that concern the SEC, a summary is given below of the reasons advanced by the SEC for issuing a stop order on the proposed sale of $10.5 million of common stock by Republic Cement Corporation to construct a cement plant in Arizona. The SEC found

> . . . that the registrant had failed to disclose that its proposed output of gray cement combined with that of a presently producing plant in its market area would far exceed any past or present market demand and that the existing plant had not been operating at full capacity. It further found that the registrant's proposed output of white cement exceeded 25 percent of the annual consumption of that product in the entire United States. The company's plant construction cost figures were determined to be much lower than those of its competitors because certain installations which are normally part of a cement plant were to be eliminated, and the registrant had not provided for sufficient storage capacity for its finished product. The Commission also found that despite the representation in the prospectus that the registrant had on its properties 1,851,300,000 tons of limestone suitable for the production of cement, only the most rudimentary type of exploration had been performed on the properties, and no systematic core drilling or sampling was used to test the continuity, depth, and quality of the limestone.[14]

Enforcement of the act is aided by the provision of civil and criminal liabilities. In addition, purchasers of securities may sue for damages suffered as a result of untrue or materially inadequate information in the prospectus. Practically everybody connected with the issue, excluding the SEC, may be sued.

A recent means of evading registration with the SEC has been the use of *letter stock*. Characteristic of small and emerging businesses, letter stock is common stock issued to 25 or fewer investors who agree in an "investment letter" that they will not resell the stock to other investors within some specified period. The buyer usually cannot resell the stock unless the firm registers the issue or until he can find another investor who will similarly agree not to sell the stock in the market. The president of a New York brokerage house doing a large letter stock business cited the advantages to corporations from selling letter stock: "Our clients sell letter stock for three reasons—speed, speed, and

[14]Securities and Exchange Commission, *23rd Annual Report*, p. 46.

speed."[15] Some deals have been concluded in as little as 48 hours, compared to the median wait with an SEC registration of 65 days.

State Regulation. Some state laws parallel the SEC approach in that they are primarily designed to prevent fraud. Others go farther and attempt to protect the investor from himself—or his own poor judgment—by prohibiting the sale of secutities deemed by some state commissions to be especially speculative, overpriced, or of very poor quality. It is entirely possible for a state commissioner to prevent the sale of a security within his state, even though the SEC has allowed its registration statement to become effective. State laws are sometimes referred to as "blue sky legislation," because they represent an attempt to prevent the sale of the "blue sky" to unwary investors. Ordinarily a corporation issuing securities may comply with these state laws by filing with the state commission information similar to that contained in its registration statement. If the securities are not to be offered in interstate commerce, the issuer need file only with the state in which the securities are offered for sale.

Existing Issues

An important aid to the original sale of new securities is the provision of fair and honest markets in which they may be subsequently sold. The Securities Exchange Act of 1934 requires the registration of security exchanges and of brokers and dealers doing business in securities traded (listed) on and outside of the exchanges. (The market in unlisted securities is called the *over-the-counter* market.) Working largely through the governing bodies of the various exchanges and the National Association of Security Dealers, the SEC attempts to prevent "fraudulent, deceptive, and manipulative acts and practices" in security transactions. Issuers of securities which are traded on the exchanges and unlisted companies with more than $1 million in assets and more than 500 shareholders are subject to regulation and reporting requirements of the SEC. Material used to solicit proxies must be filed with the SEC before being sent to stockholders. These corporations are also required to provide regular financial statements to their stockholders.

Trading by corporate officers and directors in securities of their own companies is limited to some extent, and a full report of their transactions is published monthly. In an effort to speed the flow of information to the market—and thereby make it more efficient—the SEC has filed complaints against use of inside information before it became publicly available. In the case of *S.E.C. v. Texas Gulf Sulphur Co.* the Commission alleged

> . . . that certain insiders had purchased shares of Texas Gulf stock or calls thereon [A *call* is an option to buy a specified number of shares.] on the basis of material inside information concerning the results of exploratory drilling for base metals by Texas Gulf near Timmins, Ontario; had passed this information to others and advised them to purchase Texas Gulf stock or calls; and had accepted stock options from Texas Gulf without disclosing material information to the board of directors.[16]

[15] "'Bargain' Securities," *Wall Street Journal*, November 18, 1969, p. 1.
[16] Securities and Exchange Commission, *34th Annual Report*, p. 6.

The court of appeals "unanimously held that a corporate insider in possession of important inside information about his corporation may not trade in the corporation's stock without disclosing that information. . . This duty was unanimously held to apply to employees of the corporation, as well as to its top officers."[17]

The general purpose of these regulations is to encourage the capital markets to function so that funds are channeled into their most productive uses. Deceptive practices, either in the original issue or in subsequent sale of securities, are likely to divert investors' funds from economically desirable uses to less desirable uses. Suppression of these practices is not obtained without cost, however. In addition to the resources devoted to the SEC and other regulatory bodies there are the delays and other burdens which may handicap or prevent reputable firms from seeking funds in the capital markets. Moreover, it would be asking too much to expect regulation to promote wisdom and prevent speculation. Waves of optimism and pessimism will continue to sway the securities markets, and the daily take at pari-mutuel windows across the country suggests the difficulties of preventing speculative activity. Indeed, most small businesses would find it difficult to obtain any financing if we outlawed all speculation.

Summary

An investment banker stands ready to perform three main functions: investigating, risk-bearing, and selling. We can dispense with any or all of these functions. When selling our securities on a public bid basis, we largely eliminate his investigating function. The investment banker usually makes an outright purchase of securities, but not always. When we sell securities on a best efforts basis, we assume the risk of their not being sold. On a privileged subscription we undertake most, or even all, of the selling effort. All three functions may be eliminated if we sell securities directly to an insurance company or to an individual investor. For the most part investment bankers are best able to serve the needs of large corporations. Small companies are rarely able to tap the capital markets for long-term borrowed funds, and few can offer the growth potential necessary to attract external equity capital.

Because many of the costs of floating issues of securities do not vary with the size of issue, the proportion of flotation costs to the gross proceeds ordinarily declines as the size of the issue increases. Furthermore, the cost of equity financing is typically greater than the cost of debt financing.

Federal regulation of new issues and the sale of existing securities is designed to provide investors with the information they need to make rational decisions. Contrary to the philosophy of some state laws, the SEC makes no attempt to substitute its judgment for the investor's in reaching a rational decision.

---

[17] *Ibid.*, p. 7.

Questions

1/ Do you feel that industrial corporations should be required to sell their securities on a competitive bid basis? Explain the reasons for your decision.

2/ Do you believe it is good investment policy for officers of a corporation to invest in the stock of the corporation? Explain.

3/ Under what conditions would adherence to the pre-emptive right be a hindrance to financing?

4/ In September, 1955, common stockholders of Household Finance were offered rights to subscribe to one additional share of common stock at $24 per share for each 20 shares held. The underwriters received a flat fee of $122,896.80 plus $1.10 per share for all shares the underwriters had to purchase. From January 1, 1955, through September 26, 1955, the price range was 28–34. The closing price on September 26, 1955, was 29⅝. The rights were offered to stockholders of record on September 30 and expired on October 17. The proceeds were to be used to reduce short-term bank loans. Of the 341,380 shares offered by Household, 336,900 were purchased through the exercise of rights. Do you think Household was wise to have underwritten the issue? Explain the reasons for your conclusion.

5/ "Unless the government is to assume responsibility for directing the flow of capital into industry, there are limits to what it ought to do for investors. It cannot safely act as their guardians; it cannot afford to become a bulwark of defense against all the hazards which exist in the securities markets. In a society like ours, it should regard itself as a sentry assigned to hold back the exploiter and warn the army of investors of his presence whenever he breaks through the outer defenses." (Homer V. Cherrington, *The Investor and the Securities Act.* Washington, D.C.: American Council on Public Affairs, 1942, p. 246.) Do you agree with this approach? Why or why not?

6/ Would you favor legislation limiting the underwriter's commission to 10 percent of the gross proceeds of any issue? Explain.

7/ In general, the SEC has chosen "to accept generally practiced accounting procedures, and to encourage and even enforce the conservative bias generally followed by public accountants. . . .

The insistence on conservatism is an act of commission. Failure to require possibly useful information to be provided investors, on the other hand, is an act of omission. Principally, information on unfilled orders, the current and expected market price of inventories (when greater than cost), valuable research findings, and other "favorable" data not reflected in the ordinary accounting records, need not be reported to the investor. Nor are statements about the ability and health of management, public acceptability of products, subtle changes in labor-management relations, effects of political events on the company, and other vital activities required by the SEC regulations. (That these may not be objectively determinable does not deny their usefulness to investors.)" George J. Benston, "The Effectiveness and Effects of the SEC's Accounting Disclosure Requirements," in *Economic*

Policy and the Regulation of Corporate Securities, Henry G. Manne, ed. (Washington, D.C.: American Enterprise Institute for Public Policy Research, 1969), pp. 27, 29.
  a. Are the traditional accounting reports sufficiently timely and useful for prospective investors in a corporation's securities?
  b. Should the SEC require inclusion in a prospectus of the information suggested by Benston?

8/ In the latter part of 1970, American Telephone & Telegraph Co. was considering the sale of savings bonds in $100 units through its local business offices. The president of the National Association of Home Builders warned that if the bonds were issued, "It will certainly set back the anticipated recovery of the housing industry from its recent depressed state." *Business Week,* October 24, 1970, p. 34. Do you see any basis for the assertion? Trace the effects of the proposal.

Problems

1/ From a prospectus placed on file or obtained directly from the underwriter, glean the following information:
  a. Name of issuing corporation.
  b. Amount and description of securities offered.
  c. Price to the public, underwriters' commission, proceeds to corporation (in total amounts). By what percentage could the securities decline in price from the original offering price before wiping out the underwriters' commission?
  d. The amount of additional flotation costs borne by the corporation.
  e. The percentage of total flotation costs to gross proceeds.
  f. For what purpose will the proceeds of the sale be used?
  g. To how many underwriters was the issue sold? What was the maximum and minimum participation? Who were the managing underwriters?
  h. Was this a firm underwriting or were the securities to be sold on a best efforts basis? If a firm commitment was made, under what conditions could the underwriters withdraw?
  i. What was the dealer's concession? What re-allowance (if any) was granted to members of the NASD?
  j. What provisions (if any) were made for supporting the market price at the time of issuance? Why were these provisions made? Do you think this practice should be allowed? Why or why not?

2/ On the Household Finance privileged subscription described in some detail in Question 4 above, what was the maximum and minimum amount Household could have realized on that issue? How much did Household realize, net after underwriter's commission, but before other flotation costs?

3/ The largest financing in the history of American corporate finance was the offering by American Telephone and Telegraph Co. in 1964 of 12,250,000 shares of common stock to its shareholders on the basis of stock rights. For every 20 shares of common stock held February 18, 1964, AT&T shareholders were entitled to subscribe to one additional share at $100. At the time of the announcement the stock was selling for $146. Exercise of all rights was expected to bring the corporation over $1.2 billion. The subscription period ended April 6.

a. What was the theoretical value of the stock when it was selling rights off?
b. What was the theoretical value of the rights when the stock was selling rights on?
c. After February 18, the stock and rights sold separately, and the stock presumably fell in price to the level you have calculated in part (a) — assuming no other changes in the market. If this did happen, what was the theoretical value of the rights when the stock was selling rights off?
d. What was the theoretical value of a right on April 12?
e. AT&T did not obtain a stand-by commitment from underwriters on this offering. What reasons can you suggest for this omission?

4/ Niagara Mohawk Power Co. offered rights to subscribe to its common stock at $13 a share on the basis of one new share for each 10 shares held. The rights expired September 15, 1970.

On September 1, 1970, the common stock (trading ex-rights) closed at $14\frac{3}{8}$, and the rights at $\frac{7}{64}$.

a. Does the market price reflect the theoretical value of the right?
b. If the market price rose to $15\frac{7}{8}$ (just over a 10 percent increase), by what percentage would the theoretical value of the right increase?

Selected References

BLOCH, E., "Pricing a Corporate Bond Issue: A Look behind the Scenes," *Essays in Money and Credit*, pp. 72–76, New York: Federal Reserve Bank of New York, 1964.

Brown, J. M., "Post-Offering Experience of Companies Going Public," *Journal of Business*, 43 (January, 1970), pp. 10–18.

BROWNE, D. E. "The New SEC Regulations — and the Future of Financial Relations," *Financial Executive*, 33 (July, 1965), pp. 15–16ff.

EITEMAN, D. K., "The S.E.C. Special Study and the Exchange Markets," *Journal of Finance*, 21 (May, 1966), pp. 311–23.

EVANS, G. H., Jr., "The Theoretical Value of a Stock Right," *Journal of Finance*, 10 (March, 1955), pp. 55–61.

FRIEND, I., G. W. HOFFMAN, and W. J. WINN, *The Over-the-Counter Securities Market*. New York: McGraw-Hill Book Co., Inc., 1958.

FRIEND, I. et. al., *Investment Banking and the New Issues Market*. Cleveland: The World Publishing Co., 1967.

————, *Investment Banking and the New Issues Market* (Philadelphia: Securities Research Unit, University of Pennsylvania, 1965).

MANNE, H. G., ed. *Economic Policy and the Regulation of Corporate Securities*. Washington, D.C.: American Enterprise Institute for Public Policy Research, 1969.

MILLER, G. R., "Long-Term Small Business Financing from the Underwriter's Point of View," *Journal of Finance*, 16 (May, 1961), pp. 280–90.

ROBINSON, R. I. and H. R. Bartell, "Uneasy Partnership: SEC/NYSE," *Harvard Business Review*, 43 (January-February, 1965), 76–88.

SEARS, G. A., "Public Offerings for Smaller Companies," *Harvard Business Review*, 46 (September-October, 1968), pp. 112–20.

Securities and Exchange Commision, *Annual Reports*. Washington, D.C.: U.S. Government Printing Office, 19--.

SOLDOFSKY, R. M., "The Size and Maturity of Direct Placement Loans," *Journal of Finance,* 15 (March, 1960), pp. 32–44.

STOLL, H. R. and A. J. CURLEY, "Small Business and the New Issues Market for Equities," *Journal of Financial and Quantitative Analysis,* 5 (September, 1970), pp. 309–22.

STUEBNER, E. A., "The Role of the Investment Banker in Arranging Private Financing," *Business Lawyer* 16 (January, 1961), pp. 377–85.

"Venture Capital for Small Business — A Symposium," *Business Lawyer,* 24 (April, 1969), pp. 935–66.

WHEAT, F. M. and G. A. BLACKSTONE, "Guideposts for a First Public Offering," *Business Lawyer,* 15 (April, 1960), pp. 539–64.

ZWICK, J., *A Handbook of Small Business Finance.* Washington, D.C.: Small Business Administration, 1965.

Debt

17

Long-term funds are available either in the form of debt or equity. We have already noted the relative merits of each in the discussion on planning the financial structure (Chapter 10). However, the relative advantages and disadvantages of debt depend in part on the exact nature of the bargain struck between lender and borrower. When borrowing, we will wish to draw up an agreement that is most advantageous to our interests — one that minimizes the undesirable features of debt and maximizes the desirable ones. On the other side of the bargaining table is the lender. Usually the features that make the debt issue attractive to us as a means of obtaining funds are those that make it unattractive to him as an investment. This chapter is devoted mainly to the choices that must be made among the various types of contracts, or loan-offer functions, available to long-term borrowers.

Because bondholders are located all over the country, they are in a poor position to enforce the terms of the contract once the bonds have been issued. To remedy this problem there is injected into the picture a *trustee* to represent the interests of the bondholders. The terms formulated by the corporation and the investment bankers are set forth in an *indenture*, which is a contract between the corporation and the trustee in behalf of the bondholders. The major function of the trustee is to make sure that the corporation complies with the provisions of the indenture. If the corporation fails to abide by certain specified terms of the indenture, this is considered to be a *default*. The corporation and trustee usually have a minimum grace period in which to correct a minor default. If major lapses are not remedied, the trustee is generally required to report the situation to the bondholders. With the consent of a minimum proportion of the bondholders, say 25 percent, the trustee must then take action to force the corporation to comply with the indenture or to satisfy the bondholders' demands in some other manner.[1] A summary of the essential features of the indenture is provided in fine print on the bond itself.

Forms of Long-Term Debt

The various forms of long-term debt were not dreamed up by an astute college professor who wished to have some detailed material for use in hazing students on examinations. Instead they represent the end result of intensive bargaining between borrowers and lenders. As borrowers, we will strive hardest to win those features that are of most importance to us and concede those points of least significance. Whether the bargain incorporated in the indenture is more or less in our favor will depend on our bargaining strength and ability relative to that of the lender. We have alternatives and so does the lender. The attractiveness of these alternatives depends in large part on conditions in the money and capital markets, upon the general economic outlook, and upon our financial position. Keep in mind that we bargain in a dynamic setting. Our financial position may improve between two given years, but our bargaining position may decline in relation to that of the lenders. If suppliers of borrowed funds find more alternative investments open and have a smaller amount of funds to invest over the same period, we may find the bargain less in our favor in the latter year.

It will be recalled that the distinctive features of debt as opposed to equity funds related to: maturity, claim on income, claim on assets, and voice in management. Let us see the area of bargaining for each of these features.

Maturity

One of the characteristic features of debt is that it comes due. The specified maturity is of considerable interest to both creditor and debtor, and bargaining is likely to center on provisions for compulsory repayment and provisions for voluntary repayment.

---

[1] If the bond issue exceeds $1 million and must be registered with the SEC, the indenture must comply with the requirements of the Trust Indenture Act of 1939. This act is designed to give protection to bondholders by requiring that the indenture contain certain protective features and that the trustee appointed to enforce the indenture be a party responsible only for the best interests of the bondholders.

Compulsory Repayment. One of the unfavorable aspects of incurring debt is the inherent risk that it may fall due at a time when it will be very difficult to repay. Generally, we would like to postpone this day of reckoning for as long as possible. In addition, if financial leverage is favorable, we would like to use the bondholders' money more or less indefinitely, if they would be willing. They are not. To be sure of recovering their investment they would prefer a more rapid return of their money. The greater the risk of change, the earlier the maturity they would prefer. While a telephone company might be able to issue 50-year bonds, an industrial concern may be limited to a 15-year maturity.

The desired maturity is also related to interest costs. At times "30-year money" costs much more than "20-year money." In this case we say the yield curve is very "steep"; that is, interest costs rise sharply as the maturity lengthens. We must balance the unfavorable prospect of repayment of the debt in a fairly short period of time against the higher cost of funds carrying a longer maturity. This is our familiar dilemma of risk vs. return. During the tight money period of 1969–70, a number of corporations opted for return by employing short maturities in the hope that these debt issues might be replaced by less costly debt at maturity. In order to tap sufficient funds and to "hedge their bets" some floated bond issues that tapped both the intermediate and long-term segments of the market. The $200 million issue by Weyerhaeuser mentioned in the last chapter consisted of two parts: $50 million of $8\frac{1}{8}$ percent notes of six-year maturity and $150 million of $8\frac{5}{8}$ percent bonds with a 30-year maturity. Both issues were sold at par or face value. Note the confirmation of the upward-sloping yield curve in the diagram.

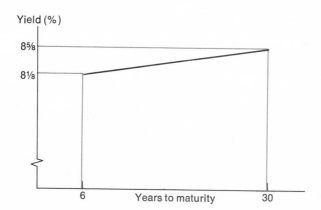

At other times the yield curve is relatively "flat" and costs of funds do not vary greatly according to maturity. Sometimes borrowers have faced a downward-sloping yield curve, wherein short-term funds were more expensive than long-term funds.

Lenders may speed the return of their money by bargaining for short maturities or by seeking a sinking fund or serial maturities. If a *sinking fund* is provided in the indenture, the corporation must usually make a periodic payment of cash to the trustee for the retirement of the bonds. A sinking fund is illustrated by the Otis Elevator Company $6\frac{1}{2}$ percent convertible subordinated debentures (a form of bond) issued in 1970 and due in 1995. To retire the $50 million issue gradually

> . . . in each year, commencing in 1981, Otis will pay to the Trustee an amount sufficient to redeem on each October 1 a principal amount of Debentures equal to not less than 5% and not more than 10% of the principal amount of Debentures outstanding at the close of business on September 15, 1980 . . . each such sinking fund payment shall be applied to the redemption of Debentures on such October 1 at 100% of their principal amount together with accrued interest to the date of redemption.[2]

Note that eleven years elapse before the first payment to the sinking fund. This is not an uncommon arrangement. It allows the corporation sufficient time to invest the funds received from the bond issue in order to increase its cash flow enough to meet the sinking fund requirements.

The amount paid to the trustee can be determined in various ways. From our point of view we would probably like to see the payment related to the amount of earnings, so that our payments into the sinking fund would rise and fall with earnings. The bondholders would ordinarily prefer a fixed payment. In some instances the amount to be paid into the sinking fund increases each year, on the theory that the corporation's ability to generate cash will improve over the years. The sinking fund may be arranged so as to retire all or only a portion of the bonds before the final maturity date. Frequently, only a portion of the bonds are retired prior to the maturity date, so that the final payment is like a "balloon payment" on an instalment contract. Whatever the method used, it is important to recognize that the sinking fund payments represent a cash drain, and that the amount of debt that we can assume will depend in part upon our ability to meet the cash payments demanded by the sinking fund. (Recall the discussion in Chapter 10.) Failure to meet these commitments will constitute an "event of default," and the trustee may call for the immediate payment of the entire bond issue.

The trustee of the Otis' bonds may *call* the bonds for redemption "at 100% of their principal amount" ($1000). Under this procedure he selects bonds at random and notifies the bondholders to send in their bonds for redemption and retirement. Alternatively, he may use the sinking fund payments received to buy the bonds in the open market if they are selling for less than 100. Had these bonds been privately placed, such open-market purchases at "bargain prices" would not be possible.

A *serial bond* differs from a bond with a sinking fund in that the bondholder knows in advance just when his bond is coming due, although these bonds may also be callable. For example, a $20 million, 20-year bond issue may be arranged so that $1 million of the bonds come due each year. Since the maturity date is stated on each bond, an investor may select the maturity that suits his needs. Serial bonds are most commonly used when the assets used to secure the bonds are real estate or railroad equipment. In these cases the annual cash flows gen-

[2]Otis Elevator Company, *Prospectus*, October 6, 1970, p. 12.

erated by the assets are thought to be sufficiently certain that the borrower can assume the risk of meeting the rigid maturity requirements of the serial bonds.

Voluntary Repayment. Rather than be forced to retire the bonds in accordance with some predetermined schedule, we would prefer to have the right to retire them at will. The time may come when the financial leverage is unfavorable. More likely, we may be able to retire 9 percent bonds and replace them with 6 percent bonds and thereby reap even greater benefit from financial leverage. This process is called *refunding* and will be discussed in greater detail at the end of the chapter. Of course, the bondholder knows that if we are allowed to repay the debt at will, we will do so when interest rates have declined. Thus the money he lent to us at 9 percent will be returned at a time when he can reinvest it with equal risk at only 6 percent. It is in his interests to prevent this sort of action or, at least, to penalize us for redeeming the bonds.

Our right to redeem the bonds is termed a *call privilege*. This right has a value to the issuing corporation and represents a possible loss of yield to the investor. To understand the investor's loss of yield assume that 20-year bonds are sold at $1000 with an 8 percent coupon. If we assume that interest is paid at the end of each year (rather than semi-annually as is customary), the present value of the bonds can be shown as follows:

$$\$1000 = \frac{\$80}{(1 + 0.08)} + \frac{\$80}{(1 + 0.08)^2} + \cdots + \frac{\$80}{(1 + 0.08)^{20}} + \frac{\$1000}{(1 + 0.08)^{20}}.$$

Should the bonds be called, the stream of $80 per year for 20 years is truncated. The bondholder receives his $1000 at the time of the call, but has no choice other than to reinvest this at a lower rate for at least some portion of the remaining years. The value to him of preventing the call depends upon his expectations of the interest he can earn during the period following the call. If he believes that interest rates will be significantly lower at a later date and remain lower thereafter, his interest in preventing or delaying the call heightens. By the same token, if we have similar expectations, our interest as an issuer of the bonds in obtaining a call privilege also heightens.

Clearly, if we are to obtain the call privilege we must offer the investor something of value to offset his expected loss of yield. At one extreme we could seek to have the bond freely callable. For this privilege we should expect to provide a higher coupon rate on the bonds, or some other attractive feature, such as the conversion option on the Otis Elevator bonds. The higher money rates are above some "normal" level, the more we must raise the coupon rate. Rather than rely entirely on the coupon rate to balance the call privilege, we can water down the call privilege. We might delay the right to call the bonds for the first five or ten years it is outstanding. Obviously, the longer the delay, the greater the value of this covenant to the bondholders. Second, we could offer a *call premium,* a penalty fee for calling the bonds. For example, the call premium on the Otis Elevator bonds was 6.5 percent ($65.00 per $1000 bond), this to apply if the bonds were called at any time during 1970. The premium declines gradually to 0.325 percent in 1989.

Since the importance of the call privilege depends upon expectations about future money rates, there is no mathematical model that will tell us just what mixture of higher coupon, delayed call privilege, and call premium is optimal. Evidence suggests that the market may undervalue the call privilege. This being the case, the optimal strategy is to pay a higher coupon rate in exchange for a full call privilege. If the research findings are correct, the market imperfection should cause the present value of the extra interest cost to be less than the present value of the call privilege to us.[3]

If money is *very* tight, we may have to give the *bondholders* a call privilege. For example, Avco Delta Corporation issued $30 million of 9¼ percent, 20-year debentures in late 1969 and gave the holders the right to turn in their bonds for cash on either September, 1973 or September, 1976. The corporation may not call the bonds until they have been outstanding for ten years. Another reason for giving bondholders a call privilege was to attract funds from individuals' savings accounts.

Claim on Income

Priority of Claim. When we borrow funds, we must allow creditors to have a claim on income prior to that of the owners. Bondholders may push their claim even further and insist upon certain restrictions on dividends very similar to those we have noted in connection with intermediate-term financing. Thus dividends might be limited to earnings realized after the date of the bond issue, or dividends may be payable only if the net working capital is maintained at or above a given level. For example, the indenture for an issue of long-term debt by Bevis Shell Homes, Inc., specifies that:

> The Company will not (a) declare or pay any dividend or make any distribution (other than stock dividends), (b) purchase, redeem or acquire or retire any shares of its stock except shares acquired upon conversion into other stock, or (c) permit a subsidiary to purchase, redeem or acquire or retire any shares of the Company's stock, if after giving effect thereto, the aggregate amount expended for such purposes subsequent to December 31, 1959, exceeds the sum of 60% of the consolidated net earnings of the Company and its subsidiaries subsequent to December 31, 1959. . . .[4]

To the extent that these restrictions are only a matter of good financial management, they are not especially onerous.

Certainty of Claim. One of the disadvantages of bonds from our point of view is the rigid requirement that interest must be paid to avoid insolvency. Failure to meet the interest payments is a serious event of default and may lead to acceleration of the debt or seizure of any assets pledged to secure the loan. Thus the terms of the indenture of the Otis Elevator issue required that:

> . . . if an event of default specified therein shall have happened and be continuing, either the Trustee or the holders of 25% in principal amount of the Debentures then outstanding may declare the principal of all such Debentures to be due and payable.[5]

---

[3] Frank C. Jen and James E. Wert, "The Effect of Call Risk on Corporate Bond Yields," *Journal of Finance,* 22 (December, 1967), pp. 637–51.

[4] Bevis Shell Homes, Inc., *Prospectus,* June 29, 1960, p. 13.

[5] Otis Elevator Co., *op. cit.,* p. 13.

As in the case of term loans, this provision is called an *acceleration clause.* If our company is in trouble now, the bondholders obviously do not wish to wait for 15 or 20 years to take legal action to collect the principal owed.

It is possible, but not very likely, that we may be able to sell *income bonds.* In this case we are obligated to pay interest only if it is earned. Typically, any unpaid interest accumulates for only three years, although some income bonds are noncumulative and others are fully cumulative. They often carry long maturities. In a few instances income bonds may be successfully issued to the public. More frequently they might be offered to preferred shareholders as a substitute for their preferred stock. In such instances, corporations trade non-deductible preferred dividends for a tax-deductible interest expense. To have a successful issue of income bonds we should expect to include at least three main features:

1/ A fairly liberal sinking fund, possibly accompanied by a pledge to make systematic improvements in plant and equipment.

2/ Interest payments, mandatory if earned.

3/ Interest cumulative for three or more years.[6]

In earlier years income bonds were issued only in the case of a reorganization: that is, a basic readjustment of the capital structure because of actual or imminent default on payments on some debt. If our position is desperate, existing bondholders may face the alternative of liquidating the company and receiving 20 cents on the dollar or of accepting income bonds in exchange for their present holdings. With the income bonds the interest charge will still be a claim on income and the principal of the debt a claim on assets prior to that of any stockholder. Consequently, bondholders may make the best of a bad situation and accept the income bonds.

Amount of Claim. One of the most crucial elements in the bargain struck with the bondholders is the amount of interest they will receive. Nonetheless, this is only one of the elements of the "package deal" we make with the bondholders. Since the interest is a tax deductible expense, it may be desirable to grant the bondholders an extra $\frac{1}{2}$ of 1 percent in order to obtain a concession from them in terms of a more distant maturity date or a more lenient call privilege.

As borrowers, we like the limitation on the amount of interest we must pay the bondholders. This is the key to successful financial leverage; we borrow at 4 percent and the bondholders' money to work at 15 percent. Bondholders take a dim view of this arrangement. They would like to share in our success in the good years and be certain of a minimum return in poor years. If we are in a relatively poor bargaining position, we may have to "sweeten the issue" by giving bondholders an opportunity for some gain over and above the stated interest charge. The extra gain for the bondholders involves some sacrifice by the owners. The chief methods whereby we may give our bond issue added zest is by making it convertible, by attaching warrants for the purchase of common stock, or by selling a package of bonds and common stocks. Let us examine each of these in turn.

A *convertible bond* is one that may be exchanged at the will of the holder

[6]Sidney M. Robbins, "A Bigger Role for Income Bonds," *Harvard Business Review,* 33 (November–December, 1955), pp. 100–14.

for a previously determined number of shares of common stock that have been authorized but unissued by the corporation. Note that to convert his bond, the bondholder must give up his position as a creditor in return for an owner's position. A convertible bond is often an indirect means of selling common stock. With the stimulation of a rising stock market and a surging demand for funds, convertible bonds became a very popular form of financing in the latter part of 1960's (Exhibit 17-1).

EXHIBIT 17-1   New Convertible Bonds Offered for Cash in the United States

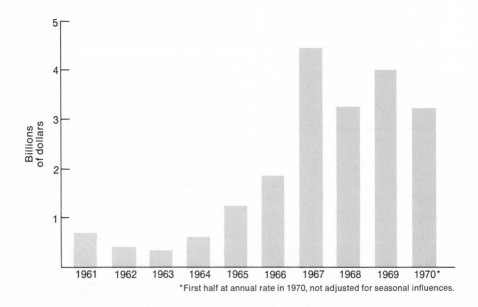

*First half at annual rate in 1970, not adjusted for seasonal influences.

Source: Securities and Exchange Commission.

The conversion privilege may be stated in two ways. On the one hand, the indenture might say that each $1000 bond is convertible into 20 shares of stock. On the other hand, it might state that the bonds are convertible into common stock at 50; that is, the conversion value of the common stock is $50. By dividing the face value (*not* the market value) of the bond ($1000) by the conversion price of the stock ($50), we can determine that 20 shares of common stock will be received upon conversion.[7] Sometimes the conversion privilege expires

[7]Sometimes exercise of the conversion privilege may require the payment of additional cash to the corporation. This requirement has frequently been adopted by the American Telephone and Telegraph Company. Terms of a 1953 issue of convertible debentures required that "the debentures will be convertible into Capital Stock, the conversion price per share being $136, payable by surrender of $100 principal amount of debentures and payment of thirty-six dollars in cash." Cited in C. James Pilcher, *Raising Capital with Convertible Securities* (Ann Arbor, Mich.: School of Business Administration, University of Michigan, 1955), p. 33.

after a certain number of years. More frequently, the conversion price rises or (the same thing) the number of shares obtainable on conversion declines over time.

The value of a convertible bond is thus made up of two parts: (1) its value as a pure bond, which we shall call the *theoretical value,* or *pure bond value,* and (2) the value of the option to convert into a fixed number of shares of common stock. As illustration, consider the 8 percent, 20-year bond for which the present-value formula was shown earlier in this chapter. Let 8 percent be the proper yield for a nonconvertible bond in this risk class. But now let us put on a 6 percent coupon, rather than an 8 percent coupon. Its value as a pure bond—its theoretical value—is then shown below:

$$\$804.08 = \frac{\$60}{(1+0.08)} + \frac{\$60}{(1+0.08)^2} + \cdots + \frac{\$60}{(1+0.08)^{20}} + \frac{\$1000}{(1+0.08)^{20}}.$$

Conversion Price. If we are to sell this bond for $1000, we must add a feature that has a market value of about $200. Let's add a conversion feature. If the common stock is selling at $45, we might set the conversion price at $50, about 11 percent above the current market price. Usually, we would set it about 10 to 15 percent above the market price of the common stock at the time the convertible bonds are issued. If we set the conversion price higher, the probabilities of the market price reaching that level within a given period of time are correspondingly diminished. That being the case, the value of the conversion privilege may not reach $200. On the other hand, if we set the conversion price below $50, we increase the value of the conversion privilege, possibly more than necessary to produce a total package worth $1000. By observation of market performance of other convertible issues in this risk class, we attempt to "fine tune" the coupon rate and conversion price (as well as other features, such as the call price) in order to hit a market value at time of issue of $1000.

Conversion Value. Let us assume that we have judged correctly and sell our convertible 6 percent bond at $1000. At the moment of sale its theoretical value, or value as a pure bond, is about $804. Since the bond is convertible into 20 shares of common stock having a market value of $45 each, the *conversion value* of the bond is $900 (20 × $45). That is to say, this is the current market value of the shares of common stock into which it may be converted.

Conversion Premium. There is one other element: the *conversion premium.* This is the difference between the market price of the bond and its theoretical or conversion value, *whichever is higher* (Exhibit 17-2). At the time of issue, the conversion premium on this bond is $100, the difference between $1000 and $900, the conversion value.

As may be seen in the exhibit, the market price of a convertible bond is constrained by two floors: the theoretical value and the conversion value. When the price of the common stock is very low, say $25 in this case, the bonds will sell at their theoretical value, and there will be little or no conversion premium. Since the price of the common stock would have to double to reach the conversion price, the conversion privilege is virtually worthless. As the price of the common stock rises, a gleam appears in the bondholder's eye as the conversion privilege acquires value, and a conversion premium appears.

EXHIBIT 17-2   Relationship of Market Price, Conversion Price, and Theoretical Value of Bond to Market Price of Common Stock (Conversion Ratio of 20 Shares of Common Stock per $1000 Bond)

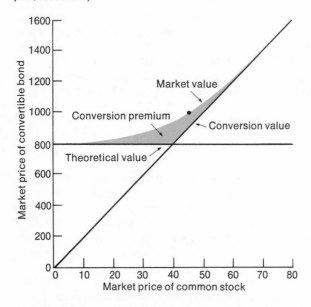

It should be noted that the floor provided by the theoretical value is not fixed. It may drop if the credit position of the firm deteriorates. If money rates should rise, the theoretical value will decline. The fixed stream of interest payments will be discounted at a higher rate, thereby producing a lower present value. For example, if yields for bonds in this risk class should rise from 8 percent to 10 percent, the theoretical value of the bond would drop from $804 to about $660.[8]

But the conversion value also provides a floor. Clearly nobody would purchase a bond at $1000 and then convert it into 20 shares of common stock worth only $900. However, if the price of the common stock should rise above $50, the market price of the bonds will move above $1000. Thus if the common stock should sell for $60, the bonds must sell for above or about $1200. Should the bonds sell for much less than $1200, people would find it profitable to buy them and convert them into common stock.[9] This possibility keeps the price of the bonds at not less than the value of the stock into which it can be converted.

However, when the market price of the common stock rises even further, the conversion premium disappears. For example, in mid-October, 1970, the convertible 5 percent debentures of Lucky Stores were selling at about 150½

[8] $\sum_{t=1}^{t=20} \dfrac{\$60}{(1+0.10)^t} + \dfrac{\$1000}{(1+0.10)^{20}} = \$659.84.$

[9] This process is called *arbitrage,* and the individuals involved in the process are referred to as *arbitrageurs.* If the bond were underpriced in relation to the common, arbitrageurs would sell common stock short and buy the bonds. (A *short sale* is basically the sale of common stock that the arbitrageur has borrowed.) Then the arbitrageur could convert the bonds into common stock and return the borrowed stock. Thus any momentary underpricing of the bond can be seized upon by the arbitrageur for a quick and certain profit. However, his action bids up the price of the bond and tends to depress the price of the stock, so that he thereby brings these prices back into their proper relationship.

($1505). Each bond was convertible into 48.57 shares of common stock. Since the common stock was selling at 31, the conversion value was also 150½ [48.57 × $31 = $150.567]. At that time the conversion premium had disappeared because Lucky Stores could have *forced conversion* of the bonds at any time. That is to say, the company could have publicly announced a call of the bonds at $1050 within 30 days. This would face the bondholder with a choice: either accept the call and receive $1050 plus accumulated interest for each bond, convert the bond into about 48.6 shares of common stock with a market price of $1505, or sell the bond on the market for that same price. Most financial decisions are not this easy.[10] Nonetheless, with the ever-present possibility of a call, buyers were unwilling to pay a premium above the conversion value and risk seeing it wiped out overnight by a call. At these rarified levels the bond is selling as if it were common stock.

Under what circumstances would a bondholder convert voluntarily? If the dividends being paid on the common are very attractive, he may sacrifice his senior position in order to obtain the higher dividends. Also, if the conversion price were scheduled to increase or the conversion privilege to expire in the near future, he might convert. However, it is important to keep in mind that the bondholder does not need to convert to realize a capital gain; he needs only to sell the bond.

Why does a conversion premium exist? Possibly the basic reason is that a convertible bond offers investors a skewed distribution of possible outcomes. Although the theoretical value is not an immovable floor, it does limit the declines on the downside that would be experienced if common stock were held. On the other hand, the conversion privilege offers an option on the common stock, thus giving the bondholders an opportunity for gain that they would not have with a pure bond. As a result of the floor and the option, the distribution of possible outcomes from a convertible issue might appear somewhat as shown below.

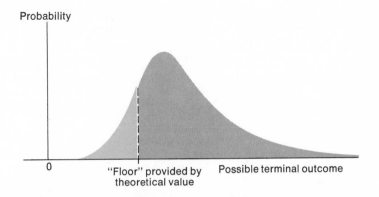

Probability

0   "Floor" provided by   Possible terminal outcome
     theoretical value

[10] Nonetheless, there remains an underprivileged segment that have not studied financial management. About two weeks prior to the redemption date, Consolidated Edison Company was still looking for holders of $440,000 face amount of its 3 percent convertible debentures who had failed to convert. The loss to these holders by failure to convert would have totalled $1,056,000. *Wall Street Journal,* May 15, 1963, p. 3.

Since investors are risk averse, they are willing to pay something for a distribution that is skewed in their favor on the upside. Other reasons advanced are that institutional investors are often limited in the amount of common stock that they may purchase, whereas they are not equally limited in purchases of convertible bonds. This imperfection in the market may partially explain the premium. Also, the margin requirements and brokerage fees are somewhat less on the purchase of bonds than for common stock. However, this is probably of minor influence.

Reasons for Issue of Convertible Bonds. It could be argued that by selling bonds convertible into common stock at 50, we are indirectly selling common stock at five points above the current market price. There is a flaw in this argument. At some later date our common stock may be selling at 80. If the bondholders convert, they will then obtain common stock at the "bargain price" of 50. Thus at the time we sell convertible bonds, it is difficult to tell who will get the better of the deal. On the one hand, we may sell the bonds at a low yield because of the conversion feature, and so obtain favorable leverage for a number of years. Even if the bondholders can ultimately convert to $80 stock at a "price" of $50, our stockholders may still benefit in the long run through the use of the low-cost funds raised by the sale of bonds in the earlier years. On the other hand, we may find we have given the bondholders a bargain. If they obtain their "bargain price" shortly after the issue, our common stockholders may have the use of favorable leverage for only a short period before being forced to share their earnings with bondholders as they convert. On balance, if the market is sensible, and financial markets tend to be, a convertible bond issue probably does not give a borrower any special advantage over a lender, or vice versa. Put another way, the borrower receives a fair price, but no more, for the commitments made. Obviously, when convertibles are popular with buyers, they should be sold, but the mere design of the debt instrument should not produce a market price that favors either buyer or seller, assuming both are intelligent financiers.

Dilution Effect of Conversion. The *dilution effect* on earnings available for common stock is illustrated below. It is assumed that an issue of $20,000,000 of 6 percent bonds is convertible at 50.

	Before conversion	After conversion
Earnings before interest and taxes	$6,000,000	$6,000,000
Bond interest	1,200,000	—0—
Earnings before taxes	4,800,000	6,000,000
Federal income taxes (50%)	2,400,000	3,000,000
Earnings after taxes	$2,400,000	$3,000,000
No. of shares of common stock outstanding	1,000,000	1,400,000
Earnings per share	$2.40	$2.14

Observe that the dilution effect occurs only if the convertible bonds have been providing favorable leverage. If we were earning less on the bondholders' funds than we were paying for them, removal of the convertible bond issue would increase earnings per share for the common stockholders. Unfortunately, this is largely wishful thinking. If this were the situation, bondholders could probably not be induced to convert.

But the dilution of *earnings* per share is not necessarily equivalent to the dilution of *price* per share. Although conversion brings a drop of earnings per share of almost 11 percent, it does not follow that the market value of the common stock will decline by the same percentage. Given the smaller financial risk attributable to the common stock because of the reduction of financial leverage, the price-earnings ratio may rise to offset in part the decline in earnings. Thus we might expect the price of the common stock not to drop by as much as 11 percent, although the actual price reaction is difficult to anticipate.

Empirical studies of the reaction of common stock prices to conversion of senior securities are hazardous because the market has very likely anticipated the potential dilution to some extent. The likelihood has recently increased with the issue by the Accounting Principles Board (APB) of *Opinion No. 15, Earnings Per Share*. In an effort to give more meaning to quoted earnings per share the APB requires that debt be treated as common stock equivalent if at the time of issuance "it has a cash yield of less than $66\frac{2}{3}$% of the then current bank prime interest rate." For example, if the prime rate were $9\frac{1}{4}$ percent and the market price of our 6 percent bonds in the illustration above were 100 at time of issuance, the cash yield would be less than two-thirds of the prime rate. Therefore, prior to conversion of the debt we would be required to show on the face of any published income statements a "primary earnings per share" of $2.14. That figure is based on the 1,000,000 shares of common stock now outstanding *plus* the 400,000 common stock equivalents of the outstanding debentures.[11] In addition, we must also present "fully diluted earnings per share." This figure must show "the amount of current earnings per share reflecting the maximum dilution that would have resulted from conversions" and all other contingent issuances of common stock that would have diluted earnings per share.[12]

Another way of offering the bondholder an opportunity to share in our good fortunes is to attach warrants to the bonds at the time of issue. *Warrants* entitle the bondholder to purchase shares of common stock from the corporation at a specified price over a stated period of time. Usually they are detachable; that is, they may be separated from the bond by the bondholder and exercised or sold separately in the market.

Warrants are similar to convertible bonds in a number of respects. First, they serve to "sweeten the issue" and enable the sale of bonds that might otherwise be marketable only at very high coupon rates. They are also useful in business combinations. In buying out another firm, we can offer the sellers warrants on our common stock as part of the purchase price, thereby enabling them to share in the later rewards of the successful merger. Warrants are also subject to APB Opinion No. 15. Warrants differ from convertible bonds in two important respects. First, the corporation receives additional cash when war-

---

[11] For a criticism of this standard, see G. F. Werner and J. J. Weygandt, "Convertible Debt and Earnings per Share: Pragmatism vs. Good Theory," *Accounting Review*, 40 (April, 1970), pp. 280–89.

[12] J. T. Ball, *Computing Earnings per Share: Unofficial Accounting Interpretations of APB Opinion No. 15* (New York: American Institute of Certified Public Accountants, 1970), p. 174.

rants are exercised, whereas that is not usually the case with convertible debentures. Second, the warrant gives the holder greater flexibility. To exercise the warrant he does not sacrifice his position as a creditor. Also, he can sell the bond and hold the warrant, or vice versa. These added options probably make the warrant more valuable than an equivalent convertible bond.

Sales of "packages" of bonds and common stock are becoming increasingly common as a means of giving bondholders a chance to share in profits. They are especially characteristic of speculative issues. A recent illustration is provided by Pocono Downs, Inc. To finance a harness racing venture the company registered a proposed offering of debentures and common shares to be offered in units of $100 of $6\frac{1}{2}$ percent subordinated debentures and $12\frac{1}{2}$ shares of common stock at a price of $150 per unit. These packages of bonds and common stock give bondholders an opportunity to share in any profits of the company as well as to maintain their senior position as creditors. Such packages are of greater interest to individuals than to institutional investors. Investments in common stock by the latter group may be prohibited or limited by law.

Claim on Assets

General Claim. Although the bondholders will have a claim on assets prior to that of the owners, it is in our interests to see that the bondholders' claim interferes as little as possible with our obtaining funds from other creditors. Any time we pledge specific assets as security for a bond issue, those assets are removed to a large extent as a means of protecting the interests of other creditors. Only if the pledged assets are more than enough to satisfy the claims of the bondholders will they benefit the unsecured creditors in case of insolvency. Consequently, if we can persuade the bondholders to accept a ranking equal to, rather than above, that of other unsecured creditors, those other creditors (trade creditors, banks, etc.) will be more willing to extend credit.

We should keep in mind that bondholders fundamentally look to our earnings to satisfy their claims, rather than to our assets. If they thought that they would ultimately have to seize our assets to enforce their rights, they would not buy the bonds in the first place. Therefore, it is entirely possible that if our earnings are clearly adequate, bondholders will forego any claim on our assets. Bonds that do not have specific assets pledged to secure payment of interest and principal are termed *debentures*. (Do not confuse with "indenture.") The holders of these securities have a claim on assets prior to that of the owners but equal to that of the other unsecured creditors. We are able to issue debentures if our credit position is so strong that purchasers believe that the claim they share with other creditors on the assets offers about as much protection as would a lien on specific assets.

Usually the indenture provides a *negative pledge clause:* that is, a promise that assets will not later be pledged to other creditors without giving the debenture holders equal security. A negative pledge clause is provided on the issue of debenture 3s due 1982 of the Dow Chemical Company:

> ... [the] company will not mortgage any assets now owned or hereafter acquired without equally securing convertible debentures, except for purchase money mortgages not exceeding 75% of cost of property hereafter acquired and to secure current loans.[13]

[13] *Moody's Industrial Manual* (1960), p. 1187.

In some cases we may even be able to persuade bondholders to accept a claim on the general assets subordinate to that of other "senior" creditors. Such securities are called *subordinated debentures*.[14] These are a particularly happy form of security from our point of view. According to the terms of the indenture, in the event of insolvency or bankruptcy the claims of senior creditors must be settled before any payment is made on the subordinated debentures. The senior debt is frequently defined as any debt coming due within nine months; hence, this would include most bank debt. There may also be some long-term debt that is defined in the indenture as senior debt. In short, the subordinated debt materially improves our borrowing power, because it serves as a base upon which we may build additional debt. In this respect it functions as preferred stock, but it has the advantage over preferred stock in that the interest payments are a tax-deductible expense, whereas preferred dividends are not.

The effect of the subordination feature in the event of insolvency or bankruptcy may be illustrated very simply. Assume that the liabilities and net worth of a corporation appear as follows:

Liabilities:		
Senior debt	$500	
Subordinated debt	200	
Other liabilities	100	$ 800
Net worth:		
Common stock & surplus		600
		$1,400

Let us also assume that only $400 is realized from the liquidation of the assets. We have $800 of creditors' claims to satisfy. Were it not for the subordination feature, all of the creditors would receive 50 cents on the dollar, and the common stockholders would have nothing. However, if $200 of the debt is subordinated to the specified senior debt, the senior creditors can enforce both their claim and that of the subordinated debtors until the full amount of the senior claims are satisfied. The claims of other creditors, such as trade creditors, are unaffected by the subordination feature and the residual owners still receive nothing. The results are summarized in the table below:

	Amount of claim	Amount realized without subordination	Amount realized with subordination
Senior debt	$ 500	$250	$350
Subordinated debt	200	100	0
Other liabilities	100	50	50
Common stock & surplus	600	0	0
Totals	$1,400	$400	$400

Calculation of share of senior debt

Without subordination: $\dfrac{\$500}{\$800} \times \$400 = \$250$

With subordination: $\dfrac{\$500 + \$200}{\$800} \times \$400 = \$350$

[14] For a more thorough discussion see Robert W. Johnson, "Subordinated Debentures: Debt that Serves as Equity," *Journal of Finance,* 10 (March, 1955), pp. 1–16.

Because of their junior position relative to senior debt, subordinated debentures involve greater risk to the bondholders. It should come as no surprise at this stage to learn that they also offer higher yields than senior debentures.

Other variations are limited only by the imagination of financial managers and what the market will bear. Additional issues of subordinated debentures may be subordinated to senior debt and other specified issues of subordinated debentures as well. These are sometimes called *junior subordinated debentures* or *capital debentures*. We may even be successful in issuing subordinated income debentures, which are about as close to a preferred stock as we can get and still carry the interest payments as a tax-deductible expense.

Specific Claim. By pledging specific assets as security, we may be able to obtain more funds than we might raise by selling debentures. In some cases a pledge of assets may be necessary to obtain any funds at all. Although bondholders rely primarily on our earnings, a lien on assets is valuable to them in that it gives them first claim on the assets and also prevents other creditors from obtaining a prior lien against those same assets. It is good to be first in line if financial disaster strikes. Should we fail to pay interest and principal when due, the bondholders, acting through the trustee, are entitled to seize the pledged assets to satisfy their claims. If the amount realized from the foreclosure sale of these assets is not sufficient to satisfy their requirements, the unpaid balance of their debt becomes part of the unsecured creditors' claims on the remaining unpledged assets of the business. If receipts from the sale of the property are more than enough to satisfy the demands of the bondholders, the surplus is applied to the claims of the unsecured creditors.

Now the area of bargaining centers on the nature of the assets pledged and the restrictiveness of the pledge. Almost any of our assets may be pledged as security. Very commonly, land and buildings may be pledged: that is, the bondholders are given a mortgage on our real estate. This form of security would be typical of industries with large amounts of fixed assets, such as the railroads and public utilities. If the claim granted is a first mortgage, the bonds are termed *first mortgage bonds*. Other claims may be ranked below that of the first mortgage bondholders, although the yields demanded by second and third mortgage bondholders may become prohibitively high.

If freight cars, diesel engines, or other equipment serve as collateral, the securities are called *equipment trust certificates*. As noted earlier, these are usually serial obligations. These bonds have proved to be almost the only source of external funds for the railroads since the end of World War II.[15] Generally, the equipment trust certificates are issued by a trustee who holds title to the equipment, or rolling stock. The equipment is then leased to a railroad in return for annual rental payments sufficient to pay interest on and retire the equipment trust obligations within about 15 years. Equipment trust obligations are usually highly regarded by investors because of the nature of the asset pledged. A railroad must keep up the lease payments on rolling stock or lose it as a source of earnings. If the trustee must reclaim the equipment, he prob-

[15]Donald M. Street, "The Role of Equipment Obligations in Postwar Railroad Financing," *Journal of Finance,* 15 (September, 1960), p. 333.

ably can lease it to some other railroad. In contrast, if a railroad does not maintain payments on a first mortgage bond issue secured by a bridge on a spur line, the bondholders are in an awkward position. The market for used bridges is very poor.

Sometimes we hold in our assets securities of other corporations. Possibly we wish to keep these to maintain control of other concerns, or the securities may not be marketable at a reasonable price. Rather than sell these to obtain funds, we may pledge them against bonds that we issue in our own right. These would be termed *collateral trust bonds.* Inventory may serve as collateral. The Barton Distilling Co. issued $1.3 million of 6-year bonds that were secured by a first lien on warehouse receipts for at least 1,625,000 original proof gallons of Kentucky bourbon whiskey.

We can best understand the nature of certain restrictions associated with the pledge of assets if we look at the matter from the point of view of the bondholders. Clearly, if they have a mortgage on a certain asset, they do not want others to obtain an equal lien on that same asset. When the provisions of the indenture close off others from obtaining an equal position, the bond issue is termed a *closed-end issue.* Under this arrangement we grant the bondholders a mortgage on certain assets and agree not to issue any additional debt equally secured by those same assets. (We might be permitted to issue second mortgage bonds.)

A closed-end issue is awkward. Every time we need long-term borrowed funds to finance a substantial addition to plant and equipment, a wholly new and separate bond issue is required. This new bond issue might be secured by a pledge of the newly acquired property or by a second mortgage on existing property. As a result we will eventually have outstanding a number of bond issues, each with its own indenture, and each with its own special provisions.

We would much prefer to issue additional bonds as needed under the provisions specified in one indenture. This is especially suitable when we are making frequent and substantial additions to our property (such as a utility might). Under this arrangement we have one mortgage encompassing all our property serving as collateral for one bond issue. However, the bond issue is composed of different series: Series A, Series B, and so on. (These should not be confused with serial bond issues.) Each series will probably have a different maturity date. As we acquire additional property we can then issue additional series of bonds under the terms of the original, single indenture.

Bondholders may agree to this arrangement provided that any newly acquired property also serves as collateral for all series and provided that certain limitations are placed on the total amount of bonds that can be issued. When the indenture for a specific issue of bonds requires that any property subsequently acquired must also be pledged as security for those bonds, the provision (or covenant) is termed an *after-acquired property clause.* The provisions that also limit the issue of additional bonds in relation to the "after-acquired property" are illustrated in the Northern Illinois Gas Company First $8\frac{1}{2}$s, due in 1976:

> . . . additional bonds of any other series may be issued in principal amount equal to $66\frac{2}{3}$% of "net property additions" not previously utilized . . .

provided, however, that no such bonds in any event may be issued . . . if the bonds to be issued bear a higher rate of interest than that borne by the bonds retired or being retired . . . unless the "net earnings" of the Company for a 12 months' period with the immediately preceding 15 months' period shall have been equal to at least two and one-half times the annual interest on all bonds then outstanding under the Indenture, including the bonds then applied for . . .[16]

Observe that the limitation on additional debt takes two forms: a restriction on the dollar amount of debt in relation to the value of the property pledged, and a provision for adequate coverage of interest charges by earnings. We should also expect that bondholders may wish to protect and maintain the property on which they have a mortgage.

From our point of view as a borrower, the worst arrangement would be a closed-end issue with an after-acquired property clause. The effect of these two provisions would be that the bondholders would not have their interest in the pledged assets diluted by the claims of additional bondholders, and that any newly acquired property would further add to their margin of safety. Although this may be fine for the bondholders, it effectively shuts us off from additional long-term borrowings.[17] If we have to agree to these terms in order to obtain funds at all, it would be wise to insist upon a call privilege, so that the bonds could be retired when desired.

Voice in Management

Although bondholders do not have a direct voice in management in terms of voting for directors, they are able to participate indirectly through their rights to limit certain activities of management. While we would probably bargain for as much freedom as possible, it cannot be said that the bondholders bargain for as many restrictions on management as possible. A management that is hamstrung at every turn by some covenant in a bond indenture is not likely to produce the sort of earnings that will protect the bondholders in the long run. Since it is impossible to predict the problems management must face over the lengthy life of a bond issue, it is foolhardy to formulate a complete set of rules to guide management over that same period. Consequently, bondholders are likely to seek only certain basic protections; if they truly believe that management needs an intricate set of rules, they are better off not to buy the bonds in the first place.

We have already observed that bondholders are likely to attempt to improve their claim on income by limiting payments of dividends to common stockholders. They may, in addition, require the maintenance of a minimum current ratio or a minimum dollar amount of net working capital. An after-acquired property clause and various limitations on additional debt also restrict management's freedom of action. On small bond issues sold to individuals there may be additional convenants restricting officer's salaries.

Lack of greater control over management's activities places bondholders

[16] Northern Illinois Gas Company, *Prospectus,* August 11, 1970, p. 15.

[17] For a discussion of the methods of removing or avoiding the after-acquired clause, see Harry G. Guthmann and Herbert E. Dougall, *Corporate Financial Policy* (Englewood Cliffs, N.J.: Prentice-Hall, Inc., 1962), pp. 183–6.

in an unfortunate position at times. So long as their interest is paid and so long as the other convenants are followed, they cannot effectively protest even the grossest mismanagement. They participate in the crash landing, but have very little to say during the flight.

Management of Debt

Most decisions having to do with long-term debt are faced at the time the bonds are issued. Once the debt is outstanding, there are two chief remaining areas where the financial manager may have some discretion: retirement of the debt ahead of schedule and refunding. Let us examine the nature of the decisions involved in each of these areas.

Retirement Ahead of Schedule

If the bond issue carries a call privilege, we may wish to consider calling in the issue more rapidly than required by the indenture. Grounds for such a decision may arise if we believe that the financial leverage is unfavorable or has an unfavorable effect upon the price-earnings ratio of the common stock. It may also be desirable to remove very restrictive provisions in the indenture, such as an after-acquired clause with a closed-end issue.

Sometimes the same purpose may be accomplished by exchanging one issue for another. As an illustration, Merritt-Chapman & Scott Corporation exchanged new 5 percent convertible debentures in July, 1964, for outstanding $4\frac{1}{2}$ percent convertible debentures. Not only was the interest rate increased, but the conversion ratio was raised as well. In return the bondholders gave up a restriction on the amounts of funds that could be used to acquire the company's own common stock. Before the end of the year Merritt-Chapman purchased about 432,000 shares of its common stock at $19 per share. The merits of this type of gambit will be discussed in Chapter 19.

At other times retirement of an issue ahead of schedule may stem from a desire to reduce the risk of being unable to repay the entire debt at maturity. This desire may be reinforced during periods when it is possible to repurchase bonds on the market at less than par. For example, if money rates increase substantially, we may be able to repurchase our bonds at 85 and retire them. If we waited for them to mature, we would have to retire them at 100. By a cash outlay now of $850 per bond, we avoid future cash outlays on interest and a future cash payment of $1000 at maturity. The value of this operation will depend in part on our cost of capital and in part on our estimate of the risk involved in waiting to repay the debt on schedule.

We may also engage in *roll-over* and *roll-down financing*. If we have an outstanding bond issue in the hands of a few institutional investors, we may be able to persuade them to trade—i.e. to roll-over—the forthcoming maturities for a new issue, typically with a higher coupon rate. The attraction to the investor is that he moves forward in time the receipt of a higher coupon rate. The advantage to us is that we can time the refinancing better and can avoid the risk of not being able to refinance if the old issue should mature at an awkward moment. By roll-down financing we trade an issue of subordinated debt for outstanding senior debt. The institutional holder obtains a significantly better yield, whereas we gain a form of debt that will serve as a base for additional issues of senior debt. The convenience of being able to negotiate such financing arrangements with a few institutional lenders explains in part the popularity of direct placement. Such arrangements would not be possible with numerous and widely scattered bondholders.

As we indicated earlier in this chapter, convertible bonds may be eliminated by forced conversion. Although this might be done to avoid undesirable financial leverage or to remove a bond issue carrying unfavorable features, it is more likely that we would force conversion to broaden the equity base. Sometimes corporations engage in "leap-frog financing." Convertible debentures are issued, and the cycle is repeated. In such cases the decision to eliminate the debt is based upon a need for additional equity, which may in turn serve as a base for further financing.

Refunding

Usually refunding is considered when the cost of borrowing has declined, either because of an improvement in our financial position or because of an increased supply of long-term loanable funds in the market place relative to the demand. Although refunding to remove objectionable provisions in an indenture is relatively rare, we must keep in mind that a new bond issue is seldom identical to an old one. While we will concentrate on the monetary aspects of refunding, these are not the only considerations. Even if the rate of return obtained through a refunding operation is no more than our cost of capital, we may still decide to refund if we obtain a more "livable" bond indenture or succeed in postponing the final maturity of the debt to a more suitable time.

How can we determine whether or not it is profitable to refund an existing bond issue? Since an initial cash outlay is typically required to effect a refunding, it is appropriate to use capital budgeting techniques to reach a decision.

Assume that there is an "old issue" of 9 percent bonds outstanding. We will need the following information:

Old Issue
Principal amount outstanding: $30,000,000
Coupon rate: 9 percent
Call premium: 4 percent
Issued: 10 years ago
Remaining years to maturity: 20 years

Unamortized bond discount: $400,000. The bonds were originally sold at 98: that is, the principal amount, or face value of the issue, was $30,000,000, but the corporation received $29,400,000 from the underwriters. Since the bond discount of $600,000 was to be amortized over the 30-year life of the bonds, it has been reduced by $200,000 during the first one-third of the life of the bonds.

Unamortized issue expense: $80,000. Costs of registration, printing and engraving, legal fees, and so on were $120,000. One-third of this has been amortized.

Occasionally a new bond issue is offered in exchange for outstanding bonds. More frequently, the new bonds are sold in the market and the proceeds used to call and retire the outstanding issue. We shall assume that the latter is the case here. The following information is available concerning a proposed new issue of 8 percent bonds:

New Issue
Principal amount to be outstanding: $30,000,000
Coupon rate: 8 percent
    Proceeds to corporation: 100. That is, the corporation will receive $30,000,000 from the underwriter.[18]
Maturity: 25 years
    Legal fees and other issue expense: $110,000. This is not the underwriters' "spread," but various fees and other costs that must be borne by the corporation.

It will also be assumed that if the 9 percent bonds were refunded, there will be an "overlap" for one month of the interest payments on the two bond issues. We could issue the call notice on the old bonds and time the sale of the new bonds so that the cash from the sale would be received just when it was needed to redeem the old bonds. However, should some delay occur in the sale of the new issue, we would be faced with finding over $30 million in a great hurry. Although the probability of such an event might be small, its occurrence would have catastrophic results. We will play it safe and issue a call for the old bonds only after we have sold the new ones. This decision will cost an extra month's interest on the old bonds.

With these facts in hand, we are now in a position to calculate the net investment required in the refunding operation and the net cash benefits that will result. Aside from minor details, the method followed is that described in Chapter 8.

A few words of explanation are needed. The call premium, the unamortized discount on the old bonds, and the unamortized issue expense on the old bonds are tax-deductible expenses for the year in which the refunding occurs. (If there were an unamortized bond premium on the old bonds, this would serve to reduce the expenses and tax savings involved in the refunding.) Observe carefully that some of the expenses are out-of-pocket, or cash expenditures, while others are book entries that affect only the amount of tax paid. Although the tax savings are not realized immediately, it is assumed that they are gained within the year.[19] Consequently, they serve to reduce the net investment required.

[18] This is clearly a simplifying assumption (and a change from the previous edition). The difficulty is that if we raise more than $30 million with a new issue, we have two decisions involved: (1) an increase in the amount of debt; and (2) a refunding. Had the bonds been sold at 104, the extra $1,200,000 should not be counted as cash inflow for the purpose of refunding, and only 30,000/31,200 of the bond premium should be considered in determining the net cash benefits obtained annually from refunding. Since the purpose of the illustration is to convey basic methodology and not mathematical erudition, the simplifying assumption has been adopted.

[19] At the time of refunding, cash outflows will exceed inflows by $1,535,000 ($31,535,000–30,000,000). When tax savings are realized, the net investment will be reduced to $620,600. To be exact, the after-tax cost of the funds needed to finance the refunding during the interval before the tax savings are realized should be added to the net investment. This adjustment has not been made in order to simplify the calculations. Note also that the expense of issuing the new bonds is not immediately deductible, but must be written off over the life of the 8% bonds.

Calculation of Net Investment

	Expense on books	Cash flow
Retirement of 9% bonds		$30,000,000
Call premium (0.04 × $30,000,000)	$1,200,000	1,200,000
Expense of issuing new bonds		110,000
Duplicate interest payments		
(0.09 × $30,000,000 × 1/12)	225,000	225,000
Write-off of remaining issue expense		
of old bonds	80,000	
Write-off of remaining bond discount		
on old bonds	400,000	
Total added expenses	1,905,000	
Total added cash outflow		31,535,000
Less: Tax savings (0.48 × $1,905,000)	914,400	914,400
Net expenses after taxes	990,600	
Net cash outflow to redeem		
old issue		30,620,600
Less: Amount raised by issue of		
8% bonds at 100		30,000,000
Net cash investment in refunding		$ 620,600

Now let us calculate the net cash benefits to be realized from the refunding. First, we shall determine the net cash outlays required if we keep the old bonds; then we shall calculate the cash outlays needed on the new bonds. The difference will represent the annual net cash benefits to be achieved by the refunding.

In connection with these calculations it might be noted that the expenses of issuing the new bonds and the bond premium are amortized over the 25-year life of the bonds. Although these adjustments do not represent cash flows, they do affect the payments on income taxes.

Should we consider that the cash benefits are realized over the remaining 20-year life of the old bonds or over the 25-year life of the new bonds? Conservatism dictates that we should consider only the benefits over the shorter time span. Moreover, we might also assume that the old bonds could be replaced by a lower-cost obligation at the end of 20 years. Fortunately, it makes little difference, since the savings gained during the 21st through 25th years have little present value. We shall assume the benefits persist for 20 years.

We can judge the gain that may be realized from refunding either (1) by calculating the rate of return represented by an annual cash benefit of $146,592 for 20 years on an investment of $620,600; or (2) by calculating the present value of the annual cash return by use of the risk-adjusted cost of capital. If the first method is used, it can be found that the discounted rate of return is about 23.3 percent.[20] As for the risk-adjusted cost of debt capital, this should be below the firm's overall cost of capital applicable to the evaluation of plant

[20] Using a 22 percent rate: 4.460 × $146,592 = $667,180
Using a 24 percent rate: 4.110 × $146,592 =   614,823
$ 52,357
By interpolation, we find the approximate discounted rate of return to be 23.3 percent.

Calculation of Annual Cash Benefits

A. Annual cash outlays required on old bonds:

	Expense on books	Cash flow
Interest expense	$2,700,000	$2,700,000
Amortization of issue expense	4,000	
Amortization of bond discount	20,000	
Total expenses	2,724,000	
Less: Taxes @ 48%	1,307,520	1,307,520
Expenses after taxes	$1,416,480	
Net cash outlay		$1,392,480

B. Annual cash outlays required on new bonds:

	Expense on books	Cash flow
Interest expense	$2,400,000	$2,400,000
Amortization of issue expense ($110,000/25)	4,400	
Total expenses	2,404,400	
Less: Taxes @ 48%	1,154,112	1,154,112
Expenses after taxes	$1,250,288	
Net cash outlay		$1,245,888

C. Net annual cash benefits from new bonds:

Net outlays required on old bonds	$1,392,480
Net outlays required on new bonds	1,245,888
Net cash benefit per year	$ 146,592

and equipment. The only risk is that the firm will retire the new issue ahead of schedule, go bankrupt, or in some other manner upset the calculated cash savings. These possibilities seem best captured by the yield to maturity on our new bonds. Consequently, the pre-tax risk-adjusted cost of capital is 8 percent, and the after-tax cost is about 4 percent. The annual return of $146,592 for 20 years, discounted at 4 percent, has a present value of about $1,992,000, well in excess of the cost of the investment of $620,600. Under either method it is obviously profitable to refund the 9 percent bonds.

Before we become too impressed with our mathematical erudition, we should observe that we have still another question to answer. We have answered the question: Is it profitable to refund the 9 percent bond issue? We have *not* dealt with the query: Should we refund the 9 percent bond issue *now?* The answer to the latter question depends upon our views of the outlook for the cost of long-term funds. Possibly by waiting even a few months, we may be able to increase the profitability of refunding quite substantially. We must, there-fore, weigh the expected value of the additional savings that might be gained by postponing the refunding against the present value of the extra costs of continuing to carry the old issue of bonds until the later refunding. While it is relatively easy to calculate the return gained from refunding, it should be clear that the timing is of crucial importance.

Summary

If we bargain from a position of strength, we should be able to borrow long-term funds under favorable terms. Although we cannot ultimately fail to repay our debt, we can sometimes arrange these payments to suit our own needs. To leave ourselves in a strong bargaining position on future issues, we should attempt to obtain terms that will interfere as little as possible in any future financing.

In our bargaining we are frequently faced with the familiar dilemma of risk versus return. Although sinking fund payments drain cash and raise liquidity problems, inclusion of that provision may enable us to obtain funds at a lower cost and so improve our profitability. Inclusion of a conversion privilege may bring us more funds now, but at a sacrifice of later dilution of the earnings per share available to present common stockholders. Subordination of debt provides a base for borrowing additional funds, but at a higher interest cost than if the debt were unsubordinated.

The terms we seek also involve prediction, implicitly or explicitly. We bargain for a call privilege because we anticipate that we may wish to retire the issue prior to maturity. In setting the conversion price, we are implicitly making predictions of the price of our common stock. Agreements on sinking funds and maturity dates involve predictions concerning the flow of funds. If we foresee a need for additional financing in the future, we will try to leave the way open by means of an open-end issue of bonds or by the sale of a convertible issue. Refunding involves a decision concerning the future course of long-term interest rates.

Questions

1/ a. Under what circumstances in the money and capital markets do you believe financial managers of corporations would be faced with a downward-sloping yield curve?

  b. Under what circumstances might it slope sharply upwards?

  c. When the yield curve does slope upwards, should corporations borrow short-term funds to meet needs ordinarily financed with long-term debt?

2/ Which possible features of a bond issue would you especially seek as a borrower and on which would you be willing to make concessions under each of the following circumstances:

  a. You expect interest rates to decline.

  b. You anticipate a weak cash position over the next 5–10 years.

  c. You anticipate a considerable expansion of short-term borrowing.

  d. You foresee a period of stable, or even declining, demand for your products with narrow profit margins.

3/ As an individual investor what provisions of a bond issue would you seek and where would you be willing to make concessions if you anticipate:

  a. A decline in interest rates.

b. A rise in interest rates.

c. A period of inflation.

d. A considerable risk that the issuing corporation might be unable to meet required payments on interest and principal.

4/ Do you see any disadvantages in having corporate financial managers draw up the terms of the indenture when bonds are offered for public bid? Are bondholders likely to recéive better or poorer protection than if terms were drawn in cooperation with an investment banker?

5/ Is the bondholders' desire to obtain a sinking fund provision inconsistent with their desire to require a high call premium or to otherwise restrict the call privilege? Explain.

6/ What justification do you see for the call price being higher for voluntary retirement of bonds than for sinking fund purposes?

7/ If the corporation has the right to call and retire bonds at will, why should not the bondholders have the right to demand repayment at will?

8/ If you buy a bond at 104 and it is called for sinking fund purposes at 102, you lose $20. How do you reconcile this result with the statement that bondholders are benefited by a sinking fund provision?

9/ Do you see any similarity between equipment trust certificates with serial maturities and the instalment note an individual signs when purchasing a new car on credit? What justification is there for the rate on the individual's instalment note being 9 to 18 percent as compared to a rate of 6 to 7 percent on the equipment trust certificates?

10/ As a common stockholder would you prefer that your corporation issue a bond that is convertible into common stock at a fixed price through the period the bond issue is outstanding, or would you prefer that the conversion price increase from time to time? Explain your conclusion.

11/ It is sometimes said that the purchaser of a convertible bond pays more for the bond than it is worth and more for the stock than it is worth. Do you believe that this is true? If it is true, how can convertible bonds be sold?

12/ At one time Texas Industries, Inc., had outstanding about $4,700,000 of 4.60 percent debentures that were convertible into common stock at the rate of $13.15 for the first $1.5 million of debentures presented for conversion; at $15.03 for the next $1.5 million; and at $16.91 a share thereafter. What appears to be the purpose of this type of conversion feature?

Problems

1/ Potash Chemical Works called its 6 percent convertible debentures for redemption on August 25, 1970, at 103 plus accrued interest. The debentures could be converted into Class A common stock at the rate of 15 shares of common stock for each $1000 principal amount of debentures. Just previous to the call the common stock was selling at 80.

a. What was the minimum market price of the debentures just prior to the call?
b. Assuming that the price of the common fell to 75 after the call, what would be the approximate market price of the debentures on August 27?
c. Given the initial price of the common of 80, by what percentage would the common stock have to decline in value before debenture holders would accept the call rather than convert their debentures to common stock?

2/ The A. C. Olson Corporation plans to finance a $40 million expansion of plant and equipment by issuing either convertible debentures or debentures with warrants. The convertible debentures would carry a 5 percent coupon and be convertible into 40 shares of common stock for each $1000 principal amount of debentures. The debentures with warrants would carry a 6 percent coupon and the holder of each $1000 principal amount would receive a warrant entitling him to subscribe to ten shares of common stock at a price of $25 per share. Both issues can be sold at par. The capital structure of the corporation ofter financing will appear as follows:

Debentures	$ 40,000,000
Common stock	
(3,000,000 sh.)	30,000,000
Retained earnings	50,000,000
	120,000,000

a. In each case how much must the corporation earn before interest and taxes, to earn a 10 percent rate of return after taxes on the book value of the common stock? Assume a 50 percent corporate income tax rate.
b. If the company has an income of $18,000,000 before interest and taxes:
   (1) What will be the income after taxes per share of common stock with convertible bonds and with bonds and warrants?
   (2) What will be the income after taxes per share of common stock if the bonds are converted?
   (3) What will be the income after taxes per share of common stock if the warrants are exercised?
c. Explain the advantages and disadvantages of each alternative from the common stockholders' point of view.

3/ Select one of the following convertible bond issues:
Allied Chemical 5.20s of 1991
Apco Oil 5s of 1988
Baxter Laboratories 4s of 1987
Burling Industry 5s of 1991
Georgia Pacific 5⅜s of 1994
Indian Head 5½s of 1993
Phillip Morris 6s or 1994
Scott Paper 8⅞s of 2000
Sears Roebuck 4¾s of 1983
Xerox 6s of 1995

a. Determine the number of shares of common stock into which one bond is convertible.

b. Determine the current market price of the bond and common stock.

c. Do you think the conversion feature has materially affected the current price of the bond? Explain the reasons for your answer. (What is the yield on nonconvertible bonds of similar quality?)

d. Aside from any costs involved, would a bondholder about break even if he converted into common stock at present? If not, by what percentage would the common stock have to rise in price before a bondholder would consider conversion, assuming that the price of the bond does not change?

e. At current market prices, can the company force conversion? Explain your answer.

4/ In the early part of 1971, the Healey-Basil Products Corp. was considering the possibility of refunding an outstanding issue of $8\frac{3}{4}$ percent debentures. The following information is available on the outstanding issue:

Principal amount: $20,000,000
Coupon rate: $8\frac{3}{4}$ percent
Call price: 104
Years to maturity: 15
Unamortized bond discount: $150,000
Unamortized bond issue expense: $45,000

Conversations with the company's investment banker have indicated the following terms may be obtained on a proposed bond issue:

Principal amount: $20,000,000
Coupon rate: 8 percent
Years to maturity: 20
Proceeds to corporation: 100
Bond issue expense: $80,000

If the bonds are refunded, the corporation will find it advisable to pay interest on both the old and new bond issues for a period of 60 days. To simplify calculations, consider that corporate income taxes are at a rate of 50 percent. The president considers the corporation's cost of capital, net after taxes, to be 10 percent.
Would it be profitable for the company to refund the debentures?

5/ Assume that you are financial vice president of a concern that now has outstanding a bond issue that may profitably be refunded. One of the directors of the corporation has urged that refunding be postponed for six months on the grounds that it will be still more profitable to refund at that later date. Prepare a careful analysis of the present and prospective market for long-term debt that either supports or refutes the director's position.

6/ The Voorheis Manufacturing Corp. has been placed in liquidation and $700,000 realized in the sale of its assets. Outstanding claims are shown below. The subordinate debentures are specifically subordinated to the senior debt.

	Amount of claim (-000)
Senior debt	$ 700
Subordinated debt	200
Other liabilities	300
Common stock and surplus	1,500
	$2,700

a. How much will each class of claimant realize under the conditions indicated?

b. How much would each class have realized without the subordination feature on one class of debt?

c. How much will each class of claimant realize, given the subordination feature, if $1,000,000 is realized in the sale of assets?

7/ Textron, Inc. has outstanding warrants, each of which entitles the holder to purchase one share of common stock at $8.75 per share to May 1, 1974, and at $10 per share thereafter.

a. For a given day look up the closing price of the common stock on the New York Stock Exchange and of the warrant (listed as "Textron wt") on the American Stock Exchange.

b. Calculate the theoretical value of the warrant by subtracting the option price of the warrant from the market price of the stock.

c. There may be a premium over theoretical value. Calculate the percentage of premium by taking the difference between the market price of the warrant and its theoretical value as a percentage of its theoretical value.

d. Why should a premium exist? Given the warrant's current theoretical value, assume a 20 percent increase in the price of the common stock. What is the new theoretical value of the warrant? How does the result of these calculations bear on the existence of a premium for the warrant?

Selected References

General

ATAMIAN, E. L., "Modifying Direct Placement Agreements," *Financial Executive,* 35 (February, 1967), pp. 16ff.

CHILDS, J. F., *Long-Term Financing.* Englewood Cliffs, N.J.: Prentice-Hall, Inc., 1961.

Corporate Debt Management. New York: National Industrial Conference Board, 1968.

HICKMAN, W. B., *The Volume of Corporate Bond Financing since 1900.* Princeton, N.J.: Princeton University Press, 1953.

VAN HORNE, J. "A Linear Programming Approach to Evaluating Restrictions under Bond Indenture of Loan Agreement," *Journal of Finance and Quantitative Analysis,* 1 (June, 1966), pp. 68–83.

Maturity (Compulsory and voluntary retirement)

COHEN, K. J. and F. S. HAMMER, "Optimal Level Debt Schedules for Municipal Bonds," *Management Science,* 13 (November, 1966), pp. 161–66.

JEN, F. C. and J. E. WERT, "The Deferred Call Provision and Corporate Bond Yields," *Journal of Financial and Quantitative Analysis*, 3 (June, 1968), pp. 157–70.

————, "The Effect of Call Risk on Corporate Bond Yields," *Journal of Finance*, 22 (December, 1967), pp. 637–52.

————, "Imputed Yields of a Sinking Fund Bond and the Term Structure of Interest Rates," *Journal of Finance*, 21 (December, 1966), pp. 697–714.

————, "The Value of the Deferred Call Privilege," *National Banking Review*, 3 (March, 1966), pp. 369–78.

PYE, G., "The Value of Call Deferment on a Bond: Some Empirical Results," *Journal of Finance*, 22 (December, 1967), pp. 623–36.

————, "The Value of the Call Option on a Bond," *Journal of Political Economy*, 74 (April, 1966), pp. 200–05.

WINN, W. J. and A. HESS, Jr., "The Value of the Call Privilege," *Journal of Finance*, 14 (May, 1959), pp. 182–95.

Claim on income (Priority, certainty, amount)

BACON, P. W. and E. L. WINN, Jr., "The Impact of Forced Conversion on Stock Prices," *Journal of Finance*, 24 (December, 1969), pp. 871–74.

BAUMOL, W. J., B. G. MALKIEL, and R. E. QUANDT, "The Valuation of Convertible Securities," *Quarterly Journal of Economics*, 80 (February, 1966), pp. 48–59.

BELL, J. T., *Computing Earnings Per Share: Unofficial Accounting Interpretations of APB Opinion No. 15*. New York: American Institute of Certified Public Accountants, 1970.

BIERMAN, H., Jr., and B. BROWN, "Why Corporations Should Consider Income Bonds," *Financial Executive*, 35 (October, 1967), pp. 74ff.

BRIGHAM, E. F., "An Analysis of Convertible Debentures: Theory and Some Empirical Evidence," *Journal of Finance*, 21 (March, 1966), pp. 35–54.

CRETIEN, P. D., Jr., "Convertible Premiums vs. Stock Prices," *Financial Analysts Journal*, 25 (November–December, 1969), pp. 90–96.

HAYES, S. L., III, "New Interest in Incentive Financing," *Harvard Business Review*, 44 (July–August, 1966), pp. 99–112.

KATZIN, J. S., "Financial and Legal Problems in the Use of Convertible Securities," *Business Lawyer*, 24 (January, 1969), pp. 359–73.

POENSGEN, O. H., "The Valuation of Convertible Bonds, Part I and II," *Industrial Management Review*, 7 (Fall, 1965 and Spring, 1966), pp. 77–92; 83–98.

POWERS, J. T., "APB Opinion No. 15 and Its Implications," *Financial Analysts Journal*, 26 (May-June, 1970), pp. 69–70.

STEVENSON, R. A. and J. LAVELY, "Why A Bond Warrant Issue?" *Financial Executive*, 38 (June, 1970), pp. 16–21.

VAN HORNE, J. C., "Warrant Valuation in Relation to Volatility and Opportunity Cost," *Industrial Management Review*, 10 (Spring, 1969), pp. 19–32.

WEIL, R. L. Jr., J. E. SEGALL and D. GREEN, Jr., "Premiums on Convertible Bonds," *Journal of Finance*, 23 (June, 1968), pp. 445–64.

WERNER, G. F. and J. J. WEYGANDT, "Convertible Debt and Earnings per Share: Pro Pragmatism vs. Good Theory," *Accounting Review*, 40 (April, 1970), pp. 280–89.

Claim on assets (general and specific)

EVERETT, E., "Subordinated Debt—Nature and Enforcement," *Business Lawyer*, 20 (July, 1965), pp. 953–87.

JOHNSON, R. W., "Subordinated Debentures: Debt that Serves as Equity," *Journal of Finance*, 10 (March, 1955). pp. 1–16.

Management of debt (Retirement and refunding)

BOWLIN, O. D., "The Refunding Decision: Another Special Case in Capital Budgeting," *Journal of Finance*, 21 (March, 1966), pp. 55–68.

WEINGARTNER, H. M., "Optimal Timing of Bond Refunding," *Management Science*, 13 (March, 1967), pp. 511–24.

Yield v. risk

BUSE, A., "Expectations, Prices, Coupons and Yields," *Journal of Finance,* 25 (September, 1970), pp. 809–18.

COHAN, A. B., *Yields on Corporate Debt Directly Placed* (New York: National Bureau of Economic Research, 1967.

FISHER, L., "Determinants of Risk Premiums on Corporate Bonds," *Journal of Political Economy,* 67 (June, 1959), pp. 217–37.

FRAINE, H. G. and R. H. MILLS, "Effect of Defaults and Credit Deterioration of Yields of Corporate Bonds," *Journal of Finance,* 16 (September, 1961), pp. 423–34.

JOHNSON, R. E., "Term Structures of Corporate Bond Yields as a Function of Risk of Default," *Journal of Finance,* 22 (May, 1967), pp. 313–45.

KESSEL, R. A., *The Cyclical Behavior of the Term Structure of Interest Rates.* New York: National Bureau of Economic Research, Occasional Paper 91, 1965.

POGUE, T. F. and R. M. SOLDOFSKY, "What's in a Bond Rating?" *Journal of Financial and Quantitative Analysis,* 4 (July, 1969), pp. 201–28.

SOLDOFSKY, R. M. and R. L. MILLER, "Risk Premium Curves for Different Classes of Long-Term Securities," *Journal of Finance,* 24 (June, 1969), pp. 429–46.

WEST, R. R., "An Alternative Approach to Predicting Corporate Bond Ratings," *Journal of Accounting Research,* 8 (Spring, 1970), pp. 118–25.

Leasing

18

We should keep in mind that the basic purpose of obtaining funds is to acquire assets. We observed in Chapter 10 that if we need fixed assets, it would probably be advisable to seek long-term sources of funds. It is unlikely that the cash receipts generated by the fixed assets will be sufficient to repay short-term loans. However, we really need only the *services* of those fixed assets; we generally do not acquire plant and equipment with the aim of reselling it at a profit. If we do not wish to have title to the assets, if it is just the services we seek, we should consider leasing the assets. Thus leasing is a means of obtaining the services of fixed assets just as the sale of bonds is usually a means of acquiring both the services of and title to various assets.

More specifically, a *lease* is a contractual arrangement whereby the owner of the property (lessor) allows another party (lessee) to use the services of the property for a specified period of time. Title to the property is retained by the lessor. Usually, the lessee may continue to use the property after the initial period of the lease at a reduced rental specified in the lease. Sometimes he may also be given an option to purchase the property.

Leasing must be regarded as equivalent to debt financing. We incur fixed obligations to a creditor, the lessor, and we must meet these obligations or lose the services of the leased assets. In essence, we have borrowed some asset other than cash. The fixed nature of our obligation under a rental contract should be emphasized. We cannot evade periodic rental payments any more than we can overlook equivalent interest and sinking fund payments on a bond issue.

Acquisition of the services of assets through lease arrangements has increased greatly, although no national figures are available on the total volume. The rapid growth of leasing has brought many new firms into the field and has created a variety of lease arrangements. We shall first discuss these developments and then examine the factors that should influence our decision to adopt this form of financing.

Sources of Lease Arrangements

There are many different types of concerns in the leasing field, although here again, as in so many areas of finance, we find a considerable degree of specialization. In the industrial field there are concerns that specialize in leasing equipment, mainly on a net, or finance, lease basis (explained later). In addition there are a large number of companies specializing in leasing vehicles, with many providing maintenance and other services in addition to the financing service.

Under a 1963 ruling of the Comptroller of the Currency national banks are permitted to acquire property upon request and lease it to customers. A number of state-chartered banks have been granted the same privilege. Because leasing requires a considerable amount of skill and "know-how," some banks have joined with existing industrial leasing companies under arrangements that consist principally of pooling the banks' money with the leasing companies' expertise. Other banks have established subsidiaries to provide leasing services. While they have not made a substantial penetration of the field to date, banks may become more potent competitors when they do not find so many customers standing in line at the loan window.

In an effort to give small business firms access to new shopping centers and industrial parks, the Small Business Administration has developed a lease guarantee program. In return for advance payment of the insurance premium and three months rent, the small businessman can obtain a direct or a SBA-participation policy written by an insurance company guaranteeing his lease payment for 5 to 15 years, or even longer. Armed with this guarantee, he is then in a position to be competitive with larger firms in leasing desirable space.

In the long-term leasing of land and buildings, the market is dominated by life insurance companies, although some pension funds have been involved in a number of transactions. Mortgage companies often act as financial intermediaries in setting up the arrangement between the lessor and lessee.

Forms of Lease Arrangements

Types of Assets Leased

At the present almost anything can be leased. One large leasing company reported that it had rented "50,000 metal beer kegs, three $100,000 tugboats, a $300,000 aluminum extrusion press and 50 hotel soap racks, worth about $5 each."[1] Trucks, autos, and computers are commonly leased. The airlines have turned to renting planes because cash flows have proved insufficient to purchase the large number of planes required, and the Illinois Central Railroad has a Rent-a-Train Plan.[2]

Lease arrangements are also common in real estate financing. An illustration is provided by the 800-room Hilton hotel in Pittsburgh. The land on which the hotel stands is owned by the Equitable Life Assurance Society and is leased to Hilton for 32 years, with three 15-year renewal options.[3] Modern shopping centers are typically financed on the basis of a complex package of various lease arrangements.

Length of Lease

The period for which equipment or buildings are leased is related to the useful economic life of the asset and the needs of the lessee. Usually the term on rented equipment runs for at least 75 percent to 80 percent on the economic life. Rapid obsolesence can considerably shorten the term of the lease. For example, cash registers may last for ten or more years. However, lessors generally write lease contracts on such equipment to grocery chains for only seven years, because grocery stores often remodel about every seven years. Similarly, electronic test equipment is frequently leased for periods of about three years because of its high rate of obsolescence.

In contrast, leases on land and buildings usually are written for much longer periods of time. The lease period often ranges from 20 to 25 years, with renewal options available to extend the lease period an additional 30 to 40 years.

The lessee may readily shorten the period of the lease. It is entirely possible to rent a car or truck for a few days if the services are needed for only that period. Manufacturers may rent machinery for just the duration of their defense contracts. Office space and office equipment may be rented for the length of a special sales campaign or a political campaign. Usually the relative cost of leasing for short periods of time is higher than if the assets were leased for a longer portion of their economic life. When we return the property to the lessor, he runs the risk of having a large portion of his investment tied up in used equipment that he may not be able to sell or rent to others at a profitable return.

[1] *Wall Street Journal,* January 22, 1959, p. 1.

[2] "Rent Your Own Freight Train," *Business Week,* October 26, 1968, pp. 104ff.

[3] "They're Building Hotels Again," *Business Week,* February 14, 1959, p. 25.

Acquisition and Maintenance of Property

Sometimes the lessor purchases general-purpose equipment that he makes available for rent. This approach is characteristic of car- and truck-rental firms. If we plan to lease machinery and equipment, we are more likely to select the desired units and then request that the lessor purchase the equipment for lease to us. Similarly, we might have the lessor construct a building to our specifications. Alternatively, we could sell to the lessor assets that we own and then lease them back. If we are faced with a shortage of funds, we may sell a portion of our equipment to a lessor and then lease that same equipment back from the lessor. For example, a company needing to expand its plant facilities sold $500,000 of its machine tools to the U.S. Leasing Corporation and then leased them back for a period of 60 months at a rental cost of $10,417 per month.[4] In this process the company converted fixed assets into cash to meet problems of liquidity. This is termed a *sale-leaseback* arrangement and is also commonly used to acquire the services of land and buildings.

When assets are leased, the question immediately arises concerning the responsibility for maintenance of the assets. Somebody, the lessor or the lessee, must assume responsibility for their maintenance. (Remember that the owner of the assets is the lessor; the user of their services is the lessee.) There are three main types of agreements in use:

1. The *Maintenance lease,* in which the lessor is required to maintain the equipment and to provide any necessary insurance or other protection. This arrangement is often found in rentals of automobiles or rentals of specialized equipment, such as electronic data-processing equipment, that require a highly trained maintenance staff. Maintenance leases are usually short-term leases. Maintenance leases may be desirable when the lessor can furnish low-cost repair services because of his size or special skills.

2. *Nonmaintenance leases* place the burden of maintenance upon the lessee. They are more typical of long-term contracts, such as leases of land and buildings. Should we sell and lease back a plant or store to an insurance company, we would probably be responsible for maintenance and repairs, insurance, and taxes.

3. *Net or finance leases* are limited mainly to fleet leasing: that is, the rental of large numbers of automobiles to corporations. Usually the lessor furnishes no maintenance or other services other than at the lessee's expense. Moreover, the lessee must absorb any loss incurred when the vehicles are sold. Thus the lessor provides only the financing service and a brokerage function in buying and selling cars. The monthly rental charge reflects depreciation, financing charges, and the lessor's overhead and profit.

Security

Under what circumstances might we expect to be able to lease the services of assets? Let us look at the situation from the point of view of the lessor. Since the principles hold for all forms of leasing, consider for illustrative purposes

[4] U.S. Leasing Corporation, "Leasing: A Source of Potential Profit," p. 8.

a sale-leaseback arrangement with an insurance company. The insurance company must rely on two factors: the value of the structure financed and our credit standing. Greater emphasis will be placed on our credit standing.

The significant value of the property is not its cost of construction but its economic value, its income-producing capabilities. The proposed size of the structure must be related to the economic needs of the area. An insurance company might finance a small department store for a small city, but be unwilling to finance an identical structure in a large city. Multiple-purpose property is preferable to single-purpose property. Thus a modern, general-purpose plant is easier to finance than a parking ramp. If we are unable to succeed in making washing machines in our leased plant and fail to meet our rental payments, the insurance company may lease the plant in turn to a manufacturer of radio tubes. In contrast, if our parking venture is a failure, the structure cannot readily be converted into a department store or office building. Yet the insurance company has no reason to believe it will succeed as a parking ramp operator where we have failed. Consequently, insurance companies favor general-purpose structures such as warehouses, rental stores in shopping plazas, and general purpose industrial plants.

In viewing our credit standing, the insurance company places special emphasis on the stability of our earnings and the margin between earnings and rental payments. Is the demand for our products stable and will the demand be sustained over the period of the lease? Have we been in the business long enough to test management's ability to produce earnings under adverse conditions? Can we be assured of having sound management over the period of the lease? The more specialized the structure financed, the more reliance the insurance company must place upon our financial standing and ability to meet the rental payments.

Because the types of property leased and the lease arrangements vary so widely, it is not possible to suggest any uniform rentals. In recent years lessors have evidently relied more on recapturing the full cost of the equipment during the lease and less on selling the used equipment at a profit when the lease expires. In addition to recouping his investment, the lessor will expect to earn a suitable return in profits or interest on the use of funds that he has invested in the property. If he provides a maintenance lease, he will also expect to receive his costs of maintenance.

The calculations made by the lessor are quite simple to understand. Assume that he agrees to acquire a machine costing $10,000 and to lease it for five years, after which time it will have a residual value of $1000. If he wishes to gross 8 percent on the lease, he will need to set an annual rental such that the present value of that rental (x) plus the present value of $1000 to be received at the end of five years, both discounted at 8 percent, equal $10,000. He would use Appendices A-1 and A-2 to find the appropriate discount factors:

$$\underbrace{\$10,000}_{\text{Purchase price}} = \underbrace{3.993x}_{\text{P.V. of annual rent}} + \underbrace{(0.681)(\$1000)}_{\text{P.V. of residual value}}$$

$$x = \$2,334 \text{ per year}$$

This calculation assumes that the rental payment is to be made at the end of each year. If rental payments are to be made at the *beginning* of each year,

$$\$10,000 = \sum_{t=0}^{t=4} \frac{x}{(1.08)^t} + \frac{\$1000}{(1.08)^5}.$$

$$\$10,000 = x + 3.312x + 0.681(\$1000)$$

$$x = \$2,161 \text{ per year.}$$

The rapid growth of computer-leasing firms can be attributed to their willingness to gamble that the economic life of computers will be longer than assumed by the manufacturer in pricing his own lease contracts. By using such an assumption in the calculation shown above, computer-leasing companies have been able to cut their rentals 10 to 20 percent below those charged by IBM and other manufacturers. Although the stretching out of rentals might appear to lower the current income of computer-leasing firms, through the alchemy of bookkeeping some have reported handsome profits.[5]

When land and buildings are leased, the annual rental payments are likely to be higher in the early years on property of a specialized nature. This is because in the early years a high proportion of the rental payments are returned as interest and a relatively low proportion as a write-down of the initial investment. Since the economic value of specialized property is likely to decline more rapidly in the early part of its life than in the latter part, an insurance company is likely to prefer the high-low pattern of rental payments to a level rental. The advisability of obtaining an option to purchase a property at the end of an initial rental period is debatable. If an option is provided, it should be clear from the agreement that no part of the rentals are applicable to the purchase price and that the purchase price is to be based on the appraised value of the property at the time of sale. Unless carefully drawn, options to purchase may jeopardize the tax-deductibility of the rental payments. The tax collector may argue that the sale-leaseback arrangement is merely a form of instalment purchase and that we are entitled to deduct for tax purposes only the depreciation on the property and the interest charges involved.

Reasons Given for Leasing

In some cases we may have no choice between leasing or purchasing the services of assets. Owners of certain assets may simply refuse to sell us the assets, because they wish to reserve for their own benefit any capital gains that may be realized as the property appreciates. For this reason we may find it necessary to lease land to obtain the mineral or oil rights or the privilege of cutting timber. Similarly we may obtain the right to use certain patents only through lease rather than purchase.

At other times we will lease property because we seek only a small portion of the facility or wish to use it for only a short period of time. Thus if we wish office space in midtown Manhattan, we must either rent the space or buy a skyscraper. Should we wish a truck to help move furniture into our new quarters, it is clearly inadvisable to buy a truck to obtain its services for that one day.

However, in most cases we can rent or buy property. Then our true alterna-

---

[5] Alvin Zises, "Law and Order in Lease Accounting," *Financial Executive*, 38 (July, 1970), pp. 46–54ff.

tive becomes: lease or borrow. Note that we did not say: lease or buy. We are comparing two methods of *financing;* hence, the comparison is between leasing and borrowing. In either case we obtain the services of some asset. Some of the advantages claimed for lease financing are in large part fallacious; others are valid. Let us examine both the supportable and unsupportable claims made in behalf of leasing as opposed to borrowing.

Shift in Risks of Ownership to Lessor

If we hold title to a machine, we bear the risk of obsolescence. Would it not be better to shift this risk to somebody else and rent the services of the machine until it is superseded by more modern equipment? Consequently, when faced with a lease-or-borrow decision on equipment subject to a high rate of obsolescence, leasing should be viewed favorably.

This is all very well and a valid argument if the lessor is not very intelligent. However, it is likely that he is as aware as we are of the rate of innovation in the field. Indeed, since he is a specialist, he may be in a better position than we are to judge the rate of obsolescence. Consequently, he will include in his rental fee a charge for obsolescence and for other risks of owning property. It will not be an explicit charge, but may be reflected in especially high payments during the early period of the lease, so that the lessor recovers his investment as rapidly as possible. If the rate of obsolescence is higher than the lessor had anticipated we will benefit by having shifted the risk to him. Also, if the lessor can spread the risk of obsolescence over many lease contracts, we may benefit just as we do from purchasing fire insurance. The hazard of sudden obsolescence may be a greater individual risk than we can safely assume.

Flexibility

A related argument sometimes advanced for leasing is that it provides greater flexibility. Presumably if we borrowed funds to purchase a store that subsequently proved to be poorly located, we would be bound to that location. Were we to lease the property, we could depart when the lease expired.

This argument assumes that the lessor has drawn the lease so that he does not recover his investment in the property during the term of the lease. This may be true of leases of equipment, but it is generally not the case on long-term leases of land and buildings. Thus by the time a lease expires we should expect to have paid, in addition to interest and service charges, most, if not all, of the cost of equipment leased and all of the cost of any real estate leased. We are forced to continue to make rental payments for the full term of the lease, unless we can sublease the property to some other unwary soul. Whether we borrow to buy the property or whether we lease it, we will have paid for it—either directly in cash or over time through the lease payments. If we cannot profitably use the property, we have lost money.

Piecemeal Financing

Companies expanding in relatively small "jumps" may find leasing useful. Chain stores might not need enough additional funds for new stores each year to make it worthwhile to float a bond issue. By financing new stores through lease arrangements, these concerns may obtain funds at a lower cost than if they attempted to sell numerous small bond issues. Very suitable alternatives are available, however. A company could temporarily finance its needs with short-term debt and then fund the short-term loans with long-term bonds. Another possibility would be to obtain a commitment for a long-term loan from an insurance company with a take-down agreement. This would allow us to use and pay for the money only as we needed it. Thus we would "take down" portions of the loan until the full amount of the loan was outstanding.

Avoidance of Restrictions Accompanying Debt

We saw in the preceding chapter that the indentures of most bond issues contain various covenants restricting the actions of the borrower. Similar limitations are sometimes found in lease arrangements, but they are not as common or as restrictive in many cases. Indeed, many indentures provide bondholders with inadequate protection from the dangers of the company's assuming burdensome lease obligations. Thus leasing is regarded as one of the standard means of avoiding the after acquired property clause. Although earlier studies showed that bond indentures did not provide adequate protection against incurring implicit debt via lease obligations,[6] more recent indentures apply restrictions to leases as well as to explicit debt. There has been a growth in the use of leasing by state and local governments to reverse an unfavorable vote on a bond issue or to avoid having to secure approval of a bond issue.[7]

Although leasing may enable us to avoid some of the restrictions that accompany the sale of bonds, it may bring with it restrictions on the use of the property leased. For example, in leasing equipment, we may be limited in the number of hours per day that it can be operated or prohibited from making changes or adjustments. Tenants in shopping plazas are frequently closely restricted concerning such matters as the size and character of signs that they display. Even if leasing is not accompanied by such restrictions, it is inevitable that lawyers who draft bond indentures will learn to prevent the use of leasing as a means of avoiding restrictions on additional debt. Thus this is at best a temporary advantage of leasing.

Evasion of Budgetary Restrictions

In some companies it may be easier for a division head to lease machinery than to buy it. Where the lease is not classed as a capital expenditure, it does not need to pass the review of the capital budgeting process. Evidently, it was largely for this reason that Electric Storage Battery Co. has now offered to lease its industrial batteries and chargers, rather than to sell them. This substantially reduces the high initial cost of battery-powered trucks because management no longer regards "purchase of the battery as a capital expense."[8] While evasion

---

[6] R. F. Vancil and R. N. Anthony, "The Financial Community Looks at Leases," *Harvard Business Review*, 37 (November-December, 1959), p. 130.

[7] For example, after five unfavorable votes on a proposed bond issue to build a new county court house, officials of Sonoma County, California, established a non-profit corporation "to borrow money, build the facility, and lease it to the county." *Wall Street Journal*, September 22, 1964, p. 1.

[8] "Switching the Charge on Batteries," *Business Week*, March 13, 1965, p. 132.

of budgetary restrictions is advanced (by leasing companies) as a reason for leasing, probably the lesson to be gained is that some firms need to improve their budget processes.

Of a somewhat similar nature is the practice of some private utilities of leasing fuel cores for nuclear energy plants. Whereas the core would be counted as an asset if purchased, leasing fees are treated as an operating expense and directly affect rates. Also, the utility avoids an outlay ranging up to $50 million in a period of capital shortages and high interest rates.

Freedom of Cash for More Profitable Investment

The gist of this argument is that if we can only free our funds from fixed assets, which have a low turnover, and invest in current assets, which have a high turnover, we will improve the earning power of the entire business. The claim is sometimes reinforced by pointing out that retailers should specialize in retailing and leave the real estate business to others. Thus department stores should rent their premises, invest their funds in inventory and accounts receivable, and concentrate on the merchandising business that is their specialty. The argument is most frequently cited for sale-leaseback arrangements.

Unfortunately, this argument is not valid. The confusion arises because we are assuming that our method of financing determines the mixture of assets that we acquire. Thus if we borrow, we acquire fixed assets; but if we lease, we can avoid acquiring fixed assets and invest only in current assets with a high turnover. This is putting the cart before the horse. We must start on the left-hand side of the balance sheet. To operate our business we need a certain mixture of assets — both fixed and current. There is no point in saying that some assets "earn" more than others. We need the services of all. Whether we have title to all the assets is beside the point.

Once we determine the assets needed, we then turn to the available methods for financing these assets. Among the possible methods are leasing and borrowing. We will not vary the total earnings that we derive from the predetermined mixture of assets by changing our methods of financing, except insofar as one method of financing is more expensive than the other. In short, leasing does "free cash," but so does borrowing. The real question is whether one method of financing is more expensive than the other.

The deceptive improvement in turnover of assets produced by leasing is illustrated in Table 18–1. The only difference between the two companies shown is that one has obtained $400 by selling debentures, and the other has borrowed $400 worth of assets. Note that the debentures are based on the general credit of the firm, just as are the lease payments. Assume that the debentures carry a sinking fund requirement, such that they are retired uniformly over ten years. Sinking fund payments are made to return to the debenture holders their investment. Similarly, the rental payments made to the lessor are large enough to return the sum that he has paid for the assets. The fixed assets are assumed to have no residual value at the end of ten years. Both the debenture holders and the lessor will also expect to receive interest on their investments. It is assumed that the interest rates charged are the same, and that the repayment of the debt and the lessor's investment are made at the same pace. Consequently, the total interest cost is identical in each situation. Since each concern repays the $400 gradually, on the average it has the use of about $200. Thus the average annual interest is $12 (0.06 × $200) and the total cost for ten years is $120. In summary, the cost of obtaining the services of $400 worth of assets in this example is exactly the same over the ten years, whether those services are secured by borrowing the money to buy the asset or by borrowing the asset.

TABLE 18-1   Effect of Leasing vs. Borrowing on Balance Sheet and Income Statement

Opening Balance Sheet or Position Statement		Borrowing	Leasing
Current assets		$ 600	$600
Fixed assets		400	—
Total		$1,000	$600
Debentures		400	—
Net worth		600	600
		$1,000	$600

Ten-year Income Statement — Borrower

			Ten-year turnover of assets:
Sales		$4,000	
Operating expenses	$2,820	3,220	$\dfrac{\$4000}{1000} = 4.00$
Depreciation	400		
Net operating income		780	
Interest on debentures		120	
Net profit before taxes		$ 660	

Ten-year Income Statement — Lessee

			Ten-year turnover of assets:
Sales		$4,000	
Operating expenses	$2,820		$\dfrac{\$4000}{600} = 6.67$
Lease payments to compensate lessor for:			
Cost of assets	$400		
Interest	120	520	3,340
Net profit before taxes		$ 660	

However, observe the effect of leasing vs. borrowing on the turnover of assets. The lessee reports a much higher turnover — 6.67 times, compared to only 4.00 times on a ten-year basis. Nonetheless, in each case the owners receive a total of $660 before taxes over the ten years on their original net worth of $600. Why is this so? Why does not the higher turnover for the lessee produce a higher rate of return for the owners? Essentially, it does not because the lease is really a form of debt. We could in fact reconstitute the balance sheet for the lessee and show the present value of the lease payments as a debt and the rented assets as an asset. This is not accepted accounting practice, but it has been considered by the accounting profession as one means of demonstrating the impact of substantial lease obligations on the position of a concern. The effect

of leasing on customary financial ratios suggests that we will need to be careful in analyzing the financial statements of any of our customers who obtain
part of their assets through leases.

Cost of Leasing Versus Owning

To decide between leasing or owning, we must first determine the comparative
costs. Assume that we have tentatively decided to acquire the services of a
$10,000 machine for five years.[9] Note that the decision to acquire the machine
precedes the choice between owning and leasing. That decision is reached by
the usual capital-budgeting procedures described in Chapter 8. Having made
that decision, we must now select the method of acquiring its services.

We may either lease the $10,000 machine for $2920 per year or borrow
$10,000 on a term loan at 8 percent. The loan is to be repaid in equal annual
instalments.[10] To focus on the methodology rather than computational aspects,
we will assume that both lease payments and loan payments are due at the
end of each of the five years. As another simplifying assumption, we shall use
straight-line depreciation and assume no salvage value. On this basis depreciation is $2000 per year.

The problem is to determine the relative costs of owning versus leasing. If
we own the machine, the cost is composed of (1) the initial outlay of $10,000,
less (2) the present value of the tax shield provided by depreciation. If we assume a 50 percent tax rate, the tax shield (reduction in taxes) is $1000 per year.
But what discount rate should be used? We are facing a decision similar to a
bond refunding. When we decided to acquire the services of the machine, we
used a cost of capital appropriate to the risk associated with the machine.
However, we are now choosing between methods of financing the machine.
The lease payments and loan payments (but not depreciation expense) have a
high degree of certainty, or at least the lessor and lender hope they have. Their
evaluation of the risk of receiving regular annual payments is best captured
by the firm's borrowing rate: 8 percent. Since this is a *pre*-tax rate and we are
discounting *after*-tax savings from a reduction in taxes, we must discount at

---

[9] The words "tentative decision" are used with purpose. It is possible that an acquisition of a machine
might be rejected on the basis of normal capital-budgeting procedures, but that it might be leased on
terms so favorable that its acquisition would be warranted. To see the point, carry the illustration to
the extreme. Assume that acquisition of a $10,000 machine has been rejected, because it has a nega-
tive net present value of $1000. However, if somebody were willing to lease it for $1 per year for five
years, it would then become an acceptable project.

[10] Although not germane to the problem, the annual instalments are $2505, computed by dividing
$10,000 by 3.993, the present value of $1 per year received at the end of each year for five years, discounted at 8 percent (Appendix A-2).

Also, the implicit rate of interest on the lease is about 14 percent. Let the unknown discount
factor from Appendix A-2 equal y (for a change):

$$\frac{\$2920y}{\text{P. V. of accrued rentals}} = \frac{\$10,000}{\text{Purchase price}}$$

$$y = 3.425$$

By reference to Appendix A-2, we see that the implicit rate is almost exactly 14 percent. If we
also judge that by leasing we will give up a residual value in the equipment, we must additionally
employ Appendix A-1 and find the appropriate gross yield by a series of successive approximations.

the after-tax borrowing rate, in this case 4 percent. Thus the present value of the after-tax cost of owning the machine is as follows:

Cost of owning = (Initial outlay) − $\begin{pmatrix}\text{Present value of tax shield from} \\ \text{depreciation, discounted at the} \\ \text{after-tax cost of capital}\end{pmatrix}$

↓

= (Initial outlay) − $\begin{pmatrix}\text{Annual reduction} \\ \text{in taxes resulting} \\ \text{from depreciation}\end{pmatrix} \times \begin{pmatrix}\text{Present value of \$1 per year,} \\ \text{paid at end of each year,} \\ \text{discounted at 10 percent}\end{pmatrix}$

= $10,000 − ($1,000 × 3.791)

= $6209.

Alternatively, we may acquire the services of the machine by agreeing to a stream of lease payments of $2920 per year for five years. The cost of that stream is simply the present value of the after-tax cost of the lease payments discounted at the after-tax borrowing rate:

Cost of leasing = Present value of after-tax lease payments
discounted at after-tax cost of borrowing

= Lease payments × (1 − tax rate) × $\begin{pmatrix}\text{Present value of \$1 per year,} \\ \text{paid at end of each year,} \\ \text{discounted at 4 percent}\end{pmatrix}$

= ($2920) (1 − 0.50) (4.452)

= $6500.

Since the present value of the cost of owning is $291 less than that of leasing, we should decide to own (purchase) the machine rather than lease it, unless there is some overriding non-cost advantage to leasing.

There may be other cost considerations involved. Assume that we plan to depreciate the machine fully over the five years, but that we estimate it to have a possible after-tax salvage value of $1000 at the end of the fifth year. This should be counted as a benefit of owning or an opportunity cost of leasing (but not both; that would be double-counting). Since this is probably in the same risk category as the machine and not a relatively certain financial flow, we should discount this at our after-tax cost of capital, say 10 percent. This would reduce the adjusted cost of owning:

Adjusted cost of owning = $6209 − $\begin{array}{l}\text{Present value of recovery} \\ \text{at end of fifth year}\end{array}$

= $6209 − $\begin{pmatrix}\text{Present value of \$1 received} \\ \text{at end of 5th year,} \\ \text{discounted at 10 percent}\end{pmatrix} \times$ After-tax recovery

= $6209 − (0.621 × $1000)

= $5588.

As a general rule we would expect leasing to be somewhat more expensive than owning, although the entry of commercial banks into the field has apparently brought the implicit rate on leasing down much closer to the interest rates on term loans.[11] But there are cases where the cost of leasing will be less than owning. This might be true for a small concern whose credit-standing is significantly poorer than that of the lessor. In such a case, the superior credit position of the lessor may enable the lessee to borrow assets more cheaply than if he were to borrow cash. Also, groups of wealthy professional people and business executives may form an investment partnership to purchase equipment, such as an airplane. Using the plane as security, they borrow all but the downpayment and then lease the plane to an airline. Since they are in the 60 to 70 percent tax bracket, the tax shield provided by the interest on their borrowed funds and the accelerated depreciation is more valuable to them than to the lessee, an airline paying taxes at about a 50 percent rate. By passing on part of their tax savings in the form of lower lease payments, the investment partnership may be able to offer leases at implicit rates that are competitive with interest charges on direct loans.

Depreciation of Land. It is sometimes argued that leasing has a cost advantage over owning because it enables the lessee to "depreciate land." If we borrowed to acquire title to land and a building we could depreciate only the building for Federal income tax purposes. In contrast, should we sell the land and building to an insurance company and then lease them back, our rental payments would include the cost of the land to the insurance company. Through the lease we are thus able to "depreciate" the cost of the land. As a result we would pay lower income taxes. If we are in the 48 percent income tax bracket, a $100,000 piece of land would "cost" us only $52,000. Note that the tax advantage of leasing land and buildings increases the higher the ratio of land value to the total value of the property leased.

This is fine. But we should remember that when the lease expires, we will have paid $52,000 for a piece of land that we do not own. Our real problem is to determine the present value of the expected market value of the land at the expiration of the lease. Assume that the lease is for 40 years and that the expected value of the property at the end of the fortieth year is $120,000. If our cost of capital is 10 percent, the present value of our expected loss (i.e., $120,000) is no more than $2640.[12] Nonetheless, there have been instances where the value of land has appreciated immensely over a period of years. We are risking the loss of this appreciation by leasing the property rather than borrowing to acquire title.

More Funds Available

It is sometimes argued that leasing enables us to finance 100 percent of the cost of property, as contrasted with only 50 percent to 75 percent of the cost if we were to raise the funds with a mortgage bond issue. The implication that leasing therefore provides more funds than borrowing is misleading. The con-

[11] Richard H. Pettway, "Interest Rates on Direct Leases and Secured Term Loans," *National Banking Review*, 3 (June, 1966), pp. 533–37.

[12] In other words, if we invested $2640 at 10 percent, compounded annually, we would have $120,000 at the end of 40 years. If our cost of capital is 10 percent, this is the minimum return that we would accept on an investment. Therefore the present value of having $120,000 in the 40th year is no more than $2640.

clusion that a lease provides 100 percent financing is based on an erroneous assumption that it has no effect on our general borrowing power. This is unlikely. To clarify this, assume that we issue $10 million of debentures on the basis of $100 million of net worth and use the proceeds to construct a $10 million plant. This could be termed 100 percent financing, but this would also be misleading. Whether we borrow or lease, we are "using up" some of our credit. The real question is whether a lease that is equivalent to $10 million of debentures uses up as much of our borrowing power as the issue of debentures. Or, to put it in terms of Table 18-1, the question is whether the lessee has any greater residual borrowing power after he has promised to pay $520 over ten years than the borrower who has promised to repay an equal amount at the same rate to debenture holders.

This is a key question. If leasing provides more funds than borrowing in relation to a given amount of equity, it may be desirable even if it is more costly. Analysis suggests that leasing may indeed provide more funds than borrowing in relation to equity, not because leasing is a clever way of avoiding debt, but because it is not adequately recognized as debt in the financial marketplace. This advantage of leasing may ultimately prove to be transitory.

One reason that lease obligations may not have their deserved impact on our borrowing power was demonstrated in Table 18-1. Because the $520 obligation on the lease is not shown in any manner on the balance sheet, the lessee appears to be in a much stronger position than he really is. (We should show any accrued liability on the lease.) Calculation of various ratios, such as debt to net worth, and current assets to debt, would give a financial analyst the impression that the lessee is in a much stronger financial position than the borrower. Some accountants have been concerned about the omission from the balance sheet of significant information concerning lease obligations.[13] In spite of efforts to make disclosure of leases a standard practice, many corporations still fail to provide the essential data.

Summary

Leasing is equivalent to borrowing; we borrow physical assets instead of cash. Since rental payments are a fixed obligation, we should be certain of our ability to meet these cash disbursements, just as we should be assured of meeting sinking fund requirements and interest payments on a bond issue. Although

---

[13] Recommendations by the Accounting Principles Board on the disclosure of lease obligations are as follows:

"The right to use property and a related obligation to pay specific rents over a definite future period are not considered by the Board to be assets and liabilities under present accounting concepts. . . . Leases of this type involve future rights and obligations, however, and pertinent information should be disclosed. . . . In the opinion of the Board, disclosure rather than capitalization is the correct accounting treatment of these leases. . . . The Board believes that financial statements should disclose sufficient information regarding material, noncancelable leases which are not recorded as assets and liabilities . . . to enable the reader to assess the effect of lease commitments upon the financial position and results of operations, both present and prospective, of the lessee. Consequently, the financial statements or the accompanying notes should disclose the minimum annual rentals under such leases and the period over which the outlays will be made. "Opinion No. 5: Reporting of Leases in Financial Statements of Lessee," *Journal of Accountancy,* 118 (November, 1964), p. 65.

numerous fallacious reasons have been advanced to favor leasing rather than borrowing, there are certainly instances where leasing is preferable. In specific situations leasing may enable us to avoid restrictive covenants characteristic of bonds, provide convenient piecemeal financing, or free us from unusual burdens of maintenance or risks of obsolescence. Sometimes leasing is the only means by which we can acquire the services of an asset. Faced with a choice between leasing and owning an asset, we should compare the present cost of owning (initial outlay less the present value of the tax shield from depreciation) versus the present cost of leasing (present value of after-tax rental payments). The after-tax cost of debt is the appropriate discount rate to use in these calculations, but the firm's cost of capital is applicable to more uncertain flows, such as the after-tax terminal value of the property. Leasing is likely to be more expensive than owning. We may benefit by reducing Federal income taxes by "depreciating" land, but we also forego title to the land and possible appreciation in its value. For the time being it is likely that leasing will provide us with more borrowing power than an equivalent amount of debt. The fact that these added costs and the debt that they represent are not as readily apparent as costs of borrowing suggests a special need for careful analysis of lease arrangements by the financial manager.

Questions

1/ Loblaw Leased Properties, Ltd., sold $5,400,000 of first mortgage bonds to purchase 20 store properties and two warehouses for leaseback to Loblaw Grocerterias Co., Ltd. What reasons can you suggest for this arrangement? Why would not Loblaw Grocerterias issue the bonds directly to finance its needs?

2/ The total of payments on leases extending over several years almost invariably exceeds the initial cost of the property leased. In view of this, why should the lessor be concerned with the creditworthiness of the lessee? Does not the value of the leased property provide adequate protection?

3/ Which do you suppose would be easier to finance under a sale-leaseback arrangement: a movie theater or a grocery store? Explain.

4/ If interest rates are unusually low and expected to rise, would the financial institution arranging a sale-leaseback favor a level or high-low rental plan? Which would the tenant prefer? Explain.

5/ During a recent period of very tight money, International Business Machines Corp. raised monthly rentals of most elements of its System 360 computer line by about 3 percent and reduced the purchase prices of the same items by about 3 percent. How do you explain this action?

6/ Evaluate the following statements regarding the advantages of leasing.
   a. "If, by leasing equipment which would thereby add fixed capital to the company and permit it to retain the use of its cash working capital over the term of the lease, the company can continue to earn 30 percent on its

freed working capital, then any lease agreement which costs less than 30 percent for the funds involved, is an obvious gain to that manufacturer." *The Pros and Cons of Leasing* (Chicago: Foundation for Management Research, Inc., 1963), p. 7.

b. Harvey Granat, president of Granite Equipment Leasing Corp.: "Our business is booming because we're living in an age of leverage. The companies that are most successful expand using somebody else's money." "Can Leasing Make Ownership Obsolete?" *Business Week,* March 8, 1969, p. 50.

c. "Also, during the early years of a lease arrangement, higher tax savings often can be realized, because rentals generally exceed the Internal Revenue Service guidelines for depreciation."

d. "Where obsolescence of equipment becomes a major consideration, this threat usually can be minimized through leasing, as customers often can return undepreciated equipment to the lessor." Both statements from *Continental Comment* (Continental Illinois National Bank and Trust Company of Chicago, May 8, 1970.)

7/ How would you draw up an indenture provision to protect bondholders against the corporation's incurring burdensome lease obligations? Does it make a difference that part of lease payments would be for interest and part for repayment of the lessor's investment?

Problems

1/ The Haslem Equipment Leasing Corp. has purchased a heavy extrusion press for $180,000 and plans to lease it for six years. During the period of the lease the lessor expects to recover its investment in addition to a return of 10 percent on its investment. The return is to cover both interest and service charges. Assume that the rent is collected at the end of each year.
   a. What would the annual rental have to be to accomplish the desired result?
   b. What would the annual rental have to be if the lessor expected to receive a salvage value of $30,000 on the machine at the end of the sixth year?

2/ Mr. Don Tuttle, financial vice president of Indiana Manufacturing Corp. was considering the acquisition of a large press for $60,000. The press would have an expected life of eight years. He could finance the acquisition with either an 8-year term loan at 10 percent, repayable at $11,247 per year or by a lease calling for annual payments of $11,660 per year. In both cases payments were due at the end of each year. The firm was in the 40 percent tax bracket, and Mr. Tuttle estimated his after-tax cost of capital at 14 percent.
   a. What is the implicit interest charge of the lease agreement? (See footnote 10.)
   b. On the assumption of straight-line depreciation and no salvage value, what are the proper comparative costs of owning versus leasing the press?
   c. On the assumption of sum-of-the-years'-digits depreciation and no salvage value, what are the proper comparative costs of owning versus leasing the press? (8/36th depreciation the first year.)

d. Assume that the entire investment will be depreciated over eight years on a straight-line basis, but that the press will have an after-tax salvage value of around $9000 at the end of the eighth year. What are the proper comparative costs of owning versus leasing the press?

3/ The R. H. Pettway Department Store owns a large building and the land on which it is situated. Their respective book values are $2,000,000 and $800,000. The building is being depreciated at $100,000 per year over 20 years. An insurance company has offered to buy the land and building at book value and to lease it back to the firm for 20 years at $300,000 per year, payable at the end of each year. At the end of the 20th year, it is estimated that after costs of demolishing the building the land could net about $900,000, although the degree of certainty is about the same as any investment in downtown retailing. If the sale-leaseback proposal were accepted Pettway would still be responsible for maintenance, insurance, and so on, but would have no residual claims on the property at the end of the 20th year. The financial vice president estimates the firm's after-tax cost of capital at 12 percent, and he is able to borrow long-term funds at 8 percent. The firm is in the 50 percent tax bracket.

a. Compute the difference in the net present values of the two arrangements.
b. What would the net after-tax recovery of the building and land have to be for management to be indifferent on a present-value basis between retaining or leasing the building?

Selected References

BEECHY, T. H., "Quasi-Debt Analysis of Financial Leases," *Accounting Review,* 44 (April, 1969), pp. 375–81.

BOWER, R. S., F. C. HERRINGER, and J. P. WILLIAMSON, "Lease Evaluation," *Accounting Review.* 41 (April, 1966), pp. 257–65.

BRIGHAM, E. F., "The Impact of Bank Entry on Market Conditions in the Equipment Leasing Industry," *National Banking Review,* 2 (September, 1964), pp. 11–26. R. S. BOWER, "Comment," and "Reply and Correction," *National Banking Review,* 2 (March, 1965), pp. 419–24.

COOK, D. C., "The Case Against Capitalizing Leases," *Harvard Business Review,* 41 (January–February, 1963), pp. 145–50ff.

FORD, T. C., "Another View of the SBA 'Lease' Guarantee Program," *Business Lawyer,* 25 (April, 1970), pp. 1053–65.

GANT, D. R., "Illusion in Lease Financing," *Harvard Business Review,* 37 (March–April, 1959), pp. 121–42.

MCEACHRON, W. D., "Leasing: A Discounted Cash-Flow Approach," *Controller,* 29 (May, 1961), pp. 213–19.

MCLEAN, J. H., "Economic and Accounting Aspects of Lease Financing," *Financial Executive,* 31 (December, 1963), pp. 18–23.

MITCHELL, G. B., "After-Tax Cost of Leasing," *Accounting Review,* 45 (April, 1970), pp. 308–14.

NELSON, T. A., "Capitalizing Leases—the Effect on Financial Ratios," *Journal of Accountancy,* 116 (July, 1963), pp. 49–58.

"Opinion No. 5: Reporting of Leases in Financial Statements of Lessee," *Journal of Accountancy,* 118 (November, 1964), pp. 63–66.

PETTWAY, R. H., "Interest Rates on Direct Leases and Secured Term Loans," *National Banking Review,* 3 (June, 1966), pp. 533–37.

RIORDAN, H. P. and E. C. DUFFY, "Lease Financing," *Business Lawyer,* 24 (April, 1969), pp. 763–72.

SAX, F. S., "The Lease-or-Purchase Decision—Present Value Method," *Management Accounting,* 47 (October, 1965), pp. 55–61.

THULIN, W. B., "Own or Lease? Underlying Financial Theory," *Financial Executive,* 32 (April, 1964), pp. 23–24ff.

VANCIL, R. F., "Lease or Borrow— New Method of Analysis," *Harvard Business Review,* 39 (September–October, 1961), pp. 122–36.

_____, "Lease or Borrow—Steps in Negotiation," *Harvard Business Review,* 39 (November–December, 1961), pp. 138–59.

_____, *Leasing of Industrial Equipment.* New York: McGraw Hill Book Co., Inc. 1963.

VANCIL, R. F. and R. N. ANTHONY, "The Financial Community Looks at Leasing," *Harvard Business Review,* 37 (November–December, 1959), pp. 113–30.

WEEKES, P. A., J. C. HAMBERS, and S. K. MULLICK, "Lease-Buy Planning Decisions," *Management Science,* 15 (February, 1969), pp. B-295–307.

WILHELM, M. F., Jr. "Purchase or Lease: That is the Question," *Management Accounting,* 51 (July, 1969), pp. 43–46.

ZEHNER, L. A., Jr. "Investor Leasing Programs," *Financial Executive,* 38 (July, 1970), pp. 62–64ff.

ZISES, A., "Law and Order in Lease Accounting," *Financial Executive,* 38 (July, 1970), pp. 46–54ff.

Preferred Owners

19

Let us now turn from borrowed funds to those obtained from owners. Whereas not all business concerns employ long-term debt or leases, all are financed to some extent with equity or owners' funds. There are two possible types of owners: preferred owners and residual owners. While we obtain funds directly from preferred owners, we may secure funds from residual owners in two ways: either by their direct investment or by retention of a portion of their share of the earnings. In this chapter we shall consider the variations in the bargain we might arrange with preferred owners. In the following two chapters we shall discuss the two methods of raising funds from residual owners.

Figures are not available to show the relative importance of these sources of equity among unincorporated business. Among corporations in recent years issues of preferred stock have been a considerably less important source of equity funds than issues of common stock. During the first half of 1970, for example, new issues of preferred stock of about $560 million were less than one-sixth as large as new issues of common stock.[1] However, these data represent only securities sold for cash and exclude stocks issued in exchange for other securities in mergers and acquisitions. Even considering this omission, retained earnings have generally provided even larger amounts of equity funds than both preferred and common stock issues.

Forms of Preferred Ownership

As indicated earlier, limited partnership agreements may grant limited partners a preferred position over general partners with respect to income and assets. The general philosophy of the preferred ownership position has reached its most elaborate expression in preferred stock. Because this form of preferred ownership is much more common than limited partnerships, we shall concentrate our attention on the nature of the bargain struck with this group of owners.

To a considerable extent preferred stock is a hybrid security—not quite equity, not quite debt.[2] From a legal point of view it is part of the equity. Because the dividends on preferred stock are regarded as a distribution of earnings, they are not a tax-deductible expense. Creditors correctly view preferred stock as part of the equity base that helps to support a corporation's debt. If the corporation's charter or the agreement with preferred stockholders makes no provisions to the contrary, preferred stockholders have almost the same rights as common stockholders. The only exception is the preferred stockholders' claim on cumulative dividends up to a specified amount before payment of earnings to common stockholders.

From the financial manager's point of view preferred stock is best regarded as quasi-debt. One indication of the "debt-like" position of preferred stockholders is that we bargain with them. In contrast, there should be no bargaining between the company and residual owners. The company, be it a proprietorship, partnership, or corporation, does not have interests separate from those of the residual owners. What is in the long-run interests of the enterprise should also be the long-run interests of the residual owners. Consequently, the financial manager should not bargain *for* the "company" *against* the residual owners. He bargains with creditors and preferred owners in the interests of residual owners.

In the agreement between the company and preferred shareholders the covenants that are of benefit to the preferred owners are usually detrimental to the residual owners, and vice versa. The residual owners would like the preferred owners to give up some of the rights characteristic of residual ownership, such as an unlimited claim on earnings. To persuade the preferred owners to make this sacrifice, we must give them some privileges very similar to those held by creditors. Thus the common stockholders tread a narrow line by granting limited rights of seniority to the preferred owners, while gaining for themselves the important privileges that they cherish as residual owners. To accomplish

---

[1] *Federal Reserve Bulletin*, 56 (October, 1970), p. A-46.

[2] It should be noted that sometimes a corporation will have outstanding a "Class A" common stock. Close examination of the terms of the stock may reveal it to be a preferred stock in disguise.

these aims we draw up an agreement that embodies many of the features characteristic of debt, even though the preferred stock is still part of the equity so far as the creditors are concerned. As in the case of debt, there is an area for bargaining, and the bargaining centers on provisions for retirement, claim on income, claim on assets, and voice in management. Since these features were discussed in some detail in Chapter 18, we will devote most of our attention to those aspects that are peculiar to preferred stock.

Retirement

Preferred stock does not have a "maturity date." Ordinarily, owners' investment is considered to be permanent until the ultimate failure or liquidation of the corporation. Because preferred stockholders are regarded as a special class of owners, provisions are sometimes made for compulsory repayment of their investment and are usually made for voluntary repayment.

Compulsory Retirement. Sinking fund provisions are much less characteristic of preferred stock than of bonds. Convertible preferred stock issues carry sinking fund provisions only infrequently, because of the expectations that the issue will ultimately be converted into common stock. From the standpoint of the residual owners it would be preferable not to have any provision for compulsory retirement of preferred stock. The requirement could cause considerable financial embarrassment when cash is scarce. We must balance this threat to our liquidity against the attractions the sinking fund may offer to investors. The provision favors the investors because it means a steadily diminishing supply of preferred stock in relation to available income and assets. By absorbing small amounts of preferred stock, the corporation also tends to support its market price. Thus the inclusion of a sinking fund requirement may enable us to sell the preferred stock with a lower dividend rate than might otherwise be possible.

The nature of the sinking fund requirement is also a matter of bargaining. Most favorable from our point of view would be a provision of sinking fund payments in some relation to earnings, so that the burden would be minimized during periods of low earnings. Sinking fund payments might also be related to the dividends paid on common stock during some previous period. Preferred stockholders would be more likely to seek a flat sinking fund payment amounting to, say, 2 percent of the amount outstanding. This latter provision has been common on recent issues. A corporation that is delinquent in its sinking fund payments is frequently prohibited from paying dividends on its common stock. Observe that failure to meet sinking fund requirements is not a cause of insolvency, as in the case of debt.

Voluntary Retirement. It is clearly in our interests to be able to retire the preferred stock if the financial leverage based on the fixed dividend becomes unfavorable. This is more likely than in the case of bonds, largely because the dividends on the preferred stock are not counted as a tax-exempt expense. At other times it may be possible to replace the existing preferred stock with bonds or another preferred stock issue carrying a lower interest or dividend rate or with less restrictive features. Indeed, a call feature is even more desirable than in the case of debt. Whereas we will ultimately be able to retire debt at maturity, the lack of any maturity date on preferred stock could mean a permanent millstone around our corporate neck were there also no call feature.

Since a call feature is usually included in preferred stock agreements, bargaining centers on the size of the call premium and the "call protection"; that is the number of years before the stock is first callable. The intensity of our bargaining efforts will depend largely on the probability that we will wish to retire the issue. As in the case of bonds, the call price is usually set above the issuing price of the security and is likely to decline over time, so that it becomes progressively cheaper to call and retire the stock.

When we agree to a sinking fund provision, we can expect to have a lower call price for this purpose than for voluntary retirement of the issue. Since the sinking fund is for the benefit of the preferred shareholders, they should not also expect us to pay a substantial premium to fulfill our obligations.

Claim on Income

To identify the claim on income of preferred shareholders we will need to understand a few more terms. We may issue preferred stock that has a *par value* or *no par value*. The par value is the face amount of each share as stated in the corporation's charter. It appears on the front of the stock certificate sent to purchasers of the stock and is usually the amount at which the stock is carried on the corporation's balance sheet. The par value may be $25, $50, $100, or any amount specified. What is the significance of this figure? First, we should not sell the stock at less than par when it is first offered to the public. This may be prohibited by state law, or, if it is permitted, the stockholders may be held liable to the creditors in case of insolvency for any difference between the price paid and the par value. However, once the stock is issued, it may be freely sold in the market without regard to the par value. A second aspect of par value is that we are usually prohibited by law from paying dividends that would reduce the net worth of the corporation below this par value. Except for these two legal technicalities, par value has little significance, and even these restrictions may sometimes be avoided by various legal maneuvers. Stock having no par value is just what it says; no stated value is specified in the charter and we may sell the stock in the market for what it will bring.

Dividends on preferred stock are specified either as a percentage of the par value or as an annual dollar amount. Thus if we sell a 5 percent preferred stock the annual dividend per share of stock would be $5 if the par value were $100, but only $1.00 if the par value were $20. Specification of the dividend as a dollar amount is characteristic of no par preferred. Thus the Kaiser Steel $1.46 preferred has no par value, and the holders of the stock hope to receive an annual dividend of $1.46 per share.

Priority of Claim. To strengthen their claim on income, preferred stockholders usually seek certain protective features very similar to those found in term loans and bonds. A fairly typical provision is the prohibition of dividends on common stock or purchases of common stock that would reduce the current ratio below a certain level, e.g. 2.5 to 1. In addition, restrictions are often placed on the proportion of current earnings that may be paid out for dividends on, or retirement of, common stock. The earned surplus outstanding at the time the preferred stock is issued might be "frozen" by requiring that payments to common stockholders be made out of earnings subsequently accumulated. Sometimes the percentage of current earnings that may be paid in cash dividends to the common stockholders is limited according to the proportion of the common stock equity to the total capital structure of the corporation. As the equity base increases in relation to long-term debt and preferred stock, a higher proportion of earnings may be paid to the common stockholders. We should be willing to concede to the preferred stockholders those provisions that are only an expression of good financial management.

Occasionally we may be able to issue a "first preferred" and "second preferred" stock. In this case the first preferred issue might have a claim on income and assets prior to that of the second preferred stock. Both issues would be senior to the common stock.

Certainty of Claim. Dividends on preferred stock are usually *cumulative;* that is, unpaid dividends are carried forward from year to year. Thus if the dividends are $6 per share and the company has failed to pay dividends for two years, it is said to be $12 *in arrears* on its preferred stock. Therefore, it must pay $18 per share to the preferred shareholders during the third year before it can make any payments to the common stockholders. Unpaid dividends on noncumulative preferred stock are not carried forward from one year to the next.

It should be emphasized that preferred stock is unlike debt, in that failure to pay preferred dividends does not give the preferred stockholders the right to take legal action to obtain their unpaid dividends. The only commitment made is that preferred dividends will be paid in the amounts agreed upon before any dividends are paid on common stock. Preferred stock is like debt, in that its claim on income precedes the claim of the residual owners and in that the maximum amount of the claim is usually limited. It is unlike debt, in that failure to comply with the terms of the agreement does not bring insolvency.

Although it might appear that the preferred shareholders are making a very poor bargain, such is not entirely the case. If the financial manager has the interest of the common stockholders at heart, he will recognize that failure to pay preferred dividends also means failure to pay common dividends. Consequently, contentment on the part of the common stockholders depends on prior satisfaction of the preferred shareholders. Moreover, many corporate directors believe that the terms of their agreement with the preferred stockholders carry a moral commitment to treat the obligation to pay preferred dividends with almost the same respect as they view the interest requirement on a bond issue. Nonetheless, even if we earn enough to pay dividends on the preferred stock, and even if we have sufficient cash available to make the payment, the directors are not obligated to declare the dividend payable.

If *noncumulative* dividends are not paid in one year, they lapse and are not carried forward to the following year. So far as noncumulative preferred dividends are concerned, we usually start each year with a clean slate. An exception to this general rule is found in preferred stocks that are cumulative to the extent that dividends are earned. Even without this legal requirement, corporate directors often feel a moral obligation to pay noncumulative preferred dividends to the extent that they are earned in any one year. However, problems often arise in defining earnings from an accounting standpoint.

Noncumulative preferred stock is quite rare. It is analogous to income bonds in that it is most likely to arise when our corporation is in desperate financial straits. Our bargaining position is poor, but that of our creditors and preferred owners may be even worse, since their only alternative is to liquidate the company and accept the lean pickings that will result. In such a case preferred stockholders, or even bondholders, may be persuaded to accept noncumulative preferred stock. The numerous financial difficulties of railroads have left a heritage of both income bonds and noncumulative preferred stock.

Amount of Claim. One of the important elements of our agreement with the preferred stockholders is the amount of their dividends. Since the dividend is deducted from earnings *after* taxes and is generally higher than the interest rate on bonds, we are likely to bargain more vigorously on this aspect of the agreement than in the case of bonds. Just as bondholders object to the fixed ceiling on their claim on income, so do preferred stockholders find fault with their position. Because preferred stockholders have no means of directly enforcing their claim on income, they are in a considerably poorer position than bondholders. In lean years they may receive no dividends at all; in prosperous years they are restricted to a maximum return (plus any dividends in arrears). Therefore, we are likely to find preferred shareholders striving for an extra share in earnings over and above their limited return. If their bargaining position is strong relative to ours, we may have to "sweeten the issue" by granting some additional participation in earnings.

Since the devices created to add the speculative flavor of common stock to preferred stock are similar to those found with bonds, they need not be discussed in detail here. The conversion feature is most commonly found on preferred stock issues of industrial concerns and is relatively rare on preferred stock issues of utilities. Because a preferred stockholder is already an owner whose dividends are subject to the discretion of the board of directors, he is more likely to convert voluntarily in order to obtain a higher common stock dividend than a bondholder. The bondholder sacrifices a stronger senior position when he converts. We have the same possibilities of forcing conversion of preferred stock in order to build the equity in the form of common stock that we do in the case of convertible bonds. Preferred stock may also be sold with warrants to purchase common stock or in a "package" with common stock.

Occasionally *participating preferred stock* may be issued. (Participating bonds are so uncommon that they were not discussed.) The variations in participation features are limited only by the creativeness and ingenuity of our lawyers. The agreement might provide that once the common stockholders have received the same dividends per share as preferred stockholders, both classes of owners share equally in any additional distributions of earnings. If our bargaining position is somewhat stronger, we may limit the additional participation of the preferred stock in any one year to a certain dollar amount. Clearly, we would not grant any participation if it were not necessary to sell the issue.

Claim on Assets

Although preferred shareholders have a claim on the general assets prior to that of the common stockholders, no specific assets are pledged as security for the preferred stock. Usually the amount to which preferred stockholders are entitled in liquidation is limited to the par value of their stock, or an amount slightly above the par value (plus accumulated dividends). (Recall that the *par value* is the face amount of the stock certificate and is usually the amount at which the stock is carried on the corporation's balance sheet.) In some cases preferred stockholders may be entitled to a premium in addition to the par value in voluntary liquidation, but only to par value in involuntary liquidation.

To protect their position, preferred stockholders will bargain to maintain assets at an adequate level in relation to the outstanding preferred stock and to prevent additional investors from receiving an equal or better claim against the assets. In other words, preferred stockholders will want to maintain a margin of safety between their investment and the assets in the hope that they might receive something in case of liquidation.

Provisions for maintenance of adequate assets in relation to preferred stock vary. The agreement might state that assets must be maintained at a level twice the sum of preferred stock and debt or above a certain amount or percentage of outstanding preferred stock. If such provisions are not fulfilled, dividends on common stock may be prohibited or some voting power granted to the preferred stockholders.

In addition, preferred stockholders generally seek some rights to control the issuance of additional prior or equal securities. A reasonable agreement would be to limit additional debt (excluding trade debt) or preferred stock unless certain standards are met. These are usually expressed in terms of a minimum coverage of interest plus preferred dividends by earnings and a minimum ratio of common stock equity to preferred stock and debt. For example, the agreement on preferred stock of a public utility may require that earnings before interest and taxes cover proposed interest and preferred dividends by at least $1\frac{1}{2}$ times and that debt not exceed total equity nor preferred stock the total common stock equity.

Frequently the agreement with the preferred stockholder provides that if these standards are not met, additional issues of prior or equal securities may be made only with the approval of two-thirds of the outstanding preferred stock. In other words, the end result of the agreement is that if expansion is justified by sound financial standards, it may be financed without formal approval of the preferred stockholders. If the proposed financing does not meet these standards, the proposal must be submitted to a vote of the preferred stockholders.

Voice in Management

If no specific provision is made in a corporation's charter, preferred shareholders are also entitled to voting rights. However, the typical practice is to limit the preferred shareholder's voice in management to certain powers over payment of dividends and subsequent issues of prior or equal securities. In such cases the preferred shareholders vote as a class. Thus consent of two-thirds or three-fourths of outstanding preferred may be required to approve the issue of preferred ranking ahead of or equally with the existing preferred or the issue of any long-term debt.

In addition, a company will probably have to grant preferred stockholders the right to vote or to elect a specific number of directors if it fails to abide by important features of its agreement with them. Thus the holders of the Kaiser Steel $1.46 preferred mentioned earlier have no voting power unless six quarterly dividends are in default. At that unhappy point the preferred shareholders, voting as a single class, are entitled to elect one-third of the Board of Directors. This is probably a rather hollow victory for the preferred stockholders.

Reasons for Use

Favorable Financial Leverage

In spite of the fact that dividends on preferred stock are not tax deductible, preferred stock may still provide favorable financial leverage. Since debt clearly provides lower-cost financial leverage, we might term the leverage contributed by preferred stock as "secondary financial leverage."[3] Additionally, preferred stock contributes to primary financial leverage by providing a portion of the equity base from which may build further additions to long-term debt. Thus we may not love preferred stock much for its own sake, but chiefly as a means of supporting more debt. Nonconvertible preferred stocks are particularly characteristic of utilities because of their desire to squeeze as much as possible from financial leverage. Put another way, a balanced capital structure that includes preferred stock may provide utilities with a lower cost of capital than if they relied entirely on debt and common equity.

Mergers and Acquisitions

Preferred stock has been lifted from relative obscurity as a vestigial form of finance by the recent wave of mergers and acquisitions. A substantial portion of convertible preferred has come to the market as a result of mergers. A recent case in point was the acquisition of Foster Grant Co. by Ashland Oil Inc. Common stockholders of Foster Grant received 0.825 share of Ashland convertible preferred for each of their shares. The Ashland preferred is convertible into 1.5 shares of common stock and is entitled to cumulative dividends at an annual rate of $2.20 a share until September 15, 1978, and $2.40 a share thereafter.[4]

Why might we issue convertible preferred in a merger? Let us consider that we are the Acquiring Firm, a growth-minded company paying a relatively low dividend in order to retain sufficient earnings to continue on our expan-

---

[3] Donald E. Fisher and Glenn A. Wilt, Jr., "Non-Convertible Preferred Stock as a Financing Instrument, 1950–1965," *Journal of Finance*, 23 (September, 1968), p. 620.

[4] At the time of the announcement of the merger, Ashland's common stock was selling at $25.75 per share. Thus each share of preferred was convertible into Ashland common with a market value of $38.625 (1.5 × $25.75). However, common shareholders of Foster Grant received only 0.825 shares of preferred for each of their shares, or about $32 worth (0.825 × $38.625). This was the bid price for the common stock of Foster Grant at the time of the announcement. *Wall Street Journal*, November 2, 1970, p. 10.

sionist path (Table 19-1). We are considering the acquisition of Acquired Firm. One method of effecting the merger would be to exchange one new share of our common stock for each share of Acquired Firm's common stock. Since our market price is $20 and theirs is only $15, the market-price aspects of the merger should be attractive to them. Our stockholders should be happy, because earnings per share would rise from the current $0.80 to $0.86.

TABLE 19-1   Use of Convertible Preferred Stock in a Merger

	Acquiring Firm	Acquired Firm
A. Prior to Merger		
Market price per share of common stock	$20	$15
Earning available for common stock	$800	$400
Number of shares outstanding	1000	400
Earnings per share	$0.80	$1.00
Dividends per share	$0.10	$0.60

	Share-for-share exchange of common stock	One share of $0.60 preferred stock per share of common stock
B. After Merger		
Earnings after taxes	$1200	$1200
Preferred dividends	0	240
Earnings available for common stock	$1200	$ 960
Number of shares	1400	1000
Earnings per share	$0.86	$0.96

But the merger comes unstuck when we start discussing dividends on the new total of 1400 shares of common stock. To continue our growth we would like to pay no more than $0.10 per share (our current rate), but the common stockholders of Acquired Firm take a very dim view of accepting that payment in lieu of their current $0.60 per share. But to pay $0.60 a share on all 1400 shares of common stock would require us to increase total payments on dividends from $100 to $840, while earnings available for common will grow from $800 to $1200. We are not about to increase our cash dividends by this much. We are at an impasse.

There is a solution. If we were to create an issue of $0.60 convertible preferred, we could then exchange this on a share-for-share basis for the common stock of Acquired Firm. First, this would give them their $0.60 dividend, without spreading this high rate to our own common stock. Second, by making the preferred convertible into one share of our common stock, we can still provide the Acquired Firm's stockholders with an increase in market price as a result of the merger. The new preferred should sell on a direct parity with our common stock. Our stock might even rise above $20 in view of the increase in earnings per share from $0.80 to $0.96—a 20 percent rise. (Of course, we would also have to report the fully diluted earnings per share of $0.86.)

One other thought. We may not really wish the holders of the new preferred to convert and thereby reduce earnings per share by $0.10. That is easy. We

can adopt the technique used by Ashland Oil and set the dividend on the preferred at $0.60 through December, 1978, and at $0.70 thereafter. This extra
cash inflow should make them less willing to convert voluntarily to the more
uncertain and possibly lower stream of dividends on the common stock.

Why not issue convertible debentures, rather than convertible preferred,
in order to gain the advantage of the tax-deductible interest? First, we may
have all of the debt outstanding that the market will permit us to assume.
Second, exchange of a debt instrument for their common stock will usually
result in a taxable capital gain for the Acquired Firm's shareholders. Since
they are aware of the time value of money, they would prefer to postpone the
realization of the capital gain and the payment of the tax for as long as possible.
They can do this by continuing in an equity position, since the exchange of
preferred for common in this case would not result in a taxable capital gain.

Management of Preferred Stock

Once we have sold an issue of preferred stock, our problems are not ended.
Just as in the case of bonds, occasions may arise when we will wish to recon-
sider the bargain that we have struck with the preferred owners.

Refinancing

By *refinancing* we mean the use of funds obtained from the sale of new securities to retire outstanding securities. We may refinance either callable or noncallable preferred stock.

The motives for and principles involved in replacing an issue of preferred
stock are similar to those involved in refunding bonds. The principal objective
is usually to reduce the cost of capital. A secondary purpose may be to eliminate
undesirable features, such as voting privileges. There are two important differences in the details of the calculations to determine the rate of return that
may be gained by replacement. First, the savings achieved by replacing a 9
percent issue with a 6 percent issue may be realized over a very long period of
time. If there is no sinking fund provision on either issue, the savings presumably stretch over an infinite period of time, assuming that the corporation's
life expectancy is equally optimistic. This fact enables us to avoid the use of
present value tables if we wish. For example, if we determined that the net
investment after taxes necessary to replace one preferred stock issue with
another requiring a lower dividend would be $50,000, and that the annual sav-
ings in dividends would be $5000, the rate of return after taxes would be 10
percent. If we plan gradually to retire the preferred stock, we must estimate
the rate of return over the anticipated life of the stock through the use of present
value tables.

Observe that these calculations are made on an after-tax basis because
dividends and any call premium on the preferred stock are not tax-deductible
expenses. Any expenses of retiring the old issue that are tax-deductible should
be reduced to an after-tax basis in calculating the net investment required. Thus
the rate of return that would be gained by replacing one issue of preferred with

another would be the rate after deduction of Federal income taxes. Of course, this should then be compared with the corporation's cost of capital or other cut-off rate on an after-tax basis.

Although noncallable preferred stock is rarely issued these days, some financial managers have inherited noncallable preferred stock issued in earlier years when the residual owners were in a weaker bargaining position. It becomes painful to continue to pay dividends at the high rates characteristic of the 1920's, when similar issues could be issued at a much lower rate. How can the noncallable preferred be eliminated?

One method of eliminating noncallable preferred stock is by seeking *tenders:* that is, offers to sell a definite number of shares at a specific price. For example, during 1961 the International Silver Company sold $7,822,000 of 5 percent convertible subordinated debentures. The proceeds of the sale were to be applied first toward the retirement of the outstanding noncallable 7 percent preferred stock of the company. On June 12, 1961, the company "invited tenders of its Preferred Stock at $40 per share plus dividends accrued from July 1, 1961, to the date of payment for the shares purchased."[5] The company proposed to purchase and retire all shares tendered prior to July 11, 1961. Needless to say, the price set for the tenders requested was somewhat above the market price; otherwise the company could not have expected the submission of tenders.

Recapitalization

Callable or noncallable preferred stock may also be eliminated by *recapitalization;* that is, by initiating a voluntary exchange of new securities for outstanding securities. Such an arrangement is especially useful when a dividend arrearage has accumulated on the preferred stock.

To eliminate the dividend accumulation it is customary to offer the preferred shareholders a "package" containing some combination of cash, common stock, preferred stock, or possibly even debentures. This offer is usually coupled with the suggestion that dividends can be resumed on the preferred stock once the accumulation is eliminated. At times the preferred holders may also be asked to exchange their preferred stock for another carrying a lower dividend rate. Theoretically, the value of the package should equal the value of the accumulated dividends, but the offers are usually not this generous. In part the value will depend on the laws of the state and the original agreement with the preferred stockholders. In some cases, the will of two-thirds or three-fourths of the preferred stockholders may be forced on the minority group; in other instances, those who do not accept the offer may continue to hold their stock and have a right to payment of the accumulated dividend before dividends are paid on the common stock. In the latter case, the offer to the preferred shareholders is apt to be more generous. After missing dividends for a number of years, the preferred stockholders are often lean and hungry and can be persuaded to accept a package of securities considerably less valuable than the dollar amount of their accumulated dividends. Because they cannot

[5] The International Silver Company, *Prospectus,* June 30, 1961, p. 5.

force bankruptcy, their bargaining position is weak. They can only wait out the common stockholders. Rather than pay a large accumulated dividend on the preferred stock in cash, the common stockholders may be prepared for a long wait.

Clearly, persuasion must be in concrete, monetary terms. Occasionally, a new, callable preferred is exchanged for the noncallable issue. Thus in 1964, the holders of General Baking noncallable $8 preferred stock agreed to accept 1.35 shares of a new callable $6 preferred stock plus $24 in cash (equal to the dividend arrearage on the $8 preferred). The arrangement gave the holder of one, old preferred share a claim on dividends of $8.10 (1.35 × $6.00) and stock with a call price value of $143.10 (1.35 times call price stated of $106). In return, General Baking gained maneuverability through a "modern" issue of preferred stock, and the common stockholders could scent dividends in the air for a change.[6]

A more common arrangement is to offer a bond issue (or bonds plus cash) in return for noncallable preferred stock. We might offer preferred stockholders a subordinated debenture issue providing a slightly higher interest income. This may be less costly to the common stockholders, after taxes, than the dividends on preferred stock. (See the case of Baldwin-Montrose Chemical Company, Inc., problem 4 at the end of this chapter.)

Summary

Equity funds may be provided by either preferred owners or residual owners. Although they are legally owners, preferred owners are in a class by themselves. Preferred stock is a hybrid security and presents a strange mixture of features characteristic of both equity and debt.

On the one hand, it is important to observe that payments of dividends on preferred stock are not obligatory; the only commitment is that dividends on the preferred stock must be paid before dividends are paid on common stock. Default in the payment of dividends or on other terms of the agreement with the preferred shareholders is not a cause for insolvency. Because preferred stockholders are legally owners, the earnings distributed to them are not a tax-deductible expense. Unlike creditors, preferred stockholders may also have voting privileges, although these rights are usually granted only after the corporation has proceeded some distance along the path to financial disaster.

On the other hand, preferred stockholders bargain with residual owners much in the fashion of creditors and over many of the same features of their agreement with the company. They will bargain to penalize early retirement of the securities and to strengthen or to protect their claim on income and on assets. As in the case of bargaining with creditors, the final agreement reached will represent compromises on the part of both preferred and residual owners, with the weaker party making the larger concessions.

Use of preferred stock may be justified by favorable financial leverage,

---

[6]"Notice of Special (in Lieu of Annual) Meeting of Stockholders," General Baking Company, March 27, 1964, p. 6.

although debt is more attractive if feasible. Convertible preferred stock can be a useful means of effecting a merger, especially when combining firms with very different ratios of dividends to earnings.

Management of preferred stock presents problems very similar to the management of debt. By refinancing or recapitalization, we may be able to eliminate noncallable preferred or, more commonly, preferred with an accumulation of unpaid dividends.

Questions

1/ Why should the call premium on preferred stock decline over time? Does this feature have any relationship to the time value of money?

2/ If preferred stockholders are sometimes permitted to elect several members of the board of directors after failure to receive four quarterly dividends, why should not bondholders have the same power after the omission of an interest or sinking fund payment? Explain.

3/ Consider the following protective features typically found in agreements with preferred stockholders. Why should the preferred stockholders seek these provisions? In each case why does not the prior claim on earnings provide adequate protection?
a. A lower limit to the current ratio.
b. An upper limit on the ratio of debt to net worth.
c. A limit on the earnings that may be paid out to common stock in dividends.

4/ If the arrears on preferred stock are eventually paid, can the preferred shareholders be said to have suffered any loss?

5/ Why should the arrears on preferred stock not be shown as a liability on the balance sheet or position statement? If it should not be shown as a liability, why should it be shown as a footnote?

6/ We observed that agreements with preferred stockholders of a utility might limit additional issues unless proposed interest and dividends were covered $1\frac{1}{2}$ times by earnings before interest and taxes, and that debt should not exceed the total equity nor preferred stock exceed total common equity. Why should the agreement require both the earnings test and the capital structure test? Why would not one or the other requirement provide adequate protection?

7/ Under what circumstances might you replace preferred stock with debt? Debt with preferred stock?

8/ Describe the features that make preferred stock closely resemble bonds. Describe those that make preferred stock closely resemble common stock. Which features represent the more significant sacrifices on the part of the residual owners?

9/ a. In early November, 1970, duPont's $4.50 preferred stock was selling at $63, although it had a par value of $100 and was callable at $120. How do you explain this?

b. When U.S. Steel recapitalized to eliminate its 7 percent noncallable preferred stock, it offered $175 principal amount of $4\frac{5}{8}$ debentures for each share of preferred stock. The margin of attraction is seen by the increase in the market price of the preferred from $152\frac{1}{4}$ at the time of the offer to $170\frac{1}{4}$ about a month later.[7] Why did not the market price of the preferred stock rise to 175, when it was to be exchanged for $175 principal amount of debentures?

Problems

1/ To what extent are the provisions for preferred stocks influenced by their investment quality? Listed below are preferred stocks included in two of Moody's preferred stock indexes. In May, 1970, those in the "High grade" group yielded 7.52 percent, whereas those in the "Speculative grade" yielded 8.45 percent.

High grade	Speculative grade
American Can $1.75	American Crystal Sugar Co. $4\frac{1}{2}$%
American Standard 7%	Armour & Co. $4.75
Carrier Corp. $4\frac{1}{2}$%	Celanese Corp. 4.50% Series A
Du Pont (E. I.) de	General Tire & Rubber Co. $5.00
Nemours & Co. $4.50	Gulf & Western Industries $5.75
General Motors Corp. $5	Houdaille Industries, Inc. $2.25
Ingersol-Rand Co. 6%	Kaiser Steel $1.46
Liggett & Myers Inc. 7%	Porter (H. K.) Co., Inc. $5.50
National Gypsum Co. $4.50	Stokely-Van Camp, Inc. 5%
USM Corp. 6%	U.S. Smelting $5.50
Westvaco Corp. $4\frac{1}{2}$%	

a. Summarize from investment manuals the provisions listed below for one preferred stock from each of the two lists.
  (1) Sinking fund provision, if any.
  (2) Preference as to income.
    (a) Limitations on dividends to common stock.
    (b) Cumulative or noncumulative.
    (c) Amount of claim.
  (3) Preference as to assets.
    (a) Voluntary liquidation.
    (b) Involuntary liquidation (if distinction is made).
  (4) Conversion privileges, warrants, or other special features.
b. In which case do you think the issuing corporation was in a relatively strong bargaining position? Support your position.

2/ Norgaard Insurance Co.'s $3 cumulative preferred stock has preference as to assets and is entitled to a cumulative dividend of $3 per share, and, when-

---

[7] *Wall Street Journal*, September 29, 1965, p. 2.

ever a dividend is declared on common, an additional dividend must be declared upon each preferred share in an amount equal to one-fourth of the dividend declared on each common share. Additional dividends on preferred are limited to $1 per share in any calendar year.

At the end of a recent year, approximately the following number of shares were outstanding:

Preferred stock	490,000 shares
Common stock	1,580,000 shares

What would be the dividends per share on the preferred stock and common stock in each year if the earnings available for dividends in three successive years were as follows: (a) $1,200,000, (b) $1,740,000, (c) $4,875,000? Assume that all available earnings are distributed.

3/ The following convertible preferred stocks were among those outstanding recently. In each case both common and preferred stock are listed on the New York Stock Exchange.

Amerada-Hess Corp. $3.50	Cooper Tire & Rubber $1.25
Allied Products $3.00	Duke Power Co. $6.75
Beneficial Corp. $5.50	Household Finance $4.40
Bristol-Myers $2.00	Midland-Ross Corp. $4.75
Cluett Peabody $1.00	

a. Select one issue and from investment manuals and current newspaper quotations determine the conversion price and the call price of the preferred stock, and the current market prices of both the preferred stock and the common stock.

b. Do you believe that the conversion feature presently has a material effect upon the market price of the preferred stock? Explain the reasons for your answer.

c. Aside from any minor costs involved, would a preferred stockholder about break even if he converted into common stock at present? If not, by what percentage would the common stock have to rise in price before the preferred stockholder would about break even, assuming that the price of the preferred does not change?

d. Can the company force conversion at current prices? Explain your answer.

4/ In a prospectus dated November 14, 1962, the Baldwin-Montrose Chemical Company, Inc., offered to exchange $5,952,000 of 7 percent, ten-year subordinated debentures for 372,000 shares out of 744,000 outstanding shares of its convertible preferred stock. It was proposed that the exchange be at the rate of $16 principal amount of debentures for each share exchanged.

The convertible preferred stock, without par value, carried a cumulative dividend preference of $1 per share per annum, had one vote per share, and was convertible into 1.3 shares of common stock on or before June 1, 1966, into one share of common stock from that date until June 1, 1971, after which date the conversion privilege expired. After March 1, 1963, the preferred was callable at $25 per share, plus dividends. Claims on assets in liquidation amounted to $21.50 per share plus dividends. Common stock had four votes per share.

The indenture provided a sinking fund on the debentures to retire annually the excess, up to $150,000, of net income after taxes above $750,000. (Thus if earnings after taxes were $850,000, then $100,000 of the debentures would be retired.) The debentures were redeemable, at the option of the company, at any time prior to maturity at their principal amount in addition to accrued interest.

During the second quarter of 1962, preferred stock ranged in price from $12\frac{7}{8}$ to $8\frac{1}{4}$; common from $6\frac{3}{4}$ to $3\frac{5}{8}$. In the third quarter the respective ranges were: $12\frac{5}{8}-9\frac{1}{2}$; $6\frac{7}{8}-4\frac{1}{4}$. On November 13, 1962, the closing price of the convertible preferred stock was $11\frac{1}{4}$, and the closing price of the common stock was $4\frac{7}{8}$.

The annual report for Baldwin-Montrose Chemical Co. for the period ending June 30, 1962, may be found below. (Dollar amounts in thousands.)

Assets		Liabilities and capital	
Cash & securities	$ 1,525	Notes payable	$ 1,328
Receivables	2,332	Accounts payable	1,094
Inventories	1,831	Accruals	655
Prepaid expenses	193	Current liabilities	3,076
Current assets	5,881	Long-term liabilities	2,061
Investments	10,596	Preferred stock	
		(744,015 sh.)	15,966
Property, plant (net)	4,243	Common stock (par 50¢,	
		765,824 sh.)	383
Intangibles	2,544	Capital surplus & adjust.	1,730
		Retained earnings	47
	$23,264		$23,264

Income Statement — Six Months Ended June 30, 1962

Sales and commissions		$9,915
Cost of goods sold	$7,320	
Selling, general admin. expense	2,305	9,625
Income from operations		289
Other income (less interest expense)		172
Net income before Federal income taxes*		$ 461

*Although the company had a tax-loss carry forward, analysis may be based on a 50 percent tax basis to ease calculations. Keep in mind that this is a six-month statement. Details may not add to totals because of rounding.

Discuss carefully the merits of the proposal from the point of view of (a) the preferred stockholders and (b) the common stockholders. Had you been a preferred shareholder, would you have accepted the offer?

5/ In 1959, Eastman Kodak Co. offered two shares of $3.60 cumulative preferred (par $50) in exchange for each share of outstanding noncallable 6 percent preferred stock (par $100). The new preferred was callable in five years at $100 per share. As an alternative, Kodak offered to buy the old preferred at $180 per share and dividends.

Assume that a holder of the preferred stock expects that the new stock offered will receive dividends for five years and that it will be called at the end of the fifth year. To ease computations, assume further that dividends are paid at the end of each year.

a. If the holder of the preferred stock accepts the offer of $180 per share (assume no accumulated dividends), what rate of return is he sacrificing by not accepting the $3.60 preferred stock?

b. Should Kodak have offered significantly more than $180 per share? Significantly less? Note: Just prior to the announcement of the offer the preferred stock was selling for about 156–158 per share. The following day the range was $178\frac{1}{2}$–180. During 1959, Moody's average yield on high grade preferred stocks was 4.38 percent and the yield on medium-grade preferred, 4.78 percent.

6/ The agreement of the Southstates Gas & Electric Co. preferred stock provides that additional debentures may not be issued unless earnings before interest and taxes during the previous 12 months cover proposed interest and preferred dividends by at least two times, and that debt not exceed total equity nor preferred stock the total common stock equity.

The position statement of the company at the end of the most recent year shows (in thousands of dollars):

Debentures	$240,000
Preferred stock	100,000
Common stock & surplus	180,000

A simplified income statement shows the following (in thousands of dollars):

Earnings before interest and taxes	$45,000
Interest	17,000
Earnings before taxes	28,000
Federal income taxes	14,000
Earnings after taxes	14,000
Dividends on preferred stock	5,000
Earnings available for common stock	$ 9,000

a. On the basis of the statements shown what is the maximum amount of 8 percent debentures that this company could issue?

b. If earnings before interest and taxes were $50 million, what would be the maximum amount of 8 percent debentures that could be issued?

c. Assume that earnings before interest and taxes are $50 million and that the company can issue any combination of 8 percent debentures and $8\frac{1}{2}$ percent preferred stock. What would be the largest amount (to the nearest hundred thousand dollars) that the corporation could raise, assuming that the company also wishes to obtain the maximum amount of funds at the lowest possible cost? (*Hint:* Assume that the corporation first raises as much as possible from debentures, given the present capital structure limitations. What will then be the necessary relationship between additional amounts of debentures and preferred stock? Note that the rates currently paid on existing debt and preferred stock are not the same as for the proposed issues.)

d. Assume the same situation described in part (c) above, except that earnings before interest and taxes are $60 million. What is the maximum amount and minimum-cost combination of debentures and preferred stock that may be issued?

Selected References

DONALDSON, G., "In Defense of Preferred Stock," *Harvard Business Review,* 40 (July–August, 1962), pp. 123–36.

ELSAID, H. H., "Non-Convertible Preferred Stock as a Financing Instrument, 1950–1965: Comment," *Journal of Finance,* 24 (December, 1969), pp. 939–41.

FERGUSSON, D. A., "Preferred Stock Valuation in Recapitalizations," *Journal of Finance,* 13 (March, 1958), pp. 48–69.

FISCHER, D. E. and G.A. WILT, Jr., "Non-Convertible Preferred Stock as a Financing Instrument, 1950–1965," *Journal of Finance,* 23 (September, 1968), pp. 611–24.

_____, "Recent Trends in Electric Preferred Stock Financing," *Public Utilities Fortnightly,* 78 (September 15, 1966), pp. 19–31.

MEYER, A. B., "Designing a Convertible Preferred Issue," *Financial Executive,* 36 (April, 1968), pp. 42ff.

PINCHES, G. E., "Financing with Convertible Preferred Stocks, 1960–1967," *Journal of Finance,* 25 (March, 1970), 53–64.

SOLDOFSKY, R. M. "Convertible Preferred Stock: Renewed Life in an Old Form," *Business Lawyer,* 24 (July, 1969), pp. 1385–92.

Residual Owners

20

Whereas relatively few business concerns rely on funds obtained from preferred owners, all forms of business organization obtain some portion of their funds from residual owners. There must be some group with a residual claim to income and assets; somebody must have final responsibility for management. The residual owners have these claims and responsibilities.

From the very beginning we have assumed that the financial manager makes decisions in the interest of the residual owners. Consequently, under our assumptions the rights of the residual owners are not those obtained by "bargaining" with the corporation or with the managers of the business. They are rights that remain after the financial manager has bargained for the residual owners to persuade preferred owners and creditors to invest their funds in the business.

At the time a business is formed, equity funds are directly contributed by those who are to be the residual owners. Momentarily the residual owners have an unrestricted claim on income and assets and an unchallenged voice in management. As we know, the financial manager usually finds it necessary and profitable to obtain funds from creditors and preferred owners. To do this the business must first have an equity base of sufficient size to attract these funds, because it is the equity base that provides a cushion to absorb losses and declines in the value of assets. The more likely are losses and declines in values, the greater must be the initial residual equity cushion in relation to other sources of funds. However, the mere existence of the equity base is ordinarily not enough. As we have seen, to obtain funds from creditors and preferred owners it is usually necessary to bargain away some portion of the claim on income and assets and some of the complete control of the company initially held by the residual owners.

In the first part of this chapter we shall examine the important rights that remain with the residual owners and then turn to an examination of basic decisions that must be made in the management of these residual claims. In the following chapter we shall discuss the issues involved in deciding how much income is to be retained in the business and how much is to be paid out to the residual owners.

Rights of Residual Owners

As we saw in the first chapter, the rights and privileges of a sole proprietor are seldom enumerated in a formal document. However, partners should carefully define their rights in a partnership agreement. In a corporation the claims of common stockholders on income and on assets, and to a voice in management, are defined by the laws of the state in which the corporation is chartered, in the articles of incorporation or charter, and in the bylaws of the corporation. Because the position of common stockholders in a corporation involves the most complex form of analysis, we shall devote most of our attention in this chapter to the rights of common stockholders and to the management of common stock.

Maturity

As was true of preferred stock, common stock does not have any maturity date. Common stockholders cannot be involuntarily forced to sacrifice their claims to income and assets, except in the case of reorganization or bankruptcy. In these cases the order of the court only recognizes in a formal sense that these claims are worthless, or nearly so.

In some cases a portion of the common stockholders may be persuaded to sell their common stock to the corporation. Essentially, this means that some common stockholders are buying the common stock of others through the media of the corporation. In much the same manner, some partners might purchase the ownership interests of other partners that desire to withdraw from the business. We shall discuss these arrangements later in the chapter in the section on management of common stock.

Claim on Income

The common stockholders are in much the same position as preferred stockholders with respect to their claims on income. They have no rights to profits until dividends are declared by the board of directors. Under the terms of their contract with the corporation, stockholders have delegated authority in this area to the directors. This situation is in sharp contrast to the practice in the case of proprietorships and partnerships, where the owners participate directly in determining the amount of profits to be distributed. Only in case of fraud can stockholders turn to a court of equity to force payment of dividends by the directors. Such legal action is rare, and cases where the stockholders have won are rarer still.

Pre-emptive Right. Although a common stockholder does not have the right to force the declaration of dividends, he does have the common-law right to maintain his share in the earnings and assets by purchasing proportionate amounts of any future issues of common stock. As we saw in Chapter 16, this pre-emptive right gives rise to the offering of subscription rights to common stockholders. By the exercise of these rights, the common stockholder may prevent dilution of the value of his claim on earnings and assets: that is, he may keep "outsiders" from obtaining additional shares of common stock at less than the current market value. Moreover, he also maintains his voting power relative to that of other stockholders.

Although the pre-emptive right is justified by both logic and common law, statutes of several states permit its omission from the contract with common stockholders. Moreover, it is possible for the common stockholders later to waive their pre-emptive rights. Nor does the right apply to the exchange of stock for assets of other companies. Consequently, the applicability of this common-law right has been considerably watered down in actual practice. Where the pre-emptive right does hold, it includes issues of other securities that are convertible into common stock.

Claim on Assets

The residual claim on assets of the common stockholders is represented by the *book value* of the common stock: that is, the sum of the common stock and surplus accounts. As we saw in Chapter 11, the economic value of the common stock is a function of the stream of future cash dividends and the risk of receiving those payments, rather than the dollar amount of assets presented on the balance sheet. The market price tends to reflect this economic value. Consequently, it would not be correct to assume that as a corporation accumulates wealth and as the book value of the common stock rises, the market price of the common stock will grow as well. We must ask about the cash flows produced by the accumulated assets. This measure of value is significant when we judge the worth of a going concern or when we consider joining one going concern with another.

If a corporation liquidates, the book value then assumes importance as a measure of the dollar amount of assets that common stockholders hope to receive after claims of creditors and any preferred stockholders are settled. Unfortunately, in a forced liquidation these hopes are usually forlorn. The amounts at which assets are shown on the books bear little relation to the sums that are realized when these assets are sold in liquidation. Since losses on assets are charged first against the common stockholders' equity, their claim on assets is usually reduced to zero. In the case of voluntary liquidation, common stockholders are more likely to receive something, but the amount received will seldom, if ever, match the book value prior to liquidation.

How do residual owners protect their claim on assets? Partners and proprietors generally have direct control over the management of assets. However, common stockholders must rely for the most part on the discretion of the directors. In some cases directors must secure approval of the stockholders to mortgage or to dispose of a substantial portion of the assets. This may be required by the laws of the state in which a corporation is chartered or by the charter and bylaws of the corporation. If it becomes apparent to the stockholders that there is no profitable future in a particular line of business, they may voluntarily move to liquidate the corporation to gain what salvage value they can before the assets are further dissipated. Even this privilege may be restricted if the corporation is connected with the public interest, as in the case of a railroad.

Still more weight is placed on the discretion of the directors to select the various assets to be owned by the corporation. Except in small, closely-held corporations, where the principal stockholders are also officers and directors, the common stockholder is seldom consulted on the purchase of assets. Only if the acquisition involves the issue of new stock or the exchange of stock of one concern for another would directors ordinarily seek approval of common stockholders. In other cases the common stockholders must rely on the directors to select the proper balance between risk and return in allocating the corporation's resources among various assets.

One exception to these generalizations should be noted. Stockholders have the right to prevent the use of assets for purposes other than those stated in the corporation's charter. Acts of the directors that are outside the purposes stated are called *ultra vires.* Most corporate charters are drawn so broadly these days that it would be difficult in some cases for directors to be guilty of an ultra vires act.

Voice in Management

The ultimate authority to determine the management of a business rests with the proprietor, partners, or common stockholders, depending upon the form of business organization. While this authority is exercised directly in proprietorships, partnerships, and many corporations, it is typically exercised only indirectly in a large corporation. Although this indirect control is the only feasible method of operation, it also creates problems in defining the scope of stockholders' rights to certain aspects of management. Moreover, the separation of powers gives rise to situations where management may abuse the prerogatives assigned it by the stockholders.

Right to Elect Directors. Each stockholder has the right to vote for members of the board of directors, his voting power being determined by the number of shares of stock that he holds. This right may be assigned to others. Thus at one time the Hughes Tool Co. assigned the voting rights of its TWA stock to a board of trustees in order to obtain a large loan. In a few corporations, usually small, we find two classes of common stock: one with voting power, and the other without. In all other respects the stock may be identical. Although this is a useful device to maintain control of a corporation, it is frowned upon by the Securities and Exchange Commission, and the New York Stock Exchange will not list nonvoting common stock. It is also true of many small corporations that the leading common stockholders elect themselves as directors and are appointed as officers. In such cases stockholders have a direct voice in management.

Once stockholders have elected directors, they have a right to expect them to administer the affairs of the corporation for the stockholders' benefit and not for their own. In case a director does abuse his power, even a minority stockholder may sue for the benefit of the corporation to recover any sums lost. For example, if a director caused the corporation to purchase, at an unreasonably high price, property that he owned in order to obtain a substantial profit, a stockholder might sue to recover the amount paid above the market price of the property. Any sums recovered by this *derivative suit,* as it is called, would be paid to the corporation too, and not just to the stockholder bringing the suit.[1] To prevent stockholders from making nuisances of themselves, many state laws require that stockholders who bring derivative suits put up "security for expenses" to cover the costs to the corporation of defending against the suit should the charge be found to be without merit.

Right to Inspect Books. Although the right to inspect a corporation's books is given to stockholders under common law, the right is usually satisfied by furnishing the stockholders with audited reports. Frequently the stockholders vote upon the selection of auditors. (It would be most surprising if the stockholders voted against the auditors designated by the directors.) When a stockholder presses to obtain information that is not provided in the audited statement, he may have to prove in court that he seeks the information to appraise management's ability rather than to harm the interests of the other stockholders. Were it not for this protection, competitors might easily buy a few shares of stock to obtain valuable information concerning the concern's operations. Thus the courts face a delicate task in judging whether or not the right to inspect books is being abused.

Stockholders also have the right to obtain a list of the names and addresses of their fellow stockholders. Obviously, this information is necessary if an individual stockholder is to enlist the support of others who also seek a change in management. Again, this right may be abused. Therefore, a stockholder seeking this information may have to show in court that he has no ulterior motive. Otherwise, he might obtain the list in order to sell items to the stockholders or to persuade them to switch to some other security that he is peddling.

Methods of Voting. Since it is difficult for him to attend the stockholders' meeting in person, a stockholder may vote by means of a *proxy:* that is, a written authorization that delegates to another person his rights to vote at the meeting. Proxies are usually mailed out by the group controlling the corporation.[2] If the stockholders are reasonably contented, they sign and return the proxies as a

---

[1] However, there are also "friendly" derivative suits, whereby a stockholder friendly to the board of directors institutes a suit concerning a questionable practice of the board. By adroit stupidity the stockholder loses the suit, and then, of course, the directors cannot be sued again on the same charge.

[2] Effective December 31, 1961, the New York Stock Exchange required that all actively operating companies listed on the exchange solicit proxies from their stockholders. The requirement affected about

matter of course, thus giving management the power to vote their shares. Those that fail to return their proxies make it easier for management to secure a majority of the votes of those stockholders represented at the meeting. Because of the proxy mechanism it is usually fairly simple to maintain control of a corporation by owning considerably less than 50 percent of the outstanding stock.

Ownership of less than a majority of the outstanding stock always leaves one open to a raid by outside interests seeking to seize control. In such cases both the "ins" and the "outs" may hire proxy solicitation firms to seek proxies and to bombard the stockholders with charges and countercharges. Keep in mind, however, that the "ins" have the use of corporate funds to wage their battle to maintain control. This is one reason that explains why proxy raids are often more spectacular than successful.

The Securities and Exchange Commission requires that proxy material of companies under its jurisdiction be submitted to it for approval. In general the SEC seeks full disclosure of pertinent information, and requires that stockholders be allowed to vote for or against key issues that will come before the stockholders' meeting. The problem of eliminating false or misleading information is most acute in the heat of a proxy battle. In addition to the full and truthful disclosure requirements, the regulations also provide

> . . . any security holder desiring to communicate with other security holders for a proper purpose may require the management to furnish him with a list of all security holders or to mail his communication to security holders for him. A security holder may also, subject to certain limitations, require the management to include in its proxy material any appropriate proposal which he wants to submit to a vote of security holders.[3]

Proxy contests are most frequently initiated when firms have shown relatively low rates of return on common equity. However, one study suggests that only about one out of three are successful from the point of view of the outsiders. As a general rule, the poorer the earnings performance of management, the more likely were the "outs" to overthrow the "ins."[4]

There are two systems of voting in common use. Under the majority-rule system each stockholder has one vote for each share he holds. If he holds 100 shares, he may cast that many votes for each director that he prefers. The voting is conducted for each position, one at a time — "Mr. In" versus "Mr. Out." Thus if there is a group that has 600 out of the 1000 shares outstanding of a corporation, this group will be able to elect every one of the directors that it desires. Unless the majority allows it, there will be no representation of the minority interests on the board of directors.

The alternative system is called *cumulative voting*. Corporations chartered

---

28 listed companies that did not previously seek proxies because management had "sufficient voting strength to keep itself in office." Companies affected included Johnson & Johnson, American Cable & Radio, and Anaconda Wire & Cable. *Business Week* (April 11, 1959), p. 85.

[3] Securities and Exchange Commission, *35th Annual Report, Fiscal Year Ended June 30, 1969* (Washington, D.C.: U.S. Government Printing Office, 1970), p. 45.

[4] R. M. Duvall and D. V. Austin, "Predicting the Results of Proxy Contests," *Journal of Finance,* 20 (September, 1965), pp. 464–71.

in some states are permitted to have cumulative voting; in a few states they are required to employ this system. If there were five directors to be elected, a common stockholder with 100 shares would have 500 votes; that is, the number of shares held, multiplied by the number of directors to be elected. Further, he could allot all 500 votes to one director. Ballots are cast for all five positions at the same time. A minority group controlling 400 shares out of 1000 would have a total of 2000 votes available in the election of a five-man board of directors. By allocating 1000 votes to each of two directors, they could be assured of placing them on the board and having this degree of representation. The majority with 600 shares and 3000 votes would spread their votes over three directors and be equally certain of electing them.

The two voting methods may be compared as follows:

Results of vote

Candidates	Under majority-rule voting		Under cumulative voting	
	Votes		Votes	
Majority A	600	Elected	1000	Elected
Majority B	600	Elected	1000	Elected
Majority C	600	Elected	1000	Elected
Majority D	600	Elected	0	—
Majority E	600	Elected	0	—
Minority V	400	—	1000	Elected
Minority W	400	—	1000	Elected
Minority X	400	—	—	—
Minority Y	400	—	—	—
Minority Z	400	—	—	—

To determine the number of shares we would need to control in order to elect a certain number to the board of directors, we can use the formula:

$$\frac{\text{Total number of shares outstanding} \times \text{Number of directors desired}}{\text{Total number of directors to be elected} + 1} + 1$$

If we wish to be sure of electing one director, we would need 167 shares:[5]

$$\frac{1000 \times 1}{5 + 1} + 1 = 167\tfrac{2}{3}, \text{ or } 167 \text{ (Drop any fractions.)}$$

Although cumulative voting provides the democratic flavor of proportional representation, there is no law of management that says that this is the one best way to operate a corporation. The case for or against cumulative voting depends largely on the circumstances. In some cases the minority representative has been able to bring substantial improvement in the affairs of a corporation through his managerial abilities and powers of persuasion. In other cases the minority representative has been a source of friction who used his position to gather ammunition for future proxy fights. Such activities tend to hamstring effective and aggressive management.

[5] The minority would need 167 shares and would have to cast all votes for one man to elect one director. They would cast 835 votes (5 × 167) for their candidate. If the majority tried to elect the entire board, they would spread their 4165 votes (5 × 833) over 5 candidates. This would give each man 833 votes; the minority representative would win one seat.

Cumulative voting may be thwarted by several devices. In the previous example, where the minority had 167 shares of common stock, a change in the bylaws to reduce the number of directors from five to four would keep any minority representative off the board. Although 167 shares would be just sufficient to elect one director in five, it would not be adequate to elect one in four. A similar approach is to have only a portion of the directors stand for election each year. If there were nine directors to be elected, 167 shares would be more than enough to elect one. However, if only three were elected each year for three-year terms, the minority group would again be prevented from having representation on the board. The legality of these devices depends in part upon the laws of the state in which the corporation is chartered.

Other Rights

Common stockholders have two other important legal rights: to have a stock certificate and to transfer it at will. A *stock certificate* is the evidence of ownership in the corporation. The face of the certificate shows principally the name of the owner and the number of shares. To transfer title the owner sends the certificate (usually through his broker) to a *transfer agent* designated by the corporation. Most large corporations select a bank or trust company as a transfer agent, but smaller corporations often handle this specialized function themselves. Besides making out new stock certificates, the transfer agent may also prepare lists of stockholders of record for dividend payments and send out dividends. In a large corporation, especially one with stock listed on a stock exchange, the new certificate must also be signed by a *registrar*. He checks the transfer agent and makes sure that no more stock is issued than authorized.

Sometimes the right to transfer common stock is limited. For example, in a small corporation there may be an agreement, specified in the bylaws or made among the stockholders, that a stockholder wishing to sell his stock must first offer it to the corporation. Sometimes an officer who has purchased stock under an option cannot sell it for a certain number of years. Also when one corporation absorbs another through an exchange of common stock, stockholders receiving stock in the surviving corporation may agree not to sell it for a certain period, or to sell it gradually. This prevents their dumping the stock on the market in large blocks so that the price is depressed.

A final right of common stockholders is to pass on any changes proposed in their contract with the corporation. Approval of the stockholders must be obtained to alter the charter, including any change in the purpose for which the corporation was organized, and to amend the bylaws. More than a majority vote is sometimes needed to make these changes.

Management of Common Stock

Although the technical and legal aspects are important to our understanding of common stock as a source of funds, we are more concerned with the various decisions that must be made concerning its management. Some must be made at the time the corporation is formed. Other decisions — listing of stock on an exchange, payment of stock dividends, stock splits, and retirement of stock — are generally made at later stages in the corporation's life.

Decisions at Time of Formation

At the time a corporation is formed the number of shares of common stock to be authorized and the par value, if any, must be determined. Let us consider these in order.

Authorized Shares. State incorporation taxes and annual franchise taxes necessary in order to do business within certain states are sometimes based upon the number of shares of capital stocks authorized in a corporation's charter. Consequently, it would appear to be to our advantage to keep the number of shares authorized to a bare minimum. When we need additional shares, we can obtain stockholders' approval to amend the charter to authorize more. However, in a large corporation this approval may not be given readily, and in any case it will be expensive to tell the stockholders the reasons for the desired increase in authorized shares and to obtain their permission. Since we are likely to need shares in small amounts from time to time, it may be preferable to estimate the probability of these future needs and to authorize an adequate number of shares at the time of organization.

For what purposes might we need authorized, but unissued, common stock? First, there is always the possibility that we will wish to sell more common stock to raise funds for expansion. In addition, we may need to provide stock for conversion of senior convertible issues, for options to officers, and for dividends in the form of common stock. More important is the possibility that we will have an opportunity at some future time to acquire another corporation through an exchange of stock or by the issue of some of our stock for the assets of the other concern. If we must wait to obtain approval of the stockholders to increase the number of authorized shares, somebody else could make the acquisition before we do. We must weigh the probability of these future needs and the costs of later increasing the authorized shares against the present cost of paying a somewhat higher tax on incorporation and possibly higher annual franchise taxes.

Par Value. We saw the meaning and what little significance there was to par value in the previous chapter. How should we set the par value at the time of incorporation, or should we issue *no par stock?* There are disadvantages in no par stock. Some states levy corporation taxes and annual franchise taxes on no par stock as if it carried a par of $100. If this is true of the state in which we seek our charter, we should consider issuance of a low par stock, say $1 or $5 par value per share.

There are several advantages to this low par stock besides the possible savings in corporation and franchise taxes. Should we set the par at $100, the initial and all future sales of new stock by the corporation must be at $100 or above; otherwise buyers may later be assessed for the difference between the price they paid and the par value. This requirement might seriously hamper any future financing if the market price of our stock should decline in the interim. It would be better to set the par value at $1 per share. We might sell the first offering at $100. If the price later declined to $60, we could still sell additional stock. Moreover, the initial sale of common stock at $100 provides a pleasant paid-in surplus, against which in some states we may charge losses in our early unprofitable months of operation. Thus the relevant portion of our balance sheet after the initial sale might appear as follows:

> Common stock (authorized 20,000 shares)
> Issued, 2000 shares (par value, $1) $ 2,000
> Paid-in surplus   198,000

The possibility of misleading the investor may be lessened by use of low par and no par stock. There are still investors who believe that they are getting a "bargain" if they can buy stock with a par value of $100 for only $60. A request that they pay $60 for a par value of $1 hopefully may encourage them to examine the earnings they are buying, rather than the par value of the stock certificate. By removing emphasis on the par value, we may also eliminate some of the trickery involved in "padding" the amounts paid in by the founders of the corporation to make it appear to creditors and others that they have paid the full par value, when they have not.

Going Public

A firm whose stock is held by only a few individuals, often related, is termed *closely-held*. Examples of a few large companies that are family-owned or closely-held are Hallmark, Levi Strauss, Hills Bros. Coffee, and Reader's Digest. Reasons for refusing to sell their common stock to the general public typically center on a desire for privacy and independence. Unless they have more than 500 shareholders and assets of more than $1 million, they do not need to disclose publicly their financial statements. A desire for independence is usually expressed as "not wanting to have stockholders looking over your shoulder," with the suggestion that management will be more willing to take risks when it is not going to be "second-guessed" by outside stockholders.

However, there are strong incentives for eventually *going public;* that is, for selling common stock (either new shares, shares owned by the family, or both) to the general public. Closely-held concerns find it very difficult to raise additional capital, so that expansion is largely dependent upon retained earnings. Should they wish to expand by acquiring other firms, they are handicapped by not having marketable securities to offer in exchange for those of the company to be acquired. Moreover, publicly owned firms are better able to attract and retain good management by offering stock options, retirement plans, and other benefits related to the publicly-traded stock. Finally, owners of a privately-held firm may have estate tax problems, both in terms of raising the funds to pay the taxes and in establishing a fair price for the shares in order to value the estate. These considerations have forced most closely-held firms ultimately to go public.

Listing

We pointed out earlier in this chapter that one of the rights of a stockholder is to transfer ownership of his shares to another party. He will probably find a buyer more easily if his stock is listed on a national exchange, such as the New York Stock Exchange, or on a regional exchange, such as the Boston Stock Exchange. A stock that is *listed* on an exchange may be purchased and sold on the floor of the exchange by its members. Many of these members execute orders to buy or sell which are received from customers located throughout the world.

The problem of whether or not to list securities is faced by the financial managers of relatively few corporations. On June 30, 1969, only 2,764 corporations had securities listed and registered on the 13 national securities exchanges registered with the Securities and Exchange Commission. Of this group 53 percent were on the New York Stock Exchange. On the same date the aggregate market value of stocks listed on the New York Stock Exchange amounted to $692 billion, as compared to $61 billion for the American Stock Exchange, and $6 billion for those shares listed exclusively on all other registered exchanges.[6] In view of the limited applicability of the discussion, we shall be less concerned with developing the technical aspects of listing than with gaining an understanding of the effects of listing upon financial management.

To have its stock listed on an exchange a corporation must file an application with both the exchange and the SEC. The material presented in this application is very similar to that found in a registration statement. Requirements for listing vary among the exchanges and from time to time. In general they require that a stock admitted to trading have a sufficiently broad and active market to be of national or regional interest.

The regulatory differences between listed and unlisted stocks of large corporations are minimal. We have mentioned that listed and large, unlisted corporations must submit proxy solicitations to the SEC. Officers and directors must report their transactions in the stock of the corporation to the SEC and are not allowed to make short sales in the corporation's stock. (A short sale is a sale of stock that has been borrowed for that purpose. The seller hopes to buy the stock later at a lower price to return to the lender. Thus he hopes to sell high and buy low.) Profits that they make by buying and then selling the stock within a period of less than six months may be recovered for the benefit of the corporation by a derivative suit brought by a stockholder. Specified financial information must be provided stockholders on a quarterly or annual basis.

Listing may offer advantages, although a recent study of new listings could find no statistical evidence that listing *per se* added significantly to the market value of the firm.[7] An argument sometimes cited for listing is that the ready market is an aid to future financing. Listing may provide a bargaining advantage in the acquisition of firms whose shares are unlisted or closely held. As a counter argument, managers of some companies have pointed out that a growing concern may obtain more "push" in the sale of its securities if it is unlisted. Because brokers handling securities in the over-the-counter market typically obtain a larger margin than if they were dealing in listed stocks, they are often prepared to work harder to sell them. In general, it is the pull or push problem characteristic of marketing any product. A large, well-known company, such as General Motors Corp., can sell new stock at a relatively low "markup" or margin to the underwriters. The name of the company is sufficient to pull the stock

---

[6]Securities and Exchange Commission, *35th Annual Report*, pp. 72–3.

[7]James C. Van Horne, "New Listings and Their Price Behavior," *Journal of Finance*, 25 (September, 1970), pp. 783–94.

through the market channels to the consumer. A less seasoned company may need to "push" its new stock through the market channels by offering a larger markup or margin to underwriters and brokers handling the stock.

Stock Dividends and Splits

A source of considerable confusion is the stock dividend. In fact, it is not a dividend in a true sense at all. It is really another form of *recapitalization;* that is, a change in the capital structure involving a shift in the amount or types of outstanding securities.

Ordinarily a stock dividend is payable in common stock, although preferred stock is sometimes distributed. The effect of a 10 percent stock dividend on the balance sheet accounts of a corporation is illustrated below. We assume that the "fair value" (usually market value) of the stock at the time of the dividend is $15 per share.

Before

Cash	$5,000,000	Common stock (1,000,000 shares at $10 par)	$10,000,000
		Retained earnings	$20,000,000

After

Cash	$5,000,000	Common stock (1,100,000 shares at $10 par)	$11,000,000
		Capital surplus*	500,000
		Retained earnings	18,500,000

*A more refined title would be: Capital in Excess of Par Value—From Stock Dividends.

Since accountants take the position that the transfer from retained earnings should be based on the "fair value" of the shares issued in the case of small stock dividends, it is necessary to create a new capital account to handle the difference between the fair value and the par (or stated) value of the common stock.[8] In spite of the flurry of activity in the bookkeeping department, the important point is that the net effect is only to transfer $1.5 million out of retained earnings to common stock and capital accounts. We could say that we have "capitalized" a portion of the retained earnings. Consequently, under the laws of some states, we have reduced our legal ability to pay cash dividends.

From the stockholder's point of view, he now has 110 instead of 100 shares of common stock. He is likely to feel richer. But is he? He still has the same proportionate share of the corporation that he had before the stock dividend, because all the other stockholders received one-tenth more shares. Since the transaction created no more earnings for the corporation, he has no more

[8] For stock dividends greater than about 20 percent only the legal minimum requirement (par value, for example) needs to be transferred from retained earnings. See *Restatement and Revision of Accounting Research Bulletins,* Chap. 7, Sec. B (New York: American Institute of Certified Public Accountants, 1953). The New York Stock Exchange will not approve a stock dividend of less than 25 percent unless the company deducts from retained earnings an amount equal to the fair value of the shares issued and unless the retained earnings for the period of the dividend are at least equal to the fair value of the dividends.

earnings to claim than he had before. Although he has more shares, the earnings *per share* of common stock have declined. If earnings prior to the stock dividend were $3.3 million, the earnings per share were then $3.30 ($3,300,000/1,000,000 shares). Now the earnings per share are $3.00 ($3,300,000/1,100,000 shares). These changes have no effect upon the owner's claim on current earnings, as shown in the table below:

	Number of shares owned	×	Earnings per share	=	Total claim on earnings
Before split	100	×	$3.30	=	$330
After split	110	×	$3.00	=	$330

Should dividends be reduced proportionately, it is likely that the market price per share of the common stock will also decline, because the same dollar amount of earnings and dividends is now being spread over a larger number of shares. Often the dividends are not reduced proportionately, so that the market price per share does not fall in relation to the increased number of shares outstanding. However, this price behavior is in response to an effective increase in the proportion of earnings paid out, and it should not be associated with the stock dividend. After an exhaustive study one analyst concluded that ". . . stock dividends alone, whether large or small, produce no lasting gains in market price for widely held stocks on national exchanges,"[9] Even the Internal Revenue Service recognizes that the stockholder has received nothing of value, for the stock dividend is not considered as taxable income.[10]

Why bother with a stock dividend? There is considerable doubt that we should bother. It is sometimes argued that a stock dividend is a means of conserving cash while providing tangible recognition to the stockholder that a portion of his earnings has been retained. Not only have current earnings been retained, but a portion of past retained earnings have been transferred to and frozen in the common stock account. He hardly needs the additional piece of paper to inform him of this unpleasant fact. As an intelligent investor he should be able to figure it out from the balance sheet. The stock dividend is actually a rather expensive means of communication. When a stock dividend is declared, owners of small amounts of stock receive fractional shares. They then must either buy more fractional shares to obtain full shares, or sell the fractional shares. The cost to the corporation (and ultimately, the stockholders) of handling these transactions is considerable, with the trustee's charge per account for stock dividends averaging several times the fee for cash dividends.[11] Moreover, the courts have held that the cost of issuing stock dividends is a capital outlay and not deductible as a business expense for tax purposes.

[9] Austin Barker, "Evaluation of Stock Dividends," *Harvard Business Review,* 36 (July, 1958), p. 114.

[10] If the stock dividend changes the stockholder's proportionate interest in the corporation, it would be taxable. If no preferred stock is outstanding, a dividend in common stock or preferred stock would not be taxable, since the share of the stockholder in the corporation is unchanged. However, if preferred stock is outstanding, a dividend in preferred stock would be taxable. In this case the common stockholder is increasing his share of the corporation relative to that of existing preferred stockholders.

[11] A champion of some sort is Georgia-Pacific Corp., which has declared one percent stock dividends in every quarter since 1960. Philip L. Carret, "Useless Paper Work," *Financial Analysts Journal,* 26 (September–October, 1970), pp. 48–50.

Another possible reason for a stock dividend is to reduce the market price of the stock. There is some thought that if a stock sells within a range from about $20 to $40 it will be attractive to a broader group of investors than if it sells for $80. Should our stock be selling for $80, we could readily cut the price about in half by granting a 100 percent stock dividend and cutting dividends per share in half. Just why we should wish to have a broad group of investors is sometimes not entirely clear, although generally it will be easier to maintain control if stockholders are widely scattered and hold small amounts of stock.

It should be noted that if our objective is to lower the market price of the stock, we could probably achieve the same result at a lower cost through a stock split. A *stock split* simply involves the division of the capital stock into a larger number of shares. Should we exchange two $5 par shares for each $10 par share outstanding, it would be termed a "2-for-1 stock split," and the changes in the balance sheet would appear as follows:

Before

| Cash | $5,000,000 | Common stock (1,000,000 shares at $10 par) | $10,000,000 |
| | | Retained earnings | $20,000,000 |

After

| Cash | $5,000,000 | Common stock (2,000,000 shares at $5 par) | $10,000,000 |
| | | Retained earnings | $20,000,000 |

Stock splits are almost a necessity for a growing company and a prelude to further common stock financing. If a corporation's common stock is selling for $200 per share, it may be difficult to sell additional common stock in this price range. A 4-for-1 split easily reduces the market price of the stock to a more "popular" level and paves the way for a new issue.

If our stock is selling at too low a price, we could obtain stockholders' permission for a *reverse split*. As in the case of the Studebaker Corp. in 1965, we might substitute one share in exchange for each five shares currently held. This would raise the price of our stock in the market so that it would not sell in the price range of the "cats and dogs." It might still be a poor stock, however.

Repurchase of Common Stock

The Pittsburgh and Lake Erie Railroad Company once addressed a letter to its common stockholders, saying that the company

> . . . hereby invites you to tender your share of capital stock of the Company, of the par value of $50 each, for sale to the Company at a cash price to be specified by you . . .
> The maximum number of shares to be purchased by the Company, if it should accept any tenders, will be 100,000 shares.[12]

---

[12] Pittsburgh and Lake Erie Railroad Co., *Invitation for Tenders of Shares of Capital Stock* (March 31, 1959).

The company planned to purchase the least expensive shares first and continue buying shares until it had acquired 100,000 shares, or until it judged the price asked in the tenders to be too high. Frequently companies will specify a maximum price that they are willing to pay.

We saw the use of tenders applied to the retirement of noncallable preferred stock in the preceding chapter. Why should we seek to repurchase a portion of the common stock?

One valid reason for the growing popularity of repurchases of common stock arises in a situation when a corporation has more funds than can be reinvested at a return that is equal to or better than the appropriate cost of capital. These funds should be returned to the owners, either as cash dividends or through repurchase of common stock. The entire amount of any dividends is taxed as ordinary income, whereas a lower tax rate applies on any capital gains received from the sale of securities. In addition, stockholders not selling pay no taxes, but should experience a rise in the market price of their stock. These benefits of repurchase are not evenly distributed, however. Owners holding a small number of shares benefit the least, since their tax rates are likely to be low and because transaction costs may wipe out their tax savings.

Since the Internal Revenue Service will view continued share repurchases as a form of cash dividends, repurchase of common stock is most appropriate when some unusual event has generated a large amount of excess cash. For example, after Martin Marietta Corp. sold several operating divisions, it proposed to distribute its excess cash by inviting its stockholders to tender up to two million (out of over 21 million) shares of common stock at $22 each.[13] Companies with depleting assets (such as a coal mine) or those that have encountered a long-run decline in their business may have excess cash because they have not reinvested funds in new plant and equipment. Thus, when the textile concern, Bates Manufacturing, reduced its operations from five to three mills, it acted to reduce its outstanding common stock from 1,761,750 shares to 1,500,000 shares. Reductions were also sought in its authorized common stock to save annual franchise taxes.[14]

A second valid reason for repurchase of common stock is illustrated by the offer of Pittsburgh and Lake Erie Railroad to exchange bonds for a portion of the outstanding common stock. At that time the company had about $48 million of long-term debt in relation to an equity of about $129 million. Since this was a rather low ratio of debt to equity for a railroad, the issue of at least $8.7 million of first mortgage bonds was designed to utilize more fully the firm's borrowing capacity and thereby lower its cost of capital.

Repurchase of common stock, either directly in the market or via tenders, may be justified in order to settle a struggle for control of a corporation. When a new management assumes office after a proxy battle, there are likely to be groups of stockholders favorable to the old management, possibly with representatives on the board of directors. It may be worthwhile in the interest of harmony to allow them a chance to sell their holdings. Rather than have them dump their stock on the market and depress the price, the corporation would

[13] *Wall Street Journal*, April 5, 1965, p. 9.
[14] *Wall Street Journal*, March 30, 1959, p. 20.

probably benefit the remaining stockholders more by purchasing the stock. Of course, all shareholders must be offered the same opportunity to submit tenders, but presumably only the disgruntled losers would submit tenders.

A more questionable reason for repurchase of its own shares by a corporation has been to block acquisition of control by another concern. Thus when American Steel & Pump Corp. attempted to gain control of Standard Products Co. by seeking tenders at $15 per share, Standard Products outbid its rival by offering $17.25 per share. It purchased about 37 percent of its outstanding shares.[15]

Not infrequently, we find stock repurchases justified solely on the grounds that it "is part of our program to improve our earnings per share . . . it will be held for possible use for acquisitions and to reduce long-term dividend requirements."[16] Since the increase in earnings per share is in direct proportion to the reduction in number of shares outstanding, there should be no change in the aggregate market value of the common shares. Some firms may hope to create an illusion of rising earnings per share by "swallowing their own tail," but no basic improvement in earnings has been attained. Nor is repurchase usually justifiable to accumulate stock for future acquisitions or for employees' stock options. Stock for these purposes can almost always be obtained from authorized but unissued stock.

Whatever our objective, it would be unfair to offer only selected shareholders the opportunity to sell their stock to the corporation. Similarly, it seems unethical for management to undertake a program of buying the stock on the market without notifying stockholders in advance of the plan and the reasons for its adoption. Because the solicitation of tenders inevitably pits one group of stockholders against the other, it is particularly important that all have the full information necessary to decide whether to stay with the corporation or to sell out. Thus it would be highly unethical for management to solicit tenders, while keeping from stockholders knowledge of a startling new invention or a favorable acquisition of another concern that was contemplated. In short, as much information should be provided when offering stockholders the chance to sell as when offering them the opportunity to buy.

Summary

At the time a business is founded, residual owners have the sole claim on earnings and assets, and a full voice in management. To obtain additional funds portions of these rights may be granted to creditors and preferred owners. In proprietorships, partnerships, and small corporations, the residual owners frequently participate directly in enforcing their claim on earnings and assets and in determining any distributions that they are to receive. In larger corporations, most of these matters are delegated by the stockholders to the directors. Because they are one step removed from the decision-making process, common

[15] *Wall Street Journal,* October 6, 1965, p. 4.

[16] Quotation from Willard F. Rockwell, Jr., Chairman, North American Rockwell Corporation, *Business Week,* April 25, 1970, p. 35.

stockholders in large corporations must rely in part on fairly elaborate safe-guards designed to encourage the directors to act in the interests of the residual owners. The pre-emptive right, the right to sue directors for *ultra vires* acts, the use of derivative suits, and the right to inspect the books are examples of such defenses. As an owner, the common stockholder also has the right to elect directors. Although voting by proxy is a necessary mechanism in a large corporation, it also fosters control by entrenched management. Ultimately, preservation of the rights of the common stockholders must rest in large part on the integrity of management.

At the time a corporation is formed, there are usually valid reasons for providing an ample supply of unissued common stock and for setting a relatively low par value, or no par value at all. Once a corporation has been seasoned, consideration should be given to listing the stock, in part as a means of improving the marketability of the stock. Since they do not provide income in any form to the stockholder, stock dividends are not a true dividend, but a form of recapitalization. Their chief justification seems to be that they give the stockholder a sense of well-being. It is expensive patent medicine. If the aim is to reduce the market price of the common stock, it is probably better to have a stock split.

Repurchase of its own stock by a corporation has become increasingly popular in recent years. Such action is justified because of the tax advantages of distributing an unusual surplus of cash by repurchasing shares instead of paying cash dividends. It is also a valid strategy when recapitalization will lower the firm's cost of capital. It may sometimes be justified as a means of retaining corporate control. While repurchase does raise reported earnings per share, that result offers no valid excuse for repurchase, unless investment analysts are unable to distinguish between real and contrived changes in these data.

Questions

1/ If new common stock is offered at prices just below the current market price, are present shareholders injured, even though they are not granted pre-emptive rights to the new issue?

2/ In some cases a corporation's stock is listed on more than one exchange. Why would this be done? What variations would you expect to find in the price of the stock on different exchanges?

3/ What justification do you see for the rule that a corporation or its stockholders may recover for the corporation short-run profits made by the officers or directors by trading in the company's stock?

4/ Why should officers and directors be prohibited from making short sales in their company's stock?

5/ Should stockholders have the right to vote whether their stock should be listed or removed from listing (delisted)? Explain the reasons for your conclusion.

6/ Between 1958 and 1964, Commonwealth Edison Co. paid out most of its annual earnings in cash and stock dividends. The president justified the policy by explaining that the stock dividends permitted the company to conserve cash for expansion and to retire its preferred stock, without having to sell more common stock. (*Wall Street Journal,* May 20, 1964, p. 11.) Explain why you agree or disagree with this argument.

7/ When the 3-for-1 split of AT&T was announced, trading was momentarily suspended in the stock because of the flood of orders to buy. Before trading had been suspended, it had sold at $202; after resumption of trading the first block sold at $225. Whereas one share had previously received a dividend of $9.00, the three new shares were to receive a total dividend of $9.90. Do you think that the jump in price was justified?

A spokesman for AT&T was reported as saying that the split would "help widen the base of AT&T ownership." At that time it had 1.6 million stockholders. What is the significance of this statement? Why should this be an objective of management? (*Business Week,* December 20, 1958, p. 25.)

8/ "During 1969 we added 113,950 shares to the holdings of our own Class A common stock in the treasury, making total holdings at year-end 142,600 shares. These shares may be used for stock options, acquisitions or other purposes, avoiding the dilution which would otherwise occur. We believe that purchases of treasury stock at market prices less than book value are a wise use of company funds." Inland Container Corporation, *1969 Annual Report,* p. 3. Explain why you agree or disagree with this argument.

9/ Would you believe it advisable and acceptable for a corporation with temporarily excess cash during a slack season to invest this cash in purchases of its common stock, with the aim of selling it later at a profit? Explain the reasons for your conclusion.

10/ In the *Notice of Annual Meeting of Stockholders* of Mack Trucks, Inc. we find the following:

OTHER MATTERS

Lewis D. Gilbert and John J. Gilbert of 1165 Park Avenue, New York 28, N. Y., holders of 230 shares of the Common Stock of the Company, have advised the Company that either or both of them will introduce from the floor two resolutions, as hereinafter set forth:

Resolution I:

"Resolved: That the stockholders of Mack Trucks, Inc., assembled in annual meeting in person and by proxy, hereby request the Board of Directors to take the steps necessary to provide for cumulative voting in the election of directors, which means each stockholder shall be entitled to as many votes as shall equal the number of shares he owns, multiplied by the number of directors to be elected, and he may cast all of such votes for a single candidate, or any two or more of them as he may see fit."

The following "statement of reasons" for introduction of this resolution was submitted by the Messrs. Gilbert:

"Only through cumulative voting can stockholders influence their corporation in proportion to their stockholdings. Cumulative voting does not enable the minority to block the majority; it enables the minority to be heard.

Cumulative voting is especially important at Mack Trucks in view of differences of opinion regarding proper post-meeting reports, election of auditors and options.

Stanley Penn recently reported in THE WALL STREET JOURNAL that some 400 companies listed on the New York Stock Exchange use cumulative voting, up from 350 in 1960.

At the last annual meeting 629 owners of 65,669 shares voted in favor of our similar resolution."

Management opposes the foregoing proposal and recommends a vote AGAINST it. Directors elected by cumulative voting might very well tend to regard themselves as representatives of the special group which elects them and not as representatives of all the stockholders. Cumulative voting thus tends to be divisive, facilitates special interests and dilutes responsibility. The present method of electing directors is in accord with the principle of majority rule. The management of Mack Trucks, Inc. believes that each director should be truly representative of all of the stockholders and therefore recommends a vote against cumulative voting. An identical proposal by the same stockholders was defeated at last year's meeting when 8,088 proxies, representing 1,863,307 shares, or 96.6% of the votes cast, were voted against it.

Evaluate these arguments relating to cumulative voting.

11/ In July, 1970, the Securities and Exchange Commission proposed to "limit a company's purchase of its stock on any one day to 15% of the average daily volume in the stock during the four weeks preceding the week of purchase." In addition a company could not "deal with more than one broker a day or pay more than the last sale price on the exchange or the highest current bid price." Evaluate this proposal. (*Wall Street Journal*, July 14, 1970, p. 7.)

Problems

1/ A corporation has 600,000 shares of common stock outstanding. Cumulative voting is used. (Show all calculations.)
   a. How many shares would you need to control to assure the election of 3 out of 7 directors?
   b. If only 500,000 out of the 600,000 shares were voted at the stockholders' meeting, how many shares would you have to control to assure the election of 3 out of 7 directors?

2/ At one time the board of directors of General Fireproofing Co. consisted of ten members, all elected annually by cumulative voting. Management proposed to reduce the board to nine and to elect one-third of the board each year. (*Wall Street Journal*, March 5, 1962, p. 11.) If management controlled 75 percent of the vote, how many directors could it be assured of electing prior to the change, and how many after the change had been in effect for several years?

3/ The A. C. Olson Corp. reports the following items on its position statement:

Cash	$18,000,000	Retained earnings	$42,000,000
		Common stock	
		(2,000,000 shares at	
		$25 par)	50,000,000

Show how these accounts would appear after:
a. A 5 percent stock dividend (fair value, $36 per share).
b. A 5-for-1 stock split.
c. A 2-for-1 reverse stock split.
d. Assume that prior to any of the actions noted above the market price of the common stock of A. C. Olson is $36 per share. In each case, taken separately, what will be the market price of the common stock after the action, assuming no change in the aggregate amount of cash dividends paid.

Selected References

BAKER, R. L., "Purchases by a Corporation of Its Own Shares for Employee Benefit Plans," *Business Lawyer,* 22 (January, 1967), pp. 439–48.

BIERMAN, Jr., and R. WEST, "The Acquisition of Common Stock by the Corporate Issuer," *Journal of Finance,* 21 (December, 1966), pp. 687–96. "Further Comments," *Journal of Finance,* 23 (December, 1968), pp. 865–69.

BRIGHAM, E. F., "The Profitability of a Firm's Purchase of Its Own Common Stock," *California Management Review,* 7 (Winter, 1964), pp. 69–76.

CHANG, E. C., "Accounting for Stock Splits," *Financial Executive,* 38 (March, 1969), pp. 79–80ff.

DUVALL, R. M. and D. V. AUSTIN, "Predicting the Results of Proxy Contests," *Journal of Finance,* 20 (September, 1965), pp. 464–71.

ELTON, E. J. and M. J. GRUBER, "The Cost of Retained Earnings–Implications of Share Repurchase," *Industrial Management Review,* 9 (Spring, 1968), pp. 87–104.

————, "The Effect of Share Repurchases on the Value of the Firm," *Journal of Finance,* 23 (March, 1968), pp. 135–50.

GUTHART, L. A., "More Companies Are Buying Back Their Stock," *Harvard Business Review,* 43 (March–April, 1965) pp. 40–53ff.

HAYES, S. L. III and H. B. REILING, "Sophisticated Financing Tool: The Warrant," *Harvard Business Review,* 47 (January–February, 1969), pp. 137–50.

HOLLAND, D. M. and W. G. LEWELLEN, "Probing the Record of Stock Options," *Harvard Business Review,* 40 (March–April, 1962), pp. 132–50.

HUBBARD, P. M., Jr. "The Many Aspects of Dilution," *Financial Analysts Journal,* 19 (May–June, 1963), pp. 33, 36–40.

JOHNSON, K. B., "Stock Splits and Price Change," *Journal of Finance,* 21 (December, 1966), pp. 675–86.

KERR, J. H. Jr. and J. S. LETTS, "Appraisal Procedures for Dissenting Delaware Stockholders," *Business Lawyer* 20 (July, 1965), pp. 1083–97.

MARSH, H., Jr., "Are Directors Trustees?" *Business Lawyer,* 22 (November, 1966), pp. 35–92.

MARSHALL, W. S. and A. E. YOUNG, "A Mathematical Model for Re-Acquisition of Small Shareholdings," *Journal of Financial and Quantitative Analysis,* 3 (December, 1968), pp. 463–70.

O'NEAL, F. H., "Minority Owners Can Avoid Squeeze-Outs," *Harvard Business Review,* 41 (March–April, 1963), pp. 150–52ff.

SCHWARTZ, W., "Warrants: A Form of Equity Capital," *Financial Analysts Journal,* 26 (September–October, 1970), pp. 87–101.

SOSNICK, S. H., "Stock Dividends are Lemons, Not Melons," *California Management Review,* 3 (Winter, 1961), pp. 61–82.

SUSSMAN, M. R., *The Stock Dividend.* Ann Arbor: Bureau of Business Research, University of Michigan, 1962.

VAN HORNE, J. C., "New Listings and Their Price Behavior," *Journal of Finance,* 25 (September, 1970), pp. 783–94.

YOUNG, A., "Parameters for Stock Repurchase," *Financial Analysts Journal,* 25 (July–August, 1969), pp. 123–28.

_____, "The Performance of Common Stocks Subsequent to Repurchase," *Financial Analysts Journal,* 23 (September–October, 1967), pp. 117–21.

ZWERDLING, G. H., "Stock Repurchase: Financial Issues," *California Management Review,* 11 (Winter, 1968), pp. 34–39.

Retained Earnings

21

We have observed in the preceding two chapters that funds may be obtained directly from preferred owners and residual owners by the sale of stock. Once a company has been formed and continues in operation, it should have earnings to retain or to distribute to the owners. This disposition of these earnings is a fundamental problem of financial management. Should the residual owners be permitted to withdraw their earnings or should all, or a portion of, the earnings be retained in the business? Theoretically, the choice should not be the financial manager's, but the residual owners'. The proprietor or partners will determine the size of their withdrawals, as will the few stockholders of a closely-held corporation. However, we have seen that in most large corporations the policy concerning the distribution of earnings has been delegated by the stockholders to the elected directors. It is our hope, and theoretical assumption, that these directors will determine dividend policy in the interests of the common stockholders. Although we will couch our discussion in corporate terms, the principles that apply to distribution of corporate earnings can also be related to proprietorships and partnerships. We shall consider, first, the implications of dividend policy to the economy and, second, the determinants of dividend policy.

Implications of Dividend Policy

Business concerns finance a large portion of their needs internally: that is, from retained earnings and from noncash charges, such as depreciation, to the extent that they are covered by earnings. We can see from Exhibit 21-1 that these internal funds have provided a substantial portion of outlays by U.S. business firms on new plant and equipment. The shortage of internal funds relative to outlays on new plant and equipment since 1965 has been filled by external financing.

EXHIBIT 21-1   Fixed Investment and Internal Funds

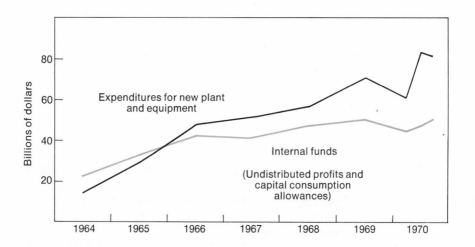

Sources: Flow of Funds, Federal Reserve Board; *Statistical Bulletin* Securities and Exchange Commission.
Fixed investments exclude those by agricultural business, real estate operators, and non-profit organizations.

   The ability of business firms to depend heavily upon internally generated funds for fixed investment has led to some concern. In a proprietorship or partnership the owners are very likely to compare the return to be gained from retaining earnings in the business and the return that they might make from some other investment of equivalent risk. Because they do not participate directly in formulating dividend policy, stockholders in large corporations do not have the chance to make this direct comparison. Thus it is alleged earnings that are retained in many corporations have not met a "market test"; we may not be sure that they should have been retained.

The absence of a direct market test for retained earnings concerns some economists because there is the inherent danger that resources will not be allocated as productively as possible. In a dynamic economic system, some industries should be contracting, while others are growing. Some companies deserve to decline or fail; others need funds. Dividend policies should divert funds from less productive operations to productive ones. Indeed, one could argue that all corporations should be treated as if they have depleting assets, as do coal mines. All cash generated from operations might be given to the owners; then they could return such funds as they think justified by the profit potential of the company. If the prospects were so much better elsewhere that the owners returned no funds at all, the concern would be unable to replace its plant and equipment and would suffer a lingering death. From an economic point of view, this fate might be well-deserved.

We should recognize that it is difficult for directors and officers of a corporation to accept their fate and to allow the gradual liquidation of their corporation. If they find themselves in a declining industry, it is more likely that they will seek out other more profitable investments for the corporation's funds. To the extent that they are successful in finding new investment outlets, they meet economists' criticisms of the procedures for determining dividends. Funds are being diverted from less profitable to more profitable enterprises. However, they are not being channeled through the stockholders. As we shall see in the following section, this may be advantageous from the stockholders' point of view.

Determinants of Dividend Policy

Theoretical Determinants

If we lived in a world without taxes, dividend policy *per se* would not be an issue. Either the firm or the owners could reinvest earnings in projects that are equally risky with corresponding returns. Aside from minor transaction costs, owners would be indifferent between having the firm retain earnings or pay out cash dividends. This indifference would be expressed by refusing to pay a market premium for shares of firms following any particular dividend policy.

However, in the real world there are taxes. As we saw in Chapter 2, tax rates applicable to capital gains are less than the rates on dividend income. Capital gains are taxed at one-half the rate employed for regular dividend income and, in general, at rates no higher than 25 percent.[1] When shareholders receive $100 in dividends, they will not *net* that amount after taxes. If one takes the average marginal tax rate of investors in common stocks to be about 35 percent, those investors on the average will retain a net increment of about $65 after taxes from a $100 dividend.[2] Had the $100 been retained in the busi-

[1] The maximum tax on capital gains in excess of $50,000 is $32\frac{1}{2}$ percent in 1971 and 35 percent beginning in 1972.

[2] Vincent Jolivet, "The Weighted Average Marginal Tax Rate on Dividends Received by Individuals in the United States," *American Economic Review,* 56 (June, 1966), pp. 473–77. E. J. Elton and M. J. Gruber, "Marginal Stockholder Tax Effects and the Clientele Effect," *Review of Economics and Statistics,* 52 (February, 1970), pp. 68–74.

ness and reinvested so that the stockholders realized instead a capital gain of $100 they would be better off net after taxes for two reasons. First, the tax rate applicable to the capital gain would be about one-half of 35 percent (on average), or 17.5 percent. Second, realization of the capital gain can be postponed, thereby delaying the cash outflow to pay taxes. As we saw in Chapter 11, the effective capital gains rate has been estimated at about 10 percent.[3] At the 10 percent rate the value of retained earnings to shareholders, net after taxes, is about $90, contrasted to only $65 for cash dividends.

This is obviously not the whole story. If it were, we would have no cash dividends. Institutional factors in the market dilute the effect of the differential in tax rates applicable to regular income and to capital gains. There is no relative tax effect of this sort for the many holders of common stock who pay no taxes: pension trusts, tax-exempt foundations, and low-income retirees. Corporate holders, such as casualty insurance companies, pay income taxes on only 15 percent of their dividend income. Indeed, these firms would often prefer current dividends to capital gains, since their tax rate on dividends would be about 7.5 percent (assuming they are in a 50 percent tax bracket), whereas they are taxed at a rate of 30 percent on their capital gains. Trust officers also prefer dividends to capital gains when the latter may not be used for distributions to the beneficiaries of the trust. These market factors reduce the relative advantage of retained earnings over dividends as a means of increasing stockholders' wealth.

Market-Related Determinants

Dividend policy must be influenced by other factors than purely theoretical considerations. These do not weaken the basic theory, but they do influence the effect of dividend policy upon the market value of the firm — and thereby upon the wealth of the owners.

Stable Dividends. There is some evidence that stockholders are willing to pay a premium for stable dividends. If so, this preference should be reflected in dividend policy. Let us assume that two streams of dividends are equally certain and that each stream is discounted at a rate of 10 percent. Other things being equal, the present value of each of the two streams of dividends shown below is about $2.487.

Dividends paid by	1st year	2nd year	3rd year
Stable Corp.	$1.00	$1.00	$1.00
Unstable Corp.	$2.00	—	$ .89

Even if these streams of income are equally certain, so that the present values of the dividends are the same, we may find that stockholders prefer the dividend payments of the Stable Corp. and will pay a higher price for its stock: that is, there is utility in stability. This utility is not shown in the discount rate of 10 percent, which reflects the certainty of receiving the dividend. To the extent that there is utility in stability, a policy of favoring relatively stable dividends would be justified.

[3]Martin J. Bailey, "Capital Gains and Income Taxation," in M. J. Bailey and A. C. Harberger, eds. *Taxation of Income from Capital* (Washington, D.C.: Brookings Institution, 1969), pp. 11–49.

The quest for stability can be overdone. Ultimately, we must adapt our dividend policy to the nature of our industry and company. If we are in a highly cyclical industry, such as the machine tool industry, we cannot create through regular dividends a stability that does not exist. In such cases a low payout in boom times can seldom be offset by continued dividends in periods of large losses. If earnings retained in good years are to provide dividends in lean years, those earnings will have to be maintained in relatively liquid form, probably not in plant and equipment. When invested in liquid assets, those retained earnings will probably earn less for the owners than in alternative investments. Given the time value of money, there are ample grounds for believing that it would be better to relate dividends to earnings and not attempt to screen stockholders from large fluctuations in earnings inherent in the business.

Efforts of corporate directors to stabilize dividends have led to the use of *regular* and *extra* dividends. Thus the directors might authorize the payment of 50 cents a quarter "regular" dividends. The implication is that insofar as possible these dividends will be maintained at this level through good times and bad. At the end of the year, if earnings are satisfactory, the directors may declare an "extra" dividend in addition to the regular one. The implication is that this dividend will fluctuate with earnings and the corporation's needs for funds. The stockholders should not count on this dividend—and they are very likely to find they cannot count on the regular dividends either when a severe recession affects the company.

Unbroken Record of Dividends. An unbroken record of dividend payments may be very important to the investment standing of a company's common stock. Some investment companies like to point out that they hold stocks of concerns that have paid dividends each year for several decades. Dissatisfaction with our dividend policies may cause some investment companies to sell their holdings of our stock and depress its price on the market. The longer an unbroken record of dividend payments, the harder it is to break the habit and the larger will be the shock to the market price of the stock from a lapse of payments.

Another factor that contributes to the desire to maintain an unbroken record of dividends is the possible effect of a lapse upon the investment standing of senior obligations. The laws of many states require that savings banks, trustees, and other institutional investors may not hold the bonds of corporations unless dividends have been paid continuously on the underlying common stock for some specified period of time, say five years. Failure to pay dividends in one year would remove the bonds from the *legal list* of obligations approved for investment by these regulated institutions for five years. Because of the narrowed market, additional debt financing would probably be more costly.

Information Content. By paying stable and consistent dividends, management hopes to convey to shareholders an appraisal of the long-run level of earnings that may not be readily apparent in the reported earnings per share. Reported earnings are subject to short-term influences, as well as to the vagaries of accounting practices. Thus, when the directors raise the "regular" dividend, it should be done with some forethought as a signal to the stockholders of the directors' belief that basic earnings have reached a new and higher level. Also, if directors plan to sell additional common stock in the near future, they sometimes raise the dividend rate just prior to the announcement of the offering. If this action is used to communicate to the prospective buyers a realistic appraisal of the anticipated level of earnings, it is entirely acceptable. If the increase is only a temporary expedient to facilitate the sale of stock, it smacks of false and misleading advertising.

Conflicting Interests

In developing dividend policies, corporate managers are faced with the problem that what is good for the stockholders may not be good for the directors and officers of the corporation. Moreover, what is good for some stockholders may not be good for others. It is in part because of these conflicting interests that a clear statement of dividend policy is desirable.

Owners Versus Managers. Although directors represent the owners, they may also be managers of the corporation. As directors and managers, their motives are not always identical with those of the owners. Because they like to be associated with a large and growing concern, directors may tend to reinvest a larger amount of earnings than is economically justified. Nor is it always clear that reinvestment of earnings in plush offices benefits the residual owners. A larger equity base reduces the risk inherent in debt, and may thereby make the directors' tasks easier. But this building of an ultra-safe equity base may substantially reduce the benefits of profitable financial leverage for the residual owners. Sometimes the market price of a corporation's common stock is so low that the stockholders would profit if the affairs of the corporation were wound up and the assets sold. (That is, the market value is less than the liquidating value.) In the eyes of investors the corporation is worth more dead than alive. However, it is clearly painful for the director-managers to close up the business, for to do so would be to recognize their failure and eliminate their jobs.

While the preceding discussion suggests that director-managers may lean towards retaining more earnings than is economically justified, there are situations in which they might tend to pay out more dividends than suitable. In a study of corporations drawn from *Fortune* magazine's tabulation of the top 500 industrial corporations, Lewellen found that since 1955 the after-tax rewards senior executives obtained from dividends, capital gains, and other compensation related to the common stock of their firms were more than four times as important as the after-tax returns from salaries, bonuses, and other fixed-dollar rewards. For the top five executives the ownership compensation was five times as important as fixed-dollar earnings.[4] There have undoubtedly been situations in which executives have caused their firms to pay an excessive dividend in order to support the market price of their personal holdings to enable them to weather some personal financial storm. Aside from such occasional aberrations, it is generally reassuring to find executives' compensation so closely tied to the market value of their firm's stock. The evidence suggests strongly that over the long run they will pursue a dividend policy that will maximize the market price of the firm's common stock.

[4]Wilbur G. Lewellen, "Management and Ownership in the Large Firm," *Journal of Finance,* 24, (May, 1969), pp. 315–19.

Owners Versus Owners. Another difficulty of establishing a dividend policy is that the interests of owners may not be uniform. Decisions on payment of earnings to owners must be tempered by considerations of the tax status of the owners. In the case of proprietorships and partnerships, the taxable income of owners is the same whether or not they withdraw earnings. The earnings of the business are counted as part of the owners' personal income. In fact, owners may have to withdraw earnings in order to pay their personal income taxes. In contrast, in the case of corporations we have seen that owners in high tax brackets will favor retention of earnings more than owners in low tax brackets. Although the *average* marginal tax rate may be about 35 percent, how can our dividend policy reflect the possible dispersion about this average?

In actual practice a clash between the interests of high-income and low-income stockholders may not occur. Stockholders seeking capital gains may gravitate towards those companies that follow a policy of building residual equity through retained earnings, while those in low tax brackets purchase stocks of firms paying out a high proportion of their earnings. This "clientele effect" has been supported by a recent study of stocks on the New York Stock Exchange by Elton and Gruber.[5] In general, the lower the dividend yield and the lower the ratio of dividends to earnings, the higher the calculated tax bracket of the shareholders. Therefore, a dividend policy need not be "all things to all people." Having established a policy, we attract those investors to whom that policy appeals.

Legal Aspects

Up to this point we have considered the interests of the owners in withdrawing earnings from a company. However, the creditors and preferred owners are also concerned with any withdrawal of earnings, since the residual equity provides a cushion to absorb declines in the values of assets. Equally important, the residual owners have financed assets whose earnings provide a margin of safety to meet the payments on the investments of creditors and preferred owners. The protection afforded creditors and preferred owners against excessive withdrawals of earnings stems from two sources: provisions in their agreement with the company and provisions of applicable state laws.

Since we have already discussed the types of restrictions on dividends that are sought by creditors and preferred owners, they need not be considered further here. A large proportion of publicly-owned corporations operate under such contractual limitations on dividends. These restrictions are often no more than would be expected of sound financial management, and in most cases "directors voluntarily reduce a dividend well before the restriction bites them."[6]

Prohibition of Capital Impairment. We saw earlier that the original investment by stockholders may be regarded as a "trust fund" contributed by the owners to establish the corporation and to provide a cushion for creditors. Since creditors have a right to expect that this original investment of stockholders will not be withdrawn, provisions prohibiting capital impairment are designed to make the

---

[5] Elton and Gruber, *op. cit.*, pp. 71–73.
[6] "Reputations and Dividends," *Fortune*, 58 (August, 1958), p. 81.

original "capital" a permanent part of the corporation's funds so long as it continues as a going concern. Problems arise in the definition of capital. In some states it is considered to be the amount originally paid in by stockholders; this might appear on the balance sheet as common stock and capital surplus. In other states "capital" is defined as the par value of the common stock: that is, the value stated on the face of the stock certificate. Whatever the definition, the capital would be impaired if we paid out so much cash as dividends to our stockholders that the difference between assets and liabilities would be less than the "capital." Not only would this practice reduce the protection for the creditors, but it would mislead the stockholders. They are only getting back their original investment—not earnings on that investment. If we encourage the stockholders to believe that the dividends represent earnings, they may be led to invest more money in our concern.

Payments Charged Only Against Retained Earnings. We should recall from our knowledge of accounting that retained earnings, or earned surplus, represents only a portion of the claim of the residual owners on assets. It is just a claim; there is no cash available in earned surplus. We could have an earned surplus of $10 million and not a nickel of cash among our assets. Since the surplus represents a claim on assets, that claim is reduced when a portion of the assets (usually cash) is turned over to the stockholders as dividends. Many state laws provide that assets may be distributed to stockholders only to the extent of the earned surplus. In other words, we cannot distribute to the stockholders any more than they have allowed to be retained in the business over the years. There are many problems of defining earned surplus which are considered in greater detail in the individual statutes.

Prevention of Insolvency. A number of states have laws prohibiting the payment of dividends if a corporation is insolvent or if payment would render the corporation insolvent. Some laws define insolvency as a condition wherein assets are less than liabilities. Other laws consider insolvency to mean technical insolvency, the inability to meet bills or other obligations as they come due. The latter definition is more realistic in view of the intent of the law to protect creditors.

Payment Out of Net Profits. A few states have laws which permit the payment of dividends even though the capital has been impaired. Under these statutes dividends may be paid from current earnings or from earnings during the preceding 12 months. Although payments which would bring on insolvency would still be prohibited, these excessively liberal statutes weaken the position of creditors.

Formulation of Policy

In theory, we might conceive of dividends as a residual payment to stockholders of those funds not needed within the firm at a particular moment of time. But this oversimplifies the problem. Since retained earnings are only *one* source of funds, a decision concerning the proper level of a quarterly dividend payment cannot be made on a marginal basis, abstracted from the effect of any additional retained earnings on the availability of other sources of funds. Therefore, short-term dividend decisions should represent a series of successive approximations to obtain the optimal financial structure of debt and equity required to meet the need for funds over the long run. In short, dividend policy is really a subset of the overall policies designed to minimize the cost of capital, as set forth in Chapter 11.

There is a significant point to add, however. Given the clientele effect observed, we can contribute to the maximization of the market price of our shares by a precise statement of dividend policy and by adherence to a consistent policy. An example of a clear statement is provided by a letter from the president of Government Employees Life Insurance Co. to the stockholders:

> Since 1956 our Company has had the following policy with respect to the declaration and payment of dividends:
>
> (A) To pay relatively small semiannual cash dividends, thus retaining the major portion of earnings in order to provide a strong capital base for growth and development;
>
> (B) To pay periodic stock dividends in order to capitalize the undistributed earnings of the preceding year or years; and
>
> (C) To split the capital stock of the Company when such action is deemed to be in the best interests of the stockholders, the policyholders and the Company, taking into account the market price of the stock, the cash dividend rate, and other pertinent factors.[7]

Having made such a statement, we should adhere to it if reasonably possible. To shift a firm's payout policy is very likely to require a shift in clientele. It is unlikely that the replacement of one clientele with another can be accomplished without at least temporarily depressing the market price of the common stock.

Dividend Policy in Practice

Dividends have been more stable than corporate profits (Exhibit 21-2). Even during the rather sharp decline in profits before taxes in 1969–70, the level of dividends was maintained. To a small extent the stability may be attributed to continued payments on preferred stock. To a much greater extent, the stability reflects a desire of corporate directors to maintain a steady payment of dividends in the face of what they perceive to be temporary financial reverses. To achieve this result corporations increased their *payout ratio* (dividends as a percentage of profits after taxes) from 48 percent in 1968 to 57 percent in the second quarter of 1970.

Contrary to what theory might suggest, studies of dividend policy followed by corporate managers suggest that dividend payments are not just a residual paid out after the need for retained earnings has been met.[8] There is a strong tendency to maintain a particular level of dividend payment and to make a change in the level only when management is convinced that a new rate can be

---

[7] Letter from Lorimer A. Davidson, President, to the stockholders of Government Employees Life Insurance Company (May 24, 1961).

[8] See especially John Lintner, "Distribution of Incomes of Corporations Among Dividends, Retained Earnings, and Taxes," *American Economic Review*, 46 (May, 1956), pp. 97–113.

EXHIBIT 21-2   Corporate Profits, Taxes, and Dividends

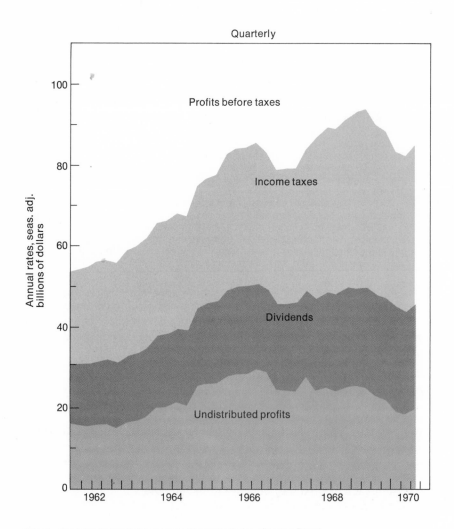

Source: Department of Commerce data charted by Federal Reserve Board.

maintained for a reasonable period of time. This policy of gradual adjustment of dividend payments to changes in earnings seems to be coupled with a *target payout ratio:* that is, the proportion of earnings that management believes is "proper" or suitable to pay out to the stockholders. This target payout ratio seems to vary from 20 percent to 80 percent, with the most common rates being from 40 percent to 60 percent. This policy suggests that directors believe stockholders are willing to pay higher prices for those stocks with a record of stable dividends.

To illustrate the effect of this policy, assume that a corporation has a target payout ratio of 60 percent and that earnings per share increase to a higher level. The annual adjustments in dividends might appear as follows:

Per share	1st year	2nd year	3rd year	4th year
Earnings	$2.00	$4.00	$4.00	$4.00
Dividends	1.20	1.50	1.50	2.40
Payout ratio				
(Target: 60%)	60%	37.5%	37.5%	60%

Thus there appears to be a lagged adjustment of dividend payments to basic changes in the level of earnings. This is not as much in conflict with the theoretical basis of dividend policy as might at first appear. Dividend policy in practice can be seen to approach dividend policy in theory if we examine the implications for dividend policy of cyclical changes in investment opportunities and the differences between accounting income and economic income.

Cyclical Changes in Investment Opportunities. During periods of expansion, as in the upward phase of a business cycle, corporations often have a relatively low payout ratio, as the dollars paid out in dividends lag behind the growth in earnings. This lowered payout ratio occurs during a period when we typically find corporations with very favorable investment opportunities. Consequently, application of capital budgeting principles would also require that corporations retain relatively large amounts of earnings. In a period of contraction, the proportion of earnings paid out tends to rise, again because of the tendency for dividends to adjust slowly to changes in earnings. Indeed, during this period there may be *corporate dissaving:* that is, there may be partial repayment of debt, payments of dividends in excess of income, or even retirement of some common stock. However, this dividend policy is again consistent with the results obtained by following normal capital budgeting procedures. In a period of recession, we have less profitable opportunities, and would expect to pay out a higher proportion of earnings.

It might be added that these alternating periods of net investment and net disinvestment tend to reinforce the movements of the business cycle. For this reason various attempts have been made, both in the United States and in other countries, to encourage more investments in periods of recession. Special tax credits for new investment in plant and equipment during a recession are one means of attempting to make the rate of return on investment more attractive.

Accounting Income Versus Economic Income. A second area of consistency between dividend policy in theory and in practice lies in the difference between accounting income and economic income. By *accounting income* we mean the profits as reported by the accountant in accordance with generally accepted accounting principles. It is not a criticism of the accountant to point out that this measure of income is expressed in terms of monetary units with changing purchasing power. We might define *economic income* as the net addition to economic power in terms of immediate command over goods and services between two points of time.[9]

A simple illustration will serve to distinguish between these two concepts of business income. Let us return to our now-famous hot dog stand. We have been buying hot dogs at 7 cents and selling them for 9 cents. Now we are informed that the cost of hot dogs is going to rise to 8 cents. In view of this we raise our selling price to 10 cents on the hot dogs we purchased for 7 cents. Our accountant comes in beaming at the end of the day and reports an accounting profit of $15.

It will be recalled that up to the time prices rose we customarily ended each day with $100 in our cash box. We would retain $10 to make change, $70 to buy more hot dogs for the following day, and then withdraw the remaining $20 in

	Yesterday		Today	
Sales (1000)		$90		$100
Operating expenses:				
Cost of goods sold	$70		$70	
Salaries	15	85	15	85
Net operating income		$ 5		$ 15

the form of salary ($15) and profits ($5). Can we do the same today? Can we pay a salary of $15 and also withdraw the $15 of net operating income reported by the accountant?

At this point we call in our economic consultant. He points out that tomorrow it is going to cost $80 to buy 1000 hot dogs. In other words, in terms of our command over goods (hot dogs) our economic power, or economic income, is better by only $5, not $15. Today $80 commands the same number of hot dogs that $70 did yesterday. We ended this day with $110, but we will have to set aside $10 for change, $80 for new inventory, and $15 for salary. The remainder, our economic income, is still only $5. If we paid out all the profits reported by the accountant, we would have only $70 to buy more hot dogs tomorrow. Since we would then be able to acquire only 875 hot dogs, we would have to reduce our scale of operations correspondingly.

The investment of the additional $10 in the business is a capital budgeting decision: that is, we should compare the return earned by the $10 with the possible return from its investment elsewhere. Since prosperity has hit the hot dog business, let us assume that we reinvest the $10 of the $15 of accounting income in higher-priced inventory. In relation to our accounting income, our payout is only $33\frac{1}{3}$ percent ($5/$15). To the uninitiated this appears to be a substantial reduction from the former payout ratio of 100 percent. However, our economist can point out that we are still withdrawing the full $5 of our *economic income.*

During periods of economic expansion and rising prices, economic income is frequently less than accounting income. Although changes in dividends may lag behind increases in accounting income, they may not fall behind economic income. Thus dividends may properly be viewed by directors and stockholders as an indication of the economic income of the going concern and

[9] See *Changing Concepts of Business Income* (New York: The Macmillan Co., 1952), pp. 5–16.

should properly be changed only when there is a significant shift in the basic earning power of the corporation.

Since it is sometimes difficult to convince stockholders that their dividends should not rise with reported earnings, the accountant's income is sometimes adjusted to approximate the economic income. Use of various systems of valuing inventory and creation of special reserves may reduce the reported income or at least conceal portions from the owners. Whether or not this approach is justified may be argued at some length, but not here.

In many cases the decision to retain earnings rather than to allow owners to withdraw them is expressed as a shortage of cash — a liquidity problem. Corporate directors frequently point to a poor current ratio or a low cash balance as justification for the payment to stockholders of a low percentage of earnings. To a considerable extent this begs the question. Very likely the corporation's liquidity position is poor because decisions were made at an earlier date to invest funds in inventory and receivables and in fixed assets. Presumably, under capital budgeting procedures we have weighed the rate of return available against the cost of the necessary funds. To say now that dividends cannot be paid because of the shortage of cash is like a student's attributing his "F" to the difficulty of the exam rather than to his earlier decision to forego studying in order to take his girl to a movie.

Methods of Paying Dividends

When directors declare a dividend, they announce that all who hold common stock on a certain date in the future are entitled to receive a specified dividend on each share. Thus on October 7, 1970, directors of Consumers Power Co. announced that *holders of record* — that is stockholders holding the stock on Monday, October 19, 1970 — would be paid dividends of $0.50 per share on November 20, 1970. Because of the time it takes to record transfers of ownership, the rules of the New York Stock Exchange and other exchanges specify that the effective date of ownership is really four full business days earlier than the date of record. Consequently, through Monday, October 12, the stock was selling *dividends-on,* and a stockholder purchasing the stock on or before that date later received the dividend. However, on the next trading day, October 13, the stock sold *ex-dividends.* On that day the stock closed at $31\frac{1}{4}$, one-half point (50 cents) less than the close the previous day. Since purchasers of the stock on October 13 were not entitled to receive 50 cents per share in dividends, we would expect them to pay that much less for the stock.[10]

Most dividends of corporations and withdrawals by proprietors and partners are in the form of cash. In the case of a corporation, a dividend that has been declared by the board of directors becomes a current liability. If we skip

---

[10] However, if stockholders were in high income brackets, we would expect them to sell the stock before it goes ex-dividend in order to reap a capital gain rather than dividend income. In this case the market price of the stock would not decline by the full amount of the dividend when it goes ex-dividend. The higher the tax bracket of shareholders, the smaller the decline in relation to the dividend. This phenomenon enabled Elton and Gruber to estimate the clientele effect of dividend policy. Elton and Gruber, *op. cit.*

this intermediate step, the ultimate effect of a dividend of $2,000,000 ($2 per share) on the pertinent accounts of a corporation is shown below:

Before

Cash	$5,000,000	Common stock (1,000,000 shares at $10 par) Retained earnings	$10,000,000 $15,000,000

After

Cash	$3,000,000	Common stock (1,000,000 shares at $10 par) Retained earnings	$10,000,000 $13,000,000

Occasionally corporations have distributed other forms of assets as dividends. When a corporation (holding company) owns stock or bonds of other corporations, it may distribute these securities to its stockholders as a dividend. For example, Prentice-Hall, Inc., distributed its common stock holdings in two textbook subsidiaries (Charles E. Merrill Books, Inc., and Wadsworth Publishing Co.) as a dividend to its stockholders on the basis of one share of each company for each ten shares of Prentice-Hall common stock. This type of distribution is called a *spin-off*. Distillers have sometimes distributed whiskey as a dividend. The effect on the balance sheet of these dividends is the same as shown above, except that some asset other than cash is affected.

Summary

If resources are to be allocated economically, earnings should be returned to owners if they can invest them elsewhere at the same risk for a better return than is offered within the business. The fact that capital gains are taxed at lower rates than dividend income introduces a bias in favor of retaining earnings. The extent of the bias is tempered by the market's esteem for steady, unbroken dividends. These dividends also convey to the market information about management's perception of the basic level of earnings. Although there may be instances when management's decisions on dividends are more in their personal interests than in the stockholder's, such cases are probably rare because of the close dependence of management's compensation upon the market performance of their firm's common stock. The fact that owners gravitate to those companies whose dividend policies are most suitable to their personal tax positions implies a strong preference for maintenance of a consistent dividend policy. Subject to these market forces, dividend policy should be a by-product of the creation of an optimal capital structure designed to meet the firm's long-term financing needs.

Whereas dividend policy in theory might suggest that cash payments to owners are a residual available after meeting the needs of a balanced capital structure, dividend policy in practice is significantly influenced by the concept of an ideal, or target, payout ratio. As it turns out, consideration of investment opportunities available over a business cycle and the differences between accounting and economic income may significantly close any gap that exists between the theory and practice of dividend policy.

Questions

1/ Would you advocate that common stockholders vote on dividend payments, as do residual owners in a proprietorship or partnership? Explain the reasons for your position.

2/ During 1960, International Paper Co. expected to spend something less than $100 million on new plant and equipment, as compared to $137 million in 1956. Even lower outlays were forecast for 1961. Profit margins were also shrinking. What effect do you anticipate these changes would have on the level of dividends per share? On the percentage of earnings paid out in dividends? (*Forbes,* November 1, 1960, p. 36.)

3/ A study by the National Industrial Conference Board showed that a dividend payout of "about half net earnings was considered the ideal figure." Would you believe it a suitable policy for all business concerns to adopt this payout ratio? Justify your position.

4/ How would accounting income and economic income differ during a period of declining prices? Explain.

5/ There has been a good deal of interest in recent years in the common stocks of "growth companies." How would you determine the price that you would be willing to pay for the stock of a growth company that was forbidden by the terms of its charter to pay out any dividends?

6/ In what areas other than those mentioned may the interests of directors and managers of a corporation differ from those of the owners? As a matter of public policy, how would you suggest dealing with these diverse interests?

7/ What are the effects on the business cycle of corporate dividend policy as illustrated in Exhibit 21-2?

8/ What are the effects on investors' real income of corporate dividend policy as illustrated in Exhibit 21-2? Make your assumptions clear.

9/ Would you advocate that the board of directors formally declare their dividend policy? Support your position.

10/ In 1916 minority stockholders of Ford Motor Company brought suit to force the payment of dividends on the common stock. Henry Ford testified that he wished to retain earnings in order to expand the business and employ more men; thus he intended to benefit the public welfare through the retention of earnings. How would you view the case (a) as judge, (b) as an economist?

11/ Do you believe it would ever be justifiable for a business concern to obtain a short-term loan from a bank to allow withdrawal of earnings by owners or to allow payment of a dividend? Justify your position.

12/ What do you judge to be the effect upon dividend policy of the introduction of various forms of accelerated depreciation and the more rapid write-off of plant and equipment permitted by the new depreciation guide-lines?

13/ A move towards lowering dividend payments by corporations "would surely have to be accompanied by a major re-education program aimed at persuading stockholders that dividend cuts are bullish, not bearish."[11] How could dividend cuts be bullish?

14/ General Public Utilities Corp. proposed to its shareholders to substitute stock dividends for three out of every four quarterly cash dividends. Any stockholder wishing to have a cash return instead of the additional stock could sell his stock dividend through the corporation for a nominal brokerage fee. Analyze the advantages and disadvantages of the plan to the stockholders.

15/ The *Wall Street Journal* showed that on a Thursday, Electric Auto-Lite Co. went ex-dividend and closed at $63\frac{5}{8}$. This price was reported as being unchanged from the previous day's closing price, in spite of the fact that the stock closed Wednesday at $64\frac{1}{4}$. How do you explain this apparent discrepancy?

Problems

1/ You are a married stockholder in the 60 percent tax bracket and hold 1000 shares of Nagata Manufacturing Corp. You anticipate a cash dividend of $2 per share. Aside from brokerage costs, what is the net dollar advantage after taxes to you of selling the stock prior to the ex-dividend date versus continuing to hold it? Assume that the stock would be sold at a long-term capital gain.

2/ At their meeting in the third quarter of 1971 the board of directors of D-C Manufacturing Co. faced the problem of whether or not to continue the quarterly dividend of $37\frac{1}{2}$ cents per share on the common stock. This was the rate that had been paid during 1970 and during the first half of 1971.

D-C was a large manufacturer of machinery and heavy electrical products. As one would expect, its earnings had been severely affected by the recession that began in mid-1970. However, economic indicators had signalled an upturn during the first quarter of 1971. The president of D-C indicated in July, 1971, that sales of equipment were "running well ahead" of sales in the previous year. Moreover, the company's "business serving the mining and cement industries has the biggest backlog it has ever had—and it's going to get bigger still." As a result of these and other improvements,

[11] Carol J. Loomis, "A Case for Dropping Dividends," *Fortune, 77* (June, 1968), p. 183.

he predicted that the second half of the year would be better than the first.

Given the following financial data that were available to the directors at the time of their meeting, what dividend should D-C pay in the third quarter of 1971? There were about 9,101,000 shares of common stock outstanding.

Earnings, Dividends, and Price Range per Share of
Common Stock, 1962–1971

Year	Earnings per share	Dividends per share	Price range
1971	$0.50[a]	$0.75[a]	$29\frac{1}{2}-19\frac{3}{8}$
1970	1.12	1.50	$40\ -22$
1969	2.47	1.25	$38\frac{3}{4}-26\frac{7}{8}$
1968	2.34	1.25	$30\frac{1}{8}-22\frac{1}{8}$
1967	2.11	2.00	$36\frac{1}{4}-20\frac{7}{8}$
1966	2.42	3.00	$37\frac{1}{4}-30\frac{1}{8}$[b]
1965	6.05	4.00	$81\frac{1}{8}-61\frac{1}{4}$
1964	7.20	4.00	$74\frac{7}{8}-45\frac{1}{8}$
1963	6.58	3.00	$59\frac{1}{2}-41\frac{1}{8}$
1962	7.98	4.00	$61\frac{5}{8}-46\frac{1}{4}$

[a]First six months.
[b]Stock was split 2-for-1 in 1966.

Consolidated Statements of D-C Manufacturing
Corporation, 1969–1971

(Dollar figures in thousands)

Assets	Year ended December 31, 1969	Year ended December 31, 1970	Six months ended June 30, 1971
Cash	$ 25,574	$ 33,375	$ 28,239
Notes, accounts rec.	156,116	139,970	144,001
Inventory	216,802	190,224	178,343
Billings on contracts	(19,856)	(19,779)	(15,818)
Other current assets	1,630	1,242	
Current assets	$380,266	$345,032	$334,796
Plant and equipment (net)	118,186	121,850	127,832
Investment in subs.	20,142	20,942	32,838
Other assets	9,293	11,631	
Totals	$527,886	$499,454	$495,466

Liabilities and Stockholders' Equity

	Year ended December 31, 1969	Year ended December 31, 1970	Six months ended June 30, 1971
Current liabilities	$ 89,298	$ 64,992	$ 66,388
Long-term debt	94,145	93,475	90,350
Capital stock and surplus	187,947	188,393	197,744
Earned surplus	146,699	143,244	140,984
Totals	$527,886	$499,454	$495,466
Sales	$539,641	$530,019	$260,088
Cost and expenses	494,585	507,986	250,229
Net earnings before taxes	$ 45,056	$ 22,033	$ 9,859
Federal and Canadian income taxes	22,200	11,450	5,100
Net profit	$ 22,865	$ 10,583	$ 4,759

Quarterly Earnings per Share

	1970	1971
First quarter	0.28	0.15
Second quarter	0.55	0.35

3/ Construct a table similar to that given in Problem 2, showing earnings, dividends, and price range per share of Babcock & Wilcox and Foster Wheeler Corp.

a. What differences do you find in dividend policy? What explanations would you advance for these differences? Do you believe each policy justified?

b. What effect does the dividend policy (or earnings) have upon the market price of the stock?

4/ The following lists are taken from Standard and Poor's year-end compilation of recommendations for "Potential price appreciation—aggressive" (List A) and "Stocks for good income return" (List B).

A	B
Ampex Corp.	Columbia Gas System
Cyclops Corp.	Duquesne Light
FAS International	Northern States Power
Microwave Associates	Pacific Lighting (NYSE)
Potter Instruments	Union Electric

All stocks are listed on the New York Stock Exchange, except the last two on List A, which are listed on the American Stock Exchange. Select one company from each list and prepare the following analysis. (The preparation time may be cut in half by two people working together.)

a. Prepare a statement of balance sheet changes from fiscal year ended 1968 to the latest available fiscal year. What proportion of the expansion was financed by short-term debt, long-term debt, preferred stock, common stock, and retained earnings?

b. Justify or criticize the methods used to finance expansion in the light of the company's present position and the nature of its industry.

c. Over the period what proportion of earnings have been paid out in dividends? How do you explain the firm's dividend policy?

d. Refer to the model from Chapter 11, footnote 6:

$$P_o = \frac{\bar{d}_1}{k_e - g}, \quad \text{where}$$

P_o = current market price of the common stock,

$\bar{d}_1$ = expected annual dividends at end of first year,

k_e = cost of common stock equity, and

g = expected annual growth of dividends per share.

P_o and $\bar{d}_1$ are available in your daily newspaper, assuming that the current rate of dividends will be continued through the remainder of the year. If k_e for List A is 12 percent and for List B, 8 percent, what is the market's implicit estimate of g?

e. Which common stock would you buy if you were in the 50 percent tax bracket? Why?

5/ Refer to Problem 3 in Chapter 20.

a. Show how each of the three accounts would appear after a cash dividend of $2 per share.

b. Assume that prior to the dividend the common stock of A. C. Olson has a market price of $36 per share. Other things being equal, what will be the market price of the common stock after it goes "ex-dividend"?

Selected References

BRIGHAM, E. F. and M. J. Gordon, "Leverage Dividend Policy, and the Cost of Capital," *Journal of Finance*, 23 (March, 1968), pp. 85–104.

BRITTAIN, J. A., *Corporate Dividend Policy*. Washington, D.C.: Brookings Institution, 1966.

DARLING, P. G., "The Influence of Expectations and Liquidity on Dividend Policy," *Journal of Political Economy*, 45 (June, 1957), pp. 209–24.

DHRYMES, P. J. and M. KURZ, "On the Dividend Policy of Electric Utilities," *Review of Economics and Statistics*, 46 (February, 1964), pp. 76–81.

ELTON, E. J. and M. J. GRUBER, "Marginal Stockholder Tax Rates and the Clientele Effect," *Review of Economics and Statistics*, 52 (February, 1970), pp. 68–74.

FAMA, E. F. and H. BABIAK, "Dividend Policy: An Empirical Analysis," *Journal of the American Statistical Association*, 63 (December, 1968), pp. 1132–61.

FRIEND, I. and M. PUCKETT, "Dividends and Stock Prices," *American Economic Review*, 54 (September, 1964), pp. 656–82.

GORDON, M. J. "Dividends, Earnings and Stock Prices," *Review of Economics and Statistics*, 41 (May, 1959), pp. 99–105.

HARKAVY, O., "The Relation Between Retained Earnings and Common Stock Prices for Large Listed Corporations," *Journal of Finance*, 8 (September, 1953), pp. 283–97.

———, "Distribution of Incomes of Corporations among Dividends, Retained Earnings, and Taxes," *American Economic Review*, 46 (May, 1956), pp. 97–113.

———, "Dividends, Earnings, Leverage, Stock Prices and the Supply of Capital to Corporations," *Review of Economics and Statistics*, 44 (August, 1962), pp. 243–69.

LINTNER, J., "Optimal Dividends and Corporate Growth Under Uncertainty," *Quarterly Journal of Economics*, 78 (February, 1964), pp. 49–95.

MACDOUGAL, G. E., "Investing in a Dividend Boost," *Harvard Business Review*, 45 (July–August, 1967), pp. 87–92.

MANNE, A. S., "Optimal Dividend and Investment Policies for a Self-Financing Business Enterprise," *Management Science*, 15 (November, 1968), pp. 119–29.

LOOMIS, C. J., "A Case for Dropping Dividends," *Fortune*, 77 (June, 1968), pp. 181–85ff.

MILLER, M. H. and F. MODIGLIANI, "Dividend Policy, Growth, and the Valuation of Shares," *Journal of Business*, 34 (October, 1961), pp. 411–33. "A Reply," *Journal of Business*, 36 (January, 1963), pp. 116–19.

SCHWARTZ, E. and J. R. ARONSON, "The Corporate Sector: A Net Exporter of Funds," *Southern Economic Journal*, 33 (October, 1961), pp. 252–57.

TURNOVSKY, S. J. "The Allocation of Corporate Profits between Dividends and Retained Earnings," *Review of Economics and Statistics*, 49 (November, 1967), pp. 583–89.

WALTER, J. E., *Dividend Policy and Enterprise Valuation*. Belmont, Calif.: Wadsworth Publishing Co., Inc., 1967.

———, "Dividend Policy: Its Influence on the Value of the Enterprise," *Journal of Finance*, 18 (May, 1963), pp. 280–91.

WILSON, R., "A Pareto-Optimal Dividend Policy," *Management Science*, 13 (May, 1967), pp. 756–64.

Part Six

Valuing of Business Enterprises

Valuation and the New Company

22

Although the financial manager devotes most of his time to problems of planning his needs for funds, acquiring those funds, and then employing them effectively within the business, he occasionally faces certain special problems of lasting importance. These problems have a common core in that they require the financial manager to determine the value of a group of assets or the value of certain claims on those assets; claims by creditors, preferred owners, or residual owners. The basic principles of valuation discussed here in Part Six do not differ from the theory of capital budgeting set forth in Chapter 8. Here we apply the principles to the valuation of a group of assets held by a going concern, rather than to determination of the present value of individual assets. As in the case of capital budgeting, valuation is difficult because it is necessarily based upon forecasts of future income and estimates of the certainty of receiving that income. In some instances the importance of individual valuation decisions to the long-range success of the company surpasses the effects of the more frequent, but less weighty, financial decisions that have been covered to this point.

Although problems of valuation arise in a great number of areas, we shall restrict our discussion to the application of the principles involved in three main areas: promotion of a new company (either by purchase of an existing business or formation of an entirely new firm); acquisition of one company by another; and exchange of new for existing securities within a single concern. In this chapter we shall develop the principles of valuation and show the application of the principles to the promotion of a new business. Applications in the other two areas will be covered in the following chapter.

It should be observed that the principles developed and illustrated in these two chapters are applicable to other situations as well. Securities left as part of an estate must be valued for estate tax purposes. Often no market quotations are available as a basis for valuation, and if they are available, they may not provide a satisfactory measure of value. When a partner withdraws or dies, the value of his share of the business must be determined to enable the remaining partners to buy his interest or pay his share of the business to his heirs. Sometimes one corporation acquires another through purchase of assets or an exchange of common stock. Stockholders who disagree with the basis of the acquisition may sue to have the value of their interests determined in court.

In certain instances the valuation principles developed here do not apply. Commissions regulating the rates charged by public utilities are given the task of valuing the assets of those companies in order to allow them to earn a "fair return on a fair value." Instead of estimating the future income to determine the present value of the assets, these commissions must estimate the "fair" value of the assets in order to fix the income that will be allowed. Similar problems arise when attempting to fix the prices charged for any services or products. For example, most states set the rates that personal loan companies may charge. We shall not be concerned with these special problems of valuation for rate-making purposes.

Principles of Valuation

Valuation is not an exact science; it is "sophisticated guess-work."[1] Not only are there many different methods of valuation, but variations in the use of each method may lead to widely different results. The one method that is theoretically sound is the capitalization of income. Other methods are sometimes used because they are easier, but ease is a poor criterion for accuracy. Consequently, our discussion of various methods of valuation should not be taken as a suggestion that all methods be used and then a final valuation figure be computed by averaging the results obtained under each method. The use of averages cannot convert basically unsound figures into sound ones.

In the following discussion a fundamental consideration is that the valuation process applies to a "going concern." We are valuing an existing mixture of assets, or an anticipated mixture, if we are forming a new business. Taken together, these assets will provide a stream of income which we expect to continue

[1] Arthur S. Dewing, *The Financial Policy of Corporations* (New York: The Ronald Press Company, 1953), p. 287.

for some time into the future. But in a going concern there are more than tangible assets. There is an *organization:* that is, the complex of relationships among the group of individuals running the company and between the company and its suppliers and customers. The existence of an organization is the distinguishing feature of a going concern. The size and reliability of the annual stream of income produced by the assets in conjunction with the organization determines the *economic value* of the going concern.

Liquidating Value

Individual assets, such as a lathe, have two values (at least). We are primarily interested in the economic value of the lathe to the company: that is, its value in use along with all other assets and the organization. It has another value because some other company would also have a use for the lathe and would be willing to pay some price for it. Each of the assets has a value in some alternative use; this value we shall define as the *liquidating value.* If we have a lot of time to look for a buyer, the liquidating value of the lathe will be higher than if we have to sell it within a matter of a week. For the company as a whole the liquidating value will be the estimated net amounts that will be received by sale of the assets, less any liabilities. The liquidating value of a company is usually less than its economic value as a going concern. In other words, the sum of the independent value of the parts is generally not equal to the value of the parts working together under an effective organization.

As we shall see in the following chapter, liquidating value does have significance in bargaining on valuation in that it represents an "upset price." Thus we would not sell our company as a unit for less than its liquidating value. Similarly, a bondholder cannot be expected to exchange his bonds for new securities if the value of the new securities is less than the bondholder might obtain through forced liquidation of the company.

Original Cost, Less Depreciation

One method of valuation is to determine the original cost of the assets and subtract valuation reserves, such as allowances for depreciation, depletion, and bad debts. If the assets are being transferred subject to various liabilities, those liabilities should be deducted from the calculated value of the assets to arrive at the net worth. In a proprietorship the net worth would be equal to the capital account of the proprietor. In the case of a corporation, the net worth figure, less any prior claims on assets of preferred stock, divided by the number of shares of common stock outstanding, would yield the book value per share of common stock. Frequently, intangible assets are deducted from total assets to determine tangible net worth and tangible book value per share. Thus under this method of valuation three figures might be produced: value of total assets, value of net worth (assets minus liabilities), and book value per share of common stock. The failings of this method apply to all three figures.

First of all, calculations are based upon the original cost of the assets. This is usually the figure shown by the accountant on the books, unless an asset has been reappraised and written down or up. Although the assets have been purchased at various times, no adjustment has been made on the books for changes in the price level. A plant built in 1939 may have cost $250,000 at the time, but could not be replaced today at less than $750,000. However, this rise is not reflected in the value placed on the plant under this method. Second, valuation reserves, especially for depreciation, are relatively arbitrary. Because several different systems of allocating depreciation expense over time may be used, companies starting out their lives at identical moments with identical assets would probably soon show different book values for assets. Moreover, individual companies often change their methods of depreciation from time to time.

Most important of all, the system gives no recognition to the economic value of the assets. Maybe we built a dam for $5 million to generate electric power. If the river has run dry, what is the value of the dam? Even though the depreciated value of the dam may be $4 million, its economic value is zero because it is not capable of producing income in the foreseeable future. The dam does not even have much in the way of a liquidating value, since it will be difficult to persuade somebody to take it off our hands; the alternative uses for a dam on a dry river bed are few. On the other hand, if we had casually purchased for $400 a plot of land that eventually develops into a busy corner in the heart of the city, can we judge its present value to be only $400? Clearly we must use some basis other than historical cost to determine present value.

For the most part, then, valuation based upon the depreciated historical cost of assets is likely to be misleading. Purchasers of common stocks usually pay little attention to book value. In their effort to appraise the economic value of a share of common stock, investors attempt to estimate the future gains to be realized from that share. Their estimates are expressed in the price they are willing to pay for the stock on the market. The great diversity between market price, or investors' estimate of economic value, and book value suggests that investors determine value on some basis other than book value. The much closer relation of market price to earnings and dividends indicates the relatively greater emphasis placed on these factors in valuing common stocks.

In the case of the common stocks of concerns such as banks, insurance companies, and finance companies there is likely to be a fairly close correlation between book value per share and stockholders' appraisal of economic value. Many of the assets are short-term obligations, such as consumer installment notes, which will soon be converted into cash. In contrast, the value of any long-term securities, such as government bonds, held by financial institutions will vary with money rates. The value of any corporate obligations held will also reflect the changing fortunes of the issuers. Any variations in the value of these securities will cause the economic values of the financial institutions holding them to depart from their book values.

Replacement Cost, Less Depreciation

In an effort to avoid the problem of changing price levels, it might be argued that assets should be valued on the basis of replacement cost, rather than historical cost. The replacement cost alone, without deduction of depreciation reserves, represents about the maximum price a buyer might pay for assets. We say "about" because when one concern buys another, it is acquiring something more than just assets; it is buying an organization. Consequently, even though it might be less expensive to buy brand new assets, a buyer may favor acquiring the "used" assets of a going concern, in order to acquire the accompanying organization.

There are several problems in using replacement cost as a method of valuation. It is often difficult to estimate cost of replacement. Generally we would not try to estimate costs of replacing identical equipment. This could be prohibitively expensive if the equipment were no longer manufactured. Instead, we should estimate the costs of providing assets to perform similar services. There remains the problem of determining depreciation on the replacement cost, and this is subject to the same difficulties of determining depreciation with historical costs. Finally, we are faced with the basic issue that estimates of replacement cost do not measure the value of assets in use. Two companies might each have a lathe with an identical replacement cost (less depreciation). Yet because of favorable relationships with suppliers and customers, one company might be able to make far more effective use of its lathe than the other. Again, we cannot for our purposes consider the value of assets as distinct from their value in use.

Market Value

Very frequently assets are transferred subject to various liabilities. This is often true when a new enterprise is started by buying an existing concern or when two existing companies merge. When the company whose value we are trying to determine has securities which are traded on some exchange or over the counter, it may be possible to estimate the value of a share in that company on the basis of the market price of the securities. Assume that Company A proposes to absorb Company B by exchanging its common stock for that of Company B. If the stock of Company A is selling for $60 and the stock of Company B for $30, would it be fair for Company A to acquire control by offering one share of its common stock for every two shares of the stock of Company B?

Unfortunately, it is difficult to base a determination of value entirely upon market value because investors' evaluation of future dividends and earnings is so volatile. For example, during 1970, the market price of the common stock of Outboard Marine varied from about 13 to 28; Xerox from 65 to 115; and Polaroid from 51 to 131. Can it really be said that the economic value of the assets of these companies changed so drastically during such a short period of time? It would hardly appear so. Basically, what we are saying is that if market value is a true measure of economic value, then the market value is always correct and we need not undertake any analysis to buy common stocks. We can buy blind. This is so obviously untrue that we must reject market value as a certain or accurate measure of economic value.

There are some other problems in using market value that might be mentioned. Attention must be paid to the breadth of the market; that is, the volume of transactions which take place in the stock. Daily quotations of stock prices often represent purchases and sales of only a few hundred shares, a small fraction of the total number of shares outstanding. For example, on November 20, 1970, 3700 shares of the common stock of American Metal Climax were sold on the New York Stock Exchange at prices ranging from $28\frac{7}{8}$ to $29\frac{1}{8}$ per share. Since there were 23,636,000 shares of the stock outstanding at the time, these transactions represent a minority opinion of the value of the stock. Holders of over 23 million other shares evidently believed the price too low to justify selling. Millions of other potential investors must have thought the price too high to warrant buying. If we use market value as a measure of economic value for purposes of a merger, we must also recognize that rumors of the merger will affect the market value of the stock. Unfortunately, it is difficult to tell whether movements on the price of a stock in response to such rumors cause the price to move towards or away from its economic value. Finally, sales of stock in a closely held corporation may not reflect fair market value. Possibly these sales are forced sales or sales between members of the same family. Although market value has deficiencies, it is probably a better measure of economic value than historical or replacement cost. For this reason and because it is easy to determine, it is often given much weight in practical valuation problems.

The Valuation Model

The conceptual approach of this method is the same as that underlying the present-value approach to capital budgeting (Chapter 8). In that case the first step was to estimate the stream of net cash benefits that a machine would produce over some specified period of time. Our problem was then to determine the present value of that stream of cash benefits discounted at the firm's estimated cost of capital. The present value was compared with the required net investment in the machine. Presumably, we would pay no more for a machine than its calculated present value. If we could buy it for less, we would raise the market value of the firm.

In most cases valuation of a going business concern or of its assets is based upon an estimate of anticipated net income after taxes, rather than net cash benefits. Because we are dealing with a going concern, it is customary to assume that (1) over time cash expenditures on replacement of equipment will about equal the noncash depreciation charges (Exhibit 21-1); (2) the stream of income will continue for an indefinite period; and (3) the incomes will be constant. Although it is not difficult to modify these assumptions, we will restrict our analysis to these assumptions in order to emphasize the underlying principles of valuation.

Assume now that we are proposing to acquire a bundle of assets that are producing a stream of incomes. At issue is the price that we should be willing to pay for that income stream. Even if the selling firm should specify a price, it is probably only a bargaining offer and has no greater significance than the price that we originally offer to pay. We are looking for the price at which we would be willing to sign.

What factors influence our valuation of that income stream? First, other things being equal, we would be willing to pay more, the higher the after-tax income stream. Second, our valuation is affected by the risks involved in realizing that income. To perceive the third factor, consider for the moment two income streams identical in all respects, except that in one case we are unable to borrow to finance our acquisition of the stream, whereas in the other case we can borrow. Clearly, we would be willing to pay more for the second stream.

Other things being equal, the more we can lever the acquisition of the income stream, the more we would be willing to pay for it.

By this point, we may begin to wonder if we have not seen this valuation model before—and of course we have. As we observed in Chapter 3:

$$V_L = \frac{Y(1 - t_c)}{k_a} + Dt_c, \quad \text{where} \tag{3-7a}$$

V_L = value of a levered firm,

Y = net operating income before interest and taxes,

t_c = corporate income tax rate

k_a = after-tax discount rate for unlevered firm, and

D = dollar amount of debt.

The model displays in symbols what has just been said in words. The market value of a firm is higher, the greater the after-tax stream of earnings, the lower the discount rate (risk), and the greater the debt capacity. Therefore, to estimate the value of a stream of income produced by a bundle of assets we must undertake four basic steps:

1. Determine the expected after-tax net operating income $[Y(1 - t_c)]$.
2. Determine the discount rate for that income (k_a).
3. Estimate the extent to which earnings may be levered (D).
4. Calculate the estimated market value of the firm from the valuation formula shown above.

Determining Expected Income. Estimates of expected "normal" net operating income before interest and taxes are usually based upon a study of past earnings, adjusted for any foreseeable changes in operations. The first step is the selection of a period of time which will represent a normal picture of both the good and bad years in the company's recent history. Although we might arbitrarily select the most recent five or ten years, it is better to base the selection of the time period upon a study of causes of variations in past earnings and the likelihood of these fluctuations being repeated in the future. Thus, if we are valuing the assets of a paint company, we should consider its earnings over a complete building cycle, so that the poor years are averaged with the good. This might cover a period as long as 10 or 15 years. Other types of business might have much shorter cycles of prosperity and recession.

Superimposed on cyclical fluctuations in earnings may be an upward or downward trend in earnings. One means of taking a trend into account is to give a greater weight to the earnings of recent years. The rather mechanical weighting system illustrated below is probably too artificial to produce desirable results, but it suggests the nature of the approach.

Year	Net income after depreciation and taxes, but before bond interest or preferred dividends (A)	Weights assigned (B)	(A) × (B)
19_5	$206,000	1	$ 206,000
19_6	180,000	2	360,000
19_7	218,000	3	654,000
19_8	220,000	4	880,000
19_9	226,000	5	1,130,000
		15	$3,230,000

$$\text{Weighted average annual income} = \frac{\$3,230,000}{15} = \$217,333.$$

(The unweighted average of the figures shown is $210,000.)

The next step is to adjust past earnings for any variations which cannot be expected to persist in the future. At some time in the past a company might have reduced its Federal income taxes by buying another concern with a large loss which was carried forward for tax purposes. Unless we expect this process to be repeated consistently in the future, it would be desirable to adjust net income downward to show the income after taxes that would have been available without the tax-loss carry-forward. Similarly, gains and losses from disposal of assets should be deleted unless these are regularly incurred in the normal course of business. Although it is sometimes suggested that inventory gains or losses should not be considered as part of normal income, these are likely to be characteristic of cyclical movements and probably should be included as part of the normal income over a cycle. In this same category of adjustments to income are expenditures which the purchasing company can avoid or reduce. For example, one large company found that salesmen's salaries in another company it proposed to buy were exorbitant. Furthermore, a rather expensive yacht was maintained by the company, and the president's son was on the payroll, although there were no benefits evident from his services. In determining the income it could expect from the purchase of the other concern, the buying company deducted these extra costs from the operating expenses of the company. Needless to say, the purchaser did not inform the seller that these costs would be pared.

In other cases past earnings may be considerably higher than probable future earnings. To illustrate, after the patent on the Ronson lighter expired, a flood of similar lighters came on the market with the result that the earnings of the Ronson Company suffered materially for a while. Projection of earnings realized during the years when its patent gave a company a strong position in the market to the years following expiration of the patent would not have been justified. Similar situations could arise when a company has a contract for the sale of its products with a large customer. If the contract is not renewed, earnings could drop precipitously. Companies may allow a trade position to slip, so that a once valuable brand name loses its significance. The classic example usually cited is Sapolio, once a nationally-known soap that is now mentioned only in textbooks. In each of these cases, historical earnings could not be projected into the future without substantial downward adjustments to reflect an estimated decline in annual net income.

An adequate evaluation of earnings cannot be made without a thorough understanding of accounting. "Generally accepted accounting principles" permit such a wide latitude in recording income that we should examine carefully the procedures used to produce reported earnings. For example, land and franchises may be sold on the instalment plan. Does the seller take in the entire gross income from the sale at the time of sale or spread it over the years during which he receives payment? What method of depreciation is used? Are research and development expenses capitalized or expensed on the books? Is the LIFO or FIFO system of accounting for inventory used? These and similar questions must be answered before we can make a proper evaluation of past earnings of a firm that we propose to purchase or before we can compare the reported earnings of two firms proposing to merge.

Let us say that after removing some non-recurring expenses and adjusting for some vagaries in accounting procedures, we judge the expected normal net operating income before interest and taxes to be $220,000. Our best estimate of future corporate tax rates is 50 percent. On these bases the expected value

$$Y(1 - t_c) = \$220,000(1 - 0.50) = \$110,000.$$

Determining Discount Rate. The discount rate reflects the degree of risk inherent in the business. By risk we mean the variance in the range of possible outcomes around an expected return. Although it is difficult to deal with statistically, we are particularly concerned with downside variance, the risk that successive months of depressed business activity could result in failure of the firm.

The discount rate, k_a, can best be estimated by examining the market valuation of firms in the same line of business. Let us consider, first, the case of firms that, by the nature of their activity, are typically unlevered and, second, levered firms.

Determination of the discount rate for an unlevered firm is relatively simple. The valuation model for an unlevered firm is simply[2]

$$V = \frac{Y(1 - t_c)}{k_a} \tag{22-1}$$

Since we are seeking to determine k_a by examining the market valuation of earnings of other firms, we can rewrite (22-1) as

$$k_a = \frac{Y(1 - t_c)}{V} \tag{22-2}$$

It may help to go one step further and convert the expression to *per share* earnings after taxes and market value per share by dividing earnings and market value by N, the number of shares of common stock outstanding:

$$k_a = \frac{Y(1 - t_c)/N}{V/N} = \frac{EPS}{P} \tag{22-3}$$

In short, the appropriate discount rate for an unlevered firm is simply the ratio of expected earnings per share, *EPS,* to the current market price, *P;* that

[2] In Chapter 3 this was shown as equation (3–6), with the adjustment here that $(1 - t_c) = \theta$.

is, the earnings-price ratio. If we are proposing to acquire a going concern in an industry that is typically unlevered, we would examine other firms in that industry and relate their *expected* earnings per share to their market price per share. To the extent that the firm we propose to acquire is more or less risky than similar firms, we should adjust the discount rate up or down.

As the appropriate discount rate for a *levered* stream of after-tax earnings, we cannot simply use the earnings-price ratios of other firms, even though they are also levered. Now the earnings-price ratio reflects not only the business risk associated with uncertain operating income, but also the financial risk added by the use of financial leverage. Since other firms may employ different degrees of financial leverage, we must allow for this by using the valuation formula for a levered firm:

$$V_L = \frac{Y(1 - t_c)}{k_a} + Dt_c \tag{3-7a}$$

It is, of course, not an easy task to find companies in the same risk class as the firm that we proposed to buy. We seek firms with the same product line, with similar cost structures and market positions. Assume that we find another firm very similar to the one that we propose to acquire. Current market values of its common stock and debt, as well as our estimates of expected earnings are shown below:

Earnings before interest and taxes	$ 200,000
Interest on debt (0.06 × $500,000)	30,000
Earnings before taxes	170,000
Taxes (50%)	85,000
Earnings after taxes	$ 85,000
Market value of debt	$ 500,000
Market value of common stock	750,000
Market value of levered firm	$1,250,000

We can insert appropriate data into formula (3-7a) and then solve for k_a:

$$V_L = \frac{Y(1 - t_c)}{k_a} + Dt_c$$

$$\$1,250,000 = \frac{\$200,000(1 - 0.50)}{k_a} + \$500,000(0.50)$$

$$\$1250 = \$100/k_a + \$250$$

$$\$1250k_a = \$100 + \$250k_a$$

$$\$1000k_a = \$100$$

$$\boxed{k_a = 0.10}$$

Ordinarily, we would make similar calculations for a number of comparable firms. As in the case of valuing an unlevered firm, we could adjust the discount rate if we have good reason to believe that the risks of the proposed acquisition do not match those of the other firms studied.

Estimate Debt Capacity. As might be suspected by now, we again turn to the marketplace to judge the debt limit supportable by the expected stream of operating from the assets that we propose to acquire. Basically, we relate cash flows of similar firms to the level of debt and debt service charges they seem able to support, as well as examine their ratios of debt to equity. In addition, consultation with investment bankers may produce rules of thumb characteristic of our industry.

What if the firm whose assets we propose to acquire already has outstanding debt? How does that affect our estimate of D, and how does it influence the maximum price that we should be willing to pay for the income stream? We should be alert to the possibility that the firm has not made adequate use of debt. If this is the case, the value we estimate for the firm may exceed its aggregate market value, and we have found a bargain. In other words, we should not assume that the firm to be acquired is making optimal use of debt without confirming this by examining comparable companies.

The effect of outstanding debt on our maximum purchase price depends upon whether we plan to acquire only the assets of the firm or its common stock. In either case our first task is to value the stream of income produced by those assets. If we are buying only the assets and do not assume any of the debts of the firm, our maximum purchase price is our valuation of the firm, V_L. If we purchase the common stock, or purchase the assets and assume certain of the debts, our maximum purchase price is then V_L *minus* the market value of the assumed debt.

Assume that examination of the debt positions of comparable firms suggests that the expected stream of operating income should be able to support $600,000 of debt. Then we have

$$D = \$600,000.$$

Calculation of Estimated Market Value. We now have all of the necessary ingredients to calculate the aggregate market value of the levered firm.

$$V_L = \frac{Y(1 - t_c)}{k_a} + Dt_c$$

$$V_L = \frac{\$220,000(1 - 0.50)}{0.10} + \$600,000(0.50)$$

$$V_L = \$1,400,000.$$

Some further adjustments in the estimated market value may be necessary. If some of the assets purchased have not contributed to the operating income, they presumably can be sold without affecting the normal operating income. There might be excessive amounts of cash, inventories, or other assets on hand. The fair market value of these assets (net after any taxes incurred by their sale) should be added to the calculated value of the assets. On the other hand, it may be necessary to pay out additional sums to operate the assets effectively. If we are buying the assets of a hardware store, it may be desirable to pay the former owner not to open another store in competition. Future earnings of a small manufacturing concern may depend upon the purchase of additional machinery or patent rights. Such payments made in order to obtain the estimated normal net income should be subtracted from the value of the assets calculated by capitalization of income. Thus our final adjusted valuation might appear as follows:

Value of levered firm, V_L	$1,400,000
Add: Net market value after taxes of excess inventory	100,000
	$1,500,000
Subtract: Necessary outlays on equipment	50,000
Net value of assets acquired	$1,450,000

Although we have adopted the point of view of an investor considering the acquisition of the assets or common stock of a firm, the same approach holds for a firm proposing to issue common stock to the public for the first time. With no market price on which to base an offering price, the company and its underwriters must value the firm by the same process described above. The aggregate market value of the firm, V_L, less the market value of any debt, yields the estimated total market value of the common stock. We then obtain the estimated market value per share by dividing that figure by the number of shares of common stock that will be outstanding. The process has a certain intuitive appeal, since we have shown this to be the form of analysis pursued by prospective purchasers of the new issue.

Valuation of the New Company

When first starting out in business, we may purchase either the assets or residual ownership of an existing business or acquire the necessary assets piecemeal to form an entirely new firm. Although the basic evaluation process is the same in either case, there are additional considerations related to the method of acquiring the new business. There are many aspects to the formation of a new business, but we shall concentrate primarily on the financial problems involved in the valuation process. Promotion of a new enterprise requires skill in many areas—marketing, finance, production, and law, to name only a few. However, experience suggests that those entering business for the first time are usually weakest in the area of financial management.

Purchase of an Existing Company

This method of entering business has both advantages and disadvantages. Probably the most important advantage is that we may be able to get off to a "fast start." We should already have suppliers and customers, as well as a mix of assets with which to work. This is important financially, because with this existing organization we can immediately begin to realize a return on our investment.

On the other hand, many businesses are offered for sale that are doomed to failure. We have all seen businesses in a poor location that pass from one hand to another. With excellent management the survival period may be stretched out a few months, but in the end another business joins the statistics of business failures. Sometimes the planned scale of operations is too large in relation to the market. A hardware store in a shopping plaza was for sale. Investigation showed that it was impossible to generate enough sales from the surrounding market area to meet the high rental payments for the large floor space occupied. A smaller store would have survived where this one could not. Because of the many opportunities for failure, the reasons for offering a business for sale should be carefully investigated. Sometimes the owner quite legitimately desires to retire or wishes to withdraw because of poor health. We should take care that his poor health is not a direct result of the frustrations of the business.

The first step in the purchase of an existing company is to make an exhaustive survey of the company's financial history to be sure that the income is accurately and fairly reported. As a second step, we must study the possibilities that these earnings will continue at the same rate in the future. Only a few of the many factors that should be investigated can be mentioned here. What about the materials used in the business? A firm manufacturing bricks was recently offered for sale. Although its monopolistic position in the community made it appear to have assured earnings, further investigation revealed that its supply of clay would shortly give out. What about the internal organization? The labor relations of the business should be examined. In some cases certain key officers are important to the future success. Can we arrange to have them continue with the company? The relations of the business with its customers and other outsiders should be ascertained. If the company has had poor customer relations in the past, it will be difficult to regain the good graces of these customers. It will not be enough just to post a sign saying, "Under New Management." What do the firm's banker and suppliers think of the concern's prospects? Will they be willing to continue to extend credit?

Although the value of the business will depend largely upon the estimated market value of the earnings, it will also be influenced by the form of the sale. If a business that is incorporated is purchased, either the assets or the common stock may be acquired. Because the method used will affect income tax payments of both buyer and seller, it will also have a bearing on the price paid. Since this is a fairly complex legal problem, we can only suggest here some of the aspects involved.

Assume first that we buy the common stock. The price paid for the stock will reflect the economic value of the assets, including, for example, the profits yet to be realized on the inventory which is on hand. Thus if $100,000 of finished goods can be sold for a net amount of $180,000, the $80,000 profit will affect the sale price of the common stock. However, when the profit is made, about one-half will be absorbed by Federal corporate income taxes; if we are paid dividends from the $40,000 income remaining after taxes, those dividends are taxed as part of our personal income. Of course, this is unfair, because the $80,000 "profit" is really just a return of part of our original investment. Nonetheless, since combined taxes may leave us with only $20,000, we should seek to adjust our purchase price downward to take account of the taxes to be paid. In contrast, we might obtain the common stock at a price much lower than its book value per share. This would imply that the assets are carried on the books at prices that are very high in relation to their earning power. As a result we might have high depreciation charges and initially realize very small profits on the sale of inventories on hand. Since this would serve to reduce our taxable income, the seller of the common stock might argue for a somewhat higher price.

When buying the assets of a business, we should seek to have the seller draw up the sales contract to allocate the amount paid among the assets acquired in such a way as to minimize later tax payments. Obviously, tax experts should be consulted at an early stage of the negotiations. For example, since land cannot be depreciated, it should be carried at a low value. Inventory should be carried at a high price to reduce the gross margin on sales, and equipment at a high price to raise depreciation charges. Another advantage of buying the assets is that we avoid any contingent liabilities of the old corporation. If somebody is about to sue the old corporation for $500,000, we are better off to buy just the assets and let the old corporation settle its own problems. The final method of sale will depend upon the bargaining powers of seller and buyer. Since both have tax considerations, the purchase price will be adjusted to reflect their respective tax gains and losses.

If we cannot agree on a selling price, it may be possible to effect the sale by offering the seller a contingent payment. If he believes the picture is rosier than we do, we could agree to purchase the firm at a fixed price reflecting our view of the future, but offer him *in addition* a percentage of earnings above some fixed level, or warrants to purchase the common stock at a given price. If his estimates are right, he will gain; if he is wrong, he gains nothing and we lose nothing.

Establishment of a New Company

The alternative to buying a company with an established organization is to set up an entirely new one and build an organization. In this particular instance the process of valuation usually proceeds from an estimate of net income to an estimate of the assets necessary to produce that income. As we shall see, estimates of income and assets may need frequent adjustment before settlement on a final plan. After the method of financing the needed assets is determined, the final step is to decide whether or not the anticipated income provides an adequate rate of return on the necessary investment of the owner.

Scale of Operations. In the establishment of a new business the first objective must be to reach some general conclusion concerning the proposed scale of operations. By *scale* we mean "the particular aggregate of fixed assets with which the enterprise operates and that is not subject to alteration in the short period."[3] From a technical or engineering point of view, there is probably some particular size of plant and mix of machinery and equipment that will enable us to turn out a product at the lowest possible unit cost. But this is only one aspect of scale. For one thing, it may be uneconomical to manage a firm of this size. The market for the product may not be that large, or it may cost too much to reach or create a market of sufficient size. Finally, we may not be able to obtain enough money to build a plant of that size. In other words, in most cases when a business is formed there are certain factors that limit its scale. The limit may be in terms of engineering, economics, managerial ability, market, labor supply,

[3]Norman S. Buchanan, *The Economics of Corporate Enterprise* (New York: Holt, Rinehart & Winston, Inc., 1940), p. 146. See also pp. 141–77.

materials, or capital. Our aim is to discover whether we can make an adequate rate of return, given the scale of operations that seems suitable or possible.

Failure to investigate these limits on scale can be disastrous. A firm was organized to make a new device which would improve the operation of a particular piece of equipment. The price of the item was reasonable in view of its undeniable advantages. The plant was built, and sales were most gratifying during the first year. However, the very poor sales of the following year touched off an investigation which revealed that the sales of the first year had almost completely met the existing need for the item. Since the device needed to be replaced only once every ten years, the company had made all of its foreseeable sales for ten years in its first year of operations. The case of the hardware store that was too large for the available market is similar, except that its death was more lingering.

Estimated Profits. Without past earnings as a guide, it is exceedingly difficult to judge the future net income for a new business. If we have an entirely new product or service, even the price that can be charged is not known, but must be estimated. In other cases, it is possible to set the price at the level prevailing in the market. For example, the prices of haircuts, milk, gasoline, and such items are usually fairly uniform in a community. There then remains the problem of estimating the volume of sales that may be expected at that price. Fortunately for the financial manager, this is primarily a marketing problem.

The costs of producing the estimated volume of sales will depend in large part on earlier decisions concerning the scale of operations, as well as on the particular mix of labor and machinery selected for that scale. Companies that need to maintain flexibility in order to meet cyclical variations in sales or changes in the mix of products will tend to avoid specialized equipment and favor the use of labor rather than machines. Given the scale of operations, total costs will then vary with the output, as indicated in Chapter 10. About the best that can be done is to develop estimates of costs in as much detail as possible at the estimated "normal" output and at the expected normal range of output. In many cases these estimates of costs in relation to sales may be checked against average expense ratios for particular lines of business. Thus if we were considering opening a hardware store, we would compare our estimated expense ratios to the ratios typical for a store of the scale that we have planned. Unusual variations may direct out attention to a need for changing the proposed scale, for revising the selected mix of assets, or for reducing certain expenses.

Estimated Investment Required. The best way to estimate the required investment is to prepare a cash budget and budget of capital expenditures. The cash budget would be based on estimated sales, and the budget of expenditures for capital equipment would depend upon the scale of operations planned. The choice between using equipment or labor, or between different types of equipment, would be based upon the analysis developed in Chapters 8 and 9 insofar as possible. The uncertainties involved in a new business make capital budgeting particularly difficult. From these budgets it should be possible to prepare pro forma balance sheets which will provide estimates of the assets required on opening day and those required six and 12 months later.

An important consideration that many prospective owners fail to realize is that more funds will be needed six months after the opening of business than at the time the business is started. During this period cash will probably flow out more rapidly than it will flow in. On opening day, we will not have any funds invested in accounts receivable, whereas receivables may constitute an important portion of the assets six months later. It will take time to build a clientele, and it will also take money in the form of advertising expenditures, special promotions, and so on. Consequently, losses are likely to occur during the first months of operation. The first year is usually crucial, and during this period the failure rate, especially of retail stores, is very high. In large part these failures are attributable to poor financial management. Funds are sufficient to finance the first week of operations, but the owners have not planned beyond that period.

Pro forma financial statements may also be checked against relationships typical for the type of business. What are the expected average sales per square foot of floor space and per dollar of assets? How does the anticipated turnover of inventory and receivables compare with average turnover of stores of similar size? Because the firms from which industry figures are drawn are not homogeneous, we cannot be slaves to these figures, which represent averages of the best and the worst. However, they may be used to point up unusual variations resulting from our plans.

At this stage we can still change our plans. Possibly the analysis reveals that we will not have enough funds to finance accounts receivable. If so, we can decide not to offer credit during the early years of operation. Maybe the figures for sales per square foot of floor space suggest that the building selected is too large for the market area. Rather than court failure, it would be preferable to wait for a better opportunity. In other words, the planning and checking of plans proceeds on a broad front. With each revision of the scale of operations there must be a change of other plans. It is a whole series of successive approximations based on sound judgment and laced with a certain degree of optimism. The entire process is beset with uncertainties, in part because it is not possible to make accurate estimates; in part because there comes a point when the cost of obtaining additional information does not justify the expected value of the information obtained.

Proposed Financial Plan. Once the need for funds has been determined, we may proceed to formulate plans for raising them. (See Chapter 10.) Because of the great uncertainties surrounding any new business, we should develop a financial structure that minimizes risk and emphasizes maneuverability. This means a reliance primarily on trade credit and equity financing. Whereas large companies will find capital markets fairly accessible, small concerns must be considered fortunate to raise anything beyond what the owner is able to scrape together.

Estimated Value of Investment. Once we have arrived at one "best plan," or maybe two or three alternative "best plans," we must determine whether it is worthwhile to go ahead with the new business. Given the discount rate, k_a, that we find applicable to this line of business and the expected level of net operating income and the debt capacity of the firm, how does the estimated market value of the residual equity $(V_L - D)$ compare to the initial equity investment that is required? By "initial investment" we mean the peak investment; that is, the largest amount of funds that will be committed during the formative months, or even years, of the new business. Usually we should employ a higher discount rate, k_a, when setting up a new business than when purchasing the common stock or assets of an existing business. Without experience as a guide there is a much greater chance of error in estimating the annual operating income and required investment. In addition, most people starting up a new concern are likely to be somewhat overcome with optimism.

If the estimated market value of the equity is less than the initial equity investment required, further revisions of the plans to reduce the scale of initial investment may be needed. We have suggested selling for cash rather than on credit in order to eliminate accounts receivable. Along the same lines we might rent the needed facilities rather than purchase them, or purchase used rather than new equipment. Inventories can be cut in spite of the obvious penalty of a greater number of stock-outs. Functions requiring a large investment in equipment can be shifted to other concerns. Thus we might assemble the final product and subcontract the manufacture of the component parts to others. Although such actions will reduce the required initial investment, they will also tend to lower net income, either by cutting sales or by raising costs of operations. By selling only for cash and reducing inventory, we will probably lower sales. Operation of second-hand equipment is usually more costly than use of new equipment, and we lose to subcontractors a portion of the profit that might have been ours. Consequently, even though we lower the initial investment required, we may not significantly better our rate of return on that investment. In this case it is probably preferable to await a more attractive opportunity to which we may entrust our life savings.

Summary

On infrequent occasions the financial manager must deal with problems of acquiring or establishing a new business, transferring assets from one business to another, or transferring creditors' or owners' claims on assets. In these instances problems of valuation arise. It may be tempting to use a figure bearing some relationship to the balance sheet, such as liquidating value; original cost, less depreciation; or replacement cost, less depreciation. However, such data do not reflect the basic fact that we should buy business assets, not for the pleasure of ownership, but for the joy of receiving income. To value the expected stream of revenues we naturally reach for our valuation model that is based on the appealing assumption that the market value of a levered firm is related directly to the expected net operating income after taxes, its debt limit, and inversely to the degree of risk involved, as explicitly revealed in the discount rate. These estimates are probably subject to greater error when setting up an entirely new business than when purchasing the assets or common stock of an existing company. In the following chapter we shall see how the valuation process is used in the case of transferring assets from one business to another and in exchanging various forms of claims on assets.

Questions

1/ Assume that you own a block of common stock in a company. The liquidating value per share (net after payment of all prior claims) is $40 and the present market value is $32. What are the various possible actions you might take? What factors would you consider in arriving at your decision?

2/ a. In determining the price you are willing to pay for a home, what are the principles upon which you would determine its value?
   b. How are these principles and procedures similar to and different from the principles described in this chapter?
   c. Is it easier or more difficult to value a home than a macaroni factory? Explain.

3/ As a general rule would you expect over the past 20 years to find the book value per share of common stock of existing corporations above or below the market value? Explain.

4/ After you purchase a home, you discover beyond any shadow of doubt that George Washington slept there. What happens to the value of your house? Why? On what basis is its new value determined?

5/ In some states personal loan companies are licensed: that is, new offices cannot be opened without approval of some state regulatory body. Frequently, new offices are prohibited in an area where a "sufficient" number already exist. How does this policy affect the value of existing offices? Explain in terms of the valuation principles set forth in this chapter.

6/ a. What is the effect of rent controls on the value of existing apartment houses subject to the controls?
   b. If building costs rise, what will happen to the value of existing apartment houses—
      (1) which are subject to rent controls?
      (2) which are not subject to rent controls? Does your answer to this latter question indicate that replacement costs determine value?

7/ Two corporations are substantially identical in all respects but one. Discuss the independent effect on the relative values of the common stock of each of the following differences:
   a. One has assets of $100 million and the other, assets of $10 million.
   b. Management is important to the success of each concern. The president of one company is 67; the president of the other, 43.
   c. The debt-to-net-worth ratio of one corporation is 0.4 to 1; of the other 0.1 to 1.
   d. One company distributes its product nationally; the other only in the New England area.

8/ You are preparing an estimate of a firm's normal earnings for valuation purposes. Indicate the adjustments, if any, that you would make in a company's net income after taxes, to take account of the following past events. Make clear any assumptions.
   a. The company lost a patent suit and was forced to pay damages.

b. A dress manufacturer had some poor designs in one year. He estimates these cost $20,000 in sales.

c. A heavy snowfall one winter added $400,000 to the cost of maintenance of a railroad.

d. The state purchased a portion of the company's property, and a substantial profit was realized.

e. The company has recently sold one of its plants.

9/ A plant in a small town in Michigan was recently offered for sale by the Federal government. (It had been a war production facility and had been idle for some time.) When the highest bidder was awarded the plant, he announced that he planned to dismantle it and sell it piecemeal. The citizens were irate and demanded that the government re-offer the plant for sale.

a. On what value did the winning bidder base his bid?

b. What value did the citizens of the community wish used?

c. What explains the differences in these values? Which basis of value would you advocate if you were the government official in charge of disposing of surplus war plants?

10/ Any stockholder-employee of Ted Bates & Co., Inc., a well-known New York advertising agency, "who retires or resigns must sell his stock back to the agency at current book value." ("Does Brainpower Require Capital?" *Business Week,* December 12, 1964, p. 84.) Comment on the suitability of this measure of value for this purpose. Have you a better alternative to propose?

11/ The Seagram Building in New York City has been generally regarded as a particularly attractive building. When it was assessed by tax appraisers at $21 million, the Regional Plan Association criticized the decision as one that "would destroy the hope of great commercial architecture in New York State." The association contended that the assessment should be based, not upon the cost of construction, but upon capitalization of rental income. This approach would have yielded an assessment of about $17 million. The court, however, stated that the building "includes a real property value not reflected in commercial rental income." (*New York Times,* June 13, 1964, p. 25.) What conflicting measures of value are present in this controversy? What approach would you advocate and why?

Problems

1/ Determine the acceptable purchase price of the assets of a corporation on the basis of the following information:

a. Estimated annual net operating income before taxes, $69,600.

b. Estimated debt capacity, $80,000.

c. Estimated discount rate, 12 percent.

d. Marketable government bonds held by company and not needed in business: cost, $80,000; net market value, $86,000.

e. Some unneeded inventory and supplies with a book value of $98,000 may be sold for $140,000. The broker's fee on the sale will be 4 percent.

f. Capital gains taxes at 25 percent apply to the sales of the bonds and regular corporate income tax rates of 48 percent to other income.

2/ Select one company from either list A or list B (Chapter 21, Problem 4).
   a. Be prepared in class to compare its yield, price-earnings ratio, book value, and market price over the past five years with the record of other firms listed.
   b. Can you explain differences between the value investors have placed on the common stock of these concerns?
   c. Would you expect the firms on list A or list B to have the more stable market value? Why? What relationship does this hypothesis have to the valuation model?

3/ Whereas the discount rate, k_a, of a nonlevered firm is merely the earnings-price ratio, we observed that this was not the case for a levered firm. It is possible, and indeed useful, to identify the relationship of the earnings-price ratio of a levered firm to the elements in the valuation model for a levered firm. This can be shown to be:

$$\frac{EPS}{P} = k_a + (k_a - i)(1 - t_c)(D/V_S),$$

where i = interest rate on debt and V_S = market value of the common stock. Show how this result can be derived from the basic valuation model (3-7a). *Hint:* Note that $V_L = V_S + D$.

4/ Clip from your local newspaper an advertisement offering a business for sale. Prepare a detailed check list of the features you would investigate before buying this business.

5/ In December, 1969, General Foods Corporation acquired all of the assets and business of Viviane Woodward Corporation, subject to all of the liabilities, for $38,865,000 in cash (equivalent to $30 per share of outstanding stock). Viviane Woodward manufactured and sold a diversified line of cosmetic and fragrance products.
   The following financial information was available at the time of the sale.

Viviane Woodward Corporation and Subsidiary
Consolidated Balance Sheet
September 30, 1969

Assets

Current Assets:	
Cash	$ 28,951
Certificates of deposit	816,675
Receivables	2,139,657
Inventories	1,699,980
Prepaid expenses	52,944
Total current assets	4,738,207
Equipment and Leasehold Improvements, Net	124,437
Other Assets	76,714
	$4,939,358

Liabilities and Stockholders' Equity

Current Liabilities
Accounts payable and accrued expenses	$ 615,784
Income taxes	412,470
Total current liabilities	1,028,254

Stockholders' Equity:
Common stock (outstanding 1,296,500 sh.)	850,361
Retained earnings	3,060,743
	$4,939,358

Consolidated Statement of Income
Five Years Ended September 30, 1969

Year Ended September 30

	1965	1966	1967	1968	1969
Net sales	$3,584,108	$4,474,458	$5,724,656	$6,845,072	$7,352,985
Cost of goods sold	1,660,721	1,850,865	2,222,375	2,641,042	2,805,625
Gross profit	1,923,387	2,623,593	3,502,281	4,204,030	4,547,360
Selling, general, and administrative expenses	1,401,983	1,783,247	2,170,628	2,689,416	2,849,037
Operating profit	521,404	840,346	1,331,653	1,514,614	1,698,323
Other income, net	29,982	54,872	60,487	100,428	143,595
	551,386	895,218	1,392,140	1,615,042	1,841,918
Interest on long-term debt	38,346	34,022	25,055	3,918	
Income before income taxes	513,040	861,196	1,367,085	1,611,124	1,841,918
Income taxes applicable to above income	271,316	420,540	684,353	817,689	953,393
Income before income tax reduction	241,724	440,656	682,732	793,435	888,525
Income tax reduction from net operating loss carryovers from prior years	4,100				
Net income	$ 245,824	$ 440,656	$ 682,732	$ 793,435	$ 888,525
Net income per share of common stock based on 1,296,500 shares outstanding at September 30, 1969	$ 0.19	$ 0.34	$ 0.53	$ 0.61	$ 0.69

Dividends paid (none)

Book value per share at September 30, 1969	$ 3.02

Market Prices

The Company's Common Stock was traded in the over-the-counter market. Set forth below are market quotations for the Company's stock since trading commenced for the periods indicated as reported by the National Quotation Bureau, Inc. These prices do not include retail markup, markdown or commissions.

	Bid		Asked	
Period	High	Low	High	Low
1967	34	$7\frac{3}{4}$	$34\frac{1}{4}$	$8\frac{1}{8}$
1968				
First Quarter	31	$19\frac{1}{2}$	$31\frac{1}{4}$	20
Second Quarter	34	24	$34\frac{1}{2}$	$24\frac{1}{4}$
Third Quarter	$30\frac{1}{2}$	$25\frac{1}{2}$	$30\frac{3}{4}$	$25\frac{3}{4}$
Fourth Quarter	34	$26\frac{1}{2}$	$34\frac{3}{4}$	27
1969				
First Quarter	28	$23\frac{3}{4}$	$28\frac{1}{2}$	$24\frac{1}{4}$
Second Quarter	28	23	$28\frac{1}{4}$	$23\frac{3}{4}$
Third Quarter	$23\frac{1}{2}$	$18\frac{3}{4}$	$20\frac{3}{4}$	$20\frac{1}{2}$
Fourth Quarter (through November 28)	28	$19\frac{3}{4}$	$28\frac{1}{4}$	$20\frac{1}{4}$

On November 5, 1969, the date of public announcement of an agreement in principle between the Company and General Foods Subsidiary, the high bid and low asked prices of the Company's Common Stock as reported by the National Quotation Bureau, Inc., were $23\frac{3}{4}$ and $24\frac{1}{4}$, respectively.

a. How do you explain the great disparity between book value and market value per share?

b. Based on the valuation formula (3-7a), how do you justify the price of $30 per share paid by General Foods? Do the assumptions on which that model rests apparently hold here? Can you change the model to make it more applicable to this situation?

Selected References

BERANEK, W., *Common Stock Financing, Book Values and Stock Dividends: The Theory and the Evidence.* Madison, Wisc.: University of Wisconsin, 1961.

BERNHARD, A., *The Evaluation of Common Stocks.* New York: Simon and Schuster, Inc., 1959.

BONBRIGHT, J. C., *The Valuation of Property.* 2 vols. New York: McGraw-Hill Book Co., 1937. The classic study on the subject of valuation.

BOSLAND, C. C., "The Valuation of Public Utility Enterprises by the Security and Exchange Commission," *Journal of Finance,* 16 (March, 1961), pp. 52–64.

————, *Valuation Theories and Decisions of the Securities and Exchange Commission.* New York: Simmons-Boardman Books, 1964.

COTTLE, S. and T. WHITMAN, *Corporate Earning Power and Market Valuation, 1935–1955.* Durham, N.C.: Duke University Press, 1959.

GORDON, M. J., *The Investment, Financing and Valuation of the Corporation.* Homewood, Ill.: Richard D. Irwin, Inc., 1962.

————, "The Savings, Investment, and Valuation of a Corporation," *Review of Economics and Statistics,* 44 (February, 1962), pp. 37–51.

HELFERT, E., *Valuation: Concepts and Practice.* Belmont, Calif.: Wadsworth Publishing Company, Inc., 1966.

JOHNSON, L. R., E. SHAPIRO and J. O'MEARA, Jr., "Valuation of Closely-Held Stock for Federal Tax Purposes: Approach to an Objective Method," *University of Pennsylvania Law Review,* 100 (November, 1951), pp. 166–95.

KOTLER, P., "Elements of a Theory of Growth Stock Valuation," *Financial Analysts Journal,* 18 (May–June, 1962), pp. 35–44.

MALKIEL, B. G., "Equity Yields, Growth and the Structure of Share Prices," *American Economic Review,* 53 (December, 1963), pp. 467–94.

MARGOSHES, S. L., " 'Present Value' Techniques of Stock Valuation," *Financial Analysts Journal,* 17 (March–April, 1961), pp. 37–42.

MOLODOVSKY, N., "Stock Values and Stock Prices," Part I, *Financial Analysts Journal,* 16 (May–June), 1960 pp. 9–12; Part II, 16 (July–August, 1960), pp. 53–64.

MOONITZ, M., "The Valuation of Business Capital: An Accounting Analysis," *American Economic Review,* 41 (May, 1951), pp. 157–65.

SCHIFF, M. and S. ARBESFELD, "Goodwill—A Make-or-Buy Approach," *Management Accounting,* 47 (August, 1966), pp. 25–35.

WEED, J. B., "Techniques in Valuation of Close Corporations," in New York University, *Proceedings of the Twentieth Annual Institute on Federal Taxation.* Albany, N.Y.: Matthew Bender & Co., 1962.

Merger and Consolidation

23 In this chapter we shall continue to demonstrate the application of the principles of valuation developed in the preceding chapter. We have pointed out that valuation is involved at the birth of a new business. Here we shall show that it must also be applied at two other possible stages in the life cycle of a company. Because one method that a business may use to expand is through combination with other concerns, we shall first consider the application of valuation principles to this situation. At the same time we shall note some of the methods or procedures used to effect business combinations. Second, many business concerns fall into financial difficulties of varying degrees. Since one way out of these difficulties is to persuade existing security holders to adjust their claims or exchange their old securities for new ones, principles of valuation must also be applied to these situations.

Companies involved in the more elaborate financial maneuvers are almost always organized as corporations. Although our discussion will be related to corporations, the approach may also be applied to other forms of business.

However, the changes described are usually facilitated by the corporate form of organization.

Forms of Combination

Let us begin with a bird's eye view of the techniques of business combination. In the first place, we may purchase either the assets or the common stock of the business that we seek to acquire. Second, we may pay for these acquisitions either with cash or with the common stock (or other securities) of our own corporation. Third, there are various possibilities concerning the final form of the combination. If we have acquired the assets of the other company, we will have merged the two companies, or at least portions of two companies. In contrast, if we acquire the common stock of another company, the resulting combination may take the form of a holding company, merger, or consolidation. These various alternatives are illustrated below:

Acquire	Means of payment	Resulting form of combination
Assets	Cash	Merger
	Stock, or other securities	
Common stock	Cash	
	Stock, or other securities	Holding company
		Merger
		Consolidation

At the outset let us also distinguish as clearly as possible between the various forms of combination. A *holding company* is a corporation that owns a controlling interest in the voting stock of one or more other corporations. The companies that are controlled are referred to as *subsidiaries*. Review of the earlier discussion of methods of voting for directors will suggest that a holding company does not need to own a majority of the voting stock or another corporation to have effective working control. Frequently, ownership of only 10 percent of the stock will be sufficient, although we then might not refer to the companies controlled as "subsidiaries." In all cases both the holding company and its subsidiaries continue to exist as separate corporations. Schematically, we might indicate a combination of two corporations via a holding company as $A + B = \dfrac{A}{B}$. A *merger* may be defined as a combination of two businesses in which only one corporation survives, while the merged corporation goes out of existence and leaves its assets (and possibly liabilities) to be combined with those of the surviving corporation. In this form of combination, $A + B = A$. *Consolidation* involves the fusion of two or more corporations into a third, entirely new corporation, which absorbs the assets (and probably liabilities) of the old corporations, which then pass out of existence. Thus, in a consolidation, $A + B = C$. In general discussions the difference between these terms is often unclear. Let us now examine these forms of combination in somewhat greater detail.

Holding Company

The first step in a combination is frequently the formation of a holding company. Common stocks of another company can be purchased without great difficulty or the need for formal approval by either group of stockholders. If purchases are made gradually, there need be no marked rise in the price of the stock, whereas if it were known that we were attempting to gain control, we might be forced to pay a much higher price. After we have acquired control we may live with the situation for a while and test the suitability of a later "marriage" between the two companies. If the trial marriage proves that the companies are incompatible, it is quite simple gradually to sell the stock that was acquired and disengage from the situation.

Another important reason for the use of the holding company device is that control over extensive amounts of assets may be achieved by a relatively small investment on the part of the residual owners. To illustrate this principle, which is really an improved version of financial leverage, let us assume that we have working control of corporations by ownership of 20 percent of their common stock. We shall assume that preferred stock is non-voting. For illustrative purposes we shall consider the possibilities with an electric utility empire and follow the characteristic capital structure proportions for electric utilities.

Under our assumptions it is possible to control the holding company with an investment of $1.2 million (20 percent of $6 million). In turn the holding com-

Holding Company
(amounts in millions of dollars)

Assets		Liabilities	
Common stock investments		Long-term debt	$ 8
Company A	$ 8	Preferred stock	2
Company B	8	Common & surplus	6
	$16		$16

Subsidiary Company A		Subsidiary Company B	
Long-term debt	$ 53	Long-term debt	$ 53
Preferred stock	13	Preferred stock	13
Common & surplus	40	Common & surplus	40
Total assets & total liabilities	$106	Total assets & total liabilities	$106

pany holds one-fifth of the common stock of the two subsidiaries. Through the device of a holding company an investment of $1.2 million controls working assets at the subsidiary level of $212 million. In other words, control is achieved by an investment amounting to about 0.6 percent of the assets at the operating level. The high degree of financial leverage embodied in this structure means that any variation in earnings at the operating level is greatly magnified at the holding company level.

In addition to the attractions of control and leverage, some holding companies are created in response to restrictive state laws. Many state laws favor domestic corporations, i.e., corporations chartered by the state, in relation to "foreign corporations" which are chartered by other states. Taxes may be lower, and there are often other differences in treatment. In such cases, it is often desirable to maintain the holding company structure when operating in a number of states. For example, when personal loan companies expand by purchasing the common stock of firms in other states, they often keep the newly acquired corporations as subsidiaries chartered in the state within which they do business. If they merged the subsidiary into the parent concern, the loan offices would then be offices of a foreign corporation (assuming the parent is chartered in some other state). Still another reason for maintaining the holding company structure is to avoid risks of lawsuits or other contingent liabilities which may be characteristic of the subsidiary's business.

There are important disadvantages to the holding company device. The parent corporation must pay a tax on 15 percent of the dividends received from subsidiaries. This tax would be avoided by a merger or consolidation. There are added costs of maintaining separate organizations and separate corporate relationships. The task of managing and coordinating the activities of two distinct corporations is usually more difficult. Because directives must pass through the board of directors of the subsidiary, response may be slow and hesitant. If the parent concern does not own 100 percent of the subsidiary's stock there are minority interests who may harry the board of directors of the subsidiary. It might be preferable to deal with these minority groups once and for all in a merger or consolidation rather than put up with their legal maneuvering over several years. Finally, holding companies are generally viewed with disfavor by the public and by some regulatory bodies, largely because the device has been so abused in the past.

Because of their disadvantages, many holding companies give way to a more formal type of combination. There are two methods by which this may take place. The two companies may be combined under the procedures described in the following section, or the subsidiary may pay over its assets to the parent company in the form of a liquidating dividend. In either case the subsidiary would be dissolved.

Merger and Consolidation

Since these methods of combination differ but slightly in their financial implications, they will be treated together. In each case the boards of directors of the companies that are about to join pass identical resolutions proposing the combination and specifying the terms. After approval of these resolutions by a majority to three-fourths of the stockholders (depending upon the state laws), the merger or consolidation may proceed. Various documents must be filed with the appropriate offices of the state, and possibly approval of some regulatory commission must be secured. Dissenting stockholders have a right to a separate determination of the value of their shares. They then sell their shares to the corporation at that price, and the shares are canceled. When these formalities are concluded, securities of the surviving corporation are given in exchange for the securities of the expiring corporation (merger); or securities of an entirely new corporation are given in exchange for the securities of both of the old corporations (consolidation).

A large and small corporation will usually be combined through a merger, whereas large companies of about equal size will adopt the consolidation device. In part the choice is based on human factors; no group of directors and officers wants to accept the "second best" implication necessarily involved in being merged into another company. Sometimes the surviving corporation has certain features in its charter that are especially desirable, or if both charters are deemed to be too restrictive, a consolidation may be chosen. In other cases we may wish to exchange new securities for existing obligations that have some especially awkward or restrictive covenants.

There are three basic types of mergers and consolidations. A *vertical merger* (or consolidation) is a combination of firms involved in different stages of production of the same product; e.g. an automobile manufacturer merging with a steel company. A *horizontal merger* is a combination of firms in the same line of business; e.g. the combination of two chains of grocery stores. Finally, a *conglomerate* is a firm that has grown through the merger of companies in unrelated lines of business.

The Merger Movement

At the beginning of 1960, Gulf & Western Industries was a rather lack-lustre manufacturer of automobile bumpers. Sales of $8,400,000 produced a slight deficit. But then Gulf & Western became a conglomerate. Eight years and 80 acquisitions later, Gulf & Western had sales of $1.3 billion and a net income of $69,800,000.[1] Many other firms, especially conglomerates, had similarly spectacular records of growth. In this section we shall review briefly the growth in the number of mergers and then examine with care the reasons for this merger movement. Finally, we shall look at the performance of merged firms to see if they have fulfilled their promises, let alone their hopes.

The Growth of Mergers

The recent decade has been marked by the greatest merger movement in history. The number of mergers occurring during 1970 was about ten times the number that took place in 1950, even though there was a slight decline in the number of mergers from the previous year. Just in the five years from 1965 to 1969, the number of mergers increased by almost three times (Exhibit 23-1). Under the pressure of tight money, low liquidity, and the depressed stocks of some of the leading conglomerates, the number of mergers during the first half of 1970 was 2719, down slightly from the 2815 that occurred during the same period in 1969.[2]

A recent feature of the merger movement has been a decrease in the size of transaction (Exhibit 23-2). This trend probably reflects a number of forces. The increased interest by the Justice Department in the growth of mergers has undoubtedly reduced the number of mergers between large firms. The decline in the stock prices of the major conglomerates made them relatively unattractive merger partners. For example, the common stock of Gulf and Western sold as high as $66 in 1968, but as low as $9.50 in 1970. Liquidity problems and high interest rates also made it difficult to combine large firms. Finally, there was an increasing tendency to merge with divisions of firms, rather than with entire companies. For example, in the first half of 1970, sales of company divisions

---

[1] Arthur M. Louis, "Ten Conglomerates and How They Grew," *Fortune,* 79 (May, 1969), p. 208.
[2] W. T. Grimm & Co., "1970 Midyear Merger Summary," p. 1.

EXHIBIT 23-1   Merger Transactions by Medium of Payment

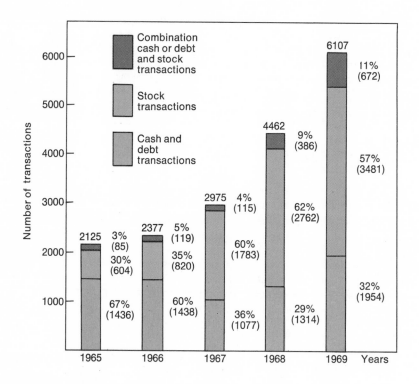

Reproduced by permission of W. T. Grimm & Co., 135 South La Salle Street, Chicago, Illinois 60603. The firm's "Merger Summary" is available on a subscription basis.

accounted for 24 percent of all merger activity, compared to only 12 percent in the same period of the previous year.[3]

Economic Reasons for Merger

Let us first examine the alleged economic reasons for mergers. To focus our analysis, we must understand that the basic objective of a merger should be to combine two or more firms so that the market value of the merged firm is greater than the market values of the firms operating as independent entities. In symbols, a merger is justified from an economic point of view only if

$$V_L(A) + V_L(B) < V_L(AB). \tag{23-1}$$

This being the case, it should be clear that a merger is economically justi-

[3] *Ibid.*

EXHIBIT 23-2   Analysis of Mergers by Size of Transactions
(First Six Months, 1970 and 1969)

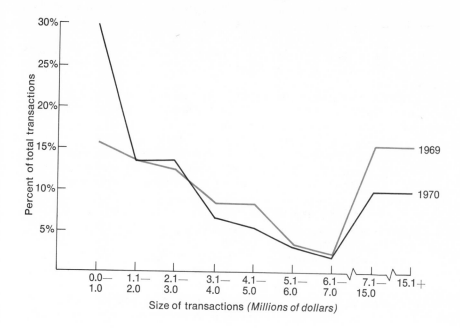

Reproduced by permission of W. T. Grimm & Co.

fied only if it raises the market value of the merged firm by affecting one or
more of the determinants of the market value made explicit in our valuation
formula:

$$V_L = \frac{Y(1 - t_c)}{k_a} + Dt_c .$$ (23-2)

Let us examine the effect of a merger on each of the components of the
valuation model.

[Y.] How can we improve the expected net operating income before interest and taxes? An improvement in Y must arise in operating advantages of some
sort. But there is no merit to a merger if the acquisition price already reflects
the anticipated operating savings. For example, it is argued that an acquisition
of another firm enables the acquiring company to enter a new field quickly,
without the delay in realizing income that would occur if it were to build a new
plan and launch a marketing effort. This is, of course, true. However, the assertion overlooks the fact that these advantages are probably already reflected
in the market value of the firm to be acquired. A firm that is currently established
in a given field will surely be valued at a relatively higher price than one that is
just beginning and must wait months or even years before it will realize a net
operating income as attractive as that enjoyed by an established firm. In short,

speed of entry is an advantage of a merger, but probably not a *net* advantage in view of the price that must be paid to achieve that result.

More persuasive arguments for merger lie in various operating economies that might generally be classified as economies of scale. A currently popular buzz word in some academic circles is *synergism,* or "2 + 2 = 5." The concept is that if we put two separate entities together, we can achieve certain operating economies such that the value of the whole is greater than the sum of its parts.

A merger does offer opportunities for economies of scale. We may be able to acquire management skills that are needed or permit the spreading of existing management skills over a larger operation — with a consequent improvement in net operating income, Y. There are opportunities to consolidate the functions of production, marketing, purchasing, personnel, and so on, in order to eliminate duplicate facilities and redundant personnel. We may be able to fill out product lines, so that the same salesmen can sell six products rather than four at no significant increase in selling cost. Theoretically, these economies of scale should be most readily available in horizontal mergers, where facilities and functions can be combined, and least accessible in conglomerate mergers, where diverse businesses are brought together.

Are the theoretical advantages of "synergism" realized in fact? The answer from available research is "Rarely." One study based upon intensive field interviews concluded that "far from producing the biggest payoff, production and technology are at the bottom of the list of dollar producers through synergy; marketing shows up better; and finance is clearly the area where synergy has the biggest payoff."[4] The advantage of combining the finance function lies in the greater ease of integrating financial activities and the lower cost of capital available to firms selling large blocks of securities. Although real, the dollar amounts of such savings are small compared to the alleged, but often unrealized, advantages of economies of scale in production and marketing.

A recent statistical study found that acquiring firms had a significantly worse performance than other firms in their industry, with a total annual gain that was five percent less than the average for their industry.[5] Thus conclusive evidence does not exist to support the realities of economies of scale — or synergism, if you insist — although there have undoubtedly been mergers where net operating income was improved by combining facilities and functional areas.

Finally, another way of raising the net operating income, Y, through merger is through greater power over the market. The alleged advantages of large size from mergers are reciprocal dealing (buying from one another), exclusive dealing (forcing customers to buy our products, rather than a competitor's), tie-in sales (if you want my product A, you must also buy my product B), predatory pricing, and prevention of potential competition.[6] Such results are indeed

[4]John Kitching, "Why Do Mergers Miscarry?" *Harvard Business Review,* 45 (November–December, 1967), p. 93.

[5]Thomas F. Hogarty, "The Profitability of Corporate Mergers," *Journal of Business,* 43 (July, 1970), pp. 317–27.

[6]James H. Lorie and Paul Halpern, "Conglomerates: The Rhetoric and the Evidence," *Journal of Law and Economics,* 13 (April, 1970), pp. 149–66.

possible from increased market power, but they are also illegal. In addition to policing these activities, the Justice Department and the Federal Trade Commission have directed increasing attention to the merger movement and have prevented a considerable number of proposed mergers. In short, if we perceive market power as a means of raising net operating income, our merger is likely to be prevented. If we are permitted to merge, we are likely to have a difficult time exercising that market power.

$\boxed{(1 - t_c).}$ Some have argued that a reason for mergers is to acquire firms with a large tax-loss carry forward. As this is applied to the acquiring firm's earnings, its effective tax rate, t_c, is reduced, with a consequent rise in net operating income after taxes. This argument overlooks two aspects. First, if tax-loss carry forwards are valuable, we can expect the market value of the acquired firm to reflect this fact. Hence, merger in itself may not result in an increase in value for the merged company. Second, we must remember that t_c also appears in the second term of the valuation model (Dt_c) preceded by a plus sign; that is, a reduction in t_c at that point lowers the market value of the firm. In other words, although a reduction in the tax rate improves the firm's net operating income after taxes, it also reduces the advantage of financial leverage by lowering the tax shield provided by interest payments.[7]

It seems more likely that the impetus to merger comes from the acquired firm. With a record of heavy losses and increasing liquidity problems, that company seeks a partner to save it from bankruptcy. To find a partner it may have to offer itself at a bargain price.

$\boxed{k_a.}$ One of the most widely asserted advantages of mergers, especially conglomerate mergers, is that through diversification a merger reduces the risk of the residual owners and thereby the discount rate, k_a. As risk is lowered, so the argument goes, the value of the merged firm exceeds the values of the companies operating independently. A variant of this is the price-earnings argument. If a high risk, low-price-earnings ratio company is acquired by a low-risk, high price-earnings firm, the common stock of the merged firm will somehow reflect the best of both possible worlds, and all stockholders will benefit. The argument is most frequently advanced with respect to conglomerates and least frequently for horizontal mergers.

The contra-argument to this assertion is precisely the same as that advanced in our discussion of capital budgeting. Unless returns are perfectly correlated, it will always be true that the merger of two firms will result in a narrower dispersion of expected net operating income. Since investors are risk averse, they view this favorably. But they can achieve this same result by diversifying their own investment portfolios. Hence, *they will not pay anything extra to have a conglomerate do this for them.*

Indeed, a valid argument can be made that a conglomerate is *less* efficient at diversification than the individual investor. Therefore, investors will pay less

[7]An interesting case is provided by the merger of Montgomery Ward and Container Corp. Because of its instalment sales, Wards was able to defer a substantial portion of its federal income taxes. However, its earnings were so low that it was unable to benefit fully from the tax shield. When the earnings of the two firms were combined in Marcor, Inc., the new firm in effect was "able to defer the federal income tax on Container's earnings for a considerable period of time." "The Tax Laws, Bless 'Em," *Forbes*, 102 (December, 1968), p. 27.

for the conglomerate than for the two firms as separate entities.[8] There are two reasons for this. First, the conglomerate's investments must necessarily be "lumpy." It must have whole companies or at least very large pieces of companies, whereas an individual investor can balance his portfolio with whatever fractional shares of companies that suit his risk-return aspirations. Second, a conglomerate cannot acquire certain companies, either because of their size (such as General Motors Corp.) or because of frowns from the Justice Department. The individual investor is not so restricted and therefore can achieve what for him is a more efficient balance of risk versus return.

In summary, the discount rates, k_a, of the individual firms prior to merger will already reflect the advantages that they offer to investors who seek diversification. By combining these firms, we do nothing for the investor that he cannot do himself. Hence, he will, if rational, pay nothing extra for the service, and he may pay somewhat less, since the conglomerate is less efficient at matching his personal requirements for diversification than he is.

$\boxed{Dt_c.}$ The possible financial advantages of merger are reflected in this second term of our valuation model. Can a merger raise Dt_c for the merged firm above the sum of Dt_c for the individual firms prior to merger? There are two possibilities.

First, it is possible that one of the firms was not making sufficient use of debt. We have seen in our discussion of cost of capital that a firm will enhance its market value by increasing its use of debt up to its debt limit. This result stems from the tax-deductibility of the interest on the debt. If a firm is not making adequate use of debt, it will be undervalued in the marketplace. We can acquire it, possibly by trading debt for its outstanding common stock. The market value of the merged firm will then exceed the market values of the firms as independent entities.

The contra-argument to this possibility applies to the general assertion that the merger movement is a result of clever acquisition-minded managers ferreting out undervalued companies. There are occasionally such discoveries, particularly among unlisted firms. But reason must suggest to us that it is not common enough to explain the great proportion of mergers. We must remember that the market is constantly being reviewed by investors, both individuals and institutions. It is hard to believe that any significant or sizeable undervaluation goes unnoticed for long, whether that undervaluation stems from an unnoticed improvement in earnings or a sub-optimal use of debt. We have no reason to believe that the managers of acquiring companies are significantly more (or less) shrewd than the managers of the numerous insurance companies, investment companies, and trust funds. But we strongly suspect that, having recognized an undervalued company, managers of conglomerates will take longer to effect a merger than it will require an investor to place an order for the stock. In fact, the announcement of the possibility of merger will attract attention to the stock and very likely cause it to be bid up to a level such that it is no longer undervalued.

Second, it is entirely possible, indeed likely, that a merger will permit the

[8] K. V. Smith and J. C. Schreiner, "A Portfolio Analysis of Conglomerate Diversification," *Journal of Finance,* 24 (June, 1969), pp. 413–28.

merged firm to borrow more than the two firms were able to borrow independently. In short, the merged firm has a relatively larger debt capacity than the independent companies. Since it can increase Dt_c, it can increase its value above the combined market values of the independent firms.[9]

Statistically, it may be shown that if we merge two streams of expected cash flows, the dispersion about the mean of the merged stream will be relatively less than the dispersion about the independent means prior to merger, unless the income streams are perfectly correlated. The amount that lenders are willing to provide a corporation is dependent upon their estimate of the likelihood that the corporation will default; that is, the probability that one or more years of insufficient cash flows will prevent its meeting required payments on the debt. Thus if iD represents the required dollar amount of interest payments on the debt, lenders are worried about the size of the shaded area, in the probability distribution function over expected before-tax cash flows, A', shown below. The larger the area, the more likely are lenders to add restrictive covenants and to reduce their loans.

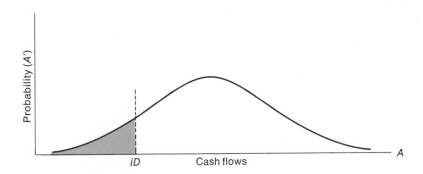

But what happens if we combine Corporation X and Corporation Y, whose cash flows are not perfectly correlated? If the merged corporation assumes the debts of its constituents, the combined cash flows will usually provide greater protection for its lenders, and never less. This is represented by the probability distributions over expected cash flows shown on the following page.

In essence, we are saying that "within the family" the merged corporation can divert cash flows from Division X to Division Y, if the latter's cash flows are insufficient to support its debt payments. The lender cannot do this when loaning to *Corporation* X and *Corporation* Y, independently. He cannot phone Corp. X and say "Corp. Y is a little short this month; would you mind making up the deficiency." He can make the call, but the answer will not be to his liking. Whereas a conglomerate's diversification does nothing for its stockholders that they cannot do for themselves, it can provide a greater certainty of cash flows to cover payments on debt than lenders can provide for themselves. Thus, lenders should

[9]This analysis is based upon W. G. Lewellen, "A Pure Financial Rationale for the Conglomerate Merger," *Journal of Finance*, 26 (May, 1971).

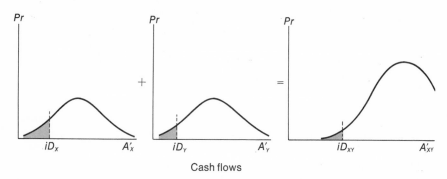

Cash flows

be willing to provide relatively more debt, *D,* to a merged firm than to the un-merged firms independently, and the evidence suggests that they do. This advantage of merger is particularly available to conglomerates, and not a significant factor in horizontal mergers, where we would expect returns to be highly correlated. With the greater debt, the value of the merged firm should be greater than the sum of its parts, and we have a rational financial justification for merger.

Non-Economic Reasons for Merger

Having explored the economic reasons for mergers, let us turn to some non-economic reasons. For the most part these must be considered as transitory, since they relate to some accounting procedures that acquisition-minded companies were permitted to use in reporting profits. In each case the procedures permitted the firms to create an apparent record of growth that attracted capital and encouraged even more mergers. In fact, in some instances the only way to maintain the fiction was to keep merging. Since a full discussion of the issues can be treated better by accountants, we shall cover them only briefly here.

One popular method of financing acquisitions has been the use of convertible debentures and convertible preferred stock. These were either issued directly for the common stock of the acquired firm or sold to purchase the common stock. Since the financial leverage was favorable, this method of financing boosted earnings per share and created an aura of rapid growth. More recently, requirements for reporting earnings on a fully diluted basis (Chapter 17) has significantly reduced the attractiveness of this method of financing. For example, in a recent prospectus AMK Corp. listed "primary" earnings at $3.36 per share, but was required also to show them at a fully diluted basis as $2.19 per share.[10]

A great deal of controversy has been generated by procedures used to report the earnings of a merged firm. In *purchase accounting* any excess of the consideration paid over the current fair value of an acquired company is shown as goodwill. Under a recent ruling of the Accounting Principles Board of the American Institute of Certified Public Accountants this goodwill must be written off over at least 40 years. Such write-offs will slightly depress earnings, although the ruling is not retroactive.

[10] "The Fine Points Have a Hefty Clout," *Business Week,* October 18, 1969, p. 130.

The more popular procedure has been a *pooling-of-interest*. Under this method the balance sheets and income statements of the merging companies are simply combined in the financial reports of the surviving firm, and the financial histories of the merged firms are combined and stated retroactively. By a judicious merger towards the end of its fiscal year a conglomerate can thus pump up its reported earnings per share and provide investors with an impression of rapid growth. Nor is the acquiring firm required to write off any excess that it may have paid over the fair value of the acquired firm. More important, since assets acquired are recorded at their book value (at most) they may later be sold at their market value, thus creating "instant profits" to add further to the semblance of growth. The Accounting Principles Board has recently limited pooling-of-interest accounting to mergers that are arranged through an exchange of stock and that meet certain other technical requirements. All other transactions must be treated as purchases. Since over half of recent mergers have been on such a basis (Exhibit 23-1), the rules provide considerable leeway and are much less strict than those originally proposed.

Deconglomeration

The gradual tightening of accounting principles will place greater emphasis on mergers that are justified on basic economic grounds. Accompanying this change is a trend apparent merely by observing executive bulletin boards. Whereas executive training programs of the 1960's were directed to the techniques of effecting successful mergers, those of the early 1970's have turned to the procedures for divestiture, or getting rid of the bad apples acquired earlier. Obviously, what is a divestiture for one firm is often an acquisition for another, but the change in emphasis is notable. Conglomerates also spin off divisions as separate companies by selling their shares to the public or by distributing their shares as dividends.

Part of the pressure for divestiture comes from a scramble for cash to meet debts. Some of the subsidiaries dumped are money losers. Others are separated under pressure from the Justice Department. Whatever the initiating force, the basic economic justification for de-merging should be the same as for merging. If the market value of the parent firm will be increased, the division should be dropped. The difference between conglomeration and deconglomeration is not a matter of theory, but more a function of popularity.

Terms of Combination

Acquisition: Assets Versus Stock

The relative merits of acquiring a business through acquisition of assets or stock has been covered for the most part in the previous chapter in the discussion relating to the establishment of a new business. In comparison with other methods of acquiring a business, purchase of assets has the merit of avoiding any or all liabilities of the selling company. When FMC Corp. purchased the operating assets of American Viscose Corp. for $116 million cash, it also assumed Avisco's liabilities, but excluded claims for income tax refunds and liabilities for income taxes. Thus any tax headaches of Avisco were not transmitted to FMC. In addition to possible tax advantages, purchase of assets also has the merit of being simple. All that is needed to effect the sale is the approval of the board of directors of both companies and the consent of the stockholders of the selling corporation. Sometimes state laws make it difficult to acquire another business through purchases of stock if the two corporations involved are chartered in different states. In other cases the purchasing corporation desires only a portion of the assets of the selling company, or the selling corporation is willing to dispose of only part of its assets.

The procedures for handling a sale of assets are quite simple. After approval by the stockholders of the selling corporation, the assets are transferred in exchange for either cash, stock, or other securities. If the selling corporation distributes the receipts from the sale to its stockholders as a liquidating dividend, it then gives up its corporate charter and ceases to exist. Occasionally, the selling corporation may continue in business with whatever portion of its assets remain. Strictly speaking, if the selling corporation continues in existence, the combination should not be termed a merger.

There are legal provisions protecting the creditors and stockholders of the selling corporation when assets are sold. Often the purchaser assumes whatever obligations attach to the assets acquired, such as mortgage bonds. The claims of any remaining creditors must be met by the selling corporation before any payments are made to the owners. Stockholders who believe that the sale does not provide a fair value for their interests may request the court to prevent the sale or ask the court to award them more for their stock.

If a holding company or consolidation is deemed to be the desirable form of combination, control of another business must be obtained through acquisition of its common stock. This method may be especially suitable when we wish to obtain a controlling interest gradually, possibly without the owners being aware of our intentions. It is sometimes easier to force combination with this procedure. Whereas dissident stockholders may succeed in blocking the sale of assets, under the laws of some states we can force a merger if we obtain a sufficiently high percentage of the voting stock (e.g., 95 percent in New York).

Payment: Cash Versus Securities

We can see in Exhibit 23-1 that in recent years about three-fifths of mergers have involved an exchange of stock, while the others have been either straight cash purchases or transactions employing a combination of cash and securities. What determines the choice of the means of payment?

The acquiring company may prefer to exchange common stock or other securities for the securities of its partner for several reasons. Although the same securities could presumably be sold on the market to the public and the acquisition made for cash, the direct exchange of securities avoids the underpricing and flotation costs that would accompany a public issue. An exchange of stock may be favored because it permits a pooling-of-interest accounting for the merger. The desirability of that approach depends in part upon the acquiring firm's objective. If it wishes to emphasize rising earnings (but also rising taxes), it will choose a pooling-of-interest. If it would prefer to acquire assets at their current market value, with a consequent increase in depreciation charges and lower future profits (and taxes), it may opt for a cash purchase and use purchase accounting for the merger.

The desires of the seller must also be considered. Let us assume that an individual originally formed a corporation and purchased the common stock for $5 a share. After operating the company with considerable success over many years, he now wishes to diversify his holdings and avoid the valuation problems that would occur upon his death. If he sells his stock to another company for cash at $65 per share, he will immediately pay a capital gains tax on the profit of $60 per share. However, if he properly carries out the transaction, he can postpone this tax by exchanging his shares for $65 worth (market value) of the common stock of the corporation that is acquiring his company. The transaction is then treated as a tax-free exchange of securities.[11] No capital gains tax is payable until the subsequent sale of the newly-acquired securities. This postponement of tax payments has merit because of the time value of money. Because of the tax advantages of the exchange we may succeed in giving the seller something less than $65 per share of market value of our stock. In other cases the seller wishes to maintain a partial ownership interest in the surviving business. If we plan to have the seller participate in the management of the new or surviving company, it would probably be advisable to offer him common stock in exchange for his assets in order to obtain his eager application to his new duties. On the other hand, if the seller desires cash to form a new business, or to refurbish his old one, then nothing but cash will do. It would probably be unwise to exchange stock for his assets or stock, because he would promptly sell the stock to raise cash. If a substantial block were involved, his sales could depress the price, or the stock might fall into the hands of a rival group.

Many other considerations may influence the choice between cash or stock in acquiring another business, but tax considerations are paramount. The brief discussion here should not be taken as definitive, but only as a note of warning to seek expert legal advice.

The Exchange Ratio

A crucial issue in a merger or consolidation is the *exchange ratio;* that is, the number of shares of common stock of the acquiring corporation that are to be exchanged for outstanding shares of the acquired corporation. Let us examine the considerations involved in setting the exchange ratio.

In applying principles of valuation to a business combination, we have the same problem that we had in acquiring a new business. We must value the stream of income that we anticipate receiving from the assets together with the organization. In the case of a business combination, there are two going concerns to

---

[11]Occasionally, even debentures may be exchanged for common stock on a tax-free basis. In the merger of Seaboard Finance Company into Avco Corporation, stockholders of Seaboard were given a choice between $5\frac{1}{2}$ percent convertible subordinated debentures or $7\frac{1}{2}$ percent subordinated debentures plus warrants to purchase common stock of Avco. Under specified conditions stockholders could elect to have any gain taxed on an instalment basis, with the result that "if a stockholder holds the Debentures until their maturity he may postpone taxation of 5% of his gain for 24 years and the remaining 95% for 25 years." *Prospectus*, "Exchange Offer to Holders of Common and Convertible Preferred Stock of Seaboard Finance Company," December 20, 1968, p. 7.

value rather than one. However, there is one further complication. Operated as independent units, each of the companies has an earning power of its own. Can we assume that the earning power of the companies joined together through a holding company, merger, or consolidation will be the sum of the earnings they would be able to achieve when operated independently? In other words, if Company A may be expected to have a normal net income of $70,000, and Company B a normal net income of $80,000, can we judge the expected earnings of Company AB to be $150,000? If so, there is hardly any operational justification for the combination, except that the president of the new company may be able to join a better country club. In short, we must first estimate the normal earnings to be expected from the *combined* business, taking into account the expected economies of operation, monopoly power, and other valid reasons for the combination. Let us say that our best estimate of expected earnings after taxes is $180,000. The next step is to estimate the contribution of the constituent companies to that income. Thus we must value the companies being fused, not as independent units, but as parts of the whole. In the same way, we value a lathe, not as an independent piece of equipment, but in terms of its contributions to earnings through operation with other pieces of equipment and the organization.

Let us follow through a consolidation to see how these principles might be applied. Consider the following information available on Corporations A and B, which are to be consolidated into Corporation AB.

	Corporation A	Corporation B
Current assets (net)	$150,000	$100,000
Fixed assets (net)	450,000	700,000
Total assets	$600,000	$800,000
Current liabilities	$ 70,000	$ 60,000
Bonds	60,000	
Preferred stock ($100 par)		100,000
Common stock ($100 par)	400,000	500,000
Earned surplus	70,000	140,000
	$600,000	$800,000
Shares of common stock outstanding	4,000	5,000
Estimated normal net income	$ 70,000	$ 80,000
Estimated combined net income	$180,000	

For the moment let us assume that we can persuade the holders of the bonds and preferred stock to exchange their securities for those of Corporation AB. In this case the combined assets, liabilities and preferred stock would appear as follows:

Corporation AB

Current assets (net)	$ 250,000	Current liabilities	$ 130,000
Fixed assets (net)	1,150,000	Bonds	60,000
		Preferred stock ($100 par)	100,000
		Common stock	?
		Capital surplus	?
	$1,400,000		$1,400,000

We can issue any number of shares in the new corporation that we wish. The number of shares issued will determine the market price of the new stock. If 1000 shares are issued, the estimated earnings per share would amount to $180 $\left(\frac{\$180,000}{1000}\right)$. Should the normal price-earnings ratio be 10 to 1, stock would sell for about $1800 a share, clearly a price that is too high for ready marketability. In contrast, if 180,000 shares were issued, the earnings per share would amount to $1, and the market price would be about $10. This price might be too low for our tastes; it gives an implication of being a "cheap" or speculative stock that we may not desire. As a compromise, let us decide to issue 60,000 shares. With this number of shares outstanding the estimated earnings will be $3 per share and the market price about $30.

We can set any par value we wish on this new stock (or have no par value). Since assets total $1,400,000 and debt and preferred stock, $290,000, the common stock portion of the equity must make up the balance of $1,110,000. We can distribute this common equity between common stock and capital surplus any way we want. If the par value is set at $1 per share, the common stock equity portion of the balance sheet would then appear as shown below:

Common stock ($1 par)	$ 60,000
Capital surplus	1,050,000
Total common stock equity	$1,110,000

Since there may be some tax advantages to having a low par value, let us settle on the $1 par figure. Furthermore, this arrangement provides the uninitiated with a healthy appearance on the balance sheet in the form of a large surplus.

Now we face the basic valuation problem: How shall the 60,000 shares of Corporation AB's common stock be distributed to the stockholders of Corporations A and B? Theoretically, the final distribution should be based upon the value of the contribution by each company to the combined net income. One firm may contribute valuable patents or fixed assets and managerial talent that have previously not been fully utilized. The value of these factors would be greater to the combination than to the company which supplied them. Consequently, the stockholders of that company should receive a greater share of the stock of the new company than might be warranted by their previous net income.

However, theory must give ground to the relative bargaining positions of the two parties. In this bargaining the officers of each company will stress the particular valuation technique that gives their company the most favorable position in the merger. Thus the stockholders of Corporation A might argue that distribution of the new stock should give weight to their favorable current ratio, whereas the stockholders of Corporation B might argue for a distribution based upon the value of fixed assets contributed. Many intangible considerations influence terms of the merger. If the chief officers of Corporation A are nearing retirement, and there are no suitable successors, stockholders of that concern may accept somewhat less than their "fair share" of the new issue. Thus the final agreement might allocate 25,000 shares to the stockholders of Corporation A and 35,000 shares to the stockholders of Corporation B. Under this exchange ratio stockholders of Corporation A would receive $6\frac{1}{4}$ shares of "AB" stock for each share of "A" stock $\left(\frac{25,000}{4000}\right)$; stockholders of Corporation B would receive 7 shares of "AB" stock for each share of "B" stock.

In a merger or consolidation it may also be possible to induce holders of bonds or preferred stock to accept less remunerative securities. This again is a matter of valuation. We might persuade the holders of 7 percent bonds in Corporation A that $6\frac{1}{2}$ percent bonds in Corporation AB would have the same value because of the more reliable interest coverage of the latter concern. If the merits of the argument failed to move them, we might be able to call the 7 percent bonds and float a less costly issue through Corporation AB. Nor is it necessary that we issue only common stock in exchange for the common stock of Corporations A and B. Some desirable leverage may be obtained by offering some bonds or preferred stock as well as common stock in exchange. Should the major stockholders of Corporation A desire a more certain income than would be provided by common stock, a combination of bonds and common, or preferred and common, might meet their needs. In each case, however, they will question whether the securities of Corporation AB that they receive are of greater value than the securities they presently hold. Unless they are convinced that the value received is greater, there is little incentive for them to proceed with the consolidation.

If we reach an impasse, the merger may be facilitated by a deferred payment plan contingent upon reaching a certain level of earnings or by issuance of stock purchase warrants. As an example of the former arrangement, CNA Financial Corp. agreed to acquire the Larwin Group (home-building and financing) for $100 million in CNA stock "and the promise of $100 million more if Larwin's earnings double over a five-year period."[12] Loew's Inc. granted over 6,470,000 warrants in the acquisition of P. Lorillard Co. Each warrant entitles the holder to buy one share of Loew's at prices ranging from $35 to $40. The Loew's common stock was selling for about $47 at the time. Such arrangements provide a hedge against too low a price having been paid at the time of the acquisition by giving the seller a contingent claim on the future earnings of the acquiring company.

Negotiations leading toward a merger or consolidation may be carried out directly between representatives of the companies involved or through an intermediary, such as an investment banker, consulting firm, commercial banker, or accounting firm. Not infrequently the "marriage broker" helps to design the financial structure, the exchange ratios, and provides advice on the legal, tax, and S.E.C. issues.

Methods of Avoiding Acquisition

Mergers are not always a result of mutual consent. If it is rebuffed in its suit to acquire another company, an acquisition-minded concern may appeal directly to the shareholders of the desired company by a public offer to purchase their

---

[12]*Wall Street Journal*, June 6, 1969, p. 20.

EXHIBIT 23-3 Offer to Exchange Shares

EXCHANGE OFFER

TO HOLDERS OF COMMON STOCK OF

AMERICAN SMELTING AND REFINING COMPANY

American Smelting and Refining Company ("Asarco"), by its Offering Circular dated July 31, 1970, is offering to exchange 2,820,590 shares of common stock of General Cable Corporation ("Cable Stock") for Asarco Common Stock on the basis of

1.35 SHARES OF COMMON STOCK OF
GENERAL CABLE CORPORATION
PLUS $8.50 IN CASH FOR
ONE SHARE OF COMMON STOCK OF ASARCO

subject to the terms and conditions set forth in the Offering Circular. The maximum number of shares of Asarco Common Stock which may be exchanged on the foregoing ratio is 2,089,325 shares.

THE EXCHANGE OFFER WILL EXPIRE AT 3:30 P.M.
NEW YORK TIME ON AUGUST 17, 1970, UNLESS EXTENDED

If more than the maximum number of shares of Asarco Common Stock are tendered prior to the expiration of the Exchange Offer on August 17, 1970, the Exchange Agent will allot the Cable Stock and cash among the tendering shareholders on a pro rata basis as provided in the Offering Circular.

Shareholders tendering on or before August 17, 1970 will retain the 47½¢ dividend per Asarco share payable August 31, 1970 to holders of record August 7, 1970.

Copies of the Offering Circular and Letter of Transmittal may be obtained from the Exchange Agent or from Kuhn, Loeb & Co., 40 Wall Street, New York, N. Y. 10005.

EXCHANGE AGENT

By Mail

The Chase Manhattan Bank N.A.
Post Office Box 2437
Church Street Station
New York, N. Y. 10008

Hand Delivery

The Chase Manhattan Bank N.A.
Corporate Agency Division
1 New York Plaza, 14th Floor
New York, N. Y.

This announcement is neither an offer nor a solicitation of an offer to acquire, dispose of or exchange any of these securities. The offer is made only by the Offering Circular.

AMERICAN SMELTING AND REFINING COMPANY
New York, N. Y.

shares. Stockholders may be asked to tender (i.e., offer to sell) their shares for cash or in exchange for securities (Exhibit 23-3). The request for tenders is preferred to a proxy contest, because it is relatively less costly and produces a quick resolution of the battle for control.

Management seldom views a raid by outsiders placidly. What methods are available to fight off an unwanted suitor? A common ploy is quickly to find an alternate marriage partner. For example, when Greatamerica Corp. sought control of Glidden Co. by asking for tenders on its common stock at $30 per share, Glidden's management quickly arranged a merger with SCM Corporation. The exchange of common stock of SCM for Glidden was valued at $35 per share.[13] Similarly, Commercial Credit Co. successfully fended off seizure by Loew's Theatres Inc. by merging with Control Data Corp. Loew's had to be content with a profit of over $20 million on the shares it had previously acquired.

Another means of avoiding a take-over is to acquire a firm that would make a merger with the raider questionable from a legal point of view. Thus, when B. F. Goodrich was attempting to fend off a tender offer from Northwest Industries, a holding company that included a railroad among its subsidiaries, it acquired Motor Freight Corp., a trucking concern. The Interstate Commerce Commission could be counted on to view a merger of a railroad and trucking company as objectionable. Similarly, a company might acquire a firm in the same line of business as that of the raider. Then it could complain plaintively to the Justice Department that a merger with the corporate raider should be blocked as a violation of anti-trust laws.

Still another ploy has been to amend articles of incorporation to require approval of a merger by a greater proportion of the shareholders. Corporations have changed the procedure for electing directors, so that only one-third are to be elected each year, thereby substantially delaying any takeover. For example, Goodrich introduced staggered terms for its directors, so that Northwest could not possibly win a majority of the board for two years. The raider's voting control may also be diluted by issuing additional common stock in exchange for securities of other companies.

Finally, management of the raided company typically engages in a vigorous campaign of letters and advertisements to its stockholders (at their expense) decrying the offer. Lawsuits against the raider are frequently instituted. For example, when Sinclair Oil "received a tender from Gulf & Western, Sinclair got an injunction in Austin, Texas, from a judge who then disappeared for days before Gulf & Western attorneys could find him."[14]

Are mergers and consolidations, whether friendly or not, in the interests of shareholders and the community at large? To the extent that they are based upon imaginative accounting practices, they are probably not warranted. However, we must recognize that acquisitions, even in the form of a corporate "raid," are likely to be more effective than proxy contests in unseating inefficient management. The often remarkable increases in the value of common stock as a result of a takeover bid (Commercial Credit from $32 to $53) suggests that

[13] *Wall Street Journal,* May 17, 1967, p. 4.

[14] "How Companies Fend off Suitors," *Business Week,* March 15, 1969, p. 88.

either value has gone unrecognized in the market or that the market looks forward eagerly to new management. In either case the shareholders are better off and resources more efficiently allocated. In this sense corporate "raids" serve as a beneficial economic force. Although efforts to fight off corporate raiders are entirely understandable, the fact remains that the best way to avoid a take-over is to run the business right in the first place.

Summary

There are three basic forms of business combination: holding companies, merger, and consolidation. Most of our discussion has centered on the latter two forms of combination.

The pace of the great merger movement of the 1960's has slackened in the early 1970's, partly as a result of more intervention by the Justice Department and partly through some tightening of accounting procedures. More than ever, mergers and acquisitions must be justified from an economic point of view. The most successful mergers are likely to result from operating economies and an enlarged capacity to bear debt. Mere diversification, as practiced by some conglomerates, should not raise the value of the merged firm, since stockholders can provide self-diversification, often more efficiently than the conglomerates.

The methods by which a combination is effected are many. The choice of acquiring assets or stock in exchange for cash, securities, or securities and cash is strongly affected by tax laws. Although the exchange ratio is similarly affected, the basis usually represents an approximation of the relative contributions of each merging firm to the market value of the surviving corporation.

In general, the possibility of merger and acquisition, of corporate raids and proxy fights, is probably a healthy influence in the market. They are means of driving actual market prices to their true values, of weeding out inefficient management, and of achieving a more efficient allocation of economic resources.

Questions

1/ Over the years, the annual number of mergers and consolidations has generally moved with the level of business activity. How would you explain this close relationship?

2/ If recognizable economies of operation can be achieved by business combination, would there still be instances in which you would wish to prevent combination from the point of view of public policy?

3/ Under the Public Utility Holding Company Act of 1935 regulated public utility holding companies are permitted to have only three "layers" — a top holding company, an intermediate company, and operating subsidiaries.

a. What benefits do you believe result from this restriction? Who benefits?

b. Should the same regulation be applied to the industrial field? Support your conclusion.

4/ If a company has suffered losses for a number of years and may be expected to do so in the future, could it have any value when merged or consolidated with another concern (aside from its tax-loss carry forward)? Explain your answer.

5/ Is it possible to form a strong company by combining two or more financially weak concerns? Explain.

6/ Would you recommend a law requiring that if owners of 95 percent of the outstanding stock approve the terms of a merger, the remaining minority group must also accept the terms of the merger? Support your position.

7/ On February 24, 1969, Rep. Wilbur Mills (D., Ark.) introduced H. R. 7489, a bill "Relating to the tax treatment of certain indebtedness incurred by corporations in acquiring stock of other corporations." The bill had two main features:

(1) "It would disallow the acquiring company's tax deduction on any more than 35 percent of the interest on debt from an acquisition by purchase of stock, where more than 35 percent of the price paid to acquire the stock consisted of bonds and debentures . . . and cash raised from borrowing."

(2) "It would prevent the sellers of the stock from deferring payment of tax on their profits from the sale by denying them the use of the installment method of reporting under Section 453 (b) of the Internal Revenue Code of 1954, where the total of cash, bonds, and debentures received in the year of the sale exceeded 30% of the sales price." *The Conglomerate Merger Tax Proposal* (Washington, D.C.: American Enterprise Institute, 1969), p. 13.

Evaluate the effects of this proposed legislation and its desirability from a standpoint of public policy.

Problems

1/ In the hypothetical illustration of a holding company shown in the text, assume that the interest paid on long-term debt is 8 percent and the dividend rate on the preferred stock is 9 percent. Assume the corporate tax rate to be 50 percent. Only 15 percent of the dividend income received by the holding company is counted as income for purposes of calculating corporate income taxes.

a. If each subsidiary had earnings before interest and taxes of 21 million, and all the earnings available were paid out, what would be the dollar amount of earnings available for the common stockholders of the holding company?

b. If EBIT of the subsidiaries fell by 10 percent, by what percentage would the earnings available for the common stockholders of the parent company decline?

2/ During 1970, the directors of Tech, Inc. proposed to acquire all of the property and assets of View Corp. by exchanging shares of Tech common stock for the outstanding shares of View Corp. Financial and other data for the two companies are provided below. On the basis of the information what should be the basis of the exchange; that is, how many shares or fractions thereof of View Corp. should be exchanged for each share of Tech, Inc. common stock?

Market Values

	View — Per Share Bid Price		Tech — Per Share Sales Price	
	High	Low	High	Low
1968:				
First Quarter	$34\frac{1}{2}$	15	$138\frac{1}{4}$	$77\frac{1}{4}$
Second Quarter	19	15	$121\frac{5}{8}$	$82\frac{1}{8}$
Third Quarter	$19\frac{1}{2}$	16	$112\frac{3}{4}$	82
Fourth Quarter	$27\frac{1}{2}$	18	$107\frac{1}{2}$	88
1969:				
First Quarter	$24\frac{3}{4}$	$16\frac{1}{2}$	$93\frac{3}{4}$	$58\frac{3}{4}$
Second Quarter	$17\frac{3}{4}$	$12\frac{3}{4}$	$80\frac{3}{4}$	$58\frac{1}{2}$
Third Quarter	$13\frac{1}{2}$	$9\frac{1}{2}$	$65\frac{3}{4}$	$47\frac{1}{2}$
Fourth Quarter	$14\frac{3}{4}$	$10\frac{1}{2}$	79	$53\frac{3}{8}$
1970:				
First Quarter	$17\frac{3}{4}$	11	$90\frac{1}{4}$	$56\frac{7}{8}$
April 2, 1970	14	$13\frac{1}{2}$	$67\frac{7}{8}$	$64\frac{3}{8}$

On Wednesday, October 29, 1969, the day preceding the first public announcement of the exploration of merger possibilities, the sales prices of Tech Common Stock on the New York Stock Exchange ranged from $70\frac{1}{8}$ to $73\frac{5}{8}$ and the bid prices for View Common Stock ranged from $11\frac{1}{4}$ to $11\frac{1}{2}$. On Monday, November 17, 1969, the day preceding the public announcement of the proposed merger, the sales prices of Tech Common Stock on the New York Stock Exchange ranged from $70\frac{5}{8}$ to $72\frac{3}{4}$ and the bid prices for View Common Stock ranged from $12\frac{1}{2}$ to $13\frac{3}{4}$.

Assets and Capitalization

On December 31, 1969, Tech had assets of $74,483,822. Tech's book value per share on that date was $21.27. Tech had a total capitalization of $54,363,609, including $938,489 of long-term debt and $3,276,427 of short-term debt.

On December 31, 1969, View had total assets of $16,321,564. Its book value per share was $5.43. It had a total capitalization of $14,106,616, including long-term debt of $2,555,357, and short-term debt of $5,444,643.

Business of Tech and View

Tech is engaged primarily in the business of designing, developing, fabricating and marketing equipment and supplies to gather, record, display or reproduce information through the application of optical, photo-optical, electro-optical and electronic technologies and systems. Tech's Government business consists principally of the design, development and production of: (1) aerial reconnaissance systems, including advanced optics and photographic and related data handling equipment, and (2) electric countermeasures systems and equipment. Its commercial business consists principally of the manufacture and distribution of (1) equipment and supplies for document copying and reproduction and (2) commercial optical products. During 1969, Tech's Government business accounted for approximately 63% of its net sales of $153,152,310; its commercial business accounted for approximately 37% of such sales.

View is engaged primarily in the manufacture of ophthalmic products and other materials used for the protection and improvement of human vision. These products and materials include principally glass and plastic lenses and frames for prescription eyeglasses. The company also distributes machines and systems (some made by itself and the balance by others) for the processing of lenses in the wholesale laboratories maintained by customers, and sells various types of supplies which these wholesale laboratories require in their regular operations.

Tech, Inc. and Subsidiaries
Consolidated Statements of Earnings (Loss)

	1965	1966	1967	1968	1969
			(Covered by Report of Independent Public Accountants)		
Net Sales and Revenues from Contracts	$79,100,114	$98,384,607	$132,885,595	$130,027,438	$153,152,310
Costs and Expenses					
Cost of Sales	58,540,462	71,961,645	97,391,387	99,221,584	110,987,732
Selling, General and Administrative Expenses	15,045,463	18,125,743	24,944,722	27,177,301	32,000,010
Total Costs and Expenses	73,585,925	90,087,388	122,336,109	126,398,885	142,987,742
Operating Income	5,514,189	8,297,219	10,549,486	3,628,553	10,164,568
Other Income (Expense)					
Interest Expense	(520,744)	(654,183)	(478,686)	(579,103)	(849,644)
Other, net	91,964	(149,351)	44,439	109,807	168,237
Income From Continuing Operations					
Before Federal Income Taxes	5,085,409	7,493,685	10,115,239	3,159,257	9,483,161
Provision for Federal Income Taxes	2,176,000	3,343,000	4,749,000	1,388,000	4,735,000
Income From Continuing Operations	2,909,409	4,150,685	5,366,239	1,771,257	4,748,161
Income (Loss) From Operations Discontinued in 1968 net of Federal income taxes	68,212	(129,368)	(480,099)	(1,000,264)	—
Income Before Extraordinary Items	2,977,621	4,021,317	4,886,140	770,993	4,748,161
Extraordinary Items, net	—	—	—	(23,017)	—
Net Income	$ 2,977,621	$ 4,021,317	$ 4,886,140	$ 747,976	$ 4,748,161
Weighted Average Number of Common and Common Equivalent Shares Outstanding	2,025,800	2,092,900	2,246,300	2,336,600	2,350,600
Earnings Per Share of Common and Common Equivalent Shares					
From Continuing Operations	$1.44	$1.98	$2.39	$1.76	$2.02
From Discontinued Operations	.03	(.06)	(.21)	(.43)	—
Extraordinary Items, net	—	—	—	(.01)	—
Net Income	$1.47	$1.92	$2.18	$ .32	$2.02

Tech, Inc. has followed a policy of investing all earnings in its business and no cash dividends have been paid. It is expected that the same policy will be followed in the foreseeable future.

View Corp. and Subsidiaries
Consolidated Statements of Earnings (Loss)

	Year Ended December 31,				
	1965	1966	1967	1968	1969
Income:					
Net Sales	$15,455,986	$16,293,043	$16,503,255	$16,403,667	$24,112,438
Other income, net	57,522	95,325	73,508	82,039	173,207
	15,513,508	16,388,368	16,576,763	16,485,706	24,285,645
Costs and Expenses:					
Cost of products sold	8,980,973	9,985,540	10,785,610	11,185,114	15,581,653
Marketing, administrative, product development, etc	4,732,096	4,537,710	4,756,278	4,504,878	7,829,354
Interest	–	–	45,978	135,324	659,446
	13,713,069	14,523,250	15,587,866	15,825,316	24,070,453
Earnings from continuing operations before taxes on income and extraordinary items	1,800,439	1,865,118	988,897	660,390	215,192
Provision (Credit) for Taxes on Income:					
Federal	721,000	743,000	558,000	299,000	136,000
Puerto Rican	121,000	117,000	(113,000)	16,000	(24,000)
	842,000	860,000	445,000	315,000	112,000
Earnings from continuing operations before extraordinary items	958,439	1,005,118	543,897	345,390	103,192
Net earnings (loss) of operations to be terminated in 1970	26,352	17,597	31,367	(6,874)	(76,593)
Earnings before extraordinary items	984,791	1,022,715	575,264	338,516	26,599
Extraordinary Items:					
Anticipated loss relating to termination of operations of the Omnitech Division	–	–	–	–	(250,000)
Costs relating to pending litigation	–	–	–	–	(89,625)
Net earnings (loss)	$ 984,791	$ 1,022,715	$ 575,264	$ 338,516	$ (313,026)
Earnings (Loss) Per Share:					
From continuing operations	$.90	$.92	$.49	$.32	$ .09
From operations to be discontinued	.02	.02	.03	(.01)	(.07)
Extraordinary items	–	–	–	–	(.31)
Net earnings (loss)	$.92	$.94	$.52	$.31	$ (.29)
Cash Dividends Per Share	$.36	$.42	$.42	$.25	$ .15

Selected References

ALBERTS, W. W. and J. E. SEGALL (eds.). *The Corporate Merger.* Chicago: University of of Chicago Press, 1966.

ARANOW, E. R. and H. A. EINHORN, "The Takeover Bid," *Financial Executive,* 36 (October, 1968), pp. 80ff.

AUSTIN, D. V., "A Defense of the Corporation Pirate," *Business Horizons* (Winter, 1964) pp. 51–58.

BOCK, B. *Mergers and Markets,* New York: National Industrial Conference Board, Inc., 1962, 1964.

BRILOFF, A. J., "The 'Funny-Money' Game," *Financial Analysts Journal,* 25 (May–June, 1969), pp. 73–79.

COHEN, M. F., "Takeover Bids," *Financial Analysts Journal,* 26 (January–February, 1970), pp. 26–29ff.

COHEN, M. H., "Tender Offers and Takeover Bids," *Business Lawyer,* 23 (April, 1968), pp. 611–20.

"Conglomerates and Other Modern Merger Movements," Proceedings, ABA National Institute, *Business Lawyer,* 25 (January, 1970), pp. 555–881.

ECONOMOS, A. M., "A Financial Simulation for Risk Analysis of a Proposed Subsidiary," *Management Science,* 15 (August, 1969), pp. 675–82.

GORT, M. and T. F. HOGARTY, "New Evidence on Mergers," *Journal of Law and Economics,* 13 (April, 1970), pp. 167–84.

HOGARTY, T. F., "The Profitability of Corporate Mergers," *Journal of Business,* 43 (July, 1970), pp. 317–27.

KEMP, B. A., *Understanding Merger Activity—Assessing the Structural Effects of Acquisitions.* New York: New York University, Institute of Finance, 1969.

JACOBY, N. H., "The Conglomerate Corporation," *Financial Analysts Journal,* 26 (May–June, 1970), pp. 35–38.

KELLY, E. M., *The Profitability of Growth through Mergers.* University Park, Pa.: Pennsylvania State University, 1967.

KENNEDY, W. M., "Tender Moment," *Business Lawyer,* 23 (July, 1968), pp. 1091–1114.

KITCHING, J., "Why Do Mergers Miscarry?" *Harvard Business Review,* 45 (November–December, 1967), pp. 84–101.

KRASIK, C., "Tender Offers: The Target Company's Duty of Disclosure," *Business Lawyer,* 25 (January, 1970), pp. 455–76.

LEONTIADES, M., "Another Look at Conglomerates," *Financial Analysts Journal,* 25 (May–June, 1969), pp. 80–86.

LEVY, H. and M. SARNAT, "Diversification, Portfolio Analysis and the Uneasy Case for Conglomerate Mergers," *Journal of Finance,* 25 (September, 1970), pp. 795–802.

LEWELLEN, W. G., "A Pure Financial Rationale for the Conglomerate Merger," *Journal of Finance,* 26 (May, 1971).

LORIE, J. H. and P. HALPERN, "Conglomerates: The Rhetoric and the Evidence," *Journal of Law and Economics,* 13 (April, 1970), pp. 149–66.

MACE, M. L. and G. G. MONTGOMERY, Jr. *Management Problems of Corporate Acquisitions.* Boston: Division of Research, Harvard Business School, 1962.

MANNE, H. G., "Mergers and the Market for Corporate Control," *Journal of Political Economy,* 73 (April, 1965), pp. 110–120.

MCCARTHY, G. D. *Acquisitions and Mergers.* New York: Ronald Press, 1963.

MEADE, W. J., "Instantaneous Merger Profit as a Conglomerate Merger Motive," *Western Economic Journal,* 7 (December, 1969), pp. 295–306.

MEYER, J. E., "Determining the Optimum Tender Offer Price," *Financial Executive,* 37 (August, 1969), p. 70ff.

O'HANLON, T., "The Odd News about Conglomerates," *Fortune,* 75 (June 1967), pp. 175–177ff.

REUM, W. R. and T. A. STEELE, III, "Contingent Payouts Cut Acquisition Risks," *Harvard Business Review,* 48 (March–April, 1970), pp. 83–91.

SEGALL, J., "Merging for Fun and Profit," *Industrial Management Review,* 9 (Winter, 1968), pp. 17–29.

SHAD, J. S. R., "The Financial Realities of Mergers," *Harvard Business Review,* 47 (November–December, 1969), 133–46.

SILBERMAN, H., "A Note on Merger Valuation," *Journal of Finance,* 23 (June, 1968), pp. 528–34.

SMALTER, D. J. and R. C. LANCEY, "P/E Analysis in Acquisition Strategy," *Harvard Business Review,* 44 (November–December, 1966), pp. 85–95.

SMITH, K. V. and J. C. SCHREINER, "A Portfolio Analysis of Conglomerate Diversification," *Journal of Finance,* 24 (June, 1969), pp. 413–28.

TINCHER, W. R., "Yardsticks for Evaluating Corporate Acquisitions," *Management Review,* (October, 1964), pp. 33–45.

VANCE, J. O., "Is Your Company a Take-Over Target?" *Harvard Business Review,* 47 (May–June, 1969), pp. 93–98.

WESTON, J. F., *Planning for Corporate Merger.* Los Angeles: Division of Research, Graduate School of Business Administration, University of California, Los Angeles, 1963.

WHITMAN, M. J., "The Strategy of Tender Solicitations," *Financial Executive,* 35 (November, 1967), pp. 63–64ff.

WYATT, A. R. and D. E. KIESO, *Business Combinations: Planning and Action.* Scranton, Pa.: International Textbook Company, 1969.

Failure and Reorganization

24 Many companies find themselves in financial difficulties at one time or another. Sometimes earnings are not as great as originally anticipated. At other times management has failed to adjust adequately to fundamental economic changes that have taken place. Not infrequently management proves to be incapable of directing the business; very often failings of managerial ability are particularly noticeable in the area of financial management. Finally, some companies are struck down by external forces, such as floods and strikes, over which they have little control and can gain no reasonable protection.

What public policies should guide the handling of these situations of financial stress? As a first objective, we should attempt to preserve as going concerns those companies which can make a significant contribution to the economy as measured by the rate of return that may be expected on the investment required. Since the value of assets in a going concern is usually considerably above their liquidating value, it is often in the interests of the economy to set up informal and formal arrangements to continue and rehabilitate financially distressed companies. In the second place, we still want to make it possible for companies to fail and go out of business. If creditors and owners are forced as a matter of public policy to keep their funds in a failing business rather than remove them for reinvestment in more attractive alternatives, resources will be poorly allocated within the economy. Furthermore, it would be difficult to finance business concerns if the suppliers of funds did not have some procedures available for withdrawing their investment if their contracts were not fulfilled. Our third objective must be to define very clearly the rights of creditors and owners in times of financial difficulty and then adhere to these definitions. For example, we cannot expect to borrow long-term funds unless we grant certain prior claims on income and assets. In the event of some financial readjustment or even liquidation of the company, these claims must be supported by the courts. Otherwise, suppliers of long-term funds will hold back from the capital market to the subsequent disadvantage of the economy. This process is illustrated by the difficulties of obtaining funds for investment in some foreign countries. Without a reasonably clear understanding of their right to withdraw profits or interest, without certainty of their claims on income and assets, investors are loath to commit funds in these countries. If they are to obtain the capital that is necessary to economic growth and development, these countries must allow the withdrawal of profits and interest, develop stable governments which can enforce the rights of creditors, and protect foreign investors against the seizure of their assets.

There are many degrees of financial difficulty. The greater the difficulty, the more drastic must be the remedy. Also, the larger the company, the more formal must be the arrangements to adjust the financial difficulties. If the company is small, or the financial problem is not especially acute, the owners may initiate the remedial action. To deal with greater financial strain, the owners may involuntarily submit to actions forced by the creditors, or occasionally they may take steps to speed the readjustments that will inevitably be sought by the creditors. We shall deal with voluntary and involuntary adjustments to deal with financial difficulty. However, we shall touch only briefly on the very complex legal issues involved.

Voluntary Adjustments

Adjustment of Cash Flows To Meet Obligations

At the first sign of impending difficulty in meeting obligations to creditors, the financial manager should take steps to adjust his cash flows to fulfill his commitments. On the one hand, we may attempt to increase cash inflow by selling accounts receivable to a factor or by reducing inventories through special sales. It may be possible to sell all or a portion of the plant and then lease the necessary facilities. In recent years some of the conglomerates that have faced difficulties in meeting payments on their debts have been forced to sell entire divisions to raise needed cash. On the other hand, it may also be possible to reduce cash outflows by cutting salaries and eliminating dividends to preferred and residual owners. Expenditures for advertising, remodeling, new equipment, and so on, should often be postponed. Payments to trade creditors may be slowed, although with the inevitable damage to our credit reputation. If the financial cancer has not progressed too far, we may be able to substitute some intermediate- or long-term debt for existing short-term debt. This process is called *funding,* in contrast with *re*funding, which involves the replacement of of one long-term debt issue with another.

Voluntary Adjustment of Obligations To Meet Financial Capabilities

In many cases the adjustments of cash flows prove to be only a temporary expedient or insufficient to deal with the financial emergency. It then becomes necessary to request creditors to adjust their claims to come within the limits of our financial abilities. As we shall see later, the creditors have the alternative of refusing our plea and forcing the liquidation or reorganization of the business.

There are several types of adjustment that we might seek. Sometimes a company has borrowed funds from its owners or officers. In order to give other creditors, such as the bank, a senior claim on assets in the event of liquidation, the owners and officers may agree to a *subordination* of their claims. This arrangement may so strengthen the position of the senior creditors that they will agree not to demand prompt settlement of their claims. This type of arrangement is the origin of the subordinated debentures discussed in Chapter 17.

In other cases we may be able to persuade short- or long-term creditors to agree to an *extension:* that is, to a postponement of the maturity of the troublesome debt. Such arrangements are most typically made by a small business with its major trade creditors. In return for their agreement to extend the term of their credit, creditors often ask for concessions and some form of assurance that the debt will be paid under the new and longer terms. For example, trade creditors may demand promissory notes which bear interest and mature at regular intervals. We may also have to agree not to increase officers' salaries or pay dividends. In the infrequent cases of extensions of long-term debt, bondholders have been offered a higher interest rate, mortgage security, conversion privileges, and other inducements.

A more extreme form of adjustment of obligations to meet financial capabilities is a *composition.* Under this type of arrangement creditors agree to accept a partial payment in final settlement of their claims, say 60 cents on the dollar. A portion of the settlement is frequently in the form of promissory notes. Compositions are most characteristic of small companies, because of the difficulty of persuading the more numerous and widely-scattered creditors of large corporations to agree to such arrangements.

Finally, we may agree to having our business operated by a *creditors' committee* until sufficient funds have been generated to repay creditors or until a satisfactory composition can be arranged. The aim of such a committee is to enable the business to recover from some random error in management, and it is seldom able to cure more fundamental managerial ills that may have led to the difficulty. For example, a creditors' committee was formed for Banner Industries, Inc. Members of the board of directors contributed about $150,000 in exchange for stock of Banner, and the creditors' committee secured acceptance from about 90 percent of the creditors for a composition for 20 cents on the dollar.[1]

[1] *Wall Street Journal,* May 24, 1965, p. 6.

In each of these cases individual creditors are not required to accept the proposed adjustment. Because these arrangements are voluntary, there is no legal means of enforcing the will of the majority upon the minority. Any one creditor is entitled to reject the proposal and, if his rightful claims are not met, to force the company into liquidation or reorganization. Rather than face this hazard, creditors agreeing to the adjustment often permit payment in full of small creditors who refuse to join the agreement. Thus there is even some incentive for small creditors to dissent. However, these selfish ends cannot be pushed too far, since the owners may always adopt the alternative of liquidation. As we shall see, the amounts creditors receive in liquidation are likely to be considerably less than the value to them of keeping the business as a going concern. While an individual creditor might prefer to be one of the minority group that has its claims paid in full, he may not wish to assume the risk of building such a large minority group that an undesirable liquidation is forced.

We have already discussed in Chapters 19 and 20 one other type of adjustment initiated by the residual owners; that is, recapitalization. This form of voluntary adjustment includes the elimination of dividend accumulations on preferred stock, stock splits, and the voluntary exchange of one type of security for another.

Forced Adjustments

The treatment of business concerns in financial distress is governed by a Federal law, the Chandler Act, or Bankruptcy Act. The objective of the act is relatively simple. Once the company is placed in the hands of the court, the situation is "frozen"; that is, the *status quo* is temporarily preserved so that no one creditor or group of creditors can make off with an unfair share of the assets. Time is granted to study the situation to determine whether the company can be preserved as a going concern or whether it should be liquidated. If it is possible to preserve the company as a going concern, an opportunity is provided to reduce the amount and cost of debt to a level that the company can manage. In this process of scaling down the claims of owners and creditors, their rights are under the protection of the court, so that the priority of their claims on income and assets are supported insofar as possible.

Arrangement

Chapter 11 of the Chandler Act is designed for "use by the modest size corporation (as well as, of course, by individuals and partnerships), where there is a substantial identity between management and dominant stockholders."[2] The chapter applies only to the settlement of unsecured debts; secured obligations are not affected. After the court has accepted a petition by the debtor for reorganization under Chapter 11, it may appoint a receiver to manage the firm or leave it in the hands of the existing management. The plan proposed by the debtor for settlement of unsecured debt must be accepted by a majority in

[2]Sydney Krause, "Chapter X and XI—A Study in Contrasts," *Business Lawyer,* 19 (January, 1964), p. 516.

number and amount of claims filed, but then the remaining creditors must accept the plan. Note the contrast with the voluntary settlements discussed earlier. In addition, the court must determine that the proposed arrangement is feasible and "for the best interest of creditors."

An example of an arrangement is afforded by the trials and tribulations of John's Bargain Stores. On August 31, 1967, the company filed a petition for reorganization under Chapter 11 following its inability to meet maturing obligations. The court subsequently appointed a receiver to operate the concern. About 16 months later, after 263 of 474 stores had been closed, the court and creditors approved a plan whereby John's was to repay 50 cents on the dollar in instalments extending through December, 1972. With that agreement the corporation was discharged from its Chapter 11 proceedings, although the plan also placed three members of the creditors' committee on John's board of directors.[3]

The Securities and Exchange Commission may intervene in a Chapter 11 proceeding to ask that it be amended to comply with the requirements of Chapter 10. Illustration of such intervention is provided by the case of the Time Sales Finance Corporation. The firm had proposed a Chapter 11 arrangement whereby all unsecured creditors would be paid in full, except for holders of the debentures, who were to receive 40 percent of their claims in the preferred stock of an unrelated corporation. The Commission moved against the planned arrangement, "urging that the proposed plan involved more than a minor adjustment of unsecured debt and that past financial activities of the debtor warranted a disinterested investigation by a Chapter X trustee."[4] The judge refused the plan of arrangement and declared the debtor a bankrupt.

Reorganization and Liquidation

When there are publicly held securities and a comprehensive reorganization is needed, adjustment usually takes place under Chapter 10 of the Chandler Act. Railroads are reorganized under Section 77 of the Act.[5]

A debtor may voluntarily petition to be adjudged a bankrupt. Alternatively, his creditors may seek to have the proper Federal district court declare him a bankrupt under the following circumstances:

1. His total debts are $1,000 or more;

2. If there are 12 or more creditors, the petition must be signed by three or more with total claims of $500 or more. (If there are fewer, any one creditor owed $500 or more may file);

3. The debtor has committed an *act of bankruptcy* within the preceding four months. The most important and common act of bankruptcy is the debtor's admission in writing that he cannot pay his debts and is willing to be adjudged a bankrupt. Others involve concealment of assets, preferential transfer of some assets to creditors, and various other actions signifying impending doom.

---

[3] *Wall Street Journal,* December 24, 1968, p. 10.

[4] Securities and Exchange Commission, *35th Annual Report, 1969* (Washington, D.C.: U. S. Government Printing Office, 1970), p. 171.

[5] The chief difference is the involvement of the Interstate Commerce Commission, rather than the Securities and Exchange Commission. The ICC must approve the trustee(s) and the reorganization plan.

If the court finds that the corporation is indeed insolvent or unable to meet maturing debts, it will appoint a trustee to administer the affairs of the corporation. When the debts are greater than $250,000, the court must appoint a trustee who has no connection with the debtor; in other cases the court may appoint either a disinterested trustee or leave the company in the hands of the current management. The trustee has four main tasks:

1. Prepare a compilation of the assets and liabilities of the corporation and guard the assets for the protection of the creditors and owners.

2. By a comparison of its going-concern value and liquidation value, determine whether or not the firm should be liquidated or reorganized.

3. If it is to be liquidated, convert the assets into cash and distribute the cash to creditors and owners in accordance with the rule of absolute priority.

4. If it is to be reorganized, draw up a plan of reorganization with the advice of creditors and stockholders that is fair and feasible.

Let us consider these duties, assuming that the tabulation of assets and liabilities has been completed.

Liquidating Value Versus Going-Concern Value. Acceptance or rejection of plans to remedy financial strain ultimately rest upon a comparison of various estimated values. It will be recalled that in the case of a proposed business combination our object was to compare the economic value of the company as an independent, going concern to its value in combination with another company. The latter value was determined by the contribution of the individual company to the earnings of the combination. In cases of financial strain the first objective is to compare the value of the going concern to its value when dismembered and liquidated. In other words, creditors who are requested to agree to a plan for relief of financial strain must ask: Is the company worth more dead than alive? If the liquidating value exceeds the going concern value, the presumption is in favor of liquidation. At times the answer to this question will not determine the final decision. For example, a trade creditor may not wish to gain a reputation for forcing customers into liquidation. However, he must first answer the question, so that he knows the cost of preserving his reputation for dealing reasonably with customers.

The answer to this valuation problem is admittedly difficult. In considering the value of the company as a going concern, a creditor must ask why the company got into financial difficulty. Was it a basic fault of management, or some situation that might be remedied, given time and understanding creditors? Will it be "throwing good money after bad" to continue with the situation? The liquidating value of the company is generally much easier to calculate. Fixed assets can usually be sold only at a considerable discount from their book value, depending upon their specialization and the nature of the market. A lead-smelting plant might bring only a few cents on the dollar, whereas multipurpose machine tools would sell for much more in relation to their depreciated cost. Inventories and accounts receivable will probably bring still more in relation to their book values.

As an application of this principle, we find that small retail stores are frequently liquidated in times of financial strain. If mismanagement has brought a small hardware store into difficulties, there is probably little hope of improvement. After the remedial action—extension, composition, reorganization—the same owner-manager may still be in control. If this is the prospect, the going-concern value cannot be very high. In contrast, most of the assets can probably be sold without excessive losses. If the store leases its space, the assets are largely in the form of inventories and accounts receivable, which may be liquidated fairly readily. Thus the creditors find that the liquidating value exceeds the going-concern value and may reject remedies which involve sacrifices on their part in order to maintain the company as a going concern. On the other hand, the liquidating value of a steel mill is very low because of the high proportion of specialized, fixed assets. Even though the going-concern value is not very high, it is still not as low as the liquidating value. As a result steel companies that fall into financial difficulties are usually reorganized rather than liquidated.

Rule of Absolute Priority. When a company falls into financial difficulties, both the liquidating value and economic or going-concern value of its assets are usually not as high as stated on the balance sheet of the company. Since the economic value of the assets on the balance sheet has shrunk, downward adjustments must be made on the claims on those assets. If the company is to be liquidated, the claims on assets must be scaled down to match the cash realized from the liquidation. If the company is to be preserved, however, the claims must be reduced to match the economic or going-concern value of the assets. How is the recognized loss in the value of the assets to be distributed among creditors and owners? To express it in a more positive sense, how should the value that remains be distributed among the creditors and owners?

In a liquidation or reorganization under Chapter 10 of the Chandler Act claims of creditors and owners must usually be satisfied in accordance with the *rule of absolute priority*.[6] Under this rule senior claims on assets must be settled in full before anything is granted to junior claimants. Thus all creditors must have their claims settled in full before any payments are made to preferred owners, and preferred owners must receive all to which they are entitled before anything is paid to the residual owners. There may also be senior and junior creditors. If there are subordinated debentures outstanding, claims of all senior creditors must be satisfied before any payments are made to the holders of subordinated debentures. The application of the rule of absolute priority is relatively simple in the case of liquidation, but involves further problems of valuation in the case of reorganization.

Let us consider first the treatment of creditors and owners in the case of liquidation. The required ordering of claims is as follows:

1. Certain priority claims in the order shown.

---

[6] It will be recalled that under Chapter 11 the plan must be "for the best interest of creditors." Because companies under this chapter are typically closely held, it may well be in the best interest of creditors to allow the managers-owners to retain a share of the business. Were the reorganization under Chapter 10, application of the rule of absolute priority would wipe them out. Some large concerns have sought refuge under Chapter 11, evidently in a attempt to preserve some portion of the common stockholders' interest. The SEC has quite properly objected to this distortion of the purposes of Chapter 11. See Krause, *op. cit.,* p. 514.

a. Costs incurred by the trustee in preserving and administering the assets.

b. Wages earned within three months before the commencement of bankruptcy proceedings, not exceeding $600 for each claimant.

c. Reasonable costs incurred by creditors to block an unjustified arrangement or discharge of the bankrupt.

d. Federal, state, and local taxes.

e. Certain debts that have been given special priority, such as unpaid rent within three months prior to bankruptcy.

2. Secured creditors. Proceeds from assets in which these creditors have a security interest are applied first to senior liens (e.g. first mortgage holders) and then in order to those having junior liens. To the extent that the proceeds are inadequate to satisfy the secured creditors, they become unsecured creditors.

3. Unsecured and subordinated creditors.[7]

4. Preferred owners.

5. Residual owners.

A simple illustration may clarify the application of the rule. Assume that the following amounts are realized from the liquidation of assets to satisfy the claims shown:

Net cash realized from sale of assets (after settlement of priority claims):		Mortgage bonds (secured by plant and equipment)	$800,000
		Unsecured debts	400,000
Plant and equipment	$600,000	Common stock & surplus	
Other assets	300,000	(deficit)	($700,000)
Cash available	$900,000		

Under the rule of absolute priority, the available cash of $900,000 would be distributed as follows:

Claim of mortgage bonds	$800,000
Cash from sale of pledged assets	600,000
Unsatisfied claim of mortgage bonds	200,000
Claims of unsecured creditors	400,000
Total unsecured claims	$600,000

Settlement of unsecured claims: $\dfrac{\$300,000}{\$600,000}$, or at rate of 50 percent.

Allocation of cash:	
Bondholders	$700,000 ($600,000 + 50% × $200,000)
Unsecured creditors	200,000 (50% × $400,000)
Common stockholders	0
Total	$900,000

Now let us turn to the adjustment of claims of creditors and owners in the case of a reorganization. We have seen that settlement of claims under the rule

[7] For the treatment of subordinated debenture holders, see Chapter 17.

of absolute priority in the case of liquidation is relatively simple. Once the claims have been verified and substantiated and the assets sold, we have two definite sets of figures—claims and cash. This simplicity is not characteristic of a reorganization. Although the claims are readily determined, the values that will be given in satisfaction of these claims are not. If we reorganize, we will not be giving cash to existing security holders; we will be exchanging a new collection of securities for an old group of securities. We give them not cash, but claims on assets. Whereas a debenture holder might be entitled to receive $1000 in cash in liquidation, he might receive ten shares of 5 percent preferred stock in a reorganization. The Bankruptcy Act states that creditors are entitled to *fair and equitable* treatment. We know that $1000 in cash is "fair and equitable," but are ten shares of preferred stock equally fair and equitable? This is our problem, and there are basically three steps involved in the application of valuation principles in reaching its solution.

First, we must determine the rate of earnings that can be expected if the company is to be maintained as a going concern. This estimate is made at an early stage in the proceedings, because it is necessary to determine whether it is better to liquidate the company or allow it to reorganize and continue in business. This process leads to the comparison of liquidating value and economic or going-concern value discussed earlier in this section.

Second, we must formulate a capital structure for the concern that can be supported by the estimated stream of earnings. In addition to requiring that the reorganization plan be fair and equitable, the Bankruptcy Act also requires that it be *feasible.* The present capital structure clearly will not do; the existing burden of debt is the cause of our financial stress. The principles upon which we might base our plans for a new financial structure were discussed in Chapter 10. In the case of a reorganization, emphasis must first be upon avoidance of risk. Fixed charges must be minimized so that the reorganized company can avoid falling back into financial difficulties. To relieve a company of fixed charges, trustees frequently propose the issue of income bonds, preferred stock, and common stock to replace a capital structure that was top-heavy with debt. The more serious the financial difficulty, the more likely are existing debts to be replaced by preferred and common stocks. Also, the planned capital structure must provide maneuverability. Since additional funds will probably be needed to rehabilitate the company, we must leave "elbow room" in the financial structure. The equity base must be large enough to support the additional borrowings which will probably be needed. In short, the financial plan must be "feasible." The reorganized company should be able to live and prosper with the proposed capital structure for the foreseeable future.

Third, we must determine the value of the new securities and then exchange them for the old securities in accordance with the rule of absolute priority. To focus our discussion on a concrete proposal, let us consider the plan advanced by the Interstate Commerce Commission on March 17, 1952, for the reorganization of the Wisconsin Central Railway Company. At that time the railroad was paying interest on only one issue of its bonds. The proposal was to offer two new bond issues—First Mortgage 4s (i.e., 4 percent coupon rate) due in 2002 and new Income $4\frac{1}{2}$s (due 2027). The old preferred and common stocks of the

Wisconsin Central Railway Company were to be wiped out, and the new securities would then be allocated to the existing bondholders as follows:

		Distribution of cash and new securities to holder of one old bond		
Old bonds	Cash	1st Mtge. 4s, 2002	Income 4½s, 2027	Common Stock
1st 4s, 1949	$100	$900	–	–
Superior & Duluth 4s, 1936		150	$ 550	8 shares
1st & ref. 4s, 1945		150	1,000	5 shares
1st & ref. 5s, 1945		150	1,050	7 shares

Because of the very low liquidating value of a railroad and the public interest involved, it had already been decided to preserve the company as a going concern. The proposed plan seemed feasible in that the projected earnings would cover the new fixed charges by almost $3\frac{1}{2}$ times and fixed and contingent charges by 1.9 times. Earnings per share of common stock were estimated at $3.15. So far so good. Is the plan "fair and equitable"? Observe the problems of valuation that are involved. First the ICC found there was insufficient value as a going concern to support existing preferred and common stocks. Under the rule of absolute priority these claims were wiped out.[8] Second, the ICC had to judge the value of the new securities. For example, there were formerly two issues due in 1945, one bearing 4 percent interest and the other 5 percent interest. Does the extra $50 of Income 4½s and the extra two shares of common stock adequately compensate a bondholder for the difference of one percentage point between the coupon rates on the old bonds? Essentially the answer to this question must be based upon a determination of the capitalized value of the estimated stream of income from the package of new securities. Such calculations obviously do not represent an exact science. The greater the probable error in estimating income, the more likely are the regulatory bodies involved to grant existing security holders some share in the new, reorganized company.

When the trustee has finally evolved a plan, he must submit it to the court for a hearing. If liabilities exceed $3 million, the judge must submit the proposal to the SEC for advice; he may request an opinion from the SEC in other cases. If the court and the SEC find the plan to be "fair, equitable, and feasible," it is then submitted to the creditors and stockholders for approval. To become effective, the plan must be accepted by two-thirds of the amount of each class of debt and by a majority of each class of stock. If the corporation is actually insolvent, that is, if liabilities exceed assets, the stockholders have no vote. When the plan is approved, minority interests must accept the proposal as well. Again, this coercion represents an important departure from voluntary readjustments, such as extensions and compositions.

[8] In contrast, because of the greater uncertainty of estimates of earnings in an industrial reorganization, preferred and common stockholders are often given a small share of the new common stock, or possibly options to buy common stock at a fixed price. If earnings later prove to be higher than estimated, these options then allow the former stockholders to recover some of their losses.

Summary

Principles of valuation are applicable to adjustments designed to relieve financial strains. In any exchange involving a sacrifice of assets or securities for cash or securities, we wish to be assured that the value received is greater than the value of our assets or claims on assets when operating as an independent concern.

Relief of financial strain involves as a first step the comparison of the value of a company as a going concern with its liquidating value. If the company is worth more alive than dead, then steps must be taken to adjust downward the various claims on its assets. If the stress is not great, creditors may merely postpone the enforcement of their claims or voluntarily reduce their claims. However, when large companies fall into financial difficulties, creditors are more likely to demand strict adherence to the terms of their contracts. Sacrifices will then be made under court supervision. In Chapter 10 reorganizations, the rule of absolute priority prevails, and the reorganization plan must be "fair, equitable, and feasible"; that is, creditors and owners must receive their fair share of a new group of securities than can be supported by projected earnings.

Since valuation must be based upon estimates of income and capitalization rates, the calculated values can be no more accurate than these estimates. Consequently proposals for business combination or for relief of financial strain generally bring forth a wide variety of estimates of income and capitalization rates. Each side determines the "value" most favorable to its interests. Although these values may differ widely, this should not detract from the validity of the principles of valuation.

Questions

1/ Insolvency has many possible origins. What type of voluntary financial adjustment, if any, would you recommend that owners seek under each of the following circumstances? Explain your reasoning and indicate any additional factors that would influence your decision.

   a. An automobile crashes into a barber shop. It will take several weeks for repairs to be made so that the shop may reopen for business. The owner has no insurance against loss of income resulting from interruption of business.

   b. A hardware store is unable to pay bills because of failure to sell its spring stock of fertilizers, seeds, etc., during a recession.

   c. A normally successful clothing store loses a large portion of its stock as a result of a flood. It carries no flood insurance.

   d. A filling station is in financial difficulties because a new thruway has diverted traffic away from the station.

2/ Might a company voluntarily liquidate, even if it were not about to fail? Explain.

3/ Assume that a company has failed to pay interest on its 5 percent bonds. As a result the bonds are selling on the market at 65. The unpaid interest on each bond amounts to $50. In reorganization, should the new securities offered in exchange for the old bonds be based on the principal and unpaid interest of each bond ($1050) or on the current market value ($650)? Explain your position.

4/ If bondholders were entitled to vote in the election of the board of directors, would you recommend any changes in the principles followed in reorganization? Explain your position.

Problem

The balance sheet of the Poor Richard Corporation prior to liquidation appears as follows:

Assets		Liabilities and capital	
Cash	$ 3,500	Common stock	$200,000
Accounts receivable	72,800	Earned surplus (deficit)	(46,500)
Inventory	153,600	Preferred stock	50,000
Plant and equipment	411,600	First Mortgage bonds	200,000
		Second mortgage bonds	80,000
		Debentures	100,000
		Accounts payable	38,000
		Notes payable—bank	20,000
	$641,500		$641,500

The amounts realized in liquidation are as follows:

Cash	$ 3,500
Accounts receivable	42,000
Inventory	46,140
Plant and equipment	208,500

Assuming that the mortgage bondholders have a mortgage on the plant and equipment, determine how much each class of creditors and owners would receive upon liquidation. The bank has the right of offset on the $3500 in cash.

Selected References

ALTMAN, E. I., "Corporate Bankruptcy Potential, Stockholder Returns and Share Valuation," *Journal of Finance,* 24 (December, 1969), pp. 887–900.

BOGEN, J. ed., *Financial Handbook,* 4th ed. New York: Ronald Press Company, 1964, section 22.

BLUM, W. J., "Full Priority and Full Compensation in Corporate Reorganization: A Reappraisal," *University of Chicago Law Review,* 25 (Spring, 1958), pp. 417–44.

CAVITCH, Z. "Reorganization Techniques in Corporate Planning," *Business Lawyer,* 19 (January, 1964), pp. 429–62.

HIRSCH, G. J. and S. KRAUSE, *Bankruptcy and Arrangements,* 3rd ed. New York: Practicing Law Institute, 1964.

KRAUSE, S., "Chapters X and XI—A Study in Contrasts," *Business Lawyer,* 19 (January, 1964), pp. 511–26.

Appendix A: Present Value Tables

Derivation of Appendix A-1

Let A equal the dollar amount realized at the end of some period of time, r represent compound rate of interest per period of time, n the number of interest periods, and P the present sum of money, or present value of the stream of income.

If P is invested for one year, the interest received is rP. Thus the total amount received at the end of the first year can be shown as:

$$A_1 = P + rP$$
$$A_1 = P(1 + r) \tag{1}$$

The interest earned on this amount (A_1) at the end of the second year is rA_1, and the total amount receivable at the end of the second year may be shown as:

$$A_2 = A_1 + rA_1$$

Substituting from (1) for A_1,

$$A_2 = P(1 + r) + rP(1 + r)$$

Factoring $P(1 + r)$,

$$A_2 = P(1 + r)(1 + r)$$
$$A_2 = P(1 + r)^2 \tag{2}$$

In the general case,

$$A_n = P(1 + r)^n \tag{3}$$

Appendix A-1 is prepared by solving for P: that is,

$$P = \frac{A_n}{(1 + r)^n} \tag{4}$$

For example, if we wish to know the present value of $1 received at the end of the second year, discounted at 10 percent, we can substitute in (4):

$$P = \frac{1.00}{(1 + 0.10)^2} = \$0.826$$

Appendix A-1

Present Value of $1 Received at the End of Period

Years Hence	1%	2%	4%	6%	8%	10%	12%	14%	15%	16%	18%	20%	22%	24%	25%	26%	28%	30%	35%	40%	45%	50%
1	0.990	0.980	0.962	0.943	0.926	0.909	0.893	0.877	0.870	0.862	0.847	0.833	0.820	0.806	0.800	0.794	0.781	0.769	0.741	0.714	0.690	0.667
2	0.980	0.961	0.925	0.890	0.857	0.826	0.797	0.769	0.756	0.743	0.718	0.694	0.672	0.650	0.640	0.630	0.610	0.592	0.549	0.510	0.476	0.444
3	0.971	0.942	0.889	0.840	0.794	0.751	0.712	0.675	0.658	0.641	0.609	0.579	0.551	0.524	0.512	0.500	0.477	0.455	0.406	0.364	0.328	0.296
4	0.961	0.924	0.855	0.792	0.735	0.683	0.636	0.592	0.572	0.552	0.516	0.482	0.451	0.423	0.410	0.397	0.373	0.350	0.301	0.260	0.226	0.198
5	0.951	0.906	0.822	0.747	0.681	0.621	0.567	0.519	0.497	0.476	0.437	0.402	0.370	0.341	0.328	0.315	0.291	0.269	0.223	0.186	0.156	0.132
6	0.942	0.888	0.790	0.705	0.630	0.564	0.507	0.456	0.432	0.410	0.370	0.335	0.303	0.275	0.262	0.250	0.227	0.207	0.165	0.133	0.108	0.088
7	0.933	0.871	0.760	0.665	0.583	0.513	0.452	0.400	0.376	0.354	0.314	0.279	0.249	0.222	0.210	0.198	0.178	0.159	0.122	0.095	0.074	0.059
8	0.923	0.853	0.731	0.627	0.540	0.467	0.404	0.351	0.327	0.305	0.266	0.233	0.204	0.179	0.168	0.157	0.139	0.123	0.091	0.068	0.051	0.039
9	0.914	0.837	0.703	0.592	0.500	0.424	0.361	0.308	0.284	0.263	0.225	0.194	0.167	0.144	0.134	0.125	0.108	0.094	0.067	0.048	0.035	0.026
10	0.905	0.820	0.676	0.558	0.463	0.386	0.322	0.270	0.247	0.227	0.191	0.162	0.137	0.116	0.107	0.099	0.085	0.073	0.050	0.035	0.024	0.017
11	0.896	0.804	0.650	0.527	0.429	0.350	0.287	0.237	0.215	0.195	0.162	0.135	0.112	0.094	0.086	0.079	0.066	0.056	0.037	0.025	0.017	0.012
12	0.887	0.788	0.625	0.497	0.397	0.319	0.257	0.208	0.187	0.168	0.137	0.112	0.092	0.076	0.069	0.062	0.052	0.043	0.027	0.018	0.012	0.008
13	0.879	0.773	0.601	0.469	0.368	0.290	0.229	0.182	0.163	0.145	0.116	0.093	0.075	0.061	0.055	0.050	0.040	0.033	0.020	0.013	0.008	0.005
14	0.870	0.758	0.577	0.442	0.340	0.263	0.205	0.160	0.141	0.125	0.099	0.078	0.062	0.049	0.044	0.039	0.032	0.025	0.015	0.009	0.006	0.003
15	0.861	0.743	0.555	0.417	0.315	0.239	0.183	0.140	0.123	0.108	0.084	0.065	0.051	0.040	0.035	0.031	0.025	0.020	0.011	0.006	0.004	0.002
16	0.853	0.728	0.534	0.394	0.292	0.218	0.163	0.123	0.107	0.093	0.071	0.054	0.042	0.032	0.028	0.025	0.019	0.015	0.008	0.005	0.003	0.002
17	0.844	0.714	0.513	0.371	0.270	0.198	0.146	0.108	0.093	0.080	0.060	0.045	0.034	0.026	0.023	0.020	0.015	0.012	0.006	0.003	0.002	0.001
18	0.836	0.700	0.494	0.350	0.250	0.180	0.130	0.095	0.081	0.069	0.051	0.038	0.028	0.021	0.018	0.016	0.012	0.009	0.005	0.002	0.001	0.001
19	0.828	0.686	0.475	0.331	0.232	0.164	0.116	0.083	0.070	0.060	0.043	0.031	0.023	0.017	0.014	0.012	0.009	0.007	0.003	0.002	0.001	
20	0.820	0.673	0.456	0.312	0.215	0.149	0.104	0.073	0.061	0.051	0.037	0.026	0.019	0.014	0.012	0.010	0.007	0.005	0.002	0.001	0.001	
21	0.811	0.660	0.439	0.294	0.199	0.135	0.093	0.064	0.053	0.044	0.031	0.022	0.015	0.011	0.009	0.008	0.006	0.004	0.002	0.001		
22	0.803	0.647	0.422	0.278	0.184	0.123	0.083	0.056	0.046	0.038	0.026	0.018	0.013	0.009	0.007	0.006	0.004	0.003	0.001	0.001		
23	0.795	0.634	0.406	0.262	0.170	0.112	0.074	0.049	0.040	0.033	0.022	0.015	0.010	0.007	0.006	0.005	0.003	0.002	0.001			
24	0.788	0.622	0.390	0.247	0.158	0.102	0.066	0.043	0.035	0.028	0.019	0.013	0.008	0.006	0.005	0.004	0.003	0.002	0.001			
25	0.780	0.610	0.375	0.233	0.146	0.092	0.059	0.038	0.030	0.024	0.016	0.010	0.007	0.005	0.004	0.003	0.002	0.001	0.001			
26	0.772	0.598	0.361	0.220	0.135	0.084	0.053	0.033	0.026	0.021	0.014	0.009	0.006	0.004	0.003	0.002	0.002	0.001				
27	0.764	0.586	0.347	0.207	0.125	0.076	0.047	0.029	0.023	0.018	0.011	0.007	0.005	0.003	0.002	0.002	0.001	0.001				
28	0.757	0.574	0.333	0.196	0.116	0.069	0.042	0.026	0.020	0.016	0.010	0.006	0.004	0.002	0.002	0.002	0.001	0.001				
29	0.749	0.563	0.321	0.185	0.107	0.063	0.037	0.022	0.017	0.014	0.008	0.005	0.003	0.002	0.002	0.001	0.001	0.001				
30	0.742	0.552	0.308	0.174	0.099	0.057	0.033	0.020	0.015	0.012	0.007	0.004	0.003	0.002	0.001	0.001	0.001	0.001				
40	0.672	0.453	0.208	0.097	0.046	0.022	0.011	0.005	0.004	0.003	0.001	0.001										
50	0.608	0.372	0.141	0.054	0.021	0.009	0.003	0.001	0.001	0.001												

Source: R. N. Anthony, *Management Accounting: Text and Cases* (Homewood, Ill., Richard D. Irwin, Inc., 1969).

Appendix A-2

Present Value of $1 Received Annually at the End of Each Period for N Periods

Years (N)	1%	2%	4%	6%	8%	10%	12%	14%	15%	16%	18%	20%	22%	24%	25%	26%	28%	30%	35%	40%	45%	50%
1	0.990	0.980	0.962	0.943	0.926	0.909	0.893	0.877	0.870	0.862	0.847	0.833	0.820	0.806	0.800	0.794	0.781	0.769	0.741	0.714	0.690	0.667
2	1.970	1.942	1.886	1.833	1.783	1.736	1.690	1.647	1.626	1.605	1.566	1.528	1.492	1.457	1.440	1.424	1.392	1.361	1.289	1.224	1.165	1.111
3	2.941	2.884	2.775	2.673	2.577	2.487	2.402	2.322	2.283	2.246	2.174	2.106	2.042	1.981	1.952	1.923	1.868	1.816	1.696	1.589	1.493	1.407
4	3.902	3.808	3.630	3.465	3.312	3.170	3.037	2.914	2.855	2.798	2.690	2.589	2.494	2.404	2.362	2.320	2.241	2.166	1.997	1.849	1.720	1.605
5	4.853	4.713	4.452	4.212	3.993	3.791	3.605	3.433	3.352	3.274	3.127	2.991	2.864	2.745	2.689	2.635	2.532	2.436	2.220	2.035	1.876	1.737
6	5.795	5.601	5.242	4.917	4.623	4.355	4.111	3.889	3.784	3.685	3.498	3.326	3.167	3.020	2.951	2.885	2.759	2.643	2.385	2.168	1.983	1.824
7	6.728	6.472	6.002	5.582	5.206	4.868	4.564	4.288	4.160	4.039	3.812	3.605	3.416	3.242	3.161	3.083	2.937	2.802	2.508	2.263	2.057	1.883
8	7.652	7.325	6.733	6.210	5.747	5.335	4.968	4.639	4.487	4.344	4.078	3.837	3.619	3.421	3.329	3.241	3.076	2.925	2.598	2.331	2.108	1.922
9	8.566	8.162	7.435	6.802	6.247	5.759	5.328	4.946	4.772	4.607	4.303	4.031	3.786	3.566	3.463	3.366	3.184	3.019	2.665	2.379	2.144	1.948
10	9.471	8.983	8.111	7.360	6.710	6.145	5.650	5.216	5.019	4.833	4.494	4.192	3.923	3.682	3.571	3.465	3.269	3.092	2.715	2.414	2.168	1.965
11	10.368	9.787	8.760	7.887	7.139	6.495	5.988	5.453	5.234	5.029	4.656	4.327	4.035	3.776	3.656	3.544	3.335	3.147	2.752	2.438	2.185	1.977
12	11.255	10.575	9.385	8.384	7.536	6.814	6.194	5.660	5.421	5.197	4.793	4.439	4.127	3.851	3.725	3.606	3.387	3.190	2.779	2.456	2.196	1.985
13	12.134	11.343	9.986	8.853	7.904	7.103	6.424	5.842	5.583	5.342	4.910	4.533	4.203	3.912	3.780	3.656	3.427	3.223	2.799	2.468	2.204	1.990
14	13.004	12.106	10.563	9.295	8.244	7.367	6.628	6.002	5.724	5.468	5.008	4.611	4.265	3.962	3.824	3.695	3.459	3.249	2.814	2.477	2.210	1.993
15	13.865	12.849	11.118	9.712	8.559	7.606	6.811	6.142	5.847	5.575	5.092	4.675	4.315	4.001	3.859	3.726	3.483	3.268	2.825	2.484	2.214	1.995
16	14.718	13.578	11.652	10.106	8.851	7.824	6.974	6.265	5.954	5.669	5.162	4.730	4.357	4.003	3.887	3.751	3.503	3.283	2.834	2.489	2.216	1.997
17	15.562	14.292	12.166	10.477	9.122	8.022	7.120	6.373	6.047	5.749	5.222	4.775	4.391	4.059	3.910	3.771	3.518	3.295	2.840	2.492	2.218	1.998
18	16.398	14.992	12.659	10.828	9.372	8.201	7.250	6.467	6.128	5.818	5.273	4.812	4.419	4.080	3.928	3.786	3.529	3.304	2.844	2.494	2.219	1.999
19	17.226	15.678	13.134	11.158	9.604	8.365	7.366	6.550	6.198	5.877	5.316	4.844	4.442	4.097	3.942	3.799	3.539	3.311	2.848	2.496	2.220	1.999
20	18.046	16.351	13.590	11.470	9.818	8.514	7.469	6.623	6.259	5.929	5.353	4.870	4.460	4.110	3.954	3.808	3.546	3.316	2.850	2.497	2.221	1.999
21	18.857	17.011	14.029	11.764	10.017	8.649	7.562	6.687	6.312	5.973	5.384	4.891	4.476	4.121	3.963	3.816	3.551	3.320	2.852	2.498	2.221	2.000
22	19.660	17.658	14.451	12.042	10.201	8.772	7.645	6.743	6.359	6.011	5.410	4.909	4.488	4.130	3.970	3.822	3.556	3.323	2.853	2.498	2.222	2.000
23	20.456	18.292	14.857	12.303	10.371	8.883	7.718	6.792	6.399	6.044	5.432	4.925	4.499	4.137	3.976	3.827	3.559	3.325	2.854	2.499	2.222	2.000
24	21.243	18.914	15.247	12.550	10.529	8.985	7.784	6.835	6.434	6.073	5.451	4.937	4.507	4.143	3.981	3.831	3.562	3.327	2.855	2.499	2.222	2.000
25	22.023	19.523	15.622	12.783	10.675	9.077	7.843	6.873	6.464	6.097	5.467	4.948	4.514	4.147	3.985	3.834	3.564	3.329	2.856	2.499	2.222	2.000
26	22.795	20.121	15.983	13.003	10.810	9.161	7.896	6.906	6.491	6.118	5.480	4.956	4.520	4.151	3.988	3.837	3.566	3.330	2.856	2.500	2.222	2.000
27	23.560	20.707	16.330	13.211	10.935	9.237	7.943	6.935	6.514	6.136	5.492	4.964	4.524	4.154	3.990	3.839	3.567	3.331	2.856	2.500	2.222	2.000
28	24.316	21.281	16.663	13.406	11.051	9.307	7.984	6.961	6.534	6.152	5.502	4.970	4.528	4.157	3.992	3.840	3.568	3.331	2.857	2.500	2.222	2.000
29	25.066	21.844	16.984	13.591	11.158	9.370	8.022	6.983	6.551	6.166	5.510	4.975	4.531	4.159	3.994	3.841	3.569	3.332	2.857	2.500	2.222	2.000
30	25.808	22.396	17.292	13.765	11.258	9.427	8.055	7.003	6.566	6.177	5.517	4.979	4.534	4.160	3.995	3.842	3.569	3.332	2.857	2.500	2.222	2.000
40	32.835	27.355	19.793	15.046	11.925	9.779	8.244	7.105	6.642	6.234	5.548	4.997	4.544	4.166	3.999	3.846	3.571	3.333	2.857	2.500	2.222	2.000
50	39.196	31.424	21.482	15.762	12.234	9.915	8.304	7.133	6.661	6.246	5.554	4.999	4.545	4.167	4.000	3.846	3.571	3.333	2.857	2.500	2.222	2.000

Source: R. N. Anthony, Management Accounting: Text and Cases (Homewood, Ill., Richard D. Irwin, Inc., 1969).

Appendix B: Guide to Notation

A_t After-tax cash flows in year t. Without the subscript, annual cash flows are assumed to be equal.

A' Level annual pre-tax cash flows.

b Cost of floating new issue of common stock expressed as a percentage of the gross proceeds.

B Net proceeds of a bond issue, or market price of a bond.

BEP Break-even point.
$$= \frac{F}{p - v}.$$

c Cash outlay on capital investment.

$\overline{d_t}$ Expected annual dividend per share of preferred stock or common stock defined in year t.

D Dollar amount of debt; face (or par) value of a bond.

DOL Degree of operating leverage.
$$= \frac{T(p - v)}{T(p - v) - F} = \frac{T}{T - BEP}.$$

E Expected present value of stream of after-tax net cash benefits.

$EBIT$ Earnings before interest and taxes. $EBIT$ differs from net operating income, Y, only if there are non-operating income or expense items, other than interest expense. In the absence of such items, net operating income equals earnings before interest and taxes, or $Y = EBIT$.

EP Earning power, or ratio of net operating income to net operating assets. $= Y/O$.

EPS Earnings per share.

F Dollar amount of fixed operating costs.

g Expected annual rate of growth of dividends per share of common stock, or of cash flow to residual owners of an unincorporated business.

i Annual rate of interest on debt, or yield. This is a *percentage* rate, in contrast to I, which represents the annual *dollar* amount of interest on debt.

I Interest on debt in dollars. $= iD$.

k Pre-tax discount rate used to discount a level annual stream of cash flows for an unlevered firm.

k_a After-tax discount rate used to discount an annual stream of level cash flows for an unlevered firm.

k_e Cost of common equity. $= \bar{d}_1/P_0 + g$.

k'_e Cost of a new issue of common stock.
$$= \frac{k_e}{1 - b}.$$

k_p Cost of preferred stock. $= \bar{d}/P_0$.

k_r Cost of retained earnings.
$$= k_e \frac{1 - t_p}{1 - t_g}.$$

K Pre-tax rate of return on the book value of the owners' equity. $= EP \cdot L$.

K_a After-tax rate of return on the book value of the owners' equity. $= EP \cdot L_a = EP \cdot L \cdot \theta$.

L Pre-tax leverage factor.
$$= \frac{1}{Q}\left(\frac{Y - 1}{Y}\right).$$

L_a After-tax leverage factor.
$$= \frac{1}{Q}\left(\frac{Y - I}{Y}\right)\theta.$$

n Number of years to maturity of a bond issue.

N Number of shares of common stock.

NPV Net present value.

O Net operating assets.

p Selling price per unit of output.

P or P_0 Current price of equity per share; either preferred stock or common stock as defined.

Q Proportion of total assets financed by residual owners' equity.

r Discounted rate of return.

ρ (Greek letter, Rho). The cost of capital or opportunity cost. The rate of return that must be earned on an investment in order to leave the residual owners as well off after the investment as before the investment.

R Accounts receivable.

S Net sales.

t_c Corporate income tax rate.

t_g Capital gains tax rate.

t_p Personal income tax rate.

θ (Greek letter, Theta). The after-tax rate; i.e. one minus the tax rate. If the corporate tax rate is 48%, θ equals 52%.

$= (1 - t_c)$, if corporate income tax rate is applicable.

T Output, or number of units produced per period of time.

v Variable costs per unit of output.

V Market value of unlevered firm.

V_L Market value of levered firm.

$$= \frac{Y(1 - t_c)}{k_a} + Dt_c .$$

V_s Aggregate market value of common stock.

Y Net operating income.

INDEX